RUDYARD KIPLING

THE COMPLETE VERSE

with a foreword by
M. M. Kaye

KYLE CATHIE LIMITED

This edition published 1990 by
Kyle Cathie Limited
3 Vincent Square, London SW1P 2LX

Reprinted 1991
Reprinted 1992 (three times)

ISBN   Hardcover edition 1 85626 009 7
        Paperback edition 1 85626 007 0

A CIP catalogue record for this book is available from the British Library.

Typeset by Invicta, Folkestone, Kent
Printed and bound in Great Britain by
Butler & Tanner Ltd, Frome and London

CONTENTS

FOREWORD

Rudyard Kipling died just after midnight on the morning of 18 January 1936. His widow, Carrie, who had once been Caroline Balestier of Vermont, New England, made a brief, poignant entry in the diary she had kept ever since she became his wife: 'Rud died at 12 a.m. Our wedding day.' They had been married for exactly forty-five years.

Kipling had come uncomfortably close to death once before, in the early months of 1899 when he and Josephine, the elder of his two little daughters, both went down with a severe attack of pneumonia, brought on by a bitterly cold and stormy voyage to New York. Kipling was then at the height of his fame, and if he had died then he would have gone out in a blaze of glory, for it seemed that the whole civilised world was holding its breath as it waited for his doctors' bulletins. In the street outside the hotel in which he and his family were staying, tanbark had been spread to lessen the noise of passing traffic and crowds knelt on the pavement to pray for the sick man's recovery.

His reputation as a living poet, fiction-writer and balladeer was at that time probably second to none – certainly among the working- and middle-class readers for whom he wrote. In the event, it was six-year-old Josephine who died – the adored little daughter who was the love of his life and whose loss was to leave an open wound in his heart for the rest of his days. Kipling recovered; and thirty-seven years later, when he died in a London hospital, his death was to go almost unnoticed. This was partly because his popularity, which had reached its peak at the turn of the century, had in the sour aftermath of the First World War begun to decline. But the lack of interest was also because the public's attention at that time was focused upon another deathbed: that of a King-Emperor, George V.

It is doubtful if anyone, bar a few close friends and a handful of the staff of Brown's Hotel, knew that the Kiplings were in London; or cared. All eyes were on the King, and silent crowds collected daily before the gates of Buckingham Palace – not because he was in residence there, for he was at Sandringham – but to show sympathy and to read the hourly bulletins that were displayed on the Palace gates. He died a few days after Kipling, whose ashes were interned in Poets' Corner at Westminster Abbey on 23 January – the same day that the body of George V, who had been a personal friend of his, was brought to London to lie in state in Westminster Hall. One of the daily newspapers wrote that 'The King has gone, and taken his trumpeter with him!' But to me, the king who had gone was Kipling.

Anyone who is interested in Rudyard Kipling as a person can now learn almost everything there is to know about him, from his birth in Bombay to the internment of his ashes in Westminster Abbey. The Tale of Rudyard has been told by any number of biographers, including the poet himself in his autobiography, *Something of Myself*, which in fact tells us almost nothing and can be regarded as a smoke-screen, timed to go off after his death and designed to lead would-be biographers astray. He also left a short verse, the last in this book and probably the last he ever wrote, entitled 'The Appeal', which is a plea to posterity to respect his private life. Considering that, as a journalist, he had never shown much respect for other people's, I don't know why he thought it would work. It didn't, of course. He, as well as his stories and verses, has been criticised, praised, attacked and dissected by scores of writers in countless reviews and essays, magazine articles and memoirs. There has even been a brilliant one-man play, subsequently filmed for television, in which the actor portraying Kipling walks up and down a mock-up of his study in his Sussex home, Batemans, and talks to the audience about himself and his work. As for biographies, they must take up a lot of space in the section devoted to that form of literature in our public libraries. The most detailed is by Professor Charles Carrington,* who was personally chosen by Kipling's daughter Elsie, Mrs Bambridge, to write her father's biography. But there are at least half a dozen others that are well worth reading and, since every self-respecting town has its library, it seems a waste of time to give even the briefest outline of Rudyard's life here. However, as certain happenings in the life of any writer obviously influence his or her work, it is worth mentioning some that undoubtedly influenced Kipling's.

To start with, both his grandfathers were Methodist ministers – as

---

***Rudyard Kipling, His Life and Work*, Macmillan, 1955.

was a great-grandfather on his mother's side, who had been converted to that faith by the great John Wesley himself. This probably accounts for Rudyard's tendency to preach, as well as for his detailed knowledge of the Bible and his love of it as literature, which often shows in the biblical lilt of his prose – just as his familiarity with hymn tunes is reflected in many of his verses. It is said that he often wrote them to some hymn tune or other that happened to be running in his head, and that he could be seen pacing up and down his study or striding about in the garden, crooning a hymn tune to which he beat time as he fitted words to it.

His scholarly father, John Lockwood Kipling, was an artist and sculptor as well as a writer of no small merit. His mother, Alice, who dabbled in writing and poetry, was one of the beautiful and remarkable Macdonald sisters,* two of whom married famous painters, Sir Edward Burne-Jones and Sir Edward Poynter, while a third married a rich iron-master, Alfred Baldwin; their son Stanley became Prime Minister and later Lord Baldwin. A fifth sister did not marry. Lockwood and Alice first met at a picnic on the shores of Lake Rudyard in Staffordshire (which accounts for the unusual name they later bestowed on their first-born) and on 18 March 1865, immediately after their wedding, they set sail for India, where Lockwood had been appointed Professor of Architectural Sculpture in the new School of Art in Bombay. It was here, in this 'blazing beauty of a city' – the description is Lockwood's – that their son, christened Joseph Rudyard but never called anything but Rud or Ruddy, was born on the last-but-one day of the same year.

The child's early recollections were of sunshine and colour, but his first visit to England at the age of three was not a success, for he had been hopelessly spoiled by his parents' Indian servants and, according to a Macdonald uncle, 'dear Alice is as wax in his small fists'. (One would have expected dear Alice, who was a pretty, witty and intelligent woman, to have more sense.) Her son's fits of screaming rage whenever he was thwarted did not endear him to his relations; nor were they amused by his habit of stamping off to the village, warning the inhabitants to clear the way because there was 'an angry Ruddy coming!' Much of his verse in future years was to be written by that same Ruddy, older and wiser of course, but still angry.

*See A. S. Baldwin, *The Macdonald Sisters*, Peter Davies, 1960.

His sister, Trix, was born during that leave; and five months later the Kiplings returned with their two children to Bombay. Here once more Ruddy was to receive, as of right, the spoiling that the East bestows on that lord of creation, the eldest son. To see again the blazing sunlight and the brilliant colours; and to hear again the drowsy, day-long chorus of the tree-frogs and, by night, the familiar lullaby of palm trees and banana fronds rustling in the wind. It was a time that Ruddy was never to forget, and which twenty-two years later he was to remember nostalgically in 'Song of the Wise Children':

> We shall go back by the boltless doors,
>   To the life unaltered our childhood knew—
> To the naked feet on the cool, dark floors,
>   And the high-ceiled rooms that the Trade blows through:
>
> To the trumpet-flowers and the moon beyond,
>   And the tree-toad's chorus drowning all—
> And the lisp of the split banana-frond
>   That talked us to sleep when we were small.

I don't think he realised, when he wrote that, that no one, except in memory, can ever go back to 'the life unaltered our childhood knew'; and he must have done that often during the bleak years that followed his return to England in 1871 . . .

He was six years old when his parents made the bitter decision that thousands of Anglo-Indian* parents, my own among them, had made before them and would make in the future: that it was time for the spoiling to stop and for their children to go back to their own country to be educated and disciplined, and to put down roots there. Kipling describes in his evasive autobiography his arrival in England, the cold grey drizzle and gaunt grey buildings of London's Tilbury Docks: 'There was next a dark land and a darker room full of cold.'

Worse was to come. Since Lockwood's salary was a meagre one even for those days, it was going to take a good five or six years to save up enough money for another voyage to England, and Alice had decided to leave her children in a narrow, chilly, terrace house in Southsea, in

---

*Anglo-Indian was, until the thirties, a term used to describe the British whose work was in India but who would return to their own country in retirement. It was not applied, as it is now, to people of mixed race, who were then known as 'Eurasians'.

the care of a total stranger who eked out her husband's pension by boarding children of parents whose work lay in distant parts of the Empire. The woman, whom they were told to call 'Auntie Rosa', took an immediate dislike to the spoilt little boy (she may have had every reason to do so) and not only punished him severely for every real or imagined fault, but also allowed her own son, who was several years older, to bully him unmercifully. The result of one of the punishments inflicted by the dreadful Auntie Rosa was to affect poor Rudyard all his life, for discovering that he had a passion for books, she would punish him by forbidding him to read. But since books had become his only escape from the harsh realities of life, he would read by stealth, of necessity in a bad light – in some shadowy corner, or by twilight, or by the flickering glow of a filched candle-end. Not unnaturally, this strained his eyesight so badly that eventually he could only read something that was held within an inch or two of his nose, and could see nothing but a blur beyond that.

In the end, one of his many aunts (all of whom had offered to take charge of the children and had been refused) wrote a letter to Alice that brought her hurrying home a year before the stipulated six were over, to find that the ebullient, noisy six-year-old whom she had left behind in Southsea had become a thin, wary, half-blind boy of eleven, who kept one anxious eye on Auntie Rosa and flinched at any sudden movements, as though in expectation of a blow.

A good many writers have come up with a variety of reasons to explain why Alice unloaded her children on strangers instead of on a relative, and I admit to having a reason of my own, based on the experience of my mother-in-law in a similar situation. I think Alice was afraid that her little son might grow to love one of her sisters more than he loved her, but felt that there was no danger of that happening where Auntie Rosa was concerned. And indeed he hated Auntie Rosa all his life. He wrote a bitter short story about his years in her house in Southsea* and returned to the subject, with unabated hatred, in the last book he ever wrote – that autobiography.

He tells us himself that one good thing that the experience did for him was to cure him for ever of Hate, because he had used it all up

---

*'Baa, Baa, Black-Sheep', *Wee Willie Winkie and Other Stories*.

on Auntie Rosa and her son. But that I do not believe. You have only to read some of the verses he writes when he has a really good target lined up in his sights and lets fly with both barrels – as, for instance, this lethal little offering which he aimed in the direction of Gladstone, whose dependence on the Irish vote in the House of Commons had led him to look the other way and pretend not to notice when a Special Commission of Inquiry cleared the Irish leaders, whose actions Kipling denounced as 'blatant traffic in murder and the Irish Land Leagues'. The verses that he wrote on the subject he called ' "Cleared" '; here are two of them:

> "Cleared," honourable gentlemen! Be thankful it's no more:—
> The widow's curse is on your house, the dead are at your door.
> On you the shame of open shame; on you from North to South
> The hand of every honest man flat-heeled across your mouth.
>
> My soul! I'd sooner lie in jail for murder plain and straight,
> Pure crime I'd done with my own hand for money, lust, or hate
> Than take a seat in Parliament by fellow-felons cheered,
> While one of those "not-provens" proved me cleared as you are
>   cleared.

There is a lot more of the same. All good ripe dynamite – but hardly, I would have said, the work of a man who could claim to have been cured of hate?

We also have it on Kipling's authority that even after his rescue from the 'House of Desolation', he was not to be free from bullying. He came in for more during his first few terms at his public school, the United Services College at Westward Ho! in Devon, where he was nicknamed 'Gig-lamps' or 'Gigger' because of those owlish, thick-lensed spectacles, life-long reminders of the untender care of Auntie Rosa. This, I think, is something that should be kept in mind by those who profess to be disgusted by the 'cruelty' in some of Kipling's work. It is not difficult for a child to be scarred for life by early ill-treatment at the hands of adults or bullies of his own age, and poor Ruddy had plenty of both.

He must have tried his hand at writing poetry at an early age, and it is my belief that in later life he actually *thought* in rhyming verse. Many of his juvenile efforts at putting his thoughts on paper were in that medium, and during his years at Westward Ho! he seems to have been the acknowledged poet laureate of his house, if not of the entire school,

and to have composed popular verses on any subject of local interest
– preferably to the disparagement of some form-master.

We get an idea of 'Gigger's' verses from his school story, *Stalky and Co.*, in which the character of 'Beetle' is plainly a self-portrait of the author. In one of the Stalky adventures, while Beetle is being dressed down by a house-master, a drunken carter from outside the study window starts pelting the teacher with stones and abuse, and advises him to 'poultice his long nose.' At this, 'Beetle's heart leapt within him . . . He would embody that suggestion about the nose in a deathless verse.' In the same book, Kipling tells us that Beetle 'applied himself most seriously throughout third lesson (algebra with little Hartopp) to composing a poem entitled "The Lazer House" '. And in another chapter he makes the school chaplain, the Rev. John Gillett, say of Beetle that 'I fancy he spends most of his time with me in writing verse.'

I fancy so too.

But young Rud must also have tried his hand at more serious work, for his headmaster, Cormell Price, recognising the boy's talent, encouraged his reading and appointed him editor of the school magazine, thereby giving him his baptism in printer's ink and a taste for journalism that was to remain with him all his life – as well as being indirectly responsible for his first employment after leaving school. For his parents having moved from Bombay to Lahore, following Lockwood's promotion to Curator of the Museum and Principal of the Mayo College of Art in that city, Lockwood was able to obtain a post for his son on the staff of one India's English-Language newspapers: the Lahore-based *Civil and Military Gazette*.

Rud, though old for his years, was still only sixteen when in 1886, after a sentimental farewell to his first love – a girl called Flo Garrard to whom he considered himself engaged – he set sail once more for India; this time to the old walled city of Lahore. There, despite his youth, he was flung in at the deep end of the newspaper business by his chief, Stephen Wheeler, who worked him hard and remorselessly from the start, and during the next few years the young Rudyard, technically an assistant editor, was by turns – and often simultaneously – editor, reporter, journalist, correspondent, compositor and printer. He learned early that a newspaper cannot go to press with blank patches in its columns, and he took to filling such gaps by writing verses and short stories exactly tailored to fit the available spaces.

These 'column-fillers' were to provide the material for his first two books to be published:* *Departmental Ditties*, a book of verse; and *Plain Tales from the Hills*, that collection of very short stories that made him instantly famous throughout India, though it would be some years before they became known to the British Public. The first appearance of 'Pagett, M.P.' was as a column-filler, one of the many that he signed with a pseudonym — in this case, 'An Englishman'.

There were a lot of Pagett M.P.s around in my day, too. They were among the major pests to infest the Raj and, as a newspaperman, Kipling met a great many of them and grew to detest the breed. Here are the first two verses:

Pagett, M.P., was a liar, and a fluent liar therewith,—
He spoke of the heat of India as "The Asian Solar Myth";
Came on a four months' visit, to "study the East" in November,
And I got him to make an agreement vowing to stay till September.

March came in with the *koil*.† Pagett was cool and gay,
Called me a "bloated Brahmin," talked of my "princely pay."
March went out with the roses. "Where is your heat?" said he.
"Coming," said I to Pagett. "Skittles!" said Pagett, M.P.

The next five verses describe the hot-weather horrors that can affect those whose work, like Rudyard's, keeps them tied to their desks in the plains throughout April, May, June and July. Pagett does not wait to see what August has up her sleeve:

We reached a hundred and twenty once in the Court at noon,
[I've mentioned Pagett was portly] Pagett went off in a swoon.
That was an end to the business. Pagett, the perjured, fled
With a practical, working knowledge of "Solar Myths" in his head.

And I laughed as I drove from the station, but the mirth died out on
     my lips
As I thought of the fools like Pagett who write of their "Eastern trips,"
And the sneers of the travelled idiots who duly misgovern the land,
And I prayed to the Lord to deliver another one into my hand.

---

*Discounting *Schoolboy Lyrics*, a selection of juvenile poetry collected by his parents, who, much to his annoyance, had them printed and bound by the Civil and Military Press.
†The Indian bell-bird, whose maddeningly monotonous hot-weather song led to its being nicknamed the 'brain-fever bird'.

The young author of these verses – that anonymous 'Englishman' – was presumably still in his teens. But his words struck a chord in the heart of every Anglo-Indian who had smarted under the lofty criticisms of visiting VIPs making their 'fact-finding' visits in the best months of the cold weather, and fleeing at the first warning breath of the heat.

It was in those Lahore days that Rudyard first came to know and to make friends with men of the British regiments stationed in the Cantonments of Mian Mir, not far from the city. In particular with the enlisted men, the ordinary rank and file of Victoria's volunteer army who served overseas. The more he saw of them and the hardships they endured so stoically, the more he came to admire them. He sang their praises and described their hardships and their tragedies in *Soldiers Three* and *Barrack-Room Ballads*, and any number of other stories and verses; and but for him we would know almost nothing about 'Tommy Atkins',* the volunteer private soldier who kept the Queen's peace in the outposts of her Empire for the sum of a shilling a day – and who frequently died there, either in action or from one of the many killer diseases endemic in India. There are few sadder ballads than his ' "Follow Me 'Ome'' ', the lament of a private soldier for a dead friend:

> There was no one like 'im, 'Orse or Foot,
>   Nor any o' the Guns I knew;
> An' because it was so, why, o' course 'e went an' died,
>   Which is just what the best men do.
>
> *So it's knock out your pipes an' follow me!*
> *An' it's finish up your swipes an' follow me!*
>   *Oh, 'ark to the big drum callin',*
>   *Follow me—follow me 'ome!*

It would be interesting to know what sort of writer Kipling would have become had he been born in England instead of India and spent his formative years in London or Yorkshire instead of Bombay and Lahore. Or if he would even have become a writer at all, for there is some evidence that he once considered taking up medicine as a career, with a view to becoming a doctor – a surgeon most likely, since he always took a great interest in complicated operations and on several occasions actually watched one being performed. Certainly without India he would

*Contemporary slang for a private soldier.

have been a totally different kind of writer. Its people, its climate, its sounds and scents and smells, and particularly its rhythms and viewpoints, helped produce the tales and verses that poured from his pen in those early years of fame. Without India there would have been no *Soldiers Three*, no 'Love Song of Har Dyal'. No *Plain Tales* or stories 'of mine own people', and no Mrs Hauksbee. No *Jungle Books* either. And, worst of all, no *Kim*.

The Raj can take credit for the success of the two earliest Kipling books, *Departmental Ditties* and *Plain Tales from the Hills*, and also for those early paperback editions of *Soldiers Three*, *Under the Deodars*, *The Phantom Rickshaw* and *Wee Willie Winkie*, which were sold for one rupee a copy on every railway bookstall in India and snapped up by the travelling 'Sahib-log' just as fast as the books could be printed. When, finally, the young Rudyard decided the time had come to try his luck in London, where despite his fame in India only a handful of people had ever heard of him and he was forced to endure an initial spell of hardship and penury, it was the publication of two of his India verses, 'The Ballad of East and West' and the spellbinding 'Danny Deever' – neither of which could have been written by someone unacquainted with the Raj – that were to make him famous. Even though he had signed both of them 'Youssef'.

The former, which tells a true story of India's North-West Frontier, has been responsible for its being labelled 'racist' by carping critics who have apparently never read beyond the first line, which ends 'and never the twain shall meet'. But on the day that 'Danny Deever' first appeared in print, a Professor Mason, well known as an authority on Milton, brought a copy of it into his classroom and, waving it at his students, shouted: 'Here's Literature! Here's Literature at last!' – an opinion that was endorsed by that greatly revered old Poet Laureate, Alfred, Lord Tennyson, who told a friend that 'young Kipling' was 'the only one of them to have the divine fire'.

'Divine fire' is probably as good a description as any of genius, a God-given gift bestowed on very few. Kipling called it his 'daemon', though it was plainly not something that he could command at will, for there were times when it would do no more than glance over his shoulder and others when it would absent itself altogether. But when it took hold of his hand the result was pure magic; the divine fire indeed:

My new-cut ashlar takes the light
Where crimson-blank the windows flare.
By my own work before the night,
Great Overseer, I make my prayer.

If there be good in that I wrought
Thy Hand compelled it, Master, Thine—
Where I have failed to meet Thy Thought
I know, through Thee, the blame was mine.*

To get the best out of Kipling's verses they should be read aloud. The cadence of each line and the sound of each word – and he chose his words with the greatest care – are part of their charm, like notes on a harp being played by a skilled musician. Some of them, like 'The Bell Buoy' seem to cry out to be declaimed, which is something I have done more than once. You need a windy autumn day on the Sussex Downs, when all the summer visitors have gone and you have the place to yourself. You are the voice of the bell buoy, comparing his work to that of his brother who hangs in the belfry of some ancient Sussex church a mile or so inland, and the warning cry of '*Shoal! 'Ware shoal!*' should be shouted at the top of your voice. It sounds wonderful. There are nine verses; here are two of them:

There was never a priest to pray,
    There was never a hand to toll,
When they made me guard of the bay,
    And moored me over the shoal.
    I rock, I reel, and I roll—
My four great hammers ply—
    Could I speak or be still at the Church's will?
(*Shoal! 'Ware shoal!*) Not I!

I dip and I surge and I swing
    In the rip of the racing tide,
By the gates of doom I sing,
    On the horns of death I ride.
    A ship-length overside,
Between the course and the sand,
    Fretted and bound I bide
    Peril whereof I cry.
Would I change with my brother a league inland?
(*Shoal! 'Ware shoal!*) Not I!

* ' "My New-Cut Ashlar" ' (L'Envoi to *Life's Handicap*).

Kipling had a great love of ships and the sea, and he made them the
subject of many of his stories and verses, one of the most famous being
'McAndrew's Hymn', the first line of which is a superb example of his
magical way with words. It sounds like a bar of music – 'Lord, Thou
has made this world below the shadow of a dream'. As the opening
line of a poem, or even as a poem by itself, that is hard to beat: and
if Kipling, as many claim, could not write poetry, what is this?—

> Then you drive out where the storm-clouds swallow,
> And the sound of your oar-blades, falling hollow,
> Is all we have left through the months to follow.*

Or try the enchanting 'Way Through the Woods' – if that is not poetry
I don't know what is. But then Kipling never claimed to write poetry.
He didn't even try and fail. There were certain things he wished to say,
'notions' that came into his head or were given to him by other people
(he said that all his best notions were given him by his father). These
he put down on paper in his own way; sometimes with the help of his
daemon, sometimes not. And sometimes just for fun. (The sheer variety
and originality of his verse is staggering, and one gets the impression
that he invented any number of new ways of constructing them, just
for the fun of it.) As for his gift of description, that alone is surely proof
that he possessed more than just a touch of 'divine fire'. Listen to these
lines on one of his favourite subjects, the sea:

> Who hath desired the Sea?—the sight of salt water unbounded—
> The heave and the halt and the hurl and the crash of the comber
>   wind-hounded?
> The sleek-barrelled swell before storm, grey, foamless, enormous, and
>   growing—
> Stark calm on the lap of the Line or the crazy-eyed hurricane
>   blowing—†

Then there is the plea of a Roman Centurion who, after a lifetime
of service in Britain, has been ordered back to his own country and
is asking to be allowed to stay on in the land that has become home
to him:

---

*'Harp Song of the Dane Women'.
†'The Sea and the Hills'.

> You'll take the old Aurelian Road through shore-descending pines
> Where, blue as any peacock's neck, the Tyrrhene Ocean shines.
> You'll go where laurel crowns are won, but—will you e'er forget
> The scent of hawthorn in the sun, or bracken in the wet?*

Yet this was a man whose sight, we are told, was so bad that even with the aid of powerful lenses he could read only something that was right under his nose! I find that hard to believe; the descriptions are too good.

Blank verse was not as popular in Kipling's day as it is know, but he could take it in his stride: though his ear for cadence was so acute that in 'Giffen's Debt' you could easily not notice that there are no rhymes. He could also make such a complicated verse-form as a sestina seem easy – as witness his delightful 'Sestina of the Tramp-Royal'. A number of his verses were intentionally modelled on the work of established nineteenth-century poets whom he had read and admired in his schooldays: Ruskin, Browning, Keats, Fitzgerald . . . Several of his long, narrative poems owe much to Browning, while 'The Exiles' Line' is Kipling taking off Fitzgerald's translation of Omar Khayyam's quatrains:

> Now the New Year reviving old desires,
> The restless soul to open sea aspires,
> Where the Blue Peter flickers from the fore,
> And the grimed stoker feeds the engine-fires.

Some of his verse, like Fitzgerald's version of the *Rubáiyát*, was based on translations from the work of Eastern poets. He credits 'The Prayer' to Kabir, and in a short story, 'Beyond the Pale', makes one of his characters, an Englishman named Trejago, quote a verse of a Pathan love song to an unseen girl behind a lattice – who caps it by quoting the fifth verse of the same song. Kipling then gives his own version of the song; taking it up at the point where the heroine of 'The Love Song of Har Dyal' calls upon her lover to return:

> Alone upon the housetops to the North
> I turn and watch the lightnings in the sky—
> The glamour of thy footsteps in the North.
> *Come back to me, Beloved, or I die.*

*'The Roman Centurion's Song' (*A History of England*, 1911).

There are two more verses, and I have never been able to discover who is supposed to have written the original song; or if Kipling invented those verses — which were presumably in Pushtu if the girl in the song is a Pathan.* Yet if that is not a translation, but an invention of Kipling's in the style of a vernacular song, it is a superb imitation. But then so is 'Gertrude's Prayer',† a poem which he wrote in the style of Chaucer, and which, in the story that went with it,‡ was supposed to have been a fake that fooled an acknowledged authority on Chaucer into thinking it was genuine. It makes one wonder which he thought of first — the story or the verse? On the evidence of 'Gertrude's Prayer' and 'The Runes on Weland's Sword',§ I imagine that as often as not it was the verse that first spoke itself in his head, and that he then worked out a story to fit it.

Kipling also wrote a good deal of political verse which, although bitingly topical when he wrote it, has become sadly out of date. Only 'Gehazi', a scathing attack on Lord Reading, who was implicated in the now forgotten Marconi Scandal, may survive as an excellent example of the savage political lampoon.

Poor Rudyard, who so loved and was loved by children, not only lost his adored first-born, Josephine, but was also to lose his only son, seventeen-year-old John, killed at the Battle of Loos in the First World War: a war with Germany that Kipling had foreseen and that in verses such as 'The Dykes' had warned his countrymen, again and again, that unless they stopped considering themselves invulnerable and neglecting their defences, they could well be overwhelmed.

> These are the dykes our fathers left, but we would not look to the same.
> Time and again were we warned of the dykes, time and again we delayed:
> Now, it may fall, we have slain our sons, as our fathers we have betrayed.

But the Islanders did not care to listen. Their Empire looked set to last for another century or two and they disliked being urged to look to

---

*Pathans are Muslims, but Har Dyal is not a Muslim name. Kipling did not usually make mistakes like that.
†*Plain Tales from the Hills.*
‡Dayspring Mishandled, *Limits and Renewals.*
§*Puck of Pook's Hill.*

their defences and being described as 'flannelled fools at the wicket' and 'muddied oafs in the goals' because they preferred playing games to building ships or enlisting in the armed forces.

Kipling's lament for his son, 'The Children',* must have been agony to write, for he makes no attempt to shroud the terrible reality of that death. Here are two of its verses, the first and the last:

> These were our children who died for our lands: they were dear in our sight.
> We have only the memory left of their home-treasured sayings and laughter.
> The price of our loss shall be paid to our hands, not another's hereafter.
> Neither the Alien nor Priest shall decide on it. That is our right.
> *But who shall return us the children?*
>
> That flesh we had nursed from the first in all cleanness was given
> To corruption unveiled and assailed by the malice of Heaven—
> By the heart-shaking jests of Decay where it lolled on the wires—
> To be blanched or gay-painted by fumes—to be cindered by fires—
> To be senselessly tossed and retossed in stale mutilation
> From crater to crater. For this we shall take expiation.
> *But who shall return us the children?*

No. Kipling was certainly not a warmonger. Nor was the dream that he followed all his life a dream of Empire – that was something he outlived; and even during his most pro-Empire period he spent far more time lambasting its failings than blowing its trumpet. It is, in fact, worth noting how many times he has given the other side's point of view rather than the accepted British one. As in 'Hadramauti', in which a desert Arab voices his dislike of the white man and all his ways:

> He invites the derision of strangers—he enters all places.
> Booted, bareheaded he enters. With shouts and embraces
> He asks of us news of the household whom *we* reckon nameless.
> Certainly Allah created him forty-fold shameless!

There are many other examples of this attitude; 'We and They' for one. And his surprising choice of one of the most humiliating episodes in English history, 'The Dutch in the Medway', which, wearing his

---

*'The Honours of War', *A Diversity of Creatures*, 1917.

historian's hat, he uses to summarise the period between 1664–72 when England was at war with Holland. No one but Rudyard would even have thought of doing that. But then he never hesitated to rub his country's nose in the mud when he felt she needed it, and he frequently used his verse to criticise bureaucrats, red tape and inefficiency in high places.

Kipling's only remaining child, Elsie Bambridge, died childless in 1976, so there were no grandchildren to carry on whatever ingredient in his make-up was responsible for his undoubted genius. Who did it come from? And did he really possess the Second Sight – that goblin-gift that is said to come through a strain of Celtic blood? It would seem so, for his predictions of the First World War were uncannily accurate; as too his tremendous hymn, 'Recessional', which foretold the dissolution of the Empire:

> Far-called, our navies melt away;
>   On dune and headland sinks the fire:
> Lo, all our pomp of yesterday
>   Is one with Nineveh and Tyre!

In the last decade of his life the Sight returned to trouble him again. While the bulk of his countrymen persisted in regarding Hitler and Mussolini as a faintly comic duo, and took to saying that at least you had to give those two credit for one thing – 'they have made their trains run on time, which is more than you can say for ours!' – Rudyard Kipling sat down once more to warn the Islanders, in one of the last verses he would ever write. And once again, for the last time, his daemon returned to him, and together they wrote 'The Storm Cone':

> This is the midnight—let no star
> Delude us—dawn is very far.
> This is the tempest long foretold—
> Slow to make head but sure to hold.
>
> Stand by! The lull 'twixt blast and blast
> Signals the storm is near, not past;
> And worse than present jeopardy
> May our forlorn to-morrow be.

He couldn't put it clearer than that, could he? But, as usual no one was prepared to listen; it was only the old warmonger again, up to his same tricks and trying to frighten people with a sheet and a turnip-lantern. There couldn't *possibly* be another war.

Luckily for him, he did not live to see it. Or the end of Empire and the 'savage wars of peace' either.

> 'How far from St. Helena to the Gate of Heaven's Grace?'
> That no one knows—that no one knows—and no one ever will.
> But fold your hands across your heart and cover up your face,
> And after all your trapesings, child, lie still!*

M.M. Kaye
April 1990

Prelude

(To "Departmental Ditties")

1885

I have eaten your bread and salt.
  I have drunk your water and wine.
The deaths ye died I have watched beside,
  And the lives ye led were mine.

Was there aught I did not share
  In vigil or toil or ease,—
One joy or woe that I did not know,
  Dear hearts across the seas?

I have written the tale of our life
  For a sheltered people's mirth,
In jesting guise—but ye are wise,
  And ye know what the jest is worth.

A General Summary

We are very slightly changed
From the semi-apes who ranged
   India's prehistoric clay;
He that drew the longest bow
Ran his brother down, you know,
   As we run men down to-day.

"Dowb," the first of all his race,
Met the Mammoth face to face
   On the lake or in the cave:
Stole the steadiest canoe,
Ate the quarry others slew,
   Died—and took the finest grave.

When they scratched the reindeer-bone,
Some one made the sketch his own,
   Filched it from the artist—then,
Even in those early days,
Won a simple Viceroy's praise
   Through the toil of other men.
Ere they hewed the Sphinx's visage
Favouritism governed kissage,
   Even as it does this age.

Who shall doubt "the secret hid
Under Cheops' pyramid"
   Was that the contractor did
   Cheops out of several millions?
Or that Joseph's sudden rise
To Comptroller of Supplies
Was a fraud of monstrous size
   On King Pharaoh's swart Civilians?

Thus, the artless songs I sing
Do not deal with anything
   New or never said before.
As it was in the beginning
Is to-day official sinning,
   And shall be for evermore.

Army Headquarters

Old is the song that I sing—
Old as my unpaid bills—
Old as the chicken that khitmutgars[1] *bring*
Men at dâk-bungalows old as the Hills.

Ahasuerus Jenkins of the "Operatic Own"
Was dowered with a tenor voice of *super*-Santley tone.
His views on equitation were, perhaps, a trifle queer.
He had no seat worth mentioning, but oh! he had an ear.

He clubbed his wretched company a dozen times a day;
He used to quit his charger in a parabolic way;
His method of saluting was the joy of all beholders;
But Ahasuerus Jenkins had a head upon his shoulders.

He took two months at Simla when the year was at the spring,
And underneath the deodars eternally did sing.
He warbled like a *bul-bul*[2] but particularly at
Cornelia Agrippina, who was musical and fat.

She controlled a humble husband, who, in turn, controlled a Dept.
Where Cornelia Agrippina's human singing-birds were kept
From April to October on a plump retaining-fee,
Supplied, of course, *per mensem*, by the Indian Treasury.

Cornelia used to sing with him, and Jenkins used to play;
He praised unblushingly her notes, for he was false as they;
So when the winds of April turned the budding roses brown,
Cornelia told her husband:—"Tom, you mustn't send him down."

They haled him from his regiment, which didn't much regret him;
They found for him an office-stool, and on that stool they set him
To play with maps and catalogues three idle hours a day,
And draw his plump retaining-fee—which means his double pay.

Now, ever after dinner, when the coffee-cups are brought,
Ahasuerus waileth o'er the grand pianoforte;
And, thanks to fair Cornelia, his fame hath waxen great,
And Ahasuerus Jenkins is a Power in the State!

[1]Waiters.   [2]Nightingale.

Study of an Elevation, in Indian Ink

This ditty is a string of lies.
But—how the deuce did Gubbins rise?

Potiphar Gubbins, C.E.,
  Stands at the top of the tree;
And I muse in my bed on the reasons that led
  To the hoisting of Potiphar G.

Potiphar Gubbins, C.E.,
  Is seven years junior to Me;
Each bridge that he makes either buckles or breaks,
  And his work is as rough as he.

Potiphar Gubbins, C.E.,
  Is coarse as a chimpanzee;
And I can't understand why you gave him your hand,
  Lovely Mehitabel Lee.

Potiphar Gubbins, C.E.,
  Is dear to the Powers that Be;
For They bow and They smile in an affable style,
  Which is seldom accorded to Me.

Potiphar Gubbins, C.E.,
  Is certain as certain can be
Of a highly paid post which is claimed by a host
  Of seniors—including Me.

Careless and lazy is he,
  Greatly inferior to Me.
What is the spell that you manage so well,
  Commonplace Potiphar G.?

Lovely Mehitabel Lee,
  Let me inquire of thee,
Should I have riz to where Potiphar is,
  Hadst thou been mated to Me?

Delilah

We have another Viceroy now,— those days are dead and done
Of Delilah Aberyswith and depraved Ulysses Gunne.

Delilah Aberyswith was a lady—not too young—
With a perfect taste in dresses and a badly-bitted tongue,
With a thirst for information, and a greater thirst for praise,
And a little house in Simla in the Prehistoric Days.

By reason of her marriage to a gentleman in power,
Delilah was acquainted with the gossip of the hour;
And many little secrets, of the half-official kind,
Were whispered to Delilah, and she bore them all in mind.

She patronised extensively a man, Ulysses Gunne,
Whose mode of earning money was a low and shameful one.
He wrote for certain papers, which, as everybody knows,
Is worse than serving in a shop or scaring off the crows.

He praised her "queenly beauty" first; and, later on, he hinted
At the "vastness of her intellect" with compliment unstinted.
He went with her a-riding, and his love for her was such
That he lent her all his horses and—she galled them very much.

One day, THEY brewed a secret of a fine financial sort;
It related to Appointments, to a Man and a Report.
'Twas almost worth the keeping,—only seven people knew it—
And Gunne rose up to seek the truth and patiently ensue it.

It was a Viceroy's Secret, but—perhaps the wine was red—
Perhaps an Aged Councillor had lost his aged head—
Perhaps Delilah's eyes were bright—Delilah's whispers sweet—
The Aged Member told her what 'twere treason to repeat.

Ulysses went a-riding, and they talked of love and flowers;
Ulysses went a-calling, and he called for several hours;
Ulysses went a-waltzing, and Delilah helped him dance—
Ulysses let the waltzes go, and waited for a chance.

The summer sun was setting, and the summer air was still,
The couple went a-walking in the shade of Summer Hill.
The wasteful sunset faded out in turkis-green and gold,
Ulysses pleaded softly, and . . . that bad Delilah told!

Next morn, a startled Empire learnt the all-important news;
Next week, the Aged Councillor was shaking in his shoes.

Next month, I met Delilah and she did not show the least
Hesitation in affirming that Ulysses was a "beast."

We have another Viceroy now, those days are dead and done—
Off, Delilah Aberyswith and most mean Ulysses Gunne!

A Legend of the Foreign Office

This is the reason why Rustum Beg,
  Rajah of Kolazai,
Drinketh the "simpkin"[1] and brandy peg,
  Maketh the money to fly,
Vexeth a Government, tender and kind,
Also—but this is a detail—blind.

Rustum Beg of Kolazai—slightly backward Native State—
Lusted for a C.S.I.[2]—so began to sanitate.
Built a Gaol and Hospital—nearly built a City drain—
Till his faithful subjects all thought their ruler was insane.

Strange departures made he then—yea, Departments stranger still:
Half a dozen Englishmen helped the Rajah with a will,
Talked of noble aims and high, hinted at a future fine
For the State of Kolazai, on a strictly Western line.

Rajah Rustum held his peace; lowered octroi dues a half;
Organised a State Police; purified the Civil Staff;
Settled cess and tax afresh in a very liberal way;
Cut temptation of the flesh—also cut the Bukhshi's[3] pay:

Roused his Secretariat to a fine Mahratta fury,
By an Order hinting at supervision of *dasturi*;[4]
Turned the State of Kolazai very nearly upside-down;
When the end of May was nigh waited his achievement's crown.

Then the Birthday Honours came. Sad to state and sad to see,
Stood against the Rajah's name and nothing more than *C.I.E.!*[5] . . .'
Things were lively for a week in the state of Kolazai,
Even now the people speak of that time regretfully.

[1]Champagne.   [2]The Order of the Star of India.   [3]The Commander in Chief.
[4]Bribes.   [5]A Companionship of the ORder of the Indian Empire.

How he disendowed the Gaol—stopped at once the City drain;
Turned to beauty fair and frail—got his senses back again;
Doubled taxes, cesses, all; cleared away each new-built *thana*;[1]
Turned the two-lakh Hospital into a superb *Zenana*;

Heaped upon the Bukhshi Sahib wealth and honours manifold;
Clad himself in Eastern garb—squeezed his people as of old.
Happy, happy Kolazai! Never more will Rustum Beg
Play to catch his Viceroy's eye. He prefers the "simpkin" peg.

The Story of Uriah

"Now there were two men in one city; the one rich, and the other poor."

Jack Barrett went to Quetta
  Because they told him to.
He left his wife at Simla
  On three-fourths his monthly screw.
Jack Barrett died at Quetta
  Ere the next month's pay he drew.

Jack Barrett went to Quetta.
  He didn't understand
The reason of his transfer
  From the pleasant mountain-land.
The reason was September,
  And it killed him out of hand.

Jack Barrett went to Quetta
  And there gave up the ghost,
Attempting two men's duty
  In that very healthy post;
And Mrs. Barrett mourned for him
  Five lively months at most.

Jack Barrett's bones at Quetta
  Enjoying profound repose;
But I shouldn't be astonished
  If *now* his spirit knows
The reason for his transfer
  From the Himalayan snows.

[1]Police station.

And, when the Last Great Bugle Call
    Adown the Hurnai throbs,
And the last grim joke is entered
    In the big black Book of Jobs,
And Quetta graveyards give again
    Their victims to the air,
I shouldn't like to be the man
    Who sent Jack Barrett there.

The Post that Fitted

Though tangled and twisted the course of true love,
    This ditty explains,
No tangle's so tangled it cannot improve
    If the Lover has brains.

Ere the steamer bore him Eastward, Sleary was engaged to marry
An attractive girl at Tunbridge, who he called "my little Carrie."
Sleary's pay was very modest; Sleary was the other way.
Who can cook a two-plate dinner on eight rupees a day?

Long he pondered o'er the question in his scantly furnished quarters—
Then proposed to Minnie Boffkin, eldest of Judge Boffkin's daughters.
Certainly an impecunious Subaltern was not a catch,
But the Boffkins knew that Minnie mightn't make another match.

So they recognised the business and, to feed and clothe the bride,
Got him made a Something Something somewhere on the Bombay side.
Anyhow, the billet carried pay enough for him to marry—
As the artless Sleary put it:—"Just the thing for me and Carrie."

Did he, therefore, jilt Miss Boffkin—impulse of a baser mind?
No! He started epileptic fits of an appalling kind.
[Of his *modus operandi* only this much I could gather:—
"Pear's shaving sticks will give you little taste and lots of lather."]

Frequently in public places his affliction used to smite
Sleary with distressing vigour—always in the Boffkins' sight.
Ere a week was over Minnie weepingly returned his ring,
Told him his "unhappy weakness" stopped all thought of marrying.

Sleary bore the information with a chastened holy joy,—
Epileptic fits don't matter in Political employ,—
Wired three short words to Carrie—took his ticket, packed his kit—
Bade farewell to Minnie Boffkin in one last, long, lingering fit.

Four weeks later, Carrie Sleary read—and laughed until she wept—
Mrs. Boffkin's warning letter on the "wretched epilept." . . .
Year by year, in pious patience, vengeful Mrs. Boffkin sits
Waiting for the Sleary babies to develop Sleary's fits.

A Code of Morals

Lest you should think this story true
I merely mention I
Evolved it lately.   'Tis a most
Unmitigated misstatement.

Now Jones had left his new-wed bride to keep his house in order,
And hied away to the Hurrum Hills above the Afghan border,
To sit on a rock with a heliograph; but ere he left he taught
His wife the working of the Code that sets the miles at naught.

And Love had made him very sage, as Nature made her fair;
So Cupid and Apollo linked, *per* heliograph, the pair.
At dawn across the Hurrum Hills, he flashed her counsel wise—
At e'en, the dying sunset bore her husband's homilies.

He warned her 'gainst seductive youths in scarlet clad and gold,
As much as 'gainst the blandishments paternal of the old;
But kept his gravest warnings for (hereby the ditty hangs)
That snowy-haired Lothario, Lieutenant-General Bangs.

'Twas General Bangs, with Aide and Staff, who tittupped on the way,
When they beheld a heliograph tempestuously at play.
They thought of Border risings, and of stations sacked and burnt—
So stopped to take the message down—and this is what they learnt—

"Dash dot dot, dot, dot dash, dot dash dot" twice.   The General swore.
"Was ever General Officer addressed as 'dear' before?
" 'My Love,' i' faith! 'My Duck,' Gadzooks! 'My darling popsy-wop!'
"Spirit of great Lord Wolseley, *who* is on the mountain top?"

The artless Aide-de-camp was mute, the gilded Staff were still,
As, dumb with pent-up mirth, they booked that message from the hill;
For clear as summer lightning-flare, the husband's warning ran:—
"Don't dance or ride with General Bangs—a most immoral man."

[At dawn, across the Hurrum Hills, he flashed her counsel wise—
But, howsoever Love be blind, the world at large hath eyes.]
With damnatory dot and dash he heliographed his wife
Some interesting details of the General's private life.

The artless Aide-de-camp was mute, the shining Staff were still,
And red and ever redder grew the General's shaven gill.
And this is what he said at last (his feelings matter not):—
"I think we've tapped a private line. Hi! Threes about there! Trot!"

All honour unto Bangs, for ne'er did Jones thereafter know
By word or act official who read off that helio.
But the tale is on the Frontier, and from Michni to Mool*tan*
They know the worthy General as "that most immoral man."

Public Waste

Walpole talks of "a man and his price."
   List to a ditty queer—
The sale of a Deputy-Acting-Vice-
   Resident-Engineer,
Bought like a bullock, hoof and hide,
By the Little Tin Gods on the Mountain Side.

By the Laws of the Family Circle 'tis written in letters of brass
That only a Colonel from Chatham can manage the Railways of State,
Because of the gold on his breeks, and the subjects wherein he must pass;
Because in all matters that deal with Railways his knowledge is great.

Now Exeter Battleby Tring had laboured from boyhood to eld
On the Lines of the East and the West, and eke of the North and South;
Many Lines had he built and surveyed—important the posts which he held;
And the Lords of the Iron Horse were dumb when he opened his mouth.

Black as the raven his garb, and his heresies jettier still—
Hinting that Railways required lifetimes of study and knowledge—
Never clanked sword by his side—Vauban he knew not nor drill—
Nor was his name on the list of the men who had passed through the "College."

Wherefore the Little Tin Gods harried their little tin souls,
Seeing he came not from Chatham, jingled no spurs at his heels,
Knowing that, nevertheless, was he first on the Government rolls
For the billet of "Railway Instructor to Little Tin Gods on Wheels."

Letters not seldom they wrote him, "having the honour to state,"
It would be better for all men if he were laid on the shelf.
Much would accrue to his bank-book, and he consented to wait
Until the Little Tin Gods built him a berth for himself,

"Special, well paid, and exempt from the Law of the Fifty and Five,
Even to Ninety and Nine"—these were the terms of the pact:
Thus did the Little Tin Gods (long may Their Highnesses thrive!)
Silence his mouth with rupees, keeping their Circle intact;

Appointing a Colonel from Chatham who managed the Bhamo State Line
(The which was one mile and one furlong—a guaranteed twenty-inch gauge),
So Exeter Battleby Tring consented his claims to resign,
And died, on four thousand a month, in the ninetieth year of his age!

What Happened

Hurree Chunder Mookerjee, pride of Bow Bazar,
Owner of a native press, "Barrishter-at-Lar,"
Waited on the Government with a claim to wear
Sabres by the bucketful, rifles by the pair.

Then the Indian Government winked a wicked wink,
Said to Chunder Mookerjee: 'Stick to pen and ink.
They are safer implements, but, if you insist,
We will let you carry arms wheresoe'er you list."

Hurree Chunder Mookerjee sought the gunsmith and
Bought the tubes of Lancaster, Ballard, Dean, and Bland,
Bought a shiny bowie-knife, bought a town-made sword,
Jingled like a carriage-horse when he went abroad.

But the Indian Government, always keen to please,
Also gave permission to horrid men like these—
Yar Mahommed Yusufzai, down to kill or steal,
Chimbu Singh from Bikaneer, Tantia the Bhil;

Killar Khan the Marri chief, Jowar Singh the Sikh,
Nubbee Baksh Punjabi Jat, Abdul Huq Rafiq—
He was a Wahabi; last, little Boh Hla-oo
Took advantage of the Act—took a Snider too.

They were unenlightened men, Ballard knew them not.
They procured their swords and guns chiefly on the spot;
And the lore of centuries, plus a hundred fights,
Made them slow to disregard one another's rights.

With a unanimity dear to patriot hearts
All those hairy gentlemen out of foreign parts
Said: "The good old days are back—let us go to war!"
Swaggered down the Grand Trunk Road into Bow Bazar.

Nubbee Baksh Punjabi Jat found a hide-bound flail;
Chimbu Singh from Bikaneer oiled his Tonk jezail[1];

[1]Native gun.

Yar Mahommed Yusufzai spat and grinned with glee
As he ground the butcher-knife of the Khyberee.

Jowar Singh the Sikh procured sabre, quoit, and mace,
Abdul Huq, Wahabi, jerked his dagger from its place,
While amid the jungle-grass danced and grinned and jabbered
Little Boh Hla-oo and cleared his dah-blade from the scabbard.

What became of Mookerjee?   Soothly, who can say?
Yar Mahommed only grins in a nasty way,
Jowar Singh is reticent, Chimbu Singh is mute,
But the belts of all of them simply bulge with loot.

What became of Ballard's guns?   Afghans black and grubby
Sell them for their silver weight to the men of Pubbi;
And the shiny bowie-knife and the town-made sword are
Hanging in a Marri camp just across the Border.

What became of Mookerjee? Ask Mahommed Yar
Prodding Siva's sacred bull down the Bow Bazar,
Speak to placid Nubbee Baksh—question land and sea—
Ask the Indian Congressmen—only don't ask me!

The Man Who Could Write

Shun—shun the Bowl! That fatal, facile drink
  Has raised many geese who dipped their quills in 't;
Bribe, murder, marry, but steer clear of Ink
  Save when you write receipts for paid-up bills in 't.
There may be silver in the "blue-black"—all
I know of is the iron and the gall.

Boanerges Blitzen, servant of the Queen,
Is a dismal failure— is a Might-have-been.
In a luckless moment he discovered men
Rise to high position through a ready pen.

Boanerges Blitzen argued therefore—"I
With the selfsame weapon, can attain as high."
Only he did not possess when he made the trial,
Wicked wit of Colvin, irony of Lyall.

[Men who spar with Government need, to back their blows,
Something more than ordinary journalistic prose.]

Never young Civilian's prospects were so bright,
Till an Indian paper found that he could write:
Never young Civilian's prospects were so dark,
When the wretched Blitzen wrote to make his mark.

Certainly he scored it, bold, and black, and firm,
In that Indian paper— made his seniors squirm,
Quoted office scandals, wrote the tactless truth—
Was there ever known a more misguided youth?

When the Rag he wrote for praised his plucky game,
Boanerges Blitzen felt that this was Fame;
When the men he wrote of shook their heads and swore,
Boanerges Blitzen only wrote the more:

Posed as Young Ithuriel, resolute and grim,
Till he found promotion didn't come to him;
Till he found that reprimands weekly were his lot,
And his many Districts curiously hot.

Till he found his furlough strangely hard to win,
Boanerges Blitzen didn't care a pin:
Then it seemed to dawn on him something wasn't right—
Boanerges Blitzen put it down to "spite";

Languished in a District desolate and dry;
Watched the Local Government yearly pass him by;
Wondered where the hitch was; called it most unfair.

That was seven years ago—and he still is there!

Pink Dominoes

"They are fools who kiss and tell"—
Wisely has the poet sung.
Man may hold all sorts of posts
If he'll only hold his tongue.

Jenny and Me were engaged, you see,
　　On the eve of the Fancy Ball;
So a kiss or two was nothing to you
　　Or any one else at all.

Jenny would go in a domino—
　　Pretty and pink but warm;
While I attended, clad in a splendid
　　Austrian uniform.

Now we had arranged, through notes exchanged
    Early that afternoon,
At Number Four to waltz no more,
    But to sit in the dusk and spoon.

I wish you to see that Jenny and Me
    Had barely exchanged our troth;
So a kiss or two was strictly due
    By, from, and between us both.

When Three was over, an eager lover,
    I fled to the gloom outside;
And a Domino came out also
    Whom I took for my future bride.

That is to say, in a casual way,
    I slipped my arm around her;
With a kiss or two (which is nothing to you),
    And ready to kiss I found her.

She turned he head and the name she said
    Was certainly not my own;
But ere I could speak, with a smothered shriek
    She fled and left me alone.

Then Jenny came, and I saw with shame
    She'd doffed her domino;
And I had embraced an alien waist—
    But I did not tell her so.

Next morn I knew that there were two
    Dominoes pink, and one
Had cloaked the spouse of Sir Julian Vouse,
    Our big Political gun.

Sir J. was old, and her hair was gold,
    And her eye was a blue cerulean;
And the name she said when she turned her head
    Was not in the least like "Julian."

Now wasn't that nice, when want of *pice*
    Forbade us twain to marry,
That old Sir J., in the kindest way,
    Made me his Secre*tarry*?

Municipal

"Why is my District death-rate low?"
Said Binks of Hezabad.
"Well, drains and sewage-outfalls are
"My own peculiar fad.
"I learnt a lesson once. It ran
"Thus," quoth that most veracious man:—

It was an August evening and, in snowy garments clad,
I paid a round of visits in the lines of Hezabad;
When, presently, my Waler saw, and did not like at all,
A commissariat elephant careering down the Mall.

I couldn't see the driver, and across my mind it rushed
That the Commissariat elephant had suddenly gone *musth*.[1]
I didn't care to meet him, and I couldn't well get down,
So I let the Waler have it, and we headed for the town.

The buggy was a new one and, praise Dykes, it stood the strain,
Till the Waler jumped a bullock just above the City Drain;
And the next that I remember was a hurricane of squeals,
And the creature making toothpicks of my five-foot patent wheels.

He seemed to want the owner, so I fled, distraught with fear,
To the Main Drain sewage-outfall while he snorted in my ear
Reached the four-foot drain-head safely and, in darkness and despair,
Felt the brute's proboscis fingering my terror-stiffened hair.

Heard it trumpet on my shoulder—tried to crawl a little higher—
Found the Main Drain sewage-outfall blocked, some eight feet up, with
    mire;
And, for twenty reeking minutes, Sir, my very marrow froze,
While the trunk was feeling blindly for a purchase on my toes!

It missed me by a fraction, but my hair was turning grey
Before they called the drivers up and begged the brute away.
Then I sought the City Elders, and my words were very plain.
They flushed that four-foot drain-head and—it never choked again!

You may hold with surface-drainage, and the sun-for-garbage cure,
Till you've been a periwinkle shrinking coyly up a sewer.
I believe in well-flushed culverts. . . .
    This is why the death-rate's small;
And if you don't believe me, get *shikarred*[2] yourself.   That's all.

[1]Mad.   [2]Hunted.

The Last Department

Twelve hundred million men are spread
About this Earth, and I and You
Wonder, when You and I are dead,
"What will those luckless millions do?"

"None whole or clean," we cry, "or free from stain
Of favour."   Wait awhile, till we attain
The Last Department where nor fraud nor fools,
Nor grade nor greed, shall trouble us again.

Fear, Favour, or Affection—what are these
To the grim Head who claims our services?
   I never knew a wife or interest yet
Delay that *pukka* step, miscalled "decease";

When leave, long overdue, none can deny;
When idleness of all Eternity
   Becomes our furlough, and the marigold
Our thriftless, bullion-minting Treasury

Transferred to the Eternal Settlement,
Each in his strait, wood-scanted office pent,
   No longer Brown reverses Smith's appeals,
Or Jones records his Minute of Dissent.

And One, long since a pillar of the Court,
As mud between the beams thereof is wrought;
   And One who wrote on phosphates for the crops
Is subject-matter of his own Report.

These be the glorious ends whereto we pass—
Let Him who Is, go call on Him who Was;
   And He shall see the *mallie*[1] steals the slab
For curry-grinder, and for goats the grass.

A breath of wind, a Border bullet's flight,
A draught of water, or a horse's fright—
   The droning of the fat *Sheristadar*[2]
Ceases, the punkah stops and falls the night

For you or Me.   Do those who live decline
The step that offers, or their work resign?
   Trust me, To-day's Most Indispensables,
Five hundred men can take your place or mine.

[1] The cemetery gardener.   [2] Clerk of the Court.

My Rival

I go to concert, party, ball—
   What profit is in these?
I sit alone against the wall
   And strive to look at ease.
The incense that is mine by right
   They burn before Her shrine;
And that's because I'm seventeen
   And she is forty-nine.

I cannot check my girlish blush,
   My colour comes and goes.
I redden to my finger-tips,
   And sometimes to my nose.
But she is white where white should be,
   And red where red should shine.
The blush that flies at seventeen
   Is fixed at forty-nine.

I wish *I* had her constant cheek:
   I wish that I could sing
All sorts of funny little songs,
   Not quite the proper thing.
I'm very *gauche* and very shy,
   Her jokes aren't in my line;
And, worst of all, I'm seventeen
   While She is forty-nine.

The young men come, the young men go,
   Each pink and white and neat,
She's older that their mothers, but
   They grovel at Her feet.
They walk beside Her *rickshaw*-wheels—
   None ever walk by mine;
Ant that's because I'm seventeen
   And she is forty-nine.

She rides with half a dozen men
   (She calls them "boys" and "mashes"),
I trot along the Mall alone;
   My prettiest frocks and sashes
Don't help to fill my programme-card,
   And vainly I repine
From ten to two A.M. Ah me!
   Would I were forty-nine.

She calls me "darling," "pet," and "dear,"
   And "sweet retiring maid."
I'm always at the back, I know—
   She puts me in the shade.
She introduces me to men—
   "Cast" lovers, I opine;
For sixty takes to seventeen,
   Nineteen to forty-nine.

But even She must older grow
   And end Her dancing days,
She can't go on for ever so
   At concerts, balls, and plays.
One ray of priceless hope I see
   Before my footsteps shine;
Just think, that She'll be eighty-one
   When I an forty-nine!

To the Unknown Goddess

Will you conquer my heart with your beauty, my soul going out from
   afar?
Shall I fall to your hand as a victim of crafty and cautious *shikar*?

Have I met you and passed you already, unknowing, unthinking, and
   blind?
Shall I meet you next season at Simla, O sweetest and best of your kind?

Does the P. & O. bear you to meward, or, clad in short frocks of the
   West,
Are you growing the charms that shall capture and torture the heart in
   my breast?

Will you stay in the Plains till September— my passion as warm as the
   day?
Will you bring me to book on the Mountains, or where the
   thermantidotes play?

When the light of your eyes shall make pallid the mean lesser lights I
   pursue,
And the charm of your presence shall lure me from love of the gay
   "thirteen-two";[1]

[1]Polo-pony.

When the "peg"[2] and the pigskin shall please not; when I buy me
  Calcutta-built clothes;
When I quit the Delight of Wild Asses, forswearing the swearing of oaths;

As a deer to the hand of the hunter when I turn 'mid the gibes of my
  friends;
When the days of my freedom are numbered, and the life of the bachelor
  ends.

Ah, Goddess! child, spinster, or widow—as of old on Mars Hill when they
  raised
To the God that they knew not an altar—so I, a young Pagan, have
  praised

The Goddess I know not nor worship; yet, if half that men tell me be
  true,
You will come in the future, and therefore these verses are written to you.

The Rupaiyat of Omar Kal'vin

[Allowing for the difference 'twixt prose and rhymed exaggeration, this ought
to reproduce the sense of what Sir Auckland (Colvin) told the nation some time
ago, when the Government struck from our income two per cent.]

> Now the New Year reviving last Year's Debt,
> The Thoughtful Fisher casteth wide his Net;
>   So I with begging Dish and ready Tongue
> Assail all Men for all that I can get.
>
> Imports indeed are gone with all their Dues—
> Lo! Salt a Lever that I dare not use,
>   Nor may I ask the Tillers in Bengal—
> Surely my Kith and Kin will not refuse
>
> Pay—and I promise by the Dust of Spring,
> Retrenchment. If my promises can bring
>   Comfort, Ye have Them now a thousand-fold—
> By Allah! I will promise *Anything*!
>
> Indeed, indeed, Retrenchment oft before
> I swore—but did I mean it when I swore?
>   And then, and then, We wandered to the Hills,
> And so the Little Less became Much More.

[2]Whisky and Soda.

Whether at Boileaugunge or Babylon,
I know not how the wretched Thing is done,
  The Items of Receipt grow surely small;
The Items of Expense mount one by one.

I cannot help it.   What have I to do
With One and Five, or Four, or Three, or Two?
  Let Scribes spit Blood and Sulphur as they please,
Or Statesmen call me foolish—Heed not you.

Behold, I promise—Anything You will.
Behold, I greet you with an empty Till—
  Ah! Fellow-Sinners, of your Charity
Seek not the Reason of the Dearth but fill.

For if I sinned and fell, where lies the Gain
Of Knowledge? Would it ease you of your Pain
  To know the tangled Threads of Revenue,
I ravel deeper in a hopeless Skein?

"Who hath no Prudence"—what was it I said,
Of Her who paints Her Eyes and tires Her Head,
  And jibes and mocks the People in the Street,
And fawns upon them for Her thriftless Bread?

Accursèd is She of Eve's daughters—She
Hath cast off Prudence, and Her End shall be
  Destruction. . . . Brethren, of your Bounty grant
Some portion of your daily Bread to *Me*!

Pagett, M.P.

*The toad beneath the harrow knows
Exactly where each tooth-point goes;
The butterfly upon the road
Preaches contentment to that toad.*

Pagett, M.P., was a liar, and a fluent liar therewith,—
He spoke of the heat of India as "The Asian Solar Myth";
Came on a four months' visit, to "study the East" in November,
And I got him to make an agreement vowing to stay till September.

March came in with the *koil*.[1] Pagett was cool and gay,
Called me a "bloated Brahmin," talked of my "princely pay."
March went out with the roses.   "Where is your heat?" said he.
"Coming," said I to Pagett.   "Skittles!" said Pagett, M.P.

[1] The Indian bell-bird.

April began with the punkah, coolies, and prickly-heat,—
Pagett was dear to mosquitoes, sandflies found him a treat.
He grew speckled and lumpy—hammered, I grieve to say,
Aryan brothers who fanned him, in an illiberal way.

May set in with a dust-storm,—Pagett went down with the sun.
All the delights of the season tickled him one by one.
Imprimis—ten days' "liver"—due to his drinking beer;
Later, a dose of fever—slight, but he called it severe.

—Dysent'ry touched him in June, after the *Chota Bursat*[1]—
Lowered his portly person—made him yearn to depart.
He didn't call me a "Brahmin," or "bloated," or "overpaid,"
But seemed to think it a wonder that any one ever stayed.

July was a trifle unhealthy,—Pagett was ill with fear,
Called it the "Cholera Morbus," hinted that life was dear.
He babbled of "Eastern exile," and mentioned his home with tears;
But I hadn't seen *my* children for close upon seven years.

We reached a hundred and twenty once in the Court at noon,
[I've mentioned Pagett was portly] Pagett went off in a swoon.
That was an end to the business.   Pagett, the perjured, fled
With a practical, working knowledge of "Solar Myths" in his head.

And I laughed as I drove from the station, but the mirth died out on my
   lips
As I thought of the fools like Pagett who write of their "Eastern trips,"
And the sneers of the travelled idiots who duly misgovern the land,
And I prayed to the lord to deliver another one into my hand.

La Nuit Blanche

A much-discerning Public hold
   The Singer generally sings
   Of personal and private things,
And prints and sells his past for gold.

Whatever I may here disclaim,
   The very clever folk I sing to
   Will most indubitably cling to
Their pet delusion, just the same.

I had seen, as dawn was breaking
   And I staggered to my rest,
Tara Devi softly shaking
   From the Cart Road to the crest.

[1]The early rains.

I had seen the spurs of Jakko
    Heave and quiver, swell and sink.
    Was it Earthquake or tobacco,
    Day of Doom or Night of Drink?

In the full, fresh fragrant morning
    I observed a camel crawl,
Laws of gravitation scorning,
    On the ceiling and the wall.
Then I watched a fender walking,
    And I heard grey leeches sing,
And a red-hot monkey talking
    Did not seem the proper thing.

Then a Creature, skinned and crimson,
    Ran about the floor and cried,
And they said I had the "jims" on,
    And they dosed me with bromide,
And they locked me in my bedroom—
    Me and one wee Blood-Red Mouse—
Though I said:—"To give my head room
    "You had best unroof the house."

But my words were all unheeded,
    Though I told the grave M.D.
That the treatment really needed
    Was a dip in open sea
That was lapping just below me,
    Smooth as silver, white as snow—
And it took three men to throw me
    When I found I could not go.

Half the night I watched the Heavens
    Fizz like '81 champagne—
Fly to sixes and to sevens,
    Wheel and thunder back again;
And when all was peace and order
    Save one planet nailed askew,
Much I wept because my warder
    Would not let me see it true.

After frenzied hours of waiting,
    When the Earth and Skies were dumb,
Pealed an awful voice dictating
    An interminable sum,
Changing to a tangled story—
    "What she said you said I said—"

Till the Moon arose in glory,
　　And I found her . . . in my head;

Then a Face came, blind and weeping,
　　And It couldn't wipe Its eyes,
And It muttered I was keeping
　　Back the moonlight from the skies;
So I patted It for pity,
　　But It whistled shrill with wrath,
And a huge, black Devil City
　　Poured its peoples on my path.

So I fled with steps uncertain
　　On a thousand-year-long race,
But the bellying of the curtain
　　Kept me always in once place,
While the tumult rose and maddened
　　To the roar of Earth on fire,
Ere it ebbed and sank and saddened
　　To a whisper tense as wire.

In intolerable stillness
　　Rose one little, little star,
And it chuckled at my illness,
　　And it rocked me from afar;
And its brethren came and eyed me,
　　Called the Universe to aid,
Till I lay, with naught to hide me,
　　'Neath the Scorn of All Things Made.

Dun and saffron, robed and splendid
　　Broke the solemn, pitying Day,
And I knew my pains were ended,
　　And I turned and tried to pray;
But my speech was shattered wholly,
　　And I wept as children weep,
Till the dawn-wind, softly, slowly,
　　Brought to burning eyelids sleep.

The Lover's Litany

Eyes of grey—a sodden quay,
Driving rain and falling tears,
As the steamer puts to sea
In a parting storm of cheers.

Sing, for Faith and Hope are high—
None so true as you and I—
Sing the Lovers' Litany:—
"Love like ours can never die!"

Eyes of black—a throbbing keel,
Milky foam to left and right;
Whispered converse near the wheel
In the brilliant tropic night.
    Cross that rules the southern Sky!
    Stars that sweep, and turn and fly
    Hear the Lovers' Litany:—
    "Love like ours can never die!

Eyes of brown—a dusty plain
Split and parched with heat of June.
Flying hoof and tightened rein,
Hearts that beat the ancient tune.
    Side by side the horses fly,
    Frame we now the old reply
    Of the Lovers' Litany:—
    "Love like ours can never die!"

Eyes of blue—the Simla Hills
Silvered with the moonlight hoar;
Pleading of the waltz that thrills,
Dies and echoes round Benmore.
    "Mabel," "Officers," "Good-bye,"
    Glamour, wine, and witchery—
    On my soul's sincerity,
    "Love like ours can never die!"

Maidens, of your charity,
Pity my most luckless state.
Four times Cupid's debtor I—
Bankrupt in quadruplicate.
    Yet, despite my evil case,
    An a maiden showed me grace,
    Four-and-forty times would I
    Sing the Lovers' Litany:—
    "Love like ours can never die!"

A Ballade of Burial

"Saint Praxed's ever was the Church for peace."

If down here I chance to die,
  Solemnly I beg you take
All that is left of "I"
  To the Hills for old sake's sake.
Pack me very thoroughly
  In the ice that used to slake
Pegs I drank when I was dry—
  This observe for old sake's sake.

To the railway station hie,
  There a single ticket take
For Umballa—goods-train—I
  Shall not mind delay or shake.
I shall rest contentedly
  Spite of clamour coolies make;
Thus in state and dignity
  Send me up for old sake's sake.

Next the sleepy Babu wake,
  Book a Kalka van "for four."
Few, I think, will care to make
  Journeys with me any more
As they used to do of yore.
  I shall need a "special brake"—
'Thing I never took before—
  Get me one for old sake's sake.

After that—arrangements make.
  No hotel will take me in,
And a bullock's back would break
  'Neath the teak and leaden skin.
Tonga-ropes are frail and thin,
  Or, did I a back-seat take,
In a tonga I might spin,—
  Do your best for old sake's sake.

After that—your work is done.
  Recollect a Padre must
Mourn the dear departed one—
  Throw the ashes and the dust.
Don't go down at once. I trust
  You will find excuse to "snake

Three days' casual on the bust,"[1]—
    Get your fun for old sake's sake.

I could never stand the Plains.
    Think of blazing June and May,
Think of those September rains
    Yearly till the Judgement Day!
I should never rest in peace,
    I should sweat and lie awake.
Rail me then, on my decease,
    To the Hills for old sake's sake!

The Overland Mail

(Foot-service to the Hills)

In the Name of the Empress of India, make way,
    O Lords of the Jungle, wherever you roam,
The woods are astir at the close of the day—
    We exiles are waiting for letters from Home.
Let the robber retreat—let the tiger turn tail—
In the name of the Empress, the Overland Mail!

With a jingle of bells as the dusk gathers in,
    He turns to the footpath that heads up the hill—
The bags on his back and a cloth round his chin,
    And, tucked in his waistband, the Post Office bill:—
"Despatched on this date, as received by the rail,
"*Per* runner, two bags of the Overland Mail."

Is the torrent in spate? He must ford it or swim.
    Has the rain wrecked the road? He must climb by the cliff.
Does the tempest cry halt? What are tempests to him?
    The service admits not a "but" or an "if."
While the breath's in his mouth, he must bear without fail,
In the Name of the Empress, the Overland Mail.

From aloe to rose-oak, from rose-oak to fir,
    From level to upland, from upland to crest,
From rice-field to rock-ridge, from rock-ridge to spur,
    Fly the soft-sandalled feet, strains the brawny, brown chest.
From rail to ravine—to the peak from the vale—
Up, up through the night goes the Overland Mail.

[1]Three days' leave.

There's a speck on the hillside, a dot on the road—
   A jingle of bells on the footpath below—
There's a scuffle above in the monkey's abode—
   The world is awake and the clouds are aglow.
For the great Sun himself must attend to the hail:—
"In the Name of the Empress, the Overland Mail!"

Divided Destinies

It was an artless *Bandar*[1] and he danced upon a pine,
And much I wondered how he lived, and where the beast might dine,
And many other things, till, o'er my morning smoke,
I slept the sleep of idleness and dreamt that *Bandar* spoke.

He said:—"O man of many clothes! Sad crawler on the Hills!
"Observe, I know not Ranken's shop, nor Ranken's monthly bills!
"I take no heed to trousers or the coats that you call dress;
"Nor am I plagued with little cards for little drinks at Mess.

"I steal the bunnia's grain at morn, at noon and eventide
"(For he is fat and I am spare), I roam the mountain-side.
"I follow no man's carriage, and no, never in my life
"Have I flirted at Peliti's with another *Bandar's* wife.

"O man of futile fopperies—unnecessary wraps;
"I own no ponies in the hills, I drive no tall-wheeled traps.
"I buy me not twelve-button gloves, 'short-sixes' eke, or rings,
"Nor do I waste at Hamilton's my wealth on 'pretty things.'

"I quarrel with my wife at home, we never fight abroad;
"But Mrs. B has grasped the fact I *am* her only lord.
"I never heard of fever—dumps nor debts depress my soul;
"And I pity and despise you!" Here he pouched my breakfast-roll.

His hide was very mangy and his face was very red,
And ever and anon he scratched with energy his head.
His manners were not always nice, but how my spirit cried
To be an artless *Bandar* loose upon the mountain-side!

So I answered:—"Gentle *Bandar*, an inscrutable Decree
"Makes thee a gleesome fleasome Thou, and me a wretched me.
"Go! Depart in peace, my brother, to thy home amid the pine;
"Yet forget not once a mortal wished to change his lot with thine."

[1]Monkey.

The Masque of Plenty

ARGUMENT.—*The Indian Government being minded to discover the economic condition of their land, sent a Committee to inquire into it; and saw that it was good.*

SCENE.—*The wooded heights of Simla.   The Incarnation of the Government of India in the raiment of the Angel of Plenty sings, to pianoforte accompaniment—*

> "How sweet is the shepherd's sweet life!
>   From the dawn to the even he strays—
> He shall follow his sheep all the day
>   And his tongue shall be fillèd with praise.
>   (*adagio dim.*) Fillèd with praise!"

> (*largendo con sp.*) Now this is the position,
>   Go make an inquisition
>   Into their real condition
>   As swiftly as ye may.
>   (*p*) Ay, paint our swarthy billions
>   The richest of vermillions
>   Ere two well-led cotillions
>   Have danced themselves away.

TURKISH PATROL, *as able and intelligent Investigators wind down the Himalayas:—*

What is the state of the Nation?   What is its occupation?
Hi! get along, get along, get along— lend us the information!
(*dim.*) Census the *byle* and the *yabu*[1]—capture a first-class Babu,
Set him to file Gazetteers—Gazetteers . . .
    (*ff*) What is the state of the Nation, etc. etc.

INTERLUDE, *from Nowhere in Particular, to stringed and Oriental instruments.*

Our cattle reel beneath the yoke they bear—
    The earth is iron and the skies are brass—
And faint with fervour of the flaming air
    The languid hours pass.

The well is dry beneath the village tree—
    The young wheat withers ere it reach a span,
And belts of blinding sand show cruelly
    Where once the river ran.

Pray, brothers, pray, but to no earthly King—
    Lift up your hands above the blighted grain,
Look westward—if they please, the Gods shall bring
    Their mercy with the rain.

[1] The ox and the pony.

Look westward—bears the blue no brown cloud-bank?
   Nay, it is written—wherefore should we fly?
On our own field and by our cattle's flank
   Lie down, lie down to die!

SEMI-CHORUS

   By the plumèd heads of Kings
     Waving high,
   Where the tall corn springs
     O'er the dead.
   If they rust or rot we die,
   If they ripen we are fed.
   Very mighty is the power of our Kings!

Triumphal return to Simla of the Investigators, attired after the manner of Dionysus, leading a pet tiger-cub in wreaths of rhubarb-leaves, symbolical of India under medical treatment. They sing:—

We have seen, we have written—behold it, the proof of our manifold toil!
In their hosts they assembled and told it—the tale of the Sons of the Soil.
We have said of the Sickness—"Where is it?"—and of Death—"It is far
   from our ken,"—
We have paid a particular visit to the affluent children of men.
We have trodden the mart and the well-curb—we have stooped to the
   bield and the byre;
And the King may the forces of Hell curb, for the People have all they
   desire!

Castanets and step-dance:—

   Oh, the *dom*[1] and the *mag* and the *thakur* and the *thag*,
     And the *nat* and the *brinjaree*,
   And the *bunnia* and the *ryot* are as happy and as quiet
     And as plump as they can be!
   Yes, the *jain* and the *jat* in his stucco-fronted hut,
     And the bounding *bazugar*,
   By the favour of the King, are as fat as anything,
     They are—they are—they are!

RECITATIVE, *Government of India, with white satin wings and electro-plated harp:—*

How beautiful upon the Mountains—in peace reclining,
Thus to be assured that our people are unanimously dining.
And though there are places not so blessed as others in natural
   advantages, which, after all, was only to be expected,

---

[1] A list of various Indian tribes and castes.

Proud and glad are we to congratulate you upon the work you have thus
    ably effected.
(*Cres.*) How be-ewtiful upon the Mountains!

HIRED BAND, *brasses only, full chorus:*—

> God bless the Squire
> And all his rich relations
> Who teach us poor people
> We eat our proper rations—
> We eat our proper rations,
> In spite of inundations,
> Malarial exhalations,
> And casual starvations,
> We have, we have, they say we have—
> We *have* our proper rations!

CHORUS OF THE CRYSTALLISED FACTS

> Before the beginning of years
> There came to the rule of the State
> Men with a pair of shears,
> Men with an Estimate—
> Strachey with Muir for leaven,
> Lytton with locks that fell,
> Ripon fooling with Heaven,
> And Temple riding like H—ll!
> And the bigots took in hand
> Cess and the falling of rain,
> And the measure of sifted sand
> The dealer puts in the grain—
> Imports by land and sea,
> To uttermost decimal worth,
> And registration—free—
> In the houses of death and of birth.
> And fashioned with pens and paper,
> And fashioned in black and white,
> With Life for a flickering taper
> And Death for a blazing light—
> With the Armed and the Civil Power,
> That his strength might endure for a span—
> From Adam's Bridge to Peshawur,
> The Much Administered Man.
>
> In the towns of the North and the East,
> They gathered as unto rule,
> They bade him starve his priest

And send his children to school.
Railways and roads they wrought,
For the needs of the soil within;
A time to squabble in court,
A time to bear and to grin.
And gave him peace in his ways,
Jails—and Police to fight,
Justice—at length of days,
And Right—and Might in the Right.
His speech is of mortgaged bedding,
On his kine he borrows yet,
At his heart is his daughter's wedding,
In his eye foreknowledge of debt.
He eats and hath indigestion,
He toils and he may not stop;
His life is a long-drawn question
Between a crop and a crop.

The Mare's Nest

Jane Austen Beecher Stowe de Rouse
    Was good beyond all earthly need;
But, on the other hand, her spouse
    Was very, very bad indeed.
He smoked cigars, called churches slow,
And raced—but this she did not know.

For Belial Machiavelli kept
    The little fact a secret, and,
Though o'er his minor sins she wept,
    Jane Austen did not understand
That Lilly—thirteen-two and bay—
Absorbed one-half her husband's pay.

She was so good she made him worse
    (Some women are like this, I think);
He taught her parrot how to curse,
    Her Assam donkey how to drink.
He vexed her righteous soul until
She went up, and he went down hill.

Then came the crisis, strange to say,
    Which turned a good wife to a better.
A telegraphic peon, one day,
    Brought her—now, had it been a letter

For Belial Machiavelli, I
Know Jane would just have let it lie—

But 'twas a telegram instead,
   Marked "urgent," and her duty plain
To open it. Jane Austen read:—
   "Your Lilly's got a cough again.
" 'Can't understand why she is kept
"At your expense." Jane Austen wept.

It was a misdirected wire,
   Her husband was at Shaitanpore.
She spread her anger, hot as fire,
   Through six thin foreign sheets or more;
Sent off that letter, wrote another
To her solicitor—and mother.

Then Belial Machiavelli saw
   Her error and, I trust, his own,
Wired to the minion of the Law,
   And travelled wifeward—not alone.
For Lilly—thirteen-two and bay—
Came in a horse-box all the way.

There was a scene—a weep or two—
   With many kisses. Austen Jane
Rode Lilly all the season through,
   And never opened wires again.
She races now with Belial . . . This
Is very sad, but so it is.

The Ballad of Fisher's Boarding-House

That night, when through the morning-chains
   The wide-eyed corpse rolled free,
To blunder down by Garden Reach
   And rot at Kedgeree,
The tale the Hughli told the shoal
   The lean shoal told me.

'Twas Fultah Fisher's boarding-house,
   Where sailor-men reside,
And there were men of all the ports
   From Mississip to Clyde,

And regally they spat and smoked,
  And fearsomely they lied.

They lied about the purple Sea
  That gave them scanty bread,
They lied about the Earth beneath,
  The heavens overhead,
For they had looked too often on
  Black rum when that was red.

They told their tales of wreck and wrong,
  Of shame and lust and fraud,
They backed their toughest statements with
  The Brimstone of the Lord,
And crackling oaths went to and fro
  Across the fist-banged board.

And there was Hans the blue-eyed Dane,
  Bull-throated, bare of arm,
Who carried on his hairy chest
  The maid Ultruda's charm—
The little silver crucifix
  That keeps a man from harm.

And there was Jake Without-the-Ears,
  And Pamba the Malay,
And Carboy Gin the Guinea cook,
  And Luz from Vigo Bay,
And Honest Jack who sold them slops
  And harvested their pay.

And there was Salem Hardieker,
  A lean Bostonian he—
Russ, German, English, Halfbreed, Finn,
  Yank, Dane, and Portugee,
At Fultah Fisher's boarding-house
  They rested from the sea.

Now Anne of Austria shared their drinks,
  Collinga knew her fame,
From Tarnau in Galicia
  To Jaun Bazar she came,
To eat the bread of infamy
  And take the wage of shame.

She held a dozen men to heel—
  · Rich spoil of war was hers,
In hose and gown and ring and chain,

From twenty mariners,
    And, by Port Law, that week, men called
Her Salem Hardieker's.

But seamen learnt—what landsmen know—
    That neither gifts nor gain
Can hold a winking Light o' Love
    Or Fancy's flight restrain,
When Anne of Austria rolled her eyes
    On Hans the blue-eyed Dane.

Since Life is strife, and strife means knife,
    From Howrah to the Bay,
And he may die before the dawn
    Who liquored out the day,
In Fultah Fisher's boarding-house
    We woo while yet we may.

But cold was Hans the blue-eyed Dane,
    Bull-throated, bare of arm,
And laughter shook the chest beneath
    The maid Ultruda's charm—
The little silver crucifix
    That keeps a man from harm.

"You speak to Salem Hardieker;
    "You was his girl, I know.
"I ship mineselfs to-morrow, see,
    "Und round the Skaw we go,
"South, down the Cattegat, by Hjelm,
    "To Besser in Saro."

When love rejected turns to hate,
    All ill betide the man.
"You speak to Salem Hardieker"—
    She spoke as woman can.
A scream—a sob—"He called me—names!"
    And then the fray began.

An oath from Salem Hardieker,
    A shriek upon the stairs,
A dance of shadows on the wall,
    A knife-thrust unawares—
And Hans came down as cattle drop,
    Across the broken chairs.

In Anne of Austria's trembling hands
    The weary head fell low:—

"I ship mineselfs to-morrow, straight
  "For Besser in Saro;
"Und there Ultruda comes to me
  "At Easter, und I go

"South, down the Cattegat.—What's here?
  "There—are—no—lights—to—guide!"
The mutter ceased, the spirit passed.
  And Anne of Austria cried
In Fultah Fisher's boarding-house
  When Hans the mighty died.

Thus slew they Hans the blue-eyed Dane,
  Bull-throated, bare of arm,
But Anne of Austria looted first
  The maid Ultruda's charm—
The little silver crucifix
  That keeps a man from harm.

Possibilities

Ay, lay him 'neath the Simla pine—
  A fortnight fully to be missed,
  Behold, we lose our fourth at whist,
A chair is vacant where we dine.

His place forgets him; other men
  Have bought his ponies, guns, and traps.
  His fortune is the Great Perhaps
And that cool rest-house down the glen,

Whence he shall hear, as spirits may,
  Our mundane revel on the height,
  Shall watch each flashing *rickshaw*-light
Sweep on to dinner, dance, and play.

Benmore shall woo him to the ball
  With lighted rooms and braying band;
  And he shall hear and understand
"Dream Faces" better than us all.

For, think you, as the vapours flee
  Across Sanjaolie after rain
  His soul may climb the hill again
To each old field of victory.

Unseen, whom women held so dear,
  The strong man's yearning to his kind
  Shall shake at most the window-blind,
Or dull awhile the card-room's cheer.

In his own place of power unknown,
  His Light o' Love another flame,
  His dearest pony galloped lame,
And he an alien and alone!

Yet may he meet with many a friend—
  Shrewd shadows, lingering long unseen
  Among us when *"God save the Queen"*
Shows even "extras" have an end.

And, when we leave the heated room,
  And, when at four the lights expire,
  The crew shall gather round the fire
And mock our laughter in the gloom;

Talk as we talked, and they ere death—
  Flirt wanly, dance in ghostly wise,
  With ghosts of tunes for melodies,
And vanish at the morning's breath!

Arithmetic on the Frontier

A great and glorious thing it is
  To learn, for seven years or so,
The Lord knows what of that and this,
  Ere reckoned fit to face the foe—
The flying bullet down the Pass,
That whistles clear: "All flesh is grass."

Three hundred pounds per annum spent
  On making brain and body meeter
For all the murderous intent
  Comprised in "villainous saltpetre"!
And after?—Ask the Yusufzaies
What comes of all our 'ologies.

A scrimmage in a Border Station—
  A canter down some dark defile—
Two thousand pounds of education
  Drops to a ten-rupee jezail—

The Crammer's boast, the Squadron's pride
Shot like a rabbit in a ride!

No proposition Euclid wrote
  No formulae the text-books know,
Will turn the bullet from your coat,
  Or ward the tulwar's downward blow.
Strike hard who cares—shoot straight who can—
The odds are on the cheaper man.

One sword-knot stolen from the camp
  Will pay for all the school expenses
Of any Kurrum Valley scamp
  Who knows no word of moods and tenses,
But, being blessed with perfect sight,
Picks off our messmates left and right.

With home-bred hordes the hillsides teem.
  The troopships bring us one by one,
A vast expense of time and steam,
  To slay Afridis where they run.
The "captives of our bow and spear"
Are cheap, alas! as we are dear.

The Song of the Women

(Lady Dufferin's Fund for medical aid to the Women of India)

How shall she know the worship we would do her?
  The walls are high and she is very far.
How shall the women's message reach unto her
  Above the tumult of the packed bazar?
    Free wind of March, against the lattice blowing,
    Bear thou our thanks lest she depart unknowing.

Go forth across the fields we may not roam in,
  Go forth beyond the trees that rim the city
To whatso'er fair place she hath her home in,
  Who dowered us with wealth of love and pity.
    Out of our shadow pass and seek her singing—
    "I have no gifts but Love alone for bringing."

Say that we be feeble folk who greet her,
  But old in grief, and very wise in tears:
Say that we, being desolate, entreat her
  That she forget us not in after-years;

For we have seen the light and it were grievous
　　To dim that dawning if our lady leave us.

By Life that ebbed with none to staunch the failing,
　　By Love's sad harvest garnered ere the spring,
When Love in Ignorance wept unavailing
　　O'er young buds dead before their blossoming;
　　　　By all the grey owl watched, the pale moon viewed,
　　In past grim years declare our gratitude!

By hands uplifted to the Gods that heard not,
　　By gifts that found no favour in their sight,
By faces bent above the babe that stirred not,
　　By nameless horrors of the stifling night;
　　　　By ills fordone, by peace her toils discover,
　　　　Bid Earth be good beneath and Heaven above her!

If she have sent her servants in our pain,
　　If she have fought with Death and dulled his sword;
If she have given back our sick again,
　　And to the breast the weakling lips restored,
　　　　Is it a little thing that she is wrought?
　　　　Then Life and Death and Motherhood be nought.

Go forth, O Wind, our message on thy wings,
　　And they shall hear thee pass and bid thee speed,
In reed-roofed hut, or white-walled home of kings,
　　Who have been holpen by her in their need.
　　　　All spring shall give thee fragrance and the wheat
　　Shall be a tasselled floorcloth to thy feet.

Haste, for our hearts are with thee, take no rest!
　　Loud-voiced ambassador, from sea to sea
Proclaim the blessing, manifold, confest,
　　Of those in darkness by her hand set free,
　　　　Then very softly to her presence move,
　　　　And whisper: 'Lady, lo, they know and love!"

The Betrothed

"You must choose between me and your cigar."—Breach of Promise Case, circa 1885.

Open the old cigar-box, get me a Cuba stout,
For things are running crossways, and Maggie and I are out.

We quarrelled about Havanas—we fought o'er a good cheroot,
And *I* know she is exacting, and she says I am a brute.

Open the old cigar-box—let me consider a space;
In the soft blue veil of the vapour musing on Maggie's face.

Maggie is pretty to look at—Maggie's a loving lass,
But the prettiest cheeks must wrinkle, the truest of loves must pass.

There's peace in a Larranaga, there's calm in a Henry Clay;
But the best cigar in an hour is finished and thrown away—

Thrown away for another as perfect and ripe and brown—
But I could not throw away Maggie for fear o' the talk o' the town!

Maggie, my wife at fifty—grey and dour and old—
With never another Maggie to purchase for love or gold!

And the light of Days that have Been the dark of the Days that Are,
And Love's torch stinking and stale, like the butt of a dead cigar—

The butt of a dead cigar you are bound to keep in your pocket—
With never a new one to light tho' it's charred and black to the socket!

Open the old cigar-box—let me consider a while.
Here is a mild Manila—there is a wifely smile.

Which is the better portion—bondage bought with a ring,
Or a harem of dusky beauties, fifty tied in a string?

Counsellors cunning and silent—comforters true and tried,
And never a one of the fifty to sneer at a rival bride?

Thought in the early morning, solace in time of woes,
Peace in the hush of the twilight, balm ere my eyelids close,

This will the fifty give me, asking nought in return,
With only a *Suttee's* passion—to do their duty and burn.

This will the fifty give me. When they are spent and dead,
Five times other fifties shall be my servants instead.

The furrows of far-off Java, the isles of the Spanish Main,
When they hear my harem is empty will send me my brides again.

I will take no heed to their raiment, nor food for their mouths withal,
So long as the gulls are nesting, so long as the showers fall.

I will scent 'em with best vanilla, with tea will I temper their hides,
And the Moor and the Mormon shall envy who read of the tale of my
    brides.

For Maggie has written a letter to give me my choice between
The wee little whimpering Love and the great god Nick o' Teen.

And I have been servant of Love for barely a twelvemonth clear,
But I have been priest of Cabanas a matter of seven year;

And the gloom of my bachelor days is flecked with the cheery light
Of stumps that I burned to Friendship and Pleasure and Work and Fight.

And I turn my eyes to the future that Maggie and I must prove,
But the only light on the marshes is the Will-o'-the-Wisp of Love.

Will it see me safe through my journey or leave me bogged in the mire?
Since a puff of tobacco can cloud it, shall I follow the fitful fire?

Open the old cigar-box—let me consider anew—
Old friends, and who is Maggie that I should abandon *you?*

A million surplus Maggies are willing to bear the yoke;
And a woman is only a woman, but a good Cigar is a Smoke.

Light me another Cuba—I hold to my first-sworn vows.
If Maggie will have no rival, I'll have no Maggie for Spouse!

A Ballade of Jakko Hill

One moment bid the horses wait,
    Since tiffin is not laid till three,
Below the upward path and strait
    You climbed a year ago with me.
    Love came upon us suddenly
    And loosed—an idle hour to kill—
A headless, harmless armoury
    That smote us both on Jakko Hill.

Ah, Heaven! we would wait and wait
    Through Time and to Eternity!
Ah, Heaven! we would conquer Fate
    With more than Godlike constancy!
    I cut the date upon a tree—
    Here stand the clumsy figures still:—
"10-7-85, A.D."
    Damp mists on Jakko Hill.

What came of high resolve and great,
    And until Death fidelity?
Whose horse is waiting at your gate?
    Whose *rickshaw*-wheels ride over me?

No Saint's, I swear; and—let me see
    To-night what names your programme fill.
We drift asunder merrily,
    As drifts the mist on Jakko Hill!

L'ENVOI

Princess, behold our ancient state
    Has clean departed; and we see
'Twas Idleness we took for Fate
    That bound light bonds on you and me
    Amen!   Here ends the comedy
    Where it began in all good will,
Since Love and Leave together flee
    As driven mist on Jakko Hill!

The Plea of the Simla Dancers

Too late, alas! the song
    To remedy the wrong—
The rooms are taken from us, swept and garnished for their fate,
    But these tear-besprinkled pages
    Shall attest to future ages
That we cried against the crime of it—too late, alas! too late!

"What have *we* ever done to bear this grudge?"
    Was there no room save only in Benmore
For docket, *duftar*,[1] and for office-drudge,
    That you usurp our smoothest dancing floor?
Must Babus do their work on polished teak?
    Are ballrooms fittest for the ink you spill?
Was there no other cheaper house to seek?
    You might have left them all at Strawberry Hill.

We never harmed you!   Innocent our guise,
    Dainty our shining feet, our voices low;
And we revolved to divers melodies.
    And we were happy but a year ago.
To-night, the moon that watched our lightsome wiles—
    That beamed upon us through the deodars—
Is wan with gazing on official files,
    And desecrating desks disgust the stars.

[1]Office.

Nay! by the memory of tuneful nights—
 Nay! by the witchery of flying feet—
Nay! by the glamour of foredone delights—
 By all things merry, musical, and meet—
By wine that sparkled, and by sparkling eye—
 By wailing waltz—by reckless galop's strain—
By dim verandahs and by soft replies.
 Give us our ravished ballroom back again!

Or—hearken to the curse we lay on you!
 The ghosts of waltzes shall perplex your brain,
And murmurs of past merriment pursue
 Your 'wildered clerks that they indite in vain;
And when you count your poor Provincial millions,
 The only figures that your pen shall frame
Shall be the figures of dear, dear cotillions
 Danced out in tumult long before you came.

Yea! "*See-Saw*" shall upset your estimates,
 "*Dream Faces*" shall your heavy heads bemuse.
Because your hand, unheeding, desecrates
 Our temple fit for higher, worthier use.
And all the long verandahs, eloquent
 With echoes of a score of Simla years,
Shall plague you with unbidden sentiment—
 Babbling of kisses, laughter, love, and tears.

So shall you mazed amid old memories stand,
 So shall you toil, and shall accomplish nought.
And ever in your ears a phantom Band
 Shall blare away the staid official thought.
Wherefore—and ere this awful curse be spoken,
 Cast out your swarthy sacrilegious train,
And give—ere dancing cease and hearts be broken—
 Give us our ravished ballroom back again!

"As the Bell Clinks"

As I left the Halls at Lumley, rose the vision of a comely
Maid last season worshipped dumbly, watched with fervour from afar;
And I wondered idly, blindly, if the maid would greet me kindly.
That was all—the rest was settled by the clinking tonga-bar.[1]
Yea, my life and hers were coupled by the tonga coupling-bar.

[1] Bar of the old-fashioned curricle that took men up to Simla before the railroad was made.

For my misty meditation, at the second changing-station,
Suffered sudden dislocation, fled before the tuneless jar
Of a Wagner *obbligato, scherzo,* double-hand *staccato,*
Played on either pony's saddle by the clacking tonga-bar—
Played with human speech, I fancied, by the jigging, jolting bar.

"She was sweet," thought I, "last season, but 'twere surely wild unreason
"Such a tiny hope to freeze on as was offered by my Star,
"When she whispered, something sadly: 'I—we feel your going badly!' "
"And let the chance escape you?" rapped the rattling tonga-bar.
"What a chance and what an idiot!" clicked the vicious tonga-bar.

Heart of man—O heart of putty! Had I gone by Kaka-hutti,
On the old Hill-road and rutty, I had 'scaped that fatal car.
But his fortune each must bide by, so I watched the mile-stones slide by
To—*"You call on Her to-morrow!"* fugue with cymbals by the bar—
"You must call on Her to-morrow!"—post-horn galop by the bar.

Yet a further stage my goal on—we were whirling down to Solon,
With a double lurch and roll on, best foot foremost, *ganz und gar*—
"She was *very* sweet," I hinted. "If I a kiss had been imprinted—?"
"'Would ha' saved a world of trouble!" clashed the busy tonga-bar.
"'Been accepted or rejected!" banged and clanged the tonga-bar.

Then a notion wild and daring, 'spite the income-tax's paring
And a hasty thought of sharing—less than many incomes are—
Made me put a question private, (you can guess what I would drive at.)
"You must work the sum to prove it," clanked the careless tonga-bar.
"Simple Rule of Two will prove it," lilted back the tonga-bar.

It was under Khyraghaut I mused:—"Suppose the maid be haughty—
"There are lovers rich—and forty; wait some wealthy Avatar?
"Answer, monitor untiring, 'twixt the ponies twain perspiring!"
"Faint heart never won fair lady," creaked straining tonga-bar.
"Can I tell you ere you ask Her?" pounded slow the tonga-bar.

Last, the Tara Devi turning showed the lights of Simla burning,
Lit my little lazy yearning to a fiercer flame by far.
As below the Mall we jingled, through my very heart it tingled—
Did the iterated order of the threshing tonga-bar:—
"Try your luck—you can't do better!" twanged the loosened tonga-bar.

Christmas in India

Dim dawn behind the tamarisks—the sky is saffron-yellow—
  As the women in the village grind the corn,

And the parrots seek the river-side, each calling to his fellow
  That the Day, the staring Eastern Day, is born.
    O the white dust on the highway! O the stenches in the byway!
      O the clammy fog that hovers over earth!
    And at Home they're making merry 'neath the white and scarlet
      berry—
      What part have India's exiles in their mirth?

Full day behind the tamarisks—the sky is blue and staring—
  As the cattle crawl afield beneath the yoke,
And they bear One o'er the field-path, who is past all hope or caring,
  To the ghat below the curling wreaths of smoke.
    Call on Rama, going slowly, as ye bear a brother lowly—
      Call on Rama—he may hear, perhaps, your voice!
    With our hymn-books and our psalters we appeal to other altars,
      And to-day we bid "good Christian men rejoice!"

High noon behind the tamarisks—the sun is hot above us—
  As at Home the Christmas Day is breaking wan.
They will drink our healths at dinner—those who tell us how they love us,
  And forget us till another year be gone!
    O the toil that knows no breaking! O the *Heimweh*, ceaseless, aching!
      O the black dividing Sea and alien Plain!
    Youth was cheap—wherefore we sold it. Gold was good—we hoped to
      hold it.
      And to-day we know the fullness of our gain!

Grey dusk behind the tamarisks—the parrots fly together—
  As the Sun is sinking slowly over Home;
And his last ray seems to mock us shackled in a lifelong tether
  That drags us back howe'er so far we roam.
    Hard her service, poor her payment—she in ancient, tattered
      raiment—
      India, she the grim Stepmother of our kind.
    If a year of life be lent her, if her temple's shrine we enter,
      The door is shut—we may not look behind.

Black night behind the tamarisks—the owls begin their chorus—
  As the conches from the temple scream and bray.
With the fruitless years behind us and the hopeless years before us,
  Let us honour, O my brothers, Christmas Day!
    Call a truce, then, to our labours—let us feast with friends and
      neighbours,
      And be merry as the custom of our caste;
    For, if "faint and forced the laughter," and if sadness follow after,
      We are richer by one mocking Christmas past.

The Grave of the Hundred Head

There's a widow in sleepy Chester
  Who weeps for her only son;
There's a grave on the Pabeng River,
  A grave that the Burmans shun;
And there's Subadar Prag Tewarri
  Who tells how the work was done.

A Snider squibbed in the jungle—
  Somebody laughed and fled,
And the men of the First Shikaris
  Picked up their Subaltern dead,
With a big blue mark in his forehead
  And the back blown out of his head.

Subadar Prag Tewarri,
  Jemada Hira Lal,
Took command of the party,
  Twenty rifles in all,
Marched them down to the river
  As the day was beginning to fall.

They buried the boy by the river,
  A blanket over his face—
They wept for their dead Lieutenant,
  The men of an alien race—
They made a *samadh*[1] in his honour,
  A mark for his resting-place.

For they swore by the Holy Water,
  They swore by the salt they ate,
That the soul of Lieutenant Eshmitt Sahib
  Should go to his God in state,
With fifty file of Burmans
  To open him Heaven's Gate.

The men of the First Shikaris
  Marched till the break of day,
Till they came to the rebel village
  The village of Pabengmay—
A *jingal*[2] covered the clearing,
  Calthrops hampered the way.

Subadar Prag Tewarri,
  Bidding them load with ball,

[1] A memorial.   [2] Native cannon.

Halted a dozen rifles
  Under the village wall;
Sent out a flanking-party
  With Jemadar Hira Lal.

The men of the First Shikaris
  Shouted and smote and slew,
Turning the grinning *jingal*
  On to the howling crew.
The Jemadar's flanking-party
  Butchered the folk who flew.

Long was the morn of slaughter,
  Long was the list of slain,
Five score heads were taken,
  Five score heads and twain;
And the men of the First Shikaris
  Went back to their grave again,

Each man bearing a basket
  Red as his palms that day,
Red as the blazing village—
  The village of Pabengmay.
And the *"drip-drip-drip"* from the baskets
  Reddened the grass by the way.

They made a pile of their trophies
  High as a tall man's chin,
Head upon head distorted,
  Set in a sightless grin,
Anger and pain and terror
  Stamped on the smoke-scorched skin.

Subadar Prag Tewarri
  Put the head of the Boh
On the top of the mound of triumph,
  The head of his son below—
With the sword and the peacock-banner
  That the world might behold and know.

Thus the *samadh* was perfect,
  Thus was the lesson plain
Of the wrath of the First Shikaris—
  The price of white man slain;
And the men of the First Shikaris
  Went back into camp again.

Then a silence came to the river,
    A hush fell over the shore,
And Bohs that were brave departed,
    And Sniders squibbed no more;
For the Burmans said
That a white man's head
Must be paid for with heads five-score.

There's a widow in sleepy Chester
    Who weeps for her only son;
There's a grave on the Pabeng River,
    A grave that the Burmans shun;
And there's Subadar Prag Tewarri
    Who tells how the work was done.

An Old Song

So long as 'neath the Kalka hills
    The tonga-horn shall ring,
So long as down the Solon dip
    The hard-held ponies swing,
So long as Tara Devi sees
    The lights of Simla town,
So long as Pleasure calls us up,
    Or Duty drives us down,
        If you love me as I love you
        What pair so happy we two?

So long as Aces take the King,
    Or backers take the bet,
So long as debt leads men to wed,
    Or marriage leads to debt,
So long as little luncheons, Love,
    And scandal hold their vogue,
While there is sport at Annandale
    Or whisky at Jutogh,
        If you love me as I love you
        What knife can cut our love in two?

So long as down the rocking floor
    The raving polka spins,
So long as Kitchen Lancers spur
    The maddened violins,
So long as through the whirling smoke

We hear the oft-told tale—
"Twelve hundred in the Lotteries,"
And *Whatshername* for sale,
    If you love me I love you
    We'll play the game and win it too.

So long as Lust or Lucre tempt
    Straight riders from the course,
So long with each drink we pour
    Black brewage of Remorse,
So long as those unloaded guns
    We keep beside the bed,
Blow off, by obvious accident
    The lucky owner's head,
        If you love me as I love you
        What can Life kill or Death undo?

So long as Death 'twixt dance and dance
    Chills best and bravest blood,
And drops the reckless rider down
    The rotten, rain-soaked *khud*,
So long as rumours from the North
    Make loving wives afraid,
So long as Burma takes the boy
    Or typhoid kills the maid,
        If you love me as I love you
        What knife can cut our love in two?

By all that lights our daily life
    Or works our lifelong woe,
From Boileaugunge to Simla Downs
    And those grim glades below,
Where, heedless of the flying hoof
    And clamour overhead,
Sleep, with the grey langur for guard,
    Our very scornful Dead,
        If you love me as I love you
        All earth is servant to us two!

By Docket, Billetdoux, and File,
    By Mountain, Cliff, and Fir,
By Fan and Sword and Office-box,
    By Corset, Plume, and Spur
By Riot, Revel, Waltz, and War,
    By Women, Work, and Bills,

By all the life that fizzes in
The everlasting Hills,
If you love me as I love you
What pair so happy as we two?

Certain Maxims of Hafiz

I

If it be pleasant to look on, stalled in the packed *serai*,
Does not the Young Man try Its temper and pace ere he buy?
If She be pleasant to look on, what does the Young Man say?
"Lo!   She is pleasant to look on.   Give Her to me to-day!"

II

Yea, though a Kafir die, to him is remitted Jehannum
If he borrowed in life from a native at sixty per cent. per annum.

III

Blister we not for *bursati*[1]?   So when the heart is vext,
The pain of one maiden's refusal is drowned in the pain of the next.

IV

The temper of chums, the love of your wife, and a new piano's tune—
Which of the three will you trust at the end of an Indian June?

V

Who are the rulers of Ind—to whom shall we bow the knee?
Make your peace with the women, and men will make you L. G.[2]

VI

Does the woodpecker flit round the young *ferash*[3]?   Does the grass clothe
  a new-built wall?
Is she under thirty, the woman who holds a boy in her thrall?

VII

If She grow suddenly gracious—reflect.   Is it all for thee?
The blackbuck is stalked through the bullock, and Man through jealousy.

VIII

Seek not for favour of women.   So shall you find it indeed.
Does not the boar break cover just when you're lighting a weed?

[1] A skin-disease of horses.   [2] Lieutenant-Govenor.   [3] Tamarisk.

IX

If He play, being young and unskilful, for shekels of silver and gold,
Take His money, my son, praising Allah.   The kid was ordained to be
   sold.

X

With a "weed" among men or horses verily this is the best,
That you work him in office or dog-cart lightly—but give him no rest.

XI

Pleasant the snaffle of Courtship, improving the manners and carriage;
But the colt who is wise will abstain from the terrible thornbit of
   Marriage.

XII

As the thriftless gold of the *babul*[1] so is the gold that we spend
On a Derby Sweep, or our neighbour's wife, or the horse that we buy
   from a friend.

XIII

The ways of man with a maid be strange, yet simple and tame
To the ways of a man with a horse, when selling or racing that same.

XIV

In public Her face turneth to thee, and pleasant Her smile when he meet.
It is ill. The cold rocks of El-Gidar smile thus on the waves at their feet.
In public Her face is averted; with anger She nameth thy name.
It is well.   Was there ever a loser content with the loss of the game?

XV

If She have spoken a word, remember thy lips are sealed,
And the Brand of the Dog is upon him by whom is the secret revealed.
If She have written a letter, delay not an instant but burn it.
Tear it in pieces, O Fool, and the wind to her mate shall return it!
If there be trouble to Herward, and a lie of the blackest can clear,
Lie, while thy lips can move or a man is alive to hear.

XVI

My Son, if a maiden deny thee and scufflingly bid thee give o'er,
Yet lip meets with lip at the lastward.   Get out!   She has been there before.
They are pecked on the ear and the chin and the nose who are lacking in lore.

[1]Acacia.

XVII

If we fall in the race, though we win, the hoof-slide is scarred on the
    course.
Though Allah and Earth pardon Sin, remaineth for ever Remorse.

XVIII

"By all I am misunderstood!" if the Matron shall say, or the Maid:—
"Alas! I do not understand," my son, be thou nowise afraid.
In vain in the sight of the Bird is the net of the Fowler displayed.

XIX

My son, if I, Hafiz, thy father, take hold of thy knees in my pain,
Demanding thy name on stamped paper, one day or one hour—refrain.
Are the links of thy fetters so light that thou cravest another man's chain?

The Moon of Other Days

Beneath the deep verandah's shade,
    When bats begin to fly,
I sit me down and watch—alas!
    Another evening die.
Blood-red behind the sere *ferash*
    She rises through the haze.
Sainted Diana! can that be
    The Moon of Other Days?

Ah! shade of little Kitty Smith,
    Sweet Saint of Kensington!
Say, was it ever thus at Home
    The Moon of August shone,
When arm in arm we wandered long
    Through Putney's evening haze,
And Hammersmith was Heaven beneath
    The Moon of Other Days?

But Wandle's stream is Sutlej now,
    And Putney's evening haze
The dust that half a hundred kine
    Before my window raise.
Unkempt, unclean, athwart the mist
    The seething city looms,
In place of Putney's golden gorse
    The sickly *babul* blooms.

Glare down, old Hecate, through the dust,
    And bid the pie-dog yell,
Draw from the drain its typhoid-germ,
    From each bazar its smell;
Yea, suck the fever from the tank
    And sap my strength therewith:
Thank Heaven, you show a smiling face
    To little Kitty Smith!

The Fall of Jock Gillespie

This fell when dinner-time was done—
    'Twixt the first an' the second rub—
That oor mon Jock cam' hame again
    To his rooms ahint the Club.

An' syne he laughed, an' syne he sang,
    An' syne we thocht him fou,
An' syne he trumped his partner's trick,
    An' garred his partner rue.

Then up and spake an elder mon,
    That held the Spade its Ace—
"God save the lad! Whence comes the licht
    "That wimples on his face?"

An' Jock he sniggered, an' Jock he smiled,
    An' ower the card-brim wunk:—
"I'm a' too fresh fra' the stirrup-peg,
    "May be that I am drunk."

"There's whusky brewed in Galashiels
    "An' L. L. L. forbye;
"But never liquor lit the lowe
    "That keeks fra' oot your eye.

"There's a thrid o' hair on your dress-coat breast,
    "Aboon the heart a wee?"
"Oh! that is fra' the lang-haired Skye
    "That slobbers ower me."

"Oh! lang-haired Skyes are lovin' beasts,
    "An' terrier-dogs are fair,
"But never yet was terrier born,
    "Wi' ell-lang gowden hair!!

"There's a smirch o' pouther on your breast,
  "Below the left lappel?"
"Oh! that is fra' my auld cigar,
  "Whenas the stump-end fell."

"Mon Jock, ye smoke the Trichi coarse,
  "For ye are short o' cash.
"An' best Havanas couldna leave
  "Sae white an' pure an ash.

"This nicht ye stopped a story braid,
  "An' stopped it wi' a curse.
"Last nicht ye told that tale yoursel'—
  "An' capped it wi' a worse!

"Oh! we're no fou! Oh! we're no fou!
  "But plainly we can ken
"Ye're fallin', fallin' fra' the band
  "O' cantie single men!"

"An' it fell when *siris*-shaws were sere,
  An' the nichts were lang and mirk,
In braw new breeks, wi' a gowden ring,
  Oor Jockie gaed to the Kirk!

What the People Said

Queen Victoria's Jubilee

JUNE 21st, 1887

By the well, where the bullocks go
  Silent and blind and slow—
By the field, where the young corn dies
In the face of the sultry skies,
They have heard, as the dull Earth hears
The voice of the wind of an hour,
The sound of the Great Queen's voice:—
  "My God hath given me years,
"Hath granted dominion and power:
"And I bid you, O Land, rejoice."

And the Ploughman settles the share
More deep in the grudging clod;
For he saith:—"The wheat is my care,

"And the rest is the will of God.
"He sent the Mahratta spear
"As He sendeth the rain,
"And the *Mlech*,[1] in the fated year,
"Broke the spear in twain,
"And was broken in turn. Who knows
"How our Lords make strife?
"It is good that the young wheat grows,
"For the bread is Life."

Then, far and near, as the twilight drew,
    Hissed up to the scornful dark
Great serpents, blazing, of red and blue,
That rose and faded, and rose anew,
    That the Land might wonder and mark.
"To-day is a day of days," they said,
"Make merry, O People, all!"
And the Ploughman listened and bowed his head.
"To-day and to-morrow God's will," he said,
As he trimmed the lamps on the wall.

"He sendeth us years that are good,
"As He sendeth the dearth.
"He giveth to each man his food,
"Or Her food to the Earth.
"Our Kings and our Queens are afar—
"On their peoples be peace—
"God bringeth the rain to the Bar,
"That our cattle increase."

And the Ploughman settled the share
More deep in the sun-dried clod:—
"Mogul, Mahratta, and *Mlech* from the North,
"And White Queen over the Seas—
"God raiseth them up and driveth them forth
"As the dust of the ploughshare flies in the breeze;
"But the wheat and the cattle are all my care,
"And the rest is the will of God."

[1]The foreigner.

The Undertaker's Horse

"To-tschin-shu is condemned to death.   How can he drink tea with the Executioner?"—
JAPANESE PROVERB.

The eldest son bestrides him,
And the pretty daughter rides him,
And I meet him oft o' mornings on the Course;
And there kindles in my bosom
An emotion chill and gruesome
As I canter past the Undertaker's Horse.

Neither shies he nor is restive,
But a hideously suggestive
Trot, professional and placid, he affects;
And the cadence of his hoof-beats
To my mind this grim reproof beats:—
"Mend your pace, my friend. I'm coming—Who's the next?"

Ah! stud-bred of ill-omen,
I have watched the strongest go—men
Of pith and might and muscle—at your heels,
Down the plantain-bordered highway,
(Heaven send it ne'er be my way!)
In a lacquered box and jetty upon wheels.

Answer, sombre beast and dreary,
Where is Brown, the young, the cheery?
Smith, the pride of all his friends and half the Force?
You were at that last dread *dak*[1]
We must cover at a walk,
Bring them back to me, O Undertaker's Horse!

With your mane unhogged and flowing,
And your curious way of going,
And that businesslike black crimping of your tail,
E'en with Beauty on your back, Sir,
Pacing as a lady's hack, Sir,
What wonder when I meet you I turn pale?

It may be you wait your time, Beast,
Till I write my last bad rhyme, Beast—
Quit the sunlight, cut the rhyming, drop the glass—
Follow after with the others,

[1] Stage of a journey.

Where some dusky heathen smothers
Us with marigolds in lieu of English grass.

Or, perchance, in years to follow,
I shall watch your plump sides hollow,
See Carnifex (gone lame) become a corse—
See old age at last o'erpower you,
And the Station Pack devour you,
I shall chuckle then, O Undertaker's Horse!

But to insult, jibe, and quest, I've
Still the hideously suggestive
Trot that hammers out the unrelenting text,
And I hear it hard behind me
In what place soe'er I find me:—
"'Sure to catch you soon or later. Who's the next?"

One Viceroy Resigns

LORD DUFFERIN TO LORD LANDSDOWNE:—

So here's your Empire.—No more wine, then? Good.
We'll clear the Aides and *khitmutgars* away.
(You'll know that fat old fellow with the knife—
He keeps the Name Book, talks in English, too,
And almost thinks himself the Government.)
O Youth, Youth, Youth! Forgive me, you're so young.
Forty from sixty—twenty years of work
And power to back the working. *Ay de mi!*
You want to know, you want to see, to touch
And, by your lights, to act.—It's natural.
I wonder can I help you?—Let me try.
You saw—what did you see from Bombay east?
Enough to frighten any one but me?
Neat that! It frightened Me in Eighty-Four!
You shouldn't take a man from Canada
And bid him smoke in powder-magazines;
Nor with a Reputation such as—Bah!
That ghost has haunted me for twenty years,
My Reputation now full-blown. Your fault!
Yours, with your stories of the strife at Home,
Who's up, who's down, who leads and who is led—
One reads so much, one hears so little here.

Well, now's your turn of exile.   I go back
To Rome and leisure. All roads lead to Rome,
Or books—the refuge of the destitute.
When you . . . that brings me back to India.   See!
    Start clear.   I couldn't.   Egypt served my turn.
You'll never plumb the Oriental mind,
And if you did, it isn't worth the toil.
Think of a sleek French priest in Canada;
Divide by twenty half-breeds.—Multiply
By twice the Sphinx's silence.—There's your East,
And you're as wise as ever.—So am I.

    Accept on trust and work in darkness, strike
At venture, stumble forward, make your mark,
(It's chalk on granite) then thank God no flame
Leaps from the rock to shrivel mark and man.
I'm clear—my mark is made.   Three months of drought
Had ruined much.   It rained and washed away
The specks that might have gathered on my Name.
I took a country twice the size of France,
And shuttered up one doorway in the North.
I stand by those.—You'll find that both will pay,
I pledged my Name on both—they're yours to-night.
Hold to them—they hold fame enough for two.
I'm old, but I shall live till Burma pays.
Men there—*not* German traders—Crosthwaite knows—
You'll find it in my papers. For the North
Guns always—quietly—but always guns.
You've seen your Council?   Yes, they'll try to rule,
And prize their Reputations.   Have you met
A grim lay-reader with a taste for coins,
And faith in Sin most men withhold from God?
He's gone to England.   Ripon knew his grip
And kicked. A Council always has its Hopes.
They look for nothing from the West but Death
Or Bath or Bournemouth.   Here's their ground.

                                              They fight

Until the Middle Classes take them back,
One of ten millions plus a C. S. I.,
Or drop in harness.   Legion of the Lost?
Not altogether.   Earnest, narrow men,
But chiefly earnest, and they'll do your work,
And end by writing letters to the *Times*.
(Shall I write letters, answering Hunter—fawn
With Ripon on the Yorkshire grocers? Ugh!)

They have their Reputations.   Look to one—
I work with him—the smallest of them all,
White-haired, red-faced, who sat the plunging horse
Out in the garden.   He's your right-hand man,
And dreams of tilting Wolseley from the throne,
But while he dreams gives work we cannot buy;
He has his Reputation—wants the Lords
By way of Frontier Roads.   Meantime, I think,
He values very much the hand that falls
Upon his shoulder at the Council table—
Hates cats and knows his business. *Which is yours.*
     Your business!   Twice a hundred million souls.
Your business! I could tell you what I did
Some nights of Eighty-five, at Simla, worth
A Kingdom's ransom.   When a big ship drives
God knows to what new reef, the man at the wheel
Prays with the passengers.   They lose their lives,
Or rescued go their way; but he's no man
To take his trick at the wheel again.   That's worse
Than drowning.   Well, a galled Mashobra mule
(You'll see Mashobra) passed me on the Mall,
And I was—some fool's wife had ducked and bowed
To show the others I would stop and speak.
Then the mule fell—three galls, a hand-breadth each,
Behind the withers.—Mrs. Whatsisname
Leers at the mule and me by turns, thweet thoul!
"How could they make him carry such a load!"
I saw—it isn't often I dream dreams—
More than the mule that minute—smoke and flame
From Simla to the haze below.   That's weak.
You're younger.   You'll dream dreams before you've done.
You've youth, that's one; good workmen—that means two
Fair chances in your favour.   Fate's the third.
I know what *I* did.   Do you ask me, "Preach?"
I answer by my past or else go back
To platitudes of rule—or take you thus
In confidence and say:—"You know the trick:
"You've governed Canada.   You know.   *You* know!"
And all the while commend you to Fate's hand
(Here at the top one loses sight o' God),
Commend you, then, to something more than you—
The Other People's blunders and . . . that's all.
I'd agonise to serve you if I could.
It's incommunicable, like the cast

That drops the hackle with the gut adry.
Too much—too little—there's your salmon lost!
And so I tell you nothing—wish you luck,
And wonder—how I wonder!—for your sake!
And triumph for my own.   You're young, you're young,
You hold to half a hundred Shibboleths.
I'm old.   I followed Power to the last,
Gave her my best, and Power followed Me.
It's worth it—on my soul I'm speaking plain,
Here by the claret glasses!—worth it all.
I gave—no matter what I gave—I win.
I know I win.   Mine's work, good work that lives!
A country twice the size of France—the North
Safeguarded.   That's my record: sink the rest
And better if you can.   The Rains may serve,
Rupees may rise—threepence will give you Fame—
It's rash to hope for sixpence.   If they rise
Get guns, more guns, and lift the salt-tax . . . Oh!
I told you what the Congress meant or thought?
I'll answer nothing.   Half a year will prove
The full extent of time and thought you'll spare
To Congress.   Ask a Lady Doctor *once*
How little Begums see the light—deduce
Thence how the True Reformer's child is born.
It's interesting, curious . . . and vile.
I told the Turk he was a gentleman.
I told the Russian that his Tartar veins
Bled pure Parisian ichor; and he purred.
The Congress doesn't purr.   I think it swears.
You're young—you'll swear too ere you've reached the end.
The End!   God help you, if there be a God.
(There must be one to startle Gladstone's soul
In that new land where all the wires are cut,
And Cross snores anthems on the asphodel.)
God help you!   And I'd help you if I could,
But that's beyond me.   Yes, your speech was crude.
Sound claret after olives—yours and mine;
But Médoc slips into vin ordinaire.
(I'll drink my first at Genoa to your health)
Raise it to Hock.—You'll never catch my style.
And, after all, the middle-classes grip
The middle-class—for Brompton talk Earl's Court.
Perhaps you're right.   I'll see you in the *Times*—
A quarter-column of eye-searing print,

A leader once a quarter—then a war;
The Strand a-bellow through the fog:—"Defeat!"
"'Orrible slaughter!"　While you lie awake
And wonder.　Oh, you'll wonder ere you're free!
I wonder now.　The four years slide away
So fast, so fast, and leave me here alone.
Reay, Colvin, Lyall, Roberts, Buck, the rest,
Princes and Powers of Darkness, troops and trains,
(I *cannot* sleep in trains), land piled on land,
Whitewash and weariness, red rockets, dust,
White snows that mocked me, palaces—with draughts,
And Westland with the drafts he couldn't pay.
Poor Wilson reading his obituary
Before he died, and Hope, the man with bones,
And Aitchison a dripping mackintosh
At Council in the Rains, his grating "Sirrr"
Half drowned by Hunter's silky: "Bât, my lahd."
Hunterian always: Marshal spinning plates
Or standing on his head; the Rent Bill's roar,
A hundred thousand speeches, much red cloth,
And Smiths thrice happy if I called them Jones,
(I can't remember half their names) or reined
My pony on the Mall to greet their wives.
More trains, more troops, more dust, and then all's done . . .
Four years, and I forget.　If I forget,
How will *they* bear me in their minds? The North
Safeguarded—nearly (Roberts knows the rest),
A country twice the size of France annexed.
That stays at least.　The rest may pass—may pass—
Your heritage and I can teach you naught.
"High trust," "vast honour," "interests twice as vast,"
"Due reverence to your Council"—keep to those.
I envy you the twenty years you've gained,
But not the five to follow.　What's that? One!
Two!—Surely not so late. Good-night. *Don't* dream.

The Galley-Slave

Oh, gallant was our galley from her carven steering-wheel
To her figurehead of silver and her beak of hammered steel.
The leg-bar chafed the ankle and we gasped for cooler air,
But no galley on the waters with our galley could compare!

Our bulkheads bulged with cotton and our masts were stepped in gold—

We ran a mighty merchandise of niggers in the hold;
The white foam spun behind us, and the black shark swam below,
As we gripped the kicking sweep-head and we made the galley go.

It was merry in the galley, for we revelled now and then—
If they wore us down like cattle, faith, we fought and loved like men!
As we snatched her through the water, so we snatched a minute's bliss,
And the mutter of the dying never spoiled the lover's kiss.

Our women and our children toiled beside us in the dark—
They died, we filed their fetters, and we heaved them to the shark—
We heaved them to the fishes, but so fast the galley sped
We had only time to envy, for we could not mourn our dead.

Bear witness, once my comrades, what a hard bit gang were we—
The servants of the sweep-head, but the masters of the sea!
By the hands that drove her forward she plunged and yawed and sheered,
Woman, Man, or God or Devil, was there anything we feared?

Was it storm? Our fathers faced it and a wilder never blew.
Earth that waited for the wreckage watched the galley struggle through.
Burning noon or choking midnight, Sickness, Sorrow, Parting, Death?
Nay, our very babes would mock you had they time for idle breath.

But to-day I leave the galley and another takes my place;
There's my name upon the deck-beam—let it stand a little space.
I am free—to watch my messmates beating out to open main,
Free of all that Life can offer—save to handle sweep again.

By the brand upon my shoulder, by the gall of clinging steel,
By the welts the whips have left me, by the scars that never heal;
By eyes grown old with staring through the sunwash on the brine,
I am paid in full for service. Would that service still were mine!

Yet they talk of times and seasons and of woe the years bring forth,
Of our alley swamped and shattered in the rollers of the North;
When the niggers break the hatches and the decks are gay with gore,
And a craven-hearted pilot crams her crashing on the shore.

She will need no half-mast signal, minute-gun, or rocket-flare.
When the cry for help goes seaward, she will find her servants there.
Battered chain-gangs of the orlop, grizzled drafts of years gone by,
To the bench that broke their manhood, they shall lash themselves and
    die.

Hale and crippled, young and aged, paid, deserted, shipped away—
Palace, cot, and lazaretto shall make up the tale that day,
When the skies are black above them, and the decks ablaze beneath,
And the top-men clear the raffle with their clasp-knives in their teeth.

It may be that Fate will give me life and leave to row once more—
Set some strong man free for fighting as I take awhile his oar.
But to-day I leave the galley.   Shall I curse her service then?
God be thanked!   Whate'er comes after, I have lived and toiled with
   Men!

A Tale of Two Cities

Where the sober-coloured cultivator smiles
   On his *byles*;[1]
Where the cholera, the cyclone, and the crow
   Come and go;
Where the merchant deals in indigo and tea,
   Hides and *ghi*;[2]
Where the Babu drops inflammatory hints
   In his prints;
Stands a City—Charnock chose it—packed away
   Near a Bay—
By the sewage rendered fetid, by the sewer
   Made impure,
By the Sunderbunds unwholesome, by the swamp
   Moist and damp;
And the City and the Viceroy, as we see,
   Don't agree.

Once, two hundred years ago, the trader came
   Meek and tame.
Where his timid foot first halted, there he stayed.
   Till mere trade
Grew to Empire, and he sent his armies forth
   South and North,
Till the country from Peshawur to Ceylon
   Was his own.
Thus the midday halt of Charnock—more's the pity!—
   Grew a City.
As the fungus sprouts chaotic from its bed,
   So it spread—
Chance-directed, chance-erected, laid and built
   On the silt—
Palace, byre, hovel—poverty and pride—
   Side by side;
And, above the packed and pestilential town,
   Death looked down.

----

[1]Cattle.   [2]Butter.

But the Rulers in that City by the Sea
   Turned to flee—
Fled, with each returning Spring-tide, from its ills
   To the Hills.
From the clammy fogs of morning, from the blaze
   Of the days,
From the sickness of the noontide, from the heat,
   Beat retreat;
For the country from Peshawur to Ceylon
   Was their own.
But the Merchant risked the perils of the Plain
   For his gain.

Now the resting-place of Charnock, 'neath the palms,
   Asks an alms,
And the burden of its lamentation is,
   Briefly, this:—
"Because, for certain months, we boil and stew,
   "So should you.
"Cast the Viceroy and his Council, to perspire
   "In our fire!"
And for answer to the argument, in vain
   We explain
That an amateur Saint Lawrence cannot cry:—
   "*All* must fry!"
That the Merchant risks the perils of the Plains
   For his gains.
Nor can Rulers rule a house that men grow rich in,
   From its kitchen.

Let the Babu drop inflammatory hints
   In his prints;
And mature—consistent soul—his plan for stealing
   To Darjeeling:
Let the Merchant seek, who makes his silver pile,
   England's isle;
Let the City Charnock pitched on—evil day!—
   Go Her way.
Though the argosies of Asia at Her doors
   Heap their stores,
Though Her enterprise and energy secure
   Income sure,
Though "out-station orders punctually obeyed"
   Swell Her trade—
Still, for rule, administration, and the rest,
   Simla's best!

In Springtime

My garden blazes brightly with the rose-bush and the peach,
　　And the *koïl* sings above it, in the *siris* by the well,
From the creeper-covered trellis comes the squirrel's chattering speech,
　　And the blue jay screams and flutters where the cheery *sat-bhai*[1] dwell.
But the rose has lost its fragrance, and the *koïl*'s note is strange;
　　I am sick of endless sunshine, sick of blossom-burdened bough.
Give me back the leafless woodlands where the winds of Springtime
　　range—
　　Give me back one day in England, for it's Spring in England now!

Through the pines the gusts are booming, o'er the brown fields blowing
　　chill,
　　From the furrow of the ploughshare streams the fragrance of the loam,
And the hawk nests on the cliffside and the jackdaw in the hill,
　　And my heart is back in England 'mid the sights and sounds of Home.
But the garland of the sacrifice this wealth of rose and peach is
　　Ah! *koïl*, little *koïl*, singing on the *siris* bough,
In my ears the knell of exile your ceaseless bell like speech is—
　　Can *you* tell me aught of England or of Spring in England now?

Giffen's Debt

Imprimis he was "broke."　Thereafter left
His Regiment and, later, took to drink;
Then, having lost the balance of his friends,
"Went Fantree"—joined the people of the land,
Turned three parts Mussulman and one Hindu,
And lived among the Gauri villagers,
Who gave him shelter and a wife or twain,
And boasted that a thorough, full-blood *sahib*
Had come among them.　Thus he spent his time,
Deeply indebted to the village *shroff*[2]
(Who never asked for payment), always drunk,
Unclean, abominable, out-at-heels;
Forgetting that he was an Englishman.

You know they dammed the Gauri with a dam,
And all the good contractors scamped their work
And all the bad material at hand
Was used to dam the Gauri—which was cheap,

---

[1]Indian starlings.　　[2]Money-lender.

And, therefore, proper.   Then the Gauri burst,
And several hundred thousand cubic tons
Of water dropped into the valley, *flop*,
And drowned some five-and-twenty villagers,
And did a lakh or two of detriment
To crops and cattle.   When the flood went down
We found him dead, beneath an old dead horse
Full six miles down the valley. So we said
He was a victim to the Demon Drink,
And moralised upon him for a week,
And then forgot him. Which was natural.

But, in the valley of the Gauri, men
Beneath the shadow of the big new dam,
Relate a foolish legend of the flood,
Accounting for the little loss of life
(Only those five-and-twenty villagers)
In this wise:—On the evening of the flood,
They heard the groaning of the rotten dam,
And voices of the Mountain Devils.   Then
An incarnation of the local God,
Mounted upon a monster-neighing horse,
And flourishing a flail-like whip, came down,
Breathing ambrosia, to the villages,
And fell upon the simple villagers
With yells beyond the power of mortal throat,
And blows beyond the power of mortal hand,

And smote them with his flail-like whip, and drove
Them clamorous with terror up the hill.
And scattered, with the monster-neighing steed,
Their crazy cottages about their ears,
And generally cleared those villages.
Then came the water, and the local God,
Breathing ambrosia, flourishing his whip,
And mounted on his monster-neighing steed,
Went down the valley with the flying trees
And residue of homesteads, while they watched
Safe on the mountain-side these wondrous things,
And knew that they were much beloved of Heaven.

Wherefore, and when the dam was newly built,
They raised a temple to the local God,
And burnt all manner of unsavoury things
Upon his altar, and created priests,
And blew into a conch and banged a bell,

And told the story of the Gauri flood
With circumstance and much embroidery . . .
So he, the whiskified Objectionable,
Unclean, abominable, out-at-heels,
Became the Tutelary Deity
Of all the Gauri valley villages,
And may in time become a Solar Myth.

Two Months

JUNE

No hope, no change!   The clouds have shut us in,
  And through the cloud the sullen Sun strikes down
  Full on the bosom of the tortured Town,
Till Night falls heavy as remembered sin
That will not suffer sleep or thought of ease,
  And, hour on hour, the dry-eyed Moon in spite
  Glares through the haze and mocks with watery light
The torment of the uncomplaining trees.
Far off, the Thunder bellows her despair
To echoing Earth, thrice parched.   The lightnings fly
In vain.   No help the heaped-up clouds afford,
But wearier weight of burdened, burning air.
What truce with Dawn?   Look, from the aching sky,
Day stalks, a tyrant with a flaming sword!

SEPTEMBER

At dawn there was a murmur in the trees,
  A ripple on the tank, and in the air
  Presage of coming coolness—everywhere
A voice of prophecy upon the breeze.
Up leapt the Sun and smote the dust to gold,
  And strove to parch anew the heedless land,
All impotently, as a King grown old
  Wars for the Empire crumbling 'neath his hand.
One after one the lotos-petals fell,
  Beneath the onslaught of the rebel year,
  In mutiny against a furious sky;
And far-off Winter whispered:— "It is well!
"Hot Summer dies.   Behold your help is near,
"For when men's need is sorest, then come I."

L'envoi

(*Departmental Ditties*)

The smoke upon your Altar dies,
  The flowers decay,
The Goddess of your sacrifice
  Has flown away.
What profit then to sing or slay
  The sacrifice from day to day?

"We know the Shrine is void," they said,
  "The Goddess flown—
"Yet wreaths are on the altar laid—
  "The Altar-Stone
"Is black with fumes of sacrifice,
"Albeit She has fled our eyes.

"For, it may be, if still we sing
  "And tend the Shrine,
"Some Deity on wandering wing
  "May there incline;
"And, finding all in order meet,
"Stay while we worship at Her feet."

(End of *Departmental Ditties*)

The Fires

Men make them fires on the hearth
  Each under his roof-tree,
And the Four Winds that rule the earth
  They blow the smoke to me.

Across the high hills and the sea
  And all the changeful skies,
The Four Winds blow the smoke to me
  Till the tears are in my eyes.

Until the tears are in my eyes
  And my heart is wellnigh broke
For thinking on old memories
  That gather in the smoke.

With every shift of every wind
  The homesick memories come,
From every quarter of mankind
  Where I have made me a home.

Four times a fire against the cold
  And a roof against the rain—

Sorrow fourfold and joy fourfold
    The Four Winds bring again!

How can I answer which is best
    Of all the fires that burn?
I have been too often host or guest
    At every fire in turn.

How can I turn from any fire,
    On any man's hearthstone?
I know the wonder and desire
    That went to build my own!

How can I doubt man's joy or woe
    Where'er his house-fires shine,
Since all that man must undergo
    Will visit me at mine?

Oh, you Four Winds that blow so strong
    And know that this is true,
Stoop for a little and carry my song
    To all the men I knew!

Where there are fires against the cold,
    Or roofs against the rain—
With love fourfold and joy fourfold,
    Take them my songs again!

Dedication from "Barrack-Room Ballads"

Beyond the path of the outmost sun rough utter darkness hurled—
Farther than ever comet flared or vagrant star-dust swirled—
Live such as fought and sailed and ruled and loved and made our world.

They are purged of pride because they died; they know the worth of their
    bays;
They sit at wine with the Maidens Nine and the Gods of the Elder
    Days—
It is their will to serve or be still as fitteth Our Father's praise.

'Tis theirs to sweep through the ringing deep where Azrael's outposts are,
Or buffet a path through the Pit's red wrath when God goes out to war,
Or hang with the reckless Seraphim on the rein of a red-maned star.

They take their mirth in the joy of the Earth—they dare not grieve for her
    pain.
They know of toil and the end of toil; they know God's Law is plain;
So they whistle the Devil to make them sport who know that Sin is vain.

And oft-times cometh our wise Lord God, master of every trade,
And tells them tales of His daily toil, of Edens newly made;
And they rise to their feet as He passes by, gentlemen un-afraid.

To these who are cleansed of base Desire, Sorrow and Lust and Shame—
Gods for they knew the hearts of men, men for they stooped to Fame—
Borne on the breath that men call Death, my brother's spirit came.

He scarce had need to doff his pride or slough the dross of Earth—
E'en as he trod that day to God so walked he from his birth,
In simpleness and gentleness and honour and clean mirth.

So cup to lip in fellowship they gave him welcome high
And made him place at the banquet board—the Strong Men ranged thereby,
Who had done his work and held his peace and had no fear to die.

Beyond the loom of the last lone star, through open darkness hurled,
Further than rebel comet dared or hiving star-swarm swirled,
Sits he with those that praise our God for that they served His world.

To the True Romance

1893

THY face is far from this our war,
   Our call and counter-cry,
I shall not find Thee quick and kind,
   Nor know Thee till I die.
Enough for me in dreams to see
   And touch Thy garments' hem:
Thy feet have trod so near to God
   I may not follow them!

Through wantonness if men profess
   They weary of Thy parts,
E'en let them die at blasphemy
   And perish with their arts;
But we that love, but we that prove
   Thine excellence august,
While we adore, discover more
   Thee perfect, wise, and just.

Since spoken word Man's Spirit stirred
   Beyond his belly-need,
What is is Thine of fair design
   In Thought and Craft and Deed.
Each stroke aright of toil and fight,
   That was and that shall be,

And hope too high, wherefore we die,
    Has birth and worth in Thee.

Who holds by Thee hath Heaven in fee
    To gild his dross thereby,
And knowledge sure that he endure
    A child until he die—
For to make plain at man's disdain
    Is but new Beauty's birth—
For to possess in singleness
    The joy of all the earth.

As Thou didst teach all lovers speech,
    And Life all mystery,
So shalt Thou rule by every school
    Till life and longing die,
Who wast, or yet the Lights were set,
    A whisper in the Void,
Who shalt be sung through planets young
    When this is clean destroyed.

Beyond the bounds our staring rounds,
    Across the pressing dark,
The children wise of outer skies
    Look hitherward and mark
A light that shifts, a glare that drifts,
    Rekindling thus and thus—
Not all forlorn, for Thou hast borne
    Strange tales to them of us.

Time hath no tide but must abide
    The servant of Thy will;
Tide hath no time, for to Thy rhyme
    The ranging stars stand still—
Regent of spheres that lock our fears,
    Our hopes invisible,
Oh, 'twas certes at Thy decrees
    We fashioned Heaven and Hell!

Pure Wisdom hath no certain path
    That lacks Thy morning-eyne,
And Captains bold by Thee controlled
    Most like to Gods design.
Thou art the Voice to kingly boys
    To lift them through the fight,

And Comfortress of Unsuccess,
   To give the Dead good-night.

A veil to draw 'twixt God His Law
   And Man's infirmity,
A shadow kind to dumb and blind
   The shambles where we die;
A rule to trick th' arithmetic,
   Too base, of leaguing odds—
The spur of trust, the curb of lust,
   Thou handmaid of the Gods!

O Charity, all patiently
   Abiding wrack and scaith!
O Faith, that meets ten thousand cheats
   Yet drops no jot of faith!
Devil and brute Thou dost transmute
   To higher, lordlier show,
Who art in sooth that lovely Truth
   The careless angels know!

Thy face is far from this our war,
   Our call and counter-cry,
I may not find Thee quick and kind,
   Nor know Thee till I die.

Yet may I look with heart unshook
   On blow brought home or missed—
Yet may I hear with equal ear
   The clarions down the List;
Yet set my lance above mischance
   And ride the barriere—
Oh, hit or miss, how little 'tis,
   My lady is not there!

Sestina of the Tramp-Royal

1896

Speakin' in general, I 'ave tried 'em all—
The 'appy roads that take you o'er the world.
Speakin' in general, I 'ave found them good
For such as cannot use one bed too long,
But must get 'ence, the same as I 'ave done,
An' go observin' matters till they die.

What do it matter where or 'ow we die,
So long as we've our 'ealth to watch it all—
The different ways that different things are done,
An' men an' women lovin' in this world;
Takin' our chances they come along,
An' when they ain't, pretendin' they are good?

In cash or credit—no, it aren't no good;
You 'ave to 'ave the 'abit or you'd die,
Unless you lived your life but one day long,
Nor didn't prophesy nor fret at all,
But drew your tucker some'ow from the world,
An' never bothered what you might ha' done.

But, Gawd, what things are they I 'aven't done?
I've turned my 'and to most, an' turned it good,
In various situations round the world—
For 'im that doth not work must surely die;
But that's no reason man should labour all
'Is life on one same shift—life's none so long.

Therefore, from job to job I've moved along.
Pay couldn't 'old me when my time was done,
For something in my 'ead upset it all,
Till I 'ad dropped whatever 'twas for good,
An', out at sea, be'eld the dock-lights die,
An' met my mate—the wind that tramps the world!

It's like a book, I think, this bloomin' world,
Which you can read and care for just so long,
But presently you feel that you will die
Unless you get the page you're readin' done,
An' turn another—likely not so good;
But what you're after is to turn 'em all.

Gawd bless this world!   Whatever she 'ath done—
Excep' when awful long—I've found it good.
So write, before I die, " 'E liked it all!"

The Miracles
1894

I sent a message to my dear—
    A thousand leagues and more to Her—
The dumb sea-levels thrilled to hear,
    And Lost Atlantis bore to Her!

Behind my message hard I came,
  And nigh had found a grave for me;
But that I launched of steel and flame
  Did war against the wave for me.

Uprose the deep, in gale on gale,
  To bid me change my mind again—
He broke his teeth along my rail,
  And, roaring, swung behind again.

I stayed the sun at noon to tell
  My way across the waste of it;
I read the storm before it fell
  And made the better haste of it.

Afar, I hailed the land at night—
  The towers I built had heard of me—
And, ere my rocket reached its height,
  Had flashed my Love the word of me.

Earth sold her chosen men of strength
  (They lived and strove and died for me)
To drive my road a nation's length,
  And toss the miles aside for me.

I snatched their toil to serve my needs—
  Too slow their fleetest flew for me.
I tired twenty smoking steeds,
  And bade them bait a new for me.

I sent the Lightnings forth to see
  Where hour by hour She waited me.
Among ten million one was She,
  And surely all men hated me!

Dawn ran to meet me at my goal—
  Ah, day no tongue shall tell again!
And little folk of little soul
  Rose up to buy and sell again!

Song of the Wise Children

1902

When the darkened Fifties dip to the North,
   And frost and the fog divide the air,
And the day is dead at his breaking-forth,
   Sirs, it is bitter beneath the Bear!

Far to Southward they wheel and glance,
   The million molten spears of morn—
The spears of our deliverance
   That shine on the house where we were born.

Flying-fish about our bows,
   Flying sea-fires in our wake:
This is the road to our Father's House,
   Whither we go for our soul's sake!

We have forfeited our birthright,
   We have forsaken all things meet;
We have forgotten the look of light,
   We have forgotten the scent of heat.

They that walk with shaded brows,
   Year by year in a shining land,
They be men of our Father's House,
   They shall receive us and understand.

We shall go back by the boltless doors,
   To the life unaltered our childhood knew—
To the naked feet on the cool, dark floors,
   And the high-ceiled rooms that the Trade blows through:

To the trumpet-flowers and the moon beyond,
   And the tree-toad's chorus drowning all—
And the lisp of the split banana-frond
   That talked us to sleep when we were small.

The wayside magic, the threshold spells,
   Shall soon undo what the North has done—
Because of the sights and the sounds and the smells
   That ran with our youth in the eye of the sun.

And Earth accepting shall ask no vows,
   Nor the Sea our love, nor our lover the Sky.
When we return to our Father's House
   Only the English shall wonder why!

Zion

1914–18

The Doorkeepers of Zion,
   They do not always stand
In helmet and whole armour,
   With halberds in their hand;
But, being sure of Zion,
   And all her mysteries,
They rest awhile in Zion,
Sit down and smile in Zion;
Ay, even jest in Zion;
   In Zion, at their ease.

The Gatekeepers of Baal,
   They dare not sit or lean,
But fume and fret and posture
   And foam and curse between;
For, being bound to Baal,
   Whose sacrifice is vain,
Their rest is scant with Baal,
They glare and pant for Baal,
They mouth and rant for Baal;
   For Baal in their pain.

But we will go to Zion,
   By choice and not through dread,
With these our present comrades
   And those our present dead;
And, being free of Zion
   In both her fellowships,
Sit down and sup in Zion—
Stand up and drink in Zion
Whatever cup in Zion
   Is offered to our lips!

Buddha at Kamakura

1892

"And there is a Japanese idol at Kamakura."

O ye who tread the Narrow Way
By Tophet-flare to Judgment Day,
Be gentle when "the heathen" pray
    To Buddha at Kamakura!

To Him the Way, the Law, apart,
Whom Maya held beneath her heart,
Ananda's Lord, the Bodhisat,
    The Buddha of Kamakura.

For though He neither burns nor sees,
Nor hears ye thank your Deities,
Ye have not sinned with such as these,
    His children at Kamakura,

Yet spare us still the Western joke
When joss-sticks turn to scented smoke
The little sins of little folk
    That worship at Kamakura—

The grey-robed, gay-sashed butterflies
That flit beneath the Master's eyes.
He is beyond the Mysteries
    But loves them at Kamakura.

And whoso will, from Pride released,
Contemning neither creed nor priest,
May feel the Soul of all the East
    About him at Kamakura.

Yea, every tale Ananda heard,
Of birth as fish or beast or bird,
While yet in lives the Master stirred,
    The warm wind brings Kamakura.

Till drowsy eyelids seem to see
A-flower 'neath her golden *htee*
The Shwe-Dagon flare easterly
    From Burma to Kamakura,

And down the loaded air there comes
The thunder of Thibetan drums,

And droned—"*Om mane padme hum's*"[1]
   A world's-width from Kamakura.

Yet Brahmans rule Benares still,
Buddh-Gaya's ruins pit the hill,
And beef-fed zealots threaten ill
   To Buddha and Kamakura.

A tourist-show, a legend told,
A rusting bulk of bronze and gold,
So much, and scarce so much, ye hold
   The meaning of Kamakura?

But when the morning prayer is prayed,
Think, ere ye pass to strife and trade,
Is God in human image made
   No nearer than Kamakura?

The Greek National Anthem

1918

We knew thee of old,
   Oh, divinely restored,
By the light of thine eyes
   And the light of thy Sword.

From the graves of our slain
   Shall thy valour prevail
As we greet thee again—
   Hail, Liberty!   Hail!

Long time didst thou dwell
   Mid the peoples that mourn,
Awaiting some voice
   That should bid thee return.

Ah, slow broke that day
   And no man dared call,
For the shadow of tyranny
   Lay over all:

And we saw thee sad-eyed,
   The tears on thy cheeks
While thy raiment was dyed
   In the blood of the Greeks.

[1] The Buddhist invocation.

Yet, behold now thy sons
  With impetuous breath
Go forth to the fight
  Seeking Freedom or Death.

From the graves of our slain
  Shall thy valour prevail
As we greet thee again—
  Hail, Liberty!   Hail!

The Sea-Wife

1893

There dwells a wife by the Northern Gate,
  And a wealthy wife is she;
She breeds a breed of roving men
  And casts them over sea.

And some are drowned in deep water,
  And some in sight o' shore,
And word goes back to the weary wife
  And ever she sends more.

For since that wife had gate or gear,
  Or hearth or garth or field,
She willed her sons to the white harvest,
  And that is a bitter yield.

She wills her sons to the wet ploughing,
  To ride the horse of tree;
And syne her sons come back again
  Far-spent from out the sea.

The good wife's sons come home again
  With little into their hands,
But the lore of men that have dealt with men
  In the new and naked lands;

But the faith of men that have brothered men
  By more than easy breath,
And the eyes of men that have read with men
  In the open books of Death.

Rich are they, rich in wonders seen,
  But poor in the goods of men;

So what they have got by the skin of their teeth
    They sell for their teeth again.

And whether they lose to the naked life
    Or win to their hearts' desire,
They tell it all to the weary wife
    That nods beside the fire.

Her hearth is wide to every wind
    That makes the white ash spin;
And tide and tide and 'tween the tides
    Her sons go out and in;

(Out with great mirth that do desire
    Hazard of trackless ways—
In with content to wait their watch
    And warm before the blaze);

And some return by failing light,
    And some in waking dream,
For she hears the heels of the dripping ghosts
    That ride the rough roof-beam.

Home, they come home from all the ports,
    The living and the dead;
The good wife's sons come home again
    For her blessing on their head!

The Broken Men

1902

For things we never mention,
    For Art misunderstood—
For excellent intention
    That did not turn to good;
From ancient tales' renewing,
    From clouds we would not clear—
Beyond the Law's pursuing
    We fled, and settled here.

We took no tearful leaving,
    We bade no long good-byes.
Men talked of crime and thieving,
    Men wrote of fraud and lies.

To save our injured feelings
    'Twas time and time to go—
Behind was dock and Dartmoor,
    Ahead lay Callao!

The widow and the orphan
    That pray for ten per cent,
They clapped their trailers on us
    To spy the road we went.
They watched the foreign sailings
    (They scan the shipping still),
And that's your Christian people
    Returning good for ill!

God bless the thoughtful islands
    Where never warrants come;
God bless the just Republics
    That give a man a home,
That ask no foolish questions,
    But set him on his feet;
And save his wife and daughters
    From the workhouse and the street!

On church and square and market
    The noonday silence falls;
You'll hear the drowsy mutter
    Of the fountain in our halls.
Asleep amid the yuccas
    The city takes her ease—
Till twilight brings the land-wind
    To the clicking jalousies.

Day long the diamond weather,
    The high, unaltered blue—
The smell of goats and incense
    And the mule-bells tinkling through.
Day long the warder ocean
    That keeps us from our kin,
And once a month our levée
    When the English mail comes in.

You'll find us up and waiting
    To treat you at the bar;
You'll find us less exclusive
    Than the average English are.
We'll meet you with a carriage,

Too glad to show you round,
But—we do not lunch on steamers,
For they are English ground.

We sail o' nights to England
And join our smiling Boards—
Our wives go in with Viscounts
And our daughters dance with Lords,
But behind our princely doings,
And behind each coup we make,
We feel there's Something Waiting,
And—we meet It when we wake.

Ah, God!   One sniff of England—
To greet our flesh and blood—
To hear the traffic slurring
Once more through London mud!
Our towns of wasted honour—
Our streets of lost delight!
How stands the old Lord Warden?
Are Dover's cliffs still white?

Gethsemane

1914–18

The Garden called Gethsemane
In Picardy it was,
And there the people came to see
The English soldiers pass.
We used to pass—we used to pass
Or halt, as it might be,
And ship our masks in case of gas
Beyond Gethsemane.

The Garden called Gethsemane,
It held a pretty lass,
But all the time she talked to me
I prayed my cup might pass.
The officer sat on the chair,
The men lay on the grass,
And all the time we halted there
I prayed my cup might pass.

It didn't pass—it didn't pass—
 It didn't pass from me.
I drank it when we met the gas
 Beyond Gethsemane!

The Song of the Banjo

1894

You couldn't pack a Broadwood half a mile—
 You mustn't leave a fiddle in the damp—
You couldn't raft an organ up the Nile,
 And play it in an Equatorial swamp.
I travel with the cooking-pots and pails—
 I'm sandwiched 'tween the coffee and the pork—
And when the duty column checks and tails,
 You should hear me spur the rearguard to a walk!

 With my *"Pilly-willy-winky-popp!"*
  [Oh, it's any tune that comes into my head!]
 So I keep 'em moving forward till they drop;
  So I play 'em up to water and to bed.

In the silence of the camp before the fight,
 When it's good to make your will and say your prayer,
You can hear my *strumpty-stumpty* overnight,
 Explaining ten to one was always fair.
I'm the Prophet of the Utterly Absurd,
 Of the Patently Impossible and Vain—
And when the Thing that Couldn't has occurred,
 Give me time to change my leg and go again.

 With my *"Tumpa-tumpa-tumpa-tumpa-tump!"*
  In the desert where the dung-fed camp-smoke curled.
 There was never voice before us till I led our lonely chorus,
  I—the war-drum of the White Man round the world!

By the bitter road the Younger Son must tread,
 Ere he win to hearth and saddle of his own,—
'Mid the riot of the shearers at the shed,
 In the silence of the herder's hut alone—
In the twilight, on a bucket upside down,
 Hear me babble what the weakest won't confess—
I am Memory and Torment—I am Town!
 I am all that ever went with evening dress!

With my *"Tunka-tunka-tunka-tunka-tunk!"*
  [So the lights—the London Lights—grow near and plain!]
So I rowel 'em afresh towards the Devil and the Flesh,
  Till I bring my broken rankers home again.

In desire of many marvels over sea,
  Where the new-raised tropic city sweats and roars,
I have sailed with Young Ulysses from the quay
  Till the anchor rumbled down on stranger shores.
He is blooded to the open and the sky,
  He is taken in a snare at shall not fail,
He shall hear me singing strongly, till he die,
  Like the shouting of a backstay in a gale.

    With my *"Hya! Heeya! Heeya! Hullah! Haul!"*
      [Oh, the green that thunders aft along the deck!]
    Are you sick o' towns and men? You must sign and sail again,
      For it's "Johnny Bowlegs, pack your kit and trek!"

Through the gorge that gives the stars at noon-day clear—
  Up the pass that packs the scud beneath our wheel—
Round the bluff that sinks her thousand fathom sheer—
  Down the valley with our guttering brakes asqueal:
Where the trestle groans and quivers in the snow,
  Where the many-shredded levels loop and twine,
Hear me lead my reckless children from below
  Till we sing the Song of Roland to the pine!

    With my *"Tinka-tinka-tinka-tinka-tink!"*
      [Oh, the axe has cleared the mountain, croup and crest!]
    And we ride the iron stallions down to drink,
      Through the cañons to the waters of the West!

And the tunes that meant so much to you alone—
  Common tunes that make you choke and blow your nose—
Vulgar tunes that bring the laugh that brings the groan—
  I can rip your very heartstrings out with those;
With the feasting, and the folly, and the fun—
  And the lying, and the lusting, and the drink,
And the merry play that drops you, when you're done,
  To the thoughts that burn like irons if you think.

    With my *"Plunka-lunka-lunka-lunka-lunk!"*
      Here's a trifle on account of pleasure past,
    Ere the wit that made you win gives you eyes to see your sin
      And—the heavier repentance at the last!

Let the organ moan her sorrow to the roof—
    I have told the naked stars the Grief of Man!
Let the trumpet snare the foeman to the proof—
    I have known Defeat, and mocked it as we ran!
My bray ye may not alter nor mistake
    When I stand to jeer the fatted Soul of Things,
But the Song of Lost Endeavour that I make,
    Is it hidden in the twanging of the strings?

        With my *"Ta-ra-rara-rara-ra-ra-rrrp!*
        [Is it naught to you that hear and pass me by?]
        But the word—the word is mine, when the order moves the line
            And the lean, locked ranks go roaring down to die!

The grandam of my grandma was the Lyre—
    [Oh, the blue below the little fisher-huts!]
That the Stealer stooping beachward filled with fire,
    Till she bore my iron head and ringing guts!
By the wisdom of the centuries I speak—
    To the tune of yestermorn I set the truth—
I, the joy of life unquestioned—I, the Greek—
    I, the everlasting Wonder-song of Youth!

        With my *"Tinka-tinka-tinka-tinka-tink!"*
        [What d'ye lack, my noble masters!   What d'ye lack?]
        So I draw the world together link by link:
            Yea, from Delos up to Limerick and back!

The Spies' March

1913

(*"The outbreak is in full swing and our death-rate would sicken Napoleon . . . Dr. M——
died last week, and C—— on Monday, but some more medicines are coming . . . We
don't seem to be able to check it at all . . . Villages panicking badly . . . In some places
not a living soul . . . But at any rate the experience gained may come in useful, so I
am keeping my notes written up to date in case of accidents . . . Death is a queer chap
to live with for steady company."*—Extract from a private letter from Manchuria.)

There are no leaders to lead us to honour, and yet without leaders we
    sally;
Each man reporting for duty alone, out of sight, out of reach, of his
    fellow.
There are no bugles to call the battalions, and yet without bugle we rally

From the ends of the earth to the ends of the earth, to follow the
    Standard of Yellow!
Fall in!   O fall in!   O fall in!

Not where the squadrons mass,
  Not where the bayonets shine,
Not where the big shell shout as they pass
  Over the firing-line;
Not where the wounded are,
  Not where the nations die,
Killed in the cleanly game of war—
  That is no place for a spy!
O Princes, Thrones and Powers, your work is less than ours—
  Here is no place for a spy!

Trained to another use,
  We march with colours furled,
Only concerned when Death breaks loose
  On a front of half a world.
Only for General Death
  The Yellow Flag may fly,
While we take post beneath—
  That is the place for a spy.
Where Plague has spread his pinions over Nations and Dominions—
  Then will be work for a spy!

The dropping shots begin,
  The single funerals pass,
Our skirmishers run in,
  The corpses dot the grass!
The howling towns stampede,
  The tainted hamlets die.
Now it is war indeed—
  Now there is room for a spy!
O Peoples, Kings and Lands, we are waiting your commands—
  What is the work for a spy?
(Drums)—Fear is upon us, spy!

"Go where his pickets hide—
  Unmask the shape they take,
Whether a gnat from the waterside,
  Or a stinging fly in the brake,
Or filth of the crowded street,
  Or a sick rat limping by,

Or a smear of spittle dried in the heat—
  That is the work for a spy!
  (Drums)—*Death is upon us, spy!*

"What does he next prepare?
  Whence will he move to attack?—
By water, earth or air?—
  How can we head him back?
Shall we starve him out if we burn
  Or bury his food-supply?
Slip through his lines and learn—
  That is the work for a spy!
  (Drums)—*Get to your business, spy!*

"Does he feint or strike in force?
  Will he charge or ambuscade?
What is it checks his course?
  Is he beaten or only delayed?
How long will the lull endure?
  Is he retreating?   Why?
Crawl to his camp and make sure—
  That is the work for a spy!
  (Drums)—*Fetch us our answer, spy!*

"Ride with him girth to girth
  Wherever the Pale Horse wheels.
Wait on his councils, ear to earth,
  And show what the dust reveals.
For the smoke of our torment rolls
  Where the burning corpses lie;
What do we care for men's bodies or souls?
  Bring us deliverance, spy!"

The Explorer

1898

"There's no sense in going further—it's the edge of cultivation,"
So they said, and I believed it—broke my land and sowed my crop—
Built my barns and strung my fences in the little border station
  Tucked away below the foothills where the trails run out and stop:

Till a voice, as bad as Conscience, rang interminable changes
  On one everlasting Whisper day and night repeated—so:

"Something hidden.   Go and find it.   Go and look behind the Ranges—
  "Something lost behind the Ranges.   Lost and waiting for you.   Go!"

So I went, worn out of patience; never told my nearest neighbours—
  Stolen away with pack and ponies—left 'em drinking in the town;
And the faith that moveth mountains didn't seem to help my labours
  As I faced the sheer main-ranges, whipping up and leading down.

March by march I puzzled through 'em turning flanks and dodging
    shoulders,
  Hurried on in hope of water, headed back for lack of grass;
Till I camped above the tree-line—drifted snow and naked boulders—
  Felt free air astir to windward—knew I'd stumbled on the Pass.

'Thought to name it for the finder: but that night the Norther found
    me—
  Froze and killed the plains-bred ponies; so I called the camp Despair
(It's the Railway Gap to-day, though). Then my Whisper waked to hound
    me:—

  "Something lost behind the Ranges.   Over yonder!   Go you there!"

Then I knew, the while I doubted—knew His Hand was certain o'er me.
  Still—it might be self-delusion—scores of better men had died—
I could reach the township living, but ... He knows what terror tore
    me ...
  But I didn't ... but I didn't. I went down the other side,

Till the snow ran out in flowers, and the flowers turned to aloes,
  And the aloes sprung to thickets and a brimming stream ran by;
But the thickets dwined to thorn-scrub, and the water drained to shallows,
  And I dropped again on desert—blasted earth, and blasting sky ...

I remember lighting fires; I remember sitting by 'em;
  I remember seeing faces, hearing voices, through the smoke;
I remember they were fancy—for I threw a stone to try 'em.
  "Something lost behind the Ranges" was the only word they spoke.

I remember going crazy.   I remember that I knew it
  When I heard myself hallooing to the funny folk I saw.
Very full of dreams that desert, but my two legs took me through it ...
  And I used to watch 'em moving with the toes all black and raw.

But at last the country altered—White Man's country past disputing—
  Rolling grass and open timber, with a hint of hills behind—
There I found me food and water, and I lay a week recruiting.
  Got my strength and lost my nightmares.   Then I entered on my find.

Thence I ran my first rough survey—chose my tree and blazed and ringed
    'em—

Week by week I pried and sampled—week by week my findings grew.
Saul he went to look for donkeys, and by God he found a kingdom!
   But by God, who sent His Whisper, I had struck the worth of two!

Up along the hostile mountains, where the hair-poised snowslide shivers—
   Down and through the big fat marshes that the virgin ore-bed stains,
Till I heard the mile-wide mutterings of unimagined rivers,
   And beyond the nameless timber saw illimitable plains!

Plotted sites of future cities, traced the easy grades between 'em;
   Watched unharnessed rapids wasting fifty thousand head an hour;
Counted leagues of water-frontage through the axe-ripe woods that screen
   'em—
   Saw the plant to feed a people—up and waiting for the power!

Well I know who'll take the credit—all the clever chaps that followed—
   Came, a dozen men together—never knew my desert-fears;
Tracked me by the camps I'd quitted, used the water-holes I'd hollowed.
   They'll go back and do the talking.   *They'll* be called the Pioneers!

They will find my sites of townships—not the cities that I set there.
   They will rediscover rivers—not my rivers heard at night.
By my own old marks and bearings they will show me how to get there,
   By the lonely cairns I builded they will guide my feet aright.

Have I named one single river?   Have I claimed one single acre?
   Have I kept one single nugget—(barring samples)?   No, not I!
Because my price was paid me ten times over by my Maker.
   But you wouldn't understand it.   You go up and occupy.

Ores you'll find there; wood and cattle; water-transit sure and steady
   (That should keep the railway-rates down), coal and iron at your doors.
God took care to hide that country till He judged His people ready,
   Then he chose me for His Whisper, and I've found it, and it's yours!

Yes, your "Never-never country"—yes, your "edge of cultivation"
   And "no sense in going further"—till I crossed the range to see.
God forgive me!   No, *I* didn't.   It's God's present to our nation.
   Anybody might have found it, but—His Whisper came to Me!

The Pro-Consuls

(LORD MILNER)

The overfaithful sword returns the user
His heart's desire at price of his heart's blood.
The clamour of the arrogant accuser

Wastes that one hour we needed to make good.
This was foretold of old at our outgoing;
This we accepted who have squandered, knowing,
The strength and glory of our reputations,
At the day's need, as it were dross, to guard
The tender and new-dedicate foundations
Against the sea we fear—not man's award.

They that dig foundations deep,
  Fit for realms to rise upon,
Little honour do they reap
  Of their generation,
Any more than mountains gain
Stature till we reach the plain.

With no veil before their face
  Such as shroud or sceptre lend—
Daily in the market-place,
  Of one height to foe and friend—
They must cheapen self to find
Ends uncheapened for mankind.

Through the night when hirelings rest,
  Sleepless they arise, alone,
The unsleeping arch to test
  And the o'er-trusted corner-stone,
'Gainst the need, they know, that lies
Hid behind the centuries.

Not by lust of praise or show,
  Not by Peace herself betrayed—
Peace herself must they forgo
  Till that peace be fitly made;
And in single strength uphold
Wearier hands and hearts acold.

On the stage their act hath framed
  For thy sports, O Liberty!
Doubted are they, and defamed
  By the tongues their act set free,
While they quicken, tend and raise
Power that must their power displace.

Lesser men feign greater goals,
  Failing whereof they may sit
Scholarly to judge the souls

That go down into the Pit
And, despite its certain clay,
Heave a new world toward the day.

These at labour make no sign,
    More than planets, tides or years
Which discover God's design,
    Not our hopes and not our fears;
Nor in aught they gain or lose
Seek a triumph or excuse!

For, so the Ark be borne to Zion, who
Heeds how they perished or were paid that bore it?
For, so the Shrine abide, what shame—what pride—
If we, the priests, were bound or crowned before it?

The Runners

Indian Frontier, 1904
("A Sahibs' War"—*Traffics and Discoveries*)

News!
What is the word that they tell now—now—now!
The little drums beating in the bazaars?
    They beat (among the buyers and the sellers)
        "*Nimrud—ah, Nimrud!*
        God sends a gnat against Nimrud!"
Watchers, O Watchers a thousand!

News!
At the edge of the crops—now—now—where the well-wheels are halted,
    One prepares to loose the bullocks and one scrapes his hoe,
    They beat (among the sowers and the reapers)
        "*Nimrud—ah, Nimrud!*
        God prepares an ill day for Nimrud!"
Watchers, O Watchers ten thousand.

News!
By the fires of the camps—now—now—where the travellers meet,
Where the camels come in and the horses, their men conferring,
    They beat (among the packmen and the drivers)
        "*Nimrud—ah, Nimrud!*
        Thus it befell last noon to Nimrud!"
Watchers, O Watchers an hundred thousand!

News!

Under the shadow of the border-peels—now—now—now!

In the rocks of the passes where the expectant shoe their horses,
　　They beat (among the rifles and the riders)
　　　"Nimrud—ah, Nimrud!
　　　Shall we go up against Nimrud?"
Watchers, O Watchers a thousand thousand!

News!

Bring out the heaps of grain—open the account-books again!

Drive forward the well-bullocks against the taxable harvest!

Eat and lie under the trees—pitch the police-guarded fairgrounds, O
　　　　dancers!

Hide away the rifles and let down the ladders from the watch-towers!
　　They beat (among all the peoples)
　　　"Now—now—now!
　　　God has reserved the Sword for Nimrud!
　　　God has given Victory to Nimrud!
　　　Let us abide under Nimrud!"
　O Well-disposed and Heedful, an hundred thousand thousand!

The Sea and the Hills

1902

Who hath desired the Sea?—the sight of salt water unbounded—

The heave and the halt and the hurl and the crash of the comber
　　wind-hounded?

The sleek-barrelled swell before storm, grey, foamless, enormous, and
　　growing—

Stark calm on the lap of the Line or the crazy-eyed hurricane blowing—

His Sea in no showing the same—his Sea and the same 'neath each
　　showing:
　His Sea as she slackens or thrills?

So and no otherwise—so and no otherwise—hillmen desire their Hills!

Who hath desired the Sea?—the immense and contemptuous surges?

The shudder, the stumble, the swerve, as the star-stabbing bowsprit
　　emerges?

The orderly clouds of the Trades, the ridged, roaring sapphire
　　thereunder—

Unheralded cliff-haunting flaws and the headsail's low-volleying thunder—

His Sea in no wonder the same—his Sea and the same through each
　　wonder:

His Sea as she rages or stills?
So and no otherwise—so and no otherwise—hillmen desire their Hills.

Who hath desired the Sea? Her menaces swift as her mercies?
The in-rolling walls of the fog and the silver-winged breeze that disperses?
The unstable mined berg going South and the calvings and groans that
    declare it—
White water half-guessed overside and the moon breaking timely to bare
    it—
His Sea as his fathers have dared—his Sea as his children shall dare it:
  His Sea as she serves him or kills?
So and no otherwise—so and no otherwise—hillmen desire their Hills.

Who hath desired the Sea? Her excellent loneliness rather
Than forecourts of kings, and her outermost pits than the streets where
    men gather
Inland, among dust, under trees—inland where the slayer may slay him—
Inland, out of reach of her arms, and the bosom whereon he must lay
    him—
His Sea from the first that betrayed—at the last that shall never betray
    him:
  His Sea that his being fulfils?
So and no otherwise—so and no otherwise—hillmen desire their Hills.

Anchor Song

1893

Heh! Walk her round. Heave, ah, heave her short again!
  Over, snatch her over, there, and hold her on the pawl.
Loose all sail, and brace your yards aback and full—
  Ready jib to pay her off and heave short all!

Well, ah, fare you well; we can stay no more with you, my love—
  Down, set down your liquor and your girl from off your knee;
    For the wind has come to say:
    "You must take me while you may,
    If you'd go to Mother Carey
    (Walk her down to Mother Carey!),
  Oh, we're bound to Mother Carey where she feeds her chicks at sea!"

Heh! Walk her round. Break, ah, break it out o' that!
  Break our starboard-bow out, apeak, awash, and clear!
Port—port she casts, with the harbour-mud beneath her foot.
  And that's the last o' bottom we shall see this year!

Well, ah, fare you well, for we've got to take her out again—
   Take her out in ballast, riding light and cargo-free.
      And it's time to clear and quit
      When the hawser grips the bitt,
  So we'll pay you with the foresheet and a promise from the sea!

Heh! Tally on. Aft and walk away with her!
   Handsome to the cathead, now; O tally on the fall!
Stop, seize and fish, and easy on the davit-guy.
   Up, well up the fluke of her, and inboard haul!

Well, ah, fare you well, for the Channel wind's took hold of us,
   Choking down our voices as we snatch the gaskets free.
      And it's blowing up for night,
      And she's dropping light on light,
  And she's snorting as she's snatching for a breath of open sea!

Wheel, full and by; but she'll smell her road alone to-night.
   Sick she is and harbour-sick—oh, sick to clear the land!
Roll down to Brest with the old Red Ensign over us—
   Carry on and thrash her out with all she'll stand!

Well, ah, fare you well, and it's Ushant slams the door on us,
   Whirling like a windmill through the dirty scud to lee,
      Till the last, last flicker goes
      From the tumbling water-rows,
    And we're off to Mother Carey
    (Walk her down to Mother Carey!),
  Oh, we're bound for Mother Carey where she feeds her chicks at sea!

The Rhyme of the Three Sealers

1893

Away by the lands of the Japanee
   Where the paper lanterns glow
And the crews of all the shipping drink
   In the house of Blood Street Joe,
At twilight, when the landward breeze
   Brings up the harbour noise,
And ebb of Yokohama Bay
   Swigs chattering through the buoys,
In Cisco's Dewdrop Dining Rooms
   They tell the tale anew

> *Of a hidden sea and a hidden fight,*
> *When the* Baltic *ran from the* Northern Light,
> *And the* Stralsund *fought the two.*

Now this is the Law of the Muscovite, that he proves with shot and steel,
When you come by his isles in the Smoky Sea you must not take the seal,
Where the grey sea goes nakedly between the weed-hung shelves,
And the little blue fox he is bred for his skin and the seal they breed for
  themselves.
For when the *matkas*[1] seek the shore to drop their pups aland,
The great man-seal haul out of the sea, aroaring, band by band.
And when the first September gales have slaked their rutting-wrath,
The great man-seal haul back to the sea and no man knows their path.
Then dark they lie and stark they lie—rookery, dune, and floe,
And the Northern Lights come down o' nights to dance with the houseless
  snow;
And God Who clears the grounding berg and steers the grinding floe,
He hears the cry of the little kit-fox and the wind along the snow.
But since our women must walk gay and money buys their gear,
The sealing-boats they filch that way at hazard year by year.
English they be and Japanee that hang on the Brown Bear's flank,
And some be Scot, but the worst of the lot, and the boldest thieves, be
  Yank!

It was the sealer *Northern Light,* to the Smoky Seas she bore,
With a stovepipe stuck from a starboard port and the Russian flag at her
  fore.
(*Baltic, Stralsund,* and *Northern Light*—oh! they were birds of a feather—
Slipping away to the Smoky Seas, three seal-thieves together!)
And at last she came to a sandy cove and the *Baltic* lay therein,
But her men were up with the herding seal to drive and club and skin.
There were fifteen hundred skins abeach, cool pelt and proper fur,
When the *Northern Light* drove into the bight and the sea-mist drove with
  her.
The *Baltic* called her men and weighed—she could not choose but run—
For a stovepipe seen through the closing mist, it shows like a four-inch
  gun
(And loss it is that is sad as death to lose both trip and ship
And lie for a rotting contraband on Vladivostok slip).
She turned and dived in the sea-smother as a rabbit dives in the whins,
And the *Northern Light* sent up her boats to steal the stolen skins.
They had not brought a load to side or slid their hatches clear,
When they were aware of a sloop-of-war, ghost-white and very near.

[1]She-seals.

Her flag she showed, and her guns she showed—three of them, black,
   abeam,
And a funnel white with the crusted salt, but never a show of steam.

There was no time to man the brakes, they knocked the shackle free,
And the *Northern Light* stood out again, goose-winged to open sea.
(For life it is that is worse than death, by force of Russian law,
To work in the mines of mercury that lose the teeth in your jaw.)
They had not run a mile from shore—they heard no shots behind—
When the skipper smote his hand on his thigh and threw her up in the
   wind:
"Bluffed—raised out on a bluff," said he, "for if my name's Tom Hall,
"You must set a thief to catch a thief—and a thief has caught us all!
"By every butt in Oregon and every spar in Maine,
"The hand that spilled the wind from her sail was the hand of Reuben
   Paine!
"He has rigged and trigged her with paint and spar, and, faith, he has
   faked her well—
"But I'd know the *Stralsund's* deckhouse yet from here to the booms
   o'Hell.
"Oh, once we ha' met at Baltimore, and twice on Boston pier,
"But the sickest day for you, Reuben Paine, was the day that you came
   here—
"The day that you came here, my lad, to scare us from our seal
"With your funnel made o' your painted cloth, and your guns o' rotten
   deal!
"Ring and blow for the *Baltic* now, and head her back to the bay,
"And we'll come into the game again—with a double deck to play!"

They rang and blew the sealers' call—the poaching-cry of the sea—
And they raised the *Baltic* out of the mist, and an angry ship was she.
And blind they groped through the whirling white and blind to the bay
   again,
Till they heard the creak of the *Stralsund's* boom and the clank of her
   mooring chain.
They laid them down by bitt and boat, their pistols in their belts,
And: "Will you fight for it, Reuben Paine, or will you share the pelts?"

A dog-toothed laugh laughed Reuben Paine, and bared his flenching-knife.
"Yea, skin for skin, and all that he hath a man will give for his life;
"But I've six thousand skins below, and Yeddo Port to see,
"And there's never a law of God or man runs north of Fifty-Three:
"So go in peace to the naked seas with empty holds to fill,
"And I'll be good to your seal this catch, as many as I shall kill!"

Answered the snap of a closing lock—the jar of a gun-butt slid,
But the tender fog shut fold on fold to hide the wrong they did.
The weeping fog rolled fold on fold the wrath of man to cloak,
As the flame-spurts pale ran down the rail and the sealing-rifles spoke.
The bullets bit on bend and butt, the splinter slivered free
(Little they trust to sparrow-dust that stop the seal in his sea!),
The thick smoke hung and would not shift, leaden it lay and blue,
But three were down on the *Baltic's* deck and two of the *Stralsund's* crew.
An arm's length out and overside the banked fog held them bound,
But, as they heard or groan or word, they fired at the sound.
For one cried out on the Name of God, and one to have him cease,
And the questing volley found them both and bade them hold their peace.
And one called out on a heathen joss and one on the Virgin's Name,
And the schooling bullet leaped across and led them whence they came.
And in the waiting silences the rudder whined beneath,
And each man drew his watchful breath slow-taken 'tween the teeth—
Trigger and ear and eye acock, knit brow and hard-drawn lips—
Bracing his feet by chock and cleat for the rolling of the ships.
Till they heard the cough of a wounded man that fought in the fog for
    breath,
Till they heard the torment of Reuben Paine that wailed upon his death:

"The tides they'll go through Fundy Race, but I'll go never more
"And see the hogs from ebb-tide mark turn scampering back to shore.
"No more I'll see the trawlers drift below the Bass Rock ground,
"Or watch the tall Fall steamer lights tear blazing up the Sound.
"Sorrow is me, in a lonely sea and a sinful fight I fall,
"But if there's law o' God or man you'll swing for it yet, Tom Hall!"

Tom Hall stood up by the quarter-rail. "Your words in your teeth," said
    he.
"There's never a law of God or man runs north of Fifty-Three.
"So go in grace with Him to face, and an ill-spent life behind,
"And I'll be good to your widows, Rube, as many as I shall find."
A *Stralsund* man shot blind and large, and a warlock Finn was he,
And he hit Tom Hall with a bursting ball a hand's-breadth over the knee.
Tom Hall caught hold by the topping-lift, and sat him down with an oath,
"You'll wait a little, Rube," he said, "the Devil has called for both.
"The Devil is driving both this tide, and the killing-grounds are close,
"And we'll go up to the Wrath of God as the holluschickie[1] goes.
"O men put back your guns again and lay your rifles by,
"We've fought our fight, and the best are down. Let up and let us die!

[1]The young seal.

"Quit firing, by the bow there—quit! Call off the *Baltic's* crew!
"You're sure of Hell as me or Rube—but wait till we get through."

There went no word between the ships, but thick and quick and loud
The life-blood drummed on the dripping decks, with the fog-dew from the shroud.
The sea-pull drew them side by side, gunnel to gunnel laid,
And they felt the sheer-strakes pound and clear, but never a word was said.

Then Reuben Paine cried out again before his spirit passed:
"Have I followed the sea for thirty years to die in the dark at last?
"Curse on her work that has nipped me here with a shifty trick unkind—
"I have gotten my death where I got my bread, but I dare not face it blind.
"Curse on the fog! Is there never a wind of all the winds I knew
"To clear the smother from off my chest, and let me look at the blue?"
The good fog heard—like a splitten sail, to left and right she tore,
And they saw the sun-dogs in the haze and the seal upon the shore.

Silver and grey ran spit and bay to meet the steel-backed tide,
And pinched and white in the clearing light the crews stared overside.
O rainbow-gay the red pools lay that swilled and spilled and spread,
And gold, raw gold, the spent shells rolled between the careless dead—
The dead that rocked so drunkenwise to weather and to lee,
And they saw the work their hands had done as God had bade them see!

And a little breeze blew over the rail that made the headsails lift,
But no man stood by wheel or sheet, and they let the schooners drift.
And the rattle rose in Reuben's throat and he cast his soul with a cry,
And "Gone already?" Tom Hall he said. "Then it's time for me to die."
His eyes were heavy with great sleep and yearning for the land,
And he spoke as a man that talks in dreams, his wound beneath his hand.

"Oh, there comes no good o' the westering wind that backs against the sun;
"Wash down the decks—they're all too red—and share the skins and run.
"*Baltic, Stralsund,* and *Northern Light*—clean share and share for all,
"You'll find the fleets off Tolstoi Mees, but you will not find Tom Hall.
"Evil he did in shoal-water and blacker sin on the deep,
"But now he's sick of watch and trick and now he'll turn and sleep.
"He'll have no more of the crawling sea that made him suffer so,
"But he'll lie down on the killing-grounds where the holluschickie go.
"And west you'll sail and south again, beyond the sea-fog's rim,
"And tell the Yoshiwara girls to burn a stick for him.

"And you'll not weight him by the heels and dump him overside,
"But carry him up to the sand-hollows to die as Bering died,
"And make a place for Reuben Paine that knows the fight was fair,
"And leave the two that did the wrong to talk it over there!"

Half-steam ahead by guess and lead, for the sun is mostly veiled—
Through fog to fog, by luck and log, sail you as Bering sailed;
And if the light shall lift aright to give your landfall plain,
North and by west, from Zapne Crest you raise the Crosses twain.
Fair marks are they to the inner bay, the reckless poacher knows,
What time the scarred see-catchie[1] lead there sleek seraglios.
Ever they hear the floe-pack clear, and the blast of the old bull-whale,
And the deep seal-roar that beats off-shore above the loudest gale.
Ever they wait the winter's hate as the thundering boorga[2] calls,
Where northward look they to St. George, and westward to St. Paul's.
Ever they greet the hunted fleet—lone keels off headlands drear—
When the sealing-schooners flit that way at hazard year by year.
Ever in Yokohama port men tell the tale anew
    Of a hidden sea and a hidden fight,
    When the Baltic *ran from the* Northern Light,
And the Stralsund *fought the two.*

McAndrew's Hymn

1893

Lord, Thou hast made this world below the shadow of a dream,
An', taught by time, I tak' it so—exceptin' always Steam.
From coupler-flange to spindle-guide I see Thy Hand, O God—
Predestination in the stride o' yon connectin'-rod.
John Calvin might ha' forged the same—enormous, certain, slow—
Ay, wrought it in the furnace-flame—*my* "Institutio."
I cannot get my sleep to-night; old bones are hard to please;
I'll stand the middle watch up here—alone wi' God an' these
My engines, after ninety days o' race an' rack an' strain
Through all the seas of all Thy world, slam-bangin' home again.
Slam-bang too much—they knock a wee—the crosshead-gibs are loose,
But thirty thousand mile o' sea has gied them fair excuse . . .
Fine, clear an' dark—a full-draught breeze, wi' Ushant out o' sight,
An' Ferguson relievin' Hay. Old girl, ye'll walk to-night!
His wife's at Plymouth . . . Seventy—One—Two—Three since he began—
Three turns for Mistress Ferguson . . . and who's to blame the man?

---

[1] The male seal.   [2] Hurricane.

There's none at any port for me, by drivin' fast or slow,
Since Elsie Campbell went to Thee, Lord, thirty years ago.
(The year the *Sarah Sands* was burned. Oh, roads we used to tread,
Fra' Maryhill to Pollokshaws—fra' Govan to Parkhead!)
Not but they're ceevil on the Board. Ye'll hear Sir Kenneth say:
"Good morrn, McAndrew! Back again? An' how's your bilge to-day?"
Miscallin' technicalities but handin' me my chair
To drink Madeira wi' three Earls—the auld Fleet Engineer
That started as a boiler-whelp—when steam and he were low.
I mind the time we used to serve a broken pipe wi' tow!
Ten pound was all the pressure then—Eh! Eh!—a man wad drive;
An' here, our workin' gauges give one hunder sixty-five!
We're creepin' on wi' each new rig—less weight an' larger power;
There'll be the loco-boiler next an' thirty mile an hour!
Thirty an' more. What I ha' seen since ocean-steam began
Leaves me na doot for the machine: but what about the man?
The man that counts, wi' all his runs, one million mile o' sea:
Four time the span from earth to moon . . . How far, O Lord, from Thee
That wast beside him night an' day? Ye mind my first typhoon?
It scoughed the skipper on his way to jock wi' the saloon.
Three feet were on the stokehold-floor just slappin' to an' fro—
An' cast me on a furnace-door. I have the marks to show.
Marks! I ha' marks o' more than burns—deep in my soul an' black,
An' times like this, when things go smooth, my wickudness comes back.
The sins o' four an' forty years, all up an' down the seas,
Clack an' repeat like valves half-fed . . . Forgie's our trespasses!
Nights when I'd come on deck to mark, wi' envy in my gaze,
The couples kittlin' in the dark between the funnel-stays;
Years when I raked the Ports wi' pride to fill my cup o' wrong—
Judge not, O Lord, my steps aside at Gay Street in Hong-Kong!
Blot out the wastrel hours of mine in sin when I abode—
Jane Harrigan's an' Number Nine, The Reddick an' Grant Road!
An' waur than all—my crownin' sin—rank blasphemy an' wild.
I was not four and twenty then—Ye wadna judge a child?
I'd seen the Tropics first that run—new fruit, new smells, new air—
How could I tell—blind-fou wi' sun—the Deil was lurkin' there?
By day like playhouse-scenes the shore slid past our sleepy eyes;
By night those soft, lasceevious stars leered from those velvet skies,
In port (we used no cargo-steam) I'd daunder down the streets—
An ijjit grinnin' in a dream—for shells an' parrakeets,
An' walkin'-sticks o' carved bamboo an' blowfish stuffed an' dried—
Fillin' my bunk wi' rubbishry the Chief put overside.
Till, off Sambawa Head, Ye mind, I heard a land-breeze ca',
Milk-warm wi' breath o' spice an' bloom: "McAndrew, come awa'!"

Firm, clear an' low—no haste, no hate—the ghostly whisper went,
Just statin' eevidential facts beyon' all argument:
"Your mither's God's a graspin' deil, the shadow o'yoursel',
"Got out o' books by meenisters clean daft on Heaven an' Hell.
'They mak' him in the Broomielaw, o' Glasgie cold an' dirt,
"A jealous, pridefu' fetich, lad, that's only strong to hurt.
"Ye'll not go back to Him again an' kiss His red-hot rod,
"But come wi' Us" (Now, who were *They?*) "an' know the Leevin' God,
'That does not kipper souls for sport or break a life in jest,
"But swells the ripenin' cocoanuts an' ripes the woman's breast."
An' there it stopped—cut off—no more—that quiet, certain voice—
For me, six months o' twenty-four, to leave or take at choice.
"Twas on me like a thunderclap—it racked me through an' through—
Temptation past the show o' speech, unnameable an' new—
The Sin against the Holy Ghost? . . . An' under all, our screw.

That storm blew by but left behind her anchor-shiftin' swell.
Thou knowest all my heart an' mind, Thou knowest, Lord, I fell—
Third on the *Mary Gloster* then, and first that night in Hell!
Yet was Thy Hand beneath my head, about my feet Thy Care—
Fra' Deli clear to Torres Strait, the trial o' despair,
But when we touched the Barrier Reef Thy answer to my prayer! . . .
We dared na run that sea by night but lay an' held our fire,
An' I was drowsin' on the hatch—sick—sick wi' doubt an' tire.
"Better the sight of eyes that see than wanderin' o' desire!"
Ye mind that word? Clear as our gongs—again, an' once again,
When rippin' down through coral-trash ran out our moorin' chain:
An', by Thy Grace, I had the Light to see my duty plain.
Light on the engine-room—no more—bright as our carbons burn.
I've lost it since a thousand times, but never past return!

Obsairve! Per annum we'll have here two thousand souls aboard—
Think not I dare to justify myself before the Lord,
But—average fifteen hunder souls safe-borne fra' port to port—
I *am* o' service to my kind. Ye wadna blame the thought?
Maybe they steam from Grace to Wrath—to sin by folly led—
It isna mine to judge their path—their lives are on my head.
Mine at the last—when all is done it all comes back to me,
The fault that leaves six thousand ton a log upon the sea.
We'll tak' one stretch—three weeks an' odd by ony road ye steer—
Fra' Cape Town east to Wellington—ye need an engineer.
Fail there—ye've time to weld your shaft—ay, eat it, ere ye're spoke;
Or make Kerguelen under sail—three jiggers burned wi' smoke!
An' home again—the Rio run: it's no child's play to go
Steamin' to bell for fourteen days o' snow an' floe an' blow.

The bergs like kelpies overside that girn an' turn an' shift
Whaur, grindin' like the Mills o' God, goes by the big South drift.
(Hail, Snow and Ice that praise the Lord. I've met them at their work,
An' wished we had anither route or they anither kirk.)
Yon's strain, hard strain, o' head an' hand, for though Thy Power brings
All skill to naught, Ye'll understand a man must think o' things.
Then, at the last, we'll get to port an' hoist their baggage clear—
The passengers, wi' gloves an' canes—an' this is what I'll hear:
"Well, thank ye for a pleasant voyage. The tender's comin' now."
While I go testin' follower-bolts an' watch the skipper bow.
They've words for every one but me—shake hands wi' half the crew,
Except the dour Scots engineer, the man they never knew.
An' yet I like the wark for all we've dam'-few pickin's here—
No pension, an' the most we'll earn's four hunder pound a year.
Better myself abroad? Maybe. *I'd* sooner starve than sail
Wi' such as call a snifter-rod *ross* . . . French for nightingale.
Commeesion on my stores? Some do; but I cannot afford
To lie like stewards wi' patty-pans. I'm older than the Board.
A bonus on the coal I save? Ou ay, the Scots are close,
But when I grudge the strength Ye gave I'll grudge their food to *those*.
(There's bricks that I might recommend—an' clink the fire-bars cruel.
No! Welsh—Wangarti at the worst—an' damn all patent fuel!)
Inventions? Ye must stay in port to mak' a patent pay.
My Deeferential Valve-Gear taught me how that business lay.
I blame no chaps wi' clearer heads for aught they make or sell.
I found that I could not invent an' look to these as well.
So, wrestled wi' Apollyon—Nah!—fretted like a bairn—
But burned the workin'-plans last run, wi' all I hoped to earn.
Ye know how hard an Idol dies, an' what that meant to me—
E'en tak' it for a sacrifice acceptable to Thee . . .
Below there! Oiler! What's your wark? Ye find it runnin' hard?
Ye needn't swill the cup wi' oil—this isn't the Cunard!
Ye thought? Ye are not paid to think. Go, sweat that off again!
Tck! Tck! It's deeficult to sweer nor tak' The Name in vain!
Men, ay, an women, call me stern. Wi' these to oversee,
Ye'll note I've little time to burn on social repartee.
The bairns see what their elders miss; they'll hunt me to an' fro,
Till for the sake of—well, a kiss—I tak' 'em down below.
That minds me of our Viscount loon—Sir Kenneth's kin—the chap
Wi' Russia-leather tennis-shoon an' spar-decked yachtin'-cap.
I showed him round last week, o'er all—an' at the last says he:
"Mister McAndrew, don't you think steam spoils romance at sea?"
Damned ijjit! I'd been doon that morn to see what ailed the throws,
Manholin', on my back—the cranks three inches off my nose.

Romance! Those first-class passengers they like it very well,
Printed an' bound in little books; but why don't poets tell?
I'm sick of all their quirks an' turns—the loves an' doves they dream—
Lord, send a man like Robbie Burns to sing the Song o' Steam!
To match wi' Scotia's noblest speech yon orchestra sublime
Whaurto—uplifted like the Just—the tail-rods mark the time.
The crank-throws give the double-bass, the feed-pump sobs an' heaves,
An' now the main eccentrics start their quarrel on the sheaves:
Her time, her own appointed time, the rocking link-head bides,
Till—hear that note?—the rod's return whings glimmerin' through the
     guides.
They're all awa'! True beat, full power, the clangin' chorus goes
Clear to the tunnel where they sit, my purrin' dynamoes.
Interdependence absolute, foreseen, ordained, decreed,
To work, Ye'll note, at ony tilt an' every rate o' speed.
Fra' skylight-lift to furnace-bars, backed, bolted, braced an' stayed,
An' singin' like the Mornin' Stars for joy that they are made;
While, out o' touch o' vanity, the sweatin' trust-block says:
"Not unto us the praise, or man—not unto us the praise!"
Now, a' together, hear them lift their lesson—theirs an' mine:
"Law, Orrder, Duty an' Restraint, Obedience, Discipline!"
Mill, forge an' try-pit taught them that when roarin' they arose,
An' whiles I wonder if a soul was gied them wi' the blows.
Oh for a man to weld it then, in one trip-hammer strain,
Till even first-class passengers could tell the meanin' plain!
But no one cares except mysel' that serve an' understand
My seven thousand horse-power here.   Eh, Lord! They're grand—they're
     grand!
Uplift am I?   When first in store the new-made beasties stood,
Were Ye cast down that breathed the Word declarin' all things good?
Not so!   O' that warld-liftin' joy no after-fall could vex,
Ye've left a glimmer still to cheer the Man—the Arrtifex!
   That holds, in spite o' knock and scale, o' friction, waste an' slip,
An' by that light—now, mark my word—we'll build the Perfect Ship.
I'll never last to judge her lines or take her curve—not I.
But I ha' lived an' I ha' worked.   Be thanks to Thee, Most High!
An' I ha done what I ha' done—judge Thou if ill or well—
Always Thy Grace preventin' me . . .
   Losh!   Yon's the "Stand-by" bell.
Pilot so soon?   His flare it is.   The mornin'-watch is set.
Well, God be thanked, as I was sayin', I'm no Pelagian yet.
Now I'll tak' on . . .
   'Morrn, Ferguson.   Man, have ye ever thought
What your good leddy costs in coal? . . . I'll burn 'em down to port.

Mulholland's Contract

1894

The fear was on the cattle, for the gale was on the sea,
An' the pens broke up on the lower deck an' let the creatures free—
An' the lights went out on the lower deck, an' no one near but me.

I had been singin' to them to keep 'em quiet there,
For the lower deck is the dangerousest, requirin' constant care,
An' give to me as the strongest man, though used to drink and swear.

I seed my chance was certain of bein' horned or trod,
For the lower deck was packed with steers thicker'n peas in a pod,
An' more pens broke at every roll—so I made a Contract with God.

An' by the terms of the Contract, as I have read the same,
If He got me to port alive I would exalt His name,
An' praise His Holy Majesty till further orders came.

He saved me from the cattle an' He saved me from the sea,
For they found me 'tween two drownded ones where the roll had landed
  me—
An' a four-inch crack on top of my head, as crazy as could be.

But that were done by a stanchion, an' not by a bullock at all,
An' I lay still for seven weeks convalescing of the fall,
An' readin' the shiny Scripture texts in the Seaman's Hospital.

An' I spoke to God of our Contract, an' He says to my prayer:
"I never puts on My ministers no more than they can bear.
"So back you go to the cattle-boats an' preach My Gospel there.

"For human life is chancy at any kind of trade,
"But most of all, as well you know, when the steers are mad-afraid;
"So you go back to the cattle-boats an' preach 'em as I've said.

"They must quit drinkin' an' swearin', they mustn't knife on a blow,
"They must quit gamblin' their wages, and you must preach it so.
"For now those boats are more like Hell than anything else I know."

I didn't want to do it, for I knew what I should get;
An' I wanted to preach Religion, handsome an' out of the wet;
But the Word of the Lord were laid on me, an' I done what was set.

I have been smit an' bruised, as warned would be the case,
An' turned my cheek to the smiter exactly as Scripture says;
But, following that, I knocked him down an' led him up to Grace.

An' we have preaching on Sundays whenever the sea is calm,
An' I use no knife or pistol an' I never take no harm;
For the Lord abideth back of me to guide my fighting arm.

An' I sign for four-pound-ten a month and save the money clear,
An' I am in charge of the lower deck, an' I never lose a steer;
An' I believe in Almighty God an' I preach His Gospel here.

The skippers say I'm crazy, but I can prove 'em wrong,
For I am in charge of the lower deck with all that doth belong—
Which they would not give to a lunatic, and the competition so strong!

The "Mary Gloster"

1894

I've paid for your sickest fancies; I've humoured your crackedest whim—
Dick, it's your daddy, dying; you've got to listen to him!
Good for a fortnight, am I? The doctor told you? He lied.
I shall go under by morning, and— Put that nurse outside.
'Never seen death yet, Dickie? Well, now is your time to learn,
And you'll wish you held my record before it comes to your turn.
Not counting the Line and the Foundry, the Yards and the village, too,
I've made myself and a million; but I'm damned if I made you.
Master at two-and-twenty, and married at twenty-three—
Ten thousand men on the pay-roll, and forty freighters at sea!
Fifty years between 'em, and every year of it fight,
And now I'm Sir Anthony Gloster, dying, a baronite:
For I lunched with his Royal 'Ighness—what was it the papers had?
"Not least of our merchant-princes." Dickie, that's me, your dad!
I didn't begin with askings. I took my job and I stuck;
I took the chances they wouldn't, an' now they're calling it luck.
Lord, what boats I've handled—rotten and leaky and old—
Ran 'em, or—opened the bilge-cock, precisely as I was told.
Grub that 'ud bind you crazy, and crews that 'ud turn you grey,
And a big fat lump of insurance to cover the risk on the way.
The others they dursn't do it; they said they valued their life
(They've served me since as skippers). I went, and I took my wife.
Over the world I drove 'em, married at twenty-three,
And your mother saving the money and making a man of me.
I was content to be master, but she said there was better behind;
She took the chances I wouldn't, and I followed your mother blind.
She egged me to borrow the money, an' she helped me to clear the loan,

When we bought half-shares in a cheap 'un and hoisted a flag of our
   own.
Patching and coaling on credit, and living the Lord knew how,
We started the Red Ox freighters—we've eight-and-thirty now.
And those were the days of clippers, and the freights were clipper-freights,
And we knew we were making our fortune, but she died in Macassar
   Straits—
By the Little Paternosters, as you come to the Union Bank—
And we dropped her in fourteen fathom: I pricked it off where she sank.
Owners we were, full owners, and the boat was christened for her,
And she died in the *Mary Gloster*. My heart, how young we were!
So I went on a spree round Java and well-nigh ran her ashore,
But your mother came and warned me and I wouldn't liquor no more:
Strict I stuck to my business, afraid to stop or I'd think,
Saving the money (she warned me), and letting the other men drink.
And I met M'Cullough in London (I'd saved five 'undred then),
And 'tween us we started the Foundry—three forges and twenty men.
Cheap repairs for the cheap 'uns. It paid, and the business grew;
For I bought me a steam-lathe patent, and that was a gold mine too.
"Cheaper to build 'em than buy 'em," *I* said, but M'Cullough he shied,
And we wasted a year in talking before we moved to the Clyde.
And the Lines were all beginning, and we all of us started fair,
Building our engines like houses and staying the boilers square.
But M'Cullough 'e wanted cabins with marble and maple and all,
And Brussels an' Utrecht velvet, and baths and a Social Hall,
And pipes for closets all over, and cutting the frames too light,
But M'Cullough he died in the Sixties, and— Well, I'm dying
   to-night . . .
I knew —*I* knew what was coming, when we bid on the *Byfleet's* keel—
They piddled and piffled with iron. I'd given my orders for steel!
Steel and the first expansions. It paid, I tell you, it paid,
When we came with our nine-knot freighters and collared the long-run
   trade!
And they asked me how I did it, and I gave 'em the Scripture text,
"You keep your light so shining a little in front o' the next!"
They copied all they could follow, but they couldn't copy my mind,
And I left 'em sweating and stealing a year and a half behind.
Then came the armour-contracts, but that was M'Cullough's side;
He was always best in the Foundry, but better, perhaps, he died.
I went through his private papers; the notes was plainer than print;
And I'm no fool to finish if a man'll give me a hint.
(I remember his widow was angry.) So I saw what his drawings meant,
And I started the six-inch rollers, and it paid me sixty per cent.
Sixty per cent *with* failures, and more than twice we could do,
And a quarter-million to credit, and I saved it all for you!

I thought—it doesn't matter—you seemed to favour your ma,
But you're nearer forty than thirty, and I know the kind you are.
Harrer an' Trinity College! I ought to ha' sent you to sea—
But I stood you an education, an' what have you done for me?
The things I knew was proper you wouldn't thank me to give,
And the things I knew was rotten you said was the way to live.
For you muddled with books and pictures, an' china an' etchin's an' fans,
And your rooms at college was beastly—more like a whore's than a
  man's;
Till you married that thin-flanked woman, as white and as stale as a bone,
An' she gave you your social nonsense; but where's that kid o' your own?
I've seen your carriages blocking the half o' the Cromwell Road,
But never the doctor's brougham to help the missus unload.
(So there isn't even a grandchild, an' the Gloster family's done.)
Not like your mother, she isn't. *She* carried her freight each run.
But they died, the pore little beggars! At sea she had 'em—they died.
Only you, an' you stood it. You haven't stood much beside.
Weak, a liar, and idle, and mean as a collier's whelp
Nosing for scraps in the galley. No help—my son was no help!
So he gets three 'undred thousand, in trust and the interest paid.
I wouldn't give it you, Dickie—you see, I made it in trade.
You're saved from soiling your fingers, and if you have no child,
It all comes back to the business. 'Gad, won't your wife be wild!
'Calls and calls in her carriage, her 'andkerchief up to 'er eye:
"Daddy! dear daddy's dyin'!" and doing her best to cry.
Grateful? Oh, yes, I'm grateful, but keep her away from here.
Your mother 'ud never ha' stood 'er, and, anyhow, women are queer . . .
There's women will say I've married a second time. Not quite!
But give pore Aggie a hundred, and tell her your lawyers'll fight.
She was the best o' the boiling—you'll meet her before it ends.
I'm in for a row with the mother—I'll leave you settle my friends.
For a man he must go with a woman, which women don't understand—
Or the sort that say they can see it they aren't the marrying brand.
But I wanted to speak o' your mother that's Lady Gloster still;
I'm going to up and see her, without its hurting the will.
Here! Take your hand off the bell-pull. Five thousand's waiting for
  you,
If you'll only listen a minute, and do as I bid you do.
They'll try to prove me crazy, and, if you bungle, they can;
And I've only you to trust to! (O God, why ain't it a man?)
There's some waste money on marbles, the same as M'Cullough tried—
Marbles and mausoleums—but I call that sinful pride.
There's some ship bodies for burial—we've carried 'em, soldered and
  packed;
Down in their wills they wrote it, and nobody called *them* cracked.

But me—I've too much money, and people might . . . All my fault:
It come o' hoping for grandsons and buying that Wokin' vault . . .
I'm sick o' the 'ole dam' business. I'm going back where I came.
Dick, you're the son o' my body, and you'll take charge o' the same!
I want to lie by your mother, ten thousand mile away,
And they'll want to send me to Woking; and that's where you'll earn your
　pay.
I've thought it out on the quiet, the same as it ought to be done—
Quiet, and decent, and proper—an' here's your orders, my son.
You know the Line? You don't, though. You write to the Board, and
　tell
Your father's death has upset you an' you're goin' to cruise for a spell,
An' you'd like the *Mary Gloster*—I've held her ready for this—
They'll put her in working order and you'll take her out as she is.
Yes, it was money idle when I patched her and laid her aside
(Thank God, I can pay for my fancies!)—the boat where your mother
　died,
By the Little Paternosters, as you come to the Union Bank,
We dropped her—I think I told you—and I pricked it off where she
　sank.
[Tiny she looked on the grating—that oily, treacly sea—]
'Hundred and Eighteen East, remember, and South just Three.
Easy bearings to carry—Three South—Three to the dot;
But I gave McAndrew a copy in case of dying—or not.
And so you'll write to McAndrew, he's Chief of the Maori Line;
They'll give him leave, if you ask 'em and say it's business o' mine.
I built three boats for the Maoris, an' very well pleased they were,
An' I've known Mac since the Fifties, and Mac knew me—and her.
After the first stroke warned me I sent him the money to keep
Against the time you'd claim it, committin' your dad to the deep;
For you are the son o' my body, and Mac was my oldest friend,
I've never asked 'im to dinner, but he'll see it out to the end.
Stiff-necked Glasgow beggar! I've heard he's prayed for my soul,
But he couldn't lie if you paid him, and he'd starve before he stole.
He'll take the *Mary* in ballast—you'll find her a lively ship;
And you'll take Sir Anthony Gloster, that goes on 'is wedding-trip,
Lashed in our old deck-cabin with all three port-holes wide,
The kick o' the screw beneath him and the round blue seas outside!
Sir Anthony Gloster's carriage—our 'ouse-flag flyin' free—
Ten thousand men on the pay-roll and forty freighters at sea!
He made himself and a million, but this world is a fleetin' show,
And he'll go to the wife of 'is bosom the same as he ought to go—
By the heel of the Paternosters—there isn't a chance to mistake—
And Mac'll pay you the money soon as the bubbles break!
Five thousand for six weeks' cruising, the staunchest freighter afloat,

And Mac he'll give you your bonus the minute I'm out o' the boat!
He'll take you round to Macassar, and you'll come back alone;
He knows what I want o' the Mary . . . I'll do what I please with my
    own.
Your mother 'ud call it wasteful, but I've seven-and-thirty more;
I'll come in my private carriage and bid it wait at the door . . .
For my son 'e was never a credit: 'e muddled with books and art,
And 'e lived on Sir Anthony's money and 'e broke Sir Anthony's heart.
There isn't even a grandchild, and the Gloster family's done—
The only one you left me—O mother, the only one!
Harrer and Trinity College—me slavin' early an' late—
An' he thinks I'm dying crazy, and you're in Macassar Strait!
Flesh o' my flesh, my dearie, for ever an' ever amen,
That first stroke come for a warning. I ought to ha' gone to you then.
But—cheap repairs for a cheap 'un—the doctors said I'd do.
Mary, why didn't *you* warn me? I've allus heeded to you,
Excep'—I know—about women; but you are a spirit now;
An' wife, they was only women, and I was a man. That's how.
An' a man 'e must go with a woman, as you *could* not understand;
But I never talked 'em secrets. I paid 'em out o' hand.
Thank Gawd, I can pay for my fancies! Now what's five thousand to
    me,
For a berth off the Paternosters in the haven where I would be?
I believe in the Resurrection, if I read my Bible plain,
But I wouldn't trust 'em at Wokin'; we're safer at sea again.
For the heart it shall go with the treasure—go down to the sea in ships.
I'm sick of the hired women. I'll kiss my girl on her lips!
I'll be content with my fountain. I'll drink from my own well,
And the wife of my youth shall charm me—an' the rest can go to Hell!
(Dickie, *he* will, that's certain.) I'll lie in our standin'-bed,
An' Mac'll take her in ballast—an' she trims best by the head . . .
Down by the head an' sinkin', her fires are drawn and cold,
And the water's splashin' hollow on the skin of the empty hold—
Churning an' choking and chuckling, quiet and scummy and dark—
Full to her lower hatches and risin' steady. Hark!
That was the after-bulkhead . . . She's flooded from stem to stern. . . .
Never seen death yet, Dickie? . . . Well, now is your time to learn!

The Ballad of the "Bolivar"

1890

Seven men from all the world back to Docks again,
Rolling down the Ratcliffe Road drunk and raising Cain.
Give the girls another drink 'fore we sign away—
We that took the Bolivar *out across the Bay!*

We put out from Sunderland loaded down with rails;
   We put back to Sunderland 'cause our cargo shifted;
We put out from Sunderland—met the winter gales—
   Seven days and seven nights to The Start we drifted.

      Racketing her rivets loose, smoke-stack white as snow,
       All the coals adrift adeck, half the rails below,
      Leaking like a lobster-pot, steering like a dray—
      Out we took the *Bolivar*, out across the Bay!

One by one the Lights came up, winked and let us by;
   Mile by mile we waddled on, coal and fo'c'sle short;
Met a blow that laid us down, heard a bulkhead fly;
   Left The Wolf behind us with a two-foot list to port.

      Trailing like a wounded duck, working out her soul;
      Clanging like a smithy-shop after every roll;
      Just a funnel and a mast lurching through the spray—
      So we threshed the *Bolivar* out across the Bay!

Felt her hog and felt her sag, betted when she'd break;
   Wondered every time she raced if she'd stand the shock;
Heard the seas like drunken men pounding at her strake;
   Hoped the Lord 'ud keep His thumb on the plummer-block!

      Banged against the iron decks, bilges choked with coal;
      Flayed and frozen foot and hand, sick of heart and soul;
      'Last we prayed she'd buck herself into Judgment Day—
      Hi! we cursed the *Bolivar* knocking round the Bay!

O her nose flung up to sky, groaning to be still—
   Up and down and back we went, never time for breath;
Then the money paid at Lloyds' caught her by the keel,
   And the stars ran round and round dancin' at our death!

      Aching for an hour's sleep, dozing 'off between:
      'Heard the rotten rivets draw when she took it green;
      'Watched the compass chase its tail like a cat at play—
      That was on the *Bolivar*, south across the Bay!

Once we saw been the squalls, lyin' head to swell—
    Mad with work and weariness, wishin' they was we—
Some damned Liner's lights go by like a grand hotel;
    'Cheered her from the *Bolivar* swampin' in the sea.

    Then a greybeard cleared us out, then the skipper laughed;
        "Boys, the wheel has gone to Hell—rig the winches aft!
    "Yoke the kicking rudder-head—get her under way!"
        So we steered her, pully-haul, out across the Bay!

Just a pack o' rotten plates puttied up with tar,
In we came, an' time enough, 'cross Bilbao Bar.
Overloaded, undermanned, meant to founder, we
Euchred God Almighty's storm, bluffed the Eternal Sea!

Seven men from all the world back to town again,
Rollin' down the Ratcliffe Road drunk and raising Cain:
Seven men from out of Hell.   Ain't the owners gay,
Cause we took the "Bolivar" safe across the Bay?

The Ballad of the "Clampherdown"

1892

This was originally written for the "St. James's Gazette" as a deliberate skit on a letter by a correspondent who seemed to believe that naval warfare of the future would be conducted on the old Nelsonic battle lines, including boarding, etc.   By some accident it was treated from the first as a serious contribution—was even, if I remember rightly, set to music as a cantata.   I never explained this till now.

It was our war-ship *Clampherdown*
    Would sweep the Channel clean,
Wherefore she kept her hatches close
When the merry Channel chops arose,
    To save the bleached Marine.

She had one bow-gun of a hundred ton
    And a great stern-gun beside.
They dipped their noses deep in the sea,
They racked their stays and stanchions free
    In the wash of the wind-whipped tide.

It was our war-ship *Clampherdown*
    Fell in with a cruiser light
That carried the dainty Hotchkiss gun

And a pair of heels wherewith to run
   From the grip of a close-fought fight.

She opened fire at seven miles—
   As ye shoot at a bobbing cork—
And once she fired and twice she fired,
Till the bow-gun dropped like a lily tired
   That lolls upon the stalk.

"Captain, the bow-gun melts apace,
   "The deck-beams break below,
" 'Twere well to rest for an hour or twain,
"And botch the shattered plates again."
   And he answered, "Make it so."

She opened fire within the mile—
   As ye shoot at the flying duck—
And the great stern-gun shot fair and true,
With the heave of the ship, to the stainless blue,
   And the great stern-turret stuck.

"Captain, the turret fills with steam,
   "The feed-pipes burst below—
"You can hear the hiss of the helpless ram,
"You can hear the twisted runners jam."
   And he answered, "Turn and go!"

It was our war-ship *Clampherdown*,
   And grimly did she roll;
Swung round to take the cruiser's fire
As the White Whale faces the Thresher's ire
   When they war by the frozen Pole.

"Captain, the shells are falling fast,
   "And faster still fall we;
"And it is not meet for English stock
"To bide in the heart of an eight-day clock
   "The death they cannot see."

"Lie down, lie down, my bold A. B.,
   "We drift upon her beam;
"We dare not ram, for she can run:
"And dare ye fire another gun,
   "And die in the peeling steam?"

It was our war-ship *Clampherdown*
   That carried an armour-belt;
But fifty feet at stern and bow

Lay bare as the paunch of the purser's sow,
   To the hail of the Nordenfeldt.

"Captain, they hack us through and through;
   "The chilled steel bolts are swift!
"We have emptied our bunkers in open sea,
   "Their shrapnel bursts where our coal should be."
   And he answered, "Let her drift."

It was our war-ship *Clampherdown*
   Swung round upon the tide,
Her two dumb guns glared south and north,
And the blood and the bubbling steam ran forth,
   And she ground the cruiser's side.

"Captain, they cry, the fight is done,
   "They bid you send your sword."
And he answered, "Grapple her stern and bow.
"They have asked for the steel.   They shall have it now;
   "Out cutlasses and board!"

It was our war-ship *Clampherdown*
   Spewed up four hundred men;
And the scalded stokers yelped delight,
As they rolled in the waist and heard the fight,
   Stamp o'er their steel-walled pen.

They cleared the cruiser end to end
   From conning-tower to hold.
They fought as they fought in Nelson's fleet;
They were stripped to the waist, they were bare to the feet
   As it was in the days of old.

It was the sinking *Clampherdown*
   Heaved up her battered side—
And carried a million pounds in steel
To the cod and the corpse-fed conger-eel,
   And the scour of the Channel tide.

It was the crew of the *Clampherdown*
   Stood out to sweep the sea,
On a cruiser won from an ancient foe,
As it was in the days of long ago,
   And as it still shall be!

Cruisers

1899

As our mother the Frigate, bepainted and fine,
Made play for her bully the Ship of the Line;
So we, her bold daughters by iron and fire,
Accost and decoy to our masters' desire.

Now, pray you, consider what toils we endure,
Night-walking wet sea-lanes, a guard and a lure;
Since half of our trade is that same pretty sort
As mettlesome wenches do practise in port.

For this is our office—to spy and make room,
As hiding yet guiding the foe to their doom;
Surrounding, confounding, we bait and betray
And tempt them to battle the sea's width away.

The pot-bellied merchant foreboding no wrong
With headlight and sidelight he lieth along,
Till, lightless and lightfoot and lurking, leap we
To force him discover his business by sea.

And when we have wakened the lust of a foe,
To draw him by flight toward our bullies we go,
Till, 'ware of strange smoke stealing nearer, he flies
Ere our billies close in for to make him good prize.

So, when we have spied on the path of their host,
One flieth to carry that word to the coast;
And, lest by false doublings they turn and go free,
One lieth behind them to follow and see.

Anon we return, being gathered again,
Across the sad valleys all drabbled with rain—
Across the grey ridges all crispèd and curled—
To join the long dance round the curve of the world.

The bitter salt spindrift, the sun-glare likewise,
The moon-track a-tremble, bewilders our eyes,
Where, linking and lifting, our sisters we hail
'Twixt wrench of cross-surges or plunge of head-gale.

As maidens awaiting the bride to come forth
Make play with light jestings and wit of no worth,
So, widdershins circling the bride-bed of death,
Each fleereth her neighbour and signeth and saith:—

"What see ye?   Their signals, or levin afar?
"What hear ye?   God's thunder, or guns of our war?
"What mark ye?   Their smoke, or the cloud-rack outblown?
"What chase ye?   Their lights, or the Daystar low down?"

So, times past all number deceived by false shows,
Deceiving we cumber the road of our foes,
For this is our virtue: to track and betray;
Preparing great battles a sea's width away.

Now peace is at end and our peoples take heart,
For the laws are clean gone that restrainèd our art;
Up and down the near headlands and against the far wind
We are loosed (O be swift!) to the work of our kind!

The Verdicts

(JUTLAND)

1916

Not in the thick of the fight,
    Not in the press of the odds,
Do the heroes come to their height,
    Or we know the demi-gods.

That stands over till peace.
    We can only perceive
Men returned from the seas,
    Very grateful for leave.

They grant us sudden days
    Snatched from their business of war;
But we are too close to appraise
    What manner of men they are.

And, whether their names go down
    With age-kept victories,
Or whether they battle and drown
    Unreckoned, is hid from our eyes.

They are too near to be great,
    But our children shall understand
When and how our fate
    Was changed, and by whose hand.

Our children shall measure their worth.
    We are content to be blind ...
But we know that we walk on a new-born earth
    With the saviours of mankind.

The Destroyers

1898

The strength of twice three thousand horse
    That seeks the single goal;
The line that holds the rending course,
    The hate that swings the whole:
The stripped hulls, slinking through the gloom,
    At gaze and gone again—
The Brides of Death that wait the groom—
    The Choosers of the Slain!

Offshore where sea and skyline blend
    In rain, the daylight dies;
The sullen, shouldering swells attend
    Night and our sacrifice.
Adown the stricken capes no flare—
    No mark on spit or bar,—
Girdled and desperate we dare
    The blindfold game of war.

Nearer the up-flung beams that spell
    The council of our foes;
Clearer the barking guns that tell
    Their scattered flank to close.
Sheer to the trap they crowd their way
    From ports for this unbarred.
    Quiet, and count our laden prey,
    The convoy and her guard!

On shoal with scarce a foot below,
    Where rock and islet throng,
Hidden and hushed we watch them throw
    Their anxious lights along.
Not here, not here your danger lies—
    (Stare hard, O hooded eyne!)
Save where the dazed rock-pigeons rise
    The lit cliffs give no sign.

Therefore—to break the rest ye seek,
    The Narrow Seas to clear—
Hark to the siren's whimpering shriek—
    The driven death is here!
Look to your van a league away,—
    What midnight terror stays
The bulk that checks against the spray
    Her crackling tops ablaze?

Hit, and hard hit!   The blow went home,
    The muffled, knocking stroke—
The steam that overruns the foam—
    The foam that thins to smoke—
The smoke that clokes the deep aboil—
    The deep that chokes her throes
Till, streaked with ash and sleeked with oil,
    The lukewarm whirlpools close!

A shadow down the sickened wave
    Long since her slayer fled:
But hear their chattering quick-fires rave
    Astern, abeam, ahead!
Panic that shells the drifting spar—
    Loud waste with none to check—
Mad fear that rakes a scornful star
    Or sweeps a consort's deck.

Now, while their silly smoke hangs thick,
    Now ere their wits they find,
Lay in and lance them to the quick—
    Our gallied whales are blind!
Good luck to those that see the end,
    Good-bye to those that drown—
For each his chance as chance shall send—
    And God for all!   *Shut down!*

The strength of twice three thousand horse
    That serve the one command;
The hand that waves the headlong force,
    The hate that backs the hand:
The doom-bolt in the darkness freed,
    The mine that splits the main;
The white-hot wake, the 'wildering speed—
    The Choosers of the Slain!

White Horses

1897

Where run your colts at pasture?
Where hide your mares to breed?
   'Mid bergs about the Ice-cap
   Or wove Sargasso weed;
By chartless reef and channel,
   Or crafty coastwise bars,
But most the ocean-meadows
   All purple to the stars!

Who holds the rein upon you?
   The latest gale let free.
What meat is in your mangers?
   The glut of all the sea.
'Twixt tide and tide's returning
   Great store of newly dead,—
The bones of those that faced us,
   And the hearts of those that fled.

Afar, off-shore and single,
   Some stallion, rearing swift,
Neighs hungry for new fodder,
   And calls us to the drift:
Then down the cloven ridges—
   A million hooves unshod—
Break forth the mad White Horses
   To seek their meat from God!

Girth-deep in hissing water
   Our furious vanguard strains—
Through mist of mighty tramplings
   Roll up the fore-blown manes—
A hundred leagues to leeward,
   Ere yet the deep is stirred,
The groaning rollers carry
   The coming of the herd!

Whose hand may grip your nostrils—
   Your forelock who may hold?
E'en they that use the broads with us—
   The riders bred and bold,
That spy upon our matings,
   That rope us where we run—

They know the strong White Horses
   From father unto son.

We breathe about their cradles,
   We race their babes ashore,
We snuff against their thresholds,
   We nuzzle at their door;
By day with stamping squadrons,
   By night in whinnying droves,
Creep up the wise White Horses,
   To call them from their loves.

And come they for your calling?
   No wit of man may save.
They hear the loosed White Horses
   Above their fathers' grave;
And, kin to those we crippled,
   And, sons of those we slew,
Spur down the wild white riders
   To school the herds anew.

What service have ye paid them,
   O jealous steeds and strong?
Save we that throw their weaklings,
   Is none dare work them wrong;
While thick around the homestead
   Our snow-backed leaders graze—
A guard behind their plunder,
   And a veil before their ways.

With march and countermarchings—
   With weight of wheeling hosts—
Stray mob or bands embattled—
   We ring the chosen coasts:
And, careless of our clamour
   That bids the stranger fly,
At peace within our pickets
   The wild white riders lie.

. . . .

Trust ye the curdled hollows—
   Trust ye the neighing wind—
Trust ye the moaning groundswell—
   Our herds are close behind!
To bray your foeman's armies—
   To chill and snap his sword—
Trust ye the wild White Horses,
   The Horses of the Lord!

A Song In Storm

1914-18

Be well assured that on our side
  The abiding oceans fight,
Though headlong wind and heaping tide
  Make us their sport to-night.
By force of weather, not of war,
  In jeopardy we steer:
Then welcome Fate's discourtesy
   Whereby it shall appear
    How in all time of our distress,
    And our deliverance too,
     The game is more than the player of the game,
     And the ship is more than the crew!

Out of the mist into the mirk
  The glimmering combers roll.
Almost these mindless waters work
  As though they had a soul—
Almost as though they leagued to whelm
  Our flag beneath their green:
Then welcome Fate's discourtesy
  Whereby it shall be seen, etc.

Be well assured, though wave and wind
  Have mightier blows in store,
That we who keep the watch assigned
  Must stand to it the more;
And as our streaming bows rebuke
  Each billow's baulked career,
Sing welcome Fate's discourtesy
  Whereby it is made clear, etc.

No matter though our decks be swept
  And mast and timber crack—
We can make good all loss except
  The loss of turning back.
So 'twixt these Devils and our deep
  Let courteous trumpets sound,
To welcome Fate's discourtesy
  Whereby it will be found, etc.

Be well assured, though in our power
  Is nothing left to give

But chance and place to meet the hour,
    And leave to strive to live,
Till these dissolve our Order holds,
    Our Service binds us here.
Then welcome Fate's discourtesy
    Whereby it is made clear
        How in all time of our distress,
        As in our triumph too,
        The game is more than the player of the game,
        And the ship is more than the crew!

The Derelict

1894

"And reports the derelict Margaret Pollock *still at sea."*—

SHIPPING NEWS.

I was the staunchest of our fleet
    Till the sea rose beneath my feet
Unheralded, in hatred past all measure.
    In his pits he stamped my crew,
    Buffeted, blinded, bound and threw,
Bidding me eyeless wait upon his pleasure.

    Man made me, and my will
    Is to my maker still,
Whom now the currents con, the rollers steer—
    Lifting forlorn to spy
    Trailed smoke along the sky,
Falling afraid lest any keel come near!

    Wrenched as the lips of thirst,
    Wried, dried, and split and burst,
Bone-bleached my decks, wind-scoured to the graining;
    And, jarred at every roll,
    The gear that was my soul
Answers the anguish of my beams' complaining.

    For life that crammed me full,
    Gangs of the prying gull
That shriek and scrabble on the riven hatches.
    For roar that dumbed the gale,
    My hawse-pipes' guttering wail,
Sobbing my heart out through the uncounted watches.

    Blind in the hot blue ring
    Through all my points I swing—

Swing and return to shift the sun anew.
  Blind in my well-known sky
  I hear the stars go by,
Mocking the prow that cannot hold one true.

  White on my wasted path
  Wave after wave in wrath
Frets 'against his fellow, warring where to send me,
  Flung forward, heaved aside,
  Witless and dazed I bide
The mercy of the comber that shall end me.

  North where the bergs careen,
  The spray of seas unseen
Smokers round my head and freezes in the falling.
  South where the corals breed,
  The footless, floating weed
Folds me and fouls me, strake on strake upcrawling.

  I that was clean to run
  My race against the sun—
Strength on the deep—am bawd to all disaster;
  Whipped forth by night to meet
  My sister's careless feet,
And with a kiss betray her to my master.

  Man made me, and my will
  Is to my maker still—
To him and his, our peoples at their pier:
  Lifting in hope to spy
  Trailed smoke along the sky,
Falling afraid lest any keel come near!

The Merchantmen

1893

  King Solomon drew merchantmen,
    Because of his desire
  For peacocks, apes, and ivory,
    From Tarnish unto Tyre,
  With cedars out of Lebanon
    Which Hiram rafted down;
  But we be only sailormen
    That use in London town.

Coastwise—cross-seas—round the world and back again—
Where the flaw shall head us or the full Trade suits—
Plain-sail—storm-sail—lay your board and tack again—
And that's the way we'll pay Paddy Doyle for his boots!

We bring no store of ingots,
    Of spice or precious stones,
But what we have we gathered
    With sweat and aching bones:
In flame beneath the Tropics,
    In frost upon the floe,
And jeopardy of every wind
    That does between them go.

And some we go by purchase,
    And some we had by trade,
And some we found by courtesy
    Of pike and carronade—
At midnight, 'mid-sea meetings,
    For charity to keep,
And light the rolling homeward-bound
    That rode a foot too deep!

By sport of bitter weather
    We're walty, strained, and scarred
From the kentledge on the kelson
    To the slings upon the yard.
Six oceans had their will of us
    To carry all away—
Our galley's in the Baltic,
    And our boom's in Mossel Bay.

We've floundered off the Texel,
    Awash with sodden deals,
We've slipped from Valparaiso
    With the Norther at our heels:
We've ratched beyond the Crossets
    That tusk the Southern Pole,
And dipped our gunnels under
    To the dread Agulhas roll.

Beyond all outer charting
    We sailed where none have sailed,
And saw the land-lights burning
    On islands none have hailed;
Our hair stood up for wonder,
    But, when the night was done,

There danced the deep to windward
   Blue-empty 'neath the sun!

Strange consorts rode beside us
   And brought us evil luck;
The witch-fire climbed our channels,
   And flared on vane and truck,
Till, through the red tornado,
   That lashed us nigh to blind,
We saw The Dutchman plunging,
   Full canvas, head to wind!

We've heard the Midnight Leadsman
   That calls the black deep down—
Ay, thrice we've heard The Swimmer,
   The Thing that may not drown.
On frozen bunt and gasket
   The sleet-cloud drave her hosts,
When, manned by more than signed with us,
   We passed the Isle of Ghosts!

And north, amid the hummocks,
   A biscuit-toss below,
We met the silent shallop
   That frighted whalers know;
For, down a cruel ice-lane,
   That opened as he sped,
We saw dead Hendrick Hudson
   Steer, North by West, his dead.

So dealt God's waters with us
   Beneath the roaring skies,
So walked His signs and marvels
   All naked to our eyes:
But we were heading homeward
   With trade to lose or make—
Good Lord, they slipped behind us
   In the tailing of our wake!

Let go, let go the anchors;
   Now shamed at heart are we
To bring so poor a cargo home
   That had for gift the sea!
Let go the great bow-anchor—
   Ah, fools were we and blind—
The worst we stored with utter toil,
   The best we left behind!

Coastwise—cross-seas—round the world and back again,
Whither flaw shall fail us or the Trades drive down:
Plain-sail—storm-sail—lay your board and tack again—
And all to bring a cargo up to London Town!

The Song Of Diego Valdez

1902

The God of Fair Beginnings
   Hath prospered here my hand—
The cargoes of my lading,
   And the keels of my command.
For out of many ventures
   That sailed with hope as high,
My own have made the better trade,
   And Admiral am I.

To me my King's much honour,
   To me my people's love—
To me the pride of Princes
   And power all pride above;
To me the shouting cities,
   To me the mob's refrain:—
"Who knows not noble Valdez
   "Hath never heard of Spain."

But I remember comrades—
   Old playmates on new seas—
Whenas we traded orpiment
   Among the savages—
A thousand leagues to south'ard
   And thirty years removed—
They knew not noble Valdez,
   But me they knew and loved.

Then they that found good liquor,
   They drank it not alone,
And they that found fair plunder,
   They told us every one,
About our chosen islands
   Or secret shoals between,
When, weary from far voyage,
   We gathered to careen.

There burned our breaming-fagots
   All pale along the shore:
There rose our worn pavilions—
   A sail above an oar:
As flashed each yearning anchor
   Through mellow seas afire'
So swift our careless captains
   Rowed each to his desire.

Where lay our loosened harness?
   Where turned our naked feet?
Whose tavern 'mid the palm-trees?
   What quenching of what heat?
Oh, fountain in the desert!
   Oh, cistern in the waste!
Oh, bread we ate in secret!
   Oh, cup we spilled in haste!

The youth new-taught of longing,
   The widow curbed and wan,
The goodwife proud at season,
   And the maid aware of man—
All souls unslaked, consuming,
   Defrauded in delays,
Desire not more their quittance
   Than I those forfeit days!

I dreamed to wait my pleasure
   Unchanged my spring would bide:
Wherefore, to wait my pleasure,
   I put my spring aside
Till, first in face of Fortune,
   And last in mazed disdain,
I made Diego Valdez
   High Admiral of Spain.

Then walked no wind 'neath Heaven
   Nor surge that did not aid—
I dared extreme occasion,
   Nor ever one betrayed.
They wrought a deeper treason—
   (Led seas that served my needs!)
They sold Diego Valdez
   To bondage of great deeds.

The tempest flung me seaward,
   And pinned and bade me hold

The course I might not alter—
   And men esteemed me bold!
The calms embayed my quarry,
   The fog-wreath sealed his eyes;
The dawn-wind brought my topsails—
   And men esteemed me wise!

Yet 'spite my tyrant triumphs,
   Bewildered, dispossessed—
My dreams held I before me—
   My vision of my rest;
But, crowned by Fleet and People,
   And bound by King and Pope—
Stands here Diego Valdez
   To rob me of my hope.

No prayer of mine shall move him.
   No word of his set free
The Lord of Sixty Pennants
   And the Steward of the Sea.
His will can loose ten thousand
   To seek their loves again—
But not Diego Valdez,
   High Admiral of Spain.

There walks no wind 'neath Heaven
   Nor wave that shall restore
The old careening riot
   And the clamorous, crowded shore—
The fountain in the desert,
   The cistern in the waste,
The bread we ate in secret,
   The cup we spilled in haste.

Now call I to my Captains—
   For council fly the sign—
Now leap their zealous galleys,
   Twelve-oared, across the brine.
To me the straiter prison,
   To me the heavier chain—
To me Diego Valdez,
   High Admiral of Spain!

The Second Voyage

1903

We've sent our little Cupids all ashore—
   They were frightened, they were tired, they were cold.
Our sails of silk and purple go to store,
   And we've cut away our mast of beaten gold.
     (Foul weather!)
Oh 'tis hemp and singing pine for to stand against the brine,
   But love he is our master as of old!
The sea has shorn our galleries away,
   The salt has soiled our gilding past remede;
Our paint is flaked and blistered by the spray,
   Our sides are half a fathom furred in weed.
     (Foul weather!)
And the Doves of Venus fled and the petrels came instead,
   But Love he was our master at our need!

'Was Youth would keep no vigil at the bow,
   'Was Pleasure at the helm too drunk to steer—
We've shipped three able quartermasters now.
   Men call them Custom, Reverence, and Fear.
     (Foul weather!)
They are old and scarred and plain, but we'll run no risk again
   From any Port o' Paphos mutineer!

We seek no more the tempest for delight,
   We skirt no more the indraught and the shoal—
We ask no more of any day or night
   Than to come with least adventure to our goal.
     (Foul weather!)
What we find we needs must brook, but we do not go to look
   Nor tempt the Lord our God that saved us whole.

Yet, caring so, not overmuch we care
   To brace and trim for every foolish blast,
If the squall be pleased to sweep us unaware,
   He may bellow off to leeward like the last.
     (Foul weather!)
We will blame it on the deep (for the watch must have their sleep),
   And Love can come and wake us when 'tis past.

Oh, launch them down with music from the beach,
   Oh, warp them out with garlands from the quays—
Most resolute—a damsel unto each—

New prows that seek the old Hesperides!
  (Foul weather!)
Though we know their voyages in vain, yet we see our path again
In the saffroned bridesails scenting all the seas!
  (Foul weather!)

The Oldest Song

"For before Eve was Lilith."—Old Tale.

"These were never your true love's eyes.
  Why do you feign that you love them?
You that broke from their constancies,
  And the wide calm brows above them!

This was never your true love's speech.
  Why do you thrill when you hear it?
You that have ridden out of its reach
  The width of the world or near it!

This was never your true love's hair,—
  You that chafed when it bound you
Screened from knowledge or shame or care,
  In the night that it made around you!"

"All these things I know, I know.
  And that's why my heart is breaking!"
"Then what do you gain by pretending so?"
  "The joy of an old wound waking."

The Liner She's A Lady

1894

The Liner she's a lady, an' she never looks nor 'eeds—
The Man-o'-War's 'er 'usband, an' 'e gives 'er all she needs;
But, oh, the little cargo-boats, that sail the wet seas roun',
They're just the same as you an' me a-plyin' up an' down!

Plyin' up an' down, Jenny, 'angin' round the Yard,
All the way by Fratton tram to Portsmouth 'Ard;
Anythin' for business, an' we're growin' old—
Plyin up an' down, Jenny, waitin' in the cold!

The Liner she's a lady by the paint upon 'er face,
An' if she meets an accident they count it sore disgrace.
The Man-o'-War's 'er 'usband, and 'e's always 'andy by,
But, oh, the little cargo-boats, they've got to load or die!

The Liner she's a lady, and 'er route is cut an' dried;
The Man-o'-War's 'er' usband, an' 'e always keeps beside
But, oh, the little cargo-boats that 'aven't any man,
They've got to do their business first, and make the most they can!

The Liner she's a lady, and if a war should come,
The Man-o'-War's 'er 'usband, and 'e'd bid 'er stay at home;
But, oh, the little cargo-boats that fill with every tide!
'E'd 'ave to up an' fight for them, for they are England's pride.

The Liner she's a lady, but if she wasn't made,
There still would be the cargo-boats for 'ome an' foreign trade.
The Man-o'-War's 'er 'usband, but if we wasn't 'ere,
'E wouldn't have to fight at all for 'ome an' friends so dear.

. . . 'Ome an' friends so dear, Jenny, 'angin round the Yard,
All the way by Fratton tram down to Portsmouth 'Ard;
Anythin' for business, an' we're growin' old—
'Ome an' friends so dear, Jenny, waitin' in the cold!

The First Chantey

1896

Mine was the woman to me, darkling I found her:
Haling her dumb from the camp, held her and bound her.
Hot rose her tribe on our track ere I had proved her;
Hearing her laugh in the gloom, greatly I loved her.

Swift through the forest we ran, none stood to guard us,
Few were my people and far; then the flood barred us—
Him we call Son of the Sea, sullen and swollen.
Panting we waited the death, stealer and stolen.

Yet ere they came to my lance laid for the slaughter,
Lightly she leaped to a log lapped in the water;
Holding on high and apart skins that arrayed her,
Called she the God of the Wind that He should aid her.

Life had the tree at that word (Praise we the Giver!),
Otter-like left he the bank for the full river.

Far fell their axes behind, flashing and ringing,
Wonder was on me and fear— yet she was singing!

Low lay the land we had left.   Now the blue bound us,
Even the Floor of the Gods level around us.
Whisper there was not, nor word, shadow nor showing,
Till the light stirred on the deep, glowing and growing.

Then did He leap to His place flaring from under,
He the Compeller, the Sun, bared to our wonder.
Nay, not a league from our eyes blinded with gazing,
Cleared He the Gate of the World, huge and amazing!

This we beheld (and we live)—the Pit of the Burning!
Then the God spoke to the tree for our returning;
Back to the beach of our flight, fearless and slowly,
Back to our slayers went he; but we were holy.

Men that were hot in that hunt, women that followed,
Babes that were promised our bones, trembled and wallowed
Over the necks of the Tribe crouching and fawning—
Prophet and priestess we came back from the dawning!

The Last Chantey

1892

"And there was no more sea."

Thus said the Lord in the Vault above the Cherubim,
    Calling to the Angels and the Souls in their degree:
    "Lo!   Earth has passed away
    On the smoke of Judgment Day.
That Our word may be established shall We gather up the sea?"

Loud sang the souls of the jolly, jolly mariners:
    "Plague upon the hurricane that made us furl and flee!
    But the war is done between us,
    In the deep the Lord hath seen us—
Our bones we'll leave the barracout', and God may sink the sea!"

Then said the soul of Judas that betrayèd Him:
    "Lord, hast Thou forgotten Thy covenant with me?
    How once a year I go
    To cool me on the floe?
And Ye take my day of mercy if Ye take away the sea."

Then said the soul of the Angel of the Off-shore Wind:
   (He that bits the thunder when the bull-mouthed breakers flee).
   "I have watch and ward to keep
   O'er Thy wonders on the deep,
And Ye take mine honour from me if Ye take away the sea!"

Loud sang the souls of the jolly, jolly mariners:
   "Nay, but we were angry, and a hasty folk are we.
   If we worked the ship together
   Till she foundered in foul weather,
Are we babes that we should clamour for a vengeance on the sea?"

Then said the souls of the slaves that men threw overboard:
   "Kennelled in the picaroon a weary band were we;
   But Thy arm was strong to save,
   And it touched us on the wave,
And we drowsed the long tides idle till Thy Trumpets tore the sea."

Then cried the soul of the stout Apostle Paul to God:
   "Once we frapped a ship, and she laboured woundily.
   There were fourteen score of these,
   And they blessed Thee on their knees,
When they learned Thy Grace and Glory under Malta by the sea!"

Loud sang the souls of the jolly, jolly mariners,
   Plucking at their harps, and they plucked unhandily:
   "Our thumbs are rough and tarred,
   And the tune is something hard—
May we lift a Deepsea Chantey such as seamen use at sea?"

Then said the souls of the gentlemen-adventurers—
   Fettered wrist to bar all for red iniquity:
   "Ho, we revel in our chains
   O'er the sorrow that was Spain's!
Heave or sink it, leave or drink it, we were masters of the sea!"

Up spake the soul of a grey Gothavn 'speckshioner—
   (He that led the flenching in the fleets of fair Dundee):
   "Oh, the ice-blink white and near,
   And the bowhead breaching clear!
Will Ye whelm them all for wantonness that wallow in the sea?"

Loud sang the souls of the jolly, jolly mariners,
   Crying: "Under Heaven, here is neither lead nor lee!
   Must we sing for evermore
   On the windless, glassy floor?
Take back your golden fiddles and we'll beat to open sea!"

Then stooped the Lord, and He called the good sea up to Him,
  And 'stablishèd its borders unto all eternity,
    That such as have no pleasure
    For to praise the Lord by measure,
They may enter into galleons and serve Him on the sea.

Sun, Wind, and Cloud shall fail not from the face of it,
  Stinging, ringing spindrift, nor the fulmar flying free;
    And the ships shall go abroad
    To the Glory of the Lord
Who heard the silly sailor-folk and gave them back their sea!

The Exiles' Line

1890

Now the New Year reviving old desires,
The restless soul to open sea aspires,
  Where the Blue Peter flickers from the fore,
And the grimed stoker feeds the engine-fires.

Coupons, alas, depart with all their rows,
And last year's sea-met loves where Grindlay knows;
  But still the wild wind wakes off Gardafui,
And hearts turn eastward with the P. & O's.

Twelve knots an hour, be they more or less—
Oh, slothful mother of much idleness,
  Whom neither rivals spur nor contracts speed!
Nay, bear us gently! Wherefore need we press?

The Tragedy of all our East is laid
O those white decks beneath the awning shade—
  Birth, absence, longing, laughter, love and tears,
And death unmaking ere the land is made.

And midnight madnesses of souls distraught
Whom the cool seas call through the open port,
  So that the table lacks one place next morn,
And for one forenoon men forgo their sport.

The shadow of the rigging to and fro
Sways, shifts, and flickers on the spar-deck's snow,
  And like a giant trampling in his chains,
The screw-blades gasp and thunder deep below;

And, leagued to watch one flying-fish's wings,
Heaven stoops to sea, and sea to Heaven clings;

While, bent upon the ending of his toil,
The hot sun strides, regarding not these things:

For the same wave that meets our stem in spray
Bore Smith of Asia eastward yesterday,
   And Delhi Jones and Brown of Midnapore
To-morrow follow on the self-same way.

Linked in the chain of Empire one by one,
Flushed with long leave, or tanned with many a sun.
   The Exiles' Line brings out the exiles' line,
And slips them homeward when their work is done.

Yea, heedless of the shuttle through the loom,
The flying keels fulfil the web of doom.
   Sorrow or shouting—what is that to them?
Make out the cheque that pays for cabin-room!

And how so many score of times ye flit
With wife and babe and caravan of kit,
   Not all thy travels past shall lower one fare,
Not all thy tears abate one pound of it.

And how so high thine earth-born dignity,
Honour and state, go sink it in the sea,
   Till that great one upon, the quarter-deck,
Brow-bound with gold, shall give thee leave to be.

Indeed, indeed from that same line we swear
Off for all time, and mean it when we swear;
   And then, and then we meet the Quartered Flag,
And, surely for the last time, pay the fare.

And Green of Kensington, estrayed to view
In three short months the world he never knew,
   Stares with blind eyes upon the Quartered Flag
And sees no more than yellow, red and blue.

But we, the gipsies of the East, but we—
Waifs of the land and wastrels of the sea—
   Come nearer home beneath the Quartered Flag
Than ever home shall come to such as we.

The camp is struck, the bungalow decays,
Dead friends and houses desert mark our ways,
   Till sickness send us down to Prince's Dock
To meet the changeless use of many days.

Bound in the wheel of Empire, one by one,
The chain-gangs of the East from sire to son,

The Exiles' Line takes out the exiles' line
And ships them homeward when their work is done.

How runs the old indictment?   "Dear and slow,"
So much and twice so much.   We gird, but go.
    For all the soul of our sad East is there,
Beneath the house-flag of the P. & O.

The Long Trail

There's a whisper down the field where the year has shot her yield,
    And the ricks stand grey to the sun,
Singing: "Over then, come over, for the bee has quit the clover,
    "And your English summer's done."
        You have heard the beat of the off-shore wind,
            And the thresh of the deep-sea rain;
        You have heard the song—how long? how long?
            Pull out on the trail again!
    Ha' done with the Tents of Shem, dear lass,
    We've seen the seasons through,
        And it's time to turn on the old trail, our own trail, the out trail,
        Pull out, pull out, on the Long Trail—the trail that is always new!

It's North you may run to the rime-ringed sun
    Or South to the blind Horn's hate;
Or East all the way into Mississippi Bay,
    Or West to the Golden Gate—
        Where the blindest bluffs hold good, dear lass,
            And the wildest tales are true,
        And the men bulk big on the old trail, our own trail, the out trail,
        And life runs large on the Long Trail—the trail that is always new.

The days are sick and cold, and the skies are grey and old,
    And the twice-breathed airs blow damp;
And I'd sell my tired soul for the bucking beam-sea roll
    Of a black Bilbao tramp,
        With her load-line over her hatch, dear lass,
            And a drunken Dago crew,
        And her nose held down on the old trail, our own trail, the out trail
        From Cadiz south on the Long Trail—the trail that is always new.

There be triple ways to take, of the eagle or the snake,
    Or the way of a man with a maid;

But the sweetest way to me is a ship's upon the sea
  In the heel of the North-East Trade.
    Can you hear the crash on her bows, dear lass,
    And the drum of the racing screw,
    As she ships it green on the old trail, our own trail, the out trail,
    As she lifts and 'scends on the Long Trail—the trail that is always
      new?

See the shaking funnels roar, with the Peter at the fore,
  And the fenders grind and heave,
And the derricks clack and grate, as the tackle hooks the crate,
  And the fall-rope whines through the sheave;
    It's "Gang-plank up and in," dear lass,
    It's "Hawsers warp her through!"
    And it's "All clear aft" on the old trail, our own trail, the out trail,
    We're backing down on the Long Trail—the trail that is always new.

O the mutter overside, when the port-fog holds us tied,
  And the sirens hoot their dread,
When foot by foot we creep o'er the hueless, viewless deep
  To the sob of the questing lead!
    It's down by the Lower Hope, dear lass,
    With the Gunfleet Sands in view,
    Till the Mouse swings green on the old trail, our own trail, the out
      trail,
    And the Gull Light lifts on the Long Trail—the trail that is always
      new.

O the blazing tropic night, when the wake's a welt of light
  That holds the hot sky tame,
And the steady fore-foot snores through the planet-powdered floors
  Where the sacred whale flukes in flame!
    Her plates are flaked by the sun, dear lass,
    And her ropes are taut with the dew,
    For we're booming down on the old trail, our own trail, the out trail,
    We're sagging south on the Long Trail—the trail that is always new.

Then home, get her home, where the drunken rollers comb,
  And the shouting seas drive by,
And the engines stamp and ring, and the wet bows reel and swing,
  And the Southern Cross rides high!
    Yes, the old lost stars wheel back, dear lass,
    That blaze in the velvet blue.
    They're all old friends on the old trail, our own tail, the out trail,
    They're God's own guides on the Long Trail—the tail that is always
      new.

Fly forward, O my heart, from the Foreland to the Start—
    We're steaming all too slow,
And it's twenty thousand mile to our little lazy isle
    Where the trumpet-orchids blow!
        You have heard the call of the off-shore wind
        And the voice of the deep-sea rain;
        You have heard the song—how long?—how long?
        Pull out on the trail again!

The Lord knows what we may find, dear lass,
And The Deuce knows what we may do—
But we're back once more on the old trail, our own trail, the out trail,
We're down, hull-down, on the Long Trail—the trail that is always new!

In the Matter of One Compass

1892
(Enlarged from "Many Inventions")

When, foot to wheel and back to wind,
The helmsman dare not look behind,
But hears beyond his compass-light,
The blind bow thunder through the night,
And, like a harpstring ere it snaps,
The rigging sing beneath the caps;
    Above the shriek of storm in sail
        Or rattle of the blocks blown free,
    Set for the peace beyond the gale,
        This song the Needle sings the Sea:

Oh, drunken Wave! Oh, driving Cloud!
    Rage of the Deep and sterile Rain,
By Love upheld, by God allowed,
    We go, but we return again!

When leagued about the 'wildered boat
The rainbow Jellies fill and float,
And, lilting where the laver lingers,
The Starfish trips on all her fingers;
Where, 'neath his myriad spines ashock,
The Sea-egg ripples down the rock,
An orange wonder dimly guessed
From darkness where the Cuttles rest,

Moored o'er the darker deeps that hide
The blind white Sea-snake and his bride,
Who, drowsing, nose the long-lost Ships
Let down through the darkness to their lips
Safe-swung above the glassy death,
Hear what the constant Needle saith:

Oh lisping Reef! Oh listless Cloud,
   In slumber on a pulseless main!
By Love upheld, by God allowed,
   We go, but we return again!

E'en so through Tropic and through Trade,
   Awed by the shadow of new skies,
As we shall watch old planets fade
   And mark the stranger stars arise,
So, surely, back through Sun and Cloud,
   So, surely, from the outward main,
By Love recalled, by God allowed,
   Shall we return—return again!
   Yea, we return—return again!

Ave Imperatrix!

(*Written on the occasion of the attempt to assassinate Queen Victoria in March 1882*)

From every quarter of your land
   They give God thanks who turned away
Death and the needy madman's hand,
   Death-fraught, which menaced you that day.

One school of many made to make
   Men who shall hold it dearest right
To battle for their ruler's sake,
   And stake their being in the fight,

Sends greeting humble and sincere—
   Though verse be rude and poor and mean
To you, the greatest as most dear—
   Victoria, by God's grace Our Queen!

Such greeting as should come from those
   Whose fathers faced the Sepoy hordes,
Or served you in the Russian snows,
   And, dying, left their sons their swords.

And some of us have fought for you
    Already in the Afghan pass—
Or where the scarce-seen smoke-puffs flew
    From Boer marksmen in the grass;

And all are bred to do your will
    By land and sea—wherever flies
The Flag,to fight and follow still,
    And work your Empire's destinies.

Once more we greet you, though unseen
    Our greeting be, and coming slow.
Trust us, if need arise, O Queen,
    We shall not tarry with the blow!

A Song of the English

1893

Fair is our lot—O goodly is our heritage!
(Humble ye, my people, and be fearful in your mirth!)
    For the lord our God Most High
    He hath made the deep as dry,
He hath smote for us a pathway to the ends of all the Earth!

Yea, though we sinned, and our rulers went from righteousness—
Deep in all dishonour though we stained our garments' hem,
    Oh, be ye not dismayed,
    Though we stumbled and we strayed,
We were led by evil counsellors—the lord shall deal with them!

Hold ye the Faith—the Faith our Fathers sealed us;
Whoring not with visions—overwise and overstale.
    Except ye pay the Lord
    Single heart and single sword,
Of your children in their bondage He shall ask them treble-tale!

Keep ye the Law—be swift in all obedience—
Clear the land of evil, drive the road and bridge the ford.
    Make ye sure to each his own
    That he reap where he hath sown;
By the peace among Our peoples let men know we serve the lord!

Hear now a song—a song of broken interludes—
A song of little cunning; of a singer nothing worth.
    Through the naked words and mean
    May ye see the truth between,
As the singer knew and touched it in the ends of all the Earth!

The Coastwise Lights

Our brows are bound with spindrift and the weed is on our knees;
Our loins are battered 'neath us by the swinging, smoking seas.
From reef and rock and skerry—over headland, ness, and voe—
The Coastwise Lights of England watch the ships of England go!

Through the endless summer evenings,on the lineless, level floors;
Through the yelling Channel tempest when the siren hoots and roars—
By day the dipping house-flag and by night the rocket's trail—
As the sheep that graze behind us so we know them where they hail.

We bridge across the dark, and bid the helmsman have a care,
The flash that, wheeling inland, wakes his sleeping wife to prayer.
From our vexed eyries, head to gale, we bind in burning chains
The lover from the sea-rim drawn—his love in English lanes.

We greet the clippers wing-and-wing that race the Southern wool;
We warn the crawling cargo-tanks of Bremen, Leith, and Hull;
To each and all our equal lamp at peril of the sea—
The white wall-sided warships or the whalers of Dundee!

Come up, come in from Eastward, from the guardports of the Morn!
Beat up, beat in from Southerly, O gipsies of the Horn!
Swift shuttles of an Empire's loom that weave us main to main,
The Coastwise Lights of England give you welcome back again!

Go, get you gone up-Channel with the sea-crust on your plates;
Go, get you into London with the burden of your freights!
Haste, for they talk of Empire there and say, if any seek,
The Lights of England sent you and by silence shall ye speak!

The Song of the Dead

Hear now the Song of the Dead—in the North by the torn berg-edges—
They that look still to the Pole, asleep by their hide-stripped sledges.
Song of the Dead in the South—in the sun by their skeleton horses,
Where the warrigal whimpers and bays through the dust of the sere river-courses.

Song of the Dead in the East—in the heat-rotted jungle-hollows,
Where the dog-ape barks in the kloof—in the brake of the buffalo-wallows.
Song of the Dead in the West—in the Barrens, the pass that betrayed them,
Where the wolverine tumbles their packs from the camp and the grave-mound they
*   made them;*
*   Hear now the Song of the Dead!*

I

We were dreamers, dreaming greatly, in the man-stifled town;
We yearned beyond the sky-line where the strange road go down.
Came the Whisper, came Vision, came the power with the Need,
Till the Soul that is not man's soul was lent us to lead.

As the deer breaks—as the steer breaks—from the herd where they graze,
In the faith of little children we went on our ways.
Then the wood failed—then the food failed—then the last water dried—
In the faith of little children we lay down and died.
On the sand-drift—on the veldt-side—in the fern-scrub we lay,
That our sons might follow after by the bones on the way.
Follow after—follow after! We have watered the root,
And the bud has come to blossom that ripens for fruit!
Follow after—we are waiting, by the trails that we lost,
For the sounds of many footsteps, for the tread of a host.
Follow after—follow after—for the harvest is sown:
By the bones about the wayside ye shall come to your own!

> When Drake went down to the Horn
>   And England was crowned thereby,
> 'Twixt seas unsailed and shores unhailed
>   Our Lodge—our Lodge was born
>   (And England was crowned thereby!)
>
> Which never shall close again
>   By day nor yet by night,
> While man shall take his life to stake
>   At risk of shoal or main
>   (By day nor yet by night)
>
> But standeth even so
>   As now we witness here,
> While men depart, of joyful heart,
>   Adventure for to know
>   (As now bear witness here!)

II

We have fed our sea for a thousand years
    And she calls us, still unfed,
Though there's never a wave of all her waves
    But marks our English dead:
We have strawed our best to the weed's unrest,
    To the shark and the sheering gull.
If blood be the price of admiralty,
    Lord God, we ha' paid in full!

There's never a flood goes shoreward now
    But lifts a keel we manned;
There's never an ebb goes seaward now
    But drops our dead on the sand—
But slinks our dead on the sands forlore,
    From the Ducies to the Swin.
If blood be the price of admiralty,
If blood be the price of admiralty,
    Lord God, we ha' paid it in!

We must feed our sea for a thousand years,
    For that is our doom and pride,
As it was when they sailed with the *Golden Hind*,
    Or the wreck that struck last tide—
Or the wreck that lies on the spouting reef
    Where the ghastly blue-lights flare.
If blood be the price of admiralty,
If blood be the price of admiralty,
If blood be the price of admiralty,
    Lord God, we ha' bought it fair!

The Deep-Sea Cables

The wrecks dissolve above us; their dust drops down from afar—
Down to the dark, to the utter dark, where the blind white sea-snakes are.
There is no sound, no echo of sound, in the deserts of the deep,
Or the grey level plains of ooze where the shell-blurred cables creep.

Here in the womb of the world—here on the tie-ribs of earth
    Words, and the words of men, flicker and flutter and beat—
Warning, sorrow, and gain, salutation and mirth—
    For a Power troubles the Still that has neither voice nor feet.

They have wakened the timeless Things; they have killed their father
    Time;
    Joining hands in the gloom, a league from the last of the sun.
Hush!   Men talk to-day o'er the waste of the ultimate slime,
    And a new Word runs between: whispering, "Let us be one!"

The Song of the Sons

One from the ends of the earth—gifts at an open door—
Treason has much, but we, Mother, thy sons have more!
From the whine of a dying man, from the snarl of a wolf-pack freed,

Turn, and the world is thine.   Mother, be proud of thy seed!
Count, are we feeble or few?   Hear, is our speech so rude?
Look, are we poor in the land?   Judge, are we men of The Blood?

Those that have stayed at thy knees, Mother, go call them in—
We that were bred overseas wait and would speak with our kin.
Not in the dark do we fight—haggle and flout and gibe;
Selling our love for a price, loaning our hearts for a bribe.
Gifts have we only to-day—Love without promise or fee—
Hear, for thy children speak, from the uttermost parts of the sea!

The Song of the Cities

BOMBAY

Royal and Dower-royal, I the Queen
  Fronting thy richest sea with richer hands—
A thousand mills roar through me where I glean
  All races from all lands.

CALCUTTA

Me the Sea-captain loved, the River built,
  Wealth sought and Kings adventured life to hold.
Hail, England!   I am Asia—Power on silt,
  Death in my hands, but Gold!

MADRAS

Clive kissed me on the mouth and eyes and brow,
  Wonderful kisses, so that I became
Crowned above Queens—a withered beldame, now,
  Brooding on ancient fame.

RANGOON

Hail, Mother!   Do they call me rich in trade?
  Little care I, but hear the shorn priest drone,
And watch my silk-clad lovers, man by maid,
  Laugh 'neath my Shwe Dagon.

SINGAPORE

Hail, Mother!   East and West must seek my aid
  Ere the spent hull may dare the ports afar.
The second doorway of the wide world's trade
  Is mine to loose or bar.

HONG-KONG

Hail, Mother! Hold me fast; my Praya sleeps
    Under innumerable keels to-day.
Yet guard (and landward), or to-morrow sweeps
    Thy warships down the bay!

HALIFAX

Into the mist my guardian prows put forth,
    Behind the mist my virgin ramparts lie,
The Warden of the Honour of the North,
    Sleepless and veiled am I!

QUEBEC AND MONTREAL

Peace is our portion. Yet a whisper rose,
    Foolish and causeless, half in jest, half hate.
Now wake we and remember mighty blows,
    And, fearing no man, wait!

VICTORIA

From East to West the circling word has passed,
    Till West is East beside our land-locked blue;
From East to West the tested chain holds fast,
    The well-forged link rings true!

CAPETOWN

Hail! Snatched and bartered oft from hand to hand,
    I dream my dream, by rock and heat and pine,
Of Empire to the northward. Ay, one land
    From Lion's Head to Line!

MELBOURNE

Greeting! Nor fear nor favour won us place,
    Got between greed of gold and dread of drouth,
Loud-voiced and reckless as the wild tide-race
    That whips our harbour-mouth!

SYDNEY

Greeting! My birth-stain have I turned to good;
    Forcing strong wills perverse to steadfastness:
The first flush of the tropics in my blood,
    And at my feet Success!

BRISBANE

The northern stock beneath the southern skies—
    I build a Nation for an Empire's need,
Suffer a little, and my land shall rise,
    Queen over lands indeed!

HOBART

Man's love first found me; man's hate made me Hell;
    For my babes' sake I cleansed those infamies.
Earnest for leave to live and labour well,
    God flung me peace and ease.

AUCKLAND

Last, loneliest, loveliest, exquisite, apart—
    On us, on us the unswerving season smiles,
Who wonder 'mid our fern why men depart
    To seek the Happy Isles!

England's Answer

Truly ye come of The Blood; slower to bless than to ban,
Little used to lie down at the bidding of any man—
Flesh of the flesh that I bred, bone of the bone that I bare;
Stark as your sons shall be—stern as your fathers were.
Deeper than speech our love, stronger than life our tether,
But we do not fall on the neck nor kiss when we come together.
My arm is nothing weak, my strength is not gone by;
Sons, I have borne many sons, but my dugs are not dry.
Look, I have made ye a place and opened wide the doors,
That ye may talk together, your Barons and Councillors—
Wards of the Outer March, Lords of the Lower Seas,
Ay, talk to your grey mother that bore you on her knees!—
That ye may talk together, brother to brother's face—
Thus for the good of your peoples—thus for the Pride of the Race.
Also, we will make promise.   So long as The Blood endures,
I shall know that your good is mine; ye shall feel that my strength is
      yours:
In the day of Armageddon, at the last great fight of all,
That Our House stand together and the pillars do not fall.
Draw now the threefold knot firm on the ninefold bands,
And the Law that ye make shall be law after the rule of your lands.
This for the waxen Heath, and that for the Wattle-bloom,
This for the Maple-leaf, and that for the Southern Broom.

The Law that ye make shall be law and I do not press my will,
Because ye are Sons of The Blood and call me Mother still.
Now must ye speak to your kinsmen and they must speak to you,
After the use of the English, in straight-flung words and few.
Go to your work and be strong, halting not in your ways,
Baulking the end half-won for an instant dole of praise.
Stand to your work and be wise—certain of sword and pen,
Who are neither children nor Gods, but men in a world of men!

The Houses

1898

(A Song of the Dominions)

'Twixt my house and thy house the pathway is broad,
In thy house or my house is half the world's hoard;
By my house and thy house hangs all the world's fate,
On thy house and my house lies half the world's hate.

For my house and thy house no help shall we find
Save thy house and my house—kin cleaving to kind;
If my house be taken, thine tumbleth anon.
If thy house be forfeit, mine followeth soon.

'Twixt my house and thy house what talk can there be
Of headship or lordship, or service or fee?
Since my house to thy house no greater can send
Than thy house to my house—friend comforting friend;
And thy house to my house no meaner can bring
Than my house to thy house—King counselling King!

To the City of Bombay

1894

(Dedication to "The Seven Seas")

The Cities are full of pride,
    Challenging each to each—
This from her mountain-side,
That from her burdened beach.

They count their ships full tale—
    Their corn and oil and wine,
Derrick and loom and bale,

And ramparts' gun-flecked line;
City by City they hail:
    "Hast aught to match with mine?"

And the men that breed from them
    They traffic up and down,
But cling to their cities' hem
    As a child to the mother's gown;

When they talk with the stranger bands,
    Dazed and newly alone;
When they walk in the stranger lands,
    By roaring streets unknown;
Blessing her where she stands
    For strength above their own.

(On high to hold her fame
    That stands all fame beyond,
By oath to back the same,
    Most faithful-foolish-fond;
Making her mere-breathed name
    Their bond upon their bond.)

So thank I God my birth
    Fell not in isles aside—
Waste headlands for the earth,
    Or warring tribes untried—
But that she lent me worth
    And gave me right to pride.

Surely in toil or fray
    Under an alien sky,
Comfort it is to say:
    "Of no mean city am I!"

(Neither by service nor fee
    Come I to mine estate—
Mother of Cities to me,
    But I was born in her gate,
Between the palms and the sea,
    Where the world-end steamers wait.)

Now for this debt I owe,
    And for her far-borne cheer
Must I make haste and go
    With tribute to her pier.

And she shall touch and remit
    After the use of kings

(Orderly, ancient fit)
   My deep-sea plunderings,
And purchase in all lands.
   And this we do for a sign
   Her power is over mine,
And mine I hold at her hands!

The Gipsy Trail

The white moth to the closing bine,
   The bee to the opened clover,
And the gipsy blood to the gipsy blood
   Ever the wide world over.

Ever the wide world over, lass
   Ever the trail held true,
Over the world and under the world,
   And back at the last to you.

Out of the dark of the gorgio camp,
   Out of the grime and the gray
(Morning waits at the end of the world),
   Gipsy, come away!

The wild boar to the sun-dried swamp,
   The red crane to her reed,
And the Romany lass to the Romany lad
   By the tie of a roving breed.

The pied snake to the rifted rock,
   The buck to the stony plain,
And the Romany lass to the Romany lad,
   And both to the road again.

Both to the road again, again!
   Out on a clean sea-track—
Follow the cross of the gipsy trail
   Over the world and back!

Follow the Romany patteran
   North where the blue bergs sail,
And the bows are gray with the frozen spray,
   And the masts are shod with mail.

Follow the Romany patteran
    Sheer to the Austral Light,
Where the besom of God is the wild South wind,
    Sweeping the sea-floors white.

Follow the Romany patteran
    West to the sinking sun,
Till the junk-sails lift through the houseless drift,
    And the east and the west are one.

Follow the Romany patteran
    East where the silence broods
By a purple wave on an opal beach
    In the hush of the Mahim woods.

"The wild hawk to the wind-swept sky,
    The deer to the wholesome wold,
And the heart of a man to the heart of a maid,
    As it was in the days of old."

The heart of a man to the heart of a maid—
    Light of my tents, be fleet.
Morning waits at the end of the world,
    And the world is all at our feet!

Our Lady of the Snows
1897

(Canadian Preferential Tariff, 1897)

A Nation spoke to a Nation,
    A Queen sent word to a Throne:
"Daughter am I in my mother's house,
    But mistress in my own.
The gates are mine to open,
    As the gates are mine to close,
And I set my house in order,"
    Said our Lady of the Snows.

"Neither with laughter nor weeping,
    Fear or the child's amaze—
Soberly under the White Man's law
    My white men to their ways.
Not for the Gentiles' clamour—
    Insult or threat of blows—
Bow we the knee to Baal,"
    Said the Lady of the Snows.

"My speech is clean and single,
   I talk of common things—
Words of the wharf and the market-place
   And the ware the merchant brings:
Favour to those I favour,
   But a stumbling-block to my foes.
Many there be that hate us,"
   Said our Lady of the Snows.

"I called my chiefs to council
   In the din of a troubled year;
For the sake of a sign ye would not see,
   And a word ye would not hear.
This is our message and answer;
   This is the path we chose:
For we be also a people,"
   Said our Lady of the Snows.

"Carry the word to my sisters—
   To the Queens of the East and the South.
I have proven faith in the Heritage
   By more than the word of the mouth.
They that are wise may follow
   Ere the world's war-trumpet blows,
But I—I am first in the battle,"
   Said our Lady of the Snows.

A Nation spoke to a Nation,
   A Throne sent word to a Throne:
"Daughter am I in my mother's house,
   But mistress in my own.
The gates are mine to open,
   As the gates are mine to close,
And I abide by my Mother's House,"
   Said our Lady of the Snows.

An American

1894

The American Spirit speaks:

If the Led Striker call it a strike,
   Or the papers call it a war,
They know not much what I am like,
   Nor what he is, my Avatar.

Through many roads by me possessed,
    He shambles forth in cosmic guise;
He is the Jester and the Jest,
    And he the Text himself applies.

The Celt is in his heart and hand,
    The Gaul is in his brain and nerve;
Where, cosmopolitanly planned,
    He guards the Redskin's dry reserve.

His easy unswept hearth he lends
    From Labrador to Guadeloupe;
Till, elbowed out by sloven friends,
    He camps, at sufferance, on the stoop.

Calm-eyed he scoffs at Sword and Crown,
    Or, panic-blinded, stabs and slays;
Blatant he bids the world bow down,
    Or cringing begs a crust of praise;

Or, sombre-drunk, at mine and mart,
    He dubs his dreary brethren Kings.
His hands are black with blood—his heart
    Leaps, as a babe's, at little things.

But, through the shift of mood and mood,
    Mine ancient humour saves him whole—
The cynic devil in his blood
    That bids him mock his hurrying soul;

That bids him flout the Law he makes,
    That bids him make the Law he flouts,
Till, dazed by many doubts, he wakes
    The drumming guns that—have no doubts;

That checks him foolish-hot and fond,
    That chuckles through his deepest ire,
That gilds the slough of his despond
    But dims the goal of his desire;

Inopportune, shrill-accented,
    The acrid Asiatic mirth
That leaves him, careless 'mid his dead,
    The scandal of the elder earth.

How shall he clear himself, how reach
    Your bar or weighed defence prefer—
A brother hedged with alien speech
    And lacking all interpreter?

Which knowledge vexes him a space;
  But, while Reproof around him rings,
He turns a keen untroubled face
  Home, to the instant need of things.

Enslaved, illogical, elate,
  He greets the embarrassed Gods, nor fears
To shake the iron hand of Fate
  Or match with Destiny for beers.

Lo, imperturbable he rules,
  Unkempt, disreputable, vast—
And, in the teeth of all the schools,
  I—I shall save him at the last!

The Choice

1917

The American Spirit speaks:

To the Judge of Right and Wrong
  With Whom fulfilment lies
Our purpose and our power belong,
  Our faith and sacrifice.

Let Freedom's Land rejoice!
  Our ancient bonds are riven;
Once more to us the eternal choice
  Of Good or Ill is given.

Not at a little cost,
  Hardly by prayer or tears,
Shall we recover the road we lost
  In the drugged and doubting years.

But, after the fires and the wrath,
  But, after searching and pain,
His Mercy opens us a path
  To live with ourselves again.

In the Gates of Death rejoice!
  We see and hold the good—
Bear witness, Earth, we have made our choice
  With Freedom's brotherhood!

Then praise the Lord Most High
  Whose Strength hath saved us whole,
Who bade us choose that the Flesh should die
  And not the living Soul!

To the God in Man displayed—
  Where'er we see that Birth,
Be love and understanding paid
  As never yet on earth!

To the Spirit that moves in Man,
  On Whom all worlds depend,
Be Glory since our world began
  And service to the end!

The Young Queen

1900

(*The Commonwealth of Australia, inaugurated New Year's Day*, 1901)

Her hand was still on her sword-hilt, the spur was still on her heel,
She had not cast her harness of grey, war-dinted steel;
High on her red-splashed charger, beautiful, bold and browned,
Bright-eyed out of the battle, the Young Queen rode to be crowned.

She came to the Old Queen's presence, in the Hall of Our Thousand
    Years—
In the Hall of the Five Free Nations that are peers among their peers:
Royal she gave the greeting, loyal she bowed the head,
Crying—"Crown me, my Mother!"   And the Old Queen rose and said—

"How can I crown thee further?   I know whose standard flies
Where the clean surge takes the Leeuwin or the coral barriers rise.
Blood of our foes on thy bridle, and speech of our friends in thy mouth—
How can I crown thee further, O Queen of the Sovereign South?

"Let the Five Free Nations witness!"   But the Young Queen answered
    swift—
"It shall be crown of Our crowning to hold Our crown for a gift.
In the days when Our folk were feeble thy sword made sure Our lands:
Wherefore We come in power to take Our crown at thy hands."

And the Old Queen raised and kissed her, and the jealous circlet prest,
Roped with the pearls of the Northland and red with the gold of the
    West,
Lit with her land's own opals, levin-hearted, alive,
And the Five-starred Cross above them, for sign of the Nations Five.

So it was done in the Presence—in the Hall of Our Thousand Years,
In the face of the Five Free Nations that have no peer but their peers;
And the Young Queen out of the Southland kneeled down at the Old
  Queen's knee,
And asked for a mother's blessing on the excellent years to be.

And the Old Queen stooped in the stillness where the jewelled head
  drooped low:—
"Daughter no more but Sister, and doubly Daughter so—
Mother of many princes—and child of the child I bore,
What good thing shall I wish thee that I have not wished before?

"Shall I give thee delight in dominion—mere pride of thy setting forth?
Nay, we be women together – we know what that lust is worth.
Peace in thy utmost borders, and strength on a road untrod?
These are dealt or diminished at the secret will of God.

"I have swayed troublous councils, I am wise in terrible things;
Father and son and grandson, I have known the hearts of the Kings.
Shall I give thee my sleepless wisdom, or the gift all wisdom above?
Ay, we be women together—I give thee thy people's love:

"Tempered, august, abiding, reluctant of prayers or vows,
Eager in face of peril as thine for thy mother's house.
God requite thee, my Sister, through the excellent years to be,
And make thy people to love thee as thou has lovèd me!"

Ode

MELBOURNE SHRINE OF REMEMBRANCE

1934

So long as memory, valour, and faith endure,
  Let these stones witness, through the years to come,
How once there was a people fenced secure
  Behind great waters girdling a far home.

Their own and their land's youth ran side by side
  Heedless and headlong as their unyoked seas—
Lavish o'er all, and set in stubborn pride
  Of judgment, nurtured by accepted peace.

Thus, suddenly, war took them—seas and skies
  Joined with the earth for slaughter.   In a breath
They, scoffing at all talk of sacrifice,
  Gave themselves without idle words to death.

Thronging as cities throng to watch a game
   Or their own herds move southward with the year,
Secretly, swiftly, from their ports they came,
So that before half earth had heard their name
   Half earth had learned to speak of them with fear;

Because of certain men who strove to reach,
   Through the red surf the crest no man might hold,
And gave their name for ever to a beach
   Which shall outlive Troy's tale when Time is old;

Because of horsemen, gathered apart and hid—
   Merciless riders whom Megiddo sent forth
When the outflanking hour struck, and bid
   Them close and bar the drove-roads to the north;

And those who, when men feared the last March flood
   Of Western war had risen beyond recall,
Stormed through the night from Amiens and made good,
   At their glad cost, the breach that perilled all.

Then they returned to their desired land—
   The kindly cities and plains where they were bred—
Having revealed their nation in earth's sight
So long as sacrifice and honour stand,
And their own sun at the hushed hour shall light
   The shrine of these their dead!

The Flowers

1895

"To our private taste, there is always something a little exotic, almost artificial, in songs which, under an English aspect and dress, are yet so manifestly the product of other skies.   They affect us like translations; the very fauna and flora are alien, remote; the dog's-tooth violet is but an ill substitute for the rathe primrose, nor can we ever believe that the wood-robin sings as sweetly in April as the English thrush."—THE ATHENAEUM.

> *Buy my English posies!*
>   *Kent and Surrey may—*
> *Violets of the Undercliff*
>   *Wet with Channel spray;*
> *Cowslips from a Devon combe—*
>   *Midland furze afire—*
> *Buy my English posies*
>   *And I'll sell your heart's desire!*

Buy my English posies!
　　You that scorn the May
Won't you greet a friend from home
　　Half the world away?
Green against the draggled drift,
　　Faint and frail but first—
Buy my Northern blood-root
　　And I'll know where you were nursed!
Robin down the logging-road whistles, "Come to me!"
Spring has found the maple-grove, the sap is running free.
All the winds of Canada call the ploughing-rain.
Take the flower and turn the hour, and kiss your love again!

Buy my English posies!
　　Here's to match your need—
Buy a tuft of royal heath,
　　Buy a bunch of weed
White as sand of Muizenberg
　　Spun before the gale—
Buy my heath and lilies
　　And I'll tell you whence you hail!
Under hot Constantia broad the vineyards lie—
Throned and throned the aching berg props the speckless sky—
Slow below the Wynberg firs trails the tilted wain—
Take the flower and turn the hour, and kiss your love again!

Buy my English posies!
　　You that will not turn—
Buy my hot-wood clematis,
　　But a frond o' fern
Gathered where the Erskine leaps
　　Down the road to Lorne—
Buy my Christmas creeper
　　And I'll say where you were born!
West away from Melbourne dust holidays begin—
They that mock at Paradise woo at Cora Lynn—
Through the great South Otway gums sings the great South Main—
Take the flower and turn the hour, and kiss your love again!

Buy my English posies!
　　Here's your choice unsold!
Buy a blood-red myrtle-bloom,
　　Buy the kowhai's gold
Flung for gift on Taupo's face,
　　Sign that spring is come—
Buy my clinging myrtle

And I'll give you back your home!
Broom behind the windy town, pollen of the pine—
Bell-bird in the leafy deep where the *ratas* twine—
Fern above the saddle-bow, flax upon the plain—
Take the flower and turn the hour, and kiss your love again!

> Buy my English posies!
>   Ye that have your own
> Buy them for a brother's sake
>   Overseas, alone!
> Weed ye trample underfoot
>   Floods his heart abrim—
> Bird ye never heeded,
>   Oh, she calls his dead to him!

Far and far our homes are set round the Seven Seas;
Woe for us if we forget, we who hold by these!
Unto each his mother-beach, bloom and bird and land—
Masters of the Seven Seas, oh, love and understand!

The Native-Born

1894

We've drunk to the Queen—God bless her!—
    We've drunk to our mothers' land;
We've drunk to our English brother,
    (But he does not understand);
We've drunk to the wide creation,
    And the Cross swings low for the morn,
Last toast, and of Obligation,
    A health to the Native-born!

They change their skies above them,
    But not their hearts that roam!
We learned from our wistful mothers
    To call old England "home";
We read of the English skylark,
    Of the spring in the English lanes,
But we screamed with the painted lorries
    As we rode on the dusty plains!

They passed with their old-world legends—
    Their tales of wrong and dearth—
Our fathers held by purchase,
    But we by the right of birth;

Our heart's where they rocked our candle,
  Our love where we spent our toil,
And our faith and our hope and our honour
  We pledge to our native soil!

I charge you charge your glasses—
  I charge you drink with me
To the men of the Four New Nations,
  And the Islands of the Sea—
To the last least lump of coral
  That none may stand outside,
And our own good pride shall teach us
  To praise our comrade's pride.
To the hush of the breathless morning
  On the thin, tin, crackling roofs,
To the haze of the burned back-ranges
  And the dust of the shoeless hoofs—
To the risk of a death by drowning,
  To the risk of a death by drouth—
To the men of a million acres,
  To the Sons of the Golden South!

To the Sons of the Golden South (Stand up!),
  And the life we live and know,
Let a fellow sing o' the little things he cares about,
If a fellow fights for the little things he cares about
  With the weight of a single blow!

To the smoke of a hundred coasters,
  To the sheep on a thousand hills,
To the sun that never blisters,
  To the rain that never chills—
To the land of the waiting springtime,
  To our five-meal, meat-fed men,
To the tall, deep-bosomed women,
  And the children nine and ten!

And the children nine and ten (Stand up!),
  And the life we live and know,
Let a fellow sing o' the little things he cares about,
If a fellow fights for the little things he cares about
  With the weight of a two-fold blow!

To the far-flung, fenceless prairie
  Where the quick, cloud-shadows trail,
To our neighbour's barn in the offing
  And the line of the new-cut rail;

To the plough in her league-long furrow
  With the grey Lake gulls behind—
To the weight of a half-year's winter
  And the warm wet western wind!

To the home of the floods and thunder,
  To her pale dry healing blue—
To the lift of the great Cape combers,
  And the smell of the baked Karroo,
To the growl of the sluicing stamp-head—
  To the reef and the water-gold,
To the last and the largest Empire,
  To the map that is half unrolled!

To our dear dark foster-mothers,
  To the heathen songs they sung—
To the heathen speech we babbled
  Ere we came to the white man's tongue.
To the cool of our deep verandahs—
  To the blaze of our jewelled main,
To the night, to the palms in the moonlight,
  And the fire-fly in the cane!

To the hearth of Our People's People—
  To her well-ploughed windy sea,
To the hush of our dread high-altar
  Where The Abbey makes us We.
To the grist of the slow-ground ages,
  To the gain that is yours and mine—
To the Bank of the Open Credit,
  To the Power-house of the Line!

We've drunk to the Queen—God bless her!
  We've drunk to our mothers' land;
We've drunk to our English brother
  (And we hope he'll understand).
We've drunk as much as we're able,
  And the Cross swings low for the morn;
Last toast—and your foot on the table!—
  A health to the Native-born!

A health to the Native-born (Stand up!),
  We're six white men arow,
All bound to sing o' the little things we care about,
All bound to fight for the little things we care about
  With the weight of a six-fold blow!

By the might of our Cable-tow (Take hands!),
  From the Orkneys to the Horn
All round the world (and a little loop to pull it by),
All round the world (and a little strap to buckle it).
  A health to the Native-born!

The Lost Legion

1895

There's a Legion that never was listed,
  That carries no colours or crest.
But, split in a thousand detachments,
  Is breaking the road for the rest.
Our fathers they left us their blessing—
  They taught us, and groomed us, and crammed;
But we've shaken the Clubs and the Messes
  To go and find out and be damned
        (Dear boys!),
  To go and get shot and be damned.

So some of us chivvy the slaver,
  And some of us cherish the black,
And some of us hunt on the Oil Coast,
  And some on the Wallaby track:
And some of us drift to Sarawak,
  And some of us drift up The Fly,
And some share our tucker with tigers,
  And some with the gentle Masai,
        (Dear boys!),
  Take tea with the giddy Masai.

We've painted The Islands vermilion,
  We've pearled on half-shares in the Bay,
We've shouted on seven-ounce nuggets,
  We've starved on a Seedeeboy's pay;
We've laughed at the world as we found it,—
  Its women and cities and men—
From Sayyid Burgash in a tantrum
  To the smoke-reddened eyes of Loben,
        (Dear boys!),
  We've a little account with Loben.

The ends of the Earth were our portion,
  The ocean at large was our share.

There was never a skirmish to windward
　　But the Leaderless Legion was there:
Yes, somehow and somewhere and always
　　We were first when the trouble began,
From a lottery-row in Manila,
　　To an I.D.B. race on the Pan
　　　　(Dear boys!),
　　With the Mounted Police on the Pan.

We preached in advance of the Army,
　　We skirmish ahead of the Church,
With never a gunboat to help us
　　When we're scuppered and left in the lurch.
But we know as the cartridges finish,
　　And we're filed on our last little shelves,
That the Legion that never was listed
　　Will send us as good as ourselves
　　　　(Good men!),
　　Five hundred as good as ourselves!

Then a health (we must drink it in whispers),
　　To our wholly unauthorized horde—
To the line of our dusty foreloopers,
　　The Gentlemen Rovers abroad—
Yes, a health to ourselves ere we scatter,
　　For the steamer won't wait for the train,
And the Legion that never was listed
　　Goes back into quarters again!
　　　　Goes back under canvas again.
　　　　Hurrah!
　　The swag and the billy again.
　　　　Here's how!
　　The trail and the packhorse again.
　　　　Salue!
　　The trek and the laager again!

The Irish Guards

1918

We're not so old in the Army List,
　　But we're not so young at our trade,
For we had the honour at Fontenoy
　　Of meeting the Guards' Brigade.

'Twas Lally, Dillon, Bulkeley, Clare,
   And Lee that led us then,
And after a hundred and seventy years
   We're fighting for France again!
     Old Days!   The wild geese are flighting,
       Head to the storm as they faced it before!
     For where there are Irish there's bound to be fighting,
       And when there's no fighting, it's Ireland no more!
     Ireland no more!

The fashion's all for khaki now,
   But once through France we went
Full-dressed in scarlet Army cloth
   The English—left at Ghent.
They're fighting on our side to-day
   But, before they changed their clothes,
The half of Europe knew our fame,
   As all of Ireland knows!
     Old Days!   The wild geese are flying,
       Head to the storm as they faced it before!
     For where there are Irish there's memory undying,
       And when we forget, it is Ireland no more!
     Ireland no more!

From Barry Wood to Gouzeaucourt,
From Boyne to Pilkem Ridge,
The ancient days come back no more
   Than water under the bridge.
But the bridge it stands and the water runs
   As red as yesterday,
And the Irish move to the sound of the guns
   Like salmon to the sea.
     Old Days!   The wild geese are ranging,
       Head to the storm as they faced it before!
     For where there are Irish their hearts are unchanging,
       And when they are changed, it is Ireland no more!
     Ireland no more!

We're not so old in the Army List,
   But we're not so new in the ring,
For we carried our packs with Marshal Saxe
   When Louis was our King.
But Douglas Haig's our Marshal now
   And we're King George's men,
And after one hundred and seventy years
   We're fighting for France again!

Ah, France!   And did we stand by you,
  When life was made splendid with gifts and rewards?
Ah, France!   And will we deny you
  In the hour of your agony, Mother of Swords?
Old Days!   The wild geese are flighting,
  Head to the storm as they faced it before!
For where there are Irish there's loving and fighting,
  And when we stop either, it's Ireland no more!
    Ireland no more!

Pharaoh and the Sergeant

1897

". . . *Consider that the meritorious services of the Sergeant Instructors attached to the Egyptian Army have been inadequately acknowledged . . . To the excellence of their work is mainly due the great improvement that has taken place in the soldiers of H.H. the Khedive.*"—EXTRACT FROM LETTER.

Said England unto Pharaoh, "I must make a man of you,
  That will stand upon his feet and play the game;
That will Maxim his oppressor as a Christian ought to do,"
  And she sent old Pharaoh Sergeant Whatsisname.
    It was not a Duke nor Earl, nor yet a *Viscount*—
      It was not a big brass General that came;
    But a man in khaki kit who could handle men a bit,
      With his bedding labelled Sergeant Whatsisname.

Said England unto Pharaoh, "Though at present singing small,
  You shall hum a proper tune before it ends,"
And she introduced old Pharaoh to the Sergeant once for all,
  And left 'em in the desert making friends.
    It was not a Crystal Palace nor Cathedral;
      It was not a public-house of common fame;
    But a piece of red-hot sand, with a palm on either hand,
      And a little hut for Sergeant Whatsisname.

Said England unto Pharaoh, "You've had miracles before,
  When Aaron struck your rivers into blood;
But if you watch the Sergeant·he can show you something more.
  He's a charm for making riflemen from mud,"
    It was neither Hindustani, French, nor Coptics;
      It was odds and ends and leavings of the same,
    Translated by a stick (which is really half the trick),
      And Pharaoh harked to Sergeant Whatsisname.

(There were years that no one talked of; there were times of horrid
        doubt—
    There was faith and hope and whacking and despair—
While the Sergeant gave the Cautions and he combed old Pharaoh out,
    And England didn't seem to know nor care.
        That is England's awful way o' doing business—
            She would serve her God (or Gordon) just the same—
        For she thinks her Empire still is the Strand and Holborn Hill,
            And she didn't think of Sergeant Whatsisname.)

Said England to the Sergeant, "You can let my people go!"
    (England used 'em cheap and nasty from the start.)
And they entered 'em in battle on a most astonished foe—
    But the Sergeant he had hardened Pharaoh's heart
        Which was broke, along of all the plagues of Egypt,
            Three thousand years before the Sergeant came—
        And he mended it again in a little more than ten,
            Till Pharaoh fought like Sergeant Whatsisname.

It was wicked bad campaigning (cheap and nasty from the first.)
    There was heat and dust and coolie-work and sun,
There were vipers, flies, and sandstorms, there was cholera and thirst,
    But Pharaoh done the best he ever done,
        Down the desert, down the railway, down the river,
            Like the Israelites from bondage so he came,
        'Tween the clouds o' dust and fire to the land of his desire,
            And his Moses, it was Sergeant Whatsisname!

We are eating dirt in handfuls for to save our daily bread,
    Which we have to buy from those that hate us most,
And we must not raise the money where the Sergeant raised the dead,
    And it's wrong and bad and dangerous to boast,
        But he did it on the cheap and on the quiet,
            And he's not allowed to forward any claim—
        Though he drilled a black man white, though he made a mummy
            fight,
        He will continue Sergeant Whatsisname—
        Private, Corporal, Colour-Sergeant, and Instructor—
            But the everlasting miracle's the same!

The Last of the Light Brigade

1891

There were thirty million English who talked of England's might,
There were twenty broken troopers who lacked a bed for the night.

They had neither food nor money, they had neither service nor trade;
They were only shiftless soldiers, the last of the Light Brigade.

They felt that life was fleeting; they knew not that art was long,
That though they were dying of famine, they lived in deathless song.
They asked for a little money to keep the wolf from the door;
And the thirty million English sent twenty pounds and four!

They laid their heads together that were scarred and lined and grey;
Keen were the Russian sabres, but want was keener than they;
And an old Troop-Sergeant muttered, "Let us go to the man who writes
The things on Balaclava the kiddies at school recites."

They went without bands or colours, a regiment ten-file strong,
To look for the Master-singer who had crowned them all in his song;
And, waiting his servant's order, by the garden gate they stayed,
A desolate little cluster, the last of the Light Brigade.

They strove to stand to attention, to straighten the toil-bowed back;
They drilled on an empty stomach, the loose-knit files fell slack;
With stooping of weary shoulders, in garments tattered and frayed,
They shambled into his presence, the last of the Light Brigade.

The old Troop-Sergeant was spokesman, and "Beggin' your pardon," he
    said,
"You wrote o' the Light Brigade, sir.   Here's all that isn't dead.
An' it's all come true what you wrote, sir, regardin' the mouth of hell;
For we're all of us nigh to the workhouse, an' we thought we'd call an'
    tell.

"No, thank you, we don't want food, sir; but couldn't you take an' write
A sort of 'to be continued' and 'see next page' o' the fight?
We think that someone has blundered, an' couldn't you tell 'em how?
You wrote we were heroes once, sir.   Please, write we are starving now."

The poor little army departed, limping and lean and forlorn.
And the heart of the Master-singer grew hot with "the scorn of scorn."
And he wrote for them wonderful verses that swept the land like flame,
Till the fatted souls of the English were scourged with the thing called
    Shame.

O thirty million English that babble of England's might,
Behold there are twenty heroes who lack their food to-night;
Our children's children are lisping to "honour the charge they made—"
And we leave to the streets and the workhouse the charge of the Light
    Brigade!

Kitchener's School

1898

Being a translation of the song that was made by a Mohammedan schoolmaster of Bengal Infantry (some time on service at Suakim) when he heard that Kitchener was taking money from the English to build a Madrissa for Hubshees—or a college for the Sudanese at Khartoum.

Oh, Hubshee, carry your shoes in your hand and bow your head on your breast!
This is the message of Kitchener who did not break you in jest.
It was permitted to him to fulfil the long-appointed years;
Reaching the end ordained of old over your dead Emirs.

He stamped only before your walls, and the Tomb ye knew was dust:
He gathered up under his armpits all the swords of your trust:
He set a guard on your granaries, securing the weak from the strong:
He said:—"Go work the waterwheels that were abolished so long."

He said:—"Go safely, being abased.   I have accomplished my vow."
That was the mercy of Kitchener.   Cometh his madness now!
He does not desire as ye desire, nor devise as ye devise:
He is preparing a second host—an army to make you wise.

Not at the mouth of his clean-lipped guns shall ye learn his name again,
But letter by letter, from Kaf to Kaf, at the mouths of his chosen men.
He has gone back to his own city, not seeking presents or bribes,
But openly asking the English for money to buy you Hakims and scribes.

Knowing that ye are forfeit by battle and have no right to live,
He begs for money to bring you learning—and all the English give.
It is their treasure—it is their pleasure—thus are their hearts inclined:
For Allah created the English mad— the maddest of all mankind!

They do not consider the Meaning of Things; they consult not creed nor clan.
Behold, they clap the slave on the back, and behold, he ariseth a man!
They terribly carpet the earth with dead, and before their cannon cool,
The walk unarmed by twos and three to call the living to school.

How is this reason (which is their reason) to judge a scholar's worth,
By casting a ball at three straight sticks and defending the same with a fourth!
But this they do (which is doubtless a spell) and other matters more strange,
Until, by the operation of years, the hearts of their scholars change:

Till these make come and go great boats or engines upon the rail
(But always the English watch near by to prop them when they fail);
Till these make laws of their own choice and Judges of their own blood;
And all the mad English obey the Judges and say that that Law is good.

Certainly they were mad from of old; but I think one new thing,
That the magic whereby they work their magic—wherefrom their fortunes
    spring—
May be that they show all peoples their magic and ask no price in return.
Wherefore, since ye are bond to that magic, O Hubshee, make haste and
    learn!

Certainly also is Kitchener mad.   But one sure thing I know—
If he who broke you be minded to teach you, to his Madrissa go!
Go, and carry your shoes in your hand and bow your head on your
    breast,
For he who did not slay you in sport, he will not teach you in jest.

Lord Roberts

(*Died in France* 1914)

He passed in the very battle-smoke
    Of the war that he had descried.
Three hundred mile of cannon spoke
    When the Master-Gunner died.

He passed to the very sound of the guns;
    But, before his eyes grew dim,
He had seen the faces of the sons
    Whose sires had served with him.

He touched their sword-hilts and greeted each
    With the old sure word of praise;
And there was virtue in touch and speech
    As it had been in old days.

So he dismissed them and took his rest,
    And the steadfast spirit went forth
Between the adoring East and West
    And the tireless guns of the North.

Clean, simple, valiant, well-loved.
    Flawless in faith and fame,
Whom neither ease nor honours moved
    An hair's-breadth from his aim.

Never again the war-wise face,
  The weighed and urgent word
That pleaded in the market-place—
  Pleaded and was not heard!

Yet from his life a new life springs
  Through all the hosts to come,
And Glory is the least of things
  That follows this man home.

Bridge-Guard in the Karroo

1901

". . . and will supply details of the Blood River Bridge."
District Orders: Lines of Communication—South African War.

Sudden the desert changes,
  The raw glare softens and clings,
Till the aching Oudtshoorn ranges
  Stand up like the thrones of Kings—

Ramparts of slaughter and peril—
  Blazing, amazing, aglow—
'Twixt the sky-line's belting beryl
  And the wine-dark flats below.

Royal the pageant closes,
  Lit by the last of the sun—
Opal and ash-of-roses,
  Cinnamon, umber, and dun.

The twilight swallows the thicket,
  The starlight reveals the ridge.
The whistle shrills to the picket—
  We are changing guard on the bridge.

(Few, forgotten and lonely,
  Where the empty metals shine—
No, not combatants—only
  Details guarding the line.)

We slip through the broken panel
  Of fence by the ganger's shed;
We drop to the waterless channel
  And the lean track overhead;

We stumble on refuse of rations,
    The beef and the biscuit-tins;
We take our appointed stations,
    And the endless night begins.

We hear the Hottentot herders
    As the sheep click past to the fold—
And the click of the restless girders
    As the steel contracts in the cold—

Voices of jackals calling
    And, loud in the hush between,
A morsel of dry earth falling
    From the flanks of the scarred ravine.

And the solemn firmament marches,
    And the hosts of heaven rise
Framed through the iron arches—
    Banded and barred by the ties,

Till we feel the far track humming,
    And we see her headlight plain,
And we gather and wait her coming—
    The wonderful north-bound train.

(Few, forgotten and lonely,
    Where the white car-windows shine—
No, not combatants—only
    Details guarding the line.)

Quick, ere the gift escape us!
    Out of the darkness we reach
For a handful of week-old papers
    And a mouthful of human speech.

And the monstrous heaven rejoices,
    And the earth allows again
Meetings, greetings, and voices
    Of women talking with men.

So we return to our places,
    As out on the bridge she rolls;
And the darkness covers our faces,
    And the darkness re-enters our souls.

More than a little lonely
    Where the lessening tail-lights shine.
No—not combatants only
    Details guarding the line!

South Africa

1903

Lived a woman wonderful,
  (May the Lord amend her!)
Neither simple, kind, nor true,
But her Pagan beauty drew
Christian gentlemen a few
  Hotly to attend her.

Christian gentlemen a few
  From Berwick unto Dover;
For she was South Africa,
And she was South Africa,
She was Our South Africa,
  Africa all over!

Half her land was dead with drouth,
  Half was red with battle;
She was fenced with fire and sword,
Plague on pestilence outpoured,
Locusts on the greening sward
  And murrain on the cattle!

True, ah, true, and overtrue.
  That is why we love her!
For she is South Africa,
And she is South Africa,
She is Our South Africa,
  Africa all over!

Bitter hard her lovers toiled,
  Scandalous their payment,—
Food forgot on trains derailed;
Cattle-dung where fuel failed;
Water where the mules had staled;
  And sackcloth for their raiment!

So she filled their mouths with dust
  And their bones with fever;
Greeted them with cruel lies;
Treated them despiteful-wise;
Meted them calamities
  Till they vowed to leave her!

They took ship and they took sail,
  Raging from her borders—
In a little, none the less,
They forgat their sore duresse,
They forgave her frowardness
  And returned for orders!

They esteemed her favour more
  Than a Throne's foundation.
For the glory of her face
Bade farewell to breed and race—
Yea, and made their burial-place
  Altar of a Nation!

Wherefore, being bought by blood,
  And by blood restorèd
To the arms that nearly lost,
She, because of all she cost,
Stands, a very woman, most
  Perfect and adored!

On your feet, and let them know
  This is why we love her!
For she is South Africa,
She is Our South Africa,
Is Our Own South Africa,
  Africa all over!

The Burial

(C. J. RHODES, BURIED IN THE MATOPPOS, APRIL 10, 1902)

1902

When that great Kings return to clay,
  Or Emperors in their pride,
Grief of a day shall fill a day,
  Because its creature died.
But we—we reckon not with those
  Whom the mere Fates ordain,
This Power that wrought on us and goes
  Back to the Power again.

Dreamer devout, by vision led
  Beyond our guess or reach,

The travail of his spirit bred
    Cities in place of speech.
So huge the all-mastering thought that drove—
    So brief the term allowed—
Nations, not words, he linked to prove
    His faith before the crowd.

It is his will that he look forth
    Across the world he won—
The granite of the ancient North—
    Great spaces washed with sun.
There shall he patient take his seat
    (As when the Death he dared),
And there await a people's feet
    In the paths that he prepared.

There, till the vision he foresaw
    Splendid and whole arise,
And unimagined Empires draw
    To council 'neath his skies,
The immense and brooding Spirit still
    Shall quicken and control.
Living he was the land, and dead,
    His soul shall be her soul!

Rhodes Memorial, Table Mountain

1905

(From a letter written to Sir Herbert Baker, R. A., when the form of the Memorial was under discussion)

As tho' again—yea, even once again,
    We should rewelcome to our stewardship
The rider with the loose-flung bridle-rein
    And chance-plucked twig for whip,

The down-turned hat-brim, and the eyes beneath
Alert, devouring—and the imperious hand
Ordaining matters swiftly to bequeath
    Perfect the work he planned.

Things and the Man

(IN MEMORIAM, JOSEPH CHAMBERLAIN)

1904

"And Joseph dreamed a dream, and he told it to his brethren and they hated him yet the more."—GENESIS xxxvii. 5.

Oh, ye who hold the written clue
    To all save all unwritten things,
And, half a league behind, pursue
    The accomplished Fact with flouts and flings,
    Look! To your knee your baby brings
      The oldest tale since Earth began—
    The answer to your worryings:
      "Once on a time there was a Man."

He, single-handed, met and slew
    Magicians, Armies, Ogres, Kings.
He lonely 'mid his doubting crew—
    "In all the loneliness of wings" –
    He fed the flame, he filled the springs,
      He locked the ranks, he launched the van
    Straight at the grinning Teeth of Things,
      "Once on a time there was a man."

The peace of shocked Foundations flew
    Before his ribald questionings.
He broke the Oracles in two,
    And bared the paltry wires and strings.
    He headed desert wanderings;
      He led his soul, his cause, his clan
    A little from the ruck of Things.
      "Once on a time there was a man."

Thrones, Powers, Dominions block the view
    With episodes and underlings—
The meek historian deems them true
    Nor heeds the song that Clio sings—
    The simple central truth that stings
      The mob to boo, the priest to ban;
    Things never yet created things—
      "Once on a time there was a Man."

A bolt is fallen from the blue.
  A weakened realm full circle swings
Where Dothan's dreamer dreams anew
  Of vast and far-borne harvesting;
  And unto him an Empire clings
    That grips the purpose of his plan.
  My Lords, how think you of these things?
    Once—in our time—is there a Man?

The Settler

1903

(*South African War ended, May* 1902)

Here, where my fresh-turned furrows run,
  And the deep soil glistens red,
I will repair the wrong that was done
  To the living and the dead.
Here, where the senseless bullet fell,
  And the barren shrapnel burst,
I will plant a tree, I will dig a well,
  Against the heat and the thirst.

Here, in a large and a sunlit land,
  Where no wrong bites to the bone,
I will lay my hand in my neighbour's hand,
  And together we will atone
For the set folly and the red breach
  And the black waste of it all;
Giving and taking counsel each
  Over the cattle-kraal.

Here will we join against our foes—
  The hailstroke and the storm,
And the red and rustling cloud that blows
  The locust's mile-deep swarm.
Frost and murrain and flood let loose
  Shall launch us side by side
In the holy wars that have no truce
  'Twixt seed and harvest-tide.

Earth, where we rode to slay or be slain,
  Our love shall redeem unto life.
We will gather and lead to her lips again
  The waters of ancient strife,

From the far and the fiercely guarded streams
    And the pools where we lay in wait,
Till the corn cover our evil dreams
    And the young corn our hate.

And when we bring old fights to mind,
    We will not remember the sin—
If there be blood on his head of my kind,
    Or blood on my head of his kin—
For the ungrazed upland, the untilled lea
    Cry, and the fields forlorn:
"The dead must bury their dead, but ye—
    Ye serve an host unborn."

Bless then, Our God, the new-yoked plough
    And the good beasts that draw,
And the bread we eat in the sweat of our brow
    According to Thy Law.
After us cometh a multitude—
    Prosper the work of our hands,
That we may feel with our land's food
    The fol of all our lands!

Here, in the waves and the troughs of the plains,
    Where the healing stillness lies,
And the vast, benignant sky restrains
    And the long days make wise—
Bless to our use the rain and the sun
    And the blind see in its bed,
That we may repair the wrong that was done
    To the living and the dead!

Sussex

1902

God gave all men all earth to love,
    But, since our hearts are small,
Ordained for each one spot should prove
    Belovèd over all;
That, as He watched Creation's birth,
    So we, in godlike mood,
May of our love create our earth
    And see that it is good.

So one shall Baltic pines content,
  As one some Surrey glade,
Or one the palm-grove's droned lament
  Before Levuka's Trade.
Each to his choice, and I rejoice
  The lot has fallen to me
In a fair ground—in a fair ground—
  Yea, Sussex by the sea!

No tender-hearted garden crowns,
  No bosomed woods adorn
Our blunt, bow-headed, whale-backed Downs,
  But gnarled and writhen thorn—
Bare slopes where chasing shadows skim,
  And, through the gaps revealed,
Belt upon belt, the wooded, dim,
  Blue goodness of the Weald.

Clean of officious fence or hedge,
  Half-wild and wholly tame,
The wise turf cloaks the white cliff-edge
  As when the Romans came.
What sign of those that fought and died
  At shift of sword and sword?
The barrow and the camp abide,
  The sunlight and the sward.

Here leaps ashore the full Sou'west
  All heavy-winged with brine,
Here lies above the folded crest
  The Channel's leaden line;
And here the sea-fogs lap and cling,
  And here, each warning each,
The sheep-bells and the ship-bells ring
  Along the hidden beach.

We have no waters to delight
  Our broad and brookless vales—
Only the dewpond on the height
  Unfed, that never fails—
Whereby no tattered herbage tells
  Which way the season flies—
Only our close-bit thyme that smells
  Like dawn in Paradise.

Here through the strong and shadeless days
    The tinkling silence thrills;
Or little, lost, Down churches praise
    The Lord who made the hills:
But here the Old Gods guard their round,
    And, in her secret heart,
The heathen kingdom Wilfrid found
    Dreams, as she dwells, apart.

Though all the rest were all my share,
    With equal soul I'd see
Her nine-and-thirty sisters fair,
    Yet none more fair than she.
Choose ye your need from Thames to Tweed,
    And I will choose instead
Such lands as lie 'twixt Rake and Rye,
    Black Down and Beachy Head.

I will go out against the sun
    Where the rolled scarp retires,
And the Long Man of Wilmington
    Looks naked toward the shires;
And east till doubling Rother crawls
    To find the fickle tide,
By dry and sea-forgotten walls,
    Our ports of stranded pride.

I will go north about the shaws
    And the deep ghylls that breed
Huge oaks and old, the which we hold
    No more than Sussex weed;
Or south where windy Piddinghoe's
    Begilded dolphin veers,
And red beside wide-bankèd Ouse
    Lie down our Sussex steers.

So to the land our hearts we give
    Till the sure magic strike,
And Memory, Use, and Love make live
    Us and our fields alike—
That deeper than our speech and thought,
    Beyond our reason's sway,
Clay of the pit whence we were wrought
    Yearns to its fellow-clay.

God gives all men all earth to love,
  But since man's heart is small,
Ordains for each one spot shall prove
  Belovèd over all.
Each to his choice, and I rejoice
  The lot has fallen to me
In a fair ground—in a fair ground—
  Yea, Sussex by the sea!

My Boy Jack

1914–18

"Have you news of my boy Jack?"
  Not this tide.
"When d'you think that he'll come back?"
  Not with this wind blowing, and this tide.

"Has any one else had word of him?"
  Not this tide.
For what is sunk will hardly swim,
  Not with this wind blowing, and this tide.

"Oh, dear, what comfort can I find!"
  None this tide,
  Nor any tide,
Except he did not shame his kind—
  Not even with that wind blowing, and that tide.

Then hold your head up all the more,
  This tide,
  And every tide;
Because he was the son you bore,
  And gave to that wind blowing and that tide!

A Nativity

1914–18

The Babe was laid in the Manger
  Between the gentle kine—
All safe from cold and danger—
  "But it was not so with mine,
      (With mine!   With mine!)

"Is it well with the child, is it well?"
    The waiting mother prayed.
"For I know not how he fell,
    And I know not where he is laid."

A Star stood forth in Heaven;
    The watchers ran to see
The Sign of the Promise given—
    "But there comes no sign to me.
        (To me!   To me!)
"My child died in the dark.
    Is it well with the child, is it well?
There was none to tend him or mark,
    And I know not how he fell."

The cross was raised on high:
    The Mother grieved beside—
"But the Mother saw Him die
    And took Him when He died.
        (He died!   He died!)
"Seemly and undefiled
    His burial-place was made—
Is it well, is it well with the child?
    For I know not where he is laid."

On the dawning of Easter Day
    Comes Mary Magdalene;
But the Stone was rolled away,
    And the Body was not within—
        (Within!   Within!)
"Ah, who will answer my word?"
    The broken mother prayed.
"They have taken my Lord,
    And I know not where He is laid."

"The Star stands forth in Heaven.
    The watchers watch in vain
For Sign of the Promise given
    Of peace on Earth again—
        (Again!   Again!)
"But I know for Whom he fell"—
    The steadfast mother smiled,
"Is it well with the child—is it well?
    It is well—it is well with the child!"

Dirge of Dead Sisters

1902

(For the Nurses who died in the South African War)

Who recalls the twilight and the rangèd tents in order
(Violet peaks uplifted through the crystal evening air?)
And the clink of iron teacups and the piteous, noble laughter,
And the faces of the Sisters with the dust upon their hair?

(Now and not hereafter, while the breath is in our nostrils,
Now and not hereafter, ere the meaner years go by—
Let us now remember many honourable women,
Such as bade us turn again when we were like to die.)

Who recalls the morning and the thunder through the foothills,
(Tufts of fleecy shrapnel strung along the empty plains?)
And the sun-scarred Red-Cross coaches creeping guarded to the culvert,
And the faces of the Sisters looking gravely from the trains?

(When the days were torment and the nights were clouded terror,
When the Powers of Darkness had dominion on our soul—
When we fled consuming through the Seven Hells of Fever,
These put out their hands to us and healed and made us whole.)

Who recalls the midnight by the bridge's wrecked abutment,
(Autumn rain that rattled like a Maxim on the tin?)
And the lightning-dazzled levels and the streaming, straining wagons,
And the faces of the Sisters as they bore the wounded in?

(Till the pain was merciful and stunned us into silence—
When each nerve cried out on God that made the misused clay;
When the Body triumphed and the last poor shame departed—
These abode our agonies and wiped the sweat away.)

Who recalls the noontide and the funerals through the market,
(Blanket-hidden bodies, flagless, followed by the flies?)
And the footsore firing-party, and the dust and stench and staleness,
And the faces of the Sisters and the glory in their eyes?

(Bold behind the battle, in the open camp all-hallowed,
Patient, wise, and mirthful in the ringed and reeking town,
These endured unresting till they rested from their labours—
Little wasted bodies, ah, so light to lower down!)

Yet their graves are scattered and their names are clean forgotten,
    Earth shall not remember, but the Waiting Angel knows
Them that died at Uitvlugt when the plague was on the city—
    Her that fell at Simon's Town[1] in service on our foes.

Wherefore we they ransomed, while the breath is in our nostrils,
Now and not hereafter—ere the meaner years go by—
Praise with love and worship many honourable women,
    Those that gave their lives for us when we were like to die!

The Vampire

1897

A fool there was and he made his prayer
(Even as you and I!)
To a rag and a bone and a hank of hair
(We called her the woman who did not care)
But the fool he called her his lady fair—
(Even as you and I!)

Oh, the years we waste and the tears we waste
And the work of our head and hand
Belong to the woman who did not know
(And now we know that she never could know)
And did not understand!

A fool there was and his goods he spent
(Even as you and I!)
Honour and faith and a sure intent
(And it wasn't the least what the lady meant)
But a fool must follow his natural bent
(Even as you and I!)

Oh, the toil we lost and the spoil we lost
And the excellent things we planned
Belong to the woman who didn't know why
(And now we know that she never knew why)
And did not understand!

The fool was stripped to his foolish hide
(Even as you and I!)
Which she might have seen when she threw him aside—

[1]Mary Kingsley

(But it isn't on record the lady tried)
So some of him lived but the most of him died—
(Even as you and I!)

And it isn't the shame and it isn't the blame
That stings like a white-hot brand—
It's coming to know that she never knew why
(Seeing, at last, she could never know why)
And never could understand!

The English Flag

1891

Above the portico a flag-staff, bearing the Union Jack, remained fluttering in the flames for some time, but ultimately when it fell the crowds rent the air with shouts, and seemed to see significance in the incident.

DAILY PAPERS.

Winds of the World, give answer!   They are whimpering to and fro—
And what should they know of England who only England know?—
The poor little street-bred people that vapour and fume and brag,
They are lifting their heads in the stillness to yelp at the English Flag!

Must we borrow a clout from the Boer—to plaster anew with dirt?
An Irish liar's bandage, or an English coward's shirt?
We may not speak of England; her Flag's to sell or share.
What is the Flag of England?   Winds of the World, declare!

The North Wind blew:—"From Bergen my steel-shod vanguards go:
"I chase your lazy whalers home from the Disko floe.
"By the great North Lights above me I work the will of God,
"And the liner splits on the ice-field or the Dogger fills with cod.

"I barred my gates with iron, I shuttered my doors with flame,
"Because to force my ramparts your nutshell navies came.
"I took the sun from their presence, I cut them down with my blast.
"And they died, but the Flag of England blew free ere the spirit passed.

"The lean white bear hath seen it in the long, long Arctic nights,
"The musk-ox knows the standard that flouts the Northern Lights:
"What is the Flag of England?   Ye have but my bergs to dare,
"Ye have but my drifts to conquer.   Go forth, for it is there!"

The South Wind sighed:—"From the Virgins my mid-sea course was ta'en
"Over a thousand islands lost in an idle main,
"Where the sea-egg flames on the coral and the long-backed breakers
    croon
"Their endless ocean legends to the lazy, locked lagoon.

"Strayed amid lonely islets, mazed amid outer keys,
"I waked the palms to laughter—I tossed the scud in the breeze.
"Never was isle so little, never was sea so lone,
"But over the scud and the palm-trees an English flag was flown.

"I have wrenched it free from the halliards to hang for a wisp on the
    Horn;
"I have chased it north to the Lizard—ribboned and rolled and torn;
"I have spread its folds o'er the dying, adrift in a hopeless sea;
"I have hurled it swift on the slaver, and seen the slave set free.

"My basking sunfish know it, and wheeling albatross,
"Where the lone wave fills with fire beneath the Southern Cross.
"Where is the Flag of England? Ye have but my reefs to dare,
"Ye have but my seas to furrow. Go forth, for it is there!"

The East Wind roared:—"From the Kuriles, the Bitter Seas, I come,
"And me men call the Home-Wind, for I bring the English home.
"Look—look well to your shipping! By the breath of my mad typhoon
"I swept your close-packed Praya and beached your best at Kowloon!

"The reeling junks behind me and the racing seas before,
"I raped your richest roadstead—I plundered Singapore!
"I set my hand on the Hoogli; as a hooded snake she rose;
"And I flung your stoutest steamers to roost with the startled crows.

"Never the lotos closes, never the wild-fowl wake,
"But a soul goes out on the East Wind that died for England's sake—
"Man or woman or suckling, mother or bride or maid—
"Because on the bones of the English the English Flag is stayed.

"The desert-dust hath dimmed it, the flying wild-ass knows,
"The scared white leopard winds it across the taintless snows.
"What is the Flag of England? Ye have but my sun to dare,
"Ye have but my sands to travel. Go forth, for it is there!"

The West Wind called:—"In squadrons the thoughtless galleons fly
"That bear the wheat and cattle lest street-bred people die.
"They make my might their porter, they make my house their path,
"Till I loose my neck from their rudder and whelm them all in my wrath.

"I draw the gliding fog-bank as a snake is drawn from the whole.
"They bellow one to the other, the frightened ship-bells toll;
"For day is a drifting terror till I raise the shroud with my breath,
"And they see strange bows above them and the two go locked to death.

"But whether in calm or wrack-wreath, whether by dark or day,
"I heave them whole to the conger or rip their plates away,
"First of the scattered legions, under a shrieking sky,
"Dipping between the rollers, the English Flag goes by.

"The dead dumb fog hath wrapped it—the frozen dews have kissed—
"The naked stars have seen it, a fellow-star in the mist.
"What is the Flag of England?   Ye have but my breath to dare,
"Ye have but my waves to conquer.   Go forth, for it is there!"

The Dead King

(EDWARD VII.)

1910

Who in the Realm to-day lays down dear life for the sake of a land more dear?
  And, unconcerned for his own estate, toils till the last grudged sands have run?
    Let him approach.   It is proven here
Our King asks nothing of any man more than Our King himself has done.

For to him, above all, was Life good, above all he commanded
Her abundance full-handed.
The peculiar treasure of Kings was his for the taking.
All that men come to in dreams he inherited waking:—

His marvel of world-gathered armies—one heart and all races;
His seas 'neath his keels when his war-castles foamed to their places;
The thundering foreshores that answered his heralded landing;
The huge lighted cities adoring, the assemblies upstanding;
The Councils of Kings called in haste to learn how he was minded—
The Kingdoms, the Powers, and the Glories he dealt with unblinded.

To him came all captains of men, all achievers of glory,
Hot from the press of their battles they told him their story.
They revealed him their lives in an hour and, saluting, departed,
Joyful to labour afresh—he had made them new-hearted.
And, since he weighed men from his youth, and no lie long deceived him,
He spoke and exacted the truth, and the basest believed him.

And God poured him an exquisite wine that was daily renewed to him,
In the clear-welling love of his peoples which daily accrued to him.
Honour and service we gave him, rejoicingly fearless;
Faith absolute, trust beyond speech and a friendship as peerless,
And since he was Master and Servant in all that we asked him,
We leaned hard on his wisdom in all things, knowing not how we tasked
    him.

For on him each new day laid command, every tyrannous hour,
To confront, or confirm, or make smooth some dread issue of power;
To deliver true judgment aright on the instant, unaided,
In the strict, level, ultimate phrase that allowed or dissuaded;
To foresee, to allay, to avert from us perils unnumbered,
To stand guard on our gates when he guessed that the watchmen had
    slumbered;
To win time, to turn hate, to woo folly to service and, mightily schooling
His strength to the use of his Nations, to rule as not ruling.

These were the works of our King; Earth's peace was the proof of them.
God gave him great works to fulfil, and to us the behoof of them.
We accepted his toil as our right—none spared, none excused him.
When he was bowed by his burden his rest was refused him.
We troubled his age with our weakness—the blacker our shame to us!
Hearing his People had need of him, straightway he came to us.

As he received so he gave—nothing grudged, naught denying;
Not even the last gasp of his breath when he strove for us, dying.
For our sakes, without question, he put from him all that he cherished.
Simply as any that serve him he served and he perished.
All that Kings covet was his, and he flung it aside for us.
Simply as any that die in his service he died for us!

Who in the Realm to-day has choice of the easy road or the hard to tread?
  And, much concerned for his own estate, would sell his soul to remain in the
    sun?
      Let him depart nor look on Our dead.
Our King asks nothing of any man more than Our King himself has done.

When Earth's Last Picture is Painted

1892

(L'Envoi to "The Seven Seas")

When Earth's last picture is painted and the tubes are twisted and dried,
When the oldest colours have faded, and the youngest critic has died,

We shall rest, and, faith, we shall need it—lie down for an aeon or two,
Till the Master of All Good Workmen shall put us to work anew.

And those that were good shall be happy: they shall sit in a golden chair;
They shall splash at a ten-league canvas with brushes of comets' hair.
They shall find real saints to draw from—Magdalene, Peter, and Paul;
They shall work for an age at a sitting and never be tired at all!

And only The Master shall praise us, and only The Master shall blame;
And no one shall work for money, and no one shall work for fame,
But each for the joy of the working, and each, in his separate star,
Shall draw the Thing as he sees It for the God of Things as They are!

"Cleared"

1890

(In memory of the Parnell Commission)

Help for a patriot distressed, a spotless spirit hurt,
Help for an honourable clan sore trampled in the dirt!
From Queenstown Bay to Donegal, oh, listen to my song,
The honourable gentlemen have suffered grievous wrong.

Their noble names were mentioned—Oh, the burning black disgrace!—
By a brutal Saxon paper in an Irish shooting-case;
They sat upon it for a year, then steeled their heart to brave it,
And "coruscating innocence" the learned Judges gave it.

Bear witness, Heaven, of that grim crime beneath the surgeon's knife,
The "honourable gentlemen" deplored the loss of life!
Bear witness of those chanting choirs that burke and shirk and snigger,
No man laid hand upon the knife or finger to the trigger!

Cleared in the face of all mankind beneath the winking skies,
Like phoenixes from Phoenix Park (and what lay there) they rise!
Go shout it to the emerald seas—give word to Erin now,
Her honourable gentlemen are cleared—and this is how:—

They only paid the Moonlighter his cattle-hocking price,
They only helped the murderer with counsel's best advice,
But—sure it keeps their honour white—the learned Court believes
They never give a piece of plate to murderers and thieves.

They never told the ramping crowd to card a woman's hide,
They never marked a man for death—what fault of theirs he died?—
They only said 'intimidate," and talked and went away—
By God, the boys that did the work were braver men than they!

Their sin it was that fed the fire—small blame to them that heard—
The boys get drunk on rhetoric, and madden at a word—
They knew whom they were talking at, if they were Irish too,
The gentlemen that lied in Court, they knew, and well they knew!

They only took the Judas-gold from Fenians out of jail,
They only fawned for dollars on the blood-dyed Clan-na-Gael.
If black is black or white is white, in black and white it's down,
They're only traitors to the Queén and rebels to the Crown.

"Cleared," honourable gentlemen!   Be thankful it's no more:—
The widow's curse is on your house, the dead are at your door.
On you the shame of open shame; on you from North to South
The hand of every honest man flat-heeled across your mouth.

"Less black than we were painted"?—Faith, no word of black was said;
The lightest touch was human blood, and that, you know, runs red.
It's sticking to your fist to-day for all your sneer and scoff,
And by the Judge's well-weighed word you cannot wipe it off.

Hold up those hands of innocence—go, scare your sheep together,
The blundering, tripping tups that bleat behind the old bell-wether;
And if they snuff the taint and break to find another pen,
Tell them it's tar that glistens so, and daub them yours again!

"The charge is old"?—As old as Cain—as fresh as yesterday;
Old as the Ten Commandments—have ye talked those laws away?
If words are words, or death is death, or powder sends the ball,
You spoke the words that sped the shot—the curse be on you all!

"Our friends believe"?   Of course they do—as sheltered women may;
But have they seen the shrieking soul ripped from the quivering clay?
They!—If their own front door is shut, they'll swear the whole world's
    warm;
What do they know of dread of death or hanging fear of harm?

The secret half a county keeps, the whisper in the lane,
The shriek that tells the shot went home behind the broken pane,
The dry blood crisping in the sun that scares the honest bees,
And show the boys have heard your talk—what do they know of these?

But you—you know—ay, ten times more; the secrets of the dead,
Black terror on the country-side by word and whisper bred,
The mangled stallion's scream at night. the tail-cropped heifer's low.
Who set the whisper going first?   You know, and well you know!

My soul!   I'd sooner lie in jail for murder plain and straight,
Pure crime I'd done with my own hand for money, lust, or hate
Than take a seat in Parliament by fellow felons cheered,
While one of those "not provens" proved me cleared as you are cleared.

Cleared—you that "lost" the League accounts—go, guard our honour still,
Go, help to make our country's laws that broke God's law at will—
One hand stuck out behind the back, to signal "strike again";
The other on your dress-shirt-front to show your heart is clane.

If black is black or white is white, in black and white it's down,
You're only traitors to the Queen and rebels to the Crown.
If print is print or words are words, the learned Court perpends:—
We are not ruled by murderers, but only—by their friends.

The Ballad of the Red Earl

1891

(*It is not for them to criticize too minutely the methods the Irish followed, though they might deplore some of their results.   During the past few years Ireland had been going through what was tantamount to a revolution.*—EARL SPENCER.)

Red Earl, and will ye take for guide
    The silly camel-birds,
That ye bury your head in an Irish thorn,
    On a desert of drifting words?

Ye have followed a man for a God, Red Earl,
    As the Lord o' Wrong and Right;
But the day is done with the setting sun—
    Will ye follow into the night?

He gave you your own old words, Red Earl,
    For food on the wastrel way;
Will ye rise and eat in the night, Red Earl,
    That fed so full in the day?

Ye have followed fast, ye have followed far,
   And where did the wandering lead?
From the day that ye praised the spoken word
   To the day ye must gloss the deed.

And as ye have given your hand for gain,
   So must ye give in loss;
And as ye ha' come to the brink of the pit,
   So must ye loup across.

For some be rogues in grain, Red Earl,
   And some be rogues in fact,
And rogues direct and rogues elect;
   But all be rogues in pact.

Ye have cast your lot with these, Red Earl;
   Take heed to where ye stand.
Ye have tied a knot with your tongue, Red Earl,
   That ye cannot loose with your hand.

Ye have travelled fast, ye have travelled far,
   In the grip of a tightening tether,
Till ye find at the end ye must take for friend
   The quick and their dead together.

Ye have played with the Law between your lips,
   And mouthed it daintilee;
But the gist o' the speech is ill to teach,
   For ye say: "Let wrong go free."

Red Earl, ye wear the Garter fair,
   And gat your place from a King:
Do ye make Rebellion of no account,
   And Treason a little thing?

And have ye weighed your words, Red Earl,
   That stand and speak so high?
And is it good that the guilt o' blood
   Be cleared at the cost of a sigh?

And is it well for the sake of peace,
   Our tattered Honour to sell,
And higgle anew with a tainted crew—
   Red Earl, and is it well?

Ye have followed fast, ye have followed far,
  On a dark and doubtful way,
And the road is hard, is hard, Red Earl,
  And the price is yet to pay.

Ye shall pay that price as ye reap reward
  For the toil of your tongue and pen—
In the praise of the blamed and the thanks of the shamed,
  And the honour o' knavish men.

They scarce shall veil their scorn, Red Earl,
  And the worst at the last shall be,
When you tell your heart that it does not know
  And your eye that it does not see.

Ulster

1912

*"Their webs shall not become garments, neither shall they cover themselves with their
works: their works are works of iniquity, and the act of violence is in their hands."*—
                        Isaiah lix. 6.

          The dark eleventh hour
          Draws on and sees us sold
          To every evil power
          We fought against of old.
          Rebellion, rapine, hate,
          Oppression, wrong and greed
          Are loosed to rule our fate,
          By England's act and deed.

          The Faith in which we stand,
          The laws we made and Guard—
          Our honour, lives, and land—
          Are given for reward
          To Murder done by night,
          To Treason taught by day,
          To folly, sloth, and spite,
          And we are thrust away.

          The blood our fathers spilt,
          Our love, our toils, our pains.
          Are counted us for guilt,
          And only bind our chains.
          Before an Empire's eyes

The traitor claims his price.
What need of further lies?
We are the sacrifice.

We asked no more than leave
To reap where we bad sown,
Through good and ill to cleave
To our own flag and throne.
Now England's shot and steel
Beneath that flag must show
How loyal hearts should kneel
To England's oldest foe.

We know the wars prepared
On every peaceful home,
We know the hells declared
For such as serve not Rome—
The terror, threats, and dread
In market, hearth, and field—
We know, when all is said,
We perish we yield.

Believe, we dare not boast,
Believe, we do not fear—
We stand to pay the cost
In all that men hold dear.
What answer from the North?
One Law, one Land, one Throne.
If England drive us forth
We shall not fall alone!

The Ballad of East and West

1889

Oh, East is East, and West is West, and never the twain shall meet,
Till Earth and Sky stand presently at God's great Judgment Seat;
But there is neither East nor West, Border, nor Breed, nor Birth,
When two strong men stand face to face, though they come from the
    ends of the earth!

Kamal is out with twenty men to raise the Border-side,
    And he has lifted the Colonel's mare that is the Colonel's pride.
He has lifted her out of the stable-door between the dawn and the day,
And turned the calkins upon her feet, and ridden her far away.
Then up and spoke the Colonel's son that led a troop of the Guides:

"Is there never a man of all my men can say where Kamal hides?"
Then up and spoke Mohammed Khan, the son of the Ressaldar:
"If ye know the track of the morning-mist, ye know where his pickets are.
"At dusk he harries the Abazai—at dawn he is into Bonair,
"But he must go by Fort Bukloh to his own place to fare.
"So if ye gallop to Fort Bukloh as fast as a bird can fly,
"By the favour of God ye may cut him off ere he win to the Tongue of Jagai.
"But if he be past the Tongue of Jagai, right swiftly turn ye then,
"For the length and the breadth of that grisly plain is sown with Kamal's men.
"There is rock to the left, and rock to the right, and low lean thorn between,
"And ye may hear a breech-bolt snick where never a man is seen."

The Colonel's son has taken horse, and a raw rough dun was he,
With the mouth of a bell and the heart of Hell and the head of a gallows-tree.
The Colonel's son to the Fort has won, they bid him stay to eat—
Who rides at the tail of a Border thief, he sits not long at his meat.
He's up and away from Fort Bukloh as fast as he can fly,
Till he was aware of his father's mare in the gut of the Tongue of Jagai,
Till he was aware of his father's mare with Kamal upon her back,
And when he could spy the white of her eye, he made the pistol crack.
He has fired once, he has fired twice, but the whistling ball went wide.
"Ye shoot like a soldier," Kamal said. 'Show now if ye can ride!"
It's up and over the Tongue of Jagai, as blown dust-devils go
The dun he fled like a stag of ten, but the mare like a barren doe.
The dun he leaned against the bit and slugged his head above,
But the red mare played with the snaffle-bars, as a maiden plays with a glove.
There was rock to the left and rock to the right, and low lean thorn between,
And thrice he heard a breech-bolt snick tho' never a man was seen.
They have ridden the low moon out of the sky, their hoofs drum up the dawn,
The dun he went like a wounded bull, but the mare like a new-roused fawn.
The dun he fell at a water-course—in a woeful heap fell he,
And Kamal has turned the red mare back, and pulled the rider free.
He has knocked the pistol out of his hand—small room was there to strive,
"'Twas only by favour of mine," quoth he, "ye rode so long alive:
"There was not a rock for twenty mile, there was not a clump of tree,
"But covered a man of my own men with his rifle cocked on his knee.

"If I had raised my bridle-hand, as I have held it low,
"The little jackals that flee so fast were feasting all in a row.
"If I had bowed my head on my breast, as I have held it high,
"The kite that whistles above us now were gorged till she could not fly."
Lightly answered the Colonel's son: "Do good to bird and beast,
"But count who come for the broken meats before thou makest a feast.
"If there should follow a thousand swords to carry my bones away,
"Belike the price of a jackal's meal were more than a thief could pay.
"They will feed their horse on the standing crop, their men on the
    garnered grain.
"The thatch of the byres will serve their fires when all the cattle are slain.
"But if thou thinkest the price be fair,—thy brethren wait to sup,
"The hound is kin to the jackal-spawn,—howl, dog, and call them up!
"And if thou thinkest the price be high, in steer and gear and stack,
"Give me my father's mare again, and I'll fight my own way back!"
Kamal has gripped him by the hand and set him upon his feet.
"No talk shall be of dogs," said he, "when wolf and grey wolf meet.
"May I eat dirt if thou has hurt of me in deed or breath;
"What dam of lances brought thee forth to jest at the dawn with Death?"
Lightly answered the Colonel's son: "I hold by the blood of my clan:
"Take up the mare for my father's gift—by God, she has carried a man!"
The red mare ran to the Colonel's son, and nuzzled against his breast;
"We be two strong men," said Kamal then, "but she loveth the younger
    best.
"So she shall go with a lifter's dower, my turquoise-studded rein,
"My 'broidered saddle and saddle-cloth, and silver stirrups twain."
The Colonel's son a pistol drew, and held it muzzle-end,
"Ye have taken the one from a foe," said he.   "Will ye take the mate
    from a friend?"
"A gift for a gift," said Kamal straight; "a limb for the risk of a limb.
"Thy father has sent his son to me, I'll send my son to him!"
With that he whistled his only son, that dropped from a mountain crest—
He trod the ling like a buck in spring, and he looked like a lance in rest.
"Now here is they master," Kamal said, "who leads a troop of the
    Guides,
"And thou must ride at his left side as shield on shoulder rides.
"Till Death or I cut loose the tie, at camp and board and bed,
"Thy life is his—thy fate it is to guard him with thy head.
"So, thou must eat the White Queen's meat, and all her foes are thine,
"And thou must harry thy father's hold for the peace of the Border-line.
"And thou must make a trooper tough and hack thy way to power—
"Belike they will raise thee to Ressaldar when I am hanged in Peshawur!"

They have looked each other between the eyes, and there they found no
    fault.

They have taken the Oath of the Brother-in-Blood on leavened bread and
    salt:
They have taken the Oath of the Brother-in-Blood on fire and
    fresh-cut sod,
On the hilt and the haft of the Khyber knife, and the Wondrous Names
    of God.
The Colonel's son he rides the mare and Kamal's boy the dun,
And two have come back to Fort Bukloh where there went forth but one.
And when they drew to the Quarter-Guard, full twenty swords flew
    clear—
There was not a man but carried his feud with the blood of the
    mountaineer.
"Ha' done! ha' done!" said the Colonel's son.   "Put up the steel at your
    sides!
"Last night ye had struck at a Border thief—to-night 'tis a man of the
    Guides!"

Oh, East is East, and West is West, and never the twain shall meet,
Till Earth and Sky stand presently at God's great Judgment Seat;
But there is neither East nor West, Border, nor Breed, nor Birth,
When two strong men stand face to face, though they come from the ends of the
    earth!

The Last Suttee
1889

*Not many years ago a King died in one of the Rajpoot States.   His wives, disregarding
the orders of the English against Suttee, would have broken out of the palace and burned
themselves with the corpse, had not the gates been barred. But one of them, disguised as
the King's favourite dancing-girl, passed through the line of guards and reached the
pyre.   There, her courage failing, she prayed her cousin, a baron of the King's court,
to kill her.   This he did, not knowing who she was.*

        Udai Chand lay sick to death
           In his hold by Gungra hill.
        All night we heard the death-gongs ring,
        For the soul of the dying Rajpoot King,
        All night beat up from the women's wing
           A cry that we could not still.

        All night the barons came and went,
           The Lords of the Outer Guard.
        All night the cressets glimmered pale

On Ulwar sabre and Tonki jezail
Mewar headstall and Marwar mail,
    That clinked in the palace yard.

In the Golden Room on the palace roof
    All night he fought for air:
And there were sobbings behind the screen,
Rustle and whisper of women unseen,
And the hungry eyes of the Boondi Queen
    On the death she might not share.

He passed at dawn—the death-fire leaped
    From ridge to river-head,
From the Malwa plains to the Abu scars:
And wail upon wail went up to the stars
Behind the grim zenana-bars,
    When they knew that the King was dead.

The dumb priest knelt to tie his mouth
    And robe him for the pyre.
The Boondi Queen beneath us cried:
"See, now, that we die as our mothers died
"In the bridal-bed by our master's side!
    "Out, women!—to the fire!"

We drove the great gates home apace—
    White hands were on the sill—
But ere the rush of the unseen feet
Had reached the turn to the open street,
The bars shot down, the guard-drum beat—
    We held the dovecot still!

A face looked down in the gathering day,
    And laughing spoke from the wall:
"Ohé, they mourn here: let me by—
"Azizun, the Lucknow nautch-girl, I!
"When the house is rotten, the rats must fly,
    "And I seek another thrall.

"For I ruled the King as ne'er did Queen,—
    "To-night the Queens rule me!
"Guard them safely, but let me go,
"Or ever they pay the debt they owe
"In scourge and torture!"   She leaped below,
    And the grim guard watched her flee.

They knew that the King had spent his soul
    On a North-bred dancing-girl:

That he prayed to a flat-nosed Lucknow god,
And kissed the ground where her feet had trod,
And doomed to death at her drunken nod,
   And swore by her lightest curl.

We bore the King to his father's place,
   Where the tombs of the Sun-born stand:
Where the grey apes swing, and the peacocks preen
On fretted pillar and jewelled screen,
And the wild boar couch in the house of the Queen
   On the drift of the desert sand.

The herald read his titles forth
   We set the logs aglow:
"Friend of the English, free from fear,
"Baron of Luni to Jeysulmeer,
"Lord of the Desert of Bikaneer,
   "King of the Jungle,—go!"

All night the red flame stabbed the sky
   With wavering wind-tossed spears:
And out of a shattered temple crept
A woman who veiled her head and wept,
And called on the King—but the great King slept,
   And turned not for her tears.

One watched, a bow-shot from the blaze.
   The silent streets between,
Who had stood by the King in sport and fray,
To blade in ambush or boar at bay,
And he was a baron old and grey,
   And kin to the Boondi Queen.

Small thought had he to mark the strife—
   Cold fear with hot desire—
When thrice she leaped from the leaping flame,
And thrice she beat her breast for shame,
And thrice like a wounded dove she came
   And moaned about the fire.

He said: "O shameless, put aside
   "The veil upon thy brow!
"Who held the King and all his land
"To the wanton will of a harlot's hand!
"Will the white ash rise from the blistered brand?
   "Stoop down, and call him now!"

Then she: "By the faith of my tarnished soul,
   "All things I did not well
"I had hoped to clear ere the fire died,
"And lay me down by my master's side
"To rule in Heaven his only bride,
   "While the others howl in Hell.

"But I have felt the fire's breath,
   "And hard it is to die!
"Yet if I may pray a Rajpoot lord
"To sully the steel of a Thakur's sword
"With base-born blood of a trade abhorred . . ."
   And the Thakur answered, "Ay."

He drew and struck: the straight blade drank
   The life beneath the breast.
"I had looked for the Queen to face the flame,
"But the harlot dies for the Rajpoot dame—
"Sisters of mine, pass, free from shame,
   "Pass with thy King to rest!"

The black log crashed above the white:
   The little flames and lean,
Red as slaughter and blue as steel,
That whistled and fluttered from head to heel,
Leaped up anew, for they found their meal
   On the heart of—the Boondi Queen!

General Joubert

1900

(Died, South African War, March 27, 1900)

With those that bred, with those that loosed the strife
   He had no part whose hands were clear of gain;
But subtle, strong, and stubborn, gave his life
   To a lost cause, and knew the gift was vain.

Later shall rise a people, sane and great,
   Forged in strong fires, by equal war made one;
Telling old battles over without hate—
   Not least his name shall pass from sire to son.

He may not meet the onsweep of our van
  In the doomed city when we close the score;
Yet o'er his grave—his grave that holds a Man—
  Our deep-tongued guns shall answer his once more!

Gehazi

1915

Whence comest thou, Gehazi,
  So reverend to behold,
In scarlet and in ermines
  And chain of England's gold?
"From following after Naaman
  To tell him all is well,
Whereby my zeal hath made me
  A Judge in Israel."

Well done, well done, Gehazi!
  Stretch forth thy ready hand.
Thou barely 'scaped from judgment,
  Take oath to judge the land
Unswayed by gift of money
  Or privy bribe, more base,
Of knowledge which is profit
  In any market-place

Search out and probe, Gehazi,
  As thou of all canst try,
The truthful, well-weighed answer
  That tells the blacker lie—
The loud, uneasy virtue,
  The anger feigned at will,
To overbear a witness
  And make the Court keep still.

Take order now, Gehazi,
  That no man talk aside
In secret with his judges
  The while his case is tried.
Lest he should show them—reason
  To keep a matter hid,
And subtly lead the questions
  Away from what he did.

Thou mirror of uprightness,
   What ails thee at thy vows?
What means the risen whiteness
   Of the skin between thy brows?
The boils that shine and burrow,
   The sores that slough and bleed—
The leprosy of Naaman
   On thee and all thy seed?
     Stand up, stand up, Gehazi,
       Draw close thy robe and go,
     Gehazi, Judge in Israel,
       A leper white as snow!

The Ballad of the King's Mercy

1889

Abdhur Rahman, the Durani Chief, of him is the story told.
His mercy fills the Khyber hills—his grace is manifold;
He has taken toll of the North and the South—his grace reacheth far,
And they tell the tale of his charity from Balkh to Kandahar.

Before the old Peshawur Gate, where Kurd and Kafir meet,
The Governor of Kabul dealt the Justice of the Street,
And that was strait as running noose and swift as plunging knife,
Tho' he who held the longer purse might hold the longer life.
There was a hound of Hindustan had struck a Yusufzai,
Wherefore they spat upon his face and led him out to die.
It chanced the King went forth that hour when throat was bared to knife;
The Kafir grovelled under-hoof and clamoured for his life.

Then said the King: "Have hope, O friend! Yea, Death disgraced is hard.
Much honour shall be thine"; and called the Captain of the Guard,
Yar Khan, a bastard of the Blood, so city-babble saith,
And he was honoured of the King—the which is salt to Death;
And he was son of Daoud Shah, the Reiver of the Plains,
And blood of old Durani lords ran fire in his veins;
And 'twas to tame an Afghan pride nor Hell nor Heaven could bind,
The King would make him butcher to a yelping cur of Hind.

"Strike!" said the King.   "King's blood art thou—his death shall be his
   pride!"
Then louder, that the crowd might catch: "Fear not—his arms are tied!"
Yar Khan drew clear the Khyber knife, and struck, and sheathed again.
"O man, thy will is done," quoth he; "A King this dog hath slain."

Abdhur Rahman, the Durani Chief, to the North and the South is sold.
The North and the South shall open their mouth to a Ghilzai flag unrolled.
When the big guns speak to the Khyber peak and his dog-Heratis fly:
Ye have heard the song—How long? How long? Wolves of the Abazai!

That night before the watch was set, when all the streets were clear,
The Governor of Kabul spoke: "My King, hast thou no fear?
"Thou knowest—thou hast heard,"—his speech died at his master's face.
And grimly said the Afghan King: "I rule the Afghan race.
"My path is mine—see thou to thine. To-night upon thy bed
"Think who there be in Kabul now that clamour for thy head."

That night when all the gates were shut to City and to throne,
Within a little garden-house the King lay down alone.
Before the sinking of the moon, which is the Night of Night,
Yar Khan came softly to the King to make his honour white.
(The children of the town had mocked beneath his horse's hoofs,
The harlots of the town had hailed him "butcher!" from their roofs.)

But as he groped against the wall, two hands upon him fell,
The King behind his shoulder spake: "Dead man, thou dost not well!
"'Tis ill to jest with King by day and seek a boon by night;
"And that thou bearest in thy hand is all too sharp to write.
"But three days hence, if God be good, and if thy strength remain,
"Thou shalt demand one boon of me and bless me in thy pain.
"For I am merciful to all, and most of all to thee.
My butcher of the shambles, rest—no knife hast thou for me!"

Abdhur Rahman, the Durani Chief, holds hard by the South and the North;
But the Ghilzai knows, ere the melting snows, when the swollen banks break forth,
When the red-coats crawl to the sungar wall, and his Usbeg lances fail:
Ye have heard the song How long? How long? Wolves of the Zukka Kheyl!

They stoned him in the rubbish-field when dawn was in the sky,
According to the written word, "See that he do not die."
They stoned him till the stones were piled above him on the plain,
And those the labouring limbs displaced they tumbled back again.
One watched beside the dreary mound that veiled the battered thing,
And him the King with laughter called the Herald of the King.

It was upon the second night, the night of Ramazan,
The watcher leaning earthward heard the message of Yar Khan.
From shattered breast through shrivelled lips broke forth the rattling
  breath,
"Creature of God, deliver me from agony of Death."

They sought the King among his girls, and risked their lives thereby:
"Protector of the Pitiful, give orders that he die!"

"Bid his endure until the day," a lagging answer came;
"The night is short, and he can pray and learn to bless my name."

Before the dawn three times he spoke, and on the day once more:
"Creature of God, deliver me, and bless the King therefor!"

They shot him at the morning prayer, to ease him of his pain,
And when he heard the matchlocks clink, he blessed the King again.

Which thing the singers made a song for all the world to sing
So that the Outer Seas may know the mercy of the King.

Abdhur Rahman, the Durani Chief, of him is the story told,
He has opened his mouth to the North and the South, they have stuffed his mouth
  with gold.
Ye know the truth of his tender ruth—and sweet his favours are:
Ye have heard the song—How long? How long?—from Balkh to Kandahar.

The Ballad of the King's Jest

1890

When spring-time flushes the desert grass,
Our kafilas[1] wind through the Khyber Pass.
Lean are the camels but fat the frails,
Light are the purses but heavy the bales,
As the snowbound trade of the North comes down
To the market-square of Peshawur town.

In a turquoise twilight, crisp and chill,
A kafila camped at the foot of the hill.
Then blue smoke-haze of the cooking rose,
And tent-peg answered to hammer-nose;
And the picketed ponies, shag and wild,
Strained at their ropes as the feed was piled;
And the bubbling camels beside the load
Sprawled for a furlong adown the road;
And the Persian pussy-cats, brought for sale,
Spat at the dogs from the camel-bale;
And the tribesmen bellowed to hasten the food;
And the camp-fires twinkled by Fort Jumrood;
And there fled on the wings of the gathering dusk
A savour of camels and carpets and musk,
A murmur of voices, a reek of smoke,
To tell us the trade of the Khyber woke.

[1]Caravans.

The lid of the flesh-pot chattered high,
The knives were whetted and—then came I
To Mahbub Ali, the muleteer,
Patching his bridles and counting his gear,
Crammed with the gossip of half a year.
But Mahbub Ali the kindly said,
"Better is speech when the belly is fed."
So we plunged the hand to the mid-wrist deep
In a cinnamon stew of the fat-tailed sheep,
And he who never hath tasted the food,
By Allah! he knoweth not bad from good.
We cleansed our beards of the mutton-grease,.
We lay on the mats and were filled with peace,
And the talk slid north, and the talk slid south,
With the sliding puffs from the hookah-mouth.

Four things greater than all things are,—
Women and Horses and Power and War.
We spake of them all, but the last the most.
For I sought a word of a Russian post,
Of a shifty promise, an unsheathed sword,
And a grey-coat on the Helmund ford.
Then Mahbub Ali lowered his eyes
In the fashion of one who is weaving lies.
Quoth he: "Of the Russians who can say?
"When the night is gathering all is grey.
"But we look that the gloom of the night shall die
"In the morning flush of a blood-red sky.
"Friend of my heart, is it meet or wise
"To warn a King of his enemies?
"We know what Heaven or Hell may bring,
"But no man knoweth the mind of the King.
"That unsought counsel is cursed of God
"Attesteth the story of Wali Dad.

"His sire was leaky of tongue and pen,
"His dam was a clucking Khattack hen;
"And the colt bred close to the vice of each,
"For he carried the curse of an unstaunched speech.
"Therewith madness—so that he sought
"The favour of kings at the Kabul Court;
"And travelled, in hope of honour, far
"To the line where the grey-coat squadrons are.
"There have I journeyed too—but I
"Saw naught, said naught, and—did not die!
"*He* hearked to rumour, and snatched at a breath

"Of 'this one knoweth,' and 'that one saith,'—
"Legends that ran from mouth to mouth
"Of a grey-coat coming, and sack of the South.
"These have I also heard—they pass
"With each new spring and the winter grass.

"Hot-foot southward, forgotten of God,
"Back to the city ran Wali Dad,
"Even to Kabul—in full durbar
"The King held talk with his Chief in War.
"Into the press of the crowd he broke,
"And what he had heard of the coming spoke.
"Then Gholam Hyder, the Red Chief, smiled,
"As a mother might on a babbling child;
"But those who would laugh restrained their breath,
"When the face of the King showed dark as death.
"Evil it is in full durbar
"To cry to a ruler of gathering war!
"Slowly he led to a peach-tree small,
"That grew by a cleft of the city wall.
"And he said to the boy: 'They shall praise thy zeal
" 'So long as the red spurt follows the steel.
" 'And the Russ is upon us even now?
" 'Great is thy prudence—wait them, thou.
" 'Watch from the tree. Thou art young and strong.
" 'Surely the vigil is not for long.
" 'The Russ is upon us, thy clamour ran?
" 'Surely an hour shall bring their van.
" 'Wait and watch. When the host is near,
" 'Shout aloud that my men may hear."

"Friend of my heart, is it meet or wise
"To warn a King of his enemies?
"A guard was set that he might not flee—
"A score of bayonet ringed the tree.
"The peach-bloom fell in showers of snow,
"When he shook at his death as he looked below.
"By the power of God, Who alone is great,
"Till the seventh day he fought with his fate.
"Then madness took him, and men declare
"He mowed in the branches as ape and bear,
"And last as a sloth, ere his body failed,
And he hung like a bat in the forks, and wailed,
"And sleep the cord of his hands untied,
"And he fell, and was caught on the points and died.

"Heart of my heart, is it meet or wise
"To warn a King of his enemies?
"We know what Heaven or Hell may bring,
"But no man knoweth the mind of the king.
"Of the grey-coat coming who can say?
"When the night is gathering all is grey.
"Two things greater than all things are,
"The first is Love, and the second War.
"And since we know not how War may prove,
"Heart of my heart, let us talk of Love!"

With Scindia to Delhi

1890

More than a hundred years ago, in a great battle fought near Delhi, an Indian Prince rode fifty miles after the day was lost, with a beggar-girl, who had loved him and followed him in all his camps, on his saddle-bow. He lost the girl when almost within sight of safety. A Mahratta trooper tells the story:—

The wreath of banquet overnight lay withered on the neck,
    Our hands and scarves were saffron-dyed for signal of despair,
When we went forth to Paniput to battle with the *Mlech*,—
    Ere we came back from Paniput and left a kingdom there.

Thrice thirty thousand men were we to force the Jumna fords—
    The hawk-winged horse of Damajee, mailed squadrons of the Bhao,
Stark levies of the southern hills, the Deccan's sharpest swords,
    And he, the harlot's traitor-son, the goatherd Mulhar Rao!

Thrice thirty thousand men were we before the mists had cleared.
    The low white mist of morning heard the war-conch scream and bray.
We called upon Bhowani and we gripped them by the beard,
    We rolled upon them like a flood and washed their ranks away.

The children of the hills of Khost before our lances ran,
    We drove the black Rohillas back as cattle to the pen.
'Twas then we needed Mulhar Rao to end what we began,
    A thousand men had saved the charge; he fled the field with ten!

There was no room to clear a sword—no power to strike a blow,
    For foot to foot, ay, breast to breast, the battle held us fast—
Save where the naked hill-men ran, and stabbing from below
    Brought down the horse and rider, and we trampled them and passed.

To left the roar of musketry rang like a falling flood—
    To right the sunshine rippled red from redder lance and blade—

Above the dark *Upsaras*[1] flew, beneath us plashed the blood,
    And, bellying black against the dust, the Bhagwa Jhanda swayed.

I saw it fall in smoke and fire, the Banner of the Bhao;
    I heard a voice across the press of one who called in vain:—
"Ho!   Anand Rao Nimbalkhur, ride!   Get aid of Mulhar Rao!
    "Go shame his squadrons into fight—the Bhao—the Bhao is slain!"

Thereat, as when a sand-bar breaks in clotted spume and spray,
    When rain of later autumn sweeps the Jumna water-head,
Before their charge from flank to flank our riven ranks gave way—
    But of the waters of that flood the Jumna fords ran red.

I held by Scindia, my lord, as close as man might hold;
    A Soobah of the Deccan asks no aid to guard his life;
But Holkar's Horse were flying, and our chiefest chiefs were cold,
    And like a flame among us leapt the long lean Northern knife.

I held by Scindia—my lance from butt to tuft was dyed,
    The froth of battle bossed the shield and roped the bridle-chain—
What time beneath our horses' feet a maiden rose and cried,
    And clung to Scindia, and I turned a sword-cut from the twain.

(He set a spell upon the maid in woodlands long ago:
    A hunter by the Tapti banks, she gave him water there:
He turned her heart to water, and she followed to her woe.
    What need had he of Lalun who had twenty maids as fair?)

Now in that hour strength left my lord: he wrenched his mare aside;
    He bound the girl behind him and we slashed and struggled free.
Across the reeling wreck of strife we rode as shadows ride
    From Paniput to Delhi town, but not alone were we.

'Twas Lutif-Ullah Populzai laid horse upon our track,
    A swine-fed reiver of the North that lusted for the maid;
I might have barred his path awhile, but Scindia called me back,
    And I—O woe for Scindia!—I listened and obeyed.

League after league the formless scrub took shape and glided by—
    League after league the white road swirled behind the white mare's
        feet—
League after league, when leagues were done, we heard the Populzai,
    Where sure as Time and swift as Death the tireless footfall beat.

Noon's eye beheld that shame of flight; the shadows fell, we fled
    Where steadfast as the wheeling kite he followed in our train;
The black wolf warred where we had warred, the jackal mocked our dead,
    And terror born of twilight-tide made mad the labouring brain.

[1] The Choosers of the Slain.

I gasped:—'A kingdom waits my lord; her love is but her own.
    "A day shall mar, a day shall cure, for her—but what for thee?
"Cut loose the girl: he follows fast. Cut loose and ride alone!"
    Then Scindia 'twixt his blistered lips:—"My Queens' Queen shall she
    be!

"Of all who ate my bread last night 'twas she alone that came
    "To seek her love between the spears and find her crown therein!
"One shame is mine to-day. What need the weight of double shame?
    "If once we reach the Delhi Gate, though all be lost, I win!"

We rode—the white mare failed—her trot a staggering stumble grew,—
    The cooking-smoke of even rose and weltered and hung low;
And still we heard the Populzai and still we strained anew,
    And Delhi town was very near, but nearer was the foe.

Yea, Delhi town was very near when Lalun whispered:—'Slay!
    "Lord of my life, the mare sinks fast—stab deep and let me die!"
But Scindia would not, and the maid tore free and flung away,
    And turning as she fell we heard the clattering Populzai.

Then Scindia checked the gasping mare that rocked and groaned for
        breath,
    And wheeled to charge and plunged the knife a hands-breadth in her
        side—
The hunter and the hunted know how that last pause is death—
    The blood had chilled about her heart, she reared and fell and died.

Our Gods were kind. Before he heard the maiden's piteous scream
    A log upon the Delhi road, beneath the mare he lay—
Lost mistress and lost battle passed before him like a dream;
    The darkness closed about his eyes. I bore my King away.

The Dove of Dacca

1892

    The freed dove flew to the Rajah's tower—
        Fled from the slaughter of Moslem kings—
    And the thorns have covered the city of Gaur.
        Dove—dove—oh, homing dove!
    Little white traitor, with woe on thy wings!

    The Rajah of Dacca rode under the wall;
        He set in his bosom a dove of flight—
    "If she return, be sure that I fall."
        Dove—dove—oh, homing dove!
    Pressed to his heart in the thick of the fight.

"Fire the palace, the fort, and the keep—
    Leave to the foeman no spoil at all.
In the flame of the palace lie down and sleep
    If the dove—if the dove—if the homing dove
Come, and alone, to the palace wall."

The Kings of the North they were scattered abroad—
    The Rajah of Dacca he slew them all.
Hot from slaughter he stooped at the ford,
    And the dove—the dove—oh, the homing dove!
She thought of her cote on the palace wall.

She opened her wings and she flew away—
    Fluttered away beyond recall;
She came to the palace at break of day.
    Dove—dove—oh, homing dove,
Flying so fast for a kingdom's fall!

The Queens of Dacca they slept in flame—
    Slept in the flame of the palace old—
To save their honour from Moslem shame.
    And the dove—the dove—oh, the homing dove,
She cooed to her young where the smoke-cloud rolled;

The Rajah of Dacca rode far and fleet,
    Followed as fast as a horse could fly,
He came and the palace was black at his feet;
    And the dove—the dove—the homing dove
Circled alone in the stainless sky.

So the dove flew to the Rajah's tower—
    Fled from the slaughter of Moslem kings;
So the thorns covered the city of Gaur,
    And Dacca was lost for a white dove's wings.
Dove—dove—oh, homing dove,
    Dacca is lost from the Roll of the Kings!

The Ballad of Boh Da Thone

1888

(Burma War, 1833–85)

This is the ballad of Boh Da Thone,
Erst a Pretender to Theebaw's throne,
Who harried the District of Alalone:

How he met with his fate and the V.P.P.[1]
At the hand of Harendra Mukerkji,
Senior Gomashta, G.B.T.[2]

Boh Da Thone was a warrior bold:
His sword and his rifle were bossed with gold,

And the Peacock Banner his henchman bore
Was stiff with bullion but stiffer with gore.

He shot at the strong and he slashed at the weak
From the Salween scrub to the Chindwin teak:

He crucified noble, he scarified mean,
He filled old ladies with kerosene:

While over the water the papers cried,
"The patriot fights for his countryside!"

But little they cared for the Native press,
The worn white soldiers in khaki dress,

Who tramped through the jungle and camped in the byre,
Who died in the swamp and were tombed in the mire,

Who gave up their lives, at the Queen's Command,
For the Pride of their Race and the Peace of the Land.

Now, first of the foemen of Boh Da Thone
Was Captain O'Neil of the Black Tyrone,

And his was a Company, seventy strong,
Who hustled that dissolute Chief along.

There were lads from Galway and Louth and Meath
Who went to their death with a joke in their teeth,

And worshipped with fluency, fervour, and zeal
The mud on the boot-heels of "Crook" O'Neil.

But ever a blight on their labours lay,
And ever their quarry would vanish away,

Till the sun-dried boys of the Black Tyrone
Took a brotherly interest in Boh Da Thone,

And, sooth, if pursuit in possession ends,
The Boh and his trackers were best of friends.

[1]Value Payable Post = Collect on Delivery.
[2]Head Clerk, Government Bullock Train.

The word of a scout—a march by night—
A rush through the mist—a scattering fight—

A volley from cover—a corpse in the clearing—
A glimpse of a loin-cloth and heavy jade earring-

The flare of a village—the tally of slain—
And ... the Boh was abroad on the raid again!

They cursed their luck, as the Irish will,
They gave him credit for cunning and skill,

They buried their dead, they bolted their beef,
And started anew on the track of the thief,

Till, in place of the "Kalends of Greece," men said,
"When Crook and his darlings come back with the head."

They had hunted the Boh from the hills to the plain—
He doubled and broke for the hills again:

They had crippled his power for rapine and raid,
They had routed him out of his pet stockade,

And at last, they came, when the Daystar tired,
To a camp deserted—a village fired.

A black cross blistered the morning-gold,
But the body upon it was stark and cold.

The wind of the dawn went merrily past,
The high grass bowed her plumes to the blast,

And out of the grass, on a sudden, broke
A spirtle of fire, a whorl of smoke—

And Captain O'Neil of the black Tyrone
Was blessed with a slug in the ulnar-bone—
The gift of his enemy Boh Da Thone.

(Now a slug that is hammered from telegraph-wire
Is a thorn in the flesh and a rankling fire.)

The shot-wound festered—as shot-wounds may
In a steaming barrack at Mandalay.

The left arm throbbed, and the Captain swore,
"I'd like to be after the Boh once more!"

The fever held him—the Captain said,
"I'd give a hundred to look at his head!"

The Hospital punkahs creaked and whirred,
But Babu Harendra (Gomashta) heard.

He thought of the cane-brake, green and dank,
That girdled his home by the Dacca tank.

He thought of his wife and his High School son,
He thought—but abandoned the thought—of a gun.

His sleep was broken by visions dread
Of a shining Boh with a silver head.

He kept his counsel and went his way,
And swindled the cartmen of half their pay.

And the months went on, as the worst must do,
And the Boh returned to the raid anew.

But the Captain had quitted the long-drawn strife,
And in far Simoorie had taken a wife;

And she was a damsel of delicate mould,
With hair like the sunshine and heart of gold,

And little she knew the arms that embraced
Had cloven a man from the brow to the waist:

And little she knew that the loving lips
Had ordered a quivering life's eclipse,

Or the eye that lit at her lightest breath
Had glared unawed in the Gates of Death.

(For these be matters a man would hide,
As a general rule, from an innocent Bride.)

And little the Captain thought of the past,
And, of all men, Babu Harendra last.

But slow, in the sludge of the Kathun road,
The Government Bullock Tain toted its load.

Speckless and spotless and shining with *ghi*,
In the rearmost cart sat the Babu-jee;

And ever a phantom before him fled
Of a scowling Boh with a silver head.

Then the lead-cart stuck, though the coolies slaved,
And the cartmen flogged and the escort raved,

And out of the jungle, with yells and squeals,
Pranced Boh Da Thone, and his gang at his heels!

Then belching blunderbuss answered back
The Snider's snarl and the carbine's crack,

And the blithe revolver began to sing
To the blade that twanged on the locking-ring,

And the brown flesh blued where the bayonet kissed,
As the steel shot back with a wrench and a twist,

And the great white oxen with onyx eyes
Watched the souls of the dead arise,

And over the smoke of the fusillade
The Peacock Banner staggered and swayed.

The Babu shook at the horrible sight,
And girded his ponderous loins for flight,

But Fate had ordained that the Boh should start
On a lone-hand raid of the rearmost cart,

And out of that cart, with a bellow of woe,
The Babu fell—flat on the top of the Boh!

For years had Harenda served the State,
To the growth of his purse and the girth of his *pêt*.[1]

There were twenty stone, as the tally-man knows,
On the broad of the chest of this best of Bohs.

And twenty stone from a height discharged
Are bad for a Boh with a spleen enlarged.

Oh, short was the struggle—severe was the shock—
He dropped like a bullock—he lay like a block;

And the Babu above him, convulsed with fear,
Heard the labouring life-breath hissed out in his ear.

And thus in a fashion undignified
The princely pest of the Chindwin died.

Turn now to Simoorie, where, all at his ease,
The Captain is petting the Bride on his knees,

Where the *whit* of the bullet, the wounded man's scream
Are mixed as the mist of some devilish dream—

[1] Stomach.

Forgotten, forgotten the sweat of the shambles
Where the hill-daisy blooms and the grey monkey gambols,

From the sword-belt set free and released from the steel,
The Peace of the Lord is on Captain O'Neil!

Up the hill to Simoorie—most patient of drudges—
The bags on his shoulder, the mail-runner trudges.

"For Captain O'Neil Sahib. One hundred and ten
"Rupees to collect on delivery."

Then

(Their breakfast was stopped while the screw-jack and hammer
Tore waxcloth, split teak-wood, and chipped out the dammer;[1])

Open-eyed, open-mouthed, on the napery's snow,
With a crash and a thud, rolled—the Head of the Boh!

And gummed to the scalp was a letter which ran:—
  "In Fielding Force Service
    "*Encampment*,
      10th Jan.

"Dear Sir,—I have honour to send, as you said,
"For final approval (see under) Boh's Head:

"Was took by myself in most bloody affair.
"By High Education brought pressure to bear.

"Now violate Liberty, time being bad,
"To mail V.P.P (rupees hundred) Please add

"Whatever Your Honour can pass.   Price of Blood
"Much cheap at one hundred, and children want food.

"So trusting Your Honour will somewhat retain
"True love and affection for Govt. Bullock Train,

"And show awful kindness to satisfy me,

  'I am,
    "Graceful Master,
      "Your
        "H. Mukerji."

As the rabbit is drawn to the rattlesnake's power,
As the smoker's eye fills at the opium hour,

---

[1]Native sealing-wax.

As a horse reaches up to the manger above,
As the waiting ear yearns for the whisper of love,

From the arms of the Bride, iron-visaged and slow,
The Captain bent down to the Head of the Boh.

And e'en as he looked on the Thing where It lay
'Twixt the winking new spoons and the napkins' array,

The freed mind fled back to the long-ago days—
The hand-to-hand scuffle—the smoke and the blaze—

The forced march at night and the quick rush at dawn—
The banjo at twilight, the burial ere morn—

The stench of the marshes—the raw, piercing smell
When the overhand stabbing-cut silenced the yell—

The oaths of his Irish that surged when they stood
Where the black crosses hung o'er the Kuttamow flood.

As a derelict ship drifts away with the tide
The Captain went out on the Past from his Bride,

Back, back, through the springs to the chill of the year,
When he hunted the Boh from Maloon to Tsaleer.

As the shape of a corpse dimmers up through deep water,
In his eye lit the passionless passion of slaughter,

And men who had fought with O'Neil for the life
Had gazed on his face with less dread than his wife.

For she who had held him so long could not hold him—
Though a four-month Eternity should have controlled him!—

But watched the twin Terror—the head turned to head—
The scowling, scarred Black, and the flushed savage Red—

The spirit that changed from her knowing and flew to
Some grim hidden Past she had never a clue to.

But It knew as It grinned, for he touched it unfearing,
And muttered aloud, "So you kept that jade earring!"

Then nodded, and kindly, as friend nods to friend,
"Old man, you fought well, but you lost in the end."

The visions departed, and Shame followed Passion:—
"He took what I said in this horrible fashion?

"*I'll* write to Harendra!"   With language unsainted
The Captain came back to the Bride . . . who had fainted

And this is fiction? No. Go to Simoorie
And look at their baby, a twelve-month old Houri,

A pert little, Irish-eyed Kathleen Mavournin—
She's always about on the Mall of a mornin'—

And you'll see, if her right shoulder-strap is displaced,
This: *Gules* upon *argent*, a Boh's Head, *erased!*

The Sacrifice of Er-Heb

1887

Er-Heb beyond the Hills of Ao-Safai
Bears witness to the truth, and Ao-Safai
Hath told the men of Gorukh. Thence the tale
Comes westward o'er the peaks to India.

The story of Bisesa, Armod's child,—
A maiden plighted to the Chief in War,
The Man of Sixty Spears, who held the Pass
That leads to Thibet, but to-day is gone
To seek his comfort of the God called Budh
The Silent—showing how the Sickness ceased
Because of her who died to save the tribe.

Taman is One and greater than us all.
Taman is One and greater than all Gods:
Taman is Two in One and rides the sky,
Curved like a stallion's croup, from dusk to dawn,
And drums upon it with his heels, by which
Is bred the neighing thunder in the Hills.

This is Taman, the God of all Er-Heb,
Who was before all Gods, and made all Gods,
And presently will break the Gods he made,
And step upon the Earth to govern men
Who give him milk-dry ewes and cheat his Priests,
Or leave his shrine unlighted—as Er-Heb
Left it unlighted and forgot Taman,
When all the Valley followed after Kysh
And Yabosh, little Gods but very wise,
And from the sky Taman beheld their sin.

He sent the Sickness out upon the hills,
The Red Horse Sickness with the iron hooves,
To turn the Valley to Taman again.

And the Red Horse snuffed thrice into the wind,
The naked wind that had no fear of him;
And the Red Horse stamped thrice upon the snow,
The naked snows that had no fear of him;
And the Red Horse went out across the rocks,
The ringing rocks that had no fear of him;
And downward, where the lean birch meets the snow,
And downward, where the grey pine meets the birch,
And downward, where the dwarf oak meets the pine,
Till at his feet our cup-like pastures lay.

That night, the slow mists of the evening dropped,
Dropped as a cloth upon a dead man's face,
And weltered in the Valley, bluish-white
Like water very silent—spread abroad,
Like water very silent, from the Shrine
Unlighted of Taman to where the stream
Is dammed to fill our cattle-troughs—sent up
White waves that rocked and heaved and stilled themselves,
Till all the Valley glittered like a marsh,
Beneath the moonlight, filled with sluggish mist
Knee-deep, so that men waded as they walked.

That night, the Red Horse grazed above the Dam,
Beyond the cattle-troughs.   Men heard him feed,
And those that heard him sickened where they lay.
Thus came the Sickness to Er-Heb, and slew
Ten men, strong men, and of the women four;
And the Red Horse went hillward with the dawn,
But near the cattle-troughs his hoofprints lay.

That night, the slow mists of the evening dropped,
Dropped as a cloth upon the dead, but rose
A little higher, to a young girl's height;
Till all the Valley glittered like a lake,
Beneath the moonlight, filled with sluggish mist.

That night, the Red Horse grazed beyond the Dam
A stone's-throw from the troughs.   Men heard him feed,
And those that heard him sickened where they lay.
Thus came the Sickness to Er-Heb, and slew
Of man a score, and of the women eight,
And of the children two.

      Because the road
To Gorukh was a road of enemies,
And Ao-Safai was blocked with early snows,
We could not flee from out the Valley.   Death
Smote at us in a slaughter-pen, and Kysh
Was mute as Yabosh, though the goats were slain;
And the Red Horse grazed nightly by the stream,
And later, outward, towards the Unlighted Shrine,
And those that heard him sickened where they lay.

Then said Bisesa to the Priests at dusk,
When the white mist rose up breast-high, and choked
The voices in the houses of the dead:—
"Yabosh and Kysh avail not.   If the Horse
"Reach the Unlighted Shrine we surely die.
"Ye have forgotten of all Gods the chief,
"Taman!"   Here rolled the thunder through the Hills,
And Yabosh shook upon his pedestal.
"Ye have forgotten of all Gods the chief
"Too long."   And all were dumb save one, who cried
On Yabosh with the Sapphire 'twixt His knees,
But found no answer in the smoky roof,
And, being smitten of the sickness, died
Before the altar of the Sapphire Shrine.

Then said Bisesa:—"I am near to Death,
"And have the Wisdom of the Grave for gift
"To bear me on the path my feet must tread.
"If there be wealth on earth, then I am rich,
"For Armod is the first of all Er-Heb;
"If there be beauty on the earth,"—her eyes
Dropped for a moment to the temple floor,—
"Ye know that I am fair.   If there be Love,
"Ye know that love is mine."   The Chief in War,
The Man of Sixty Spears, broke from the press,
And would have clasped her, but the priests withstood,
Saying:—"She has a message from Taman."
Then said Bisesa:—"By my wealth and love
"And beauty, I am chosen of the God
"Taman."   Here rolled the thunder through the Hills
And Kysh fell forward on the Mound of Skulls.

In darkness, and before our Priests, the maid
Between the altars cast her bracelets down,
Therewith the heavy earrings Armod made,
When he young, out of the water-gold

Of Gorukh—threw the breast-plate thick with jade
Upon the turquoise anklets—put aside
The bands of silver on her brow and neck;
And as the trinkets tinkled on the stones,
The thunder of Taman lowed like a bull.

Then said Bisesa, stretching out her hands,
as one in darkness fearing Devils:—"Help!
"O Priests, I am a woman very weak.
"And who am I to know the will of Gods?
"Taman hath called me—whither shall I go?"
The Chief in War, the Man of Sixty Spears,
Howled in his torment, fettered by the Priests,
But dared not come to her to drag her forth,
And dared not lift his spear against the Priests.
Then all men wept.

                        There was a Priest of Kysh
Bent with a hundred winters, hairless, blind,
And taloned as the great Snow-Eagle is.
His seat was nearest to the altar-fires,
And he was counted dumb among the Priests.
But, whether Kysh decreed, or from Taman
The impotent tongue found utterance we know
As little as the bats beneath the eaves.
He cried so that they heard who stood without:—
"To the Unlighted Shrine!" and crept aside
Into the shadow of his fallen God
And whimpered, and Bisesa went her way.

That night, the slow mist of the evening dropped,
Dropped as a cloth upon the dead, and rose
Above the roofs, and by the Unlighted Shrine
Lay as the slimy water of the troughs
When murrain thins the cattle of Er-Heb.
And through the mist men heard the Red Horse feed.

In Armod's house they burned Bisesa's dower,
And killed her black bull Tor, and broke her wheel,
And loosed her hair, as for the marriage-feast,
With cries more loud than mourning for the dead.

Across the fields, from Armod's dwelling-place,
We heard Bisesa weeping where she passed
To seek the Unlighted Shrine; the Red Horse neighed
And followed her, and on the river-mint
His hooves struck dead and heavy in our ears.

Out of the mists of evening, as the star
Of Ao-Safai climbs through the black snow-blurs
To show the Pass is clear, Bisesa stepped
Upon the great grey slope of mortised stone,
The Causeway of Taman.   The Red Horse neighed
Behind her to the Unlighted Shrine—then fled
North to the Mountain where his Stable lies.

They know who dared the anger of Taman,
And watched that night above the clinging mists,
Far up the hill, Bisesa's passing in.

She set her hand upon the cavern door,
 Fouled by a myriad bats and black with time,
Whereon is graved the Glory of Taman
In letters older than the Ao-Safai;
And twice she turned aside and twice she wept,
Cast down upon the threshold, clamouring
For him she loved—the Man of Sixty Spears,
And for her father,—and the black bull Tor,
Hers and her pride.   Yea, twice she turned away
Before the awful darkness of the door,
And the great horror of the Wall of Man
Where Man is made the plaything of Taman,
An Eyeless Face that waits above and laughs.

But the third time she cried and put her palms
Against the hewn stone leaves, and prayed Taman
To spare Er-Heb and take her life for price.

They know who watched, the doors were rent apart
And closed upon Bisesa, and the rain
Broke like a flood across the Valley, washed
The mist away; but louder than the rain
The thunder of Taman filled men with fear.

Some say that from the Unlighted Shrine she cried
For succour, very pitifully, thrice,
And others that she sang and had no fear.
And some that there was neither song nor cry,
But only thunder and the lashing rain.

Howbeit, in the morning men rose up,
Perplexed with horror, crowding to the shrine.
And when Er-Heb was gathered at the doors
The Priests made lamentation and passed in
To a strange Temple and a God they feared
But knew not.

From the crevices the grass
Had thrust the altar-slabs apart, the walls
Were grey with stains unclean, the roof-beams swelled
With many-coloured growth of rottenness,
And lichen veiled the Image of Taman
In leprosy.   The Basin of the Blood
Above the altar held the morning sun:
A winking ruby on its heart.   Below,
Face hid in hands, the maid Bisesa lay.

Er-Heb beyond the Hill of Ao-Safai
Bears witness to the truth, and Ao-Safai
Hath told the men of Gorukh.   Thence the tale
Comes westward o'er the peaks to India.

The Lament of the Border Cattle Thief

1888

O woe is me for the merry life
    I led beyond the Bar,
And a treble woe for my winsome wife
    That weeps at Shalimar.

They have taken away my long jezail,
    My shield and sabre fine,
And heaved me into the Central Jail
    For lifting of the kine.

The steer may low within the byre,
    The Jat may tend his grain,
But there'll be neither loot nor fire
    Till I come back again.

And God have mercy on the Jat
    When once more fetters fall,
And Heaven defend the farmer's hut
    When I am loosed from thrall.

It's woe to bend the stubborn back
    Above the grinching quern,
It's woe to hear the leg-bar clack
    And jingle when I turn!

But for the sorrow and the shame,
    The brand on me and mine,
I'll pay you back in leaping flame
    And loss of the butchered kine.

For every cow I spared before—
    In charity set free—
If I may reach my hold once more
    I'll reive an honest three.

For every time I raised the lowe
    That scared the dusty plain,
By sword and cord, by torch and tow
    I'll light the land with twain!

Ride hard, ride hard to Abazai,
    Young Sahib with the yellow hair—
Lie close, lie close as Khattacks[1] lie,
    Fat herds below Bonair!

The one I'll shoot at twilight-tide,
    At dawn I'll drive the other;
The black shall mourn for hoof and hide,
    The white man for his brother.

'Tis war, red war, I'll give you then,
    War till my sinews fail;
For the wrong you have done to a chief of men,
    And a thief of the Zukka Kheyl.

And if I fall to your hand afresh
    I give you leave for the sin,
That you cram my throat with the foul pig's flesh,
    And swing me in the skin!

The Feet of the Young Men

1897

Now the Four-way Lodge is opened, now the Hunting Winds are loose—
    Now the Smokes of Spring go up to clear the brain;
Now the Young Men's hearts are troubled for the whisper of the Trues,
    Now the Red Gods make their medicine again!
Who hath seen the beaver busied?   Who hath watched the black-tail
    mating?
    Who hath lain alone to hear the wild-goose cry?
Who hath worked the chosen water where the ouananiche is waiting,
    Or the sea-trout's jumping-crazy for the fly?

---

[1] A tribe on the Indian frontier.

He must go—go—go away from here?
  On the other side the world he's overdue.
Send your road is clear before you when the old Spring-fret comes o'er you.
  And the Red Gods call for you!

So for one the wet sail arching through the rainbow round the bow,
  And for the creak of snow-shoes on the crust;
And for one the lakeside lilies where the bull-moose waits the cow,
  And for one the mule-train coughing in the dust.

Who hath smelt wood-smoke at twilight?   Who hath heard the birch-log
    burning?
  Who is quick to read the noises of the night?
Let him follow with the others, for the Young Men's feet are turning
  To the camps of proved desire and known delight!

Let him go—go, etc.

I

Do you know the blackened timber—do you know that racing stream
  With the raw, right-angled log-jam at the end;
And the bar of sun-warmed shingle where a man may bask and dream
  To the click of shod canoe-poles round the bend?
It is there that we are going with our rods and reels and traces,
  To a silent, smoky Indian that we know—
To a couch of new-pulled hemlock, with the starlight on our faces,
  For the Red Gods call us out and we must go!

They must go—go, etc.

II

Do you know the shallow Baltic where the seas are steep and short,
  Where the bluff, lee-boarded fishing-luggers ride?
Do you know the joy of threshing leagues to leeward of your port
  On a coast you've lost the chart of overside?
It is here that I am going, with an extra hand to bale her—
  Just one able long-shore loafer, that I know.
He can take his chance of drowning, while I sail and sail and sail her,
  For the Red Gods call me out and I must go!

He must go—go, etc.

III

Do you know the pile-built village where the sago-dealers trade—
  Do you know the reek of fish and wet bamboo?
Do you know the streaming stillness of the orchid-scented glade
  When the blazoned, bird-winged butterflies flap through?

It is there that I am going with my camphor, net, and boxes,
    To a gentle, yellow pirate that I know—
To my little wailing lemurs, to my palms and flying-foxes,
    For the Red Gods call me out and I must go!

He must go—go, etc.

IV

Do you know the world's white roof-tree—do you know that windy rift
    Where the baffling mountain-eddies chop and change?
Do you know the long day's patience, belly-down on frozen drift,
    While the heads of heads is feeding out of range?
It is there that I am going, where the boulders and the snow lie,
    With a trusty, nimble tracker that I know.
I have sworn an oath, to keep it on the Horns of Ovis Poli,
    And the Red Gods call me out and I must go!

He must go—go, etc.

Now the Four-way Lodge is opened—now the Smokes of Council rise—
    Pleasant smokes, ere yet 'twixt trail and trail they choose—
Now the girths and ropes are tested: now they pack their last supplies:
    Now our Young Men go to dance before the Trues!
Who shall meet them at those altars—who shall light them to that shrine?
    Velvet-footed, who shall guide them to their goal?
Unto each the voice and vision: unto each his spoor and sign—
Lonely mountain in the Northland, misty sweat-bath 'neath the Line—
    And to each a man that knows his naked soul!

White or yellow, black or copper, he is waiting, as a lover,
    Smoke of funnel, dust of hooves, or beat of train—
Where the high grass hides the horseman or the glaring flats discover—
Where the steamer hails the landing, or the surf-boat brings the rover—
Where the rails run out in sand-drift . . . Quick! ah, heave the camp-kit
        over,
    For the Red Gods make their medicine again!

And we go—go—away from here!
    On the other side the world we're overdue!
Send the road is clear before you when the old Spring-fret comes o'er you.
    And the Red Gods call for you!

A Boy Scouts' Patrol Song

1913

These are *our* regulations—
   There's just one law for the Scout
And the first and the last, and the present and the past,
And the future and the perfect is "Look out!"
   I, thou and he, look out!
   We, ye and they, look out!
   Though you didn't or you wouldn't
   Or you hadn't or you couldn't;
   You jolly well *must* look out!

Look out, when you start for the day,
   That your kit is packed to your mind;
There is no use going away
   With half of it left behind.
Look out that your laces are tight,
   And your boots are easy and stout,
Or you'll end with a blister at night.
   (Chorus) *All* Patrols look out!

Look out for the birds of the air,
   Look out for the beasts of the field—
They'll tell you how and where
   The other side's concealed.
When the blackbird bolts from the copse,
   Or the cattle are staring about,
The wise commander stops
   And *(chorus)* All Patrols look out!

Look out when your front is clear,
   And you feel you are bound to win.
Look out for your flank and your rear—
   That's where surprises begin.
For the rustle that isn't a rat,
   For the splash that isn't a trout,
For the boulder that may be a hat
   (Chorus) All Patrols look out!

For the innocent knee-high grass,
   For the ditch that never tells,
Look out! Look out ere you pass—
   And look out for everything else!
A sign mis-read as you run

May turn retreat to a rout—
For all things under the sun
   (Chorus)   All Patrols look out!

Look out when your temper goes
   At the end of a losing game;
When your boots are too tight for your toes;
   And you answer and argue and blame.
It's the hardest part of the Law,
   But it has to be learnt by the Scout—
For whining and shirking and "jaw"
   (Chorus)   All Patrols look out!

The Truce Of The Bear

1898

Yearly, with tent and rifle, our careless white men go
By the Pass called Muttianee, to shoot in the vale below.
Yearly by Muttianee he follows our white men in—
Matun, the old blind beggar, bandaged from brow to chin.

Eyeless, noseless, and lipless—toothless, broken of speech,
Seeking a dole at the doorway he mumbles his tale to each;
Over and over the story, ending as he began:
"Make ye no truce with Adam-zad—the Bear that walks like a Man!

"There was a flint in my musket—pricked and primed was the pan,
When I went hunting Adam-zad—the Bear that stands like a Man.
I looked my last on the timber, I looked my last on the snow,
When I went hunting Adam-zad fifty summers ago!

"I knew his times and his seasons, as he knew mine, that fed
By night in the ripened maizefield and robbed my house of bread.
I knew his strength and cunning, as he knew mine, that crept
At dawn to the crowded goat-pens and plundered while I slept.

"Up from his stony playground—down from his well-digged lair—
Out on the naked ridges ran Adam-zad the Bear—
Groaning, grunting, and roaring, heavy with stolen meals,
Two long marches to northward, and I was at his heels!

Two long marches to northward, at the fall of the second night,
I came on mine enemy Adam-zad all panting from his flight.
There was a charge in the musket—pricked and primed was the pan—
My finger crooked on the trigger—when he reared up like a man.

"Horribly, hairy, human, with paws like hands in prayer,
Making his supplication rose Adam-zad the Bear!
I looked at the swaying shoulders, at the paunch's swag and swing,
And my heart was touched with pity for the monstrous, pleading thing.

"Touched with pity and wonder, I did not fire then . . .
I have looked no more on women—I have walked no more with men.
Nearer he tottered and nearer, with paws like hands that pray—
From brow to jaw that steel-shod paw, it ripped my face away!

"Sudden, silent, and savage, searing as flame the blow—
Faceless I fell before his feet, fifty summers ago.
I heard him grunt and chuckle—I heard him pass to his den.
He left me blind to the darkened years and the little mercy of men.

"Now ye go down in the morning with guns of the newer style,
That load (I have felt) in the middle and range (I have heard) a mile?
Luck to the white man's rifle, that shoots so fast and true,
But—pay, and I lift my bandage and show what the Bear can do!"

(Flesh like a slag in the furnace, knobbed and withered and grey—
Matun, the old blind beggar, he gives good worth for his pay.)
"Rouse him at noon in the bushes, follow and press him hard—
Not for his raging and roarings flinch ye from Adam-zad.

"But (pay, and I put back the bandage) *this* is the time to fear,
When he stands up like a tired man, tottering near and near;
When he stands up as pleading, in wavering, man-brute guise,
When he veils the hate and cunning of his little, swinish eyes;

"When he shows as seeking quarter, with paws like hands in prayer,
That is the time of peril—the time of the Truce of the Bear!"

Eyeless, noseless, and lipless, asking a dole at the door,
Matun, the old blind beggar, he tells it o'er and o'er;
Fumbling and feeling the rifles, warming his hands at the flame,
Hearing our careless white men talk of the morrow's game;

Over and over the story, ending as he began:—
"There is no truce with Adam-zad, the Bear that looks like a Man!"

Russia To The Pacifists

1918

God rest you, peaceful gentlemen, let nothing you dismay,
But—leave your sports a little while—the dead are borne this way!
Armies dead and Cities dead, past all count or care.

God rest you, merry gentlemen, what portent see you there?
  Singing:—Break ground for a wearied host
  That have no ground to keep.
  Give them the rest that they covet most . . .
  And who shall be next to sleep, good sirs,
  In such a trench to sleep?

God rest you, peaceful gentlemen, but give us leave to pass.
We go to dig a nation's grave as great as England was.
For this Kingdom and this Glory and this Power and this Pride,
Three hundred years it flourished—in three hundred days it died.
  Singing:—Pour oil for a frozen throng
  That lie about the ways.
  Give them the warmth they have lacked so long . . .
  And what shall be next to blaze, good sirs,
  On such a pyre to blaze?

God rest you, thoughtful gentlemen, and send your sleep is light!
Remains of this dominion no shadow, sound, or sight,
Except the sound of weeping and the sight of burning fire,
And the shadow of a people that is trampled into mire.
  Singing:—Break bread for a starving folk
  That perish in the field.
  Give them their food as they take the yoke . . .
  And who shall be next to yield, good sirs,
  For such a bribe to yield?

God rest you, merry gentlemen, and keep you in your mirth!
Was ever Kingdom turned so soon to ashes, blood, and earth?
'Twixt the summer and the snow—seeding-time and frost—
Arms and victual, hope and counsel, name and country lost!
  Singing:—*Let down by the foot and the head—*
  Shovel and smooth it all!
  So do we bury a Nation dead . . .
  And who shall be next to fall, good sirs,
  With your good help to fall?

The Peace Of Dives

1903

The word came down to Dives in Torment where he lay:
"Our World is full of wickedness, My Children maim and slay,
  "And the Saint and Seer and Prophet
  "Can make no better of it
"Than to sanctify and prophesy and pray.

"Rise up, rise up, thou Dives, and take again thy gold,
"And thy women and thy housen as they were to thee of old.
  "It may be grace hath found thee
  "In the furnace where We bound thee,
"And that thou shalt bring the peace My Son foretold."

Then merrily rose Dives and leaped from out his fire,
And walked abroad with diligence to do the Lord's desire;
  And anon the battles ceased,
  And the captives were released,
And earth had rest from Goshen to Gadire.

The Word came down to Satan that raged and roared alone,
'Mid the shouting of the peoples by the cannon overthrown
  (But the Prophets, Saints, and Seers
  Set each other by the ears,
For each would claim the marvel as his own):

"Rise up, rise up, thou Satan, upon the Earth to go,
"And prove the Peace if it be good or no:
  "For all that he hath planned
  "We deliver to thy hand,
"As thy skill shall serve, to break it or bring low."

Then mightily rose Satan and about the Earth he hied,
And breathed on Kings in idleness and Princes drunk with pride.
  But for all the wrong he breathed
  There was never sword unsheathed,
And the fires he lighted flickered out and died.

Then terribly rose Satan, and darkened Earth afar,
Till he came on cunning Dives where the money-changers are;
  And he saw men pledge their gear
  For the gold that buys the spear,
And the helmet and the habergeon of war.

Yea, to Dives came the Persian and the Syrian and the Mede—
And their hearts were nothing altered, nor their cunning nor their greed—
  And they pledged their flocks and farms
  For the King-compelling arms,
And Dives lent according to their need.

Then Satan said to Dives:—"Return again with me,
"Who hast broken His Commandment in the day He set thee free,
  "Who grindest for thy greed
  "Man's belly-pinch and need,
"And the blood of Man to filthy usury!"

Then softly answered Dives where the money-changers sit:—
"My Refuge is Our Master, O My Master in the Pit.
   "But behold all Earth is laid
   "In the Peace which I have made,
"And behold I wait on thee to trouble it!"

Then angrily turned Satan, and about the Seas he fled,
To shake the new-sown peoples with insult, doubt, and dread;
   But, for all the sleight he used,
   There was never squadron loosed,
And the brands he flung flew dying and fell dead.

But to Dives came Atlantis and the Captains of the West—
And their hates were nothing weakened nor their angers nor their unrest—
   And they pawned their utmost trade
   For the dry, decreeing blade;
And Dives lent and took of them their best.

Then Satan said to Dives:—"Declare thou by The Name,
"The secret of thy subtlety that turneth mine to shame.
   "It is known through all the Hells
   "How my peoples mocked my spells,
"And my faithless Kings denied me ere I came."

Then answered cunning Dives: "Do not gold and hate abide
"At the heart of every Magic, yea, and senseless fear beside?
   "With gold and fear and hate
   "I have harnessed state to state,
"And by hate and fear and gold their hates are tied.

"For hate men seek a weapon, for fear they seek a shield—
"Keener blades and broader targes than their frantic neighbours wield—
   "For gold I arm their hands,
   "And for gold I buy their lands,
"And for gold I sell their enemies the yield.

"Their nearest foes may purchase, or their furthest friends may lease,
"One by one from Ancient Accad to the Islands of the Seas.
   "And their covenants they make
   "For the naked iron's sake,
"But I—I trap them armoured into peace.

"The flocks that Egypt pledged me to Assyria I drave,
"And Pharaoh hath the increase of the herds that Sargon gave.
   "Not for Ashdod overthrown
   "Will the Kings destroy their own,
"Or their peoples wake the strife they feign to brave.

"Is not Carchemish like Calno? For the steeds of their desire
"They have sold me seven harvests that I sell to Crowning Tyre;
   "And the Tyrian sweeps the plains
   "With a thousand hired wains,
"And the Cities keep the peace and—share the hire.

"Hast thou seen the pride of Moab? For the swords about his path,
"His bond is to Philistia, in half of all he hath.
   "And he dare not draw the sword
   "Till Gaza give the word,
"And he show release from Askalon and Gath.

"Wilt thou call again thy peoples, wilt thou craze anew thy Kings?
"Lo! my lightnings pass before thee, and their whistling servant brings,
   "Ere the drowsy street hath stirred,
   "Every masked and midnight word,
"And the nations break their fast upon these things.

"So I make a jest of Wonder, and a mock of Time and Space,
"The roofless Seas an hostel, and the Earth a market-place,
   "Where the anxious traders know
   "Each is surety for his foe,
"And none may thrive without his fellow's grace.

"Now this is all my subtlety and this is all my wit,
"God give thee good enlightenment, My Master in the Pit.
   "But behold all Earth is laid
   "In the Peace which I have made,
"And behold I wait on thee to trouble it!"

A Song Of The White Men

1899

Now, this is the cup the White Men drink
   When they go to right a wrong,
And that is the cup of the old world's hate—
   Cruel and strained and strong.
We have drunk that cup—and a bitter, bitter cup—
   And tossed the dregs away.
But well for the world when the White Men drink
   To the dawn of the White Man's day!

Now, this is the road that the White Men tread
   When they go to clean a land—

Iron underfoot and levin overhead
  And the deep on either hand.
We have trod that road—and a wet and windy road—
  Our chosen star for guide.
Oh, well for the world when the White Men tread
  Their highway side by side!

Now, this is the faith that the White Men hold
  When they build their homes afar—
"Freedom for ourselves and freedom for our sons
  And, failing freedom, War."
We have proved our faith—bear witness to our faith,
  Dear souls of freemen slain!
Oh, well for the world when the White Men join
  To prove their faith again!

The Rowers

1902

(When Germany proposed that England should help her in a naval demonstration to collect debts from Venezuela.)

The banked oars fell an hundred strong,
  And backed and threshed and ground,
But bitter was the rowers' song
  As they brought the war-boat round.

They had no heart for the rally and roar
  That makes the whale-bath smoke—
When the great blades and hold and leave
  As one on the racing stroke.

They sang:—"What reckoning do you keep,
  And steer her by what star,
If we come unscathed from the Southern deep
  To be wrecked on a Baltic bar?

"Last night you swore our voyage was done,
  But seaward still we go.
And you tell us now of a secret vow
  You have made with an open foe!

"That we must lie off a lightless coast
  And haul and back and veer,
At the will of the breed that have wronged us most
  For a year and a year and a year!

"There was a never a shame in Christendie
　　They laid not to our door—
And you say we must take the winter sea
　　And sail with them once more?

"Look South! The gale is scarce o'erpast
　　That stripped and laid us down,
When we stood forth but they stood fast
　　And prayed to see us drown.

"Our dead they mocked are scarcely cold,
　　Our wounds are bleeding yet—
And you tell us now that our strength is sold
　　To help them press for a debt!

"'Neath all the flags of all mankind
　　That use upon the seas,
Was there no other fleet to find
　　That you strike hands with these?

"Of evil times that men can choose
　　On evil fate to fall,
What brooding Judgment let you choose
　　To pick the worst of all?

"In sight of peace—from the Narrow Seas
　　O'er half the world to run—
With a cheated crew, to league anew
　　With the Goth and the shameless Hun!"

An Imperial Rescript

1890

Now this is the tale of the Council the German Kaiser decreed,
To ease the strong of their burden, to help the weak in their need,
He sent a word to the peoples, who struggle, and pant, and sweat,
That the straw might be counted fairly and the tally of bricks be set.

The Lords of Their Hands assembled. From the East and the West they drew—
Baltimore, Lille, and Essen, Brummagem, Clyde, and Crewe.
And some were black from the furnace, and some were brown from the soil,
And some were blue from the dye-vat; but all were wearied of toil.

And the young King said:—"I have found it, the road to the rest ye seek:
"The strong shall wait for the weary, the hale shall halt for the weak:
"With the even tramp of an army where no man breaks from the line,
"Ye shall march to peace and plenty in the bond of brotherhood—sign!"

The paper lay on the table, the strong heads bowed thereby,
And a wail went up from the peoples:—"Ay, sign—give rest, for we die!"
A hand was stretched to the goose-quill, a fist was cramped to scrawl,
When—the laugh of a blue-eyed maiden ran clear through the
    Council-hall.

And each one heard Her laughing as each one saw Her plain—
Sadie, Mimi, or Olga, Gretchen, or Mary Jane.
And the Spirit of Man That is in Him to the light of the vision woke;
And the men drew back from the paper, as Yankee delegate spoke:—

"There's a girl in Jersey City who works on the telephone;
"We're going to hitch our horses and dig for a house of our own,
"With gas and water connections, and steam-heat through to the top;
"And, W. Hohenzollern, I guess I shall work till I drop."

And an English delegate thundered:—"The weak an' the lame be blowed!
"I've a berth in the Sou'-West workshops, a home in the Wandsworth
    Road;
"And till the 'sociation has footed my buryin' bill,
"I work for the kids an' the missus. Pull up! I'll be damned if I will!"

And over the German benches the bearded whisper ran:—
"Lager, der girls und der dollars, dey makes or dey breaks a man.
"If Schmitt haf collared der dollars, he collars der girl deremit;
"But if Schmitt bust in der pizness, we collars der girl from Schmitt."

They passed one resolution:—"Your sub-committee believe
"You can lighten the curse of Adam when you've lifted the curse of Eve.
"But till we are built like the angels—with hammer and chisel and pen,
"We will work for ourselves and a woman, for ever and ever, amen."

Now this is the tale of the Council the German Kaiser held—
The day that they razored the Grindstone, the day that the Cat was belled,
The day of the Figs from Thistles, the day of the Twisted Sands,
The day that the laugh of a maiden made light of the Lords of Their
    Hands.

A Death-Bed

1918

"This is the State above the Law.
  The State exists for the State alone."
[*This is a gland at the back of the jaw,*
  And an answering lump by the collar-bone.]

Some die shouting in gas or fire;
  Some die silent, by shell and shot.
Some die desperate, caught on the wire;
  Some die suddenly. This will not.

"Regis suprema voluntas Lex"
  [*It will follow the regular course of—throats.*]
Some die pinned by the broken decks,
  Some die sobbing between the boats.

Some die eloquent, pressed to death
  By the sliding trench, as their friends can hear.
Some die wholly in half a breath.
  Some—give trouble for half a year.

"There is neither Evil nor Good in life.
  Except as the needs of the State ordain."
[*Since it is rather too late for the knife,*
  All we can do is to mask the pain.]

Some die saintly in faith and hope—
  Some die thus in a prison-yard—
Some die broken by rape or the rope;
  Some die easily. This dies hard.

"I will dash to pieces who bar my way.
  Woe to the traitor! Woe to the weak!"
[*Let him write what he wishes to say.*
  It tires him out if he tries to speak.]

Some die quietly.   Some abound
  In loud self-pity.   Others spread
Bad morale through the cots around . . .
  This is a type that is better dead.

"The war was forced on me by my foes.
  All that I sought was the right to live."
[*Don't be afraid of a triple dose;*
  The pain will neutralize half we give.

Here are the needles.   See that he dies
  While the effects of the drug endure . . .
What is the question he asks with his eyes?—
  Yes, All-Highest, to God, be sure.]

Et Dona Ferentes

1896

In extended observation of the ways and works of man,
From the Four-mile Radius roughly to the Plains of Hindustan:
I have drunk with mixed assemblies, seen the racial ruction rise.
And the men of half Creation damning half Creation's eyes.

I have watched them in their tantrums, all that pentecostal crew,
French, Italian, Arab, Spaniard, Dutch and Greek, and Russ and Jew,
Celt and savage, buff and ochre, cream and yellow, mauve and white,
But it never really mattered till the English grew polite;

Till the men with polished toppers, till the men in long frock-coats,
Till the men who do not duel, till the men who war with votes,
Till the breed that takes their pleasure as Saint Lawrence took his grid,
Began to "beg your pardon" and—the knowing croupier hid.

Then the bandsmen with their fiddles, and the girls that bring the beer,
Felt the psychological moment, left the lit Casino clear;
But the uninstructed alien, from the Teuton to the Gaul,
Was entrapped, once more, my country, by that suave, deceptive drawl.

As it was in ancient Suez or 'neath wilder, milder skies,
I "observe with apprehension" how the racial ructions rise;
And with keener apprehension, if I read the times aright,
Hear the Old Casino order: "Watch your man, but be polite.

"Keep your temper.   Never answer (*that* was why they spat and swore).
Don't hit first, but move together (there's no hurry) to the door.
Back to back, and facing outward while the linguist tells 'em how—
'Nous sommes allong ar notre batteau, nous ne voulong pas un row.' "

So the hard, pent rage ate inward, till some idiot went too far . . .
"Let 'em have it!" and they had it, and the same was merry war—
Fist, umbrella, cane, decanter, lamp and beer-mug, chair and boot—
Till behind the fleeing legions rose the long, hoarse yell for loot.

Then the oil-cloth with its numbers, like a banner fluttered free;
Then the grand piano cantered, on three castors, down the quay;
White, and breathing through their nostrils, silent, systematic, swift—
They removed, effaced, abolished all that man could have or lift.

Oh, my country, bless the training that from cot to castle runs—
The pitfall of the stranger but the bulwark of thy sons—
Measured speech and ordered action, sluggish soul and unperturbed,
Till we wake our Island-Devil—nowise cool for being curbed!

When the heir of all the ages "has the honour to remain,"
When he will not hear an insult, though men make it ne'er so plain,
When his lips are schooled to meekness, when his back is bowed to
    blows—
Well the keen *aas-vogels* know it—well the waiting jackal knows.

Build on the flanks of Etna where the sullen smoke-puffs float—
Or bathe in tropic waters where the lean fin dogs the boat—
Cock the gun that is not loaded, cook the frozen dynamite—
But oh, beware my Country, when my Country grows polite!

The Holy War

1917

("*For here lay the excellent wisdom of him that built Mansoul, that the walls could never be broken down nor hurt by the most mighty adverse potentate unless the townsmen gave their consent thereto.*"—BUNYAN'S *Holy War*.)

A Tinker out of Bedford,
    A vagrant oft in quod,
A private under Fairfax,
    A minister of God—
Two hundred years and thirty
    Ere Armageddon came
His single hand portrayed it,
    And Bunyan was his name!

He mapped for those who follow,
    The world in which we are—
"This famous town of Mansoul"
    That takes the Holy War.
Her true and traitor people,
    The Gates along her wall,
From Eye Gate unto Feel Gate,
    John Bunyan showed them all.

All enemy divisions,
   Recruits of every class,
And highly screened positions
   For flame or poison-gas;
The craft that we call modern,
   The crimes that we call new,
John Bunyan had 'em typed and filed
   In Sixteen Eighty-two.

Likewise the Lords of Looseness
   That hamper faith and works,
The Perseverance-Doubters,
   And Present-Comfort shirks,
With brittle intellectuals
   Who crack beneath a strain—
John Bunyan met that helpful set
   In Charles the Second's reign.

Emmanuel's vanguard dying
   For right and not for rights,
My Lord Appollyon lying
   To the State-kept Stockholmites,
The Pope, the swithering Neutrals,
   The Kaiser and his Gott—
Their rôles, their goals, their naked souls—
   He knew and drew the lot.

Now he hath left his quarters,
   In Bunhill Fields to lie,
The wisdom that he taught us
   Is proven prophecy—
One watchword through our Armies,
   One answer from our Lands:—
"No dealings with Diabolus
   As long as Mansoul stands!"

A pedlar from a hovel,
   The lowest of the low—
The Father of the Novel,
   Salvation's first Defoe—
Eight blinded generations
   Ere Armageddon came.
He showed us how to meet it.
   And Bunyan was his name!

France

1913

Broke to every known mischance, lifted over all
By the light sane joy of life, the buckler of the Gaul;
Furious in luxury, merciless in toil,
Terrible with strength that draws from her tireless soil;
Strictest judge of her own worth, gentlest of man's mind,
First to follow Truth and last to leave old Truths behind—
France, beloved of every soul that loves its fellow-kind!

Ere our birth (rememberest thou?) side by side we lay
Fretting in the womb of Rome to begin our fray.
Ere men knew our tongues apart, our one task was known—
Each to mould the other's fate as he wrought his own.
To this end we stirred mankind till all Earth was ours,
Till our world-end strifes begat wayside Thrones and Powers—
Puppets that we made or broke to bar the other's path—
Necessary, outpost-folk, hirelings of our wrath.
To this end we stormed the seas, tack for tack, and burst
Through the doorways of new worlds, doubtful which was first,
Hand on hilt (rememberest thou?) ready for the blow—
Sure, whatever else we met, we should meet our foe.
Spurred or balked at every stride by the other's strength,
So we rode the ages down and every ocean's length!

Where did you refrain from us or we refrain from you?
Ask the wave that has not watched war between us two!
Others held us for a while, but with weaker charms,
These we quitted at the call for each other's arms.
Eager toward the known delight, equally we strove—
Each the other's mystery, terror, need, and love.
To each other's open court with our proofs we came.
Where could we find honour else, or men to test our claim?
From each other's throat we wrenched—valour's last reward—
That extorted word of praise gasped 'twixt lunge and guard.
In each other's cup we poured mingled blood and tears,
Brutal joys, unmeasured hopes, intolerable fears—
All that soiled or salted life for a thousand years.
Proved beyond the need of proof, matched in every clime,
O Companion, we have lived greatly through all time!

Yoked in knowledge and remorse, now we come to rest,
Laughing at old villainies that Time has turned to jest;

Pardoning old necessities no pardon can efface—
That undying sin we shared in Rouen market-place.

Now we watch the new year shape, wondering if they hold
Fiercer lightnings in their heart than we launched of old.
Now we hear new voices rise, question, boast or gird,
As we raged (rememberest thou?) when our crowds were stirred.
Now we count new keels afloat, and new hosts on land,
Massed like ours (rememberest thou?) when our strokes were planned.
We were schooled for dear life's sake, to know each other's blade.
What can Blood and Iron make more than we have made?
We have learned by keenest use to know each other's mind.
What shall Blood and Iron loose that we cannot bind?
We who swept each other's coast, sacked each other's home,
Since the sword of Brennus clashed on the scales at Rome,
Listen, count and close again, wheeling girth to girth,
In the linked and steadfast guard set for peace on earth!

Broke to every known mischance, lifted over all
By the light sane joy of life, the buckler of the Gaul;
Furious in luxury, merciless in toil,
Terrible with strength renewed from a tireless soil;
Strictest judge of her own worth, gentlest of man's mind,
First to face the Truth and last to leave old Truths behind—
France, beloved of every soul that loves or serves its kind!

"Before A Midnight Breaks In Storm"

1903

Before a midnight breaks in storm,
   Or herded sea in wrath,
Ye know what wavering gusts inform
   The greater tempest's path;
     Till the loosed wind
     Drive all from mind,
Except Distress, which, so will prophets cry,
O'ercame them, houseless, from the unhinting sky.

Ere rivers league against the land
   In piratry of flood,
Ye know what waters steal and stand
   Where seldom water stood.
     Yet who will note,
     Till fields afloat,

And washen carcass and the returning well,
Trumpet what these poor heralds strove to tell?

Ye know who use the Crystal Ball
  (To peer by stealth on Doom),
The Shade that, shaping first of all,
  Prepares an empty room.
    When doth It pass
    Like breath from glass,
But, on the extorted Vision bowed intent,
No man considers why It came or went.

Before the years reborn behold
  Themselves with stranger eye,
And the sport-making Gods of old,
  Like Samson slaying, die,
    Many shall hear
    The all-pregnant sphere,
Bow to the birth and sweat, but—speech denied—
Sit dumb or—dealt in part—fall weak and wide.

Yet instant to fore-shadowed need
  The eternal balance swings;
That wingèd men the Fates may breed
  So soon as Fate hath wings.
    These shall possess
    Our littleness,
And in the imperial task (as worthy) lay
Up our lives' all to piece one giant Day.

The Bell Buoy

1896

They christened my brother of old—
  And a saintly name he bears—
They gave him his place to hold
  At the head of the belfry-stairs,
  Where the minster-towers stand
And the breeding kestrels cry.
  Would I change with my brother a league inland?
(*Shoal!* *'Ware shoal!*) Not I!

In the flush of the hot June prime,
  O'er sleek flood-tides afire,

I hear him hurry the chime
  To the bidding of checked Desire;
  Till the sweated ringers tire
And the wild bob-majors die.
  Could I wait for my turn in the godly choir?
(*Shoal!*—'*Ware shoal!*) Not I!

When the smoking scud is blown—
  When the greasy wind-rack lowers—
Apart and at peace and alone,
  He counts the changeless hours.
  He wars with darkling Powers
(I war with a darkling sea);
  Would he stoop to my work in the gusty mirk?
(*Shoal!* '*Ware shoal!*) Not he!

There was never a priest to pray,
  There was never a hand to toll,
When they made me guard of the bay,
  And moored me over the shoal.
  I rock, I reel, and I roll—
My four great hammers ply—
  Could I speak or be still at the Church's will?
(*Shoal!* '*Ware shoal!*) Not I!

The landward marks have failed,
  The fog-bank glides unguessed,
The seaward lights are veiled,
  The spent deep feigns her rest:
  But my ear is laid to her breast,
I lift to the swell—I cry!
  Could I wait in sloth on the Church's oath?
(*Shoal!* '*Ware shoal!*) Not I!

At the careless end of night
  I thrill to the nearing screw;
I turn in the clearing light
  And I call to the drowsy crew;
  And the mud boils foul and blue
As the blind bows backs away.
  Will they give me their thanks if they clear the banks?
(*Shoal!* '*Ware shoal!*) Not they!

The beach-pools cake and skim,
  The bursting spray-heads freeze,
I gather on crown and rim
  The grey, grained ice of the seas,

Where, sheathed from bitt to trees,
The plunging colliers lie.
Would I barter my place for Church's grace?
(*Shoal!   'Ware shoal!*)   Not I!

Through the blur of the whirling snow,
    Or the black of the inky sleet,
The lanterns gather and grow,
    And I look for the homeward fleet.
    Rattle of block and sheet—
"Ready about—stand by!"
    Shall I ask them a fee ere they fetch the quay?
(*Shoal!   'Ware shoal!*)   Not I!

I dip and I surge and I swing
    In the rip of the racing tide,
By the gates of doom I sing,
    On the horns of death I ride.
    A ship-length overside,
Between the course and the sand,
    Fretted and bound I bide
        Peril whereof I cry.
Would I change with my brother a league inland?
(*Shoal!   'Ware shoal!*)   Not I!

The Old Issue

OCTOBER 9, 1899

(*Outbreak of Boer War*)

"Here is nothing new nor aught unproven," say the Trumpets,
    "Many feet have worn it and the road is old indeed.
"It is the King—the King we schooled aforetime!"
    (Trumpets in the marshes—in the eyot at Runnymede!)

"Here is neither haste, nor hate, nor anger," peal the Trumpets,
    "Pardon for his penitence or pity for his fall.
"It is the King!"—inexorable Trumpets—
    (Trumpet round the scaffold at the dawning by Whitehall!)

"He hath veiled the Crown and his the Sceptre," warn the Trumpets,
    "He hath changed the fashion of the lies that cloak his will.
"Hard die the Kings—ah, hard—dooms hard!" declare the Trumpets,
    (Trumpet at the gang-plank where the brawling troop-decks fill!)

Ancient and Unteachable, abide—abide the Trumpets!
  Once again the Trumpets, for the shuddering ground-swell brings
Clamour over ocean of the harsh, pursuing Trumpets—
  Trumpets of the Vanguard that have sworn no truce with Kings!

All we have of freedom, all we use or know—
This our fathers bought for us long and long ago.

Ancient Right unnoticed as the breath we draw—
Leave to live by no man's leave, underneath the Law—

Lance and torch and tumult, steel and grey-goose wing,
Wrenched it, inch and ell and all, slowly from the King.

Till our fathers 'stablished, after bloody years,
How our King is one with us, first among his peers.

So they bought us freedom—not at little cost—
Wherefore must we watch the King, lest our gain be lost.

Over all things certain, this is sure indeed,
Suffer not the old King: for we know the breed.

Give no ear to bondsmen bidding us endure,
Whining "He is weak and far"; crying "Time shall cure."

(Time himself is witness, till the battle joins,
Deeper strikes the rottenness in the people's loins.)

Give no heed to bondsmen masking war with peace.
Suffer not the old King here or overseas.

They that beg us barter—wait his yielding mood—
Pledge the years we hold in trust—pawn our brother's blood—

Howso' great their clamour, whatsoe'er their claim,
Suffer not the old King under any name!

Here is naught unproven—here is naught to learn.
It is written what shall fall if the King return.

He shall mark our goings, question whence we came,
Set his guards about us, as in Freedom's name.

He shall take a tribute; toll of all our ware;
He shall change our gold for arms—arms we may not bear.

He shall break his Judges if they cross his word;
He shall rule above the Law calling on the Lord.

He shall peep and mutter; and the night shall bring
Watchers 'neath our window, lest we mock the King—

Hate and all division; hosts of hurrying spies;
Money poured in secret; carrion breeding flies.

Strangers of his counsel, hirelings of his pay,
These shall deal our Justice: sell—deny—delay.

We shall drink dishonour, we shall eat abuse
For the Land we took to—for the Tongue we use.

We shall take our station, dirt beneath his feet,
While his hired captains jeer us in the street.

Cruel in the shadow, crafty in the sun,
Far beyond his borders shall his teachings run.

Sloven, sullen, savage, secret, uncontrolled,
Laying on a new land evil of the old—

Long forgotten bondage, dwarfing heart and brain—
All our fathers died to loose he shall bind again.

Here is naught at venture, random nor untrue—
Swings the wheel full-circle, brims the cup anew.

Here is naught unproven, here is nothing hid:
Step for step and word for word—so the old Kings did!

Step by step, and word by word: who is ruled may read.
Suffer not the old Kings: for we know the breed—

All the right they promise—all the wrong they bring.
Stewards of the Judgment, suffer not this King!

The Lesson

1899–1902

(Boer War)

Let us admit it fairly, as a business people should,
We have no end of a lesson: it will do us no end of good.

Not on a single issue, or in one direction or twain,
But conclusively, comprehensively, and several times and again,
Were all our most holy illusions knocked higher than Gilderoy's kite.
We have a jolly good lesson, and it serves us jolly well right!

This was not bestowed us under the trees, nor yet in the shade of a tent,
But swingingly, over eleven degrees of a bare brown continent.
From Lamberts to Delagoa Bay, and from Pietersburg to Sutherland,

Fell the phenomenal lesson we learned—with a fulness accorded no other land.

It was our fault, and our very great fault, and *not* the judgment of Heaven.
We made an Army in our image, on an island nine by seven,
Which faithfully mirrored its maker's ideals, equipment, and mental attitude—
And so we got our lesson: and we ought to accept it with gratitude.

We have spent two hundred million pounds to prove the fact once more,
That horses are quicker than men afoot, since two and two make four;
And horses have four legs, and men have two legs, and two into four goes twice,
And nothing over except our lesson—and very cheap at the price.

For remember (this our children shall know: we are too near for that knowledge)
Not our mere astonied camps, but Council and Creed and College—
All the obese, unchallenged old things that stifle and overlie us—
Have felt the effects of the lesson we got—an advantage no money could buy us!

Then let us develop this marvellous asset which we alone command,
And which, it may subsequently transpire, will be worth as much as the Rand.
Let us approach this pivotal fact in a humble yet hopeful mood—
We have had no end of a lesson. It will do us no end of good!

It was our fault, and our very great fault—and now we must turn it to use.
We have forty million reasons for failure, but not a single excuse.
So the more we work and the less we talk the better results we shall get.
We have had an Imperial lesson. It may make us an Empire yet!

Mesopotamia

1917

They shall not return to us, the resolute, the young,
    The eager and whole-hearted whom we gave:
But the men who left them thriftily to die in their own dung,
    Shall they come with years and honour to the grave?

They shall not return to us, the strong men coldly slain
    In sight of help denied from day to day:

But the men who edged their agonies and chid them in their pain,
  Are they too strong and wise to put away?

Our dead shall not return to us while Day and Night divide—
  Never while the bars of sunset hold.
But the idle-minded overlings who quibbled while they died,
  Shall they thrust for high employments as of old?

Shall we only threaten and be angry for an hour?
  When the storm is ended shall we find
How softly but how swiftly they have sidled back to power
  By the favour and contrivance of their kind?

Even while they soothe us, while they promise large amends,
  Even while they make a show of fear,
Do they call upon their debtors, and take counsel with their friends,
  To confirm and re-establish each career?

Their lives cannot repay us—their death could not undo—
  The shame that they have laid upon our race.
But the slothfulness that wasted and the arrogance that slew,
  Shall we leave it unabated in its place?

The Islanders

1902

No doubt but ye are the People—your throne is above the King's.
Whoso speaks in your presence must say acceptable things:
Bowing the head in worship, bending the knee in fear—
Bringing the word well smoothen—such as a King should hear.

Fenced by your careful fathers, ringed by your leaden seas,
Long did ye wake in quiet and long lie down at ease;
Till ye said of Strife, "What is it?" of the Sword, "It is far from our
  ken";
Till ye made a sport of your shrunken hosts and a toy of your armèd
  men.
Ye stopped your ears to the warning—ye would neither look nor heed—
Ye set your leisure before their toil and your lusts above their need.
Because of your witless learning and your beasts of warren and chase,
Ye grudged your sons to their service and your fields for their
  camping-place.
Ye forced them glean in the highways the straw for the bricks they
  brought;
Ye forced them follow in byways the craft that ye never taught.

Ye hampered and hindered and crippled; ye thrust out of sight and away
Those that would serve you for honour and those that served you for pay.
Then were the judgments loosened; then was your shame revealed,
At the hands of a little people, few but apt in the field.

Yet ye were saved by a remnant (and your land's long-suffering star),
When your strong men cheered in their millions while your striplings
    went to the war.

Sons of the sheltered city—unmade, unhandled, unmeet—
Ye pushed them raw to the battle as ye picked them raw from the street.

And what did you look they should compass?   Warcraft learned in a
    breath,
Knowledge unto occasion at the first far view of Death?

So? And ye train your horses and the dogs ye feed and prize?
How are the beasts more worthy than the souls, your sacrifice?

But ye said, "Their valour shall show them"; but ye said, "The end is
    close."

And ye sent them comfits and pictures to help them harry your foes:

And ye vaunted your fathomless power, and ye flaunted your iron pride,
Ere—ye fawned on the Younger Nations for the men who could shoot
    and ride!

Then ye returned to your trinkets; then ye contented your souls
With the flannelled fools at the wicket or the muddied oafs at the goals.

Given to strong delusion, wholly believing a lie,
Ye saw that the land lay fenceless, and ye let the months go by
Waiting some easy wonder, hoping some saving sign—
Idle—openly idle—in the lee of the forespent Line.

Idle—except for your boasting—and what is your boasting worth
If ye grudge a year of service to the lordliest life on earth?

Ancient, effortless, ordered, cycle on cycle set,
Life so long untroubled, that ye who inherit forget
It was not made with the mountains, it is not one with the deep.
Men, not gods, devised it.   Men, not gods, must keep.

Men, not children, servants, or kinsfolk called from afar,
But each man born in the Island broke to the matter of war.

Soberly and by custom taken and trained for the same,
Each man born in the Island entered at youth to the game—
As it were almost cricket, not to be mastered in haste,
But after trial and labour, by temperance, living chaste.

As it were almost cricket—as it were even your play,
Weighed and pondered and worshipped, and practised day and day.

So ye shall bide sure-guarded when the restless lightnings wake
In the womb of the blotting war-cloud, and the pallid nations quake.

So, at the haggard trumpets, instant your soul shall leap
Forthright, accoutred, accepting—alert from the wells of sleep.

So at the threat ye shall summon—so at the need ye shall send

Men, not children or servants, tempered and taught to the end;
Cleansed of servile panic, slow to dread or despise,
Humble because of knowledge, mighty by sacrifice . . .
But ye say, "It will mar our comfort." Ye say, "It will minish our
    trade."
Do ye wait for the spattered shrapnel ere ye learn how a gun is laid?
(For the low, red glare to southward when the raided coast-towns burn?
Light ye shall have on that lesson, but little time to learn.)
Will ye pitch some white pavilion, and lustily even the odds,
With nets and hoops and mallets, with rackets and bats and rods?
Will the rabbit war with your foemen—the red deer horn them for hire?
Your kept cock-pheasant keep you?—he is master of many a shire.
Arid, aloof, incurious, unthinking, unthanking, gelt,
Will ye loose your schools to flout them till their brow-beat columns melt?
Will ye pray them or preach them, or print them, or ballot them back
    from your shore?
Will your workmen issue a mandate to bid them strike no more?
Will ye rise and dethrone your rulers? (Because ye were idle both?
Pride by Insolence chastened? Indolence purged by Sloth?)
No doubt but ye are the People; who shall make you afraid?
Also your gods are many; no doubt but your gods shall aid.
Idols of greasy altars built for the body's ease;
Proud little brazen Baals and talking fetishes;
Teraphs of sept and party and wise wood-pavement gods—
These shall come down to the battle and snatch you from under the rods?
From the gusty, flickering gun-roll with viewless salvoes rent,
And the pitted hail of the bullets that tell not whence they were sent.
When ye are ringed as with iron, when ye are scourged as with whips,
When the meat is yet in your belly, and the boast is yet on your lips;
When ye go forth at mornings and the noon beholds you broke,
Ere ye lie down at even, your remnant, under the yoke?

No doubt but ye are the People—absolute, strong, and wise;
Whatever your heart has desired ye have not withheld from your eyes.
On your own heads, in your own hands, the sin and the saving lies!

The Veterans

(*Written for the gathering of survivors of the Indian Mutiny. Albert Hall,* 1907)

To-day, across our fathers' graves,
    The astonished years reveal
The remnant of that desperate host
    Which cleansed our East with steel.

Hail and farewell!   We greet you here,
  With tears that none will scorn—
O Keepers of the House of old,
  Or ever we were born!

One service more we dare to ask—
  Pray for us, heroes, pray,
That when Fate lays on us our task
  We do not shame the Day!

The Dykes

1902

We have no heart for the fishing—we have no hand for the oar—
All that our fathers taught us of old pleases us now no more.
All that our own hearts bid us believe we doubt where we do not deny—
There is no proof in the bread we eat nor rest in the toil we ply.

Look you, our foreshore stretches far through sea-gate, dyke, and groin—
Made land all, that our fathers made, where the flats and the fairway join.
They forced the sea a sea-league back.   They died, and their work stood
     fast.
We were born to peace in the lee of the dykes, but the time of our peace
   is past.

Far off, the full tide clambers and slips, mouthing and testing all,
Nipping the flanks of the water-gates, baying along the wall;
Turning the shingle, returning the shingle, changing the set of the
     sand . . .
We are too far from the beach, men say, to know how the outworks
     stand.

So we come down, uneasy, to look; uneasily pacing the beach.
These are the dykes our fathers made: we have never known a breach.
Time and again has the gale blown by and we were not afraid;
Now we come only to look at the dykes—at the dykes our fathers made.

O'er the marsh where the homesteads cower apart the harried sunlight
     flies,
Shifts and considers, wanes and recovers, scatters and sickens and dies—
An evil ember bedded in ash—a spark blown west by the wind . . .
We are surrendered to night and the sea—the gale and the tide behind!

At the bridge of the lower saltings the cattle gather and blare,
Roused by the feet of running men, dazed by the lantern-glare.
Unbar and let them away for their lives—the levels drown as they stand,

Where the flood-flash forces the sluices aback and the ditches deliver
  inland.

Ninefold deep to the top of the dykes the galloping breakers stride,
And their overcarried spray is a sea—a sea on the landward side.
Coming, like stallions they paw with their hooves, going they snatch with
  their teeth,
Till the bents and the furze and the sand are dragged out, and the old-
  time hurdles beneath.

Bid men gather fuel for fire, the tar, the oil, and the tow—
Flame we shall need, not smoke, in the dark if the riddled sea-banks go.
Bid the ringers watch in the tower (who knows how the dawn shall
  prove?)
Each with his rope between his feet and the trembling bells above.

Now we can only wait till the day, wait and apportion our shame.
These are the dykes our fathers left, but we would not look to the same.
Time and again were we warned of the dykes, time and again we delayed:
Now, it may fall, we have slain our sons, as our fathers we have betrayed.

Walking along the wrecks of the dykes, watching the work of the seas!
These were the dykes our fathers made to our great profit and ease.
But the peace is gone and the profit is gone, with the old sure days
  withdrawn . . .
That our own houses show as strange when we come back in the dawn!

The Declaration of London

JUNE 29, 1911

*(On the reassembling of Parliament after the Coronation, the Government have no intention
of allowing their followers to vote according to their convictions on the Declaration of London,
but insist on a strictly party vote.—*DAILY PAPERS.*)*

> We were all one heart and one race
>   When the Abbey trumpets blew.
> For a moment's breathing-space
>   We had forgotten you.
> Now you return to your honoured place
>   Panting to shame us anew.
>
> We have walked with the Ages dead—
>   With our Past alive and ablaze.
> And you bid us pawn our honour for bread,
>   This day of all the days!

And you cannot wait till our guests are sped,
 Or last week's wreath decays?

The light is still in our eyes
 Of Faith and Gentlehood,
Of Service and Sacrifice;
 And it does not match our mood,
To turn so soon to your treacheries
 That starve our land of her food.

Our ears still carry the sound
 Of our once-Imperial seas,
Exultant after our King was crowned,
 Beneath the sun and the breeze.
It is too early to have them bound
 Or sold at your decrees.

Wait till the memory goes,
 Wait till the visions fade,
We may betray in time, God knows,
 But we would not have it said,
When you make report to our scornful foes,
 That we kissed as we betrayed!

The Wage-Slaves

1902

Oh, glorious are the guarded heights
 Where guardian souls abide—
Self-exiled from our gross delights—
 Above, beyond, outside:
An ampler arc their spirit swings—
 Commands a juster view—
We have their word for all these things,
 No doubt their words are true.

Yet we, the bondslaves of our day,
 Whom dirt and danger press—
Co-heirs of insolence, delay,
 And leagued unfaithfulness—
Such is our need must seek indeed
 And, having found engage
The men who merely do the work
 For which they draw the wage.

From forge and farm and mine and bench,
  Deck, altar, outpost lone—
Mill, school, battalion, counter, trench,
  Rail, senate, sheepfold, throne—
Creation's cry goes up on high
  From age to cheated age:
"Send us the men who do the work
  "For which they draw the wage!"

Words cannot help nor wit achieve,
  Nor e'en the all-gifted fool,
Too weak to enter, bide, or leave
  The lists he cannot rule.
Beneath the sun we count on none
  Our evil to assuage,
Except the men that do the work
  For which they draw the wage.

When through the Gates of Stress and Strain
  Comes forth the vast Event—
The simple, sheer, sufficing, sane
  Result of labour spent—
They that have wrought the end unthought
  Be neither saint nor sage,
But only men who did the work
  For which they drew the wage.

Wherefore to these the Fates shall bend
  (And all old idle things)
Wherefore on these shall Power attend
  Beyond the grip of kings:
Each in his place, by right, not grace,
  Shall rule his heritage—
The men who simply do the work
  For which they draw the wage.

Not such as scorn the loitering street,
  Or waste, to earn its praise,
Their noontide's unreturning heat
  About their morning ways;
But such as dower each mortgaged hour
  Alike with clean couràge—
Even the men who do the work
  For which they draw the wage—
Men, like to Gods, that do the work
  For which they draw the wage—
Begin—continue—close that work
  For which they draw the wage!

The Song of the Lathes

1918

(Being the words of the tune hummed at her lathe by Mrs. L Embsay, widow)

The fans and the beltings they roar round me.
  The power is shaking the floor round me
Till the lathes pick up their duty and the midnight-shift takes over.
      It is good for me to be here!

Guns in Flanders—Flanders guns!
(I had a man that worked 'em once!)
Shells for guns in Flanders, Flanders!
Shells for guns in Flanders, Flanders!
    Shells for guns in Flanders!   Feed the guns!

The cranes and the carriers they boom over me,
The bays and the galleries they loom over me,
With their quarter-mile of pillars growing little in the distance—
      It is good for me to be here!

The Zeppelins and Gothas they raid over us.
Our lights give warning, and fade over us.
(Seven thousand women keeping quiet in the darkness!)
        Oh, it's good for me to be here!

The roofs and the buildings they grow round me,
Eating up the fields I used to know round me;
And the shed that I began in is a sub-inspector's office—
      So long have I been here!

I've seen six hundred mornings make our lamps grow dim,
Through the bit that isn't painted round our sky-light rim,
And the sunshine through the window slope according to the seasons,
        Twice since then I've been here.

The trains on the sidings they call to us
With the hundred thousand blanks that they haul to us;
And we send 'em what we've finished, and they take it where it's wanted,
        For that is why we are here!

Man's hate passes as his love will pass.
God made Woman what she always was.
Them that bear the burden they will never grant forgiveness
        So long as they are here!

Once I was a woman, but that's by with me.
All I loved and looked for, it must die with me;

But the lord has left me over for a servant of the Judgment,
  And I serve His Judgments here!

Guns in Flanders—Flanders guns!
(I had a son that worked 'em once!)
Shells for guns in Flanders, Flanders!
Shells for guns in Flanders, Flanders!
  Shells for guns in Flanders!   Feed the guns!

Rimmon

1903

(After Boer War)

Duly with knees that feign to quake—
  Bent head and shaded brow,—
Yet once again, for my father's sake,
  In Rimmon's House I bow.

The curtains part, the trumpet blares,
  And the eunuchs howl aloud;
And the gilt, swag-bellied idol glares
  Insolent over the crowd.

"This is Rimmon, Lord of the Earth—
  "Fear Him and bow the knee!"
And I watch my comrades hide their mirth
  That rode to the wars with me.

For we remember the sun and the sand
  And the rocks whereon we trod,
Ere we came to a scorched and a scornful land
  That did not know our God;

As we remember the sacrifice,
  Dead men an hundred laid—
Slain while they served His mysteries,
  And that He would not aid—

Not though we gashed ourselves and wept,
  For the high-priest bade us wait;
Saying He went on a journey or slept,
  Or was drunk or had taken a mate.

(Praise ye Rimmon, King of Kings,
  Who ruleth Earth and Sky!
And again I bow as the censer swings
  And the God Enthroned goes by.)

Ay, we remember His sacred ark
  And the virtuous men that knelt
To the dark and the hush behind the dark
  Wherein we dreamed He dwelt;

Until we entered to hale Him out,
  And found no more than an old
Uncleanly image girded about
  The loins with scarlet and gold.

Him we o'erset with the butts of our spears—
  Him and his vast designs—
To be the scorn of our muleteers
  And the jest of our halted lines.

By the picket-pins that the dogs defile,
  In the dung and the dust He lay,
Till the priests ran and chattered awhile
  And wiped Him and took Him away.

Hushing the matter before it was known,
  They returned to our fathers afar,
And hastily set Him afresh on His throne
  Because He had won us the war.

Wherefore with knees that feign to quake—
  Bent head and shaded brow—
To this dead dog, for my father's sake,
  In Rimmon's House I bow!

The Song of the Old Guard

Army Reform—After Boer War

("The Army of a Dream"—*Traffics and Discoveries*)

"Know this, my brethren, Heaven is clear
  And all the clouds are gone—
The Proper Sort shall flourish now,
  Good times are coming on"—
The evil that was threatened late
  To all of our degree
Hath passed in discord and debate,
  And, *Hey then up go we!*

A common people strove in vain
  To shame us into toil,

But they are spent and we remain,
  And we shall share the spoil
According to our several needs
  As Beauty shall decree,
As Age ordains or Birth concedes,
  And, *Hey then up go we!*

And they that with accursèd zeal
  Our Service would amend,
Shall own the odds and come to heel
  Ere worse befall their end:
For though no naked word be wrote
  Yet plainly shall they see
What pinneth Orders on their coat,
  And, *Hey then up go we!*

Our doorways that, in time of fear,
  We opened overwide
Shall softly close from year to year
  Till all be purified;
For though no fluttering fan be heard
  Nor chaff be seen to flee—
The Lord shall winnow the Lord's Preferred—
  And, *Hey then up go we!*

Our altars which the heathen brake
  Shall rankly smoke anew,
And anise, mint and cummin take
  Their dread and sovereign due,
Whereby the buttons of our trade
  Shall soon restorèd be
With curious work in gilt and braid,
  And, *Hey then up go we!*

Then come, my brethren, and prepare
  The candle sticks and bells,
The scarlet, brass, and badger's hair
  Wherein our Honour dwells,
And straitly fence and strictly keep
  The Ark's integrity
Till Armageddon break our sleep . . .
  And, *Hey then up go we!*

"The City of Brass"

1909

"Here was a people whom after their works thou shalt see wept over for their lost dominion: and in this palace is the last information respecting lords collected in the dust."—
THE ARABIAN NIGHTS.

In a land that the sand overlays—the ways to her gates are untrod—
A multitude ended their days whose fates were made splendid by God,
Till they grew drunk and were smitten with madness and went to their fall,
And of these is a story written: but Allah Alone knoweth all!

When the wine stirred in their heart their bosoms dilated.
They rose to suppose themselves kings over all things created—
To decree a new earth at a birth without labour or sorrow—
To declare: "We prepare it to-day and inherit to-morrow."
They chose themselves prophets and priests of minute understanding,
Men swift to see done, and outrun, their extremest commanding—
Of the tribe which describe with a jibe the perversions of Justice—
Panders avowed to the crowd whatsoever its lust is.

Swiftly these pulled down the walls that their fathers had made them—
The impregnable ramparts of old, they razed and relaid them
As playgrounds of pleasure and leisure, with limitless entries,
And havens of rest for the wastrels where once walked the sentries;
And because there was need of more pay for the shouters and marchers,
They disbanded in face of their foemen their yeomen and archers.
They replied to their well-wishers' fears—to their enemies' laughter,
Saying: "Peace! We have fashioned a God Which shall save us hereafter.
We ascribe all dominion to man in his factions conferring,
And have given to numbers the Name of the Wisdom unerring."

They said: "Who has hate in his soul? Who has envied his neighbour?
Let him arise and control both that man and his labour."
They said: "Who is eaten by sloth? Whose unthrift has destroyed him?
He shall levy a tribute from all because none have employed him."
They said: "Who hath toiled, who hath striven, and gathered possession?
Let him be spoiled. He hath given full proof of transgression."
They said: "Who is irked by the Law? *Though we may not remove it,*
If he lend us his aid in this raid, we will set him above it!"
So the robber did judgment again upon such as displeased him,
The slayer, too, boasted his slain, and the judges released him.

As for their kinsmen far off, on the skirts of the nation,
They harried all earth to make sure none escaped reprobation.
They awakened unrest for a jest in their newly-won borders,
And jeered at the blood of their brethren betrayed by their orders.

They instructed the ruled to rebel, their rulers to aid them;
And, since such as obeyed them not fell, their Viceroys obeyed them.
When the riotous set them at naught they said: "Praise the upheaval!
For the show and the word and the thought of Dominion is evil!"

They unwound and flung from them with rage, as a rag that defiled them,
The imperial gains of the age which their forefathers piled them.
They ran panting in haste to lay waste and embitter for ever
The wellsprings of Wisdom and Strength which are Faith and Endeavour.
They nosed out and digged up and dragged forth and exposed to derision
All doctrine of purpose and worth and restraint and prevision:

And it ceased, and God granted them all things for which they had
    striven,
And the heart of a beast in the place of a man's heart was given . . .

When they were fullest of wine and most flagrant in error,
Out of the sea rose a sign—out of Heaven a terror.
Then they saw, then they heard, then they knew—for none troubled to
    hide it,
An host had prepared their destruction, but still they denied it.
They denied what they dared not abide if it came to the trial;
But the Sword that was forged while they lied did not heed their denial.
It drove home, and no time was allowed to the crowd that was driven.
The preposterous-minded were cowed—they thought time would be given.
There was no need of a steed nor a lance to pursue them;
It was decreed their own deed, and not chance, should undo them.
The tares they had laughingly sown were ripe to the reaping.
The trust they had leagued to disown was removed from their keeping.
The eater of other men's bread, the exempted from hardship,
The excusers of impotence fled, abdicating their wardship,
For the hate they had taught through the State brought the State no
    defender,
And it passed from the roll of the Nations in headlong surrender!

The Hyaenas

After the burial-parties leave
  And the baffled kites have fled;
The wise hyaenas come out at eve
  To take account of our dead.

How he died and why he died
  Troubles them not a whit.

They snout the bushes and stones aside
   And dig till they come to it.

They are only resolute they shall eat
   That they and their mates may thrive,
And they know that the dead are safer meat
   Than the weakest thing alive.

(For a goat may butt, and a worm may sting,
   And a child will sometimes stand;
But a poor dead soldier of the King
   Can never lift a hand.)

They whoop and halloo and scatter the dirt
   Until their tushes white
Take good hold of the Army shirt,
   And tug the corpse to light,

And the pitiful face is shewn again
   For an instant ere they close;
But it is not discovered to living men—
   Only to God and to those

Who, being soulless, are free from shame,
   Whatever meat they may find.
Nor do they defile the dead man's name—
   That is reserved for his kind.

The Reformers

1901

Not in the camp his victory lies
   Or triumph in the market-place,
Who is his Nation's sacrifice
   To turn the judgment from his race.

Happy is he who, bred and taught
   By sleek, sufficing Circumstance—
Whose Gospel was the apparelled thought,
   Whose Gods were Luxury and Chance—

Sees, on the threshold of his days,
   The old life shrivel like a scroll,
And to unheralded dismays
   Submits his body and his soul:

The fatted shows wherein he stood
  Forgoing and the idiot pride,
That he may prove with his own blood
  All that his easy sires denied—

Ultimate issues, primal springs,
  Demands, abasements, penalties—
The imperishable plinth of things
  Seen and unseen, that touch our peace.

For, though ensnaring ritual dim
  His vision through the after-years,
Yet virtue shall go out of him—
  Example profiting his peers.

With great things charged he shall not hold
  Aloof till great occasion rise,
But serve, full-harnessed, as of old,
  The Days that are the Destinies.

He shall forswear and put away
  The idols of his sheltered house:
And to Necessity shall pay
  Unflinching tribute of his vows.

He shall not plead another's act,
  Nor bind him in another's oath
To weigh the Word above the Fact,
  Or make or take excuse for sloth.

The yoke he bore shall press him still,
  And, long-ingrainèd effort goad
To find, to fashion, and fulfil
  The cleaner life, the sterner code.

Not in the camp his victory lies—
  The world (unheeding his return)
Shall see it in his children's eyes
  And from his grandson's lips shall learn.

The Covenant

1914

We thought we ranked above the chance of ill.
  Others might fall, not we, for we were wise—
Merchants in freedom. So, of our free-will

We let our servants drug our strength with lies.
The pleasure and the poison had its way
    On us as on the meanest, till we learned
That he who lies will steal, who steals will slay.
    Neither God's judgment nor man's heart was turned.

Yet there remains His Mercy—to be sought
Through wrath and peril till we cleanse the wrong
By that last right which our forefathers claimed
When their Law failed them and its stewards were bought.
This is our cause.   God help us, and make strong
Our will to meet Him later, unashamed!

The Old Men

1902

This is our lot if we live so long and labour unto the end—
That we outlive the impatient years and the much too patient friend:
And because we know we have breath in our mouth and think we have thoughts in
    our head,
We shall assume that we are alive, whereas we are really dead.

We shall not acknowledge that old stars fade or stronger planets arise
(That the sere bush buds or the desert blooms or the ancient well-head
    dries),
Or any new compass wherewith new men adventure 'neath new skies.

We shall lift up the ropes that constrained our youth, to bind on our
    children's hands;
We shall call to the water below the bridges to return and replenish our
    lands;
We shall harness horses (Death's own pale horses) and scholarly plough
    the sands.

We shall lie down in the eye of the sun for lack of a light on our way—
We shall rise up when the day is done and chirrup, "Behold, it is
    day!"
We shall abide till the battle is won ere we amble into the fray.

We shall peck out and discuss and dissect, and evert and extrude to our
    mind,
The flaccid tissues of long-dead issues offensive to God and mankind—
(Precisely like vultures over an ox that the Army has left behind).

We shall make walk preposterous ghosts of the glories we once created—

Immodesty smearing from muddled palettes amazing pigments
    mismated—
And our friends will weep when we ask them with boasts if our natural
    force be abated.

The Lamp of our Youth will be utterly out, but we shall subsist on the
    smell of it;
And whatever we do, we shall fold our hands and suck our gums and
    think well of it.
Yes, we shall be perfectly pleased with our work, and that is the Perfect
    Hell of it!

This is our lot if we live so long and listen to those who love us—
That we are shunned by the people about and shamed by the Powers above us.
Wherefore be free of your harness; but, being free, be assured,
That he who hath not endured to the death, from his birth he hath never endured!

The Outlaws

1914

Through learned and laborious years
    They set themselves to find
Fresh terrors and undreamed-of fears
    To heap upon mankind.

All that they drew from Heaven above
    Or digged from earth beneath,
They laid into their treasure-trove
    And arsenals of death:

While, for well-weighed advantage sake,
    Ruler and ruled alike
Built up the faith they meant to break
    When the fit hour should strike.

They traded with the careless earth,
    And good return it gave:
They plotted by their neighbour's hearth
    The means to make him slave.

When all was ready to their hand
    They loosed their hidden sword,
And utterly laid waste a land
    Their oath was pledged to guard.

Coldly they went about to raise
　　To life and make more dread
Abominations of old days,
　　That men believed were dead.

They paid the price to reach their goal
　　Across a world in flame;
But their own hate slew their own soul
　　Before that victory came.

The White Man's Burden

1899

(The United States and the Philippine Islands)

Take up the White Man's burden—
　　Send forth the best ye breed—
Go bind your sons to exile
　　To serve your captives' need;
To wait in heavy harness
　　On fluttered folk and wild—
Your new-caught, sullen peoples,
　　Half devil and half child.

Take up the White Man's Burden—
　　In patience to abide,
To veil the threat of terror
　　And check the show of pride;
By open speech and simple,
　　An hundred times made plain,
To seek another's profit,
　　And work another's gain.

Take up the White Man's burden—
　　The savage wars of peace—
Fill full the mouth of Famine
　　And bid the sickness cease;
And when your goal is nearest
　　The end for others sought,
Watch Sloth and heathen Folly
　　Bring all your hope to nought.

Take up the White Man's burden—
　　No tawdry rule of kings,
But toil of serf and sweeper—
　　The tale of common things.

The ports ye shall not enter,
    The roads ye shall not tread,
Go make them with your living,
    And mark them with your dead!

Take up the White Man's burden—
    And reap his old reward:
The blame of those ye better,
    The hate of those ye guard—
The cry of hosts ye humour
    (Ah, slowly!) toward the light:—
"Why brought ye us from bondage,
    "Our loved Egyptian night?"

Take up the White Man's burden—
    Ye dare not stoop to less—
Nor call too loud on Freedom
    To cloak your weariness;
By all ye cry or whisper,
    By all ye leave or do,
The silent, sullen peoples
    Shall weigh your Gods and you.

Take up the White Man's burden—
    Have done with childish days—
The lightly proffered laurel,
    The easy, ungrudged praise.
Comes now, to search your manhood
    Through all the thankless years,
Cold-edged with dear-bought wisdom,
    The judgment of your peers!

Hymn Before Action

1896

The earth is full of anger,
    The seas are dark with wrath,
The Nations in their harness
    Go up against our path:
Ere yet we loose the legions—
    Ere yet we draw the blade,
Jehovah of the Thunders,
    Lord God of Battles, aid!

High lust and froward bearing,
   Proud heart, rebellious brow—
Deaf ear and soul uncaring,
   We seek Thy mercy now!
The sinner that forswore Thee,
   The fool that passed Thee by,
Our times are known before Thee—
   Lord, grant us strength to die!

For those who kneel beside us
   At altars not Thine own,
Who lack the lights that guide us,
   Lord, let their faith atone!
If wrong we did to call them,
   By honour bound they came;
Let not Thy Wrath befall them,
   But deal to us the blame.

From panic, pride, and terror,
   Revenge that knows no rein—
Light haste and lawless error,
   Protect us yet again.
Cloke Thou our undeserving,
   Make firm the shuddering breath,
In silence and unswerving
   To taste Thy lesser death.

Ah, Mary pierced with sorrow,
   Remember, reach and save
The soul that comes to-morrow
   Before the God that gave!
Since each was born of woman,
   For each at utter need—
True comrade and true foeman—
   Madonna, intercede!

E'en now their vanguard gathers,
   E'en now we face the fray—
As Thou didst help our fathers,
   Help Thou our host to-day.
Fulfilled of signs and wonders,
   In life, in death made clear—
Jehovah of the Thunders,
   Lord God of Battles, hear!

A Song At Cock-Crow

1918

"Ille auterum negavit."

The first time that Peter denièd his Lord
He shrank from the cudgel, the scourge and the cord,
But followed far off to see what they could do,
Till the cock crew—till the cock crew—
After Gethsemane, till the cock crew!

The first time that Peter denièd his Lord
'Twas only a maid in the palace who heard,
As he sat by the fire and warmed himself through.
Then the cock crew!   Then the cock crew!
("Thou also art one of them.")   Then the cock crew!

The first time that Peter denièd his Lord
He had neither the Throne, nor the Keys nor the Sword—
A poor silly fisherman, what could he do,
When the cock crew—when the cock crew—
But weep for his wickedness when the cock crew?

The next time that Peter denièd his Lord
He was Fisher of Men, as foretold by the Word,
With the Crown on his brow and the Cross on his shoe,
When the cock crew—when the cock crew—
In Flanders and Picardy when the cock crew!

The next time that Peter denièd his Lord
'Twas Mary the Mother in Heaven Who heard,
And She grieved for the maidens and wives that they slew
When the cock crew—when the cock crew—
At Tirmonde and Aerschott when the cock crew!

The next time that Peter denièd his Lord
The Babe in the Manger awakened and stirred,
And He stretched out His arms for the playmates He knew—
When the cock crew—when the cock crew—
But the waters had covered them when the cock crew!

The next time that Peter denièd his Lord
'Twas Earth in her agony waited his word,
But he sat by the fire and naught would he do,
Though the cock crew—though the cock crew—
Over all Christendom, though the cock crew!

The last time that Peter denièd his Lord,
The Father took from him the Keys and the Sword,
And the Mother and Babe brake his Kingdom in two,
When the cock crew—when the cock crew—
(Because of his wickedness) when the cock crew!

The Question

1916 [1]

Brethren, how shall it fare with me
    When the war is laid aside,
If it be proven that I am he
    For whom a world has died?

If it be proven that all my good,
    And the greater good I will make,
Were purchased me by a multitude
    Who suffered for my sake?

That I was delivered by mere mankind
    Vowed to one sacrifice,
And not, as I hold them, battle-blind,
    But dying with open eyes?

That they did not ask me to draw the sword
    When they stood to endure their lot—
That they only looked to me for a word,
    And I answered I knew them not?

If it be found, when the battle clears,
    Their death has set me free,
Then how shall I live with myself through the years
    Which they have bought for me?

Brethren, how must it fare with me,
    Or how am I justified,
If it be proven that I am he
    For whom mankind has died—
If it be proven that I am he
    Who, being questioned, denied?

[1] Attitude of the United States of America during the first two years, seven months and four days of the Great War.

Recessional

1897

God of our fathers, known of old,
  Lord of our far-flung battle-line,
Beneath whose awful Hand we hold
  Dominion over palm and pine—
Lord God of Hosts, be with us yet,
Lest we forget—lest we forget!

The tumult and the shouting dies;
  The Captains and the Kings depart:
Still stands Thine ancient sacrifice,
  An humble and a contrite heart.
Lord God of Hosts, be with us yet,
Lest we forget—lest we forget!

Far-called, our navies melt away;
  On dune and headland sinks the fire:
Lo, all our pomp of yesterday
  Is one with Nineveh and Tyre!
Judge of the Nations, spare us yet,
Lest we forget—lest we forget!

If, drunk with sight of power, we loose,
  Wild tongues that have not Thee in awe,
Such boastings as the Gentiles use,
  Or lesser breeds without the Law—
Lord God of Hosts, be with us yet,
Lest we forget—lest we forget!

For heathen heart that puts her trust
  In reeking tube and iron shard,
All valiant dust that builds on dust,
  And guarding, calls not Thee to guard,
For frantic boast and foolish word—
Thy mercy on Thy People, Lord!

"For All We Have And Are"

1914

For all we have and are,
For all our children's fate,
Stand up and take the war.
The Hun is at the gate!
Our world has passed away,
In wantonness o'erthrown.
There is nothing left to-day
But steel and fire and stone!
   Though all we knew depart,
   The old Commandments stand:—
   "In courage kept your heart,
   In strength lift up your hand."

Once more we hear the word
That sickened earth of old:—
"No law except the Sword
Unsheathed and uncontrolled."
Once more it knits mankind,
Once more the nations go
To meet and break and bind
A crazed and driven foe.

Comfort, content, delight,
The ages' slow-bought gain,
They shrivelled in a night.
Only ourselves remain
To face the naked days
In silent fortitude,
Through perils and dismays
Renewed and re-renewed.
   Though all we made depart,
   The old Commandments stand:—
   "In patience keep your heart,
   In strength lift up your hand."

No easy hope or lies
Shall bring us to our goal,
But iron sacrifice
Of body, will, and soul.
There is but one task for all—
One life for each to give.
What stands if Freedom fall?
Who dies if England live?

The Three-Decker

1894

"The three-volume novel is extinct."

Full thirty foot she towered from waterline to rail.
It took a watch to steer her, and a week to shorten sail;
But, spite all modern notions, I've found her first and best—
The only certain packet for the Islands of the Blest.

Fair held the breeze behind us—'twas warm with lovers' prayers.
We'd stolen wills for ballast and a crew of missing heirs.
The shipped as Able Bastards till the Wicked Nurse confessed,
And they worked the old three-decker to the Islands of the Blest.

By ways no gaze could follow, a course unspoiled of Cook,
Per Fancy, fleetest in man, our titled berths we took,
With maids of matchless beauty and parentage unguessed,
And a Church of England parson for the Islands of the Blest.

We asked no social questions—we pumped no hidden shame—
We never talked obstetrics when the Little Stranger came:
We left the Lord in Heaven, we left the fields in Hell.
We weren't exactly Yussufs, but—Zuleika didn't tell.

No moral doubt assailed us, so when the port we neared,
The villain had his flogging at the gangway, and we cheered.
'Twas fiddle in the foc's'le—'twas garlands on the mast,
For every one got married, and I went ashore at last.

I left 'em all in couples a-kissing on the decks.
I left the lovers loving and the parents signing cheques.
In endless English comfort, by county-folk caressed,
I left the old three-decker at the Islands of the Blest! . . .

That route is barred to steamers: you'll never lift again
Our purple-painted headlands or the lordly keeps of Spain.
They're just beyond your skyline, howe'er so far you cruise
In a ram-you-damn-you liner with a brace of bucking screws.

Swing round your aching searchlight—'twill show no haven's peace.
Ay, blow your shrieking sirens at the deaf, grey-bearded seas!
Boom out the dripping oil-bags to skin the deep's unrest—
And you aren't one knot nearer to the Islands of the Blest.

But when you're threshing, crippled, with broken bridge and rail,
At a drogue of dead convictions to hold you head to gale,
Calm as the Flying Dutchman, from truck to taffrail dressed,
You'll see the old three-decker for the Islands of the Blest.

You'll see her tiering canvas in sheeted silver spread;
You'll hear the long-drawn thunder 'neath her leaping figure-head;
While far, so far above you, her tall poop-lanterns shine
Unvexed by wind or weather like the candles round a shrine!

Hull down—hull down and under—she dwindles to a speck,
With noise of pleasant music and dancing on her deck.
All's well—all's well aboard her—she's left you far behind,
With a scent of old-world roses through the fog that ties you blind.

Her crews are babes or madmen?   Her port is all to make?
You're manned by Truth and Science, and you steam for steaming's sake?
Well, tinker up your engines—you know your business best—
She's taking tired people to the Islands of the Blest!

The Rhyme Of The Three Captains

1890

[*This ballad appears to refer to one of the exploits of the notorious Paul Jones, an American pirate. It is founded on fact.*]

. . . At the close of a winter day,
Their anchors down, by London town, the Three Great Captains lay;
And one was Admiral of the North from Solway Firth to Skye,
And one was Lord of the Wessex coast and all the lands thereby,
And one was Master of the Thames from Limehouse to Blackwall,
And he was Chaplain of the Fleet—the bravest of them all.
Their good guns guarded their great grey sides that were thirty foot in the sheer,
When there came a certain trading brig with news of a privateer.
Her rigging was rough with the clotted drift that drives in a Northern breeze,
Her sides were clogged with the lazy weed that spawns in the Eastern seas.
 Light she rode in the rude tide-rip, to left and right she rolled,
And the skipper sat on the scuttle-butt and stared at an empty hold.
"I ha' paid Port dues for your Law," quoth he, "and where is the Law ye boast
"If I sail unscathed from a heathen port to be robbed on a Christian coast?
"Ye have smoked the hives of the Laccadives as we burn the lice in a bunk,
"We tack not now for a Gallang prow or a plunging Pei-ho junk;
"I had no fear but the seas were clear as far as a sail might fare
"Till I met with a lime-washed Yankee brig that rode off Finisterre.

"There were canvas blinds to his bow-gun ports to screen the weight he
bore,
"And the signals ran for a merchantman from Sandy Hook to the Nore.
"He would not fly the Rovers' flag—the bloody or the black,
"But now he floated the Gridiron and now he flaunted the Jack.
"He spoke of the Law as he crimped my crew—he swore it was only a
loan;
"But when I would ask for my own again, he swore it was none of my
own.
"He has taken my little parrakeets that nest beneath the Line.
"He has stripped my rails of the shaddock-frails and the green unripened
pine.
"He has taken my bale of dammer and spice I won beyond the seas,
"He has taken my grinning heathen gods—and what should he want o'
these?
"My foremast would not mend his boom, my deck-house patch his boats;
"He has whittled the two, this Yank Yahoo, to peddle for shoe-peg oats.
"I could not fight for the failing light and a rough beam-sea beside,
"But I hulled him once for a clumsy crimp and twice because he lied.
"Had I had guns (as I had goods) to work my Christian harm,
"I had run him up from his quarter-deck to trade with his own yard-arm;
"I had nailed his ears to my capstan-head, and ripped them off with a
saw,
"And soused them in the bilgewater, and served them to him raw;
"I had flung him blind in a rudderless boat to rot in the rocking dark,
"I had towed him aft of his own craft, a bait for his brother shark;
"I had lapped him round with cocoa-husk, and drenched him with the oil,
"And lashed him fast to his own mast to blaze above my spoil;
"I had stripped his hide for my hammock-side, and tasselled his beard
in the mesh,
"And spitted his crew on the live bamboo that grows through the
gangrened flesh;
"I had hove him down by the mangroves brown, where the mud-reef
sucks and draws,
"Moored by the heel to his own keel to wait for the land-crab's claws.
"He is lazar within and lime without; ye can nose him far enow,
"For he carries the taint of a musky ship—the reek of the slaver's dhow."
The skipper looked at the tiering guns and the bulwarks tall and cold,
And the Captains Three full courteously peered down at the gutted hold,
And the Captains Three called courteously from deck to scuttle-butt:—
"Good Sir, we ha' dealt with that merchantman or ever your teeth were
cut.
"Your words be words of a lawless race, and the Law it standeth thus:
"He comes of a race that have never a Law, and he never has boarded
us.

"We ha' sold him canvas and rope and spar—we know that his price is
  fair,
"And we know that he weeps for the lack of the Law as he rides off
  Finisterre.
"And since he is damned for a gallows-thief by you and better than you,
"We hold it meet that the English fleet should know that we hold him
  true."
The skipper called to the tall taffrail:—"And what is that to me?
"Did ever you hear of a Yankee brig that rifled a Seventy-three?
"Do I loom so large from your quarter-deck that I lift like a ship o' the
  Line?
"He has learned to run from a shotted gun and harry such craft as mine.
"There is never a law on the Cocos Keys, to hold a white man in,
"But we do not steal the niggers' meal, for that is a nigger's sin.
"Must he have his Law as a quid to chaw, or laid in brass on his wheel?
"Does he steal with tears when he buccaneers?   'Fore Gad, then, why
  does he steal?"
The skipper bit on a deep-sea word, and the word it was not sweet,
For he could see the Captains Three had signalled to the Fleet.
But three and two, in white and blue, the whimpering flags began:—
"We have heard a tale of a—foreign sail, but he is a merchantman."
The skipper peered beneath his palm and swore by the Great Horn
  Spoon:—
"'Fore Gad, the Chaplain of the Fleet would bless my picaroon!"
By two and three the flags blew free to lash the laughing air:—
"We have sold our spars to the merchantman—we know that his price is
  fair."
The skipper winked his Western eye, and swore by a China storm:—
"They ha' rigged him a Joseph's jury-coat to keep his honour warm."
The halliards twanged against the tops, the bunting bellied broad,
The skipper spat in the empty hold and mourned for a wasted cord.
Masthead—masthead, the signal sped by the line o' the British craft:
The skipper called to his Lascar crew, and put her about and laughed:—
"It's mainsail haul, my bully boys all—we'll out to the seas again—
"Ere they set us to paint their pirate saint, or scrub at his grapnel-chain.
"It's fore-sheet free, with her head to the sea, and the swing of the
  unbought brine—
"We'll make no sport in an English court till we come as a ship o' the
  Line:
"Till we come as a ship o' the Line, my lads, of thirty foot in the sheer,
"Lifting again from the outer main with news of a privateer;
"Flying his pluck at our mizzen-truck for weft of Admiralty,
"Heaving his head for our dipsy-lead in sign that we keep the sea.
"Then fore-sheet home as she lifts to the foam—we stand on the outward
  tack,

"We are paid in the coin of the white man's trade— the bezant is hard, ay, and black.
"The frigate-bird shall carry my word to the King about the Orang-Laut
"How a man may sail from a heathen coast to be robbed in a Christian port;
"How a man may be robbed in Christian port while Three Great Captains there
"Shall dip their flag to a slaver's rag—to show that his trade is fair!"

The Conundrum of the Workshops

1890

When the flush of a new-born sun fell first on Eden's green and gold,
Our father Adam sat under the Tree and scratched with a stick in the mould:
And the first rude sketch that the world had seen was joy to his mighty heart,
Till the Devil whispered behind the leaves, "It's pretty, but is it Art?"

Wherefore he called to his wife, and fled to fashion his work anew—
The first of his race who cared a fig for the first, most dread review;
And he left his lore to the use of his sons—and that was a glorious gain
When the Devil chuckled "Is it Art?" in the ear of the branded Cain.

They builded a tower to shiver the sky and wrench the stars apart,
Till the Devil grunted behind the bricks: "It's striking, but is it Art?"
The stone was dropped at the quarry-side and the idle derrick swung,
While each man talked of the aims of Art, and each in an alien tongue.

They fought and they talked in the North and the South; they talked and they fought in the West,
Till the waters rose on the pitiful land, and the poor Red Clay had rest—
Had rest till that dank blank-canvas dawn when the Dove was preened to start,
And the Devil bubbled below the keel: "It's human, but is it Art?"

The tale is as old as the Eden Tree—and new as the new-cut tooth—
For each man knows ere his lip-thatch grows he is master of Art and Truth;
And each man hears as the twilight nears, to the beat of his dying heart,
The Devil drum on the darkened pane: "You did it, but was it Art?"

We have learned to whittle the Eden Tree to the shape of a surplice-peg,
We have learned to bottle our parents twain in the yelk of an addled egg,
We know that the tail must wag the dog, for the horse is drawn by the cart;
But the Devil whoops, as he whooped of old: "It's clever, but is it Art?"

When the flicker of London sun falls faint on the Club-room's green and
  gold,
The sons of Adam sit them down and scratch with their pens in the
  mould—
They scratch with their pens in the mould of their graves, and the ink
  and the anguish start,
For the Devil mutters behind the leaves: "It's pretty, but is it Art?"

Now, if we could win to the Eden Tree where the Four Great Rivers flow,
And the Wreath of Eve is red on the turf as she left it long ago,
And if we could come when the sentry slept and softly scurry through,
By the favour of God we might know as much—as our father Adam
  knew!

Evarra and his Gods

1890

Read here:
This is the story of Evarra—man—
Maker of Gods in the lands beyond the sea.
  Because the city gave him of her gold,
  Because the caravans brought turquoises,
  Because his life was sheltered by the King,
  So that no man should maim him, none should steal,
  Or break his rest with babble in the streets
  When he was weary after toil, he made
  An image of his God in gold and pearl,
  With turquoise diadem and human eyes,
  A wonder in the sunshine, known afar,
  And worshipped by the King; but, drunk with pride,
  Because the city bowed to him for God,
  He wrote above the shrine: *"Thus Gods are made,*
  "And whoso makes them otherwise shall die."
  And all the city praised him ... Then he died.

Read here the story of Evarra—man—
Maker of Gods in lands beyond the sea.
  Because the city had no wealth to give,
  Because the caravans were spoiled afar,
  Because his life was threatened by the King,
  So that all men despised him in the streets,
  He hewed the living rock, with sweat and tears,
  And reared a God against the morning-gold,
  A terror in the sunshine, seen afar,

And worshipped by the King; but, drunk with pride,
Because the city fawned to bring him back,
He carved upon the plinth: *"Thus Gods are made,*
"And whoso makes them otherwise shall die."
And all the people praised him . . . Then he died.

Read here the story of Evarra—man—
Maker of Gods in lands beyond the sea.
Because he lived among a simple folk,
Because his village was between the hills,
Because he smeared his cheeks with blood of ewes,
He cut an idol from a fallen pine,
Smeared blood upon its cheeks, and wedged a shell
Above its brow for eye, and gave it hair
Of trailing moss, and plaited straw for crown.
And all the village praised him for his craft,
And brought him butter, honey, milk, and curds.
Wherefore, because the shoutings drove him mad,
He scratched upon that log: *"Thus Gods are made,*
"And whoso makes them otherwise shall die."
And all the people praised him . . . Then he died.

Read here the story of Evarra—man—
Maker of Gods in lands beyond the sea.
Because his God decreed one clot of blood
Should swerve one hair's-breadth from the pulse's path,
And chafe his brain, Evarra mowed alone,
Rag-wrapped, among the cattle in the fields,
Counting his fingers, jesting with the trees,
And mocking at the mist, until his God
Drove him to labour.   Out of dung and horns
Dropped in the mire he made a monstrous God,
Uncleanly, shapeless, crowned with plantain tufts,
And when the cattle lowed at twilight-time,
He dreamed it was the clamour of lost crowds,
And howled among the beasts: *"Thus Gods are made,*
"And whoso makes them otherwise shall die."
Thereat the cattle bellowed . . . Then he died.

Yet at the last he came to Paradise,
And found his own four Gods, and that he wrote;
And marvelled, being very near to God,
What oaf on earth had made his toil God's law,
Till God said mocking: "Mock not.   These be thine."
Then cried Evarra: "I have sinned!"   "Not so.
"If thou hadst written otherwise, thy Gods

"Had rested in the mountain and the mine,
"And I were poorer by four wondrous Gods,
"And thy more wondrous law, Evarra.   Thine,
"Servant of shouting crowds and lowing kine!"
Thereat, with laughing mouth, but tear-wet eyes,
Evarra casts his Gods from paradise.

This is the story of Evarra—man—
Maker of Gods in lands beyond the sea.

The Benefactors

Ah!   What avails the classic bent
    And what the cultured word,
Against the undoctored incident
    That actually occurred?

And what is Art whereto we press
    Through paint and prose and rhyme—
When Nature in her nakedness
    Defeats us every time?

It is not learning, grace nor gear,
    Nor easy meat and drink,
But bitter pinch of pain and fear
    That makes creation think.

When in this world's unpleasing youth
    Our godlike race began,
The longest arm, the sharpest tooth,
    Gave man control of man;

Till, bruised and bitten to the bone
    And taught by pain and fear,
He learned to deal the far-off stone,
    And poke the long, safe spear.

So tooth and nail were obsolete
    As means against a foe,
Till, bored by uniform defeat,
    Some genius built the bow.

Then stone and javelin proved as vain
    As old-time tooth and nail;
Till, spurred anew by fear and pain,
    Man fashioned coats of mail.

Then was there safety for the rich
    And danger for the poor,
Till someone mixed a powder which
    Redressed the scale once more.

Helmet and armour disappeared
    With sword and bow and pike,
And, when the smoke of battle cleared,
    All men were armed alike . . .

And when ten million such were slain
    To please one crazy king,
Man, schooled in bulk by fear and pain,
    Grew weary of the thing;

And, at the very hour designed
    To enslave him past recall,
His tooth-stone-arrow-gun-shy-mind
    Turned and abolished all.

All Power, each Tyrant, every Mob
    Whose head has grown too large,
Ends by destroying its own job
    And works its own discharge;

And Man whose mere necessities
    Move all things from his path,
Trembles meanwhile at their decrees,
    And deprecates their wrath!

In the Neolithic Age

1895

In the Neolithic Age savage warfare did I wage
    For food and fame and woolly horses' pelt.
I was singer to my clan in that dim, red Dawn of Man,
    And I sang of all we fought and feared and felt.

Yea, I sang as now I sing, when the Prehistoric spring
    Made the piled Biscayan ice-pack split and shove;
And the troll and gnome and dwerg, and the Gods of Cliff and Berg
    Were about me and beneath me and above.

But a rival, of Solutré, told the tribe my style was *outré*—
    'Neath a tomahawk, of diorite, he fell.
And I left my views on Art, barbed and tanged, below the heart
    Of a mammothistic etcher at Grenelle.

Then I stripped them, scalp from skull, and my hunting-dogs fed full,
   And their teeth I threaded neatly on a thong;
And I wiped my mouth and said, "It is well that they are dead,
   "For I know my work is right and theirs was wrong."

But my Totem saw the shame; from his ridgepole-shrine he came.
   And he told me in a vision of the night:—
"There are nine and sixty ways of constructing tribal lays,
   "And every single one of them is right!"

Then the silence closed upon me till They put new clothing on me
   Of whiter, weaker flesh and bone more frail;
And I stepped beneath Time's finger, once again a tribal singer,
   And a minor poet certified by Traill!

Still they skirmish to and fro, men my messmates on the snow,
   When we headed off the aurochs turn for turn;
When the rich Allobrogenses never kept amanuenses,
   And our only plots were piled in lakes at Berne.

Still a cultured Christian age sees us scuffle, squeak, and rage,
   Still we pinch and slap and jabber, scratch and dirk;
Still we let our business slide—as we dropped the half-dressed hide—
   To show a fellow-savage how to work.

Still the world is wondrous large,—seven seas from marge to marge—
   And it holds a vast of various kinds of man;
And the wildest dreams of Kew are the facts of Khatmandhu,
   And the crimes of Clapham chaste in Martaban.

Here's my wisdom for your use, as I learned it when the moose
   And the reindeer roamed where Paris roars to-night:—
"There are nine and sixty ways of constructing tribal lays,
   "And—every—single—one—of— them—is—right!"

Natural Theology

PRIMITIVE

I ate my fill of a whale that died
   And stranded after a month at sea . . .
There is a pain in my inside.
   Why have the Gods afflicted me?
Ow! I am purged till I am a wraith!
   Wow! I am sick till I cannot see!
What is the sense of Religion and Faith?
   Look how the Gods have afflicted me!

PAGAN

How can the skin of rat or mouse hold
    Anything more than a harmless flea? . . .
The burning plague has taken my household.
    Why have my Gods afflicted me?
All my kith and kin are deceased,
    Though they were as good as good could be.
I will out and batter the family priest,
    Because my Gods have afflicted me!

MEDIAEVAL

My privy and well drain into each other
    After the custom of Christendie . . .
Fevers and fluxes are wasting my mother.
    Why has the Lord afflicted me?
The Saints are helpless for all I offer—
    So are the clergy I used to fee.
Henceforward I keep my cash in my coffer,
    Because the Lord has afflicted me.

MATERIAL

I run eight hundred hens to the acre.
    They die by dozens mysteriously . . .
I am more than doubtful concerning my Maker.
    Why has the Lord afflicted me?
What a return for all my endeavour—
    Not to mention the L. S. D.!
I am an atheist now and for ever,
    Because this God has afflicted me!

PROGRESSIVE

Money spent on an Army or Fleet
    Is homicidal lunacy . . .
My son has been killed in the Mons retreat.
    Why is the Lord afflicting me?
Why are murder, pillage and arson
    And rape allowed by the Deity?
I will write to the *Times*, deriding our parson,
    Because my God has afflicted me.

CHORUS

We had a kettle: we let it leak:
    Our not repairing it made it worse.
We haven't had any tea for a week . . .
    The bottom is out of the Universe!

CONCLUSION

This was none of the good Lord's pleasure,
    For the Spirit He breathed in Man is free;
But what comes after is measure for measure
    And not a God that afflicteth thee.
As was the sowing so the reaping
    Is now and evermore shall be.
Thou art delivered to thine own keeping.
    Only Thyself hath afflicted thee!

The Story of Ung

1894

Once, on a glittering ice-field, ages and ages ago,
Ung, a maker of pictures, fashioned an image of snow.
Fashioned the form of a tribesman—gaily he whistled and sung,
Working the snow with his fingers.   *Read ye the story of Ung!*

Pleased was his Tribe with that image—came in their hundreds to scan,
Handled it, smelt it, and grunted: "Verily, this is a man!
"Thus do we carry our lances—thus is a war-belt slung.
"Lo! it is even as we are.   Glory and honour to Ung!"

Later he pictured an aurochs—later he pictured a bear—
Pictured the sabre-tooth tiger dragging a man to his lair—
Pictured the mountainous mammoth, hairy, abhorrent, alone—
Out of the love that he bore them, scriving them clearly on bone.

Swift came his Tribe to behold them, peering and pushing and still—
Men of the berg-battered beaches, men of the boulder-hatched hill—
Hunters and fishers and trappers, presently whispering low:
"Yea, they are like—and it may be.   But how does the Picture-man
    know?

"Ung—hath he slept with the Aurochs—watched where the Mastodon
    roam?
"Spoke on the ice with the Bow-head—followed the Sabre-tooth home?
"Nay!   These are toys of his fancy!   If he have cheated us so,
"How is there truth in his image—the man that he fashioned of snow?"

Wroth was that maker of pictures—hotly he answered the call:
"Hunters and fishers and trappers, children and fools are ye all!
"Look at the beasts when ye hunt them!"   Swift from the tumult he
    broke,
Ran to the cave of his father and told him the shame that they spoke.

And the father of Ung gave answer, that was old and wise in the craft,
Maker of pictures aforetime, he leaned on his lance and laughed:
"If they could see as thou seest they would do what thou hast done,
"And each man would make him a picture, and—what would become of
    my son?

"There would be no pelts of the reindeer, flung down at thy cave for a
    gift,
"Nor dole of the oily timber that comes on the Baltic drift;
"No store of well-drilled needles, nor ouches of amber pale;
"No new-cut tongues of the bison, nor meat of the stranded whale.

"*Thou* has not toiled at the fishing when the sodden trammels freeze,
"Nor worked the war-boats outward through the rush of the rock-staked
    seas,
"Yet they bring thee fish and plunder—full meal and an easy bed—
"And all for the sake of thy pictures."   And Ung held down his head.

"*Thou* has not stood to the Aurochs when the red snow reeks of the fight.
"Men have no time at the houghing to count his curls aright.
"And the heart of the hairy Mammoth, thou sayest, they do not see,
"Yet they save it whole from the beaches and broil the best for thee.

"And now do they press to thy pictures, with opened mouth and eye,
"And a little gift in the doorway, and the praise no gift can buy:
"But—sure they have doubted thy pictures, and that is a grievous stain—
"Son that can see so clearly, return them their gifts again!"

And Ung looked down at his deerskins—their broad shell-tasselled
    bands—
And Ung drew forward his mittens and looked at his naked hands;
And he gloved himself and departed, and he heard his father, behind:
"Son that can see so clearly, rejoice that thy Tribe is blind!"

Straight on the glittering ice-field, by the caves of the lost Dordogne,
Ung, a maker of pictures, fell to his scriving on bone—
Even to mammoth editions.   Gaily he whistled and sung,
Blessing his Tribe for their blindness.   *Heed ye the Story of Ung!*

The Craftsman

Once, after long-dawn revel at The Mermaid,
He to the overbearing Boanerges
Jonson, uttered (if half of it were liquor,
        Blessed be the vintage!)

Saying how, at an alehouse under Cotswold,
He had made sure of his very Cleopatra
Drunk with enormous, salvation-contemning
     Love for a tinker.

How, while he hid from Sir Thomas's keepers,
Crouched in a ditch and drenched by the midnight
Dews, he had listened to gipsy Juliet
     Rail at the dawning.

How at Bankside, a boy drowning kittens
Winced at the business; whereupon his sister—
Lady Macbeth aged seven—thrust 'em under,
     Sombrely scornful.

How on a Sabbath, hushed and compassionate—
She being known since her birth to the townsfolk—
Stratford dredged and delivered from Avon
     Dripping Ophelia.

So, with a thin third finger marrying
Drop to wine-drop domed on the table,
Shakespeare opened his heart till the sunrise
     Entered to hear him.

London waked and he, imperturbable,
Passed from waking to hurry after shadows . . .
Busied upon shows of no earthly importance?
     Yes, but he knew it!

Samuel Pepys

1933

Like the Oak whose roots descend
   Through earth and stillness seeking food
Most apt to furnish in the end
   That dense, indomitable wood

Which, felled, may arm a seaward flank
   Of Ostia's mole or—bent to frame
The beaked Liburnian's triple bank—
   Carry afar the Roman name;

But which, a tree, the season moves
   Through gentler Gods than Wind or Tide,
Delightedly to harbour doves,
   Or take some clasping vine for bride;

So this man—prescient to ensure
  (Since even now his orders hold)
A little State might ride secure
  At sea from foes her sloth made bold,—

Turned in his midmost harried round,
  As Venus drove or Liber led,
And snatched from any shrine he found
  The Stolen Draught, the Secret Bread.

Nor these alone. His life betrayed
  No gust unslaked, no pleasure missed.
He called the obedient Nine to aid
  The varied chase. And Clio kissed;

Bidding him write each sordid love,
  Shame, panic, stratagem, and lie
In full, that sinners undiscov-
  ered, like ourselves, might say:—"'Tis I!"

The Bonfires

1933

"Gesture . . . outlook . . . vision . . . avenue . . . example . . . achievement . . . appeasement . . . limit of risk."—COMMON POLITICAL FORM.

We know the Rocket's upward whizz;
  We know the Boom before the Bust.
We know the whistling Wail which is
  The Stick returning to the Dust.
  We know how much to take on trust
Of any promised Paradise
  We know the Pie—likewise the Crust.
We know the Bonfire on the Ice.

We know the Mountain and the Mouse.
  We know Great Cry and Little Wool.
We know the purseless Ears of Sows.
  We know the Frog that aped the Bull.
  We know, whatever Trick we pull,
(Ourselves have gambled once or twice)
  A Bobtailed Flush is not a Full.
We know the Bonfire on the Ice.

We know that Ones and Ones make Twos—
  Till Demos votes them Three or Nought.
We know the Fenris Wolf is loose.

We know what Fight has not been fought.
　　We know the Father to the Thought
Which argues Babe and Cockatrice
　　Would play together, were they taught.
We know *that* Bonfire on the Ice.

We know that Thriving comes by Thrift.
　　We know the Key must keep the Door.
We know his Boot-straps cannot lift
　　The frightened Waster off the Floor.
　　We know these things, and we deplore
That not by any Artifice
　　Can they be altered.　Furthermore
We know the Bonfires on the Ice!

"When 'Omer Smote 'Is Bloomin' Lyre"

(Introduction to the Barrack-Room Ballads in "The Seven Seas")

When 'Omer smote 'is bloomin' lyre,
　　He'd 'eard men sing by land an' sea;
An' what he thought 'e might require,
　　'E went an' took—the same as me!

The market-girls an' fishermen,
　　The shepherds an' the sailors, too,
They 'eard old songs turn up again,
　　But kep' it quiet—same as you!

They knew 'e stole; 'e knew they knowed.
　　They didn't tell, nor make a fuss,
But winked at 'Omer down the road,
　　An' 'e winked back—the same as us!

The Files

1903

(The Sub-editor speaks)

Files—
The files—
Office Files!
Oblige me by referring to the Files.
Every question man can raise,

Every phrase of every phase
Of that question is on record in the Files—
(Threshed out threadbare—fought and finished in the Files).
Ere the Universe at large
Was our new-tipped arrows' targe—
Ere we rediscovered Mammon and his wiles—
Faenza, gentle reader, spent her—five-and-twentieth leader—
(You will find him, and some others, in the Files).
Warn all coming Robert Brownings and Carlyles,
It will interest them to hunt among the files
Where unvisited, a-cold
Lie the crowded years of old
In that Kensal-Green of greatness called the Files
(In our newspaPère-la-Chaise the Office Files),
Where the dead men lay them down
Meekly sure of long renown,
And above them, sere and swift,
Packs the daily deepening drift
Of the all-recording, all-effacing Files—
The obliterating, automatic Files.
Count the mighty men who slung
Ink, Evangel, Sword, or Tongue
When Reform and you were young—
Made their boasts and spake according in the Files—
(Hear the ghosts that wake applauding in the Files!)
Trace each all-forgot career
From long primer through brevier
Unto Death, a para minion in the Files
(Para minion—solid—bottom of the files) . . .
Some successful Kings and Queens adorn the Files
They were great, their views were leaded,
And their deaths were triple-headed,
So they catch the eye in running through the Files
(Show as blazes in the mazes of the Files);
And their gross, jack-booted feasts,
And their "epoch-marking actions" see the Files.
Was it Bomba fled the blue Sicilian isles?
Was it Saffi, a professor
Once of Oxford, brought redress or
Garibaldi? Who remembers
Forty-odd-year-old Septembers?—
Only sextons paid to dig among the Files
(Such as I am, born and bred among the Files).
You must hack through much deposit
Ere you know for sure who was it

Came to burial with such honour in the Files
(Only seven seasons back beneath the Files).
"Very great our loss and grievous—
"So our best and brightest leave us,
"And it ends the Age of Giants," say the Files;
All the '60—'70—'80—'90 Files
(The open-minded, opportunist Files—
The easy "O King, live for ever" Files).
It is good to read a little in the Files;
'Tis a sure and sovereign balm
Unto philosophic calm,
Yea, and philosophic doubt when Life beguiles.
When you know Success is Greatness,
When you marvel at your lateness
In apprehending facts so plain to Smiles
(Self-helpful, wholly strenuous Samuel Smiles).
When your Imp of Blind Desire
Bids you set the Thames afire,
You'll remember men have done so—in the Files.
You'll have seen those flames transpire—in the Files
(More than once that flood has run so—in the Files).
When the Conchimarian horns
Of the reboantic Norns
Usher gentlemen and ladies
With new lights on Heaven and Hades,
Guaranteeing to Eternity
All yesterday's modernity;
When Brocken-spectres made by
Some one's breath on ink parade by,
Very earnest and tremendous,
Let not shows of shows offend us.
When of everything we like we
Shout ecstatic: "*Quod ubique*,
"*Quod ab omnibus* means *semper!*"
Oh, my brother, keep your temper!
Light your pipe and take a look along the Files.
You've a better chance to guess
At the meaning of Success
(Which is Greatness—*vide* Press)
When you've seen it in perspective in the Files!

The Virginity

Try as he will, no man breaks wholly loose
　　From his first love, on matter who she be.
Oh, was there ever sailor free to choose,
　　That didn't settle somewhere near the sea?

Myself, it don't excite me nor amuse
　　To watch a pack o' shipping on the sea;
But I can understand my neighbour's views
　　From certain things which have occurred to me.

Men must keep touch with things they used to use
　　To earn their living, even when they are free;
And so come back upon the least excuse—
　　Same as the sailor settled near the sea.

He knows he's never going on no cruise—
　　He knows he's done and finished with the sea;
And yet he likes to feel she's there to use—
　　If he should ask her—as she used to be.

Even though she cost him all he had to lose,
　　Even though she made him sick to hear or see,
Still, what she left of him will mostly choose
　　Her skirts to sit by.　How come such to be?

Parsons in pulpits, tax-payers in pews,
　　Kings on your thrones, you know as well as me,
We've only one virginity to lose,
　　And where we lost it there our hearts will be!

The Legends of Evil

1890

I

This is the sorrowful story
　　Told as the twilight fails
And the monkeys walk together
　　Holding their neighbours' tails:—

"Our fathers lived in the forest,
　　"Foolish people were they,
They went down to the cornland
　　"To teach the farmers to play.

"Our fathers frisked in the millet,
　　"Our fathers skipped in the wheat;

"Our father hung from the branches,
　"Our fathers danced in the street.

Then came the terrible farmers,
　"Nothing of play they knew,
Only . . . they caught our fathers
　"And set them to labour too!

"Set them to work in the cornland
　　"With ploughs and sickles and flails,
"Put them in mud-walled prisons,
　"And—cut off their beautiful tails!

"Now, we can watch our fathers,
　"Sullen and bowed and old,
"Stooping over the millet,
　"Sharing the silly mould;

"Driving a foolish furrow,
　"Mending a muddy yoke,
"Sleeping in mud-walled prisons,
　"Steeping their food in smoke.

"We may not speak with our fathers,
　"For if the farmers knew
"They would come up to the forest
　"And set us to labour too."

This is the horrible story
　Told as the twilight fails
And the monkeys walk together
　Holding their neighbours' tails.

II

'Twas when the rain fell steady an' the Ark was pitched an' ready,
　That Noah got his orders for to take the bastes below;
He dragged them all together by the horn an' hide an' feather'
　An' all excipt the Donkey was agreeable to go.

First Noah spoke him fairly, thin talked to him sevairely,
　An' thin he cursed him squarely to the glory av the Lord:—
"Divil take the ass that bred you, and the greater ass that fed you!
　"Divil go wid ye, ye spalpeen!" an' the Donkey wint aboard.

But the wind was always failin', an' 'twas most onaisy sailin',
　An' the ladies in the cabin couldn't stand the stable air;
An' the bastes betwuxt the hatches, they tuk an' died in batches,
　Till Noah said:—"There's wan av us that hasn't paid his fare!"

For he heard a flusteration 'mid the bastes av all creation—
　The trumpetin' av elephints an' bellowin' av whales;
An' he saw forninst the windy whin he wint to stop the shindy
　The Divil wid a stable-fork bedivillin' their tails.

The Divil cursed outrageous, but Noah said umbrageous:—
　"To what am I indebted for this tenant-right invasion"
An' the Divil gave for answer:"Evict me if you can, sir,
　"For I came in wid the Donkey—on your Honour's invitation"

Pan in Vermont
1893

*(About the 15th of this month you may expect our Mr.——, with the usual Spring Seed,
etc., Catalogues.*—FLORISTS' ANNOUNCEMENT)

It's forty in the shade to-day, the spouting eaves declare;
The boulders nose above the drift, the southern slopes are bare;
Hub-deep in slush Apollo's car swings north along the Zodiac.
Good lack, the Spring is back, and Pan is on the road!

His house is Gee & Tellus' Sons,—so goes his jest with men—
He sold us Zeus knows what year; he'll take us in again.
Disguised behind a livery-team, fur-coated, rubber-shod—
Yet Apis from the bull-pen lows—he knows his brother God!

Now down the lines of tasselled pines the yearning whispers wake—
Pithys of old thy love behold!　Come in for Hermes' sake!
How long since that so-Boston boot with reeling Maenads ran?
Numen adest! Let be the rest.　Pipe and we pay, O Pan.

(What though his phlox and hollyhocks ere half a month demised?
What though his ampelopsis clambered not as advertised?
Though every seed was guaranteed and every standard true—
Forget, forgive they did not live!　Believe, and buy anew!)

Now o'er a careless knee he flings the painted page abroad—
Such bloom hath never eye beheld this side the Eden Sword;
Such fruit Pomona marks her own, yea, Liber oversees,
That we may reach (one dollar each) the Lost Hesperides!

Serene, assenting, unabashed, he writes our orders down:—
Blue Asphodel on all our paths—a few true bays for crown—
Uncankered bud, immortal flower, and leaves that never fall—
Apples of Gold, of Youth, of Health—and—thank you, Pan, that's all

He's off along the drifted pent to catch the Windsor train,
And swindle every citizen from Keene to Lake Champlain;
But where his goat's-hoof cut the crust—beloved, look below—
He's left us (I'll forgive him all) the may-flower 'neath her snow!

Verses On Games

(To "An Almanac of Twelve Sports", by W. Nicholson, 1898)

> Here is a horse to tame—
>   Here is a gun to handle—
> God knows you can enter the game
>   If you'll only pay for the same,
> And the price of the game is a candle—
>   A single flickering candle!

JANUARY
(*Hunting*)

Certes, it is a noble sport,
  And the men have quitted selle and swum for't.
But I am of the meeker sort
  And I prefer Surtees in comfort.

Reach me my *Handley Cross* again,
  My run, where never danger lurks, is
With Jorrocks and his deathless train—
  Pigg, Binjimin, and Artaxerxes.

FEBRUARY
(*Coursing*)

Most men harry the world for fun—
  Each man seeks it a different way,
But "of all the daft devils under the sun,
  A greyhound's the daftest," says Jorrocks J.

MARCH
(*Racing*)

The horse is ridden—the jockey rides—
  The backers back—the owners own—
But . . . there are lots of things besides,
  And *I* should let this game alone.

APRIL
(*Rowing*)

The Pope of Rome he could not win
From pleasant meats and pleasant sin
These who, replying not, submit
Unto the curses of the Pit
Which that stern Coach (oh, greater shame)
Flings forth by number not by name.
Can Triple Crown or Jesuit's oath
Do what one wrathful trainer doth?

MAY
(*Fishing*)

Behold a parable.   A fished for B
C took her bait; her heart being set on D.
Thank Heaven who cooled your blood and
    cramped your wishes,
Men and not Gods torment you, little fishes!

JUNE
(*Cricket*)

Thank God who made the British Isles
    And taught me how to play,
I do not worship crocodiles,
    Or bow the knee to clay!
Give me a willow wand and I
    With hide and cork and twine
From century to century
    Will gambol round my shrine!

JULY
(*Archery*)

The child of the Nineties considers with laughter
The maid whom his sire in the Sixties ran after,
While careering himself in pursuit of a girl whom
The Twenties will dub a "last-century heirloom."

AUGUST
(*Coaching*)

The Pious Horse to church may trot,
    A maid may work a man's salvation . . .
Four horses and a girl are not,
    However, roads to reformation.

SEPTEMBER
(*Shooting*)

"Peace upon Earth, Goodwill to men"
    So greet we Christmas Day!
Oh, Christian, load your gun and then,
    Oh, Christian, out and slay.

OCTOBER
(*Golf*)

Why Golf is Art and Art is Golf
    We have not far to seek—
So much depends upon the lie,
    So much upon the cleek.

NOVEMBER
(*Boxing*)

Read here the moral roundly writ
    For him who into battle goes—
Each soul that, hitting hard or hit,
    Endureth gross or ghostly foes.
    Prince, blown by many overthrows
Half blind with shame, half choked with dirt,
    Man cannot tell, but Allah knows
How much the other side was hurt!

DECEMBER
(*Skating*)

Over the ice she flies
    Perfect and poised and fair.
Stars in my true-love's eyes ·
    Teach me to do and dare.
Now will I fly as she flies—
    Woe for the stars that misled.
Stars I beheld in her eyes
    Now do I see in my head!

> *Now we must come away.*
> *What are you out of pocket?*
> *Sorry to spoil your play*
> *But somebody says we must pay,*
> *And the candle's down to the socket—*
> *Its horribly tallowy socket.*

Tomlinson

1891

Now Tomlinson gave up the ghost at his house in Berkeley Square,
And a Spirit came to his bedside and gripped him by the hair—
A Spirit gripped him by the hair and carried him far away,
Till he heard as the roar of a rain-fed ford the roar of the Milky Way:
Till he heard the roar of the Milky Way die down and drone and cease,
And they came to the Gate within the wall where Peter holds the keys.
"Stand up, stand up now, Tomlinson, and answer loud and high
"The good that ye did for sake of men or ever ye came to die—
"The good that ye did for the sake of men on little Earth so lone!"
And the naked soul of Tomlinson grew white as a rain-washed bone.

"Oh I have a friend on Earth," he said, "that was my priest and guide,
"And well would he answer all for me if he were at my side."
—"For that ye strove in neighbour-love it shall be written fair,
"But now ye wait at Heaven's Gate and not in Berkeley Square:
"Though we called your friend from his bed this night, he could not
  speak for you,
"For the race is run by one and one and never by two and two."
Then Tomlinson looked up and down, and little gain was there,
For the naked stars grinned overhead, and he saw that his soul was bare.
The Wind that blows between the Worlds, it cut him like a knife,
And Tomlinson took up the tale and spoke of his good in life.
"O this I have read in a book," he said, "and that was told to me,
"And this I have thought that another man thought of a Prince in
  Muscovy."
The good souls flocked like homing doves and bade him clear the path,
And Peter twirled the jangling keys in weariness and wrath.
"Ye have read, ye have heard, ye have thought," he said, "and the tale is
  yet to run:
"By the worth of the body that once ye had, give answer—what ha'ye
  done?"
Then Tomlinson looked back and forth, and little good it bore,

For the darkness stayed at his shoulder-blade and Heaven's Gate before:—
"O this I have felt, and this I have guessed, and this I have heard men
  say,
"And this they wrote that another man wrote of a carl in Norroway."
"Ye have read, ye have felt, ye have guessed, good lack! Ye have
  hampered Heaven's Gate;
"There's little room between the stars in idleness to prate!
"For none may reach by hired speech of neighbour, priest, and kin
"Through borrowed deed to God's good meed that lies so fair within;
"Get hence, get hence to the Lord of Wrong, for the doom has yet to run,
"And . . . the faith that ye share with Berkeley Square uphold you,
  Tomlinson!"

The Spirit gripped him by the hair, and sun by sun they fell
Till they came to the belt of Naughty Stars that rim the mouth of Hell.
The first are red with pride and wrath, the next are white with pain,
But the third are black with clinkered sin that cannot burn again.
They may hold their path, they may leave their path, with never a soul to
  mark:
They may burn or freeze, but they must not cease in the Scorn of the
  Outer Dark.
The Wind that blows between the Worlds, it nipped him to the bone,
And he yearned to the flare of Hell-gate there as the light of his own
  hearth-stone.
The Devil he sat behind the bars, where the desperate legions drew,
But he caught the hasting Tomlinson and would not let him through.
"Wot ye the price of good pit-coal that I must pay?" said he,
"That ye rank yoursel' so fit for Hell and ask no leave of me?
"I am all o'er-sib to Adam's breed that ye should give me scorn,
"For I strove with God for your First Father the day that he was born.
"Sit down, sit down upon the slag, and answer loud and high
"That harm that ye did to the Sons of Men or ever you came to die."
And Tomlinson looked up and up, and saw against the night
The belly of a tortured star blood-red in Hell-Mouth light;
And Tomlinson looked down and down, and saw beneath his feet .
The frontlet of a tortured star milk-white in Hell-Mouth heat.
"O I had a love on earth," said he, "that kissed me to my fall;
"And if ye would call my love to me I know she would answer all."
—"All that ye did in love forbid it shall be written fair,
"But now ye wait at Hell-Mouth Gate and not in Berkeley Square:
"Though we whistled your love from her bed to-night, I trow she would
  not run,
"For the sin ye do by two and two ye must pay for one by one!"
The Wind that blows between the Worlds, it cut him like a knife,
And Tomlinson took up the tale and spoke of his sins in life:—

"Once I ha' laughed at the power of Love and twice at the grip of the
    Grave,
"And thrice I ha' patted my God on the head that men might call me
    brave."
The Devil he blew on a brandered soul and set it aside to cool:—
"Do ye think I would waste my good pit-coal on the hide of a brain-sick
    fool?
"I see no worth in the hobnailed mirth or the jolthead jest ye did
"That I should waken my gentlemen that are sleeping three on a grid."
Then Tomlinson looked back and forth, and there was little grace,
For Hell-Gate filled the houseless soul with the Fear of Naked Space.
"Nay, this I ha' heard," quo' Tomlinson, "and this was noised abroad,
"And this I ha' got from a Belgian book on the word of a dead French
    lord."
—"Ye ha' heard, ye ha' read, ye ha' got, good lack! and the tale begins afresh—
"Have ye sinned one sin for the pride o' the eye or the sinful lust of the
    flesh?"
Then Tomlinson he gripped the bars and yammered, "Let me in—
"For I mind that I borrowed my neighbour's wife to sin the deadly sin."
The Devil he grinned behind the bars, and banked the fires high:
"Did ye read of that sin in a book?" said he; and Tomlinson said, "Ay!"
The Devil he blew upon his nails, and the little devils ran,
And he said: "Go husk this whimpering thief that comes in the guise of a
    man:
"Winnow him out 'twixt star and star, and sieve his proper worth:
"There's sore decline in Adam's line if this be spawn of Earth."
Empusa's crew, so naked-new they may not face the fire,
But weep that they bin too small to sin to the height of their desire,
Over the coal they chased the Soul, and racked it all abroad;
As children rifle a caddis-case or the raven's foolish hoard.
And back they came with the tattered Thing, as children after play,
And they said: "The soul that he got from God he has bartered clean
    away.
"We have threshed a stook of print and book, and winnowed a chattering
    wind,
"And many a soul wherefrom he stole, but his we cannot find.
"We have handled him, we have dandled him, we have seared him to the
    bone,
"And, Sire, if tooth and nail show truth he has no soul of his own."
The Devil he bowed his head on his breast and rumbled deep and low:—
"I'm all o'er-sib to Adam's breed that I should bid him go.
"Yet close we lie, and deep we lie, and if I gave him place,
"My gentlemen that are so proud would flout me to my face;
"They'd call my house a common stews and me a careless host,
"And—I would not anger my gentlemen for the sake of a shiftless ghost."

The Devil he looked at the mangled Soul that prayed to feel the flame,
And he thought of Holy Charity, but he thought of his own good name:—
"Now ye could haste my coal to waste, and sit ye down to fry.
"Did ye think of that theft for yourself?" said he; and Tomlinson said,
    "Ay!"
The Devil he blew an outward breath, for his heart was free from care:—
"Ye have scarce the soul of a louse," he said, "but the roots of sin are
    there,
"And for that sin should ye come in were I the lord alone,
"But sinful pride has rule inside—ay, mightier than my own.
"Honour and Wit, for-damned they sit, to each his Priest and Whore;
"Nay, scarce I dare myself go there, and you they'd torture sore.
"Ye are neither spirit nor spirk," he said; "ye are neither book nor
    brute—
"Go, get ye back to the flesh again for the sake of Man's repute.
"I'm all o'er-sib to Adam's breed that I should mock your pain,
"But look that ye win to worthier sin ere ye come back again.
"Get hence, the hearse is at your door—the grim black stallions wait—
"They bear your clay to place to-day. Speed, lest ye come too late!
"Go back to Earth with a lip unsealed—go back with an open eye,
"And carry my word to the Sons of Men or ever ye come to die:
"That the sin they do by two and two they must pay for one by one,
"And . . . the God that you took from a printed book be with you,
    Tomlinson!"

En-dor

1914-19—?

"Behold there is a woman that hath a familiar spirit at En-dor."

1 SAMUEL xxviii.7.

The road to En-dor is easy to tread
    For Mother or yearning Wife.
There, it is sure, we shall meet our Dead
    As they were even in life.
Earth has not dreamed of the blessing in store
For desolate hearts on the road to En-dor.

Whispers shall comfort us out of the dark—
    Hands—ah, God!—that we knew!
Visions and voices—look and hark!—
    Shall prove that the tale is true,
And that those who have passed to the further shore
May be hailed—at a price—on the road to En-dor.

But they are so deep in their new eclipse
   Nothing they can say can reach
Unless it be uttered by alien lips
   And framed in a stranger's speech.
The son must send word to the mother that bore,
Through an hireling's mouth. 'Tis the rule of En-dor.

And not for nothing these gifts are shown
   By such as delight our Dead.
They must twitch and stiffen and slaver and groan
   Ere the eyes are set in the head,
And the voice from the belly begins. Therefore,
We pay them a wage where they ply at En-dor.

Even so, we have need of faith
   And patience to follow the clue.
Often, at first, what the dear one saith
   Is babble, or jest, or untrue.
(Lying spirits perplex us sore
Till our loves—and their lives—are well known at En-dor) . . .

Oh, the road to En-dor is the oldest road
   And the craziest road of all!
Straight it runs to the Witch's abode,
   As it did in the days of Saul,
And nothing has changed of the sorrow in store
For such as go down on the road to En-dor!

The Female Of The Species

1911

When the Himalayan peasant meets the he-bear in his pride,
He shouts to scare the monster, who will often turn aside.
But the she-bear thus accosted rends the peasant tooth and nail.
For the female of the species is more deadly than the male.

When Nag the basking cobra hears the careless foot of man,
He will sometimes wriggle sideways and avoid it if he can.
But his mate makes no such motion where she camps beside the trail.
For the female of the species is more deadly than the male.

When the early Jesuit fathers preached to Hurons and Chóctaws,
They prayed to be delivered from the vengeance of the squaws.
'Twas the women, not the warriors, turned those stark enthusiasts pale.
For the female of the species is more deadly than male.

Man's timid heart is bursting with the things he must not say,
For the Woman that God gave him isn't his to give away;
But when hunter meets with husband, each confirms the other's tale—
The female of the species is more deadly than the male.

Man, a bear in most relations—worm and savage otherwise,—
Man propounds negotiations, Man accepts the compromise.
Very rarely will he squarely push the logic of a fact
To its ultimate conclusion in unmitigated act.

Fear, or foolishness, impels him, ere he lay the wicked low,
To concede some form of trial even to his fiercest foe.
Mirth obscene diverts his anger—Doubt and Pity oft perplex
Him in dealing with an issue—to the scandal of The Sex!

But the Woman that God gave him, every fibre of her frame
Proves her launched for one sole issue, armed and engined for the same;
And to serve that single issue, lest the generations fail,
The female of the species must be deadlier than the male.

She who faces Death by torture for each life beneath her breast
May not deal in doubt or pity—must not swerve for fact or jest.
These be purely male diversions—not in these her honour dwells.
She the Other Law we live by, is that Law and nothing else.

She can bring no more to living than the powers that make her great
As the Mother of the Infant and the Mistress of the Mate.
And when Babe and Man are lacking and she strides unclaimed to claim
Her right as femme (and baron), her equipment is the same.

She is wedded to convictions—in default of grosser ties;
Her contentions are her children, Heaven help him who denies!—
He will meet no suave discussion, but the instant, white-hot, wild,
Wakened female of the species warring as for spouse and child.

Unprovoked and awful charges—even so the she-bear fights,
Speech that drips, corrodes, and poisons—even so the cobra bites,
Scientific vivisection of one nerve till it is raw
And the victim writhes in anguish—like the Jesuit with the squaw!

So it comes that Man, the coward, when he gathers to confer
With his fellow-braves in council, dare not leave a place for her
Where, at war with Life and Conscience, he uplifts his erring hands
To some God of Abstract Justice—which no woman understands.

And Man knows it!   Knows, moreover, that the Woman that God gave
    him
Must command but may not govern—shall enthral but not enslave him.
And *She* knows, because She warns him, and Her instincts never fail,
That the Female of Her Species is more deadly than the Male.

A Recantation

1917

(TO LYDE OF THE MUSIC HALLS)

What boots it on the Gods to call?
Since, answered or unheard,
We perish with the Gods and all
Things made—except the Word.

Ere certain Fate had touched a heart
    By fifty years made cold,
I judged thee, Lyde, and thy art
    O'erblown and over-bold.

But he—but he, of whom bereft
    I suffer vacant days—
He on his shield not meanly left—
    He cherished all thy lays.

Witness the magic coffer stocked
    With convoluted runes
Wherein thy very voice was locked
    And linked to circling tunes.

Witness thy portrait, smoke-defiled,
    That decked his shelter-place.
Life seemed more present, wrote the child,
    Beneath thy well-known face.

And when the grudging days restored
    Him for a breath to home,
He, with fresh crowds of youth, adored
    Thee making mirth in Rome.

Therefore, I humble, join the hosts,
    Loyal and loud, who bow
To thee as Queen of Song—and ghosts,
    For I remember how

Never more rampant rose the Hall
    At thy audacious line
Than when the news came in from Gaul
    Thy son had—followed mine.

But thou didst hide it in thy breast
    And, capering, took the brunt
Of blaze and blare, and launched the jest
    That swept next week the Front.

Singer to children!   Ours possessed
   Sleep before noon—but thee,
Wakeful each midnight for the rest,
   No holocaust shall free!

Yet they who use the Word assigned,
   To hearten and make whole,
Not less than Gods have served mankind,
   Though vultures rend their soul.

The Explanation

1890

Love and Death once ceased their strife
At the Tavern of Man's Life.
Called for wine, and threw—alas!—
Each his quiver on the grass.
When the bout was o'er they found
Mingled arrows strewed the ground.
Hastily they gathered then
Each the loves and lives of men.
Ah, the fateful dawn deceived!
Mingled arrows each one sheaved.
Death's dread armoury was stored
With the shafts he most abhorred;
Love's light quiver groaned beneath
Venom-headed darts of Death.
Thus it was they wrought our woe
At the Tavern long ago.
Tell me, do our masters know,
Loosing blindly as they fly,
Old men love while young men die?

A Pilgrim's Way

I do not look for holy saints to guide me on my way,
Or male and female devilkins to lead my feet astray.
If these are added, I rejoice—if not, I shall not mind,
So long as I have leave and choice to meet my fellow-kind.
   For as we come and as we go (and deadly-soon go we!)
   The people, Lord, Thy people, are good enough for me!

Thus I will honour pious men whose virtue shines so bright
(Though none are more amazed than I when I by chance do right),
And I will pity foolish men for woe their sins have bred
(Though ninety-nine per cent. of mine I brought on my own head).
    And, Amorite or Eremite, or General Averagee,
    The people, Lord, Thy people, are good enough for me!

And when they bore me overmuch, I will not shake mine ears,
Recalling many thousand such whom I have bored to tears.
And when they labour to impress, I will not doubt nor scoff;
Since I myself have done no less and—sometimes pulled it off!
    Yea, as we are and we are not, and we pretend to be,
    The people, Lord, Thy people, are good enough for me!

And when they work me random wrong, as oftentimes hath been,
I will not cherish hate too long (my hands are none too clean).
And when they do me random good I will not feign surprise;
No more than those whom I have cheered with wayside courtesies.
    But, as we give and as we take—whate'er our takings be—
    The people, Lord, Thy people, are good enough for me!

But when I meet with frantic folk who sinfully declare
There is no pardon for their sin, the same I will not spare
Till I have proved that Heaven and Hell which in our hearts we have
Show nothing irredeemable on either side the grave.
    For as we live and as we die—if utter Death there be—
    The people, Lord, Thy people, are good enough for me!

Deliver me from every pride—the Middle, High, and Low—
That bars me from a brother's side, whatever pride he show.
And purge me from all heresies of thought and speech and pen
That bid me judge him otherwise than I am judged.   *Amen!*
That I may sing of Crowd or King or road-borne company,
That I may labour in my day, vocation and degree,
To prove the same by deed and name, and hold unshakenly
(Where'er I go, whate'er I know, whoe'er my neighbour be)
This single faith in Life and Death and to Eternity:
"The people, Lord, Thy people, are good enough for me!"

The Answer

1892

A rose, in tatters on the garden path,
    Cried out to God and murmured 'gainst His Wrath,
Because a sudden wind at twilight's hush

Had snapped her stem alone of all the bush.
And God, Who hears both sun-dried dust and sun,
Had pity, whispering to that luckless one.
"Sister, in that thou sayest We did not well—
"What voices heardst thou when thy petals fell?"
And the Rose answered, "In that evil hour
"A voice said, 'Father, wherefore falls the flower?
" 'For lo, the very gossamers are still,'
"And a voice answered, 'Son, by Allah's Will!' "

Then softly as a rain-mist on the sward,
Came to the Rose the Answer of the Lord:
"Sister, before We smote the Dark in twain,
"Ere yet the Stars saw one another plain,
"Tim, Tide, and Space, We bound unto the task
"That thou shouldst fall, and such an one should ask."
Whereat the withered flower, all content,
Died as they die whose days are innocent;
While he who questioned why the flower fell
Caught hold of God and saved his soul from Hell.

Mary's Son

1911

If you stop to find out what your wages will be
    And how they will clothe and feed you,
Willie, my son, don't you go on the Sea,
    For the Sea will never need you.

If you ask for the reason of every command,
    And argue with people about you,
Willie, my son, don't go on the Land,
    For the Land will do better without you.

If you stop to consider the work you have done
    And to boast what your labour is worth, dear,
Angels may come for you, Willie, my son,
    But you'll never be wanted on Earth, dear!

The Gift Of The Sea

1890

The dead child lay in the shroud,
  And the widow watched beside;
And her mother slept, and the Channel swept
  The gale in the teeth of the tide.

But the mother laughed at all.
  "I have lost my man in the sea,
"And the child is dead.   Be still," she said.
  "What more can ye do to me?"

The widow watched the dead,
  And the candle guttered low,
And she tried to sing the Passing Song
  That bids the poor soul go.

And "Mary take you now," she sang,
  "That lay against my heart,"
And "Mary smooth your crib to-night,"
  But she could not say "Depart."

Then came a cry from the sea,
  But the sea-rime blinded the glass,
And "Heard ye nothing, mother?" she said,
  "'Tis the child that waits to pass."

And the nodding mother sighed:
  "'Tis a lambing ewe in the whin,
"For why should the christened soul cry out
  "That never knew of sin?"

"O feet I have held in my hand,
  "O hands at my heart to catch,
"How should they know the road to go,
  "And how should they lift the latch?"

They laid a sheet to the door,
  With the little quilt atop,
That it might not hurt from the cold or the dirt,
  But the crying would not stop.

The widow lifted the latch
  And strained her eyes to see,
And opened the door on the bitter shore
  To let the soul go free.

There was neither glimmer nor ghost,
 There was neither spirit nor spark,
And "Heard ye nothing, mother?" she said,
 "'Tis crying for me in the dark."

And the nodding mother sighed:
 "'Tis sorrow makes ye dull;
"Have ye yet to learn the cry of the tern,
 "Or the wail of the wind-blown gull?"

"The terns are blown inland,
 "The grey gull follows the plough.
"'Twas never a bird, the voice I heard,
 "O mother, I heard it now!"

"Lie still, dear lamb, lie still;
 "The child is passed from harm,
"'Tis the ache in your breast that broke your rest,
 "And the feel of an empty arm."

She put her mother aside,
 "In Mary's name let be!
"For the peace of my soul I must go," she said,
 And she went to the calling sea.

In the heel of the wind-bit pier,
 Where the twisted weed was piled,
She came to the life she had missed by an hour,
 For she came to a little child.

She laid it into her breast,
 And back to her mother she came,
But it would not feed and it would not heed,
 Though she gave it her own child's name.

And the dead child dripped on her breast,
 And her own in the shroud lay stark;
And "God forgive us, mother," she said,
 "We let it die in the dark!"

The King

1894

"Farewell, romance!" the Cave-men said;
 "With bone well carved He went away.
"Flint arms the ignoble arrowhead,

"And jasper tips the spear to-day.
"Changed are the Gods of Hunt and Dance,
"And He with these.   Farewell, Romance!"

"Farewell, Romance!" the Lake-folk sighed;
    "We lift the weight of flatling years;
"The caverns of the mountain-side
    "Hold Him who scorns our hutted piers.
"Lost hills whereby we dare not dwell,
"Guard ye His rest.   Romance, Farewell!"

"Farewell, Romance!" the Soldier spoke;
    "By sleight of sword we may not win,
"But scuffle 'mid uncleanly smoke
    "Of arquebus and culverin.
"Honour is lost, and none may tell
"Who paid good blows.   Romance, farewell!"

"Farewell, Romance!" the Traders cried;
    "Our keels have lain with every sea.
"The dull-returning wind and tide
    "Heave up the wharf where we would be;
"The known and noted breezes swell
"Our trudging sails.   Romance, farewell!"

"Goodbye, Romance!" the Skipper said;
    "He vanished with the coal we burn.
"Our dial marks full-steam ahead,
    "Our speed is timed to half a turn.
"Sure as the ferried barge we ply
"'Twixt port and port.   Romance, goodbye!"

"Romance!" the season-tickets mourn,
    "*He* never ran to catch His train,
"But passed with coach and guard and horn—
    "And left the local—late again!
"Confound Romance!". . . And all unseen
Romance brought up the nine-fifteen.

His hand was on the lever laid,
    His oil-can soothed the worrying cranks,
His whistle waked the snowbound grade,
    His fog-horn cut the reeking Banks;
By dock and deep and mine and mill
The Boy-god reckless laboured still!

Robed, crowned and throned, He wove His spell,
  Where heart-blood beat or hearth-smoke curled,
With inconsidered miracle,
  Hedged in a backward-gazing world:
Then taught His chosen bard to say:
"Our King was with us—yesterday!"

The Last Rhyme Of True Thomas

1893

The King has called for priest and cup,
  The King has taken spur and blade
To dub True Thomas a belted knight,
  And all for the sake of the songs he made.

They have sought him high, they have sought him low,
  They have sought him over down and lea.
They have found him by the milk-white thorn
  That guards the Gates of Faerie.

'Twas bent beneath and blue above:
  Their eyes were held that they might not see
The kine that grazed beneath the knowes,
  Oh, they were the Queens of Faerie!

"Now cease your song," the King he said,
  "Oh, cease your song and get you dight
"To vow your vow and watch your arms,
  "For I will dub you a belted knight.

"For I will give you a horse o' pride,
  "Wi' blazon and spur and page and squire;
"Wi' keep and tail and seizin and law,
  "And land to hold at your desire."

True Thomas smiled above his harp,
  And turned his face to the naked sky,
Where, blown before the wastrel wind,
  The thistle-down she floated by.

"I ha' vowed my vow in another place,
  "And bitter oath it was on me.
"I ha' watched my arms the lee-long night,
  "Where five-score fighting men would flee.

"My lance is tipped o' the hammered flame,
    "My shield is beat o' the moonlight cold;
"And I won my spurs in the Middle World,
    "A thousand fathom beneath the mould.

"And what should I make wi' a horse o' pride,
    "And what should I make wi' a sword so brown,
"But spill the rings of the Gentle Folk
    "And flyte my kin in the Fairy Town?

"And what should I make wi' blazon and belt,
    "Wi' keep and tail and seizin and fee,
"And what should I do wi' page and squire
    "That am a king in my own countrie?

"For I send east and I send west,
    "And I send far as my will may flee,
"By dawn and dusk and the drinking rain,
    "And syne my Sendings return to me.

"They come wi' news of the groanin' earth,
    "They come wi' news of the roarin' sea.
"Wi' word of Spirit and Ghost and Flesh,
    "And man, that's mazed among the three."

The King he bit his nether lip,
    And smote his hand upon his knee:
"By the faith of my soul, True Thomas,' he said,
    "Ye waste no wit in courtesie!

"As I desire, unto my pride,
    "Can I make Earls by three and three,
"To run before and ride behind
    "And serve the sons o' my body."

"And what care I for your row-foot earls,
    "Or all the sons o' your body?
"Before they win to the Pride o' Name,
    "I trow they all ask leave o' me.

"For I make Honour wi' muckle mouth,
    "As I make Shame wi' mincing feet,
"To sing wi' the priests at the market-cross,
    "Or run wi' the dogs in the naked street.

"And some they give me the good red gold,
    "And some they give me the white money,
"And some they give me a clout o' meal,
    "For they be people of low degree.

"And the song I sing for the counted gold
  "The same I sing for the white money,
"But best I sing for the clout o' meal
  "That simple people have given me."

The King cast down a silver groat,
  A silver groat o' Scots money,
"If I come wi' a poor man's dole," he said,
  "True Thomas, will ye harp to me?"

"Whenas I harp to the children small,
  "They press me close on either hand.
"And who are you," True Thomas said,
  "That you should ride while they must stand?

"Light down, light down from your horse o' pride,
  "I trow ye talk too loud and hie,
"And I will make you a triple word,
  "And syne, if ye dare, ye shall 'noble me."

He has lighted down from his horse o' pride,
  And set his back against a stone.
"Now guard you well," True Thomas said,
  "Ere I rax your heart from your breast-bone!"

True Thomas played upon his harp,
  The fairy harp that couldna lee,
And the first least word the proud King heard,
  Its harpit the salt tear out o' his e'e.

"Oh, I see the love that I lost long syne,
  "I touch the hope that I may not see,
"And all that I did of hidden shame,
  "Like little snakes they hiss at me.

"The sun is lost at noon—at noon!
  "The dread of doom has grippit me.
"True Thomas, hide me under your cloak,
  "God wot, I'm little fit to dee!"

'Twas bent beneath and blue above—
  'Twas open field and running flood—
Where, hot on heath and dyke and wall,
  The high sun warmed the adder's brood.

"Lie down, lie down," True Thomas said.
  "The God shall judge when all is done,
"But I will bring you a better word
  "And lift the cloud that I laid on."

True Thomas played upon his harp,
    That birled and brattled to his hand,
And the next least word True Thomas made,
    It garred the King take horse and brand.

"Oh, I hear the tread o' the fighting-men,
    "I see the sun on splent and spear.
"I mark the arrow outen the fern
    "That flies so low and sings so clear!

"Advance my standards to that war,
    "And bid my good knights prick and ride;
"The gled shall watch as fierce a fight
    'As e'er was fought on the Border-side!"

'Twas bent beneath and blue above,
    'Twas nodding grass and naked sky,
Where, ringing up the wastrel wind,
    The eyass stooped upon the pye.

True Thomas sighed above his harp,
    And turned the song on the midmost string;
And the last least word True Thomas made,
    He harpit his dead youth back to the King.

"Now I am prince, and I do well
    "To love my love withouten fear;
"To walk with man in fellowship,
    "And breathe my horse behind the deer.

"My hounds they bay unto thy death,
    "The buck has couched beyond the burn,
"My love she waits at her window
    "To wash my hands when I return.

"For that I live am I content
    "(Oh! I have seen my true love's eyes)
"To stand with Adam in Eden-glade,
    "And run in the woods o' Paradise!"

'Twas naked sky and nodding grass,
    'Twas running flood and wastrel wind,
Where, checked against the open pass,
    The red deer turned to wait the hind.

True Thomas laid his harp away,
    And louted low at the saddle-side;
He has taken stirrup and hauden rein,
    And set the King on his horse o' pride.

"Sleep ye or wake," True Thomas said,
  "That sit so still, that muse so long?
"Sleep ye or wake?—till the Latter Sleep
  "I trow ye'll not forget my song.

"I ha' harpit a Shadow out o' the sun
  "To stand before your face and cry;
"I ha' armed the earth beneath your heel,
  "And over your head I ha' dusked the sky.

"I ha' harpit ye up to the Throne o' God,
  "I ha' harpit your midmost soul in three.
"I ha' harpit ye down to the Hinges o' Hell,
  "And—ye—would—make— a Knight o' me!"

The Sons Of Martha

1907

The sons of Mary seldom bother, for they have inherited that good part;
But the Sons of Martha favour their Mother of the careful soul and the troubled heart.
And because she lost her temper once, and because she was rude to the Lord her Guest,
Her Sons must wait upon Mary's Sons, world without end, reprieve, or rest.

It is their care in all the ages to take the buffet and cushion the shock.
It is their care that the gear engages; it is their care that the switches lock.
It is their care that the wheels run truly; it is their care to embark and entrain,
Tally, transport, and deliver duly the Sons of Mary by land and main.

They say to mountains, "Be ye removèd." They say to the lesser floods, "Be dry."
Under their rods are the rocks reprovèd—they are not afraid of that which is high.
Then do the hill-tops shake to the summit—then is the bed of the deep laid bare,
That the Sons of Mary may overcome it, pleasantly sleeping and unaware.

They finger death at their gloves' end where they piece and repiece the living wires.
He rears against the gates they tend: they feed him hungry behind their fires.
Early at dawn, ere men see clear, they stumble into his terrible stall,

And hale him forth like a haltered steer, and goad and turn him till
    evenfall.

To these from birth is Belief forbidden; from these till death is Relief afar.
They are concerned with matters hidden—under the earth-line their altars
    are—
The secret fountains to follow up, waters withdrawn to restore to the
    mouth,
And gather the floods as in a cup, and pour them again at a city's
    drouth.

They do not preach that their God will rouse them a little before the nuts
    work loose.
They do not teach that His Pity allows them to drop their job when they
    dam'-well choose.
As in the thronged and the lighted ways, so in the dark and the desert
    they stand,
Wary and watchful all their days that their brethren's days may be long in
    the land.

Raise ye the stone or cleave the wood to make some a path more fair or
    flat—
Lo, it is black already with blood some Son of Martha spilled for that!
Not as a ladder from earth to Heaven, not as a witness to any creed,
But simple service simply given to his own kind in their common need.

And the Sons of Mary smile and are blessèd—they know the Angels are
    on their side.
They know in them is the Grace confessed, and for them are the Mercies
    multiplied.
They sit at the Feet—they hear the Word—they see how truly the Promise
    runs.
They have cast their burden upon the Lord, and—the Lord He lays it on
    Martha's Sons!

Hymn Of Breaking Strain

1935

The careful text-books measure
    (Let all who build beware!)
The load, the shock, the pressure
    Material can bear.
So, when the buckled girder
    Lets down the grinding span,

The blame of loss, or murder,
　　Is laid upon the man.
　　　　Not on the Stuff—the Man!

But, in our daily dealing
　　With stone and steel, we find
The Gods have no such feeling
　　Of justice toward mankind.
To no set gauge they make us,—
　　For no laid course prepare—
And presently o'ertake us
　　With loads we cannot bear:
　　　　Too merciless to bear.

The prudent text-books give it
　　In tables at the end—
The stress that shears a rivet
　　Or makes a tie-bar bend—
What traffic wrecks macadam—
　　What concrete should endure—
But we, poor Sons of Adam,
　　Have no such literature,
　　　　To warn us or make sure!

We hold all Earth to plunder—
　　All Time and Space as well—
Too wonder-stale to wonder
　　At each new miracle;
Till, in the mid-illusion
　　Of Godhead 'neath our hand,
Falls multiple confusion
　　On all we did or planned—
　　　　The mighty works we planned.

We only of Creation
　　(Oh, luckier bridge and rail!)
Abide the twin-damnation—
　　To fail and know we fail.
Yet we—by which sole token
　　We know we once were Gods—
Take shame in being broken
　　However great the odds—
　　　　The Burden or the Odds.

Oh, veiled and secret Power
　　Whose paths we seek in vain,

Be with us in our hour
  Of overthrow and pain;
That we—by which sure token
  We know Thy ways are true—
In spite of being broken,
  Because of being broken,
    May rise and build anew.
    Stand up and build anew!

The Palace

1902

When I was King and a Mason— a Master proven and skilled—
I cleared me ground for a Palace such as a King should build.
I decreed and dug down my levels.   Presently under the silt,
I came on the wreck of a Palace such as a King had built.

There was no worth in the fashion—there was no wit in the plan—
Hither and thither, aimless, the ruined footings ran—
Masonry, brute, mishandled, but carven on every stone:
"*After me cometh a Builder.   Tell him, I too have known.*"

Swift to my use in my trenches, where my well-planned ground-works
    grew,
I tumbled his quoins and his ashlars, and cut and reset them anew.
Lime I milled of his marbles; burned it, slacked it, and spread;
Taking and leaving at pleasure the gifts of the humble dead.

Yet I despised not nor gloried; yet, as we wrenched them apart,
I read in the razed foundations the heart of that builder's heart.
As he had risen and pleaded, so did I understand
The form of the dream he had followed in the face of the thing he had
    planned.

When I was a King and a Mason—in the open noon of my pride,
They sent me a Word from the Darkness.   They whispered and called me
    aside.
They said—"The end is forbidden."   They said—"Thy use is fulfilled.
"Thy Palace shall stand as that other's—the spoil of a King who shall
    build."
I called my men from my trenches, my quarries, my wharves, and my
    sheers.
All I had wrought I abandoned to the faith of the faithless years.
Only I cut on the timber—only I carved on the stone:
"*After me cometh a Builder.   Tell him, I too have known!*"

Epitaphs of the War

1914–18

"EQUALITY OF SACRIFICE"

A. "I was a Have."   B. "I was a 'have-not.' "
    (*Together*). "What has thou given which I gave not?"

A SERVANT

We were together since the War began.
He was my servant—and the better man.

A SON

My son was killed while laughing at some jest.   I would I knew
What it was, and it might serve me in a time when jests are few.

AN ONLY SON

I have slain none except my Mother.   She
(Blessing her slayer) died of grief for me.

EX-CLERK

Pity not!   The Army gave
Freedom to a timid slave:
In which Freedom did he find
Strength of body, will, and mind:
By which strength he came to prove
Mirth, Companionship, and Love:
For which Love to Death he went:
In which Death he lies content.

THE WONDER

Body and Spirit I surrendered whole
To harsh Instructors—and received a soul . . .
If mortal man could change me through and through
From all I was—what may The God not do?

HINDU SEPOY IN FRANCE

This man in his own country prayed we know not to what Powers.
We pray Them to reward him for his bravery in ours.

THE COWARD

I could not look on Death, which being known,
Men led me to him, blindfold and alone.

SHOCK

My name, my speech, my self I had forgot.
My wife and children came—I knew them not.
I died. My Mother followed. At her call
And on her bosom I remembered all.

A GRAVE NEAR CAIRO

Gods of the Nile, should this stout fellow here
Get out—get out! He knows not shame nor fear.

PELICANS IN THE WILDERNESS

A Grave near Halfa

The blown sand heaps on me, that none may learn
Where I am laid for whom my children grieve . . .
O wings that beat at dawning, ye return
Out of the desert to your young at eve!

TWO CANADIAN MEMORIALS

I

We giving all gained all.
Neither lament us nor praise.
Only in all things recall,
It is Fear, not Death that slays.

II

From little towns in a far land we came,
To save our honour and a world aflame.
By little towns in a far land we sleep;
And trust that world we won for you to keep!

THE FAVOUR

Death favoured me from the first, well knowing I could not endure
To wait on him by day by day. He quitted by betters and came
Whistling over the fields, and, when he had made all sure,
"Thy line is at end," he said, "but at least I have saved its name."

THE BEGINNER

On the first hour of my first day
In front the trench I fell.
(Children in boxes at a play
Stand up to watch it well.)

R.A.F. (AGED EIGHTEEN)

Laughing through clouds, his milk-teeth still unshed,
Cities and men he smote from overhead.
His deaths delivered, he returned to play
Childlike, with childish things now put away.

THE REFINED MAN

I was of delicate mind.   I stepped aside for my needs,
   Disdaining the common office.   I was seen from afar and killed . . .
How is this matter for mirth?   Let each man be judged by his deeds.
   I have paid my price to live with myself on the terms that I willed.

NATIVE WATER-CARRIER (M.E.F.)

Prometheus brought down fire to men,
   This brought up water.
The Gods are jealous—now, as then,
   Giving no quarter.

BOMBED IN LONDON

On land and sea I strove with anxious care
To escape conscription.   It was in the air!

THE SLEEPY SENTINEL

Faithless the watch that I kept: now I have none to keep.
I was slain because I slept: now I am slain I sleep.
Let no man reproach me again, whatever watch is unkept—
I sleep because I am slain.   They slew me because I slept.

BATTERIES OUT OF AMMUNITION

If any mourn us in the workshop, say
We died because the shift kept holiday.

COMMON FORM

If any question why we died,
Tell them, because our fathers lied.

A DEAD STATESMAN

I could not dig: I dared not rob:
Therefore I lied to please the mob.
Now all my lies are proved untrue
And I must face the men I slew.
What tale shall serve me here among
Mine angry and defrauded young?

THE REBEL

If I had clamoured at Thy Gate
    For gift of Life on Earth,
And, thrusting through the souls that wait,
    Flung headlong into birth—
Even then, even then, for gin and snare
    About my pathway spread,
Lord, I had mocked Thy thoughtful care
    Before I joined the Dead!
But now? . . . I was beneath Thy Hand
    Ere yet the Planets came.
And now—though Planets pass, I stand
    The witness to Thy shame!

THE OBEDIENT

Daily, though no ears attended,
    Did my prayers arise.
Daily, though no fire descended,
    Did I sacrifice.
Though my darkness did not lift,
    Though I faced no lighter odds,
Though the Gods bestowed no gift,
        None the less,
    None the less, I served the Gods!

A DRIFTER OFF TARENTUM

He from the wind-bitten North with ship and companions descended,
    Searching for eggs of death spawned by invisible hulls.
Many he found and drew forth.   Of a sudden the fishery ended
    In flame and a clamours breath known to the eye-pecking gulls.

DESTROYER IN COLLISION

For Fog and Fate no charm is found
    To lighten or amend.
I, hurrying to my bride, was drowned—
    Cut down by my best friend.

CONVOY ESCORT

I was a shepherd to fools
    Causelessly bold or afraid.
They would not abide by my rules.
    Yet they escaped.   For I stayed.

UNKNOWN FEMALE CORPSE

Headless, lacking foot and hand,
Horrible I come to land.
I beseech all women's sons
Know I was a mother once.

RAPED AND REVENGED

One used and butchered me: another spied
Me broken—for which thing an hundred died.
So it was learned among the heathen hosts
How much a freeborn woman's favour costs.

SALONIKAN GRAVE

I have watched a thousand days
Push out and crawl into night
Slowly as tortoises.
Now I, too, follow these.
It is fever, and not the fight—
Time, not battle,—that slays.

THE BRIDEGROOM

Call me not false, beloved,
    If, from thy scarce-known breast
So little time removed,
    In other arms I rest.

For this more ancient bride,
    Whom coldly I embrace,
Was constant at my side
    Before I saw thy face.

Our marriage, often set—
    By miracle delayed—
At last is consummate,
    And cannot be unmade.

Live, then, whom Life shall cure,
    Almost, of Memory,
And leave us to endure
    Its immortality.

V.A.D. (MEDITERRANEAN)

Ah, would swift ships had never been, for then we ne'er had found,
These harsh Aegean rocks between, this little virgin drowned,
Whom neither spouse nor child shall morn, but men she nursed through
  pain
And—certain keels for whose return the heathen look in vain.

*On a Memorial Tablet in Holy Trinity Church,
Stratford-on-Avon*

We counterfeited once for your disport
　Men's joy and sorrow: but our day has passed.
We pray you pardon all where we fell short—
　Seeing we were your servants to this last.

JOURNALISTS

On a Panel in the Hall of the Institute of Journalists

We have served our day.

Justice

OCTOBER, 1918

*Across a world where all men grieve
　And grieving strive the more,
The great days rang like tides and leave
　Our dead on every shore.
Heavy the load we undergo,
　And our own hands prepare,
If we have parley with the foe,
　The load our sons must bear.*

Before we loose the word
　That bids new worlds to birth,
Needs must we loosen first the sword
　Of Justice upon earth;
Or else all else is vain
　Since life on earth began,
And the spent world sinks back again
　Hopeless of God and Man.

A People and their King
　Through ancient sin grown strong,
Because they feared no reckoning
　Would set no bound to wrong;
But now their hour is past,
　And we who bore it find
Evil Incarnate held at last
　To answer to mankind.

For agony and spoil
   Of nations beat to dust,
For poisoned air and tortured soil
   And cold, commanded lust,
And every secret woe
   The shuddering waters saw—
Willed and fulfilled by high and low—
   Let them relearn the Law:

That when the dooms are read,
   Not high nor low shall say:—
"My haughty or my humble head
   Has saved me in this day."
That, till the end of time,
   Their remnant shall recall
Their fathers' old, confederate crime
   Availed them not at all:

That neither schools nor priests,
   Nor Kings may build again
A people with the heart of beasts
   Made wise concerning men.
Whereby our dead shall sleep
   In honour, unbetrayed,
And we in faith and honour keep
   That peace for which they paid.

Seven Watchmen

1918

Seven Watchmen sitting in a tower,
   Watching what had come upon mankind,
Showed the Man the Glory and the Power,
   And bade him shape the Kingdom to his mind.
"All things on Earth your will shall win you"
   ('Twas so their counsel ran).
"But the Kingdom—the Kingdom is within you,"
   Said the Man's own mind to the Man.
     For time—and some time—
As it was in the bitter years before
   So it shall be in the over-sweetened hour—
That a man's mind is wont to tell him more
   Than Seven Watchmen sitting in a tower.

To Thomas Atkins

(Prelude to Barrack-Room Ballads which follow)

I have made for you a song,
And it may be right or wrong,
But only you can tell me if it's true.
I have tried for to explain
Both your pleasure and your pain,
And, Thomas, here's my best respects to you!

O there'll surely come a day
When they'll give you all your pay,
And treat you as a Christian ought to do;
So, until that day comes around,
Heaven keep you safe and sound,
And, Thomas, here's my best respects to you!

"Bobs"

1898

(Field-Marshal Lord Roberts of Kandahar: died in France 1914)

There's a little red-faced man,
　　Which is Bobs,
Rides the tallest 'orse 'e can—
　　Our Bobs.
If it bucks or kicks or rears,
'E can sit for twenty years
With a smile round both 'is ears—
　　Can't yer, Bobs?

Then 'ere's to Bobs Bahadur—little Bobs, Bobs, Bobs!
'E's our pukka Kandaharder—
　　Fightin' Bobs, Bobs, Bobs!
'E's the Dook of *Aggy Chel*;[1]
'E's the man that done us well,
An' we'll follow 'im to 'ell—
　　Won't we, Bobs?

If a limber's slipped a trace,
　　'Ook on Bobs.
If a marker's lost 'is place,
　　Dress by Bobs.

[1] Get ahead.

For 'e's eyes all up 'is coat,
An' a bugle in 'is throat,
An' you will not play the goat
  Under Bobs.

'E's a little down on drink,
  Chaplain Bobs;
But it keeps us outer Clink—
  Don't it Bobs?
So we will not complain
Tho' 'e's water on the brain,
If 'e leads us straight again—
  Blue-light[1] Bobs.

If you stood 'im on 'is head,
  Father Bobs,
You could spill a quart of lead
  Outer Bobs.
'E's been at it thirty years,
An-amassin' souveneers
In the way o' slugs an' spears—
  Ain't yer Bobs?

What 'e does not know o' war,
  Gen'ral Bobs,
You can arst the shop next door—
  Can't they Bobs?
Oh, 'e's little but he's wise,
'E's terror for 'is size,
An'—'e—*does—not—advertise*—
  Do yer, Bobs?

Now they've made a bloomin' Lord
  Outer Bobs,
Which was but 'is fair reward—
  Weren't it, Bobs?
So 'e'll wear a coronet
Where 'is 'elmet used to set;
But we know you won't forget—
  Will yer, Bobs?

Then 'ere's to Bobs Bahadur—little Bobs, Bobs, Bobs,
Pocket-Wellin'ton an' *arder*[2]—
  Fightin' Bobs, Bobs, Bobs!

---

[1]Temperance.   [2]And a half.

> This ain't no bloomin' ode,
> But you've 'elped the soldier's load,
> An' for benefits bestowed,
> > Bless yer, Bobs!

Danny Deever

"What are the bugles blowin' for?" said Files-on-Parade.
"To turn you out, to turn you out," The Colour-Sergeant said.
"What makes you look so white, so white?" said Files-on-Parade.
"I'm dreadin' what I've got to watch," the Colour-Sergeant said.
> For they're hangin' Danny Deever, you can hear the Dead March play,
> The Regiment's in 'ollow square—they're hangin' him to-day;
> They've taken of his buttons off an' cut his stripes away,
> An' they're hangin' Danny Deever in the mornin'.

"What makes the rear-rank breathe so 'ard?" said Files-on-Parade.
"It's bitter cold, it's bitter cold," the Colour-Sergeant said.
"What makes that front-rank man fall down?" said Files-on-Parade.
"A touch o' sun, a touch o' sun," the Colour-Sergeant said.
> They are hangin' Danny Deever, they are marchin' of 'im round,
> They 'ave 'alted Danny Deever by 'is coffin on the ground;
> An' 'e'll sing in 'arf a minute for a sneakin' shootin' hound—
> O they're hangin' Danny Deever in the mornin'!

"'Is cot was right-'and cot to mine," said Files-on-Parade.
"'E's sleepin' out an' far to-night," The Colour-Sergeant said.
"I've drunk 'is beer a score o' times," said Files-on-Parade.
"'E's drinkin' bitter beer alone," the Colour-Sergeant said.
> They are hangin' Danny Deever, you must mark 'im to 'is place,
> For 'e shot a comrade sleepin'—you must look 'im in the face;
> Nine 'undred of 'is county an' the Regiment's disgrace,
> While they're hangin' Danny Deever in the mornin'.

"What's that so black agin the sun?" said Files-on-Parade.
"It's Danny fightin' 'ard for life," the Colour-Sergeant said.
"What's that that whimpers over 'ead?" said Files-on-Parade.
"It's Danny's soul that's passin' now," the Colour-Sergeant said.
> For they're done with Danny Deever, you can 'ear the quickstep play,
> The Regiment's in column, an' they're marchin' us away;
> Ho! the young recruits are shakin', an' they'll want their beer to-day,
> After hangin' Danny Deever in the mornin'!

Tommy

I went into a public-'ouse to get a pint o' beer,
The publican 'e up an' sez, "We serve no red-coats here."
The girls be'ind the bar they laughed an' giggled fit to die,
I outs into the street again an' to myself sez I:
    O it's Tommy this, an' Tommy that, an' "Tommy, go away";
    But it's "Thank you, Mister Atkins," when the band begins to play—
    The band begins to play, my boys, the band begins to play,
    O it's "Thank you, Mister Atkins," when the band begins to play.

I went into a theatre as sober as could be,
They gave a drunk civilian room, but 'adn't none for me;
They sent me to the gallery or round the music-'alls,
But when it comes to fightin', Lord! they'll shove me in the stalls!
    For it's Tommy this, an' Tommy that, an' "Tommy, wait outside";
    But it's "Special train for Atkins" when the trooper's on the tide—
    The troopship's on the tide, my boys, the troopship's on the tide,
    O it's "Special train for Atkins" when the trooper's on the tide.

Yes, makin' mock o' uniforms that guard you while you sleep
Is cheaper than them uniforms, an' they're starvation cheap;
An' hustlin' drunken soldiers when they're goin' large a bit
Is five times better business than paradin' in full kit.
    Then it's Tommy this an' Tommy that, an' "Tommy, 'ow's yer soul?"
    But it's "Thin red line of 'eroes" when the drums begin to roll—
    The drums begin to roll, my boys, the drums begin to roll,
    O it's "Thin red line of 'eroes" when the drums begin to roll.

We aren't no thin red 'eroes, nor we aren't no blackguards too,
But single men in barricks, most remarkable like you;
An' if sometimes our conduck isn't all your fancy paints,
Why, single men in barricks don't grow into plaster saints;
    While it's Tommy this, an' Tommy that, an' "Tommy, fall be'ind,"
    But it's "Please to walk in front, sir," when there's trouble in the
        wind—
    O it's "Please to walk in front, sir," when there's trouble in the wind.

You talk o' better food for us, an' schools, an' fires, an' all:
We'll wait for extry rations if you treat us rational.
Don't mess about the cook-room slops, but prove it to our face
The Widow's Uniform is not the soldier-man's disgrace.
    For it's Tommy this an' Tommy that, an' "Chuck him out, the brute!"
    But it's "Saviour of 'is country" when the guns begin to shoot;
    An' it's Tommy this, an' Tommy that, an' anything you please;
    An' Tommy ain't a bloomin' fool—you bet that Tommy sees!

"Fuzzy-Wuzzy"

(Soudan Expeditionary Force.   Early Campaigns)

We've fought with many men acrost the seas,
   An' some of 'em was brave an' some was not:
The Paythan an' the Zulu an' Burmese;
   But the Fuzzy was the finest o' the lot.
We never got a ha'porth's change of 'im:
   'E squatted in the scrub an' 'ocked our 'orses,
'E cut our sentries up at Suakim,
   An' 'e played the cat an' banjo with our forces.

     So 'ere's *to* you, Fuzzy-Wuzzy, at your 'ome in the Soudan;
     You're a pore benighted 'eathen but a first-class fightin' man;
     We gives you your certificate, an' if you want it signed
     We'll come an' 'ave a romp with you whenever you're inclined.

We took our chanst among the Kyber 'ills,
   The Boers knocked us silly at a mile,
The Burman give us Irriwaddy chills,
   An' a Zulu *impi* dished us up in style:
But all we ever got from such as they
   Was pop to what the Fuzzy made us swaller;
We 'eld our bloomin' own, the papers say,
   But man for man the Fuzzy knocked us 'oller.

     Then 'ere's *to* you, Fuzzy-Wuzzy, an' the missis and the kid:
     Our orders was to break you, an' of course we went an' did.
     We sloshed you with Martinis, an' it wasn't 'ardly fair;
     But for all the odds agin' you, Fuzzy-Wuz, you broke the square.

'E 'asn't got no papers of 'is own,
   'E 'asn't got no medals nor rewards,
So *we* must certify the skill 'e's shown
   In usin' of 'is long two-'anded swords:
When 'e's 'oppin' in an' out among the bush
   With 'is coffin-'eaded shield an' shovel-spear,
An 'appy day with Fuzzy on the rush
   Will last an 'ealthy Tommy for a year.

     So 'ere's *to* you, Fuzzy-Wuzzy, an' your friends which are no more,
     If we 'adn't lost some messmates we would 'elp you to deplore.
     But give an' take's the gospel, an' we'll call the bargain fair,
     For if you 'ave lost more than us, you crumpled up the square!

'E rushes at the smoke when we let drive,
   An', before we know, 'e's 'ackin' at our 'ead;
'E's all 'ot sand an' ginger when alive,

An' 'e's generally shammin' when 'e's dead.
'E's a daisy, 'e's a ducky, 'e's a lamb!
'E's a injia-rubber idiot on the spree,
'E's the on'y thing that doesn't give a damn
    For a Regiment o' British Infantree!
    So 'ere's *to* you, Fuzzy-Wuzzy, at your 'ome in the Soudan;
    You're a pore benighted 'eathen but a first-class fightin' man;
    An' 'ere's *to* you, Fuzzy-Wuzzy, with your 'ayrick 'ead of 'air—
    You big black boundin' beggar—for you broke a British square!

Soldier, Soldier

"Soldier, soldier come from the wars,
"Why don't you march with my true love?"
"We're fresh from off the ship an' 'e's, maybe, give the slip,
"An' you'd best go look for a new love."

    New love! True love!
    Best go look for a new love,
    The dead they cannot rise, an' you'd better dry your eyes,
    An' you'd best go look for a new love.

"Soldier, soldier come from the wars,
"What did you see o' my true love?"
"I seen 'im serve the Queen in a suit o' rifle-green,
"An' you'd best go look for a new love."

"Soldier, soldier come from the wars,
"Did ye see no more o' my true love?"
"I seen 'im runnin' by when the shots begun to fly—
"But you'd best go look for a new love."

"Soldier, soldier come from the wars,
"Did aught take 'arm to my true love?"
"I couldn't see the fight, for the smoke it lay so white—
"And you'd best go look for a new love."

"Soldier, soldier come from the wars,
"I'll up an' tend to my true love!"
"'E's lying on the dead with a bullet through 'is 'ead,
"An' you'd best go look for a new love."

"Soldier, soldier come from the wars,
"I'll down an' die with my true love!"
"The pit we dug'll 'ide 'im an' the twenty more beside 'im—
"An' you'd best go look for a new love."

"Soldier, soldier come from the wars,
"Do you bring no sign from my true love?"
"I bring a lock of 'air that 'e allus used to wear,
"An' you'd best go look for a new love."

"Soldier, soldier come from the wars,
"O then I know it's true I've lost my true love!"
"An' I tell you truth again—when you've lost the feel o' pain
"You'd best take me for your new love."

True love!   New love!
Best take 'im for a new love,
The dead they cannot rise, an' you'd better dry your eyes
An' you'd best take 'im for your new love.

Screw-Guns

Smokin' my pipe on the mountings, sniffin' the mornin'-cool,
I walks in my old brown gaiters along o' my old brown mule,
With seventy gunners be'ind me, an' never a beggar forgets
It's only the pick of the Army that handles the dear little pets—'Tss! 'Tss!
  For you all love the screw-guns—the screw-guns they all love you!
  So when we call round with a few guns, o' course you will know what
    / to do—hoo! hoo!
  Jest send in your Chief an' surrender—it's worse if you fights or you
    runs:
  You can go where you please, you can skid up the trees, but you don't
    get away from the guns!

They sends us along where the roads are, but mostly we goes where they
  ain't.
We'd climb up the side of a sign-board an' trust to the stick o' the paint:
We've chivied the Naga an' Looshai; we've give the Afreedeeman fits;
For we fancies ourselves at two thousand, we guns that are built in two
    bits—'Tss! 'Tss!
  For you all love the screw-guns . . .

If a man doesn't work, why, we drills 'im an' teaches 'im 'ow to behave.
If a beggar can't march, why, we kills 'im an' rattles 'im into 'is grave.
You've got to stand up to our business an' spring without snatchin' or
  fuss.
D'you say that you sweat with the field-guns?   By God, you must lather
    with us—'Tss! 'Tss!
  For you all love the screw-guns . . .

The eagles is screamin' around us, the river's a-moanin' below,
We're clear o' the pine an' the oak-scrub, we're out on the rocks an' the
    snow,
An' the wind is as thin as a whip-lash what carries away to the plains
The rattle an' stamp o' the lead mules—the jinglety-jink o' the chains—
    'Tss! 'Tss!
  For you all love the screw-guns . . .

There's a wheel on the Horns o' the Mornin', an' a wheel on the edge o'
    the Pit,
An' a drop into nothin' beneath you as straight as a beggar can spit:
With the sweat runnin' out o' your shirt-sleeves, an' the sun off the snow
    in your face,
An' 'arf o' the men on the drag-ropes to hold the old gun in 'er place—
    'Tss! 'Tss!
  For you all love the screw-guns . . .

Smokin' my pipe on the mountings, sniffin' the mornin'-cool,
    I climbs in my old brown gaiters along o' my old brown mule.
The monkey can say what our road was—the wild-goat 'e knows where we
    passed.
Stand easy, you long-eared old darlin's!   Out drag-ropes! With shrapnel!
    Hold fast—'Tss! 'Tss!
  For you all love the screw-guns—the screw-guns they all love you!
  So when we take tea with a few guns, o' course you will know what to
    do—hoo! hoo!
  Jest send in your Chief an' surrender—it's worse if you fights or you
    runs:
  You may hide in the caves, they'll be only your graves, but you can't
    get away from the guns!

Cells

I've a head like a concertina, I've a tongue like a button-stick,
I've a mouth like an old potato, and I'm more than a little sick,
But I've had my fun o' the Corp'ral's Guard; I've made the cinders fly,
And I'm here in the Clink for a thundering drink and blacking the
    Corporal's eye.

            With a second-hand overcoat under my head,
                And a beautiful view of the yard,
        O it's pack-drill for me and a fortnight's C.B.
                For "drunk and resisting the Guard!"
                Mad drunk and resisting the Guard—
                'Strewth, but I socked it them hard!

> So it's pack-drill for me and a fortnight's C.B.
> For "drunk and resisting the Guard."

I started o' canteen porter, I finished o' canteen beer,
But a dose o' gin that a mate slipped in, it was that that brought me
here.
'Twas that and an extry double Guard that rubbed my nose in the dirt—
But I fell away with the Corp'ral's stock and the best of the Corp'ral's
shirt.

I left my cap in a public-house, my boots in the public road,
And Lord knows where—and I don't care—my belt and my tunic goed.
They'll stop my pay, they'll cut away the stripes I used to wear,
But I left my mark on the Corp'ral's face, and I think he'll keep it there!

My wife she cries on the barrack-gate, my kid in the barrack-yard.
It ain't that I mind the Ord'ly-room—its *that* that cuts so hard.
I'll take my oath before them both that I will sure abstain,
But as soon as I'm in with a mate and gin, I know I'll do it again!

> With a second-hand overcoat under my head,
> And a beautiful view of the yard,
> Yes, it's pack-drill for me and a fortnight's C.B.
> For "drunk and resisting the Guard!"
> Mad drunk and resisting the Guard—
> 'Strewth, but I socked it them hard!
> So it's pack-drill for me and a fortnight's C.B.
> For "drunk and resisting the Guard."

Gunga Din

You may talk o' gin and beer
When you're quartered safe out 'ere,
An' you're sent to penny-fights an' Aldershot it;
But when it comes to slaughter
You will do your work on water,
An' you'll lick the bloomin' boots of 'im that's got it.
Now in Injia's sunny clime,
Where I used to spend my time
A-servin' of 'Er Majesty the Queen,
Of all them blackfaced crew
The finest man I knew
Was our regimental bhisti, Gunga Din.
He was "Din! Din! Din!

"You limpin' lump o' brick-dust, Gunga Din!
  "Hi' Slippy *hitherao!*
  "Water, get it! *Panee lao,*[1]
"You squidgy-nosed old idol, Gunga Din."

The uniform 'e wore
Was nothin' much before,
An' rather less than 'arf o' that be'ind,
For a piece o' twisty rag
An' a goatskin water-bag
Was all the field-equipment 'e could find.
When the sweatin' troop-train lay
In a sidin' through the day,
Where the 'eat would make your bloomin' eyebrows crawl,
We shouted "Harry By!"[2]
Till our throats were brick-dry,
Then we wopped 'im 'cause 'e couldn't serve us all.
      It was "Din! Din! Din!
  "You 'eathin, where the mischief 'ave you been?
    "You put some *juldee*[3] in it
      "Or I'll *marrow*[4] you this minute
  "If you don't fill up my helmet, Gunga Din!"

'E would dot an' carry one
Till the longest day was done;
An' 'e didn't seem to know the use o' fear.
If we charged or broke or cut,
You could bet your bloomin' nut,
'E'd be waitin' fifty paces right flank rear.
With 'is mussick[5] on 'is back,
'E would skip with our attack,
An' watch us till the bugles made "Retire,"
An' for all 'is dirty 'ide
'E was white, clear white, inside
    When 'e went to tend the wounded under fire!
      It was "Din! Din! Din!"
  With the bullets kickin' dust-spots on the green.
      When the cartridges ran our,
        You could hear the front-ranks shout,
  "Hi! ammunition-mules an' Gunga Din!"

I shan't forgit the night
When I dropped be'ind the fight
With a bullet where my belt-plate should 'a' been.
I was chokin' mad with thirst,

---

[1]Bring water swiftly.   [2]O brother.   [3]Be quick.   [4]Hit you.   [5]Water-skin.

An' the man that spied me first
Was our good old grinnin', gruntin' Gunga Din.
'E lifted up my 'ead,
An' he plugged me where I bled,
An' 'e guv me 'arf-a-pint o' water green.
It was crawlin' and it stunk,
But of all the drinks I've drunk,
I'm gratefullest to one from Gunga Din.
    It was "Din! Din! Din!
  "'Ere's a beggar with a bullet through 'is spleen;
    "'E's chawin' up the ground.
    "An' 'e's kickin' all around:
  "For Gawd's sake git the water, Gunga Din!"

'E carried me away
To where a dooli lay,
An' a bullet come an' drilled the beggar clean.
'E put me safe inside,
An' just before 'e died,
"I 'ope you liked your drink," sez Gunga Din.
So I'll meet 'im later on
At the place where 'e is gone—
Where it's always double drill and no canteen.
'E'll be squattin' on the coals
Givin' drink to poor damned souls,
An' I'll get a swig in hell from Gunga Din!
    Yes, Din! Din! Din!
  You Lazarushian-leather Gunga Din!
    Though I've belted you and flayed you,
    By the livin' Gawd that made you,
  You're a better man than I am, Gunga Din!

Oonts

(Northern India Transport Train)

Wot makes the soldier's 'eart to penk, wot makes 'im to perspire?
It isn't standin' up to charge nor lyin' down to fire;
But it's everlastin' waitin' on a everlastin' road
For the commissariat camel an' 'is commissariat load.
  O the oont,[1] O the oont, O the commissariat oont!
    With 'is silly neck a-bobbin' like a basket full o' snakes;

[1]Camel:—*oo* is pronounced like *u* in "bull," but by Tommy Atkins to rhyme with "front."

We packs 'im like an idol, an' you ought to 'ear 'im grunt,
  An' when we get 'im loaded up 'is blessed girth-rope breaks.

Wot makes the rear-guard swear so 'ard when night is drorin' in,
An' every native follower is shiverin' for 'is skin?
It ain't the chanst o' being rushed by Paythans from the 'ills,
It's the commissariat camel puttin' on 'is bloomin' frills!
    O the oont, O the oont, O the hairy scary oont!
      A-trippin' over tent-ropes when we've got the night alarm!
    We socks 'im with a stretcher-pole an' 'eads 'im off in front,
      An' when we've saved 'is bloomin' life 'e chaws our bloomin' arm.

The 'orse 'e knows above a bit, the bullock's but a fool,
The elephant's a gentleman, the battery-mule's a mule;
But the commissariat cam-u-el, when all is said an' done,
'E's a devil an' a ostrich an' a orphan-child in one.
    O the oont, O the oont, O the Gawd-forsaken oont!
      The lumpy-'umpy 'ummin'-bird a-singin' where 'e lies,
    'E's blocked the whole division from the rear-guard to the front,
      An' when we get him up again—the beggar goes an' dies!

'E'll gall an' chafe an' lame an' fight—'e smells most awful vile.
'E'll lose 'isself for ever if you let 'im stray a mile.
'E's game to graze the 'ole day long an' 'owl the 'ole night through,
An' when 'e comes to greasy ground 'e splits 'isself in two.
    O the oont, O the oont, O the floppin', droppin' oont,
      When 'is long legs give from under an' 'is meltin' eye is dim!
    The Tribes is up be'ind us, and the Tribes is out in front—
      It ain't no jam for Tommy, but it's kites an' crows for 'im.

So when the cruel march is done, an' when the roads is blind.
An' when we sees the camp in front an' 'ears the shots be'ind,
Ho! then we strips 'is saddle off, and all 'is woes is past.
'E thinks on us that used 'im so, and gets revenge at last.
    O the oont, O the oont, O the floatin', bloatin' oont!
      The late lamented camel in the water-cut 'e lies;
    We keeps a mile be'ind 'im an' we keeps a mile in front,
      But 'e gets into the drinkin'-casks, and then o' course we dies!

Loot

If you've ever stole a pheasant-egg be'ind the keeper's back,
  If you've ever snigged the washin' from the line,
If you've ever crammed a gander in your bloomin' 'aversack,
  You will understand this little song o' mine.

But the service rules are 'ard, an' from such we are debarred,
  For the same with English morals does not suit.
    (*Cornet*: Toot! toot!)
Why, they call a man a robber if 'e stuffs 'is marchin' clobber[1]
  With the—
(*Chorus*) Loo! loo!   Lulu! lulu!   Loo! loo!   Loot! loot! loot!
      Ow, the loot!
      Bloomin' loot!
    That's the thing to make the boys git up an' shoot!
      It's the same with dogs and' men,
      If you'd make 'em come again
    Clap 'em forward with a Loo! loo!   Lulu!   Loot!~
(*ff*) Whoopee!   Tear 'im puppy!   Loo! loo!   Lulu!   Loot! loot! loot!

If you've knocked a nigger edgeways when 'e's thrustin' for your life,
  You must leave 'im very careful where 'e fell;
An' may thank your stars an' gaiters if you didn't feel 'is knife
  That you ain't told off to bury 'im as well.
Then the sweatin' Tommies wonder as they spade the beggars under
  Why lootin' should be entered as a crime.
So, if my song you'll 'ear, I will learn you plain an' clear
  'Ow to pay yourself for fightin' overtime.
(*Chorus*) With the loot, . . .

Now remember when you're 'acking round a gilded Burma god
  That 'is eyes is very often precious stones;
An' if you treat a nigger to a dose o' cleanin'-rod
  'E's like to show you everything 'e owns.
When 'e won't prodooce no more, pour some water on the floor
  Where you 'ear it answer 'ollow to the boot
    (*Cornet*: Toot! toot!)
When the ground begins to sink, shove your baynick down the chink,
  An' you're sure to touch the—
(*Chorus*) Loo! loo!   Lulu!   Loot! loot! loot!
      Ow, the loot! . . .

When from 'ouse to 'ouse you're 'unting, you must always work in
  pairs—
  It 'alves the gain, but safer you will find—
For a single man gets bottled on them twisty-twisty stairs,
  An' a woman comes and clobs 'im from be'ind.
When you've turned 'em inside out, an' it seems beyond a doubt
  As if there weren't enough to dust a flute
    (*Cornet*: Toot! toot!)—

[1]Clothes.

Before you sling your 'ook, at the 'ousetops take a look,
 For it's underneath the tiles they 'ide the loot.
(*Chorus*) Ow, the loot! . . .

You can mostly square a Sergint an' a Quartermaster too,
 If you only take the proper way to go.
I could never keep my pickin's, but I've learned you all I knew—
 But don't you never say I told you so.
An' now I'll bid good-bye, for, I'm gettin' rather dry,
 An' I see another tunin' up to toot
   (*Cornet*: Toot! toot!)
So 'ere's good-luck to those that wears the Widow's clo'es,
 An' the Devil send 'em al they want o' loot!
 (*Chorus*) Yes, the loot,
    Bloomin' loot!
   In the tunic an' the mess-tin an' the boot!
   It's the same with dogs an' men,
   If you'd make 'em come again
(*fff*) Whoop 'em forward with a Loo! loo!–Lulu! Loot! loot! loot!
 Heeya! Sick 'im puppy! Loo!loo!–Lulu! Loot! loot!loot!

"*Snarleyow*"

This 'appened in a battle to a batt'ry of the corps
Which is first among the women an' amazin' first in war;
An' what the bloomin' battle was I don't remember now,
But Two's off-lead[1] 'e answered to the name o' *Snarleyow*.
 Down in the Infantry, nobody cares;
 Down in the Cavalry, Colonel 'e swears;
 But down in the lead with the wheel at the flog
 Turns the bold Bombardier to a little whipped dog!

They was movin' into action, they was needed very sore,
To learn a little schoolin' to a native army-core,
They 'ad nipped against an uphill, they was tuckin' down the brow,
When a tricky trundlin' roundshot give the knock to *Snarleyow*.

They cut 'im loose an' left 'im—'e was almost tore in two—
But he tried to follow after as a well-trained 'orse should do;
'E went an' fouled the limber, an' the Driver's Brother squeals:
"Pull up, pull up for *Snarleyow*—'is head's between 'is 'eels!"

[1]The leading right-hand horse of No. 2 gun.

The Driver 'umped 'is shoulder, for the wheels was goin' round,
An' there ain't no "Stop, conductor!" when a batt'ry's changin' ground;
Sez 'e: "I broke the beggar in, an' very sad I feels,
"But I couldn't pull up, not for *you*—your 'ead between your 'eels!"

'E 'adn't 'ardly spoke the word, before a droppin' shell
A little right the batt'ry an' between the sections fell;
An' when the smoke 'ad cleared away, before the limber-wheels,
There lay the Driver's Brother with 'is 'ead between 'is 'eels.

Then sez the Driver's Brother, an' 'is words was very plain,
"For Gawd's own sake get over me, an' put me out o' pain."
They saw 'is wounds was mortal, an' they judged that it was best,
So they took an' drove the limber straight across 'is back 'an chest.

The Driver 'e give nothin' 'cept a little coughin' grunt,
But 'e swung 'is 'orses 'andsome when it came to "Action Front!"
An' if one wheel was juicy, you may lay your Monday head
'Twas juicier for the niggers when the case begun to spread.

The moril of this story, it is plainly to be seen:
You 'aven't got no families when servin' of the Queen—
You 'aven't got no brother, fathers, sisters, wives, or sons—
If you want to win your battles take an' work your bloomin' guns!
    Down in the Infantry, nobody cares;
    Down in the Cavalry, Colonel 'e swears;
    But down in the lead with the wheel at the flog
    Turns the bold Bombardier to a little whipped dog!

The Widow at Windsor

    'Ave you 'eard o' the Widow at Windsor
      With a hairy gold crown on 'er head?
    She 'as ships on the foam—she 'as millions at 'ome,
      An' she pays us poor beggars in red.
        (Ow, poor beggars in red!)
    There's 'er nick on the cavalry 'orses,
      There's 'er mark on the medical stores—
    An' 'er troopers you'll find with a fair wind be'ind
      That takes us to various wars.
        (Poor beggars!—barbarious wars!)
        Then 'ere's to the Widow at Windsor,
          An' 'ere's to the stores an' the guns,
        The men an' the 'orses what makes up the forces
          O' Missis Victorier's sons.
        (Poor beggars!   Victorier's sons!)

Walk wide o' the Widow at Windsor,
  For 'alf o' Creation she owns:
We 'ave bought 'er the same with the sword an' the flame,
  An' we've salted it down with out bones.
    (Poor beggars!—it's blue with our bones!)
Hands off o' the sons o' the Widow,
  Hands off o' the goods in 'er shop,
For the Kings must come down an' the Emperors frown
  When the Widow at Windsor says "Stop!"
    (Poor beggars!—we're sent to say "Stop!")
      Then 'ere's to the Lodge o' the Widow,
        From the Pole to the Tropics it runs—
        To the Lodge that we tile with the rank an' the file,
          An' open in form with guns.
        (Poor beggars!—it's always they guns!)

We 'ave 'eard o' the Widow at Windsor,
  It's safest to leave 'er alone:
For 'er sentries we stand by the sea an' the land
  Wherever the bugles are blown.
    (Poor beggars!—an' don't we get blown!)
Take 'old o' the Wings o' the Mornin',
  An' flop round the earth till you're dead;
But you won't get away from the tune that they play
  To the bloomin' old rag over'ead.
    (Poor beggars!—it's 'ot over'ead!)
      Then 'ere's to the Sons o' the Widow,
        Wherever, 'owever they roam.
      'Ere's all they desire, an' if they require
        A speedy return to their 'ome.
        (Poor beggars!—they'll never see 'ome!)

Belts

There was a row in Silver Street that's near to Dublin Quay
Between an Irish regiment an' English cavalree;
It started at Revelly an' it lasted on till dark:
The first man dropped at Harrison's, the last forninst the Park.
  For it was:—"Belts, belts, belts, an' that's one for you!"
  An' it was "Belts, belts, belts, an' that's done for you!"
  O buckle an' tongue
  Was the song that we sung
  From Harrison's down to the Park!

There was a row in Silver Street—the regiments was out,
They called us "Delhi Rebels," an' we answered "Threes about!"
That drew them like a hornets' nest—we met them good an' large,
The English at the double an' the Irish at the charge.
    Then it was:—"Belts, &c."

There was a row in Silver Street—an' I was in it too:
We passed the time o' day, an' then the belts went whirraru!
I misremember what occurred, but, subsequint the storm,
A *Freeman's Journal Supplemint* was all *my* uniform.
    O it was:—"Belts, &c."

There was a row in Silver Street—they sent the Polis there,
The English were too drunk to know, the Irish didn't care;
But when they grew impertinint we simultaneous rose,
Till half o' them was Liffey mud an' half was tatthered clo'es.
    For it was:—"Belts, &c."

There was a row in Silver Street—it might ha' raged till now,
But some one drew his side-arm clear, an' nobody knew how;
'Twas Hogan took the point an' dropped; we saw the red blood run:
An' so we all was murderers that started out in fun.
    While it was: "Belts, &c."

There was a row in Silver Street—but that put down the shine,
Wid each man whisperin' to his next:—"'Twas never work o' mine!"
We went away like beaten dogs, an' down the street we bore him,
The poor dumb corpse that couldn't tell the bhoys were sorry for him.
    When it was:—"Belts, &c."

There was a row in Silver street—it isn't over yet,
For half of us are under guard wid punishments to get;
'Tis all a miracle to me as in the Clink I lie:
There was a row in Silver Street—begod, I wonder why!
    But it was:—"Belts, belts, belts, an' that's one for you!"
    An' it was "Belts, belts, belts, an' that's done for you!"
    O buckle an' tongue
    Was the song that we sung
    From Harrison's down to the Park!

The Young British Soldier

When the 'arf-made recruity goes out to the East
    'E acts like a babe an' e' drinks like a beast,
An' 'e wonders because 'e is frequent deceased
    Ere 'e's fit for to serve as a soldier.

> Serve, serve, serve as a soldier,
> Serve, serve, serve as a soldier,
> Serve, serve, serve as a soldier,
>   So-oldier *of* the Queen!

Now all you recruities what's drafted to-day,
You shut up your rag-box an' 'ark to my lay,
An' I'll sing you a soldier as far as I may:
    A soldier what's fit for a soldier.
      Fit, fit, fit for a soldier . . .

First mind you steer clear o' the grog-sellers' huts,
For they sell you Fixed Bay'nets that rots out your guts—
Ay, drink that 'ud eat the live steel from your butts—
    An' its bad for the young British soldier.
      Bad, bad, bad, for the soldier . . .

When the cholera comes—as it will past a doubt—
Keep out of the wet and don't go on the shout,
For the sickness gets in as the liquor dies out,
    An' it crumples the young British soldier.
      Crum-, crum-, crumples the soldier . . .

But the worst o' your foes is the sun over'ead:
You *must* wear your 'elmet for all that is said:
If 'e finds you uncovered 'e'll knock you down dead,
    An; you'll die like a fool of a soldier.
      Fool, fool, fool of a soldier . . .

If you're cast for fatigue by a sergeant unkind,
Don't grouse like a woman nor crack on nor blind;
Be handy and civil, and then you will find
    That it's beer for the young British soldier.
      Beer, beer, beer for the soldier . . .

Now, if you must marry, take care she is old—
A troop-sergeant's widow's the nicest, I'm told,
For beauty won't help if your rations is cold,
    Nor love ain't enough for a soldier.
      'Nough, 'nough, 'nough for a soldier . . .

If the wife should go wrong with a comrade, be loth
To shoot when you catch 'em—you'll sing, on my oath!—
Make 'im take 'er and keep 'er: that's Hell for them both,
    An' you're shut o' the curse of a soldier.
      Curse, curse, curse of a soldier . . .

When first under fire an' you're wishful to duck
Don't look nor take 'eed at the man that is struck.

Be thankful you're livin', and trust to your luck
   And march to your front a like a soldier.
      Front, front, front like a soldier . . .

When 'arf of your bullets fly wide in the ditch,
Don't call your Martini a cross-eyed old bitch;
She's human as you are— you treat her as sich,
   An' she'll fight for the young British soldier.
      Fight, fight, fight for the soldier . . .

When shakin' their bustles like ladies so fine,
The guns o' the enemy wheel into line,
Shoot low at the limbers an' don't mind the shine,
   For the noise never startles the soldier.
      Start-, start-, startles the soldier . . .

If your officer's dead and the sergeants look white,
Remember it's ruin to run from a fight:
So take open order, lie down, and sit tight,
   And wait for supports like a soldier.
      Wait, wait, wait like a soldier . . .

When you're wounded and left on Afghanistan's plains,
And the women come out to cut up what remains,
Jest roll to your rifle and blow out your brains
   An' go to your Gawd like a soldier.
      Go, go, go like a soldier,
      Go, go, go like a soldier,
      Go, go, go like a soldier,
        So-oldier *of* the Queen!

Mandalay

By the old Moulmein Pagoda, lookin' lazy at the sea,
There's a Burma girl a-settin', and I know she thinks o' me;
For the wind is in the palm-trees, and the temple-bells they say:
"Come you back, you British soldier; come you back to Mandalay!"
   Come you back to Mandalay,
   Where the old Flotilla lay:
   Can't you 'ear their paddles chunkin' from Rangoon to Mandalay?
   On the road to Mandalay,
   Where the flyin'-fishes play,
   An' the dawn comes up like thunder outer China 'crost the Bay!

'Er petticoat was yaller an' 'er little cap was green,
An' 'er name was Supi-yaw-lat—jes' the same as Theebaw's Queen,

An' I seed her first a-smokin' of a whackin' white cheroot,
An' a-wastin' Christian kisses on an 'eathen idol's foot:
   Bloomin' idol made o' mud—
   Wot they called the Great Gawd Budd—
   Plucky lot she cared for idols when I kissed 'er where she stud!
   On the road to Mandalay . . .

When the mist was on the rice-fields an' the sun was droppin' slow,
She'd git 'er little banjo an' she'd sing "*Kulla-lo-lo!*"
With 'er arm upon my shoulder an' 'er cheek agin my cheek
We useter watch the steamers an' the *hathis* pilin' teak.
   Elephints a-pilin' teak
   In the sludgy, squdgy creek,
   Where the silence 'ung that 'eavy you was 'arf afraid to speak!
   On the road to Mandalay . . .

But that's all shove be'ind me—long ago an' fur away,
An' there ain't no 'buses runnin' from the Bank to Mandalay;
An' I'm learnin' 'ere in London what the ten-year soldier tells:
"If you've 'eard the East a-callin', you won't never 'eed naught else."
   No! you won't 'eed nothin' else
   But them spicy garlic smells,
   An' the sunshine an' the palm-trees an' the tinkly temple-bells;
   On the road to Mandalay . . .

I am sick o' wastin' leather on these gritty pavin'-stones,
An' the blasted English drizzle wakes the fever in my bones;
Tho' I walks with fifty 'ousemaids outer Chelsea to the Strand,
An' they talks a lot o' lovin', but wot do they understand?
   Beefy face an' grubby 'and—
   Law! wot do they understand?
   I've a neater, sweeter maiden in a cleaner, greener land!
   On the road to Mandalay . . .

Ship me somewheres east of Suez, where the best is like the worst,
Where there aren't no Ten Commandments an' a man can raise a thirst;
For the temple-bells are callin', an' it's there that I would be—
By the old Moulmein Pagoda, looking lazy at the sea,
   On the road to Mandalay,
   Where the old Flotilla lay,
   With our sick beneath the awnings when we went to Mandalay!
   O the road to Mandalay,
   Where the flyin'-fishes play,
   An' the dawn comes up like thunder outer China 'crost the Bay!

Troopin'

(*Old English Army in the East*)

Troopin', troopin', troopin' to the sea:
'Ere's September come again—the six-year men are free.
O leave the dead be'ind us, for they cannot come away
To where the ship's a-coalin' up that takes us 'ome to-day.
    We're goin' 'ome, we're goin' 'ome,
      Our ship is *at* the shore,
    An' you must pack your 'aversack,
      For we won't come back no more.
    Ho, don't you grieve for me,
      My lovely Mary-Ann!
    For I'll marry you yit on a fourp'ny bit
      As a time-expired man.

The *Malabar's* in 'arbour with the *Jumner* at 'er tail,
An' the time-expired's waitin' of 'is orders for to sail.
Ho! the weary waitin' when on Khyber 'ills we lay,
But the time-expired's waitin' of 'is orders 'ome to-day.

They'll turn us out at Portsmouth wharf in cold an' wet an' rain,
All wearin' Injian cotton kit, but we will not complain.
They'll kill us of pneumonia—for that's their little way—
But damn the chills and fever, men, we're goin' 'ome to-day!

Troopin', troopin', winter's round again!
See the new draft's pourin' in for the old campaign;
Ho, you poor recruities, but you've got to earn your pay—
What's the last from Lunnon, lads?   We're goin' there to-day.

Troopin', troopin', give another cheer—
'Ere's to English women an' a quart of English beer.
The Colonel an' the Regiment an' all who've got to stay,
Gawd's Mercy strike 'em gentle!   Whoop! we're goin' 'ome to-day.
    We're goin' 'ome, we're goin' 'ome,
      Our ship is *at* the shore,
    An' you must pack your 'aversack,
      For we won't come back no more.
    Ho, don't you grieve for me,
      My lovely Mary-Ann!
    For I'll marry you yit on a fourp'ny bit
      As a time-expired man.

The Widow's Party

"Where have you been this while away,
  Johnnie, Johnnie?"
Out with the rest on a picnic lay.
  Johnnie, my Johnnie, aha!
They called us out of the barrack-yard
To Gawd knows where from Gosport Hard,
And you can't refuse when you get the card,
  And the Widow gives the party.
    (*Bugle*: Ta—rara—ra-ra-rara!)

"What did you get to eat and drink,
  Johnnie, Johnnie?"
Standing water as thick as ink,
  Johnnie, my Johnnie, aha!
A bit o' beef that were three year stored,
A bit o' mutton as tough as board,
And a fowl we killed with a sergeant's sword,
  When the Widow give the party.

"What did you for knives and forks,
  Johnnie, Johnnie?"
We carries 'em with us wherever we walks,
  Johnnie, my Johnnie, aha!
And some was sliced and some was halved,
And some was crimped and some was carved,
And some was gutted and some was starved,
  When the Widow give the party.

"What ha' you done with half your mess,
  Johnnie, Johnnie?"
They couldn't do more and they wouldn't do less.
  Johnnie, my Johnnie, aha!
They ate their whack and they drank their fill,
And I think the rations had made them ill,
For half my comp'ny's lying still
  Where the Widow give the party.

"How did you get away—away,
  Johnnie, Johnnie?"
On the broad o' my back at the end o' the day,
  Johnnie, my Johnnie, aha!
I comed away like a bleedin' toff,
For I got four niggers to carry me off,
As I lay in the bight of a canvas trough,
  When the Widow give the party.

"What was the end of all the show,
  Johnnie, Johnnie?"
Ask my Colonel, for I don't know,
  Johnnie, my Johnnie, aha!
We broke a King and we built a road—
A court-house stands where the Reg'ment goed.
And the river's clean where the raw blood flowed
  When the Widow give the party.
    (*Bugle*: Ta—rara—ra-ra-rara!)

Ford o' Kabul River

Kabul town's by Kabul river—
  Blow the trumpet, draw the sword—
There I lef' my mate for ever,
  Wet an' drippin' by the ford.
    Ford, ford, ford, o' Kabul river,
      Ford o' Kabul river in the dark!
    There's the river up and brimmin', an' there's 'arf a squadron
        swimmin'
      'Cross the ford o' Kabul river in the dark.

Kabul town's a blasted place—
  Blow the trumpet, draw the sword—
'Strewth I shan't forget 'is face
  Wet an' drippin' by the ford!
    Ford, ford, ford o' Kabul river,
      Ford o' Kabul river in the dark!
    Keep the crossing-stakes beside you, an' they will surely guide you
      'Cross the ford o' Kabul river in the dark.

Kabul town is sun and dust—
  Blow the trumpet, draw the sword—
I'd ha' sooner drownded fust
  'Stead of 'im beside the ford.
    Ford, ford, ford o' Kabul river,
      Ford o' Kabul river in the dark!
    You can 'ear the 'orses threshin'; you can 'ear the men a-splashin',
      'Cross the ford o' Kabul river in the dark.

Kabul town was ours to take—
  Blow the trumpet, draw the sword—
I'd ha' left it for 'is sake—
  'Im that left me by the ford.
    Ford, ford, ford o' Kabul river,
      Ford o' Kabul river in the dark!

It's none so bloomin' dry there; ain't you never comin' nigh there,
    'Cross the ford o' Kabul river in the dark?

Kabul town'll go to hell—
  Blow the trumpet, draw the sword—
'Fore I see him 'live an' well—
  'Im the best beside the ford.
    Ford, ford, ford o' Kabul river,
      Ford o' Kabul river in the dark!
    Gawd 'elp 'em if they blunder, for their boots'll pull 'em under,
      By the ford o' Kabul river in the dark.

Turn your 'orse from Kabul town—
  Blow the trumpet, draw the sword—
'Im an' 'arf my troop is down,
  Down and drownded by the ford.
    Ford, ford, ford o' Kabul river,
      Ford o' Kabul river in the dark!
    There's the river low an' fallin', but it ain't no use a-callin'
      'Cross the ford o' Kabul river in the dark!

Gentlemen-Rankers

To the legion of the lost ones, to the cohort of the damned,
    To my brethren in their sorrow overseas,
Sings a gentleman of England cleanly bred, machinely crammed,
    And a trooper of the Empress, if you please.
Yes a trooper of the forces who has run his own six horses,
    And faith he went the pace and went it blind,
And the world was more than kin while he held the ready tin,
    But to-day the Sergeant's something less than kind.
        We're poor little lambs who've lost our way,
            Baa! Baa! Baa!
        We're little black sheep who've gone astray,
            Baa—aa—aa!
        Gentlemen-rankers out on the spree,
        Damned from here to Eternity,
        God ha' mercy on such as we,
            Baa! Yah! Bah!

Oh, it's sweet to sweat through stables, sweet to empty kitchen slops,
    And it's sweet to hear the tales the troopers tell,
To dance with blowzy housemaids at the regimental hops
    And thrash the cad who says you waltz too well.

Yes, it makes you cock-a-hoop to be "Rider" to your troop,
 And branded with a blasted worsted spur,
When you envy, O how keenly, one poor Tommy living cleanly
 Who blacks your boots and sometimes calls you "Sir."

If the home we never write to, and the oaths we never keep,
 And all we know most distant and most dear,
Across the snoring barrack-room return to break our sleep,
 Can you blame us if we soak ourselves in beer?
When the drunken comrade mutters and the great guard-lantern gutters
 And the horror of our fall is written plain,
Every secret, self-revealing on the aching whitewashed ceiling,
 Do you wonder that we drug ourselves from pain?

We have done with Hope and Honour, we are lost to Love and Truth,
 We are dropping down the ladder rung by rung,
And the measure of our torment is the measure of our youth.
 God help us, for we knew the worst too young!
Our shame is clean repentance for the crime that brought the sentence,
 Our pride it is to know no spur of pride,
And the Curse of Reuben holds us till an alien turf enfolds us
 And we die, and none can tell Them where we died.
  We're poor little lambs who've lost our way,
   Baa! Baa! Baa!
  We're little black sheep who've gone astray,
   Baa—aa—aa!
  Gentlemen-rankers out on the spree,
  Damned from here to Eternity,
  God ha' mercy on such as we,
   Baa! Yah! Bah!

Route Marchin'

 We're marchin' on relief over Injia's sunny plains,
 A little front o' Christmas-time an' just be'ind the Rains;
 Ho! get away, you bullock-man, you've 'eard the bugle blowed,
 There's a regiment a-comin' down the Grand Trunk Road;
  With its best foot first
  And the road a-sliding past,
  An' every bloomin' campin'-ground exactly like the last;
  While the Big Drum says,
  With 'is *"rowdy-dowdy-dow!"* —
  "Kiko kissywarsti don't you *hamsher argy jow?"* [1]

    [1] Why don't you get on?

Oh, there's them Injian temples to admire when you see.
There's the peacock round the corner an' the monkey up the tree,
An' there's that rummy silver-grass a-wavin' in the wind,
An' the old Grand Trunk a-trailin' like a rifle-sling be'ind.
    While it's best foot first, . . .

At half-past five's Revelly, an' our tents they down must come,
Like a lot of button-mushrooms when you pick 'em up at 'ome.
But it's over in a minute, an' at six the column starts,
While the women and kiddies sit an' shiver in the carts.
    An' it's best foot first, . . .

Oh, then it's open order, an' we lights our pipes an' sings,
An' we talks about our rations an' a lot of other things,
An' we thinks o' friends in England, an' we wonders what they're at,
An' 'ow they would admire for to hear us sling the *bat*.[1]
    An' it's best foot first, . . .

It's none so bad o' Sundays, when you're lyin' at your ease,
To watch the kites a-wheelin' round them feather-'eaded trees,
For although there ain't no women, yet there ain't no barrick-yards,
So the orficers goes shootin' an' the men they plays at cards.
    Till it's best foot first, . . .

So 'ark an' 'eed, you rookies, which is always grumblin' sore,
There's worser things than marchin' from Umballa to Cawnpore;
An' if your 'eels are blistered an' they feels to 'urt like 'ell,
You drop some tallow in your socks an' that will make 'em well.
    For it's best foot first, . . .

We're marchin' on relief over Injia's coral strand,
Eight 'undred fightin' Englishmen, the Colonel, and the Band;
Ho! get away, you bullock-man, you've 'eard the bugle blowed,
There's a regiment a-comin' down the Grand Trunk Road;
    With its best foot first
    And the road a-sliding past,
    An' every bloomin' campin'-ground exactly like the last;
    While the Big Drum says,
    With 'is *"rowdy-dowdy-dow!"* —
    "Kiko kissywarsti don't you *hamsher argy jow?"*

---

[1] Language. Thomas's first and firmest conviction is that he is a profound Orientalist and a fluent speaker of Hindustani. As a matter of fact, he depends largely on the sign-language.

Private Ortheris's Song

("The Courting of Dinah Shadd"—*Life's Handicap*)

My girl she give me the go onest,
    When I was a London lad;
An' I went on the drink for a fortnight,
    An' then I went to the bad.
The Queen she gave me a shillin'
    To fight for 'er over the seas;
But the Guv'ment built me a fever-trap,
    An' Injia give me disease.

(*Chorus*) Ho! don't you 'eed what a girl says,
        An' don't you go for the beer;
        But I was an ass when I was at grass,
        An' that is why I'm 'ere.

I fired a shot at a Afghan,
    The beggar 'e fired again,
An' I lay on my bed with a 'ole in my 'ed,
    An' missed the next campaign!
I up with my gun at a Burman
    Who carried a bloomin' *dah*,
But the cartridge stuck and the bay'nit bruk,
    An' all I got was the scar.

(*Chorus*) Ho! don't you aim at a Afghan,
        When you stand on the skyline clear;
        An' don't you go for a Burman
        If none o' your friends is near.

    I served my time for a Corp'ral,
        An' wetted my stripes with pop,
    For I went on the bend with a intimate friend,
        An' finished the night in the "shop."
    I served my time for a Sergeant;
        The Colonel 'e sez "No!
    The most you'll see is a full C.B."
        An' . . . very next night 'twas so!

(*Chorus*) Ho! don't you go for a Corp'ral
        Unless your 'ed is clear;
        But I was an ass when I was at grass,
        An' that is why I'm 'ere.

I've tasted the luck o' the Army
    In barrack an' camp an' clink,

An' I lost my tip through the bloomin' trip
  Along o' the women an' drink.
I'm down at the heel o' my service,
  An' when I am laid on the shelf,
My very worst friend from beginning to end
  By the blood of a mouse was myself!

(*Chorus*) Ho! don't you 'eed what a girl says,
        An' don't you go for the beer;
      But I was an ass when I was at grass,
        An' that is why I'm 'ere!

Shillin' a Day

My name is O'Kelly, I've heard the Revelly
From Birr to Bareilly, from Leeds to Lahore,
Hong-Kong and Peshawur,
Lucknow and Etawah,
And fifty-five more all endin' in "pore."
Black Death and his quickness, the depth and the thickness
Of sorrow and sickness I've known on my way,
But I'm old and I'm nervis,
I'm cast from the Service,
And all I deserve is a shillin' a day.

        (*Chorus*) Shillin' a day,
                Bloomin' good pay—
                Lucky to touch it, a shillin' a day!

Oh, it drives me half crazy to think of the days I
Went slap for the Ghazi, my sword at my side,
When we rode Hell-for-leather
Both squadrons together,
That didn't care whether we lived or we died.
But it's no use despairin', my wife must go charin'
An' me commissairin', the pay-bills to better,
So if me you be'old
In the wet and the cold,
By the Grand Metropold, won't you give me a letter?

(*Full chorus*)   Give 'im a letter—
                'Can't do no better,
                Late Troop-Sergeant-Major an'—runs
                    with a letter!

Think what 'e's been,
Think what 'e's seen.
Think of his pension an'—
GAWD SAVE THE QUEEN!

"Back to the Army Again"

I'm 'ere in a ticky ulster an' a broken billycock 'at,
A-layin' on the sergeant I don't know a gun from a bat;
My shirt's doin' duty for jacket, my sock's stickin' out o' my boots,
An' I'm learnin' the damned old goose-step along o' the new recruits!

    Back to the Army again, sergeant,
      Back to the Army again.
    Don't look so 'ard, for I 'aven't no card,
      I'm back to the Army again!

I done my six years' service.   'Er Majesty sez: "Good day—
You'll please to come when you're rung for, an' 'ere's your 'ole back-pay;
An' fourpence a day for baccy—an' bloomin' gen'rous, too;
An, now you can make your fortune—the same as your orf'cers do."

    Back to the Army again, sergeant,
      Back to the Army again.
    'Ow did I learn to do right-about turn?
      I'm back to the Army again!

A man o' four-an'-twenty that 'asn't learned of a trade—
Beside "Reserve" agin' him—'ed better be never made.
I tried my luck for a quarter, an' that was enough for me,
An' I thought of 'Er Majesty's barricks, an' I thought I'd go an' see.

    Back to the Army again, sergeant,
      Back to the Army again.
    'Tisn't my fault if I dress when I 'alt—
      I'm back to the Army again!

The sergeant arst no questions, but 'e winked the other eye'
'E sez to me, "Shun!" an' I shunted, the same as in days gone by;
For 'e saw the set o' my shoulders, an' I couldn't 'elp 'oldin' straight
When me an' the other rookies come under the barrick-gate.

    Back to the Army again, sergeant,
      Back to the Army again.

'Oo would ha' thought I could carry an' port?[1]
      I'm back to the Army again!

I took my bath, an' I wallered—for Gawd, I needed it so!
I smelt the smell o' the barricks, I 'eard the bugles go.
I 'eard the feet on the gravel—the feet o' the men what drill—
An' I sez to my flutterin' 'eart-strings, I sez to 'em, "Peace, be still!"

            Back to the Army again, sergeant,
                  Back to the Army again.
            'Oo said I knew when the troopship was due?
                  I'm back to the Army again!

I carried my slops to the tailor; I sez to 'im, "None o' your lip!
You tight 'em over the shoulders, an' loose 'em over the 'ip,
For the set o' the tunic's 'orrid."   An' 'e sez to me, "Strike me dead,
But I thought you was used to the business!" an' so 'e done what I said.

            Back to the Army again, sergeant,
                  Back to the Army again.
            Rather too free with my fancies?   Wot—me?
                  I'm back to the Army again!

Next week I'll 'ave 'em fitted; I'll buy me a swagger-cane;
They'll let me free o' the barricks to walk on the Hoe again,
In the name o' William Parsons, that used to be Edward Clay,
An'—any pore beggar that wants it can draw my fourpence a day!

            Back to the Army again, sergeant,
                  Back to the Army again.
            Out o' the cold an' the rain, sergeant,
                  Out o' the cold an' the rain.
                        'Oo's there?
            A man that's too good to be lost to you,
                  A man that is 'andled an' made—
            A man that will pay what 'e cost you
                  In learnin' the others their trade—parade!
            You're droppin' the pick o' the Army
                  Because you don't 'elp 'em remain,
            But drives 'em to cheat to get out o' the street
                  An' back to the Army again!

_____

[1]Carry and port his rifle.

"Birds Of Prey" March

(Troops for Foreign Service)

March! The mud is cakin' good about our trousies.
    Front!—eyes front, an' watch the Colour-casin's drip.
Front! The faces of the women in the 'ouses
    Ain't the kind o' things to take aboard the ship.

Cheer! An' we'll never march to victory.
Cheer! An' we'll never live to 'ear the cannon roar!
    The Large Birds o' Prey
    They will carry us away,
An' you'll never see your soldiers any more!

Wheel! Oh, keep your touch; we're goin' round a corner.
    Time!—mark time, an' let the men be'ind us close.
Lord! The transport's full, an' 'alf our lot not on 'er—
    Cheer, Oh, cheer! We're going off where no one knows.

March! The Devil's none so black as 'e is painted!
    Cheer! We'll 'ave some fun before we're put away.
'Alt an' 'and 'er out—a woman's gone and fainted!
    Cheer! Get on!—Gawd 'elp the married men to-day!

Hoi! Come up, you 'ungry beggars, to yer sorrow.
    ('Ear them say they want their tea, an' want it quick!)
You won't have no mind for slingers,[1] not to-morrow—
    No; you'll put the 'tween-decks stove out, bein' sick!

'Alt! The married kit 'as all to go before us!
    'Course it's blocked the bloomin' gangway up again!
Cheer, Oh, cheer the 'Orse Guards watchin' tender o'er us,
    Keepin' us since eight this mornin' in the rain!

Stuck in 'eavy marchin'-order, sopped and wringin'—
    Sick, before our time to watch 'er 'eave an' fall,
'Ere's your 'appy 'ome at last, an' stop your singin'.
    'Alt! Fall in along the troop-deck! Silence all!

Cheer! For we'll never live to see no bloomin' victory!
Cheer! An' we'll never live to 'ear the cannon roar!
    (One cheer more!)
    The jackal an' the kite
    'Ave an 'ealthy appetite,
An' you'll never see your soldiers any more! ('Ip! Urroar!)
    The eagle an' the crow
    They are waitin' ever so,

[1] Bread soaked in tea.

An' you'll never see your soldiers any more! ('Ip! Urroar!)
   Yes, the Large Birds o' Prey
   They will carry us away,
An' you'll never see your soldiers any more!

"Soldier An' Sailor Too"

(The Royal Regiment of Marines)

As I was spittin' into the Ditch aboard o' the *Crocodile*,
I seed a man on a man-o'-war got up in the Reg'lars' style.
'E was scrapin' the paint from off of 'er plates, an' I sez to 'im, "'Oo are you?"
Sez 'e "I'm a jolly—'Er Majesty's Jolly—soldier an' sailor too!"
Now 'is work begins by Gawd knows when, and 'is work is never through;
'E isn't one o' the reg'lar Line, nor 'e isn't one of the crew.
'E's a kind of a giddy harumfrodite—soldier an' sailor too!
An' after, I met 'im all over the world, a-doin' all kinds of things,
Like landin' 'isself with a Gatlin' gun to talk to them 'eathen kings;
'E sleeps in an 'ammick instead of a cot, an' 'e drills with the deck on a slew,
An' 'e sweats like a Jolly—' Er Majesty's Jolly—soldier an' sailor too!

For there isn't a job on the top o' the earth the beggar don't know, nor do—
You can leave 'im at night on a bald man's 'ead, to paddle 'is own canoe—
'E's a sort of a bloomin' cosmopolouse—soldier an' sailor too.

We've fought 'em in trooper, we've fought 'em in dock, and drunk with 'em in betweens,
When they called us the seasick scull'ry-maids, an' we called 'em the Ass-Marines;
But, when we was down for a double fatigue, from Woolwich to Bernardmyo,
We sent for the Jollies—'Er Majesty's—Jollies—soldier an' sailor too!
They think for 'emselves, an' they steal for 'emselves, and they never ask what's to do,
But they're camped an' fed an' they're up an' fed before our bugle's blew.
Ho! they ain't no limpin' procrastitutes—soldier an' sailor too!

You may say we are fond of an 'arness-cut, or 'ootin' in barrick-yards,
Or startin' a Board School mutiny along o' the Onion Guards;[1]

[1] Long ago, a battalion of the Guards was sent to Bermuda as a punishment for riotous conduct in barracks.

But once in a while we can finish in style for the ends of the earth to
    view,
The same as the Jollies—'Er Majesty's Jollies—soldier an' sailor too!
They come of our lot, they was brothers to us; they was beggars we'd met
    an' knew;
Yes, barrin' an inch in the chest an' the arm, they was doubles o' me an'
    you;
For they weren't no special chrysanthemums—soldier an' sailor too!

To take your chance in the thick of a rush, with firing all about,
Is nothing so bad when you've cover to 'and, an' leave an' likin' to shout;
But to stand an' be still to the *Birken'ead* drill[1] is a damn' tough bullet to
    chew,
An' they done it, in the Jollies—'Er Majesty's Jollies—soldier an' sailor
    too!
Their work was done when it 'adn't begun; they was younger nor me an'
    you;
Their choice it was plain between drownin' in 'eaps an' bein' mopped by
    the screw,
So they stood an' was still to the *Birken'ead* drill, soldier an' sailor too!

We're most of us liars, we're 'arf of us thieves, an' the rest are as rank as
    can be,
But once in a while we can finish in style (which I 'ope it won't 'appen to
    me).
But it makes you think better o' you an' your friends, an' the work you
    may 'ave to do,
When you think o' the sinkin' *Victorier's*[2] Jollies—soldier an' sailor too!
Now there isn't no room for to say ye don't know—they 'ave proved it
    plain and true—
That, whether it's Widow, or whether it's ship, Victorier's work is to do,
An' they done it, the Jollies—'Er Majesty's Jollies—soldier an' sailor too!

Sappers

(Royal Engineers)

When the Waters were dried an' the Earth did appear, ("It's all one,"
    says the Sapper),
The Lord He created the Engineer,
    Her Majesty's Royal Engineer,
    With the rank and pay of a Sapper!

[1]In 1852 the *Birkenhead* transport was sunk off Simon's Bay. The Marines aboard her went down
as drawn up on her deck.

[2]Admiral Tryon's flagship, sunk in collision in 1893.

When the Flood come along for an extra monsoon,
'Twas Noah constructed the first pontoon
   To the plans of Her Majesty's, etc.

But after fatigue in the wet an' the sun,
Old Noah got drunk, which he wouldn't ha' done
   If he'd trained with, etc.

When the Tower o' Babel had mixed up men's *bat*,[1]
Some clever civilian was managing that,
   An' none of, etc.

When the Jews had a fight at the foot of a hill,
Young Joshua ordered the sun to stand still,
   For he was a Captain of Engineers, etc.

When the Children of Israel made bricks without straw,
They were learnin' the regular work of our Corps,
   The work of, etc.

For ever since then, if a war they would wage,
Behold us a-shinin' on history's page—
   First page for, etc.

We lay down their sidings an' help 'em entrain,
An' sweep up their mess through the bloomin' campaign
   In the style of, etc.

They send us in front with a fuse an' a mine
To blow up the gates that are rushed by the Line,
   But bent by, etc.

They send us behind with a pick an' a spade,
To dig for the guns of a bullock-brigade
   Which has asked for, etc.

We work under escort in trousers and shirt,
An' the heathen they plug us tail-up in the dirt,
   Annoying, etc.

We blast out the rock an' we shovel the mud,
We make em' good roads an'—they roll down the *khud*,[2]
   Reporting, etc.

We make 'em their bridges, their wells, an' their huts,
An' the telegraph-wire the enemy cuts,
   An' it's blamed on, etc.

[1]Talk.   [2]Hillside.

An' when we return, an from war we would cease,
They grudge us adornin' the billets of peace,
  Which are kept for, etc.

We build 'em nice barracks—they swear they are bad,
That out Colonels are Methodist, married or mad,
  Insultin', etc.

They haven't no manners nor gratitude too,
For the more that we help 'em, the less will they do,
  But mock at, etc.

Now the Line's but a man with a gun in his hand,
An' Cavalry's only what horses can stand,
  When helped by, etc.

Artillery moves by the leave o' the ground,
But *we* are the men that do something all round,
  For *we* are, etc.

I have stated it plain, an' my argument's thus
  ("It's all one," says the Sapper)
There's only one Corps which is perfect—that's us;
  An' they call us Her Majesty's Engineers,
  Her Majesty's Royal Engineers,
  With the rank and pay of a Sapper!

That Day

It got beyond all orders an' it got beyond all 'ope;
  It got to shammin' wounded an' retirin' from the 'alt
'Ole companies was lookin' for the nearest road to slope;
  It were just a bloomin' knock-out—an' our fault!

> *Now there ain't no chorus 'ere to give,*
>   *Nor there ain't no band to play;*
> *An' I wish I was dead' fore I done what I did,*
>   *Or seen what I seed that day!*

We was sick o' bein' punished, an' we let 'em know it, too;
  An' a company-commander up an' 'it us with a sword,
An' some one shouted "'Ook it!" an' it come to *sove-ki-poo*,
  An' we chucked our rifles from us—O my Gawd!

There was thirty dead an' wounded on the ground we wouldn't keep—
  No, there wasn't more than twenty when the front begun to go—
But, Christ! along the line o' flight they cut us up like sheep,
  An' that was all we gained by doin' so!

I 'eard the knives be'ind me, but I dursn't face my man,
　　Nor I don't know where I went to, 'cause I didn't 'alt to see,
Till I 'eard a beggar squealin' out for quarter as 'e ran,
　　An' I thought I knew the voice an'—it was me!

We was 'idin under bedsteads more than 'arf a march away:
　　We was lyin' up like rabbits all about the country-side;
An' the Major cursed 'is Maker 'cause 'e'd lived to see that day,
　　An' the Colonel broke 'is sword acrost, an' cried.

We were rotten 'fore we started—we was never disci*plined*;
　　We made it out a favour if an order was obeyed.
Yes, every little drummer 'ad 'is rights an' wrongs to mind,
　　So we had to pay for teachin'—an' we paid!

The papers 'id it 'andsome, but you know the Army knows;
　　We was put to groomin' camels till the regiments withdrew,
An' they gave us each a medal for subduin' England's foes,
　　An' I 'ope you like my song—because it's true!

> *An' there ain't no chorus 'ere to give,*
> *Nor there ain't no band to play;*
> *But I wish I was dead 'fore I done what I did,*
> *Or seen what I seed that day!*

"The Men That Fought At Minden"

(In the Lodge of Instruction)

The men that fought at Minden, they was rookies in their time—
　　So was them that fought at Waterloo!
All the 'ole command, yuss, from Minden to Maiwand,
　　They was once dam' sweeps like you!

> *Then do not be discouraged, 'Eaven is your 'elper,*
> *We'll learn you not to forget;*
> *An' you mustn't swear an' curse, or you'll only catch it worse,*
> *For we'll make you soldiers yet!*

The men that fought at Minden, they 'ad stocks beneath their chins,
　　Six inch 'igh an' more;
But fatigue it was their pride, and they *would* not be denied
　　To clean the cook-'ouse floor.

The men that fought at Minden, they had anarchistic bombs
　　Served to 'em ny name of 'and-grenades;
But they got it in the eye (same as you will by-an'-by)
　　When they clubbed their field-parades.

The men that fought at Minden, they 'ad buttons up an' down,
  Two-an'-twenty dozen of 'em told;
But they didn't grouse an' shirk at an hour's extry work,
  They kept 'em bright as gold.

The men that fought at Minden, they was armed with musketoons,
  Also, they was drilled by 'alberdiers.
I didn't know what they were, but the sergeants took good care
  They washed be'ind their ears.

The men that fought at Minden, they 'ad ever cash in 'and
  Which they did not bank nor save,
But spent it gay an' free on their betters—such as me—
  For the good advice I gave.

The men that fought at Minden, they was civil—yuss, they was—
  Never didn't talk o' rights an' wrongs,
But they got it with the toe (same as you will get it—so!)—
  For interrupting songs.

The men that fought at Minden, they was several other things
  Which I don't remember clear;
But *that's* the reason why, now the six-year men are dry,
  The rooks will stand the beer!

> *Then do not be discouraged, 'Eaven is your 'elper,*
>   *We'll learn you not to forget.*
> *An' you mustn't swear an' curse, or you'll only catch it worse,*
>   *An' we'll make you soldiers yet!*
>
> *Soldiers yet, if you've got it in you—*
>   *All for the sake of the Core;*
> *Soldiers yet, if we 'ave to skin you—*
>   *Run an' get the beer, Johnny Raw—Johnny Raw!*
>   *Ho! run an' get the beer, Johnny Raw!*

Cholera Camp

(Infantry in India)

We've got the cholerer in camp—it's worse than forty fights;
We're dyin' in the wilderness the same as Isrulites.
It's before us, an' be'ind us, an' we cannot get away,
An' the doctor's just reported we've ten more to-day!

> *Oh, strike your camp an' go, the bugle's callin',*
>   *The Rains are fallin'—*
> *The dead are bushed an' stoned to keep 'em safe below.*

> *The Band's a-doin' all she knows to cheer us;*
> *The Chaplain's gone and prayed to Gawd to 'ear us—*
>   *To 'ear us—*
> *O Lord, for it's a-killin' of us so!*

Since August, when it started, it's been stickin' to our tail,
Though they've 'ad us out by marches an' they've 'ad us back by rail;
But it runs as fast as troop trains, and we cannot get away,
An' the sick-list to the Colonel makes ten more to-day.

There ain't no fun in women nor there ain't no bite to drink;
It's much too wet for shootin'; we can only march and think;
An' at evenin', down the *nullahs*, we can 'ear the jackals say,
"Get up, you rotten beggars, you've ten more to-day!"

'Twould make a monkey cough to see our way o' doin' things—
Lieutenants takin' companies an' Captains takin' wings,
An' Lances actin' Sergeants—eight file to obey—
For we've lots o' quick promotion on ten deaths a day!

Our Colonel's white an' twitterly—'e gets no sleep nor food,
But mucks about in 'orspital where nothing does no good.
'E sends us 'eaps o' comforts, all bought from 'is pay—
But there aren't much comfort 'andy on ten deaths a day.

Our Chaplain's got a banjo, an' a skinny mule 'e rides,
An' the stuff he says an' sings us, Lord, it makes us split our sides!
With 'is black coat-tails a-bobbin' to *Ta-ra-ra Boom-der-ay!*
'E's the proper kind o' *padre* for ten deaths a day.

An' Father Victor 'elps 'im with our Roman Catholicks—
He knows an' eap of Irish songs an' rummy conjurin'-tricks;
An' the two they works together when it comes to play or pray.
So we keep the ball a-rollin' on ten deaths a day.

We've got the cholerer in camp—we've got it 'ot an' sweet.
It ain't no Christmas dinner, but it's 'elped an' we must eat.
We've gone beyond the funkin', 'cause we've found it doesn't pay,
An' we're rockin' round the Districk on ten deaths a day!

> *Then strike your camp an' go, the Rains are fallin',*
>   *The Bugle's callin'!*
> *The dead are bushed an' stoned to keep 'em safe below!*
> *An' them that do not like it they can lump it,*
> *An' them that cannot stand it they can jump it;*
> *We've got to die somewhere—some way—some'ow—*
> *We might as well begin to do it now!*
> *Then, Number One, let down the tent-pole slow,*
> *Knock out the pegs an' 'old the corners—so!*
> *Fold in the flies, furl up the ropes, an' stow!*
> *Oh, strike—oh, strike your camp an' go!*
>   *(Gawd 'elp us!)*

The Ladies

I've taken my fun where I've found it:
  I've rogued an' I've ranged in my time;
I've 'ad my pickin' o' sweethearts,
  An' four o' the lot was prime.
One was an 'arf-caste widow,
  One was a woman at Prome,
One was the wife of a *jemadar-sais*,[1]
  An' one is a girl at 'ome.

Now I aren't no 'and with the ladies,
  For, takin' 'em all along,
You never can say till you've tried 'em,
  An' then you are like to be wrong.
There's times when you'll think that you mightn't,
  There's times when you'll know that you might;
But the things you will learn from the Yellow an' Brown,
  They'll 'elp you a lot with the White!

I was a young un at 'Oogli,
  Shy as a girl to begin;
Aggie de Castrer she made me,
  An' Aggie was clever as sin;
Older than me, but my first un—
  More like a mother she were—
Showed me the way to promotion an' pay,
  An' I learned about women from 'er!

Then I was ordered to Burma,
  Actin' in charge o' Bazar,
An' I got me a tiddy live 'eathen
  Through buyin' supplies off 'er pa.
Funny an' yellow an' faithful—
  Doll in a teacup she were—
But we lived on the square, like a true-married pair,
  An' I learned about women from 'er!

Then we was shifted to Neemuch
  (Or I might ha' been keepin' 'er now),
An' I took with a shiny she-devil,
  The wife of a nigger at Mhow;
Taught me the gipsy-folks' *bolee*;[2]
  Kind o' volcano she were,

---

[1]Head-groom.   [2]Slang.

For she knifed me one night 'cause I wished she was white,
    And I learned about women from 'er!

Then I come 'ome in a trooper,
    'Long of a kid o' sixteen—
Girl from a convent at Meerut,
    The straightest I ever 'ave seen.
Love at first sight was 'er trouble,
    She didn't know what it were;
An' I wouldn't do such, 'cause I liked 'er too much,
    But—I learned about women from 'er!

I've taken my fun where I've found it,
    An' now I must pay for my fun,
For the more you 'ave known o' the others
    The less will you settle to one;
An' the end of it's sittin' and thinkin',
    An' dreamin' Hell-fires to see;
So be warned by my lot (which I know you will not),
    An' learn about women from me!

What did the Colonel's Lady think?
    Nobody never knew.
Somebody asked the Sergeant's Wife,
    An' she told 'em true!
When you get to a man in the case,
    They're like as a row of pins—
For the Colonel's Lady an' Judy O'Grady
    Are sisters under their skins!

Bill 'Awkins

"'As anybody seen Bill 'Awkins?"
    "Now 'ow in the devil would I know?"
"'E's taken my girl out walkin',
    An' I've got to tell 'im so—
        Gawd—bless—'im!
    I've got to tell 'im so."

"D'yer know what 'e's like, Bill 'Awkins?"
    "Now what in the devil would I care?"
"'E's the livin', breathin' image of an organ-grinder's monkey,
    With a pound of grease in 'is 'air—
        Gawd—bless—'im!
    An' a pound o' grease in 'is 'air."

"An' s'pose you met Bill 'Awkins,
   Now what in the devil 'ud ye do?"
"I'd open 'is cheek to 'is chin-strap buckle,
   An' bung up 'is both eyes, too—
      Gawd—bless—'im!
   An' bung up 'is both eyes, too!"

"Look 'ere, where 'e comes, Bill 'Awkins!
   Now, what in the devil will you say?"
"It isn't fit and proper to be fightin' on a Sunday,
   So I'll pass 'im the time o'day—
      Gawd—bless—'im!
   I'll pass 'im the time o' day!"

The Mother-Lodge

There was Rundle, Station Master,
   An' Beazeley of the Rail,
An' 'Ackman, Commissariat,
   An' Donkin o' the Jail;
An' Blake, Conductor-Sergeant,
   Our Master twice was 'e,
With 'im that kept the Europe-shop,
   Old Framjee Eduljee.

  Outside—"Sergeant! Sir! Salute! Salaam!"
  Inside—"Brother," an' it doesn't do no 'arm.
  We met upon the Level an' we parted on the Square,
  An' I was Junior Deacon in my Mother-Lodge out there!

We'd Bola Nath, Accountant,
   An' Saul the Aden Jew,
An' Din Mohammed, draughtsman
   Of the Survey Office too;
There was Babu Chuckerbutty,
   An' Amir Singh the Sikh,
An' Castro from the fittin'-sheds,
   The Roman Catholick!

We 'adn't good regalia,
   An' Our Lodge was old an' bare,
But we knew the Ancient Landmarks,
   An' we kep' 'em to a hair;
An' lookin' on it backwards
   It often strikes me thus,

There ain't such things as infidels,
    Excep', per'aps, it's us.

For monthly, after Labour,
    We'd all sit down and smoke
(We dursn't give no banquets,
    Lest a Brother's caste were broke),
An' man on man got talkin'
    Religious an' the rest,
An' every man comparin'
    Of the God 'e knew the best.

So man on man got talkin',
    An' not a Brother stirred
Till mornin' waked the parrots
    An' that dam' brain-fever-bird;
We'd say 'twas 'ighly curious,
    An' we'd all ride 'ome to bed,
With Mo'ammed, God, an' Shiva
    Changin' pickets in our 'ead.

Full oft on Guv'ment service
    This rovin' foot 'ath pressed,
An' bore fraternal greetin's
    To the Lodges east an' west,
Accordin' as commanded,
    From Kohat to Singapore,
But I wish that I might see them
    In my Mother-Lodge once more!

I wish that I might see them,
    My Brethren black an' brown,
With the trichies smellin' pleasant
    An' the *hog-darn*[1] passin' down;
An' the old khansamah[2] snorin'
    On the bottle-khana[3] floor,
Like a Master in good standing
    With my Mother-Lodge once more.

Outside—"*Sergeant! Sir! Salute! Salaam!*"
Inside—"*Brother," an' it doesn't do no 'arm.*
We met upon the Level an' we parted on the Square,
An' I was Junior Deacon in my Mother-Lodge out there!

---

[1]Cigar-lighter.   [2]Butler.   [3]Pantry.

"Follow Me 'Ome"

There was no one like 'im, 'Orse or Foot,
   Nor any 'o the Guns I knew;
An' because it was so, why, o' course 'e went an' died,
   Which is just what the best men do.

> *So it's knock out your pipes an' follow me!*
> *An' it's finish up your swipes an' follow me!*
>   *Oh, 'ark to the big drum callin',*
>   *Follow me—follow me 'ome!*

'Is mare she neighs the 'ole day long,
   She paws the 'ole night through,
An' she won't take 'er feed 'cause o' waitin' for 'is step,
   Which is just what a beast would do.

'Is girl she goes with a bombardier
   Before 'er month is through;
An' the banns are up in church, for she's got the beggar hooked,
   Which is just what a girl would do.

We fought 'bout a dog—last week it were—
   No more than a round or two;
But I strook 'im cruel 'ard, an' I wish I 'adn't now,
   Which is just what a man can't do.

'E was all that I 'ad in the way of a friend,
   An' I've 'ad to find one new;
But I'd give my pay an' stripe for to get the beggar back,
   Which it's just too late to do!

> *So it's knock out your pipes an' follow me!*
> *An' it's finish up your swipes an' follow me!*
>   *Oh, 'ark to the fifes a-crawlin'!*
>   *Follow me—follow me 'ome!*

> *Take 'im away!*   *'E's gone where the best men go.*
> *Take 'im away!*   *An' the gun-wheels turnin' slow.*
> *Take 'im away!*   *There's more from the place 'e come.*
> *Take 'im away, with the limber an' the drum.*

> *For it's "Three rounds blank" an' follow me,*
> *An' it's "Thirteen rank" an' follow me;*
>   *Oh, passin' the love o' women,*
>   *Follow me—follow me 'ome!*

The Sergeant's Weddin'

'E was warned agin 'er—
　　That's what made 'im look:
She was warned agin' 'im—
　　That is why she took.
Wouldn't 'ear no reason,
　　Went an' done it blind;
We know all about 'em,
　　They've got all to find!

Cheer for the Sergeant's weddin'—
　　Give 'em one cheer more!
Grey gun-'orses in the lando,
　　An' a rogue is married to, etc.

What's the use 'o tellin'
　　'Arf the lot she's been?
'E's a bloomin' robber,
　　An' 'e keeps canteen.
'Ow did 'e get 'is buggy?
　　Gawd, you needn't ask!
Made 'is forty gallon
　　Out of every cask!

Watch 'im, with 'is 'air cut,
　　Count us filin' by—
Won't the Colonel praise 'is
　　Pop—u—lar—i—ty!
We 'ave scores to settle—
　　Scores for more than beer;
She's the girl to pay 'em—
　　That is why we're 'ere!

See the Chaplain thinkin'?
　　See the women smile?
Twig the married winkin'
　　As they take the aisle?
Keep your side-arms quiet,
　　Dressin' by the Band.
Ho! You 'oly beggars,
　　Cough be'ind your 'and!

Now it's done 'an over,
　　'Ear the organ squeak,
"Voice that breathed o'er Eden"—
　　Ain't she got the cheek!

White an' laylock ribbons,
    'Think yourself so fine!
I'd pray Gawd to take yer
    'Fore I made yer mine!

Escort to the kerridge,
    Wish 'im luck, the brute!
Chuck the slippers after—
    (Pity 'tain't a boot!)
Bowin' like a lady,
    Blushin' like a lad—
'Oo would say to see 'em
    Both is rotten bad?

Cheer for the Sergeant's weddin'—
    Give 'em one cheer more!
Grey gin-'orses in the lando,
    An' a rogue is married to, etc.

The Jacket

(Royal Horse Artillery)

Through the Plagues of Egyp' we was chasin' Arabi,
    Gettin' down an' shovin' in the sun;
An' you might 'ave called us dirty, an' you might ha' called us dry,
    An' you might 'ave 'eard us talkin' at the gun.
But the Captain 'ad 'is jacket, an' the jacket it was new—
    ('Orse Gunners, listen to my song!)
An' the wettin' of the jacket is the proper thing to do.
    Nor we didn't keep 'im waiting very long.

One day they gave us orders for to shell a sand redoubt,
    Loadin' down the axle-arms with case;
But the Captain knew 'is dooty, an' he took the crackers out
    An' he put some proper liquor in its place.
An' the Captain saw the shrapnel, which is six-an'-thirty clear.
    ('Orse Gunners, listen to my song!)
"Will you draw the weight," sez 'e, "or will you draw the beer?"
    An' we didn't keep 'im waiting very long.

    For the Captain 'ad 'is jacket, etc.

Then we trotted gentle, not to break the bloomin' glass,
    Though the Arabites 'ad all their ranges marked;
But we dursn't 'ardly gallop, for the most was bottled Bass,
    An' we'd dreamed of it since we was disembarked.

So we fired economic with the shells we 'ad in 'and,
   ('Orse Gunners, listen to my song!)
But the beggars under cover 'ad the impidence to stand,
   An' we couldn't keep 'em waitin' very long.

   And the Captain, etc.

So we finished 'arf the liquor (an' the Captain took champagne),
   An' the Arabites was shootin' all the while;
   An' we left our wounded 'appy with the empties on the plain,
   An' we used the bloomin' guns for projec*tile*!
We limbered up an' galloped—there were nothin' else to do—
   ('Orse Gunners, listen to my song!)
An' the Battery come a-boundin' like a boundin' kangaroo,
   But they didn't watch us comin' very long.

   As the Captain, etc.

We was goin' most extended—we was drivin' very fine,
   An' the Arabites were loosin' 'igh an' wide.
Till the Captain took the glacis with a rattlin' "right incline,"
   An' we dropped upon their 'eads the other side.
Then we give 'em quarter—such as 'adn't up and cut
   ('Orse Gunners, listen to my song!)
An' the Captain stood a limberful of fizzy somethin' Brutt,
   But we didn't leave it fizzing very long.

   For the Captain, Etc.

We might ha' been court-martialled, but it all come out all right.
   When they signalled us to join the main command,
There was every round expended, there was every gunner tight,
   An' the Captain waved a corkscrew in 'is 'and!

But the Captain 'ad 'is jacket, etc.

The 'Eathen

The 'eathen in 'is blindness bows down to wood an' stone;
'E don't obey no orders unless they is 'is own;
'E keeps 'is side-arms awful: 'e leaves 'em all about,
An' then comes up the Regiment an' pokes the 'eathen out.

All along o' dirtiness, all along o' mess,
All along o' doin' things rather-more-or-less,
All along of abby-nay,[1] kul,[2] an' hazar-ho,[3]
Mind you keep your rifle an' yourself jus' so!

   [1]Not now.   [2]To-morrow.   [3]Wait a bit.

The young recruit is 'aughty—'e draf's from Gawd knows where;
They bid 'im show 'is stockin's an' lay 'is mattress square;
'E calls it bloomin' nonsense—'e doesn't know, no more—
An' then up comes 'is Company an' kicks 'im round the floor!

The young recruit is 'ammered—'e takes it very hard;
'E 'angs 'is 'ead an' mutters—'e sulks about the yard;
'E talks o' "cruel tyrants" which 'e'll swing for by-an'-by,
An' the others 'ears an' mocks 'im, an' the boy goes orf to cry.

The young recruit is silly—'e thinks o' suicide.
'E's lost 'is gutter-devil; 'e 'asn't got 'is pride;
But day by day they kicks 'im, which 'elps 'im on a bit,
Till 'e finds 'isself one mornin' with a full an' proper kit.

Gettin clear o' dirtiness, gettin' done with mess,
Gettin' shut o' doin' things rather more-or-less;
Not so fond of abby-nay, kul, nor hazar-ho,
Learns to keep 'is rifle an' 'isself jus' so!

The young recruit is 'appy—'e throws a chest to suit;
You see 'im grow mustaches; you 'ear 'im slap 'is boot.
'E learns to drop the "bloodies" from every word 'e slings,
An' 'e shows an 'ealthy brisket when 'e strips for bars an' rings.

The cruel-tyrant sergeants they watch 'im 'arf a year;
They watch 'im with 'is comrades, they watch 'im with 'is beer;
They watch 'im with the women at the regimental dance,
And the cruel-tyrant-sergeants send 'is name along for "Lance."

An' now 'e's 'arf o' nothin', an' all a private yet,
'Is room they up an' rags 'im to see what they will get.
They rags 'im low an' cunnin', each dirty trick they can,
But 'e learns to sweat 'is temper an' 'e learns to sweat 'is man.

An', last, a Colour-Sergeant, as such to be obeyed,
'E schools 'is men at cricket, 'e tells 'em on parade;
They sees 'im quick an' 'andy, uncommon set an' smart,
An' so 'e talks to orficers which 'ave the Core at 'eart.

'E learns to do 'is watchin' without it showin' plain;
'E learns to save a dummy, an' shove 'im straight again;
'E learns to check a ranker that's buyin' leave to shirk;
An' 'e learns to make men like 'im so they'll learn to like their work.

An' when it comes to marchin' he'll see their socks are right,
An' when it comes to action 'e shows 'em how to sight.
'E knows their ways of thinkin' and just what's in their mind;
'E knows when they are takin' on an' when they've fell be'ind.

'E knows each talkin' corp'ral that leads a squad astray;
'E feels 'is innards 'eavin', 'is bowels givin' way;
'E sees the blue-white faces all tryin' 'ard to grin,
An' 'e stands an' waits an' suffers till it's time to cap 'em in.

An' now the hugly bullets come peckin' through the dust,
An' no one wants to face 'em, but every beggar must;
So, like a man in irons, which isn't glad to go,
They moves 'em off by companies uncommon stiff an' slow.

Of all 'is five years' schoolin' they don't remember much
Except' the not retreatin', the step an' keepin' touch.
It looks like teachin' wasted when they duck an' spread an' 'op—
But if 'e 'adn't learned 'em they'd be all about the shop.

An' now it's "'Oo goes backward?" an' now it's "'Oo comes on?"
And now it's "Get the doolies," an' now the Captain's gone;
An' now it's bloody murder, but all the while they 'ear
'Is voice, the same as barrick-drill, a-shepherdin' the rear.

'E's just as sick as they are, 'is 'eart is like to split,
But 'e works 'em, works 'em, works 'em till he feels 'em take the bit;
The rest is 'oldin steady till the watchful bugles play,
An' 'e lifts 'em, lifts 'em, lifts 'em through the charge that wins the day!

The 'eathen in 'is blindness bows down to wood an' stone;
'E don't obey no orders unless they is 'is own.
The 'eathen in 'is blindness must end where 'e began,
But the backbone of the Army is the Non-commissioned Man!

Keep away from dirtiness—keep away from mess,
Don't get into doin' things rather-more-or-less!
Let's ha' done with abby-nay, kul, and hazar-ho;
Mind you keep your rifle an' yourself jus' so!

The Shut-Eye Sentry

Sez the Junior Orderly Sergeant
    To the Senior Orderly Man:
"Our Orderly Orf'cer's *hokee-mut*,[1]
    "You 'elp 'im all you can.
"For the wine was old and the night is cold,
    "An' the best we may go wrong;
"So, 'fore e' gits to the sentry-box,
    "You pass the word along."

[1]Very drunk.

So it was "Rounds! What Rounds?" at two of a frosty night,
  'E's 'oldin on by the sergeant's sash, but, sentry, shut your eye.
An' it was "Pass! All's well! Oh, ain't 'e drippin' tight!
  'E'll need an affidavit pretty badly by-an'-by."

      The moon was white on the barricks,
          The road was white an' wide,
      An' the Orderly Orf'cer took it all,
          An' the ten-foot ditch beside.
      An' the corporal pulled an' the sergeant pushed,
          An' the three they danced along,
      But I'd shut my eyes in the sentry-box,
          So I didn't see nothin' wrong.

Though it was "Rounds! What Rounds?" O corporal, 'old 'im up!
  'E's usin' 'is cap as it shouldn't be used, but, sentry, shut your eyes.
An' it was "Pass! All's well! Ho, shun the foamin' cup!
  'E'll need,"etc.

      'Twas after four in the mornin';
          We 'ad to stop the fun,
      An' we sent 'im 'ome on a bullock-cart,
          With 'is belt an' stock undone;
      But we sluiced 'im down an' we washed 'im out,
          An' a first-class job we made,
      When we saved 'im, smart as a bombardier,
          For six o'clock parade.

It 'ad been "Rounds! What Rounds? Oh, shove 'im straight again!
  'E's usin' 'is sword for a bicycle, but, sentry, shut your eye."
An' it was "Pass! All's well! 'E's called me 'Darlin' Jane!'
  'E'll need,"etc.

      The drill was long an' 'eavy,
          The sky was 'ot an' blue.
      An' 'is eye was wild an' 'is 'air was wet,
          But 'is sergeant pulled 'im through.
      Our men was good old trusties—
          They'd done it on their 'ead—
      But you ought to 'ave 'eard 'em markin' time
          To 'ide the things 'e said!

For it was "Right flank—wheel!" for "'Alt, an' stand at ease!"
  An' "Left extend!" for "Centre close!" O marker, shut your eye!
An' it was, "'Ere, sir, 'ere! before the Colonel sees!"
  So he needed affidavits pretty badly by-an'-by.

There was two-an'-thirty sergeants,
      There was corp'rals forty-one,
There was just nine 'undred rank an' file
      To swear to a touch o' sun.
There was me 'e'd kissed in the sentry-box,
      As I 'ave not told in my song,
But I took my oath, which were Bible-truth,
      I 'adn't seen nothin' wrong.

There's them that's 'ot an' 'aughty,
      There's them that's cold an' 'ard,
But there comes a night when the best gets tight,
      And then turns out the Guard.
I've seen them 'ide their liquor
      In every kind o' way,
But most depends on makin' friends
      With Privit Thomas A.!

When it is "Rounds!   What Rounds?   'E's breathin' through 'is nose.
  'E's reelin', rollin', roarin', tight, but, sentry, shut your eye."
An' it is "Pass!   All's well!"   An' that's the way it goes:
  We'll 'elp 'im for 'is mother, an' 'e'll 'elp us by-an'-by!

"Mary, Pity Women!"

You call yourself a man,
      For all you used to swear,
An' leave me, as you can,
      My certain shame to bear?
I 'ear! You do not care—
You done the worst you know.
      I 'ate you, grinnin' there . . .
Ah, Gawd, I love you so!

Nice while it lasted, an' now it is over—
Tear out your 'eart an' good-bye to your lover!
What's the use o' grievin', when the mother that bore you
(Mary, pity women!) knew it all before you?

It aren't no false alarm,
      The finish to your fun;
You—you 'ave brung the 'arm,
      An' I'm the ruined one!
An' now you'll off an' run

With some new fool in tow.
   Your 'eart? You 'aven't none . . .
Ah, Gawd, I love you so!

When a man is tired there is naught will bind 'im;
All 'e solemn promised 'e will shove be'ind 'im.
What's the good o' prayin' for The Wrath to strike 'im
(Mary, pity women!), when the rest are like 'im?

What 'ope for me or—it?
   What's left for us to do?
I've walked with men a bit,
   But this—but this is you.
   So 'elp me, Christ, it's true!
Where can I 'ide or go?
   You coward through and through! . . .
Ah, Gawd, I love you so!

All the more you give 'em the less are they for givin'—
Love lies dead, an' you cannot kiss 'im livin'.
Down the road 'e led you there is no returnin'
(Mary, pity women!), but you're late in learnin'!

You'd like to treat me fair?
   You can't, because we're pore?
We'd starve? What do I care!
   We might, but *this* is shore!
   I want the name—no more—
The name, an' lines to show,
   An' not to be an 'ore . . .
Ah, Gawd, I love you so!

What's the good o' pleadin', when the mother that bore you
(Mary, pity women!) knew it all before you?
Sleep on 'is promises an' wake to your sorrow
(Mary, pity women!), for we sail to-morrow!

"For To Admire"

The Injian Ocean sets an' smiles
   So sof', so bright, so bloomin' blue;
There aren't a wave for miles an' miles
   Excep' the jiggle from the screw.
The ship is swep', the day is done,
   The bugle's gone for smoke and play;

An' black ag'in in the settin' sun
   The Lascar sings, "*Hum deckty hai!*"[1]

For to admire an' for to see,
   For to be'old this world so wide—
It never done no good to me,
   But I can't drop it if I tried!

I see the sergeants pitchin' quoits,
   I 'ear the women laugh an' talk,
I spy upon the quarter-deck
   The orficers an' lydies walk.
I thinks about the things that was,
   An' leans an' looks acrost the sea,
Till, spite of all the crowded ship,
   There's no one lef' alive but me.

The things that was which I 'ave seen,
   In barrick, camp, an' action too,
I tells them over by myself,
   An' sometimes wonders if they're true;
For they was odd—most awful odd—
   But all the same, now they are o'er,
There must be 'eaps o' plenty such,
   An' if I wait I'll see some more.

Oh, I 'ave come upon the books,
   An' frequent broke a barrick-rule,
An' stood beside an' watched myself
   Be'avin like a bloomin' fool.
I paid my price for findin' out,
   Nor never grutched the price I paid,
But sat in Clink without my boots,
   Admirin' 'ow the world was made.

Be'old a cloud upon the beam,
   An' 'umped above the sea appears
Old Aden, like a barrick-stove
   That no one's lit for years an' years.
I passed by that when I began,
   An' I go 'ome the road I came,
A time-expired soldier-man
   With six years' service to 'is name.

My girl she said, "Oh, stay with me!"
   My mother 'eld me to 'er breast.

[1] I'm looking out.

They've never written none, an' so
    They must 'ave gone with all the rest—
With all the rest which I 'ave seen
    An' found an' known an' met along.
I cannot say the things I feel,
    And so I sing my evenin' song:

For to admire an' for to see,
    For to be'old this world so wide—
It never done no good to me,
    But I can't drop it if I tried!

"The Service Man"

(Prelude to "Service Songs" in "The Five Nations")

"Tommy" you was when it began,
    But now that it is o'er
You shall be called The Service Man
    'Enceforward, evermore.

Batt'ry, brigade, flank, centre, van,
    Defaulter, Army-corps—
From first to last, The Service Man
    'Enceforward, evermore.

From 'Alifax to 'Industan,
    From York to Singapore—
'Orse, foot, an' guns, The Service Man
    'Enceforward, evermore!

The Absent-Minded Beggar

When you've shouted "Rule Britannia," when you've sung "God Save the
        Queen,"
    When you've finished killing Kruger with your mouth,
Will you kindly drop a shilling in my little tambourine
    For a gentleman in khaki ordered South?
He's an absent-minded beggar, and his weaknesses are great—
    But we and Paul must take him as we find him—
He is out on active service, wiping something off a slate—
    And he's left a lot of little things behind him!
Duke's son—cook's son—son of a hundred kings—
    (Fifty thousand horse and foot going to Table Bay!)

Each of 'em doing his country's work
 (and who's to look after their things?)
Pass the hat for your credit's sake,
 and pay—pay—pay!

There are girls he married secret, asking no permission to,
 For he knew he wouldn't get it if he did.
There is gas and coals and vittles, and the house-rent falling due,
 And it's more than rather likely there's a kid.
There are girls he walked with casual.   They'll be sorry now he's gone,
 For an absent-minded beggar they will find him,
But it ain't the time for sermons with the winter coming on.
 We must help the girl that Tommy's left behind him!
Cook's son—Duke's son—son of a belted Earl—
 Son of a Lambeth publican—it's all the same to-day!
Each of 'em doing his country's work
 (and who's to look after the girl?)
Pass the hat for your credit's sake,
 and pay—pay—pay!

There are families by thousands, far too proud to beg or speak,
 And they'll put their sticks and bedding up the spout,
And they'll live on half o' nothing, paid 'em punctual once a week,
 'Cause the man that earns the wage is ordered out.
He's an absent-minded beggar, but he heard his country call,
 And his reg'ment didn't need to send to find him!
He chucked his job and joined it—so the job before us all
 Is to help the home that Tommy's left behind him!
Duke's job—cook's job—gardner, baronet, groom,
 Mews or palace or paper-shop, there's someone gone away!
Each of 'em doing his country's work
 (and who's to look after the room?)
Pass the hat for your credit's sake,
 and pay—pay—pay!

Let us manage so as, later, we can look him in the face,
 And tell him—what he'd very much prefer—
That, while he saved the Empire, his employer saved his place,
 And his mates (that's you and me) looked out for *her*.
He's an absent-minded beggar and he may forget it all,
 But we do not want his kiddies to remind him
That we sent 'em to the workhouse while their daddy hammered Paul,
 So we'll help the homes that Tommy left behind him!
Cook's home—Duke's home—home of a millionaire,
 (Fifty thousand horse and foot going to Table Bay!)

Each of 'em doing his country's work
    (and what have you got to spare?)
Pass the hat for your credit's sake,
    and pay—pay—pay!

Chant-Pagan

(English Irregular, discharged)

Me that 'ave been what I've been—
Me that 'ave gone where I've gone—
Me that 'ave seen what I've seen—
   'Ow can I ever take on
With awful old English again,
An' 'ouses both sides of the street,
And 'edges two sides of the lane,
And the parson an' gentry between,
An' touchin' my 'at when we meet—
   Me that 'ave been what I've been?

Me that 'ave watched 'arf a world
'Eave up all shiny with dew,
Kopje on kop to the sun,
An' as soon as the mist let 'em through
Our 'elios winkin' like fun—
Three sides of a ninety-mile square,
Over valleys as big as a shire—
'Are ye there? Are ye there? Are ye there?'
An' then the blind drum of our fire . . .
An' I'm rollin' 'is lawns for the Squire,

                Me!

Me that 'ave rode through the dark
Forty mile, often, on end,
Along the Ma'ollisberg Range,
With only the stars for my mark
An' only the night for my friend,
An' things runnin' off as you pass,
An' things jumpin' up in the grass,
An' the silence, the shine an' the size
Of the 'igh, unexpressible skies—
I am takin' some letters almost
As much as a mile to the post,
An' "mind you come back with the change!"

                Me!

Me that saw Barberton took
When we dropped through the clouds on their 'ead,
An' they 'ove the guns over and fled—
Me that was through Di'mond 'Ill,
An' Pieters an' Springs an' Belfast—
From Dundee to Vereeniging all—
Me that stuck out to the last
(An' five bloomin' bars on my chest)—
I am doin' my Sunday-school best,
By the 'elp of the Squire an' 'is wife
(Not to mention the 'ousemaid an' cook),
To come in an' 'ands up an' be still,
An' honestly work for my bread,
My livin' in that state of life
To which it shall please God to call
                                            Me!

Me that 'ave followed my trade
In the place where the Lightnin's are made;
'Twixt the Rains and the Sun and the Moon—
Me that lay down an' got up
Three years with sky for my roof—
That 'ave ridden my 'unger an' thirst
Six thousand raw mile on the hoof,
With the Vaal and the Orange for cup,
An' the Brandwater Basin for dish,—
Oh! it's 'ard to be'ave as they wish
(Too 'ard, an' a little too soon),
I'll 'ave to think over it first—
                                            Me!

I will arise an' get 'ence—
I will trek South and make sure
If it's only my fancy or not
That the sunshine of England is pale,
And the breezes of England are stale,
An' there's somethin' gone small with the lot.
For *I* know of a sun an' a wind,
An' some plains and a mountain be'ind,
An' some graves by a barb-wire fence,
An' a Dutchman I've fought 'oo might give
Me a job were I ever inclined
To look in an' offsaddle an' live
Where there's neither a road nor a tree—

But only my Maker an' me,
And I think it will kill me or cure,
So I think I will go there an' see.

Me!

M. I.

(Mounted Infantry of the Line)

I wish my mother could see me now, with a fence-post under my arm,
And a knife and a spoon in my putties that I found on a Boer farm,
Atop of a sore-backed Argentine, with a thirst that you couldn't buy.
    I used to be in the Yorkshires once
      (Sussex, Lincolns, and Rifles once),
      Hampshires, Glosters, and Scottish once!   (*ad lib.*)
          But now I am M. I.

This is what we are known as—that is the name you must call
If you want officers' servants, pickets an' 'orseguards an' all—
Details for buryin'-parties, company-cooks or supply—
Turn out the chronic Ikonas!   Roll up the——[1] M. I.!

My 'ands are spotty with veldt-sores, my shirt is a button an' frill,
An' the things I've used my bay'nit for would make a tinker ill!
An' I don't know whose dam' column I'm in, nor where we're trekkin'
      nor why
    I've trekked from the Vaal to the Orange once—
      From the Vaal to the greasy Pongolo once—
      (Or else it was called the Zambesi once)—
          For now I am M. I.

That is what we are known as—we are the push you require
For outposts all night under freezin', an' rearguard all day under fire.
Anything 'ot or unwholesome?   Anything dusty or dry?
Borrow a bunch of Ikonas!   Trot out the ——M. I.!

Our Sergeant-Major's a subaltern, our Captain's a Fusilier—
Our Adjutant's "late of Somebody's 'Orse," an' a Melbourne auctioneer;
But you couldn't spot us at 'arf a mile from the crackest cavl-ry.
    They used to talk about Lancers once,
      Hussars, Dragoons, an' Lancers once,
      'Elmets, pistols, an' carbines once,
          But now we are M. I.!

[1] Number according to taste and service of audience.

That is what we are known as—we are the orphans they blame
For beggin' the loan of an 'ead-stall an' makin' a mount to the same.
'Can't even look at their 'orselines but some one goes bellerin' "Hi!"
"'Ere comes a burglin' Ikona!   Footsack, you——M. I.!"

We're trekkin' our twenty miles a day an' bein' loved by the Dutch,
But we don't hold on by the mane no more, nor lose our stirrups—much;
An' we scout with a senior man in charge where the 'oly white flags fly.
   We used to think they were friendly once,
   Didn't take any precautions once
   (Once, my ducky, an' only once!)
      But now we are M. I.!

That is what we are known as—we are the beggars that got
Three days "to learn equitation," an' six month o' bloomin' well trot!
Cow-guns, an' cattle, an' convoys—an' Mister De Wet on the fly—
We are the rollin' Ikonas!   We are the——M. I.
The new fat regiments come from home, imaginin' vain V.C.'s
(The same as your talky-fighty men which are often Number Threes[1]),

But our words o' command are "Scatter" an' "Close" an' "Let your
   wounded lie."
   We used to rescue 'em noble once,—
   Givin' the range we raised 'em once—
   Gettin' 'em killed as we saved 'em once—
      But now we are M. I.

That is what we are known as—we are the lanterns you view
After a fight round the kopjes, lookin' for men that we knew;
Whistlin' an' callin' together, 'altin' to catch the reply:—
"'Elp me!   O 'elp me, Ikonas!   This way, the——M. I.!"

I wish my mother could see me now, a-gatherin' news on my own,
When I ride like a General up to the scrub and ride back like Tod Sloan,
Remarkable close to my 'orse's neck to let the shots go by.
   We used to fancy it risky once
   (Called it a reconnaissance once),
   Under the charge of an orf'cer once,
      But now we are M.I.!

That is what we are known as—that is the song you must say
When you want men to be Mausered at one and a penny a day;
We are no five-bob Colonials—we are the 'ome-made supply,
Ask for the London Ikonas!   Ring up the——M. I.!

[1] Horse-holders when in action, and therefore generally under cover.

I wish myself could talk to myself as I left 'im a year ago;
I could tell 'im a lot that would save 'im a lot on the things that 'e ought
    to know!
When I think o' that ignorant barrack-bird, it almost makes me cry,
    I used to belong in an Army once
    (Gawd! what a rum little Army once),
    Red little, dead little Army once!
        But now I am M. I.!

That is what we are known as—we are the men that have been
Over a year at the business, smelt it an' felt it an' seen.
We 'ave got 'old of the needful—*you* will be told by and by;
Wait till you've 'eard the Ikonas, spoke to the old M. I.!

Mount—march, Ikonas! Stand to your 'orses again!
Mop off the frost on the saddles, mop up the miles on the plain.
Out go the stars in the dawnin', up goes our dust to the sky,
Walk—trot, Ikonas! Trek jou,[1] the old M. I.!

Columns

(Mobile Columns of the Boer War)

Out o' the wilderness, dusty an' dry
  (*Time, an' 'igh time to be trekkin' again!*)
'Oo is it 'eads to the Detail Supply?
  A section, a pompom,[2] an' six 'undred men.

'Ere comes the clerk with 'is lantern an' keys
  (*Time, an' 'igh time to be trekkin' again!*
"Surplus of everything—draw what you please
  "For the section, the pompom, an' six 'undred men."

"What are our orders an' where do we lay?"
  (*Time, an' 'igh time to be trekkin' again!*)
"You came after dark— you will leave before day,
  "You section, you pompom, you six 'undred men!"

Down the tin street, 'alf awake an' unfed,
'Ark to 'em blessin' the Gen'ral in bed!

Now by the church an' the outspan they wind—
Over the ridge an' it's all lef' be'ind
  For the section, etc.

---

[1] Get ahead.   [2] One-pounder q.f. gun.

Soon they will camp as the dawn's growin' grey.
Roll up for coffee an' sleep while they may—
      The section, etc.

Read their 'ome letters, their papers an' such,
For they'll move after dark to astonish the Dutch
      With a section, etc.

'Untin' for shade as the long hours pass—
Blankets on rifles or burrows in grass,
      Lies the section, etc.

Dossin' or beatin' a shirt in the sun,
Watching chameleons or cleanin' a gun,
      Waits the section, etc.

With nothin' but stillness as far as you please,
An' the silly mirage stringin' islands an' seas
      Round the section, etc.

So they strips off their hide an' they grills in their bones,
Till the shadows crawl out from beneath the pore stones
      Towards the section, etc.

An' the Mauser-bird stops an' the jackals begin,
An' the 'orse-guard comes up and the Gunners 'ook in
      As a 'int to the pompom an' six 'undred men . . .

Off through the dark with the stars to rely on—
(Alpha Centauri an' somethin' Orion)
      Moves the section, etc.

Same bloomin' 'ole which the ant-bear 'as broke,
Same bloomin' stumble an' same bloomin' joke
      Down the section, etc.

Same "Which is right" where the cart-tracks divide,
Same "Give it up" from the same clever guide
      To the section, etc.

Same tumble-down on the same 'idden farm,
Same white-eyed Kaffir 'oo gives the alarm
      Of the section, etc.

Same shootin' wild at the end o' the night,
Same flyin'-tackle, an' same messy fight,
      By the section, etc.

Same ugly 'iccup an' same 'orrid squeal,
When it's too dark to see an' it's too late to feel
      In the section, etc.

(Same batch of prisoners, 'airy an' still,
Watchin' their comrades bolt over the 'ill
  From the section, etc.)

Same chilly glare in the eye of the sun
As 'e gets up displeasured to see what was done
  By the section, etc.

Same splash o' pink on the stoep or the kraal,
An' the same quiet face which 'as finished with all
  In the section, the pompom, an' six 'undred men.

Out o' the wilderness, dusty an' dry
  (Time, an' 'igh time to be trekkin' again!
'Oo is it 'eads to the Detail Supply?
  A section, a pompom, an' six 'undred men.

The Parting of the Columns

"... *On the —th instant a mixed detachment of Colonials left ——for Cape Town, there to rejoin their respective homeward-bound contingents, after fifteen months' service in the field. They were escorted to the station by the regular troops in garrison and the bulk of Colonel ——'s column, which has just come in to refit, preparatory to further operations. The leave-taking was of the most cordial character, the men cheering each other continuously.*"

Any Newspaper, during the South African War.

We've rode and fought and ate and drunk as rations[1] come to hand,
Together for a year and more around this stinkin' land:
Now you are goin' home again, but we must see it through,
We needn't tell we liked you well. Good-bye good luck to you!

You 'ad no special call to come, and so you doubled out,
And learned us how to camp and cook an' steal a horse and scout.
Whatever game we fancied most, you joyful played it too,
And rather better on the whole. Good-bye—good luck to you!

There isn't much we 'aven't shared, since Kruger cut and run,
The same old work, the same old skoff,[2] the same old dust and sun;
The same old chance that laid us out, or winked an' let us through;
The same old Life, the same old Death. Good-bye—good luck to you!

---

[1]Convoys were not seldom captured by the Boers.   [2]Food.

Our blood 'as truly mixed with yours—all down the Red Cross train.
We've bit the same thermometer in Bloeming-typhoidtein.[1]
We've 'ad the same old temp'rature—the same relapses too,
The same old saw-backed fever chart. Good-bye—good luck to you!

But 'twasn't merely this an' that (which all the world may know),
'Twas how you talked an' looked at things which made us like you so.
All independent, queer an' odd, but most amazin' new.
My word! you shook us up to rights. Good-bye—good luck to you!

Think o' the stories round the fire, the tales along the trek—
O' Calgary an' Wellin'ton, an' Sydney and Quebec;
Of mine an' farm, an' ranch an' run, an' moose an' caribou,
An' parrots peckin' lambs to death! Good-bye—good luck to you!

We've seen your 'ome by word o' mouth, we've watched your rivers
shine,
We've heard your bloomin' forests blow of eucalyp' and pine;
Your young, gay countries north and south, we feel we own 'em too,
For they was made by rank an' file. Good-bye—good luck to you!

We'll never read the papers now without inquirin' first
For word from all those friendly dorps where you was born an' nursed.
Why, Dawson, Galle, an' Montreal—Port Darwin—Timaru,
They're only just across the road! Good-bye—good luck to you!

Good-bye!—So-long! Don't lose yourselves—nor us, nor all kind friends,
But tell the girls your side the drift we're comin'—when it ends!
Good-bye, you bloomin' Atlasses! You've taught us somethin' new:
The world's no bigger than a kraal. Good-bye—good luck to you!

Two Kopjes

(*Made Yeomanry towards the end of the Boer War*)

Only two African kopjes,
Only the cart-tracks that wind
Empty and open between 'em,
Only the Transvaal behind;
Only an Aldershot column
Marching to conquer the land . . .
Only a sudden and solemn
Visit, unarmed, to the Rand.

---

[1] There were several thousands of typhoid cases in Bloemfontein. Hence its name among the troops.

Then scorn not the African kopje,
  The kopje that smiles in the heat,
The wholly unoccupied kopje,
  The home of Cornelius and Piet.
You can never be sure of your kopje,
  But of this be you blooming well sure,
A kopje is always a kopje,
  And a Boojer is always a Boer!

Only two African kopjes,
  Only the virtues above,
Only baboons—at the bottom,[1]
  Only some buck on the move;
Only a Kensington draper
  Only pretending to scout . . .
Only bad news for the paper,
  Only another knock-out.

Then mock not the African kopje,
  And rub not your flank on its side,
The silent and simmering kopje,
  The kopje beloved by the guide.
You can never be, etc.

Only two African kopjes,
  Only the dust of their wheels,
Only a bolted commando,
  Only our guns at their heels . . .
Only a little barb-wire,
  Only a natural fort,
Only "by sections retire,"
  Only "regret to report!"

Then mock not the African kopje—
  Especially when it is twins,
One sharp and one table-topped kopje—
  For that's where the trouble begins.
You can never be, etc.

Only two African kopjes
  Baited the same as before—
Only we've had it so often,
  Only we're taking no more . . .
Only a wave to our troopers,
  Only our flanks swinging past,
Only a dozen voorloopers,[2]
  Only *we*'ve learned it at last!

[1] Showing that men are at the top.   [2] Leading horseman of the Boers.

Then mock not the African kopje,
    But take off your hat to the same,
The patient, impartial old kopje,
    The kopje that taught us the game!
For all that we knew in the Columns,
    And all they've forgot on the Staff,
We learned at the Fight o' Two Kopjes,
    Which lasted two years an' a half.

O mock not the African kopje,
    Not even when peace has been signed—
The kopje that isn't a kopje—
    The kopje that copies its kind.
You can never be sure of your kopje,
    But of this be you blooming well sure,
That kopje is always a kopje,
    And a Boojer is always a Boer!

The Instructor

(*Non-commissioned Officers of the Line*)

At times when under cover I 'ave said,
To keep my spirits up an' raise a laugh,
'Earin' 'im pass so busy over-'ead—
Old Nickel-Neck, 'oo isn't on the Staff—
"There's one above is greater than us all."

Before 'im I 'ave seen my Colonel fall,
An' watched 'im write my Captain's epitaph,
So that a long way off it could be read—
He *'as* the knack o' makin' men feel small—
Old Whistle-Tip, 'oo isn't on the Staff.

There is no sense in fleein' (I 'ave fled),
Better go on an' do the belly-crawl,
An' 'ope 'e'll 'it some other man instead
Of you 'e seems to 'unt so speshual—
Fitzy van Spitz, 'oo isn't on the Staff.

An' thus in mem'ry's cinematograph,
Now that the show is over, I recall
The peevish voice an' 'oary mushroom 'ead
Of 'im we owned was greater than us all,
'Oo give instruction to the quick an' the dead—
The Shudderin' Beggar—not upon the Staff!

Boots

(Infantry Columns)

We're foot—slog—slog—slog—sloggin' over Africa—
Foot—foot—foot—foot—sloggin' over Africa—
(Boots—boots—boots—boots—movin' up and down again!)
  There's no discharge in the war!

Seven—six—eleven—five—nine-an'-twenty mile to-day—
Four—eleven—seventeen—thirty-two the day before—
(Boots—boots—boots—boots—movin' up an' down again);
  There's no discharge in the war!

Don't—don't—don't—don't—look at what's in front of you.
(Boots—boots—boots—boots—movin' up an' down again);
Men—men—men—men—men go mad with watchin' 'em,
  An' there's no discharge in the war!

Try—try—try—try—to think o' something different—
Oh—my—God—keep—me from goin' lunatic!
(Boots—boots—boots—boots—movin' up an' down again!)
  There's no discharge in the war!

Count—count—count—count—the bullets in the bandoliers.
If—your—eyes—drop—they will get atop o' you!
(Boots—boots—boots—boots—movin' up and down again)—
  There's no discharge in the war!

We—can—stick—out—'unger, thirst, an' weariness,
But—not—not—not—not the chronic sight of 'em—
Boots—boots—boots—boots—movin' up an' down again,
  An' there's no discharge in the war!

'Tain't—so—bad—by—day because o' company,
But night—brings—long—strings—o' forty thousand million
Boots—boots—boots—boots—movin' up an' down again.
  There's no discharge in the war!

I – 'ave—marched—six—weeks in 'Ell an' certify
It—is—not—fire—devils, dark, or anything,
  But boots—boots – boots—boots—movin' up an' down again,
  An' there's no discharge in the war!

The Married Man

(Reservist of the Line)

The bachelor 'e fights for one
    As joyful as can be;
But the married man don't call it fun,
    Because 'e fights for three—
For 'Im an' 'Er an' It
    (An' Two an' One make Three)
'E wants to finish 'is little bit,
    An' 'e wants to go 'ome to 'is tea!

The bachelor pokes up 'is 'ead
    To see if you are gone;
But the married man lies down instead,
    An' waits till the sights come on,
For 'Im an' 'Er an' a hit
    (Direct or ricochee)
'E wants to finish 'is little bit,
    An' 'e wants to go 'ome to 'is tea.

The bachelor will miss you clear
    To fight another day;
But the married man, 'e says "No fear!"
    'E wants you out of the way
Of 'Im an' 'Er an' It
    (An' 'is road to 'is farm or the sea),
'E wants to finish 'is little bit,
    An' 'e wants to go 'ome to 'is tea.

The bachelor 'e fights 'is fight
    An' stretches out an' snores;
But the married man sits up all night—
    For 'e don't like out-o'-doors.
'E'll strain an' listen an' peer
    An' give the first alarm—
For the sake o' the breathin' 'e's used to 'ear,
    An' the 'ead on the thick of 'is arm.

The bachelor may risk 'is 'ide
    To 'elp you when you're downed;
But the married man will wait beside
    Till the ambulance comes round.
'E'll take your 'ome address
    An' all you've time to say,

Or if 'e sees there's 'ope, 'e'll press
   Your art'ry 'alf the day—

—For 'Im an' 'Er an' It
   (An' One from Three leaves Two),
For 'e knows you wanted to finish your bit,
   An' 'e knows 'oo's wantin' you.
Yes, 'Im an' 'Er an' It
   (Our 'oly One in Three),
We're all of us anxious to finish our bit,
   An' we want to get 'ome to our tea!

Yes, It an' 'Er an' 'Im,
   Which often makes me think
The married man must sink or swim
   An'—'e can't afford to sink!
Oh, 'Im an' It an' 'Er
   Since Adam an' Eve began!
So I'd rather fight with the bacheler
   An' be nursed by the married man!

Lichtenberg

(*New South Wales Contingent*)

Smells are surer than sounds or sights
   To make your heart-strings crack—
They start those awful voices o' nights
   That whisper, "Old man, come back!"
That must be why the big things pass
   And the little things remain,
Like the smell of the wattle by Lichtenberg,
   Riding in, in the rain.

There was some silly fire on the flank
   And the small wet drizzling down—
There were the sold-out shops and the bank
   And the wet, wide-open town;
And we were doing escort-duty
   To somebody's baggage-train,
And I smelt wattle by Lichtenberg—
   Riding in, in the rain.

It was all Australia to me—
   All I had found or missed:

Every face I was crazy to see,
    And every woman I'd kissed:
All that I shouldn't ha' done, God knows!
    (As He knows I'll do it again),
That smell of the wattle round Lichtenberg,
    Riding in, in the rain!

And I saw Sydney the same as ever,
    The picnics and brass-bands;
And my little homestead on Hunter River
    And my new vines joining hands.
It all came over me in one act
    Quick as a shot through the brain—
With the smell of the wattle round Lichtenberg,
    Riding in, in the rain.

I have forgotten a hundred fights,
    But one I shall not forget—
With the raindrops bunging up my sights
    And my eyes bunged up with wet;
And through the crack and the stink of the cordite,
    (Ah, Christ!   My country again!)
The smell of the wattle by Lichtenberg,
    Riding in, in the rain!

Stellenbosch

(Composite Columns)

The General 'eard the firin' on the flank
    An' 'e sent a mounted man to bring 'im back
The silly, pushin' person's name an' rank
    'Oo'd dared to answer Brother Boer's attack:
For there might 'ave been a serious engagement,
    An' 'e might 'ave wasted 'alf a dozen men;
So 'e ordered 'im to stop 'is operations round the kopjes,
    An' 'e told 'im off before the Staff at ten!

And it all goes into the laundry,
But it never comes out in the wash,
'Ow we're sugared about by the old men
('Eavy-sterned amateur old men!)
That 'amper an' 'inder an' scold men
For fear o' Stellenbosch![1]

---

[1] The more notoriously incompetent commanders used to be sent to the town of Stellenbosch, which name presently became a verb.

The General 'ad "produced a great effect,"
  The General 'ad the country cleared—almost;
The General " 'ad no reason to expect,"
  And the Boers 'ad us bloomin' well on toast!
For we might 'ave crossed the drift before the twilight,
  Instead o' sitting down an' takin' root;
But we was not allowed, so the Boojers scooped the crowd,
  To the last survivin' bandolier an' boot.

The General saw the farm'ouse in 'is rear,
  With its stoep so nicely shaded from the sun;
Sez 'e, "I'll pitch my tabernacle 'ere,"
  An' 'e kept us muckin' round till 'e 'ad done.
For 'e might 'ave caught the confluent pneumonia
  From sleepin' in his gaiters in the dew;
So 'e took a book an' dozed while the other columns closed,
  And De Wet's commando out an' trickled through!

The General saw the mountain-range ahead,
  With their 'elios showin' saucy on the 'eight,
So 'e 'eld us to the level ground instead.
  An' telegraphed the Boojers wouldn't fight.
For 'e might 'ave gone an' sprayed 'em with a pompom,
  Or 'e might 'ave slung a squadron out to see—
But 'e wasn't takin' chances in them 'igh an' 'ostile kranzes—
  He was markin' time to earn a K.C.B.

The General got 'is decorations thick
  (The men that backed 'is lies could not complain),
The Staff 'ad D.S.O.'s till we was sick,
  An' the soldier—'ad the work to do again!
For 'e might 'ave known the District was an 'otbed,
  Instead of 'andin' over, upside down,
To a man 'oo 'ad to fight 'alf a year to put it right,
  While the General sat an' slandered 'im in town!

An' it all went into the laundry,
But it never came out in the wash.
We were sugared about by the old men
(Panicky, pershin' old men)
That 'amper an' 'inder an' scold men
For fear o' Stellenbosch!

Half-Ballade of Waterval

(Non-commissioned Officers in Charge of Prisoners)

When by the labour of my 'ands
  I've 'elped to pack a transport tight
With prisoners for foreign lands,
  I ain't transported with delight.
  I know it's only just an' right,
    But yet it somehow sickens me,
Fir I 'ave learned at Waterval[1]
    The meanin' of captivity.

Be'ind the pegged barb-wire strands.
  Beneath the tall electric light,
We used to walk in bare-'ead bands,
  Explainin' 'ow we lost our fight;
  An' that is what they'll do to-night
    Upon the steamer out at sea,
If I 'ave learned at Waterval
    The meanin' of captivity.

They'll never know the shame that brands—
  Black shame no livin' down makes white—
The mockin' from the sentry-stands,
  The women's laugh, the gaoler's spite.
  We are too bloomin'-much polite,
    But that is 'ow I'd 'ave us be . . .
Since I 'ave learned at Waterval
    The meanin' of captivity.

They'll get those draggin' days all right,
  Spent as a foreigner commands,
An' 'orrors of the locked-up night,
  With 'Ell's own thinkin' on their 'ands.
  I'd give the gold o' twenty Rands
    (If it was mine) to set 'em free,
For I 'ave learned at Waterval
    The meanin' of captivity!

[1] Where the majority of English prisoners were kept by the Boers.

Piet

(Regular of the Line)

I do not love my Empire's foes,
  Nor call 'em angels; still,
What *is* the sense of 'atin' those
  'Oom you are paid to kill?
So, barrin' all that foreign lot
  Which only joined for spite,
Myself, I'd just as soon as not
  Respect the man I fight.

Ah, there, Piet—'is trousies to 'is knees,
'Is coat-tails lyin' level in the bullet-sprinkled breeze;
'E does not lose 'is rifle an' 'e does not lose 'is seat.
I've known a lot o' people ride a dam' sight worse than Piet.

I've 'eard 'im cryin' from the ground
  Like Abel's blood of old,
An' skirmished out to look, an' found
  The beggar nearly cold.
I've waited on till 'e was dead
  (Which couldn't 'elp 'im much),
But many grateful things 'e's said
  To me for doin' such.

    Ah, there, Piet! whose time 'as come to die,
    'Is carcase past rebellion, but 'is eyes inquirin' why.
    Though dressed in stolen uniform with badge o' rank complete,
    I've known a lot o' fellers go a dam' sight worse than Piet.

An' when there wasn't aught to do
  But camp and cattle-guards,
I've fought with 'im the 'ole day through
  At fifteen 'undred yards;
Long afternoons o' lyin' still,
  An' 'earin' as you lay
The bullets swish from 'ill to 'ill
  Like scythes among the 'ay.

    Ah, there, Piet!—be'ind 'is stony kop—
    With 'is Boer bread an' biltong,[1] an' 'is flask of awful Dop;[2]
    'Is Mauser for amusement an' 'is pony for retreat,
    I've known a lot o' fellers shoot a dam' sight worse than Piet.

[1] Dried meat.   [2] Cape brandy.

He's shoved 'is rifle 'neath my nose
  Before I'd time to think,
An' borrowed all my Sunday clo'es
  An' sent me 'ome in pink;
An' I 'ave crept (Lord, 'ow I've crept!)
  On 'ands an' knees I've gone,
And spoored and floored and caught and kept
  An' sent him to Ceylon![1]
    Ah, there, Piet!—you've sold me many a pup,
    When week on week alternate is was you an' me "'ands up!"
    But though I never made *you* walk man-naked in the 'eat,
    I've known a lot of fellows stalk a dam' sight worse than Piet.

From Plewman's to Marabastad,
  From Ookiep to De Aar,
Me an' my trusty friend 'ave 'ad,
  As you might say, a war;
But seein' what both parties done
  Before 'e owned defeat,
I ain't more proud of 'avin' won
  Than I am pleased with Piet.
    Ah, there, Piet!—picked up be'ind the drive!
    The wonder wasn't 'ow 'e fought, but 'ow 'e kep' alive,
    With nothin' in 'is belly, on 'is back, or to 'is feet—
    I've known a lot o' men behave a dam' sight worse than Piet.

No more I'll 'ear 'is rifle crack
  Along the block'ouse fence—
The beggar's on the peaceful tack,
  Regardless of expense;
For countin' what 'e eats an' draws,
  An' gifts an' loans as well,
'E's gettin' 'alf the Earth, because
  'E didn't give us 'Ell!
    Ah, there, Piet! with your brand-new English plough,
    Your gratis tents an' cattle, an' your most ungrateful frow,
    You've made the British taxpayer rebuild your country-seat—
    I've known some pet battalions charge a dam' sight less than Piet.

[1]One of the camps for prisoners of this war was in Ceylon.

"Wilful-Missing"

(Deserters of the Boer War)

There is a world outside the one you know,
    To which for curiousness 'Ell can't compare—
It is the place where "wilful-missings" go,
    As we can testify, for we are there.

You may 'ave read a bullet laid us low,
    That we was gathered in "with reverent care"
And buried proper.   But it was not so,
    As we can testify,—for we are there!

They can't be certain—faces alter so
    After the old aasvogel[1]'s 'ad 'is share.
The uniform's the mark by which they go—
    And—ain't it odd?—the one we best can spare.

We might 'ave seen our chance to cut the show—
    Name, number, record, an' begin elsewhere—
Leavin' some not too late-lamented foe
    One funeral—private—British—for 'is share.

We may 'ave took it yonder in the low
    Bush-veldt that sends men stragglin' unaware
Among the Kaffirs, till their columns go,
    An' they are left past call or count or care.

We might 'ave been your lovers long ago,
    'Usbands or children—comfort or despair.
Our death (an') burial settles all we owe,
    An' why we done it is our own affair.

Marry again, and we will not say no,
    Nor come to barstardise the kids you bear.
Wait on in 'ope—you've all your life below
    Before you'll ever 'ear us on the stair.

There is no need to give our reasons, though
    Gawd knows we all 'ad reasons which were fair;
But other people might not judge 'em so—
    And now it doesn't matter what they were.

What man can weigh or size another's woe?
    There are some things too bitter 'ard to bear.
Suffice it we 'ave finished—Domino!
    As we can testify, for we are there,
In the side-world where "wilful-missings" go.

[1] Vulture.

Ubique

(Royal Artillery)

There is a word you often see, pronounce it as you may—
"You bike," "you bykwee," "ubbikwe"—alludin' to R.A.
It serves, 'Orse, Field, an' Garrison as motto for a crest;
An' when you've found out all it means I'll tell you 'alf the rest.

Ubique means the long-range Krupp be'ind the low-range 'ill—
Ubique means you'll pick it up an', while you do, stand still.
Ubique means you've caught the flash an' timed it by the sound.
Ubique means five gunners' 'ash before you've loosed a round.

Ubique means Blue Fuse,[1] an' make the 'ole to sink the trail.
Ubique means stand up an' take the Mauser's 'alf-mile 'ail.
Ubique means the crazy team not God nor man can 'old.
Ubique means that 'orse's scream which turns your innards cold!

Ubique means "Bank, 'Olborn, Bank—a penny all the way"—
The soothin', jingle-bump-an'-clank from day to peaceful day.
Ubique means "They've caught De Wet, an' now we shan't be long."
Ubique means "I much regret, the beggar's goin' strong!"

Ubique means the tearin' drift where, breech-blocks jammed with mud,
The khaki muzzles duck an' lift across the khaki flood.
Ubique means the dancing plain that changes rocks to Boers.
Ubique means mirage again an' shellin' all outdoors.

Ubique means "Entrain at once for Grootdefeatfontein."
Ubique means "Off-load your guns"—at midnight in the rain!
Ubique means "More mounted men.   Return all guns to store."
Ubique means the R.A.M.R. Infantillery Corps.[2]

Ubique means that warnin' grunt the perished linesman knows,
When o'er 'is strung an' sufferin' front the shrapnel sprays 'is foes;
An' as their firin' dies away the 'usky whisper runs
From lips that 'aven't drunk all day: "The Guns!   Thank Gawd, the
    Guns!"

Extreme, depressed, point-blank or short, end-first or any'ow,
From Colesberg Kop to Quagga's Poort—from Ninety-Nine till now—
By what I've 'eard the others tell an' I in spots 'ave seen,
There's nothin' this side 'Eaven or 'Ell Ubique doesn't mean!

---

[1] Extreme range.
[2] The Royal Artillery Mounted Rifles—when mounted infantry were badly needed.

The Return

(All Arms)

Peace is declared an' I return
    To 'Ackneystadt, but not the same;
Things 'ave transpired which made me learn
    The size and meanin' of the game.
I did no more than others did,
    I don't know where the change began.
I started as a average kid,
    I finished as a thinkin' man.

If England was what England seems,
    An' not the England of our dreams,
But only putty, brass, an' paint,
    'Ow quick we'd drop 'er!   But she ain't!

Before my gappin' mouth could speak
    I 'eard it in my comrade's tone.
I saw it on my neighbour's cheek
    Before I felt it flush my own.
An' last it come to me—not pride,
    Nor yet conceit, but on the 'ole
(If such a term may be applied),
    The makin's of a bloomin' soul.

Rivers at night that cluck an' jeer,
    Plains which the moonshine turns to sea,
Mountains which never let you near,
    An' stars to all eternity;
An' the quick-breathin' dark that fills
    The 'ollows of the wilderness,
When the wind worries through the 'ills—
    These may 'ave taught me more or less.

Towns without people, ten times took,
    An' ten times left an' burned at last;
An' starvin' dogs that come to look
    For owners when a column passed;
An' quiet, 'omesick talks between
    Men, met by night, you never knew
Until—'is face—by shellfire seen—
    Once—an' struck off.   *They* taught me too.

The day's lay-out—the mornin' sun
    Beneath your 'at-brim as you sight;

The dinner-'ush from noon till one,
   An' the full roar that lasts till night;
An' the pore dead that look so old
   An' was so young an hour ago,
An' legs tied down before they're cold—
   These are the things which make you know.

Also Time runnin' into years—
   A thousand Places left be'ind—
An' Men from both two 'emispheres
   Discussin' things of every kind;
So much more near than I 'ad known,
   So much more great than I 'ad guessed—
An' me, like all the rest, alone—
   But reachin' out to all the rest!

So 'ath it come to me—not pride,
   Nor yet conceit, but on the 'ole
(If such a term may be applied),
   The makin's of a bloomin' soul.
But now, discharged, I fall away
   To do with little things again . . .
Gawd, 'oo knows all I cannot say,
   Look after me in Thamesfontein![1]

If England was what England seems,
   An' not the England of our dreams,
But only putty, brass, an' paint,
   'Ow quick we'd chuck 'er!   But she ain't!

"Cities and Thrones and Powers"

("A Centurion of the Thirtieth"—*Puck of Pook's Hill*)

Cities and Thrones and Powers
   Stand in Time's eye,
Almost as long as flowers,
   Which daily die:
But, as new buds put forth
   To glad new men,
Out of the spent and unconsidered Earth
   The Cities rise again.

[1]London.

This season's Daffodil,
  She never hears
What change, what chance, what chill,
  Cut down last year's;
But with bold countenance,
  And knowledge small,
Esteems her seven days' continuance
  To be perpetual.

So Time that is o'er-kind
  To all that be,
Ordains us e'en as blind,
  As bold as she:
That in our very death,
  And burial sure,
Shadow to shadow, well persuaded, saith,
  "See how our works endure!"

The Recall

("An Habitation Enforced"—*Actions and Reactions*)

I am the land of their fathers.
In me the virtue stays.
I will bring back my children,
After certain days.

Under their feet in the grasses
My clinging magic runs.
They shall return as strangers.
They shall remain as sons.

Over their heads in the branches
Of their new-bought, ancient trees,
I weave an incantation,
And draw them to my knees.

Scent of smoke in the evening,
Smell of rain in the night—
The hours, the days and the seasons,
Order their souls aright,

Till I make plain the meaning
Of all my thousand years—
Till I fill their hearts with knowledge,
While I fill their eyes with tears.

Puck's Song

(Enlarged from "Puck of Pook's Hill")

See you the ferny ride that steals
Into the oak-woods far?
O that was whence they hewed the keels
That rolled to Trafalgar.

And mark you where the ivy clings
To Bayham's mouldering walls?
O there we cast the stout railings
That stand around St. Paul's.

See you the dimpled track that runs
All hollow through the wheat?
O that was where they hauled the guns
That smote King Philip's fleet.

(Out of the Weald, the secret Weald,
Men sent in ancient years
The horse-shoes red at Flodden Field,
The arrows at Poitiers!)

See you our little mill that clacks,
So busy by the brook?
She has ground her corn and paid her tax
Ever since Domesday Book.

See you our stilly woods of oak,
And the dread ditch beside?
O that was where the Saxons broke
On the day that Harold died.

See you the windy levels spread
About the gates of Rye?
O that was where the Northmen fled,
When Alfred's ships came by.

See you our pastures wide and lone,
Where the red oxen browse?
O there was a City thronged and known,
Ere London boasted a house.

And see you, after rain, the trace
Of mound and ditch and wall?
O that was a Legion's camping-place,
When Caesar sailed from Gaul.

And see you marks that show and fade,
Like shadows on the Downs?
O they are the lines the Flint Men made,
To guard their wondrous towns.

Trackway and Camp and City lost,
Salt Marsh where now is corn—
Old Wars, old Peace, old Arts that cease,
And so was England born!

She is not any common Earth,
Water or wood or air,
But Merlin's Isle of Gramarye,
Where you and I will fare!

The Way Through The Woods

("Marklake Witches"—*Rewards and Fairies*)

They shut the road through the woods
Seventy years ago.
Weather and rain have undone it again,
And now you would never know
There was once a road through the woods
Before they planted the trees.
It is underneath the coppice and heath
And the thin anemones.
Only the keeper sees
That, where the ring-dove broods,
And the badgers roll at ease,
There was once a road through the woods.

Yet, if you enter the woods
Of a summer evening late,
When the night-air cools on the trout-ringed pools
Where the otter whistles his mate,
(They fear not men in the woods,
Because they see so few.)
You will hear the beat of a horse's feet,
And the swish of a skirt in the dew,
Steadily cantering through
The misty solitudes,
As though they perfectly knew
The old lost road through the woods . . .
But there is no road through the woods.

A Three-Part Song

(" 'Dymchurch Flit' "—*Puck of Pook's Hill*)

I'm just in love with all these three,
The Weald and Marsh and the Down countree.
Nor I don't know which I love the most,
The Weald or the Marsh or the white Chalk coast!

I've buried my heart in a ferny hill,
Twixt' a liddle low shaw an' a great high gill.
Oh, hop-bine yaller an' wood-smoke blue,
I reckon you'll keep her middling true!

I've loosed my mind for to out and run
On a Marsh that was old when Kings begun.
Oh, Romney Level and Brenzett reeds,
I reckon you know what my mind needs!

I've given my soul to the Southdown grass,
And sheep-bells tinkled where you pass.
Oh, Firle an' Ditchling an' sails at sea,
I reckon you keep my soul for me!

The Run Of The Downs

("The Knife and the Naked Chalk"—*Rewards and Fairies*)

The Weald is good, the Downs are best—
I'll give you the run of 'em, East to West.
Beachy Head and Winddoor Hill,
They were once and they are still.
Firle, Mount Caburn and Mount Harry
Go back as far as sums'll carry.
Ditchling Beacon and Chanctonbury Ring,
They have looked on many a thing,
And what those two have missed between 'em,
I reckon Truleigh Hill has seen 'em.
Highden, Bignor and Duncton Down
Knew Old England before the Crown.
Linch Down, Treyford and Sunwood
Knew Old England before the Flood;
And when you end on the Hampshire side—
Butser's old as Time and Tide.
The Downs are sheep, the Weald is corn,
You be glad you are Sussex born!

Brookland Road

("Marklake Witches"—*Rewards and Fairies*)

I was very well pleased with what I knowed,
I reckoned myself no fool—
Till I met with a maid on the Brookland Road
That turned me back to school.

Low down—low down!
Where the liddle green lanterns shine—
O maids, I've done with 'ee all but one,
And she can never be mine!

'Twas right in the middest of a hot June night,
With thunder duntin' round,
And I see her face by the fairy-light
That beats from off the ground.

She only smiled and she never spoke,
She smiled and went away;
But when she'd gone my heart was broke
And my wits was clean astray.

O, stop your ringing and let me be—
Let be, O Brookland bells!
You'll ring Old Goodman[1] out of the sea
Before I wed one else!

Old Goodman's Farm is rank sea-sand,
And was this thousand year;
But it shall turn to rich plough-land
Before I change my dear.

O, Fairfield Church is water-bound
From autumn to the spring;
But it shall turn to high hill-ground
Before my bells do ring.

O, leave me walk on Brookland Road,
In the thunder and warm rain—
O, leave me look where my love goed,
And p'raps I'll see her again!

Low down—low down!
Where the liddle green lanterns shine—
O maids, I've done with 'ee all but one,
And she can never be mine!

[1] Earl Godwin of the Goodwin Sands?

The Sack Of The Gods

(*Enlarged from "The Naulahka"*)

Strangers drawn from the ends of the earth, jewelled and plumed were we;
I was Lord of the Inca race, and she was Queen of the Sea.
Under the stars beyond our stars where the new-forged meteors glow,
Hotly we stormed Valhalla, a million years ago!

Ever 'neath high Valhalla Hall the well-tuned horns begin,
When the swords are out in the underworld, and the weary Gods come in.
Ever through high Valhalla Gate the Patient Angel goes.
He opens the eyes that are blind with hate—he joins the hands of foes.

Dust of the stars was under our feet, glitter of stars above—
Wrecks of our wrath dropped reeling down as we fought and we spurned and
    we strove.
Worlds upon worlds we tossed aside, and scattered them to and fro,
The night that we stormed Valhalla, a million years ago!

They are forgiven as they forgive all those dark wounds and deep.
Their beds are made on the Lap of Time and they lie down and sleep.
They are forgiven as they forgive all those old wounds that bleed.
They shut their eyes from their worshippers; they sleep till the world has need.

She with the star I had marked for my own—I with my set desire—
Lost in the loom of the Night of Nights—lighted by worlds afire—
Met in a war against the Gods where the headlong meteors glow,
Hewing our way to Valhalla, a million years ago!

They will come back—come back again—as long as the red Earth rolls.
He never wasted a leaf or a tree. Do you think He would squander souls?

The Kingdom

(*Enlarged from "The Naulahka"*)

Now we are come to our Kingdom,
And the State is thus and thus;
Our legions wait at the Palace gate—
Little it profits us.
Now we are come to our Kingdom!

Now we are come to our Kingdom,
And the Crown is ours to take—
With a naked sword at the Council board,
And under the throne the snake.
Now we are come to our Kingdom!

Now we are come to our Kingdom,
And the Realm is ours by right,
With shame and fear for our daily cheer,
And heaviness at night.
Now we are come to our Kingdom!

Now we are come to our Kingdom,
But my love's eyelids fall.
All that I wrought for, all that I fought for.
Delight her nothing at all.
My crown is of withered leaves,
For she sits in the dust and grieves.
Now we are come to our Kingdom!

Tarrant Moss

(*Enlarged from "Plain Tales from the Hills"*)

I closed and drew for my love's sake
That now is false to me,
And I slew the Reiver of Tarrant Moss
And set Dumeny free.

They have gone down, they have gone down,
They are standing all arow—
Twenty knights in the peat-water,
That never struck a blow!

Their armour shall not dull nor rust,
Their flesh shall not decay,
For Tarrant Moss holds them in trust
Until the Judgment Day.

Their soul went from them in their youth,
Ah, God, that mine had gone,
Whenas I leaned on my love's truth
And not on my sword alone!

Whenas I leaned on lad's belief
And not on my naked blade—
And I slew a thief, and an honest thief,
For the sake of a worthless maid.

They have laid the Reiver low in his place,
They have set me up on high.
But the twenty knights in the peat-water
Are luckier than I!

And ever they give me gold and praise
And ever I mourn my loss—
For I struck the blow for my false love's sake
And not for the Men of the Moss!

Sir Richard's Song

(A.D. 1066)

("Young Men at the Manor"—*Puck of Pook's Hill*)

I followed my Duke ere I was a lover,
   To take from England fief and fee;
But now this game is the other way over—
   But now England hath taken me!

I had my horse, my shield and banner,
   And a boy's heart, so whole and free;
But now I sing in another manner—
   But now England hath taken me!

As for my Father in his tower,
   Asking news of my ship at sea,
He will remember his own hour—
   Tell him England hath taken me!

As for my Mother in her bower,
   That rules my Father so cunningly,
She will remember a maiden's power—
   Tell her England hath taken me!

As for my brother in Rouen City,
   A nimble and naughty page is he,
But he will come to suffer and pity—
   Tell him England hath taken me!

As for my little Sister waiting
   In the pleasant orchards of Normandie,
Tell her youth is the time for mating—
   Tell her England hath taken me!

As for my comrades in camp and highway,
   That lift their eyebrows scornfully,
Tell them their way is not my way—
   Tell them England hath taken me!

Kings and Princes and Barons famèd,
   Knights and Captains in your degree;

Hear me a little before I am blamèd—
   Seeing England hath taken me!

Howso great man's strength be reckoned,
   There are two things he cannot flee.
Love is the first, and Death is the second—
   And Love in England hath taken me!

A Tree Song

(A.D. 1200)

("Weland's Sword"—*Puck of Pook's Hill*)

Of all the trees that grow so fair,
   Old England to adorn,
Greater are none beneath the Sun
   Than Oak, and Ash, and Thorn.
Sing Oak, and Ash, and Thorn, good sirs,
   (All of a Midsummer morn!)
Surely we sing no little thing
   In Oak, and Ash, and Thorn!

Oak of the Clay lived many a day
   Or ever Aeneas began.
Ash of the Loam was a lady at home
   When Brut was an outlaw man.
Thorn of the Down saw New Troy Town
   (From which was London born);
Witness hereby the ancientry
   Of Oak, and Ash, and Thorn!

Yew that is old in churchyard-mould,
   He breedeth a mighty bow.
Alder for shoes do wise men choose,
   And beech for cups also.
But when ye have killed, and your bowl is spilled,
   And your shoes are clean outworn,
Back ye must speed for all that ye need
   To Oak, and Ash, and Thorn!

Ellum she hateth mankind, and waiteth
   Till every gust be laid
To drop a limb on the head of him
   That anyway trusts her shade.

But whether a lad be sober or sad,
   Or mellow with ale from the horn,
He will take no wrong when he lieth along
   'Neath Oak, and Ash, and Thorn!

Oh, do not tell the Priest our plight,
   Or he would call it a sin;
But—we have been out in the woods all night,
   A-conjuring Summer in!
And we bring you news by word of mouth—
   Good news for cattle and corn—
Now is the Sun come up from the South
   With Oak, and Ash, and Thorn!

Sing Oak, and Ash, and Thorn, good sirs
   (All of a Midsummer morn)!
England shall bide till Judgment Tide
   By oak, and Ash, and Thorn!

The Floods

("My Son's Wife"—A *Diversity of Creatures*)

The rain it rains without a stay
   In the hills above us, in the hills;
And presently the floods break away
   Whose strength is in the hills.
The trees they suck from every cloud,
The valley brooks they roar aloud—
Bank-high for the lowlands, lowlands,
   Lowlands under the hills!

The first wood down is sere and small,
   From the hills— the brishings off the hills;
And then come by the bats and all
   We cut last year in the hills;
And then the roots we tried to cleave
But found too tough and had to leave—
Polting down through the lowlands, lowlands,
   Lowlands under the hills!

The eye shall look, the ear shall hark
   To the hills, the doings in the hills!
And rivers mating in the dark
   With tokens from the hills.

Now what is weak will surely go,
And what is strong must prove it so—
Stand fast in the lowlands, lowlands,
   Lowlands under the hills!

The floods they shall not be afraid—
   Nor the hills above 'em, nor the hills—
Of any fence which man has made
   Betwixt him and the hills.
The waters shall not reckon twice
For any work of man's device,
But bid it down to the lowlands, lowlands,
   Lowlands under the hills!

The floods shall sweep corruption clean—
   By the hills, the blessing of the hills—
That more the meadows may be green
   New-mended from the hills.
The crops and cattle shall increase,
Nor little children shall not cease.
Go—plough the lowlands, lowlands,
   Lowlands under the hills!

Cuckoo Song

(Spring begins in Southern England on the 14th April, on which date the Old Woman lets the Cuckoo out of her basket at Heathfield Fair—locally known as Heffle Cuckoo Fair.)

   Tell it to the locked-up trees,
   Cuckoo, bring your song here!
   Warrant, Act and Summons, please,
   For Spring to pass along here!
   Tell old Winter, if he doubt,
   Tell him squat and square—a!
   Old Woman!
   Old Woman!
   Old Woman's let the Cuckoo out
   At Heffle Cuckoo Fair—a!

   March has searched and April tried—
   'Tisn't long to May now.
   Not so far to Whitsuntide
   And Cuckoo's come to stay now!
   Hear the valiant fellow shout

Down the orchard bare—a!
Old Woman!
Old Woman!
Old Woman's let the Cuckoo out
At Heffle Cuckoo Fair—a!

When your heart is young and gay
And the season rules it—
Work your works and play your play
'Fore the Autumn cools it!
Kiss you turn and turn-about,
But, my lad, beware—a!
Old Woman!
Old Woman!
Old Woman's let the Cuckoo out
At Heffle Cuckoo Fair—a!

A Charm

(Introduction to "Rewards and Fairies")

Take of English earth as much
As either hand may rightly clutch.
In the taking of it breathe
Prayer for all who lie beneath.
Not the great nor well-bespoke,
But the mere uncounted folk
Of whose life and death is none
Report or lamentation.
   Lay that earth upon thy heart,
   And thy sickness shall depart!

It shall sweeten and make whole
Fevered breath and festered soul.
It shall mightily restrain
Over-busied hand and brain.
It shall ease thy mortal strife
'Gainst the immortal woe of life,
Till thyself, restored, shall prove
By what grace the Heavens do move.

Take of English flowers these—
Spring's full-facèd primroses,
Summer's wild wide-hearted rose,
Autumn's wall-flower of the close,

And, thy darkness to illume,
Winter's bee-thronged ivy-bloom.
Seek and serve them where they bide
From Candlemas to Christmas-tide,
     For these simples, used aright,
     Can restore a failing sight.

These shall cleanse and purify
Webbed and inward-turning eye;
These shall show thee treasure hid
Thy familiar fields amid;
And reveal (which is thy need)
Every man a King indeed!

The Prairie

(Canada)

"I see the grass shake in the sun for leagues on either hand,
I see a river loop and run about a treeless land—
An empty plain, a steely pond, a distance diamond-clear,
And low blue naked hills beyond.   And what is that to fear?"

"Go softly by that river-side or, when you would depart,
You'll find its every winding tied and knotted round your heart.
Be wary as the seasons pass, or you may ne'er outrun
The wind that sets that yellowed grass a-shiver 'neath the sun."

"I hear the summer storm outblown—the drip of the grateful wheat.
I hear the hard trail telephone a far-off horse's feet.
I hear the horns of Autumn blow to the wild-fowl overhead;
And I hear the hush before the snow.   And what is that to dread?"

"Take heed what spell the lightning weaves—what charm the echoes
    shape—
Or, bound among a million sheaves, your soul shall not escape.
Bar home the door of summer nights lest those high planets drown
The memory of near delights in all the longed-for town."

"What need have I to long or fear?   Now, friendly, I behold
My faithful seasons robe the year in silver and in gold.
Now I possess and am possessed of the land where I would be,
And the curve of half Earth's generous breast shall soothe and ravish me!"

Jobson's Amen

("In the Presence"—*A Diversity of Creatures*)

"Blessèd be the English and all their ways and works.
Cursèd be the Infidels, Hereticks, and Turks!"
"Amen," quo' Jobson, "But where I used to lie
Was neither Candle, Bell nor Book to curse my brethren by,

"But a palm-tree in full bearing, bowing down, bowing down,
To a surf that drove unsparing at the brown, walled town—
Conches in a temple, oil-lamps in a dome—
And a low moon out of Africa said: 'This way home!' "

"Blessèd be the English and all they profess.
Cursèd be the Savages that prance in nakedness!"
"Amen," quo' Jobson, "but where I used to lie
Was neither shirt nor pantaloons to catch my brethren by:

"But a well-wheel slowly creaking, going round, going round,
By a water-channel leaking over drowned, warm ground—
Parrots very busy in the trellised pepper-vine—
And a high sun over Asia shouting: 'Rise and shine!' "

"Blessèd be the English and everything they own.
Cursèd be the Infidels that bow to wood and stone!"
"Amen," quo' Jobson, "But where I used to lie
Was neither pew nor Gospelleer to save my brethren by:

"But a desert stretched and stricken, left and right, left and right,
Where the piled mirages thicken under white-hot light—
A skull beneath a sand-hill and a viper coiled inside—
And a red wind out of Libya roaring: 'Run and hide!' "

"Blessèd be the English and all they make or do.
Cursèd be the Hereticks who doubt that this is true!"
"Amen," quo' Jobson, "but where I mean to die
Is neither rule nor calliper to judge the matter by:

"But Himalaya heavenward-heading, sheer and vast, sheer and vast,
In a million summits bedding on the last world's past—
A certain sacred mountain where the scented cedars climb,
And—the feet of my belovèd hurrying back through Time!"

Chapter Headings

Look, you have cast out Love!   What Gods are these
    You bid me please?
The Three in One, the One in Three?   Not so!
To my own Gods I go.
It may be they shall give me greater ease
Than your cold Christ and tangled Trinities.

Lispeth.

When the earth was sick and the skies were grey,
And the woods were rotted with rain,
The Dead Man rode through the autumn day
To visit his love again.

His love she neither saw nor heard,
So heavy was her shame;
And tho' the babe within her stirred
She knew not that he came.

The Other Man.

Cry "Murder" in the market-place, and each
Will turn upon his neighbour anxious eyes
Asking: "Art thou the man?"   We hunted Cain
Some centuries ago across the world.
This bred the fear our own misdeeds maintain
To-day.

His Wedded Wife.

Go, stalk the red deer o'er the heather,
Ride, follow the fox if you can!
But, for pleasure and profit together,
Allow me the hunting of Man—
The chase of the Human, the search for the Soul
To its ruin—the hunting of Man.

Pig.

"Stopped in the straight when the race was his own—
Look at him cutting in—cur to the bone!"
Ask ere the youngster be rated and chidden
What did he carry and how was he ridden?
Maybe they used him too much at the start.
Maybe Fate's weight-cloth is breaking his heart.

In the Pride of his Youth.

"And some are sulky, while some will plunge.
(*So ho!   Steady!   Stand still, you!*)
Some you must gentle, and some you must lunge.
(*There!   There!   Who wants to kill you?*)
Some—there are losses in every trade—
Will break their hearts ere bitted and made,
Will fight like fiends as the rope cuts hard,
And die dumb-mad in the breaking-yard."

Thrown Away.

The World hath set its heavy yoke
Upon the old white-bearded folk
Who strive to please the King.
God's mercy is upon the young,
God's wisdom in the baby tongue
That fears not anything.

Tods' Amendment.

Not though you die to-night, O Sweet, and wail,
A spectre at my door,
Shall mortal Fear make Love immortal fail—
I shall but love you more,
Who, from Death's House returning, give me still
One moment's comfort in my matchless ill.

By Word of Mouth.

They burnt a corpse upon the sand—
The light shone out afar;
It guided home the plunging dhows
That beat from Zanzibar.
Spirit of Fire, where'er Thy altars rise,
Thou are the Light of Guidance to our eyes!

In Error.

Ride with an idle whip, ride with an unused heel,
But, once in a way, there will come a day
When the colt must be taught to feel
The lash that falls, and the curb that galls, and the
    sting of the rowelled steel.

The Conversion of Aurelian McGoggin.

It was not in the open fight
We threw away the sword,
But in the lonely watching
In the darkness by the ford.
The waters lapped, the night-wind blew,
Full-armed the Fear was born and grew,

And we were flying ere we knew
From panic in the night.

The Rout of the White Hussars.

In the daytime, when she moved about me,
In the night, when she was sleeping at my side,—
I was wearied, I was wearied of her presence.
Day by day and night by night I grew to hate her—
Would God that she or I had died!

The Bronckhorst Divorce Case.

A stone's throw out on either hand
From that well-ordered road we tread,
And all the world is wild and strange;
Churel[1] and ghoul and Djinn and sprite
Shall bear us company to-night,
For we have reached the Oldest Land
Wherein the Powers of Darkness range.

In the House of Suddhoo.

To-night, God knows what thing shall tide,
The Earth is racked and fain—
Expectant, sleepless, open-eyed;
And we, who from the Earth were made,
Thrill with our Mother's pain.

False Dawn.

Pit where the buffalo cooled his hide,
By the hot sun emptied, and blistered and dried;
Log in the plume-grass, hidden and lone;
Bund where the earth-rat's mounds were strown;
Cave in the bank where the sly stream steals;
Aloe that stabs at the belly and heels,
Jump if you dare on a steed untried—
Safer it is to go wide—go wide!
Hark, from in front where the best men ride;—
"Pull to the off, boys! Wide! Go wide!"

Cupid's Arrows.

He drank strong waters and his speech was coarse;
He purchased raiment and forbore to pay;
He stuck a trusting junior with a horse,
And won gymkhanas in a doubtful way.
Then, 'twixt a vice and folly, turned aside
To do good deeds—and straight to cloak them, lied.

A Bank Fraud.

[1] The ghost of a woman who has died in childbirth.

Thus, for a season, they fought it fair—
  She and his cousin May—
Tactful, talented, debonair,
  Decorous foes were they;
But never can battle of man compare
With merciless feminine fray.

The Rescue of Pluffles.

Then a pile of heads he laid—
  Thirty thousand heaped on high—
All to please the Kafir maid
  Where the Oxus rippled by.
Grimly spake Atulla Khan:—
  'Love hath made this thing a Man.'

His Chance in Life.

Rosicrucian subtleties
In the Orient had rise,
Ye may find their teachers still
Under Jacatâlâ's Hill.
Seek ye Bombast Paracelsus,
Read what Fludd the Seeker tells us
Of the Dominant that runs
Through the cycle of the Suns.
Read my story last and see
Luna at her apogee.

Consequences.

So we loosed a bloomin' volley
  An' we made the beggars cut,
An' when our pooch was emptied out
  We used the bloomin' butt
Ho! My! Don't you come anigh
When Tommy is a-playin' with the bay'nit
  an' the butt!

The Taking of Lungtungpen.

Pleasant it is for the Little Tin Gods
When great Jove nods;
But Little Tin Gods make their little mistakes
In missing the hour when great Jove wakes.

A Germ-Destroyer.

There is a tide in the affairs of men
Which, taken any way you please, is bad,
And strands them in forsaken guts and creeks
No decent soul would think of visiting.

You cannot stop the tide; but, now and then,
You may arrest some rash adventurer,
Who—h'm—will hardly thank you for your pains.

Kidnapped.

While the snaffle holds or the long-neck stings,
While the big beam tilts or the last bell rings,
While horses are horses to train and to race,
Then women and wine take a second place
   For me—for me—
    While a short 'ten-three'
Has a field to squander or fence to face.

The Broken-Link Handicap.

Little Blind Fish, thou art marvellous wise!
Little Blind Fish, who put out thy eyes?
Open thy ears while I whisper my wish.
Bring me a lover, thou little Blind Fish!

The Bisara of Pooree.

Cold Iron

("Cold Iron"—*Rewards and Fairies*)

"Gold is for the mistress—silver for the maid—
Copper for the craftsman cunning in his trade."
"Good!" said the Baron, sitting in his hall,
"But Iron—Cold Iron— is master of them all."

So he made rebellion 'gainst the King his liege,
Camped before his citadel and summoned it to siege.
"Nay!" said the cannoneer on the castle wall,
"But Iron—Cold Iron—shall be master of you all!"

Woe for the Baron and his knights so strong,
When the cruel cannon-balls laid 'em all along;
He was taken prisoner, he was cast in thrall,
And Iron—Cold Iron—was master of it all!

Yet his King spake kindly (ah, how kind a Lord!)
"What if I release thee now and give thee back thy sword?"
"Nay!" said the Baron, "mock not at my fall,
For Iron—Cold Iron—is master of men all."

"Tears are for the craven, prayers are for the clown—
Halters for the silly neck that cannot keep a crown."

"As my loss is grievous, so my hope is small,
For Iron—Cold Iron—must be master of men all!"

Yet his King made answer (few such Kings there be!)
"Here is Bread and here is Wine—sit and sup with me.
Eat and drink in Mary's Name, the whiles I do recall
How Iron—Cold Iron—can be master of men all!"

He took the Wine and blessed it.   He blessed and brake the Bread.
With His own Hands He served Them, and presently He said:
"See! These Hands they pierced with nails, outside My city wall,
Show Iron—Cold Iron—to be master of men all.

"Wounds are for the desperate, blows are for the strong.
Balm and oil for weary hearts all cut and bruised with wrong.
I forgive thy treason—I redeem thy fall—
For Iron—Cold Iron—must be master of men all!"

"Crowns are for the valiant—sceptres for the bold!
Thrones and powers for mighty men who dare to take and hold!"
"Nay!" said the Baron, kneeling in his hall,
"But Iron—Cold Iron—is master of men all!
Iron out of Calvary is master of men all!"

A Song Of Kabir

("The Miracle of Purun Bhagat"—*The Second Jungle Book*)

Oh, light was the world that he weighed in his hands!
Oh, heavy the tale of his fiefs and his lands!
He has gone from the *guddee*[1] and put on the shroud,
And departed in guise of *bairagi*[2] avowed!

Now the white road to Delhi is mat for his feet.
The *sal* and the *kikar*[3] must guard him from heat.
His home is the camp, and the waste, and the crowd—
He is seeking the Way as *bairagi* avowed!

He has looked upon Man, and his eyeballs are clear—
(There was One; there is One, and but One, saith Kabir);
The Red Mist of Doing has thinned to a cloud—
He has taken the Path for *bairagi* avowed!

[1]Seat of Justice.   [2]Wandering holy man.   [3]Wayside trees.

To learn and discern of his brother the clod,
Of his brother the brute, and his brother the God,
He has gone from the council and put on the shroud,
("Can ye hear?" saith Kabir), a *bairagi* avowed!

A Carol

("The Tree of Justice"—*Rewards and Fairies*)

Our Lord Who did the Ox command
    To kneel to Judah's King,
He binds His frost upon the land
    To ripen it for Spring—
To ripen it for Spring, good sirs,
    According to His Word.
Which well must be as ye can see—
    And who shall judge the Lord?

When we poor fenmen skate the ice
    Or shiver on the wold,
We hear the cry of a single tree
    That breaks her heart in the cold—
That breaks her heart in the cold, good sirs,
    And rendeth by the board.
Which well must be as ye can see—
    And who shall judge the Lord?

Her wood is crazed and little worth
    Excepting as to burn,
That we may warm and make our mirth
    Until the Spring return—
Until the Spring return, good sirs,
    When Christians walk abroad;
Which well must be as ye can see—
    And who shall judge the Lord?

God bless the master of this house,
    And all who sleep therein!
And guard the fens from pirate folk,
    And keep us all from sin,
To walk in honesty, good sirs,
    Of thought and deed and word!
Which shall befriend our latter end . . .
    And who shall judge the Lord?

"My New-Cut Ashlar"

(L'Envoi to "Life's Handicap")

My new-cut ashlar takes the light
Where crimson-blank the windows flare.
By my own work before the night,
Great Overseer, I make my prayer.

If there be good in that I wrought
Thy Hand compelled it, Master, Thine—
Where I have failed to meet Thy Thought
I know, through Thee, the blame was mine.

One instant's toil to Thee denied
Stands all Eternity's offence.
Of that I did with Thee to guide,
To Thee, through Thee, be excellence.

The depth and dream of my desire,
The bitter paths wherein I stray—
Thou knowest Who hast made the Fire,
Thou knowest Who hast made the Clay.

Who, lest all thought of Eden fade,
Bring'st Eden to the craftsman's brain—
Godlike to muse o'er his own Trade
And manlike stand with God again!

One stone the more swings into place
In that dread Temple of Thy worth.
It is enough that, through Thy Grace,
I saw nought common on Thy Earth.

Take not that vision from my ken—
Oh, whatsoe'er may spoil or speed.
Help me to need no aid from men
That I may help such men as need!

"Non Nobis Domine!"

(Written for "The Pageant of Parliament," 1934)

Non nobis Domine!—
Not unto us, O Lord!
The Praise or Glory be
Of any deed or word;

For in Thy Judgment lies
   To crown or bring to nought
All knowledge or device
   That Man has reached or wrought.

And we confess our blame—
   How all too high we hold
That noise which men call Fame,
   That dross which men call Gold.
For these we undergo
   Our hot and godless days,
But in our hearts we know
   Not unto us the Praise.

O Power by Whom we live—
   Creator, Judge, and Friend,
Upholdingly forgive
   Nor fail us at the end:
But grant us well to see
   In all our piteous ways—
Non nobis Domine!—
   Not unto us the Praise!

Eddi's Service

(A.D. 687)

("The Conversion of St. Wilfrid"—*Rewards and Fairies*)

Eddi, priest of St. Wilfrid
   In his chapel at Manhood End,
Ordered a midnight service
   For such as cared to attend.

But the Saxons were keeping Christmas,
   And the night was stormy as well.
Nobody came to service,
   Though Eddi rang the bell.

"Wicked weather for walking,"
   Said Eddi of Manhood End
"But I must go on with the service
   For such as care to attend."

The altar-lamps were lighted,—
   An old marsh-donkey came,
Bold as a guest invited,
   And stared at the guttering flame.

The storm beat on at the windows,
  The water splashed on the floor,
And a wet, yoke-weary bullock
  Pushed in through the open door.

"How do I know what is greatest,
  How do I know what is least?
That is My Father's business,"
  Said Eddi, Wilfrid's priest.

"But—three are gathered together—
  Listen to me and attend.
I bring good news, my brethren!"
  Said Eddi of Manhood End.

And he told the Ox of a Manger
  And a Stall in Bethlehem,
And he spoke to the Ass of a Rider
  That rode to Jerusalem.

They steamed and dripped in the chancel,
  They listened and never stirred,
While, just as though they were Bishops,
  Eddi preached them The Word,

Till the gale blew off on the marshes
  And the windows showed the day,
And the Ox and the Ass together
  Wheeled and clattered away.

And when the Saxons mocked him,
  Said Eddi of Manhood End,
"I dare not shut His chapel
  On such as care to attend."

Our Lady Of The Sackcloth

(Ethiopic Version: founded on Brit. Mus. M.S. Orient No 652, Folio 9)

There was a Priest at Philae,
  Tongue-tied, feeble, and old;
And the daily prayer to the Virgin
  Was all the Office he could.

The others were ill-remembered,
  Mumbled and hard to hear;
But to Mary, the two-fold Virgin,
  Always his voice rang clear.

And the congregation mocked him,
  And the weight of the years he bore,
And they sent word to the Bishop
  That he should not serve them more.

(Never again at the Offering
  When the Bread and the Body are one:
Oh, never the picture of Mary
  Watching him serve her Son!)

Kindly and wise was the Bishop.
  Unto the Priest said he:—
"Patience till thou art stronger,
  And keep meantime with me.

"Patience a little; it may be
  The Lord shall loosen thy tongue
And then thou shalt serve at the Offering
  As it was when we were young."

And the Priest obeyed and was silent,
  And the Bishop gave him leave
To walk alone in the desert
  Where none should see him grieve.

(Never again at the Offering
  When the Wine and the Blood are one!
Oh, never the picture of Mary
  Watching him honour her Son!)

Saintly and clean was the Bishop,
  Ruling himself aright
With prayer and fast in the daytime
  And scourge and vigil at night.

Out of his zeal he was minded
  To add one penance the more—
A garment of harshest sackcloth
  Under the robes he wore.

He gathered the cloth in secret
  Lest any should know and praise—
The shears, the palm and the packthread—
  And laboured it many ways.

But he had no skill in the making,
  And failed and fretted the while;
Till there stood a Woman before him,
  Smiling as Mothers smile.

Her feet were burned by the desert—
　　Like a desert-dweller she trod—
Even the two-fold Virgin,
　　Spouse and Bearer of God!

She took the shears and the sacking,
　　The needle and stubborn thread,
She cut, she shaped, and she sewed them,
　　And, "This shall be blessed," she said.

She passed in the white hot noontide,
　　On a wave of the quivering air;
And the Bishop's eyes were opened,
　　And he fell on his face in prayer.

But—*far from the smouldering censers—*
　　Far from the chanted praise—
Oh, far from the pictures of Mary
　　That had watched him all his days—

Far in the desert by Philae,
　　The old Priest walked forlorn,
Till he saw at the head of her Riders
　　A Queen of the Desert-born.

High she swayed on her camel,
　　Beautiful to behold:
And her beast was belled with silver,
　　And her veils were spotted with gold!

Low she leaned from her litter—
　　Soft she spoke in his ear:—
"Nay, I have watched thy sorrow!
　　Nay, but the end is near!

"For again thou shalt serve at the Offering
　　And thy tongue shall be loosed in praise,
And again thou shalt sing unto Mary
　　Who has watched thee all thy days.

"Go in peace to the Bishop,
　　Carry him word from me—
That the Woman who sewed the sackcloth
　　Would have him set thee free!"

The Legend Of Mirth

("The Horse Marines"—*A Diversity of Creatures*)

The four Archangels, so the legends tell,
Raphael, Gabriel, Michael, Azrael,
Being first of those to whom the Power was shown,
Stood first of all the Host before The Throne,
And, when the Charges were alloted, burst
Tumultuous-winged from out the assembly first.
Zeal was their spur that bade them strictly heed
Their own high judgment on their lightest deed.
Zeal was their spur that, when relief was given,
Urged them unwearied to new toils in Heaven;
For Honour's sake perfecting every task
Beyond what e'en Perfection's self could ask . . .
And Allah, Who created Zeal and Pride,
Knows how the twain are perilous-near allied.

It chanced on one of Heaven's long-lighted days,
The Four and all the Host being gone their ways
Each to his Charge, the shining Courts were void
Save for one Seraph whom no charge employed,
With folden wings and slumber-threatened brow,
To whom The Word: "Belovèd, what dost thou?"
"By the Permission," came the answer soft,
"Little I do nor do that little oft.
As is The Will in Heaven so on Earth
Where by The Will I strive to make men mirth."
He ceased and sped, hearing The Word once more:
"Belovèd, go thy way and greet the Four."

Systems and Universes overpast,
The Seraph came upon the Four, at last,
Guiding and guarding with devoted mind
The tedious generations of mankind
Who lent at most unwilling ear and eye
When they could not escape the ministry . . .
Yet, patient, faithful, firm, persistent, just
Toward all that gross, indifferent, facile dust,
The Archangels laboured to discharge their trust
By precept and example, prayer and law,
Advice, reproof, and rule, but, labouring, saw
Each in his fellows' countenance confessed,
The Doubt that sickens: "Have I done my best?"

Even as they sighed and turned to toil anew,
The Seraph hailed them with observance due:
And, after some fit talk of higher things,
Touched tentative on mundane happenings.
This they permitting, he, emboldened thus,
Prolused of humankind promiscuous.
And, since the large contention less avails
Than instances observed, he told them tales—
Tales of the shop, the bed, the court, the street,
Intimate, elemental, indiscreet:
Occassion where Confusion smiting swift
Piles jest on jest as snow-slides pile the drift
Whence, one by one, beneath deriding skies,
The victims' bare, bewildered heads arise—
Tales of the passing of the spirit, graced
With humour blinding as the doom it faced—
Stark tales of ribaldry that broke aside
To tears, by laughter swallowed ere they dried—
Tales to which neither grace nor gain accrue,
But only (Allah be exalted!) true,
And only, as the Seraph showed that night,
Delighting to the limits of delight.

These he rehearsed with artful pause and halt,
And such pretence of memory at fault,
That soon the Four—so well the bait was thrown—
Came to his aid with memories of their own—
Matters dismissed long since as small or vain,
Whereof the high significance had lain
Hid, till the ungirt glosses made it plain.
Then, as enlightenment came broad and fast,
Each marvelled at his own oblivious past,
Until—the Gates of Laughter opened wide—
The Four, with that bland Seraph at their side,
While they recalled, compared, and amplified,
In utter mirth forgot both Zeal and Pride!

High over Heaven the lamps of midnight burned
Ere, weak with merriment, the Four returned,
Not in that order they were wont to keep—
Pinion to pinion answering, sweep for sweep,
In awful diapason heard afar—
But shoutingly adrift 'twixt star and star;
Reeling a planet's orbit left or right
As laughter took them in the abysmal Night;
Or, by the point of some remembered jest,

Winged and brought helpless down through gulfs unguessed,
Where the blank worlds that gather to the birth
Leaped in the Womb of Darkness at their mirth,
And e'en Gehenna's bondsmen understood
They were not damned from human brotherhood . . .

Not first nor last of Heaven's high Host, the Four
That night took place beneath The Throne once more.
O lovelier than their morning majesty,
The understanding light behind the eye!
O more compelling than their old command,
The new-learned friendly gesture of the hand!
O sweeter than their zealous fellowship,
The wise half-smile that passed from lip to lip!
O well and roundly, when Command was given,
They told their tale against themselves to Heaven,
And in silence, waiting on The Word,
Received the Peace and Pardon of The Lord!

Shiv And The Grasshopper

("Toomai of the Elephants"—*The Jungle Book*)

Shiv, who poured the harvest and made the winds to blow,
Sitting at the doorways of a day of long ago,
Gave to each his portion, food and toil and fate,
From the King upon the *guddee*[1] to the Beggar at the gate.
  All things made he—Shiva the Preserver.
  Mahadeo! Mahadeo! He made all,—
  Thorn for the camel, fodder for the kine,
  And Mother's heart for sleepy head, O little Son of mine!

Wheat he gave to rich folk, millet to the poor,
Broken scraps for holy men that beg from door to door;
Cattle to the tiger, carrion to the kite,
And rags and bones to wicked wolves without the wall at night.
Naught he found too lofty, none he saw too low—
Parbati beside him watched them come and go;
Thought to cheat her husband, turning Shiv to jest—
Stole the little grasshopper and hid it in her breast.
  So she tricked him, Shiva the Preserver.
  Mahadeo! Mahadeo, turn and see!
  Tall are the camels, heavy are the kine,
  But this was Least of Little Things, O little Son of mine!

[1] Throne.

When the dole was ended, laughingly she said,
"Master, of a million mouths is not one unfed?"
Laughing, Shiv made answer, "All have had their part,
Even he, the little one, hidden, 'neath thy heart."
From her breast she plucked it, Parbati the thief,
Saw the Least of Little Things gnawed a new-grown leaf!
Saw and feared and wondered, making prayer to Shiv,
Who hath surely given meat to all that live!

    All things made he—Shiva the Preserver.
    Mahadeo! Mahadeo! He made all,—
    Thorn for the camel, fodder for the kine,
    And Mother's heart for sleepy head, O little Son of mine!

The Fairies' Siege

(Enlarged from "Kim")

I have been given my charge to keep—
Well have I kept the same!
Playing with strife for the most of my life,
But this is a different game.
I'll not fight against swords unseen,
Or spears that I cannot view—
Hand him the keys of the place on your knees—
'Tis the Dreamer whose dreams come true!

Ask him his terms and accept them at once.
Quick, ere we anger him, go!
Never before have I flinched from the guns,
But this is a different show.
I'll not fight with the Herald of God
(I know what his Master can do!)
Open the gate, he must enter in state,
'Tis the Dreamer whose dreams come true!

I'd not give way for an Emperor,
I'd hold my road for a King—
To the Triple Crown I would not bow down—
But this is a different thing.
I'll not fight with the Powers of Air,
Sentry, pass him through!
Drawbridge let fall, 'tis the Lord of us all,
The Dreamer whose dreams come true!

The Quest

The Knight came home from the quest,
  Muddied and sore he came.
Battered of shield and crest,
  Bannerless, bruised and lame.
  Fighting we take no shame,
  Better is man for a fall.
Merrily borne, the bugle-horn
  Answered the warder's call:—
"Here is my lance to mend (Haro!),
  Here is my horse to be shot!
Ay, they were strong, and the fight was long;
  But I paid as good as I got!"

"Oh, dark and deep their van,
  That mocked my battle-cry.
I could not miss my man,
  But I could not carry by:
  Utterly whelmed was I,
  Flung under, horse and all."
Merrily borne, the bugle-horn
  Answered the warder's call!

"My wounds are noised abroad;
  But theirs my foemen cloaked.
Ye see my broken sword—
  But never the blades she broke;
  Paying them stroke for stroke,
  Good handsel over all."
Merrily borne, the bugle-horn
  Answered the warder's call!

"My shame ye count and know.
  Ye say the quest is vain.
Ye have not seen my foe.
  Ye have not told his slain.
  Surely he fights again, again;
  But when ye prove his line,
There shall come to your aid my broken blade
  In the last, lost fight of mine!
And here is my lance to mend (Haro!),
  And here is my horse to be shot!
Ay, they were strong, and the fight was long;
  But I paid as good as I got!"

The Children

1914-18

("The Honours of War"—*A Diversity of Creatures*)

These were our children who died for our lands: they were dear in our
     sight.
  We have only the memory left of their home-treasured sayings and
     laughter.
  The price of our loss shall be paid to our hands, not another's
     hereafter.
Neither the Alien nor Priest shall decide on it.   That is our right.
     But who shall return us the children?

At the hour the Barbarian chose to disclose his pretences,
  And raged against Man, they engaged, on the breasts that they bared
     for us,
  The first felon-stroke of the sword he had long-time prepared for us—
Their bodies were all our defence while we wrought our defences.

They bought us anew with their blood, forbearing to blame us,
Those hours which we had not made good when the Judgment o'ercame us.
They believed us and perished for it.   Our statecraft, our learning
Delivered them bound to the Pit and alive to the burning
Whither they mirthfully hastened as jostling for honour—
Not since her birth has our Earth seen such worth loosed upon her.

Nor was their agony brief, or once only imposed on them.
  The wounded, the war-spent, the sick received no exemption:
  Being cured they returned and endured and achieved our redemption,
Hopeless themselves of relief, till Death, marvelling, closed on them.

That flesh we had nursed from the first in all cleanness was given
To corruption unveiled and assailed by the malice of Heaven—
By the heart-shaking jests of Decay where it lolled on the wires—
To be blanched or gay-painted by fumes—to be cindered by fires—
To be senselessly tossed and retossed in stale mutilation
From crater to crater.   For this we shall take expiation.
     But who shall return us our children?

A Song To Mithras

Hymn of the XXX Legion: circa A.D. 350

("On the Great Wall"—*Puck of Pook's Hill*)

Mithras, God of the Morning, our trumpets waken the Wall!
"Rome is above the Nations, but Thou art over all!"

Now as the names are answered, and the guards are marched away,
Mithras, also a soldier, give us strength for the day!

Mithras, God of the Noontide, the heather swims in the heat.
Our helmets scorch our foreheads, our sandals burn our feet.
Now in the ungirt hour—now lest we blink and drowse,
Mithras, also a soldier, keep us true to our vows!

Mithras, God of the Sunset, low on the Western main—
Thou descending immortal, immortal to rise again!
Now when the watch is ended, now when the wine is drawn,
Mithras, also a soldier, keep us pure till the dawn!

Mithras, God of the Midnight, here where the great Bull dies,
Look on Thy children in darkness.   Oh, take our sacrifice!
Many roads Thou hast fashioned—all of them lead to the Light!
Mithras, also a soldier, teach us to die aright!

The New Knighthood

("A Deal in Cotton"—*Actions and Reactions*)

Who gives him the Bath?
"I," said the wet,
Rank Jungle-sweat,
"I'll give him the Bath!"

Who'll sing the psalms?
"We," said the Palms.
"As the hot wind becalms,
"We'll sing the psalms."

Who lays on the sword?
"I," said the Sun,
"Before he has done,
"I'll lay on the sword."

Who fastens his belt?
"I," said Short-Rations,
"I know all the fashions
"Of tightening a belt!"

Who gives him his spur?
"I," said his Chief,
Exacting and brief,
"I'll give him the spur."

Who'll shake his hand?
"I," said the Fever,

"And I'm no deceiver,
"I'll shake his hand."

Who brings him the wine?
"I," said Quinine,
"It's a habit of mine.
'I'll come with his wine.

Who'll put him to proof?
'I," said All Earth.
"Whatever he's worth,
"I'll put to the proof."

Who'll choose him for Knight?
"I," said his Mother,
"Before any other,
"My very own Knight."

And after this fashion, adventure to seek,
Was Sir Galahad made—as it might be last week!

The Waster

1930

From the date that the doors of his prep-school close
    On the lonely little son
He is taught by precept, insult, and blows
    The Things that Are Never Done.
Year after year, without favour or fear,
    From seven to twenty-two,
His keepers insist he shall learn the list
    Of things no fellow can do.
(They are not so strict with the average Pict
    And it isn't set to, etc.)

For this and not for the profit it brings
    Or the good of his fellow-kind
He is and suffers unspeakable things
    In body and soul and kind.
But the net result of that Primitive Cult,
    Whatever else may be won,
Is definite knowledge ere leaving College
    Of the Things that Are Never Done.
(An interdict which is strange to the Pict
    And was never revealed to, etc.)

Slack by training and slow by birth,
  Only quick to despise,
Largely assessing his neighbour's worth
  By the hue of his socks or ties,
A loafer-in-grain, his foes maintain,
  And how shall we combat their view
When, atop of his natural sloth, he holds
  There are Things no Fellow can do?
(Which is why he is licked from the first by the Pict
  And left at the post by, etc.)

Outsong in the Jungle

("The Spring Running"—*The Second Jungle Book*)

BALOO

For the sake of him who showed
One wise Frog the Jungle-Road,
Keep the Law the Man-Pack make
For thy blind old Baloo's sake!
Clean or tainted, hot or stale,
Hold it as it were the Trail,
Through the day and through the night,
Questing neither left nor right.
For the sake of him who loves
Thee beyond all else that moves,
When thy Pack would make thee pain,
Say: "Tabaqui sings again."
When thy Pack would work thee ill,
Say: "Shere Khan is yet to kill."
When the knife is drawn to slay,
Keep the Law and go thy way.
(Root and honey, palm and spathe,
Guard a cub from harm and scathe!)
Wood and Water, Wind and Tree,
Jungle-Favour go with thee!

KAA

Anger is the egg of Fear—
Only lidless eyes see clear.
Cobra-poison none may leech—
Even so with Cobra-speech.
Open talk shall call to thee
Strength, whose mate is Courtesy.

Send no lunge beyond thy length.
Lend no rotten bough thy strength.
Gauge thy gape with buck or goat,
Lest thine eye should choke thy throat.
After gorging, wouldst thou sleep?
Look thy den be hid and deep,
Lest a wrong, by thee forgot,
Draw thy killer to the spot.
East and West and North and South,
Wash thy hide and close thy mouth.
(Pit and rift and blue pool-brim,
Middle-Jungle follow him!)
Wood and Water, Wind and Tree,
Jungle-Favour go with thee!

BAGHEERA

In the cage my life began;
Well I know the worth of Man.
By the Broken Lock that freed—
Man-cub, 'ware the Man-cub's breed!
Scenting-dew or starlight pale,
Choose no tangled tree-cat trail.
Pack or council, hunt or den,
Cry no truce with Jackal-Men.
Feed them silence when they say:
"Come with us an easy way."
Feed them silence when they seek
Help of thine to hurt the weak.
Make no *bandar's* boast of skill;
Hold thy peace above the kill.
Let nor call nor song nor sign
Turn thee from thy hunting-line.
(Morning mist or twilight clear,
Serve him, Wardens of the Deer!)
Wood and Water, Wind and Tree,
Jungle-Favour go with thee!

THE THREE

On the trail that thou must tread
To the thresholds of our dread,
Where the Flower blossoms red;
Through the night when thou shalt lie
Prisoned from our Mother-sky,
Hearing us, thy lovers, go by;
In the dawns when thou shalt wake

To the toil thou canst not break,
Heartsick for the Jungle's sake;
Wood and Water, Wind and Tree,
Wisdom, Strength, and Courtesy,
Jungle-Favour go with thee!

Harp Song of the Dane Women

("The Knights of the Joyous Venture"— *Puck of Pook's Hill*)

What is a woman that you forsake her,
And the hearth-fire and the home-acre,
To go with the old grey Widow-maker?

She has no house to lay a guest in—
But one chill bed for all to rest in,
That the pale suns and the stray bergs nest in.

She has no strong white arms to fold you,
But the ten-times-fingering weed to hold you—
Out on the rocks where the tide has rolled you.

Yet, when the signs of summer thicken,
And the ice breaks, and the birch-buds quicken,
Yearly you turn from our side, and sicken—

Sicken again for the shouts and the slaughters.
You steal away to the lapping waters,
And look at your ship in her winter-quarters.

You forget our mirth, and talk at the tables,
The kine in the shed and the horse in the stables—
To pitch her sides and go over her cables.

Then you drive out where the storm-clouds swallow,
And the sound of your oar-blades, falling hollow,
Is all we have left through the months to follow.

Ah, what is Woman that you forsake her,
And the hearth-fire and the home-acre,
To go with the old grey Widow-maker?

The Thousandth Man

("Simple Simon"—*Rewards and Fairies*)

One man in a thousand, Solomon says,
Will stick more close than a brother.
And it's worth while seeking him half your days
If you find him before the other.
Nine hundred and ninety-nine depend
On what the world sees in you,
But the Thousandth Man will stand your friend
With the whole round world agin you.

'Tis neither promise nor prayer nor show
Will settle the finding for 'ee.
Nine hundred and ninety-nine of 'em go
By your looks, or your acts, or your glory.
But if he finds you and you find him,
The rest of the world don't matter;
For the Thousandth Man will sink or swim
With you in any water.

You can use his purse with no more talk
Than he uses yours for his spendings,
And laugh and meet in your daily walk
As though there had been no lendings.
Nine hundred and ninety-nine of 'em call
For silver and gold in their dealings;
But the Thousandth Man he's worth 'em all,
Because you can show him your feelings.

His wrong's your wrong, and his right's your right,
In season or out of season.
Stand up and back it in all men's sight—
With *that* for your only reason!
Nine hundred and ninety-nine can't bide
The shame or mocking or laughter,
But the Thousandth Man will stand by your side
To the gallows-afoot—and after!

The Winners

("The Story of the Gadsbys")

What is the moral? Who rides may read
When the night is thick and the tracks are blind
A friend at a pinch is a friend indeed,

But a fool to wait for the laggard behind.
Down to Gehenna or up to the Throne,
He travels the fastest who travels alone.

White hands cling to the tightened rein,
Slipping the spur from the booted heel,
Tenderest voices cry "Turn again!"
Red lips tarnish the scabbarded steel.
High hopes faint on a warm hearth-stone—
He travels the fastest who travels alone.

One may fall but he falls by himself—
Falls by himself with himself to blame.
One may attain and to him is pelf –
Loot of the city in Gold or Fame.
Plunder of earth shall be all his own
Who travels the fastest and travels alone.

Wherefore the more ye be holpen and stayed,
Stayed by a friend in the hour of toil,
Sing the heretical song I have made—
His be the labour and yours be the spoil.
Win by his aid and the aid disown—
He travels the fastest who travels alone!

A St. Helena Lullaby

("A Priest in spite of Himself"—*Rewards and Fairies*)

"How far is St. Helena from a little child at play?"
What makes you want to wander there with all the world between?
Oh, Mother, call your son again or else he'll run away.
(*No one thinks of winter when the grass is green!*)

"How far is St. Helena from a fight in Paris Street?"
I haven't time to answer now—the men are falling fast.
The guns begin to thunder, and the drums begin to beat.
(*If you take the first step, you will take the last!*)

"How far is St. Helena from the field of Austerlitz?"
You couldn't hear me if I told—so loud the cannon roar.
But not so far for people who are living by their wits.
(*"Gay go up" means "Gay go down" the wide world o'er!*)

"How far is St. Helena from an Emperor of France?"
I cannot see—I cannot tell—the Crowns they dazzle so.
The Kings sit down to dinner, and the Queens stand up to dance.
(*After open weather you may look for snow!*)

"How far is St. Helena from the Capes of Trafalgar?"
A longish way—a longish way—with ten year more to run.
It's South across the water underneath a falling star.
(*What you cannot finish you must leave undone!*)

"How far is St. Helena from the Beresina ice?"
An ill way—a chill way—the ice begins to crack.
But not so far for gentlemen who never took advice.
(*When you can't go forward you must e'en come back!*)

"How far is St. Helena 'from the field of Waterloo?"
A near way—a clear way—the ship will take you soon.
A pleasant place for gentlemen with little left to do!
(*Morning never tries you till the afternoon!*)

"How far from St. Helena to the Gate of Heaven's Grace?"
That no one knows—that no one knows—and no one ever will.
But fold your hands across your heart and cover up your face,
After all your trapesings, child, lie still!

Chil's Song

("Red Dog"—*The Second Jungle Book*)

These were my companions going forth by night—
   (*For Chil! Look you, for Chil!*)
Now come I to whistle them the ending of the fight.
   (*Chil! Vanguards of Chil!*)
Word they gave me overhead of quarry newly slain.
Word I gave them underfoot of buck upon the plain.
Here's an end of every trail—they shall not speak again!

They that cried the hunting-cry—they that followed fast—
   (*For Chil! Look you, for Chil!*)
They that bade the sambhur wheel, or pinned him as he passed—
   (*Chil! Vanguards of Chil!*)
They that lagged behind the scent—they that ran before—
They that shunned the level horn—they that over-bore—
Here's an end of every trail—they shall not follow more.

Those were my companions. Pity 'twas they died!
   (*For Chil! Look you, for Chil!*)
Now come I to comfort them that knew them in their pride.
   (*Chil! Vanguards of Chil!*)
Tattered flank and sunken eye, open mouth and red,
Locked and lank and lone they lie, the dead upon their dead.
Here's an end of every trail—and here my hosts are fed!

The Captive

("The Captive"—*Traffics and Discoveries*)

Not with an outcry to Allah nor any complaining
He answered his name at the muster and stood to the chaining.
When the twin anklets were nipped on the leg-bars that held them,
He brotherly greeted the armourers stooping to weld them.
Ere the sad dust of the marshalled feet of the chain-gang swallowed him,
Observing him nobly at ease, I alighted and followed him.
Thus we had speech by the way, but not touching his sorrow—
Rather his red Yesterday and his regal To-morrow,
Wherein he statelily moved to the clink of his chains unregarded,
Nowise abashed but contented to drink of the potion awarded.
Saluting aloofly his Fate, he made haste with his story,
And the words of his mouth were as slaves spreading carpets of glory
Embroidered with names of the Djinns—a miraculous weaving—
But the cool and perspicuous eye overbore unbelieving.
So I submitted myself to the limits of rapture—
Bound by this man we had bound, amid captives his capture—
Till he returned me to earth and the visions departed.
But on him be the Peace and the Blessing; for he was great-hearted!

The Puzzler

("The Puzzler"—*Actions and Reactions*)

The Celt in all his variants from Builth to Ballyhoo,
His mental processes are plain—one knows what he will do,
And can logically predicate his finish by his start;
But the English—ah, the English!—they are quite a race apart.

Their psychology is bovine, their outlook crude and raw.
They abandon vital matters to be tickled with a straw;
But the straw that they were tickled with—the chaff that they were fed
    with—
They convert into a weaver's beam to break their foeman's head with.

For undemocratic reasons and for motives not of State,
They arrive at their conclusions—largely inarticulate.
Being void of self-expression they confide their views to none;
But sometimes in a smoking-room, one learns why things were done.

Yes, sometimes in a smoking-room, through clouds of "Ers" and "Ums,"
Obliquely and by inference, illumination comes,
On some step that they have taken, or some action they approve—
Embellished with the *argot* of the Upper Fourth Remove.

In telegraphic sentences, half nodded to their friends,
They hint a matter's inwardness—and there the matter ends.
And while the Celt is talking from Valencia to Kirkwall,
The English—ah, the English!—don't say anything at all.

The Press

("The Village that Voted the Earth was Flat"—*A Diversity of Creatures*)

The Soldier may forget his Sword,
   The Sailorman the Sea,
The Mason may forget the Word
   And the Priest his Litany:
The Maid may forget both jewel and gem,
   And the Bride her wedding-dress—
But the Jew shall forget Jerusalem
   Ere we forget the Press!

Who once hath stood through the loaded hour
   Ere, roaring like the gale,
The Harrild and the Hoe devour
   Their league-long paper-bale,
And has lit his pipe in the morning calm
   That follows the midnight stress—
He hath sold his heart to the old Black Art
   We call the daily Press.

Who once hath dealt in the widest game
   That all of a man can play,
No later love, no larger frame
   Will lure him long away.
As the war-horse snuffeth the battle afar,
   The entered Soul, no less,
He saith: "Ha! Ha!" where the trumpets are
   And the thunders of the Press!

Canst thou number the days that we fulfil,
   Or the *Times* that we bring forth?
Canst thou send the lightnings to do thy will,
   And cause them reign on earth?
Hast thou given a peacock goodly wings,
   To please his foolishness?

Sit down at the heart of men and things,
    Companions of the Press!

The Pope may launch his Interdict,
    The Union its decree,
But the bubble is blown and the bubble is pricked
    By Us and such as We.
Remember the battle and stand aside
    While Thrones and Powers confess
That King over all the children of pride
    Is the Press—the Press—the Press!

Hadramauti

(Enlarged from "Plain Tales from the Hills")

Who knows the heart of the Christian?   How does he reason?
What are his measures and balances?   Which is his season
For laughter, forbearance or bloodshed, and what devils move him
When he arises to smite us?   *I* do not love him.

He invites the derision of strangers—he enters all places.
Booted, bareheaded he enters.   With shouts and embraces
He asks of us news of the household whom *we* reckon nameless.
Certainly Allah created him forty-fold shameless!

So it is not in the Desert.   One came to me weeping—
The Avenger of Blood on his track—I took him in keeping.
Demanding not whom he had slain, I refreshed him, I fed him
As he were even a brother.   But Eblis had bred him.

He was the son of an ape, ill at ease in his clothing.
He talked with his head, hands and feet.   I endured him with loathing.
Whatever his spirit conceived his countenance showed it
As a frog shows in a mud-puddle.   Yet I abode it!

I fingered my beard and was dumb, in silence confronting him.
His soul was too shallow for silence, e'en with Death hunting him.
I said: "'Tis his weariness speaks," but, when he had rested,
He chirped in my face like some sparrow, and, presently, jested!

Wherefore slew I that stranger?   He brought me dishonour.
I saddled my mare, Bijli, I set him upon her.
I gave him rice and goat's flesh.   He bared me to laughter.
When he was gone from my tent, swift I followed after,
Taking my sword in my hand.   The hot wine had filled him.
Under the stars he mocked me—therefore I killed him!

Chapter Headings

THE NAULAHKA

There was a strife 'twixt man and maid—
Oh, that was at the birth of time!
But what befell 'twixt man and maid,
Oh, that's beyond the grip of rhyme.
'Twas, "Sweet, I must not bide with you,"
And "Love, I cannot bide alone";
For both were young and both were true,
And both were hard as the nether stone.

Beware the man who's crossed in love;
    For pent-up steam must find its vent.
Stand back when he is on the move,
    And lend him all the Continent.

Your patience, Sirs.   The Devil took me up
To the burned mountain over Sicily
(Fit place for me) and thence I saw my Earth—
(Not all Earth's splendour, 'twas beyond my need—)
And that one spot I love—all Earth to me,
And her I love, my Heaven.   What said I?
My love was safe from all the powers of Hell—
For you—e'en you—acquit her of my guilt—
But Sula, nestling by our sail-specked sea,
My city, child of mine, my heart, my home—
Mine and my pride—evil might visit there!
It was for Sula and her naked port,
Prey to the galleys of the Algerine,
Our city Sula, that I drove my price—
For love of Sula and for love of her.
The twain were woven—gold on sackcloth—twined
Past any sundering till God shall judge
The evil and the good.

Now it is not good for the Christian's health to hustle the Aryan brown,
For the Christian riles, and the Aryan smiles and he weareth the Christian
        down;
And the end of the fight is a tombstone white with the name of the late
        deceased,
And the epitaph drear: "A Fool lies here who tried to hustle the East."

There is pleasure in the wet, wet clay,
When the artist's hand is potting it.
There is pleasure in the wet, wet lay,

When the poet's pad is blotting it.
There is pleasure in the shine of your picture on the line
At the Royal Acade-my;
But the pleasure felt in these is as chalk to Cheddar cheese
When it comes to a well-made Lie.—
To a quite unwreckable Lie,
To a most impeccable Lie!
To a water-tight, fire-proof, angle-iron, sunk-hinge, time-lock, steel-faced
        Lie!
Not a private hansom Lie,
But a pair-and-brougham Lie,
Not a little-place-at-Tooting, but a country-house-with-shooting
And a ring-fence-deer-park Lie.

When a lover hies abroad
Looking for his love,
Azrael smiling sheathes his sword,
Heaven smiles above.
Earth and sea
His servants be,
And to lesser compass round,
That his love be sooner found!

We meet in an evil land
That is near to the gates of Hell.
I wait for thy command
To serve, to speed or withstand.
And thou sayest I do not well?

Oh, Love, the flowers so red
Are only tongues of flame,
The earth is full of the dead,
The new-killed, restless dead.
There is danger beneath and o'erhead,
And I guard thy gates in fear
Of words thou canst not hear,
Of peril and jeopardy,
Of signs thou canst not see—
And thou sayest 'tis ill that I came?

This I saw when the rites were done,
And the lamps were dead and the Gods alone,
And the grey snake coiled on the altar-stone—
Ere I fled from a Fear that I could not see,
And the Gods of the East made mouths at me.

Beat off in our last fight were we?
The greater need to seek the sea.
For Fortune changeth as the moon
To caravel and picaroon.
Then Eastward Ho! or Westward Ho!
Whichever wind may meetest blow.
Our quarry sails on either sea,
Fat prey for such bold lads as we,
And every sun-dried buccaneer
Must hand and reef and watch and steer,
And bear great wrath of sea and sky
Before the plate-ships wallow by.
Now, as our tall bows take the foam,
Let no man turn his heart to home,
Save to desire plunder more
And larger warehouse for his store,
When treasure won from Santos Bay
Shall make our sea-washed village gay.

Because I sought it far from men,
In deserts and alone,
I found it burning overhead,
The jewel of a Throne.

Because I sought—I sought it so
And spent my days to find—
It blazed one moment ere it left
The blacker night behind.

We be the Gods of the East—
Older than all—
Masters of Mourning and Feast—
How shall we fall?

Will they gape for the husks that ye proffer
Or yearn to your song?
And we— have we nothing to offer
Who ruled them so long—
In the fume of the incense, the clash of the cymbals, the blare of the
conch and the gong?

Over the strife of the schools
Low the day burns—
Back with the kine from the pools
Each one returns
To the life that he knows where the altar-flame glows and the *tulsi*[1] is
trimmed in the urns.

[1] The Holy Basil.

THE LIGHT THAT FAILED

So we settled it all when the storm was done
As comfy as comfy could be;
And I was to wait in the barn, my dears,
Because I was only three.
And Teddy would run to the rainbow's foot
Because he was five and a man—
And that's how it all began, my dears,
And that's how it all began!

Then we brought the lances down—then the trumpets blew—
  When we went to Kandahar, ridin' two an' two.
    Ridin'—ridin'—ridin'—two an' two!
      Ta-ra-ra-ra-ra-ra-a!
    All the way to Kandahar,
Ridin' two an' two.

The wolf-cub at even lay in the corn,
When the smoke of the cooking hung grey.
He knew where the doe made a couch for her fawn,
And he looked to his strength for his prey.
But the moon swept the smoke-wreaths away;
And he turned from his meal in the villager's close,
And he bayed to the moon as she rose.

  "I have a thousand men," he said,
    "To wait upon my will;
  And towers nine upon the Tyne,
    And three upon the Till."

  "And what care I for your men?" said she,
    "Or towers from Tyne to Till?
  Sith you must go with me," said she,
    "To wait upon my will.

  And you may lead a thousand men
    Nor ever draw the rein,
  But before you lead the Fairy Queen
    'Twill burst your heart in twain."

  He has slipped his foot from the stirrup-bar,
    The bridle from his hand,
  And he is bound by hand and foot
    To the Queen of Fairy Land.

  "If I have taken the common clay
    And wrought it cunningly

In the shape of a God that was digged a clod,
  The greater honour to me."

"If thou hast taken the common clay,
  And thy hands be not free
From the taint of the soil, thou has made thy spoil
  The greater shame to thee."

    The lark will make her hymn to God,
    The partridge call her brood,
    While I forget the heath I trod,
    The field wherein I stood.

    'Tis dule to know not night from morn,
    But greater dule to know
    I can but hear the hunter's horn
    That once I used to blow.

There were three friends that buried the fourth,
The mould in his mouth and the dust in his eyes,
And they went south and east and north—
The strong man fights but the sick man dies.

There were three friends that spoke of the dead—
The strong man fights but the sick man dies—
"And would he were here with us now," they said,
"The sun in our face and the wind in our eyes."

Yet at the last, ere our spearmen had found him,
Yet at the last, ere a sword-thrust could save,
Yet at the last, with his masters around him,
He spoke of the Faith as a master to slave.
Yet at the last, though the Kafirs had maimed him,
Broken by bondage and wrecked by the reiver,
Yet at the last, tho' the darkness had claimed him,
He called upon Allah, and died a Believer!

Gallio's Song

"And Gallio cared for none of these things."—ACTS xviii. 17)

("Little Foxes"—*Actions and Reactions*)

    All day long to the judgment-seat
    The crazed Provincials drew—
    All day long at their ruler's feet

Howled for the blood of the Jew.
Insurrection with one accord
Banded itself and woke,
And Paul was about to open his mouth
When Achaia's Deputy spoke—

"Whether the God descend from above
Or the Man ascend upon high,
Whether this maker of tents be Jove
Or a younger deity—
I will be no judge between your gods
And your godless bickerings.
Lictor, drive them hence with rods—
I care for none of these things!

Were it a question of lawful due
Or Caesar's rule denied,
Reason would I should bear with you
And order it well to be tried;
But this is a question of words and names.
I know the strife it brings.
I will not pass upon your claims.
I care for none of these things.

One thing only I see most clear,
As I pray you also see.
Claudius Caesar hath set me here
Rome's Deputy to be.
It is Her peace that ye go to break—
Not mine, nor any king's.
But, touching your clamour of 'Conscience sake,'
I care for none of these things.

Whether ye rise for the sake of a creed,
Or riot in hope of spoil,
Equally will I punish the deed,
Equally check the broil;
Nowise permitting injustice at all
From whatever doctrine it springs—
But—whether ye follow Priapus or Paul,
I care for none of these things!"

The Bees and the Flies

("The Mother Hive"—*Actions and Reactions*)

A farmer of the Augustan Age
Perused in Virgil's golden page
The story of the secret won
From Proteus by Cyrene's son—
How the dank sea-god showed the swain
Means to restore his hives again.
More briefly, how a slaughtered bull
Breeds honey by the bellyful.

The egregious rustic put to death
A bull by stopping of its breath,
Disposed the carcass in a shed
With fragrant herbs and branches spread,
And, having well performed the charm,
Sat down to wait the promised swarm.

Nor waited long.   The God of Day
Impartial, quickening with his ray
Evil and good alike, beheld
The carcass—and the carcass swelled.
Big with new birth the belly heaves
Beneath its screen of scented leaves.
Past any doubt, the bull conceives!

The farmer bids men bring more hives
To house the profit that arrives;
Prepares on pan, and key and kettle,
Sweet music that shall make 'em settle;
But when to crown the work he goes,
Gods!   What a stink salutes his nose!

Where are the honest toilers?   Where
The gravid mistress of their care?
A bust scene, indeed, he sees,
But not a sign or sound of bees.
Worms of the riper grave unhid
By any kindly coffin-lid,
Obscene and shameless to the light,
Seethe in insatiable appetite,
Through putrid offal, while above
The hissing blow-fly seeks his love,
Whose offspring, supping where they supt,
Consume corruption twice corrupt.

Road-Song of the Bandar-Log

("Kaa's Hunting"—*The Jungle Book*)

Here we go in a flung festoon,
Half-way up to the jealous moon!
Don't you envy our pranceful bands?
Don't you wish you had extra hands?
Wouldn't you like if your tails were—*so*—
Curved in the shape of a Cupid's bow?
    Now you're angry, but—never mind,
    Brother, thy tail hangs down behind!

Here we sit in a branchy row,
Thinking of beautiful things we know;
Dreaming of deeds that we mean to do,
All complete, in a minute or two—
Something noble and grand and good,
Won by merely wishing we could.
    Now we're going to—never mind,
    Brother, thy tail hangs down behind!

All the talk we ever have heard
Uttered by bat or beast or bird—
Hide or fin or scale or feather—
Jabber it quickly and all together!
Excellent! Wonderful! Once again!
Now we are talking just like men.
    Let's pretend we are . . . Never mind!
    Brother, thy tail hangs down behind!
    This is the way of the Monkey-kind!

Then join our leaping lines that scumfish through the pines,
That rocket by where, light and high, the wild-grape swings.
By the rubbish in our wake, and the noble noise we make,
Be sure—be sure, we're going to do some splendid things!

The Fabulists

1914-18

("The Vortex"—*A Diversity of Creatures*)

When all the world would keep a matter hid,
    Since Truth is seldom friend to any crowd,
Men write in fable, as old Aesop did,
    Jesting at that which none will name aloud.

And this they needs must do, or it will fall
Unless they please they are not heard at all.

When desperate Folly daily laboureth
   To work confusion upon all we have,
When diligent Sloth demandeth Freedom's death,
   And banded Fear commandeth Honour's grave—
Even in that certain hour before the fall'
Unless men please they are not heard at all.

Needs must all please, yet some not all for need,
   Needs must all toil, yet some not all for gain,
But that man taking pleasure may take heed,
   Whom present toil shall snatch from later pain.
Thus some have toiled, but their reward was small
Since, though they pleased, they were not heard at all.

This was the lock that lay upon our lips,
   This was the yoke that we have undergone,
Denying us all pleasant fellowships
   As in our time and generation.
Our pleasures unpursued age past recall,
And for our pains—we are not heard at all.

What man hears aught except the groaning guns?
   What man heeds aught save what each instant brings?
When each man's life all imaged life outruns,
   What man shall pleasure in imaginings?
So it hath fallen, as it was bound to fall,
We are not, nor we were not, heard at all.

"Our Fathers Also"

("Below the Mill Dam"—*Traffics and Discoveries*)

Thrones, Powers, Dominions, Peoples, Kings,
Are changing 'neath our hand.
Our fathers also see these things
But they do not understand.

By—they are by with mirth and tears,
Wit or the works of Desire—
Cushioned about on the kindly years
Between the wall and the fire.

The grapes are pressed, the corn is shocked—
Standeth no more to glean;

For the Gates of Love and Learning locked
When they went out between.

All lore our Lady Venus bares,
Signalled it was or told
By the dear lips long given to theirs
And longer to the mould.

All Profit, all Device, all Truth,
Written it was or said
By the mighty men of their mighty youth,
Which is mighty being dead.

The film that floats before their eyes
The Temple's Veil they call;
And the dust that on the Shewbread lies
Is holy over all.

Warn them of seas that slip our yoke,
Of slow-conspiring stars—
The ancient Front of Things unbroke
But heavy with new wars?

By—they are by with mirth and tears,
Wit or the waste of Desire—
Cushioned about on the kindly years
Between the wall and the fire!

A British-Roman Song

(A.D. 406)

("A Centurion of the Thirtieth"—*Puck of Pook's Hill*)

My father's father saw it not,
    And I, belike, shall never come
To look on that so-holy spot—
    The very Rome—

Crowned by all Time, all Art, all Might,
    The equal work of Gods and Man,
City beneath whose oldest height—
    The Race began!

Soon to send forth again a brood,
    Unshakeable, we pray, that clings
To Rome's thrice-hammered hardihood—
    In arduous things.

Strong heart with triple armour bound.
  Beat strongly, for thy life-blood runs,
Age after Age, the Empire round—
  In us thy Sons

Who, distant from the Seven Hills,
  Loving and serving much, require
Thee—*thee* to guard 'gainst home-born ills
  The Imperial Fire!

A Pict Song

("The Winged Hats"—*Puck of Pook's Hill*)

Rome never looks where she treads.
  Always her heavy hooves fall
On our stomachs, our hearts or our heads;
  And Rome never heeds when we bawl.
Her sentries pass on—that is all,
  And we gather behind them in hordes,
And plot to reconquer the Wall,
  With only our tongues for our swords.

We are Little Folk—we!
  Too little to love or to hate.
Leave us alone and you'll see
  How we can drag down the State!
We are the worm in the wood!
  We are the rot at the root!
We are the taint in the blood!
  We are the thorn in the foot!

Mistletoe killing an oak—
  Rats gnawing cables in two—
Moths making holes in a cloak—
  How they must love what they do!
Yes—and we Little Folk too,
  We are busy as they—
Working our works out of view—
  Watch, and you'll see it some day!

No indeed! We are not strong,
  But we know Peoples that are.
Yes, and we'll guide them along
  To smash and destroy you in War!
We shall be slaves just the same?

Yes, we have always been slaves,
But you—you will die of the shame,
  And then we shall dance on your graves!

We are the Little Folk, we, etc.

The Stranger

(Canadian)

The stranger within my gate,
  He may be true or kind,
But he does not talk my talk—
  I cannot feel his mind.
I see the face and the eyes and the mouth,
  But not the soul behind.

The men of my own stock,
  They may do ill or well,
But they tell the lies I am wonted to,
  They are used to the lies I tell;
And we do not need interpreters
  When we go to buy and sell.

The Stranger within my gates,
  He may be evil or good,
But I cannot tell what powers control—
  What reasons sway his mood;
Nor when the Gods of his far-off land
  Shall repossess his blood.

The men of my own stock,
  Bitter bad they may be,
But, at least, they hear the things I hear,
  And see the things I see;
And whatever I think of them and their likes
  They think of the likes of me.

This was my father's belief
  And this is also mine:
Let the corn be all one sheaf—
  And the grapes be all one vine,
Ere our children's teeth are set on edge
  By bitter bread and wine.

"Rimini"

Marching Song of a Roman Legion of the Later Empire

(*Enlarged from 'Puck of Pook's Hill'*)

When I left Rome for Lalage's sake,
By the Legions' Road to Rimini,
She vowed her heart was mine to take
With me and my shield to Rimini—
(Till the Eagles flew from Rimini—)
And I've tramped Britain, and I've tramped Gaul,
And the Pontic shore where the snow-flakes fall
As white as the neck of Lalage—
(As cold as the heart of Lalage!)
And I've lost Britain and I've lost Gaul,
And I've lost Rome and, worst of all,
I've lost Lalage!

When you go by the Via Aurelia,
As thousands have travelled before,
Remember the Luck of the Soldier
Who never saw Rome any more!
Oh, dear was the sweetheart that kissed him,
And dear was the mother that bore;
But his shield was picked up in the heather,
And he never saw Rome any more!

And *he* left Rome, etc.

When you go by the Via Aurelia
That runs from the City to Gaul,
Remember the Luck of the Soldier
Who rose to be master of all!
He carried the sword and the buckler,
He mounted his guard on the Wall,
Till the Legions elected him Caesar,
And he rose to be master of all!

And *he* left Rome, etc.

It's twenty-five marches to Narbo,
It's forty-five more up the Rhone,
And the end may be death in the heather
Or life on an Emperor's throne.
But whether the Eagles obey us,
Or we go to the Ravens—alone,
I'd sooner be Lalage's lover
Than sit on an Emperor's throne!

We've *all* left Rome for Lalage's sake, etc.

"Poor Honest Men"

(A.D. 1800)

("A Priest in spite of Himself"—*Rewards and Fairies*)

Your jar of Virginny
Will cost you a guinea,
Which you reckon too much by five shillings or ten;
But light your churchwarden
And judge it according,
When I've told you the troubles of poor honest men.

From the Capes of the Delaware,
As you are well aware,
We sail with tobacco for England—but then,
Our own British cruisers,
They watch us come through, sirs,
And they press half a score of us poor honest men!

Or if by quick sailing
(Thick weather prevailing)
We leave them behind (as we do now and then)
We are sure of a gun from
Each frigate we run from,
Which is often destruction to poor honest men!

Broadsides the Atlantic
We tumble short-handed,
With shot-holes to plug and new canvas to bend;
And off the Azores,
Dutch, Dons and Monsieurs
Are waiting to terrify poor honest men.

Napoleon's embargo
Is laid on all cargo
Which comfort or aid to King George may intend;
And since roll, twist and leaf,
Of all comforts is chief,
They try for to steal it from poor honest men!

With no heart for fight,
We take refuge in flight,
But fire as we run, our retreat to defend;
Until our stern-chasers
Cut up her fore-braces,
And she flies off the wind from us poor honest men!

'Twix' the Forties and Fifties,
South-eastward the drift is,
And so, when we think we are making Land's End,
Alas, it is Ushant
With half the King's Navy,
Blockading French ports against poor honest men!

But they may not quit station
(Which is our salvation)
So swiftly we stand to the Nor'ard again;
And finding the tail of
A homeward-bound convoy,
We slip past the Scillies like poor honest men.

Twix' the Lizard and Dover,
We hand our stuff over,
Though I may not inform how we do it, nor when.
But a light on each quarter,
Low down on the water,
Is well understanded by poor honest men.

Even then we have dangers,
From meddlesome strangers,
Who spy on our business and are not content
To take a smooth answer,
Except with a handspike . . .
And they say they are murdered by honest men!

To be drowned or be shot
Is our natural lot,
Why should we, moreover, be hanged on the end—
After all our great pains
For to dangle in chains
As though we were smugglers, not poor honest men?

"When The Great Ark"

When the Great Ark, in Vigo Bay,
    Rode stately through the half-manned fleet,
From every ship about her way
    She heard the mariners entreat—
"Before we take the seas again
Let down your boats and send us men!

"We have no lack of victual here
     With work—God knows!—enough for all,
To hand and reef and watch and steer,
     Because our present strength is small.
While your three decks are crowded so
Your crews can scarcely stand or go.

"In war, your numbers do but raise
     Confusion and divided will;
In storm, the mindless deep obeys
     Not multitudes but single skill.
In calm, your numbers, closely pressed,
Must breed a mutiny or pest.

"We, even on unchallenged seas,
     Dare not adventure where we would,
But forfeit brave advantages
     For lack of men to make 'em good;
Whereby, to England's double cost,
Honour and profit both are lost!"

Prophets At Home

("Hal o' the Draft"—*Puck of Pook's Hill*)

Prophets have honour all over the Earth,
     Except in the village where they were born,
Where such as knew them boys from birth
     Natur-ally hold 'em in scorn.

When Prophets are naughty and young and vain,
     They make a won'erful grievance of it;
(You can see by their writings how they complain),
     But O, 'tis won'erful good for the Prophet!

There's nothing Nineveh Town can give
     (Nor being swallowed by whales between),
Makes up for the place where a man's folk live,
     Which don't care nothing what he has been.
He might ha' been that, or he might ha' been this,
But they love and they hate him for what he is.

Jubal And Tubal Cain

(Canadian)

Jubal sang of the Wrath of God
  And the curse of thistle and thorn—
But Tubal got him a pointed rod,
  And scrabbled the earth for corn.
  Old—old as that early mould,
    Young as the sprouting grain—
  Yearly green is the strife between
    Jubal and Tubal Cain!

Jubal sang of the new-found sea,
  And the love that its waves divide—
But Tubal hollowed a fallen tree
  And passed to the further side.
  Black—black as the hurricane-wrack,
    Salt as the under-main—
  Bitter and cold is the hate they hold—
    Jubal and Tubal Cain!

Jubal sang of the golden years
  When wars and wounds shall cease—
But Tubal fashioned the hand-flung spears
  And showèd his neighbours peace.
  New—new as the Nine-point-Two,
    Older than Lamech's slain—
  Roaring and loud is the feud avowed
    Twix' Jubal and Tubal Cain!

Jubal sang of the cliffs that bar
  And the peaks that none may crown—
But Tubal clambered by jut and scar
  And there he builded a town.
  High—high as the snowsheds lie,
    Low as the culverts drain—
  Wherever they be they can never agree—
    Jubal and Tubal Cain!

The Voortrekker

The gull shall whistle in his wake, the blind wave break in fire.
He shall fulfil God's utmost will, unknowing His desire.
And he shall see old planets change and alien stars arise,

And give the gale his seaworn sail in shadow of new skies.
Strong lust of gear shall drive him forth and hunger arm his hand,
To win his food from the desert rude, his pittance from the sand.
His neighbours' smoke shall vex his eye, their voices break his rest.
He shall go forth till south is north, sullen and dispossessed.
He shall desire loneliness and his desire shall bring,
Hard on his heels, a thousand wheels, a People and a King.
He shall come back on his own track, and by his scarce-cooled camp
There shall he meet the roaring street, the derrick and the stamp:
There shall blaze a nation's ways with hatchet and with brand,
Till on his last-won wilderness an Empire's outposts stand!

A School Song

(Prelude to "Stalky & Co.")

"Let us now praise famous men"—
  Men of little showing—
For their work continueth,
And their work continueth,
Broad and deep continueth,
  Greater than their knowing!

Western wind and open surge
  Took us from our mothers—
Flung us on a naked shore
(Twelve bleak houses by the shore!
Seven summers by the shore!)
  'Mid two hundred brothers.

There we met with famous men
  Set in office o'er us;
And they beat on us with rods—
Faithfully with many rods—
Daily beat us on with rods,
  For the love they bore us!

Out of Egypt unto Troy—
  Over Himalaya—
Far and sure our bands have gone—
Hy-Brazil or Babylon,
Islands of the Southern Run,
  And Cities of Cathaia!

And we all praise famous men—
  Ancients of the College;

For they taught us common sense—
Tried to teach us common sense—
Truth and God's Own Common Sense,
    Which is more than knowledge!

Each degree of Latitude
    Strung about Creation
Seeth one or more of us
(Of one muster each of us),
Diligent in that he does,
    Keen in his vocation.

This we learned from famous men,
    Knowing not its uses,
When they showed, in daily work,
Man must finish off his work—
Right or wrong, his daily work—
    And without excuses.

Servants of the Staff and chain,
    Mine and fuse and grapnel—
Some, before the face of Kings,
Stand before the face of Kings;
Bearing gifts to divers Kings—
    Gifts of case and shrapnel.

This we learned from famous men
    Teaching in our borders,
Who declarèd it was the best,
Safest, easiest, and best—
Expeditious, wise, and best—
    To obey your orders.

Some beneath the further stars
    Bear the greater burden:
Set to serve the lands they rule,
(Save he serve no man may rule),
Serve and love the lands they rule;
    Seeking praise nor guerdon.

This we learned from famous men,
    Knowing not we learned it.
Only, as the years went by—
Lonely, as the years went by—
Far from help as years went by,
    Plainer we discerned it.

Wherefore praise we famous men
From whose bays we borrow—
They that put aside To-day—
All the joys of their To-day—
And with toil of their To-day
Bought for us To-morrow!

Bless and praise we famous men—
Men of little showing—
For their work continueth,
And their work continueth,
Broad and deep continueth,
Great beyond their knowing!

The Law Of The Jungle

("How Fear Came"—*The Second Jungle Book*)

Now this is the Law of the Jungle—as old and as true as the sky;
And the Wolf that shall keep it may prosper, but the Wolf that shall break it
must die.

As the creeper that girdles the tree-trunk the Law runneth forward and back—
For the strength of the Pack is the Wolf, and the strength of the Wolf is the Pack.

Wash daily from nose-tip to tail-tip; drink deeply, but never too deep;
And remember the night is for hunting, and forget not the day is for
sleep.

The Jackal may follow the Tiger, but, Cub, when thy whiskers are grown,
Remember the Wolf is a hunter—go forth and get food of thine own.

Keep peace with the Lords of the Jungle—the Tiger, the Panther, the
Bear;
And trouble not Hathi the Silent, and mock not the Boar in his lair.

When Pack meets with Pack in the Jungle, and neither will go from the
trail,
Lie down till the leaders have spoken—it may be fair words shall prevail.

When ye fight with a Wolf of the Pack, ye must fight him alone and afar,
Lest others take part in the quarrel, and the Pack be diminished by war.

The Lair of the Wolf is his refuge, and where he has made him his home,
Not even the Head Wolf may enter, not even the Council may come.

The Lair of the Wolf is his refuge, but where he has digged it too plain,
The Council shall send him a message, and so he shall change it again.

If ye kill before midnight, be silent, and wake not the woods with your
    bay,
Lest ye frighten the deer from the crops, and the brothers go empty away.

Ye may kill for yourselves, and your mates, and your cubs as they need,
    and ye can;
But kill not for pleasure of killing, and *seven times never kill Man!*

If ye plunder his Kill from a weaker, devour not all in thy pride;
Pack-Right is the right of the meanest; so leave him the head and the
    hide.

The Kill of the Pack is the meat of the Pack.   Ye must eat where it lies;
And no one may carry away of that meat to his lair, or he dies.

The Kill of the Wolf is the meat of the Wolf.   He may do what he will,
But, till he has given permission, the Pack may not eat of that Kill.

Cub-Right is the right of the Yearling.   From all of his Pack he may
    claim
Full-gorge when the killer has eaten; and none may refuse him the same.

Lair-Right is the right of the Mother.   From all of her year she may claim
One haunch of each kill for her litter; and none may deny her the same.

Cave-Right is the right of the Father—to hunt by himself for his own:
He is freed of all calls to the Pack; he is judged by the Council alone.

Because of his age and his cunning, because of his gripe and his paw,
In all that the Law leaveth open, the word of the Head Wolf is Law.

Now these are the Laws of the Jungle, and many and mighty are they;
But the head and the hoof of the Law and the haunch and the hump is —Obey!

"A Servant When He Reigneth"

"For three things the earth is disquieted, and for four which it cannot bear. For a
servant when he reigneth, and a fool when he is filled with meat; for an odious woman
when she is married, and an handmaid that is heir to her mistress.—PROV. XXX.
21-22-23."

Three things make earth unquiet
And four she cannot brook
The godly Agur counted them
And put them in a book—
Those Four Tremendous Curses
With which mankind is cursed:
But a Servant when He Reigneth
Old Agur entered first.

An Handmaid that is Mistress
We need not call upon.
A Fool when he is full of Meat
Will fall asleep anon.
An Odious Woman Married
May bear a babe and mend;
But a Servant when He reigneth
Is Confusion to the end.

His feet are swift to tumult,
His hands are slow to toil,
His ears are deaf to reason,
His lips are loud in broil.
He knows no use for power
Except to show his might.
He gives no heed to judgment
Unless it prove him right.

Because he served a master
Before his Kingship came,
And hid in all disaster
Behind his master's name,
So, when his Folly opens
The unnecessary hells,
A Servant when He Reigneth
Throws the blame on some one else.

His vows are lightly spoken,
His faith is hard to bind,
His trust is easy broken,
He fears his fellow-kind.
The nearest mob will move him
To break the pledge he gave—
Oh, a Servant when He Reigneth
Is more than ever slave!

Macdonough's Song

("As Easy as A B C"—*A Diversity of Creatures*)

Whether the State can loose and bind
    In Heaven as well as on Earth:
If it be wiser to kill mankind
    Before or after the birth—
These are matters of high concern
    Where State-kept schoolmen are;

But Holy State (we have lived to learn)
    Endeth in Holy War.

Whether The People be led by The Lord,
    Or lured by the loudest throat:
If it be quicker to die by the sword
    Or cheaper to die by vote—
These are things we have dealt with once,
    (And they will not rise from their grave)
For Holy People, however it runs,
    Endeth in wholly Slave.

Whatsoever, for any cause,
    Seeketh to take or give
Power above or beyond the Laws,
    Suffer it not to live!
Holy State or Holy King—
    Or Holy People's Will—
Have no truck with the senseless thing.
    Order the guns and kill!
      Saying—after—me:—

Once there was The People—Terror gave it birth;
Once there was The People and it made a Hell of Earth.
Earth arose and crushed it.   Listen, O ye slain!
Once there was The People—it shall never be again!

The Flight

1930

When the grey geese heard the Fool's tread
    Too near to where they lay,
They lifted neither voice nor head,
    But took themselves away.

No water broke, no pinion whirred—
    There went no warning call.
The steely, sheltering rushes stirred
    A little—that was all.

Only the osiers understood,
    And the drowned meadows spied
What else than wreckage of a flood
    Stole outward on that tide.

But the far beaches saw their ranks
  Gather and greet and grow
By myriads on the naked banks
  Watching their sign to go;

Till, with a roar of wings that churned
  The shivering shoals to foam,
Flight after flight took air and turned
  To find a safer home;

And, far below their steadfast wedge,
  They heard (and hastened on)
Men thresh and clamour through the sedge
  Aghast that they were gone!

And, when men prayed them come anew
  And nest where they were bred,
"Nay, fools foretell what knaves will do,"
  Was all the grey geese said.

"Our Fathers of Old"

("A Doctor of Medicine"—*Rewards and Fairies*)

Excellent herbs had our fathers of old—
  Excellent herbs to ease their pain—
Alexanders and Marigold,
  Eyebright, Orris, and Elecampane—
Basil, Rocket, Valerian, Rue,
  (Almost singing themselves they run)
Vervain, Dittany, Call-me-to-you—
  Cowslip, Melilot, Rose of the Sun,
    Anything green that grew out of the mould
    Was an excellent herb to our fathers of old.

Wonderful tales had our fathers of old,
  Wonderful tales of the herbs and the stars—
The Sun was Lord of the Marigold,
  Basil and Rocket belonged to Mars.
Pat as a sum in division it goes—
  (Every herb had a planet bespoke)—
Who but Venus should govern the Rose?
  Who but Jupiter own the Oak?
    Simply and gravely the facts are told
    In the wonderful books of our fathers of old.

Wonderful little, when all is said,
    Wonderful little our fathers knew.
Half their remedies cured you dead—
    Most of their teaching was quite untrue—
"Look at the stars when a patient is ill
    (Dirt has nothing to do with disease),
Bleed and blister as much as you will,
    Blister and bleed him as oft as you please."
        Whence enormous and manifold
        Errors were made by our fathers of old.

Yet when the sickness was sore in the land,
    And neither planets nor herbs assuaged,
They took their lives in their lancet-hand
    And, oh, what a wonderful war they waged!
Yes, when the crosses were chalked on the door—
    (Yes, when the terrible dead-cart rolled!)
Excellent courage our fathers bore—
    Excellent heart had our fathers of old.
        None too learned, but nobly bold
        Into the fight went our fathers of old.

If it be certain, as Galen says—
    And sage Hippocrates holds as much—
"That those afflicted by doubts and dismays
    Are mightily helped by a dead man's touch,"
Then, be good to us, stars above!
    Then, be good to us, herbs below!
We are afflicted by what we can prove,
    We are distracted by what we know.
        So—ah, so!
        Down from your heaven or up from your mould,
        Send us the hearts of our fathers of old!

Doctors

1923

Man dies too soon, beside his works half-planned.
    His days are counted and reprieve is vain:
Who shall entreat with Death to stay his hand,
    Or cloke the shameful nakedness of pain?

Send here the bold, the seekers of the way—
    The passionless, the unshakeable of soul,
Who serve the inmost mysteries of man's clay,
    And ask no more than leave to make them whole.

The Heritage

Our Fathers in a wondrous age,
 Ere yet the Earth was small,
Ensured to us an heritage,
 And doubted not at all
That we, the children of their heart,
 Which then did beat so high,
In later time should play like part
 For our posterity.

A thousand years they steadfast built,
 To 'vantage us and ours,
The Walls that were a world's despair,
 The sea-constraining Towers:
Yet in their midmost pride they knew,
 And unto Kings made known,
Not all from these their strength they drew,
 Their faith from brass or stone.

Youth's passion, manhood's fierce intent.
 With age's judgment wise,
They spent, and counted not they spent,
 At daily sacrifice.
Not lambs alone nor purchased doves
 Or tithe of trader's gold—
Their lives most dear, their dearer loves,
 They offered up of old.

Refraining e'en from lawful things,
 They bowed the neck to bear
The unadornèd yoke that brings
 Stark toil and sternest care.
Wherefore through them is Freedom sure;
 Wherefore through them we stand,
From all but sloth and pride secure,
 In a delightsome land.

Then, fretful, murmur not they gave
 So strength a charge to keep,
Nor dream that awestruck Time shall save
 Their labour while we sleep.
Dear-bought and clear, a thousand year,
 Our fathers' title runs.
Make we likewise their sacrifice,
 Defrauding not our sons.

Chapter Headings

written for

John Lockwood Kipling's

BEAST AND MAN IN INDIA

They killed a Child to please the Gods
In Earth's young penitence,
And I have bled in that Babe's stead
Because of innocence.

I bear the sins of sinful men
That have no sin of my own,
They drive me forth to Heaven's wrath
Unpastured and alone.

I am the meat of sacrifice,
The ransom of man's guilt,
For they give my life to the altar-knife
Wherever shrine is built.

The Goat.

Between the waving tufts of jungle-grass,
Up from the river as the twilight falls,
Across the dust-beclouded plain they pass
On to the village walls.
Great is the sword and mighty is the pen,
But over all the labouring ploughman's blade—
For on its oxen and its husbandmen
An Empire's strength is laid.

The Oxen.

The torn boughs trailing o'er the tusks aslant,
The saplings reeling in the path he trod,
Declares his might—our lord the Elephant,
Chief of the ways of God.

The black bulk heaving where the oxen pant,
The bowed head toiling where the guns careen,
Declare our might—our slave the Elephant,
And servant of the Queen.

The Elephant.

Dark children of the mere and marsh,
Wallow and waste and lea,
Outcaste they wait at the village gate
With folk of low degree.

Their pasture is in no man's land,
Their food the cattle's scorn;
Their rest is mire and their desire
The thicket and the thorn.

But woe to those that break their sleep,
And woe to those that dare
To rouse the herd-bull from his keep,
The wild boar from his lair!

Pigs and Buffaloes.

The beasts are very wise,
Their mouths are clean of lies,
They talk one to the other,
Bullock to bullock's brother
Resting after their labours,
Each in stall with his neighbours.
But man with goad and whip
Breaks up their fellowship,
Shouts in their silky ears
Filling their soul with fears.
When he has ploughed the land,
He says: "They understand."
But the beasts in stall together,
Freed from the yoke and tether,
Say as the torn flanks smoke:
"Nay, 'twas the whip that spoke."

LIFE'S HANDICAP

The doors were wide, the story saith,
Out of the night came the patient wraith.
He might not speak, and he could not stir
A hair of the Baron's miniver.
Speechless and strengthless, a shadow thin,
He roved the castle to find his kin.
And oh! 'twas a piteous sight to see
The dumb ghost follow his enemy!

The Return of Imray.

Before my Spring I garnered Autumn's gain,
Out of her time my field was white with grain,
The year gave up her secrets, to my woe.
Forced and deflowered each sick season lay,
In mystery of increase and decay;
I saw the sunset ere men see the day,
Who am too wise in all I should not know.

Without Benefit of Clergy.

There's a convict more in the Central Jail,
Behind the old mud wall;
There's a lifter less on the Border trail,
And the Queen's Peace over all,
Dear boys,
The Queen's Peace over all!

For we must bear our leader's blame,
On us the shame will fall,
If we lift our hand from a fettered land
And the Queen's Peace over all,
Dear boys,
The Queen's peace over all!

The Head of the District.

The Earth gave up her dead that tide,
Into our camp he came,
And said his say and went his way,
And left our hearts aflame.

Keep tally—on the gun-butt score
The vengeance we must take
When God shall bring full reckoning
For our dead comrade's sake!

The Man Who Was.

The sky is lead, and our faces are red,
And the Gates of Hell are opened and riven,
And the winds of Hell are loosened and driven,
And the dust flies up in the face of Heaven,
and the soul of man is turned from his meat,
Heavy to raise and hard to be borne.
and the soul of man is turned from his meat,
Turned from the trifles for which he has striven,
Sick in his body and heavy-hearted,
And his soul flies up like the dust in the street—
Breaks from his flesh and is gone and departed
Like the blasts that they blow on the cholera-horn.

At the End of the Passage.

KIM

Unto whose use the pregnant suns are poised,
With idiot moons and stars retracting stars?
Creep thou between—thy coming's all unnoised.
Heaven hath her high, as Earth her baser, wars.
Heir to these tumults, this affright, that fray

(By Adam's, fathers', own, sin bound alway);
Peer up, draw out thy horoscope and say
Which planet mends thy threadbare fate, or mars.

MANY INVENTIONS

'Less you want your toes trod off you'd better get back at once.
For the bullocks are walking two by two,
The *byles* are walking two by two,
And the elephants bring the guns.
Ho! Yuss!
Great—big—long—black—forty-pounder guns.
Jiggery-jolty to and fro,
Each as big as a launch in tow—
Blind—dumb—broad-breeched—beggars o' battering-guns!

My Lord the Elephant.

THE DAY'S WORK

We now, held in captivity,
    Spring to our bondage nor grieve—
See now, how it is blesseder,
    Brothers, to give than receive!
Keep trust, wherefore we were made,
    Paying the debt that we owe;
For a clean thrust, and the shear of the blade,
    Will carry us where we would go.

The Ship that Found Herself.

All the world over, nursing their scars,
Sit the old fighting-men broke in the wars—
Sit the old fighting-men, surly and grim
Mocking the lilt of the conquerors' hymn.

Dust of the battle o'erwhelmed them and hid.
Fame never found them for aught that they did.
Wounded and spent to the lazar they drew,
Lining the road where the Legions roll through.

Sons of the Laurel who press to your meed,
(Worthy God's pity most—you who succeed!)
Ere you go triumphing, crowned, to the stars,
Pity poor fighting-men, broke in the wars!

Collected.

Put forth to watch, unschooled, alone,
   'Twixt hostile earth and sky;
The mottled lizard 'neath the stone
   Is wiser here than I.

What stir across the haze of heat?
   What omen down the wind?
The buck that break before my feet—
   They know, but I am blind!

Collected.

1914–18

Farewell and adieu to you, Harwich ladies,
Farewell and adieu to you, ladies ashore!
For we've received orders to work to the eastward
Where we hope in a short time to strafe 'em some more.

We'll duck and we'll dive like little tin turtles,
We'll duck and we'll dive underneath the North Seas,
Until we strike something that doesn't expect us,
From here to Cuxhaven it's go as you please!

The first thing we did was to dock in a minefield,
Which isn't a place where repairs should be done;
And there we lay doggo in twelve-fathom water
With tri-nitro-toluol hogging our run.

The next thing we did, we rose under a Zeppelin,
With his shiny big belly half blocking the sky.
But what in the —Heavens can you do with six-pounders?
So we fired what we had and we bade him good-bye.
   Farewell and adieu, etc.

The Fringes of the Fleet.

Song of the Fifth River

("The Treasure and the Law"—*Puck of Pook's Hill*)

When first by Eden Tree
The Four Great Rivers ran,
To each was appointed a Man
Her Prince and Ruler to be.

But after this was ordained
(The ancient legends tell),
There came dark Israel,
For whom no River remained.

Then He Whom the Rivers obey
Said to him: "Fling on the ground
A handful of yellow clay,
And a Fifth Great River shall run,
Mightier than these Four,
In secret the Earth around;
And Her secret evermore
Shall be shown to thee and thy Race."

So it was said and done.
And, deep in the veins of Earth
And, fed by a thousand springs
That comfort the market-place,
Or sap the powers of Kings,
The fifth Great River had birth,
Even as it was foretold—
The secret River of Gold!

And Israel laid down
His sceptre and his crown,
To brood on that River bank,
Where the waters flashed and sank
And burrowed in earth and fell,
And bided a season below,
For reason that none might know,
Save only Israel.

He is Lord of the Last—
The Fifth, most wonderful, Flood.
He hears Her thunder past
And Her Song is in his blood.
He can foresay: "She will fall,"
For he knows which fountain dries
Behind which desert-belt
A thousand leagues to the South.

He can foresay: "She will rise."
He knows what far snows melt
Along what mountain-wall
A thousand leagues to the North.
He snuffs the coming drouth
As he snuffs the coming rain,
He knows what each will bring forth,
And turns it to his gain.

A Ruler without a Throne,
A Prince without a Sword,
Israel follows his quest.

In every land a guest,
Of many lands a lord,
In no land King is he.
But the Fifth Great River keeps
The secret of Her deeps
For Israel alone
As it was ordered to be.

The Children's Song

(*Puck of Pook's Hill*)

Land of our Birth, we pledge to thee
Our love and toil in the years to be;
When we are grown and take our place
As men and women with our race.

Father in Heaven who lovest all,
Oh, help Thy children when they call;
That they may build from age to age
An undefilèd heritage.

Teach us to bear the yoke in youth,
With steadfastness and careful truth;
That, in our time, Thy Grace may give
The Truth whereby the Nations live.

Teach us to rule ourselves alway,
Controlled and cleanly night and day;
That we may bring, if need arise,
No maimed or worthless sacrifice.

Teach us to look in all our ends
On Thee for judge, and not our friends;
That we, with Thee, may walk uncowed
By fear or favour of the crowd.

Teach us the Strength that cannot seek,
By deed or thought, to hurt the weak;
That, under Thee, we may possess
Man's strength to comfort man's distress.

Teach us Delight in simple things,
And Mirth that has no bitter springs;
Forgiveness free of evil done,
And Love to all men 'neath the sun!

Land of our Birth, our faith, our pride,
For whose dear sake our fathers died;
Oh, Motherland, we pledge to thee
Head, heart, and hand through the years to be!

Parade-Song of the Camp-Animals

("Her Majesty's Servants"—*The Jungle Book*)

ELEPHANTS OF THE GUN-TEAMS

We lent to Alexander the strengths of Hercules,
The wisdom of our foreheads, the cunning of our knees.
We bowed our necks to service—they ne'er were loosed again,—
Make way there, way for the ten-foot teams
  Of the Forty-Pounder train!

GUN-BULLOCKS

Those heroes in their harnesses avoid a cannon-ball,
And what they know of powder upsets them one and all;
Then *we* come into action and tug the guns again,—
Make way there, way for the twenty yoke
  Of the Forty-Pounder train!

CAVALRY HORSES

By the brand on my withers, the finest of tunes
Is played by the Lancers, Hussars, and Dragoons,
And it's sweeter than "Stables" or "Water" to me,
The Cavalry Canter of "Bonnie Dundee!"

Then feed us and break us and handle and groom,
And give us good riders and plenty of room,
And launch us in column of squadron and see
The Way of the War-horse to "Bonnie Dundee!"

SCREW-GUN MULES

As me and my companions were scrambling up a hill,
The path was lost in rolling stones, but we went forward still;
For we can wriggle and climb, my lads, and turn up everywhere,
And it's our delight on a mountain height, with a leg or two to spare!

Good luck to every sergeant, then, that lets us pick our road!
Bad luck to all the driver-men that cannot pack a load!
For we can wriggle and climb, my lads, and turn up everywhere,
And it's our delight on a mountain height, with a leg or two to spare!

COMMISSARIAT CAMELS

We haven't a camelty tune of our own
To help us trollop along,
But every neck is a hair-trombone
(*Rtt-ta-ta-ta!* is a hair-trombone!)
And this is our marching-song:
Can't! Don't! Shan't! Won't!
Pass it along the line!
Somebody's pack has slid from his back,
'Wish it were only mine!
Somebody's load has tipped off in the road—
Cheer for a halt and a row!
Urr! Yarrh! Grr! Arrh!
Somebody's catching it now!

ALL THE BEASTS TOGETHER

Children of the Camp are we,
Serving each in his degree;
Children of the yoke and goad,
Pack and harness, pad and load.
See our line across the plain,
Like a heel-rope bent again,
Reaching, writhing, rolling far,
Sweeping all away to war!
While the men that walk beside,
Dusty, silent, heavy-eyed,
Cannot tell why we or they
March and suffer day by day.
Children of the Camp are we,
Serving each in his degree;
Children of the yoke and goad,
Pack and harness, pad and load!

If—

("Brother Square-Toes"—*Rewards and Fairies*)

If you can keep your head when all about you
Are losing theirs and blaming it on you,
If you can trust yourself when all men doubt you,
But make allowance for their doubting too;
If you can wait and not be tired by waiting,
Or being lied about, don't deal in lies,

Or being hated, don't give way to hating,
  And yet don't look too good, nor walk too wise:

If you can dream—and not make dreams your master;
  If you can think—and not make thoughts your aim;
If you can meet with Triumph and Disaster
  And treat those two impostors just the same;
If you can bear to hear the truth you've spoken
  Twisted by knaves to make a trap for fools,
Or watch the things you gave your life to, broken,
  And stoop and build 'em up with worn-out tools:

If you can make one heap of all your winnings
  And risk it on one turn of pitch-and-toss,
And lose, and start again at your beginnings
  And never breathe a word about your loss;
If you can force your heart and nerve and sinew
  To serve your turn long after they are gone,
And so hold on when there is nothing in you
  Except the Will which says to them: "Hold on!"

If you can talk with crowds and keep your virtue,
  Or walk with Kings—nor lose the common touch,
If neither foes nor loving friends can hurt you,
  If all men count with you, but none too much;
If you can fill the unforgiving minute
  With sixty seconds' worth of distance run,
Yours is the Earth and everything that's in it,
  And—which is more—you'll be a Man, my son!

Great-Heart

(THEODORE ROOSEVELT)

"The interpreter then called for a man-servant of his, one Great Heart."—BUNYAN'S
Pilgrim's Progress.

          Concerning brave Captains
            Our age hath made known
          For all men to honour,
            One standeth alone,
          Of whom, o'er both oceans,
            Both peoples may say:
          "Our realm is diminished
            With Great-Heart away."

In purpose unsparing,
    In action no less,
The labours he praised
    He would seek and profess
Through travail and battle
    At hazard and pain . . .
And our world is none the braver
    Since Great-Heart was ta'en!

Plain speech with plain folk,
    And plain words for false things,
Plain faith in plain dealing
    'Twixt neighbours or kings,
He used and he followed,
    However it sped . . .
Oh, our world is none more honest
    Now Great-Heart is dead!

The heat of his spirit
    Struck warm through all lands;
For he loved such as showed
    'Emselves men of their hands;
In love, as in hate,
    Paying home to the last . . .
But our world is none the kinder
    Now Great-Heart hath passed!

Hard-schooled by long power,
    Yet most humble of mind
Where aught that he was
    Might advantage mankind.
Leal servant, loved master,
    Rare comrade, sure guide . . .
Oh, our world is none the safer
    Now Great-Heart hath died!

Let those who would handle
    Make sure they can wield
His far-reaching sword
    And his close-guarding shield;
For those who must journey
    Henceforward alone
Have need of stout convoy
    Now Great-Heart is gone.

The Prodigal Son

WESTERN VERSION

(Enlarged from "Kim")

Here come I to my own again,
Fed, forgiven and known again,
Claimed by bone of my bone again
And cheered by flesh of my flesh.
The fatted calf is dressed for me,
But the husks have greater zest for me.
I think my pigs will be best for me,
So I'm off to the Yards afresh.

I never was refined, you see,
(And it weighs on my brother's mind, you see)
But there's no reproach among swine, d'you see,
For being a bit of a swine.
So I'm off with wallet and staff to eat
The bread that is three parts chaff to wheat,
But glory be!—there's a laugh to it,
Which isn't the case when we dine.

My father glooms and advises me,
My brother sulks and despises me,
And Mother catechises me
Till I want to go out and swear.
And, in spite of the butler's gravity,
I know that the servants have it I
Am a monster of moral depravity,
And I'm damned if I think it's fair!

I wasted my substance, I know I did,
On riotous living, so I did,
But there's nothing on record to show I did
More than my betters have done.
They talk of the money I spent out there—
They hint at the pace that I went out there—
But they all forget I was sent out there
Alone as a rich man's son.

So I was a mark for plunder at once,
And lost my cash (can you wonder?) at once,
But I didn't give up and knock under at once.
I worked in the Yards, for a spell,
Where I spent my nights and my days with hogs,
And shared their milk and maize with hogs,

Till, I guess, I have learned what pays with hogs
And—I have that knowledge to sell!

So back I go to my job again,
Not so easy to rob again,
Or quite so ready to sob again
On any neck that's around.
I'm leaving, Pater.   Good-bye to you!
God bless you, Mater!   I'll write to you . . .
I wouldn't be impolite to you,
But Brother, you *are* a hound!

Cain and Abel

WESTERN VERSION

1934

Cain and Abel were brothers born.
  (*Koop-la!   Come along, cows!*)
One raised cattle and one raised corn.
  (*Koop-la!   Come along!   Co-hoe!*)

And Cain he farmed by the river-side,
So he did not care how much it dried.

For he banked, and he sluiced, and he ditched and he led
  (*And the Corn don't care for the Horn*)—
A-half Euphrates out of her bed
  To water his dam' Corn!

But Abel herded out on the plains
Where you have to go by the dams and the rains.

It happened, after a three-year drought,
The wells, and the springs, and the dams gave out.

The Herd-bulls came to Cain's new house
  (*They wanted water so!*—)
With the hot red Sun between their brows,
Sayin' "Give us water for our pore cows!"
  But Cain he told 'em—"No!"

The Cows they came to Cain's big house
With the cold white Moon between their brows,
Sayin, "Give some water to us pore cows!"
  But Cain he told 'em—"No!"

The li'l Calves came to Cain's fine house
With the Evenin' Star between their brows,
Sayin' "Give us water an' we'll be cows!"
  But Cain he told 'em—"No!"

The Herd-bulls led 'em back again,
An' Abel went an' said to Cain:—
"Oh, sell me water, my brother dear,
Or there will be no beef this year."
  And Cain he answered—"No!"

"Then draw your hatches, my brother true,
An' let a little water through."
  But Cain he answered:—"No!"

"My dams are tight an' my ditches are sound,
An' not a drop goes through or round
  Till she's done her duty by the Corn

"I will not sell, an' I will not draw,
An' if you breach, I'll have the Law,
  As sure as you are born!"

Then Abel took his best bull-goad,
An' holed a dyke on the Eden road.

He opened her up with foot an' hand,
An' let Euphrates loose on the land.

He spilled Euphrates out on the plain,
So's all his cattle could drink again.

Then Cain he saw what Abel done—
But, in those days, there was no Gun!

So he made him a club of a hickory-limb,
An' halted Abel an' said to him:—

"I did not sell an' I did not draw,
An' now you've breached I'll have the Law.

"You ride abroad in your hat an' spurs,
Hell-hoofin' over my cucumbers!

"You pray to the Lord to send you luck
An' you loose your steers in my garden-truck:

"An' now you're bust, as you ought to be,
You can keep on prayin' but not to me!"

Then Abel saw it meant the life;
But, in those days, there was no Knife:

So he up with his big bull-goad instead,
But—Cain hit first and dropped him dead!

The Herd-bulls ran then they smelt the blood,
An' horned an' pawed in that Red Mud,
The Calves they bawled, and the Steers they milled,
Because it was the First Man Killed;
An' the whole Herd broke for the Land of Nod,
An' Cain was left to be judged by God!

But, seein' all he had had to bear,
I never could call the Judgment fair!

The Necessitarian

("Steam Tactics"—*Traffic and Discoveries*)

I know not in Whose hands are laid
    To empty upon earth
From unsuspected ambuscade
    The very Urns of Mirth;

Who bids the Heavenly Lark arise
    And cheer our solemn round—
The Jest beheld with streaming eyes
    And grovellings on the ground;

Who joins the flats of Time and Chance
    Behind the prey preferred,
And thrones on Shrieking Circumstance
    The Sacredly Absurd,

Till Laughter, voiceless through excess,
    Waves mute appeal and sore,
Above the midriff's deep distress,
    For breath to laugh once more.

No creed hath dared to hail Him Lord,
    No raptured choirs proclaim,
And Nature's strenuous Overword
    Hath nowhere breathed His Name.

Yet, it must be, on wayside jape,
    The selfsame Power bestows
The selfsame power as went to shape
    His Planet or His Rose.

Rebirth

1914–18
("The Edge of the Evening"—*A Diversity of Creatures*)

If any God should say,
    "I will restore
The world her yesterday
    Whole as before
My Judgment blasted it"—who would not lift
Heart, eye, and hand in passion o'er the gift?

If any God should will
    To wipe from mind
The memory of this ill
    Which is mankind
In soul and substance now—who would not bless
Even to tears His loving-tenderness?

If any God should give
    Us leave to fly
These present deaths we live,
    And safely die
In those lost lives we lived ere we were born—
What man but would not laugh the excuse to scorn?

For we are what we are—
    So broke to blood
And the strict works of war—
    So long subdued
To sacrifice, that threadbare Death commands
Hardly observance at our busier hands.

Yet we were what we were,
    And, fashioned so,
It pleases us to stare
    At the far show
Of unbelievable years and shapes that flit,
In our own likeness, on the edge of it.

The Jester

There are three degrees of bliss
At the foot of Allah's Throne,
And the highest place is his

Who saves a brother's soul
At peril of his own.
There is the Power made known!

There are three degrees of bliss
In the Gardens of Paradise,
And the second place is his
Who saves his brother's soul
By excellent advice.
For there the Glory lies!

There are three degrees of bliss
And three abodes of the Blest,
And the lowest place is his
Who has saved a soul by a jest
And a brother's soul in sport . . .
But there do the Angels resort!

Philadelphia

("Brother Square-Toes"—*Rewards and Fairies*)

If you're off to Philadelphia in the morning,
    You mustn't take my stories for a guide.
There's little left, indeed, of the city you will read of,
    And all the folk I write about have died.

Now few will understand if you mention Talleyrand,
    Or remember what his cunning and his skill did;
And the cabmen at the wharf to not know Count Zinzendorf,
    Nor the Church in Philadelphia he builded.

It is gone, gone, gone with lost Atlantis,
(Never say I didn't give you warning).
In Seventeen Ninety-three 'twas there for all to see,
But it's not in Philadelphia this morning.

If you're off to Philadelphia in the morning,
    You mustn't go by anything I've said.
Bob Bicknell's Southern Stages have been laid aside for ages,
    But the Limited will take you there instead.
Toby Hirte can't be seen at One Hundred and Eighteen
    North Second Street—no matter when you call;
And I fear you'll search in vain for the wash-house down the lane
    Where Pharaoh played the fiddle at the ball.

It is gone, gone, gone with Thebes the Golden,
(Never say I didn't give you warning).
In Seventeen Ninety-four 'twas a famous dancing floor—
But it's not in Philadelphia this morning.

If you're off to Philadelphia in the morning,
    You must telegraph for rooms at some Hotel.
You needn't try your luck at Epply's or "The Buck,"
    Though the Father of his Country liked them well.
It is not the slightest use to inquire for Adam Goos,
    Or to ask where Pastor Meder has removed—so
You must treat as out of date the story I relate
    Of the church in Philadelphia he loved so.

He is gone, gone, gone with Martin Luther
(Never say I didn't give you warning).
In Seventeen Ninety-five he was (rest his soul!) alive,
But he's not in Philadelphia this morning.

If you're off to Philadelphia this morning,
    And wish to prove the truth of what I say,
I pledge my word you'll find the pleasant land behind
    Unaltered since Red Jacket rode that way.
Still the pine-woods scent the noon; still the catbird sings his tune;
    Still autumn sets the maple-forest blazing;
Still the grape-vine through the dusk flings her soul-compelling musk;
    Still the fire-flies in the corn make night amazing!

They are there, there, there with Earth immortal
(Citizens, I give you friendly warning).
The things that truly last when men and times have passed,
They are all in Pennsylvania this morning!

A Song of Travel

(Canadian)

Where's the lamp that Hero lit
    Once to call Leander home?
Equal Time hath shovelled it
    'Neath the wrack of Greece and Rome.
Neither wait we any more
That worn sail which Argo bore.

Dust and dust of ashes close
   All the Vestal Virgins' care;
And the oldest altar shows
   But an older darkness there.
Age-encamped Oblivion
Tenteth every light that shone.

Yet shall we, for Suns that die,
   Wall our wanderings from desire?
Or, because the Moon is high,
   Scorn to use a nearer fire?
Lest some envious Pharaoh stir,
Make our lives our sepulchre?

Nay! Though Time with petty Fate
   Prison us and Emperors,
By our Arts do we create
   That which Time himself devours—
Such machines as well may run
'Gainst the Horses of the Sun.

When we would a new abode,
   Space, our tyrant King no more,
Lays the long lance of the road
   At our feet and flees before,
Breathless, ere we overwhelm,
To submit a further realm!

The Two-Sided Man

(Enlarged from "Kim")

Much I owe to the Lands that grew—
More to the Lives that fed—
But most to Allah Who gave me two
Separate sides to my head.

Much I reflect on the Good and the True
In the Faiths beneath the sun,
But most upon Allah Who gave me two
Sides to my head, not one.

Wesley's following, Calvin's flock,
White or yellow or bronze,
Shaman, Ju-ju or Angekok,
Minister, Mukamuk, Bonze—

Here is a health, my brothers, to you,
However your prayers are said,
And praised be Allah Who gave me two
Separate sides to my head!

I would go without shirt or shoe,
Friend, tobacco or bread,
Sooner than lose for a minute the two
Separate sides of my head!

A *Translation*

HORACE Bk. V. Ode 3

("Regulus"—*A Diversity of Creatures*)

There are whose study is of smells,
    And to attentive schools rehearse
How something mixed with something else
    Makes something worse.

Some cultivate in broths impure
    The clients of our body—these,
Increasing without Venus, cure,
    Or cause, disease.

Others the heated wheel extol,
    And all its offspring, whose concern
Is how to make it farthest roll
    And fastest turn.

Me, much incurious if the hour
    Present, or to be paid for, brings
Me to Brundusium by the power
    Of wheels or wings;

Me, in whose breast no flame hath burned
    Life-long, save that by Pindar lit,
Such lore leaves cold.   I am not turned
    Aside to it

More than when, sunk in thought profound
    Of what the unaltering Gods require,
My steward (friend but slave) brings round
    Logs for my fire.

"Lukannon"

Song of the Seal-Rookeries, Aleutian Islands

("The White Seal"—*The Jungle Book*)

I met my mates in the morning (and oh, but I am old!)
Where roaring on the ledges the summer ground-swell rolled.
I hear them lift the chorus that drowned the breakers' song—
The Beaches of Lukannon—two million voices strong!

The song of pleasant stations beside the salt lagoons,
The song of blowing squadrons that shuffled down the dunes,
The song of midnight dances that churned the sea to flame—
The Beaches of Lukannon—before the sealers came!

I met my mates in the morning (I'll never meet them more!);
They came and went in legions that darkened all the shore.
And through the foam-flecked offing as far as voice could reach
We hailed the landing-parties and we sang them up the beach.

The Beaches of Lukannon—the winter-wheat so tall—
The dripping, crinkled lichens, and the sea-frog drenching all!
The platforms of our playground, all shining smooth and worn!
The Beaches of Lukannon—the home where we were born!

I meet my mates in the morning, a broken, scattered band.
Men shoot us in the water and club us on the land;
Men drive us to the Salt House like silly sheep and tame,
And still we sing Lukannon—before the sealers came.

Wheel down, wheel down to southward! Oh, Gooverooska,[1] go!
And tell the Deep-Sea Viceroys the story of our woe;
Ere, empty as the shark's egg the tempest flings ashore,
The Beaches of Lukannon shall know their sons no more!

An Astrologer's Song

("A Doctor of Medicine"—*Rewards and Fairies*)

To the Heavens above us
O look and behold
The Planets that love us
All harnessed in gold!
What chariots, what horses
Against us shall bide

[1] Sea-gull.

While the Stars in their courses
    Do fight on our side?

All thought, all desires,
    That are under the sun,
Are one with their fires,
    As we also are one.
All matter, all spirit,
    All fashion, all frame,
Receive and inherit
    Their strength from the same.

Oh, man that deniest
    All power save thine own,
Their power in the highest
    Is mightily shown.
Not less in the lowest
    That power is made clear.
(Oh, man, if thou knowest,
    What treasure is here!)

Earth quakes in her throes,
    And we wonder for why.
But the blind planet knows
    When her ruler is nigh;
And, attuned since Creation
    To perfect accord,
She thrills in her station
    And yearns to her Lord.

The waters have risen,
    The springs are unbound—
The floods break their prison,
    And ravin around.
No rampart withstands 'em,
    Their fury will last,
Till the Sign that commands 'em
    Sinks low or swings past.

Through abysses unproven,
    O'er gulfs beyond thought,
Our portion is woven,
    Our burden is brought.
Yet They that prepare it,
    Whose Nature we share,
Make us who must bear it
    Well able to bear.

Though terrors o'ertake us
  We'll not be afraid.
No Power can unmake us
  Save that which has made:
Nor yet beyond reason
  Or hope shall we fall—
All things have their season,
  And Mercy crowns all!

Then, doubt not, ye fearful—
  The Eternal is King—
Up, heart, and be cheerful,
  And lustily sing:—
What chariots, what horses,
  Against us shall bide
While the Stars in their courses
  Do fight on our side?

"The Power of the Dog"

("Garm—a Hostage"—*Actions and Reactions*)

There is sorrow enough in the natural way
From men and women to fill our day;
And when we are certain of sorrow in store,
Why do we always arrange for more?
Brothers and Sisters, I bid you beware
Of giving your heart to a dog to tear.

Buy a pup and your money will buy
Love unflinching that cannot lie—
Perfect passion and worship fed
By a kick in the ribs or a pat on the head.
Nevertheless it is hardly fair
To risk your heart for a dog to tear.

When the fourteen years which Nature permits
Are closing in asthma, or tumour, or fits,
And the vet's unspoken prescription runs
To lethal chambers or loaded guns,
Then you will find—It's your own affair—
But . . . you've given your heart to a dog to tear.

When the body that lived at your single will,
With its whimper of welcome, is stilled (how still!)
When the spirit that answered your every mood

Is gone—wherever it goes—for good,
You will discover how much you care,
And will give your heart to a dog to tear.

We've sorrow enough in the natural way,
When it comes to burying Christian clay.
Our loves are not given, but only lent,
At compound interest of cent per cent.
Though it is not always the case, I believe,
That the longer we've kept 'em, the more do we grieve:
For, when debts are payable, right or wrong,
A short-time loan is as bad as a long—
So why in—Heaven (before we are there)
Should we give our hearts to a dog to tear?

The Rabbi's Song

("The House Surgeon"—*Actions and Reactions*)

2 SAMUEL xiv. 14.

If thought can reach to Heaven,
    On Heaven let it dwell,
For fear thy Thought be given
    Like power to reach to Hell.
For fear the desolation
    And darkness of thy mind
Perplex an habitation
    Which thou hast left behind.

Let nothing linger after—
    No whimpering ghost remain,
In wall, or beam, or rafter,
    Of any hate or pain.
Cleanse and call home thy spirit,
    Deny her leave to cast,
On aught thy heirs inherit,
    The shadow of her past.

For think, in all thy sadness,
    What road our griefs may take;
Whose brain reflect our madness,
    Or whom our terrors shake:
For think, lest any languish
    By cause of thy distress—

The arrows of our anguish
  Fly farther than we guess.

Our lives, our tears, as water,
  Are spilled upon the ground;
God giveth no man quarter,
  Yet God a means hath found,
Though Faith and Hope have vanished,
  And even Love grows dim—
A means whereby His banished
  Be not expelled from Him!

The Bee-Boy's Song

(" 'Dymchurch Flit' "—*Puck of Pook's Hill*)

Bees! Bees!   Hark to your bees!
"Hide from your neighbours as much as you please,
But all that has happened, to us you must tell,
Or else we will give you no honey to sell!"

A maiden in her glory,
  Upon her wedding-day,
Must tell her Bees the story,
  Or else they'll fly away.
    Fly away—die away—
      Dwindle down and leave you!
    But if you don't deceive your Bees,
      Your Bees will not deceive you.

Marriage, birth or buryin',
  News across the seas,
All you're sad or merry in,
  You must tell the Bees.
    Tell 'em coming in an' out,
      Where the Fanners fan,
    'Cause the Bees are just about
      As curious as a man!

Don't you wait where trees are,
  When the lightnings play,
Nor don't you hate where Bees are,
  Or else they'll pine away.
    Pine away—dwine away—
      Anything to leave you!
    But if you never grieve your Bees,
      Your Bees'll never grieve you.

The Song of Seven Cities

("The Vortex"—A *Diversity of Creatures*)

I was Lord of Cities very sumptuously builded.
Seven roaring Cities paid me tribute from afar.
Ivory their outposts were—the guardrooms of them gilded,
And garrisoned with Amazons invincible in war.

All the world went softly when it walked before my Cities—
Neither King nor Army vexed my peoples at their toil.
Never horse nor chariot irked or overbore my Cities.
Never Mob nor Ruler questioned whence they drew their spoil.

Banded, mailed and arrogant from sunrise unto sunset,
Singing while they sacked it, they possessed the land at large.
Yet when men would rob them, they resisted, they made onset
And pierced the smoke of battle with a thousand-sabred charge.

So they warred and trafficked only yesterday, my Cities.
To-day there is no mark or mound of where my Cities stood.
For the River rose at midnight and it washed away my Cities.
They are evened with Atlantis and the towns before the Flood.

Rain on rain-gorged channels raised the water-levels round them,
Freshet backed on freshet swelled and swept their world from sight;
Till the emboldened floods linked arms and, flashing forward, drowned
    them—
Drowned my Seven Cities and their peoples in one night!

Low among the alders lie their derelict foundations,
The beams wherein they trusted and the plinths whereon they built—
My rulers and their treasure and their unborn populations,
Dead, destroyed, aborted and defiled with mud and silt!

The Daughters of the Palace whom they cherished in my Cities,
My silver-tongued Princesses, and the promise of their May—
Their bridegrooms of the June-tide—all have perished in my Cities,
With the harsh envenomed virgins that can neither love nor play.

I was Lord of Cities—I will build anew my Cities,
Seven, set on rocks, above the wrath of any flood.
Nor will I rest from search, till I have filled anew my Cities
With peoples undefeated of the dark, enduring blood.

To the sound of trumpets shall their seed restore my Cities,
Wealthy and well-weaponed, that once more may I behold
All the world go softly when it walks before my Cities,
And the horses and the chariots fleeing from them as of old!

The Return of the Children

("They"—*Traffics and Discoveries*)

Neither the harps nor the crowns amused, nor the cherubs' dove-winged races—
Holding hands forlornly the Children wandered beneath the Dome,
Plucking the splendid robes of the passers-by, and with pitiful faces
Begging what Princes and Powers refused:—"Ah, please will you let us go home?"

Over the jewelled floor, nigh weeping, ran to them Mary the Mother,
Kneeled and caressed and made promise with kisses, and drew them along to the gateway—
Yea, the all-iron unbribeable Door which Peter must guard and none other.
Straightway She took the Keys from his keeping, and opened and freed them straightway.

Then, to Her Son, Who had seen and smiled, She said: "On the night that I bore Thee,
What didst Thou care for a love beyond mine or a heaven that was not my arm?
Didst Thou push from the nipple, O Child, to hear the angels adore Thee
When we two lay in the breath of the kine?"   And He said:—"Thou hast done no harm."
So through the Void the Children ran homeward merrily hand in hand,
Looking neither to left nor right where the breathless Heavens stood still.
And the Guards of the Void resheathed their swords, for they heard the Command:
"Shall I that have suffered the Children to come to Me hold them against their will?"

Merrow Down

(*Just So Stories*)

I

There runs a road by Merrow Down—
    A grassy track to-day it is—
An hour out of Guildford town,
    Above the river Wey it is.

Here, when they heard the horse-bells ring,
    The ancient Britons dressed and rode

To watch the dark Phoenicians bring
   Their goods along the Western Road.

Yes, here, or hereabouts, they met
   To hold their racial talks and such—
To barter beads for Whitby jet,
   And tin for gay shell torques and such.

But long and long before that time
   (When bison used to roam on it)
Did Taffy and her Daddy climb
   That Down, and had their home on it.

Then beavers built in Broadstonebrook
   And made a swamp where Bramley stands;
And bears from Shere would come and look
   For Taffimai where Shamley stands.

The Wey, that Taffy called Wagai,
   Was more than six times bigger then;
And all the Tribe of Tegumai
   They cut a noble figure then!

II

Of all the Tribe of Tegumai
   Who cut that figure, none remain,—
On Merrow Down the cuckoos cry—
   The silence and the sun remain.

But as the faithful years return
   And hearts unwounded sing again,
Comes Taffy dancing through the fern
   To lead the Surrey spring again.

Her brows are bound with bracken-fronds,
   And golden elf-locks fly above;
Her eyes are bright as diamonds
   And bluer than the sky above.

In mocassins and deer-skin cloak,
   Unfearing, free and fair she flits,
And lights her little damp-wood smoke
   To show her Daddy where she flits.

For far—oh, very far behind,
   So far she cannot call to him,
Comes Tegumai alone to find
   The daughter that was all to him!

To James Whitcomb Riley

1890

(On receiving a copy of his "Rhymes for Children")

Your trail runs to the westward,
　　And mine to my own place;
There is water between our lodges,
　　And I have not seen your face.

But since I have read your verses
　　'Tis easy to guess the rest,—
Because in the hearts of the children
　　There is neither East nor West.

Born to a thousand fortunes
　　Of good or evil hap,
Once they were kings together,
　　Throned in a mother's lap.

Surely they know that secret—
　　Yellow and black and white—
When they meet as kings together
　　In innocent dreams at night.

By a moon they all can play with—
　　Grubby and grimed and unshod,
Very happy together,
　　And very near to God.

Your trail runs to the westward,
　　And mine to my own place:
There is water between our lodges,
　　And you cannot see my face.—

And that is well—for crying
　　Should neither be written nor seen,
Bit if I call you Smoke-in-the-Eyes,
　　I know you will know what I mean.

Old Mother Laidinwool

(Enlarged from Old Song)

Old Mother Laidinwool had nigh twelve months been dead.
She heard the hops was doing well, an' so popped up her head,
For said she: "The lads I've picked with when I was young and fair,
They're bound to be at hopping and I'm bound to meet 'em there!"

Let me up and go
Back to the work I know, Lord!
Back to the work I know, Lord!
For it's dark where I lie down, My Lord!
An' it's dark where I lie down!

Old Mother Laidinwool, she give her bones a shake,
An' trotted down the churchyard-path as fast as she could make.
She met the Parson walking, but she says to him, says she:—
"Oh, don't let no one trouble for a poor old ghost like me!"

'Twas all a warm September an' the hops had flourished grand.
She saw the folks get into 'em with stockin's on their hands;
An' none of 'em was foreigners but all which she had known,
And old Mother Laidinwool she blessed 'em every one.

She saw her daughters picking an' their children them-beside,
An' she moved among the babies an' she stilled 'em when they cried.
She saw their clothes was bought, not begged, an' they was clean an' fat,
An' Old Mother Laidinwool she thanked the Lord for that.

Old Mother Laidinwool she waited on all day
Until it come too dark to see an' people went away—
Until it come too dark to see an' lights began to show,
An' old Mother Laidinwool she hadn't where to go.

Old Mother Laidinwool she give her bones a shake,
An' trotted back to churchyard-mould as fast as she could make.
She went where she was bidden to an' there laid down her ghost, . . .
An' the Lord have mercy on you in the Day you need it most!

Let me in again,
Out of the wet an' rain, Lord!
Out of the wet an' rain, Lord!
For it's best as You shall say, My Lord!
An' it's best as You shall say!

The Land

("Friendly Brook"—*A Diversity of Creatures*)

When Julius Fabricius, Sub-Prefect of the Weald,
In the days of Diocletian owned our Lower River-field,
He called to him Hobdenius—a Briton of the Clay,
Saying: "What about that River-piece for layin' in to hay?"

And the aged Hobden answered: "I remember as a lad
My father told your father that she wanted dreenin' bad.
An' the more that you neglect her the less you'll get her clean.
Have it jest *as* you've a mind to, but, if I was you, I'd dreen."

So they drained it long and crossways in the lavish Roman style—
Still we find among the river-drift their flakes of ancient tile,
And in drouthy middle August, when the bones of meadows show,
We can trace the lines they followed sixteen hundred years ago.

Then Julius Fabricius died as even Prefects do,
And after certain centuries, Imperial Rome died too.
Then did robbers enter Britain from across the Northern main
And our Lower River-field was won by Ogier the Dane.

Well could Ogier work his war-boat—well could Ogier wield his brand—
Much he knew of foaming waters—not so much of farming land.
So he called to him a Hobden of the old unaltered blood,
Saying: "What about that River-piece; she doesn't look no good?"

And the aged Hobden answered: "'Tain't for *me* to interfere,
But I've know that bit o' meadow now for five and fifty year.
Have it *jest* as you've a mind to, but I've proved it time on time,
If you want to change her nature you have *got* to give her lime!"

Ogier sent his wains to Lewes, twenty hours' solemn walk,
And drew back great abundance of the cool, grey, healing chalk.
And old Hobden spread it broadest, never heeding what was in 't.—
Which is why in cleaning ditches, now and then we find a flint.

Ogier died.   His sons grew English—Anglo-Saxon was their name—
Till out of blossomed Normandy another pirate came;
For Duke William conquered England and divided with his men,
And our lower River-field he gave to William of Warenne.

But the Brook (you know her habit) rose one rainy autumn night
And tore down sodden flitches of the bank to left and right.
So, said William to his Bailiff as they rode their dripping rounds:
"Hob, what about that River-bit—the Brook's got up no bounds?"

And that aged Hobden answered: "'Tain't my business to advise,
But ye might ha' known 'twould happen from the way the valley lies.
Where ye can't hold back the water you must try and save the sile.
Hev it jest as you've a *mind* to, but it I was you, I'd spile!"

They spiled along the water-course with trunks of willow-trees,
And planks of elms behind 'em and immortal oaken knees.
And when the spates of Autumn whirl the gravel-beds away
You can see their faithful fragments, iron-hard in iron clay.

Georgii Quinti Anno Sexto, I, who own the River-field,
Am fortified with title-deeds, attested, signed and sealed,
Guaranteeing me, my assigns, my executors and heirs
All sorts of powers and profits which—are neither mine nor theirs.

I have rights of chase and warren, as my dignity requires.
I can fish—but Hobden tickles. I can shoot—but Hobden wires.
I repair, but he reopens, certain gaps which, men allege,
Have been used by every Hobden since a Hobden swapped a hedge.

Shall I dog his morning progress o'er the track-betraying dew?
Demand his dinner-basket into which my pheasant flew?
Confiscate his evening faggot under which my conies ran,
And summons him to judgment? I would sooner summons Pan.

His dead are in the churchyard—thirty generations laid.
Their names were old in history when Domesday Book was made;
And the passion and the piety and prowess of his line
Have seeded, rooted, fruited in some land the Law calls mine.

Not for any beast that burrows, not for any bird that flies,
Would I lose his large sound counsel, miss his keen amending eyes.
He is bailiff, woodman, wheelwright, field-surveyor, engineer,
And if flagrantly a poacher—'tain't for me to interfere.

"Hob, what about the River-bit?" I turn to him again,
With Fabricius and Ogier and William of Warenne.
"Hev it jest as you've a mind to, *but*"—and here he takes command.
For whoever pays the taxes old Mus' Hobden owns the land.

Just So Verses

When the cabin port-holes are dark green
   Because of the seas outside;
When the ship goes *wop* (with a wiggle between)
And the steward falls into the soup-tureen,
   And the trunks begin to slide;
When Nursey lies on the floor in a heap,
And Mummy tells you to let her sleep,
And you aren't waked or washed or dressed,
Why, then you will know (if you haven't guessed)
You're "Fifty North and Forty West!"

                        How the Whale Got his Throat.

The Camel's hump is an ugly lump
   Which well you may see at the Zoo;

But uglier yet is the hump we get
　　From having too little to do.

Kiddies and grown-ups too-oo-oo,
If we haven't enough to do-oo-oo,
　　We get the hump—
　　Cameelious hump—
The hump that is black and blue!

We climb out of bed with a frouzly head,
　　And a snarly-yarly voice.
We shiver and scowl and we grunt and we growl
　　At our bath and our boots and our toys;

And there ought to be a corner for me
(And I know there is one for you)
　　When we get the hump—
　　Cameelious hump—
The hump that is black and blue!

The cure for this ill is not to sit still,
　　Or frowst with a book by the fire;
But to take a large hoe and a shovel also,
　　And dig till you gently perspire;

And then you will find that the sun and the wind,
And the Djinn of the Garden too,
　　Have lifted the hump—
　　The horrible hump—
The hump that is black and blue!

I get it as well as you-oo-oo—
If I haven't enough to do-oo-oo!
　　We all get hump—
　　Cameelious hump—
Kiddies and grown-ups too!

How the Camel Got his Hump.

I am the Most Wise Baviaan, saying in most wise tones,
"Let us melt into the landscape—just us two by our lones,"
People have come—in a carriage—calling.   But Mummy is there . . .
Yes, I can go if you take me—Nurse says *she* don't care,
Let's go up to the pig-styes and sit on the farmyard rails!
Let's say things to the bunnies, and watch 'em skitter their tails!
Let's—oh, *anything*, daddy, so long as it's you and me,
And going truly exploring, and not being in till tea!
Here's your boots (I've brought 'em), and here's your cap and stick,
And here's your pipe and tobacco.   Oh, come along out of it—quick!

How the Leopard Got his Spots.

I keep six honest serving-men
   (They taught me all I knew);
Their names are What and Why and When
   And How and Where and Who.
I send them over land and sea,
   I send them east and west;
But after they have worked for me,
   I give them all a rest.

I let them rest from nine till five,
   For I am busy then,
As well as breakfast, lunch, and tea,
   For they are hungry men.
But different folk have different views.
   I know a person small—
She keeps ten million serving-men,
   Who get no rest at all!

She sends 'em abroad on her own affairs,
   From the second she opens her eyes—
One million Hows, two million Wheres,
   And seven million Whys!

                                  The Elephant's Child.

This is the mouth-filling song of the race that was run by a Boomer.
Run in a single burst—only event of its kind—
Started by Big God Nqong from Warrigaborrigarooma,
Old Man Kangaroo first, Yellow-Dog Dingo behind.

Kangaroo bounded away, his back-legs working like pistons—
Bounded from morning till dark, twenty-five feet at a bound.
Yellow-Dog Dingo lay like a yellow cloud in the distance—
Much too busy to bark.   My! but they covered the ground!

Nobody knows where they went, or followed the track that they flew in,
For that Continent hadn't been given a name.
They ran thirty degrees, from Torres Straits to the Leeuwin
(Look at the Atlas, please), then they ran back as they came.

S'posing you could trot from Adelaide to the Pacific,
For an afternoon's run—half what these gentlemen did—
You would feel rather hot, but your legs would develop terrific—
Yes, my importunate son, you'd be a Marvellous Kid!

                              The Sing-Song of Old Man Kangaroo.

        I've never sailed the Amazon,
           I've never reached Brazil;
        But the *Don* and *Magdalena*,
           They can go there when they will!

Yes, weekly from Southampton,
Great steamers, white and gold,
Go rolling down to Rio
(Roll down—roll down to Rio!).
And I'd like to roll to Rio
Some day before I'm old!

I've never seen a Jaguar,
  Nor yet an Armadill-
o dilloing in his armour,
  And I s'pose I never will,

Unless I go to Rio
These wonders to behold—
Roll down—roll down to Rio—
Roll really down to Rio!
Oh, I'd love to roll to Rio
Some day before I'm old!

The Beginning of the Armadilloes.

China-going P.& O.'s
Pas Pau Amma's playground close,
And his Pusat Tasek lies
Near the track of most B.I.'s.
N.Y.K. and N.D.L.
Know Pau Amma's home as well
As the Fisher of the Sea knows
"Bens," M.M.'s and Rubattinos.
But (and this is rather queer)
A.T.L.'s can *not* come here;
O. and O. and D.O.A.
Must go round another way.
Orient, Anchor, Bibby, Hall,
Never go that way at all.
U.C.S. would have a fit
If it found itself on it.
And if "Beavers" took their cargoes
To Penang instead of Lagos,
Or a fat Shaw-Savill bore
Passengers to Singapore,
Or a White Star where to try a
Little trip to Sourabaya,
Or a B.S.A. went on
Past Natal to Cheribon,
Then great Mr. Lloyds would come
With a wire and drag them home!

You'll know what my riddle means
When you've eaten mangosteens.

The Crab that Played with the Sea.

Pussy can sit by the fire and sing,
  Pussy can climb a tree,
Or play with a silly old cork and string
  To 'muse herself, not me.
But *I* like *Binkie* my dog, because
  He knows how to behave;
So, *Binkie's* the same as the First Friend was,
  And I am the Man in the Cave!

Pussy will play Man-Friday till
  It's time to wet her paw
And make her walk on the window-sill
  (For the footprint Crusoe saw);
Then she fluffles her tail and mews,
  And scratches and won't attend.
But *Binkie* will play whatever I choose,
  And he is my true First Friend!

Pussy will rub my knees with her head
  Pretending she loves me hard;
But the very minute I go to my bed
  Pussy runs out in the yard,
And there she stays till the morning-light;
  So I know it is only pretend;
But *Binkie*, he snores at my feet all night,
  And he is my Firstest Friend!

The Cat that Walked by Himself.

This Uninhabited Island
  Is near Cape Gardafui;
But it's hot—too hot—off Suez
  For the likes of you and me
Ever to go in a P.& O.
  To call on the Cake Parsee.

How the Rhinoceros got his Skin.

There was never a Queen like Balkis,
  From here to the wide world's end;
But Balkis talked to a butterfly
  As you would talk to a friend.

There was never a King like Solomon,
  Not since the world began;

But Solomon talked to a butterfly
As a man would talk to a man

She was Queen of Sabaea—
    And *he* was Asia's Lord—
But they both of 'em talked to butterflies
    When they took their walks abroad!
                                    The Butterfly that Stamped.

The Looking-Glass

A Country Dance

(Enlarged from "Rewards and Fairies")

Queen Bess was Harry's daughter.   Stand forward partners all!
    In ruff and stomacher and gown
She danced King Philip down-a-down,
And left her shoe to show 'twas true—
    (The very tune I'm playing you)
In Norgem at Brickwall![1]

The Queen was in her chamber, and she was middling old.
Her petticoat was satin, and her stomacher was gold.
Backwards and forwards and sideways did she pass,
Making up her mind to face the cruel looking-glass.
The cruel looking-glass that will never show a lass
As comely or as kindly or as young as what she was!

Queen Bess was Harry's daughter.   Now hand your partners all!

The Queen was in her chamber, a-combing of her hair.
There came Queen Mary's spirit and It stood behind her chair,
Singing "Backwards and forwards and sideways may you pass,
But I will stand behind you till you face the looking-glass.
The cruel looking-glass that will never show a lass
As lovely or unlucky or as lonely as I was!"

Queen Bess was Harry's daughter.   Now turn your partners all!

The Queen was in her chamber, a-weeping very sore,
There came Lord Leicester's spirit and It scratched upon the door,
Singing "Backwards and forwards and sideways may you pass,
But I will walk beside you till you face the looking-glass.
The cruel looking-glass that will never show a lass,
As hard and unforgiving or as wicked as you was!"

[1] A pair of Queen Elizabeth's shoes are still at Brickwall House, Northiam, Sussex

Queen Bess was Harry's daughter.   Now kiss your partners all!

The Queen was in her chamber, her sins were on her head.
She looked the spirits up and down and statelily she said:—
"Backwards and forwards and sideways though I've been,
Yet I am Harry's daughter and I am England's Queen!"
And she faced the looking-glass (and whatever else there was)
And she saw her day was over and she saw her beauty pass
In the cruel looking-glass, that can always hurt a lass
More hard than any ghost there is or any man there was!

The Queen's Men

("Gloriana"—*Rewards and Fairies*)

Valour and Innocence
Have latterly gone hence
To certain death by certain shame attended.
Envy—ah! even to tears!—
The fortune of their years
Which, though so few, yet so divinely ended.

Scarce had they lifted up
Life's full and fiery cup,
 Than they had set it down untouched before them.
Before their day arose
They beckoned it to close—
Close in confusion and destruction o'er them.

They did not stay to ask
What prize should crown their task—
Well sure that prize was such as no man strives for;
But passed into eclipse,
Her kiss upon their lips—
Even Belphoebe's, whom they gave their lives for!

A Pageant Of Elizabeth

(*Written for "The Pageant of Parliament,"* 1934)

Like Princes crowned they bore them—
   Like Demi-Gods they wrought,
When the New World lay before them
   In headlong fact and thought.

Fate and their foemen proved them
    Above all meed of praise,
And Gloriana loved them,
    And Shakespeare wrote them plays!

Now Valour, Youth, and Life's delight break forth
    In flames of womdrous deed, and thought sublime—
Lightly to mould new worlds or lightly loose
    Words that shall shake and shape all after-time!

Giants with giants, wits with wits engage,
    And England—England—England takes the breath
Of morning, body and soul, till the great Age
    Fulfils in one great chord:—Elizabeth!

The City Of Sleep

("The Brushwood Boy"—*The Day's Work*)

Over the edge of the purple down,
    Where the single lamplight gleams,
Know ye the road to the Merciful Town
    That is hard by the Sea of Dreams—

Where the poor may lay their wrongs away,
    And the sick may forget to weep?
But we—pity us! Oh, pity us!
    We wakeful; ah, pity us!—
We must go back with Policeman Day—
    Back from the City of Sleep!

Weary they turn from the scroll and crown,
    Fetter and prayer and plough—
They that go up to the Merciful Town,
    For her gates are closing now.
It is their right in the Baths of Night
    Body and soul to steep,
But we—pity us! ah, pity us!
    We wakeful; oh, pity us!—
We must go back with Policeman Day—
    Back from the City of Sleep!

Over the edge of the purple down,
    Ere the tender dreams begin,
Look—we may look—at the Merciful Town,
    But we may not enter in!

Outcasts all, from her guarded wall
    Back to our watch we creep:
We—pity us! ah, pity us!
    We wakeful; ah, pity us!—
We that go back with Policeman Day—
    Back from the City of Sleep!

"Helen All Alone"

("In the Same Boat"—*A Diversity of Creatures*)

There was darkness under Heaven
    For an hour's space—
Darkness that we knew was given
    Us for special grace.
Sun and moon and stars were hid,
    God had left His Throne,
When Helen came to me, she did,
    Helen all alone!

Side by side (because our fate
    Damned us ere our birth)
We stole out of Limbo Gate
    Looking for the Earth.
Hand in pulling hand amid
    Fear no dreams have known,
Helen ran with me, she did,
    Helen all alone!

When the horror passing speech
    Hunted us along,
Each laid hold on each, and each
    Found the other strong.
In the teeth of Things forbid
    And Reason overthrown,
Helen stood by me, she did,
    Helen all alone!

When, at last, we heard those Fires
    Dull and die away,
When, at last, our linked desires
    Dragged us up to day;
When, at last, our souls were rid
    Of what that Night had shown,
Helen passed from me, she did,
    Helen all alone!

Let her go and find a mate,
    As I will find a bride,
Knowing naught of Limbo Gate
    Or Who are penned inside.
There is knowledge God forbid
    More than one should own.
So Helen went from me, she did,
Oh, my soul, be glad she did!
        Helen all alone!

The Widower

For a season there must be pain—
For a little, little space
I shall lose the sight of her face,
Take back the old life again
While She is at rest in her place.

For a season this pain must endure,
For a little, little while
I shall sigh more often than smile
Till Time shall work me a cure,
And the pitiful days beguile.

For that season we must be apart,
For a little length of years,
Till my life's last hour nears,
And, above the beat of my heart,
I hear Her voice in my ears.

But I shall not understand—
Being set on some later love,
Shall not know her for whom I strove,
Till she reach me forth her hand,
Saying, "Who but I have the right?"
And out of a troubled night
Shall draw me safe to the land.

The Prayer Of Miriam Cohen

(Enlarged from "Many Inventions")

From the wheel and the drift of Things
Deliver us, Good Lord,
And we will face the wrath of Kings,
The faggot and the sword!

Lay not Thy Works before our eyes
Nor vex us with Thy Wars,
Lest we should feel the straining skies
O'ertrod by trampling stars.

Hold us secure behind the gates
Of saving flesh and bone,
Lest we should dream what Dream awaits
The Soul escaped alone.

Thy Path, Thy Purposes conceal
From our beleaguered realm,
Lest any shattering whisper steal
Upon us and o'erwhelm.

A veil 'twixt us and Thee, Good Lord,
A veil 'twixt us and Thee—
Lest we should hear too clear, too clear,
And unto madness see!

The Comforters

("The Dog Hervey"—A Diversity of Creatures)

Until thy feet have trod the Road
　　Advise not wayside folk,
Nor till thy back has borne the Load
　　Break in upon the broke.

Chase not with undesired largesse
　　Of sympathy the heart
Which, knowing her own bitterness,
　　Presumes to dwell apart.

Employ not that glad hand to raise
　　The God-forgotten head
To Heaven and all the neighbours' gaze—
　　Cover thy mouth instead.

The quivering chin, the bitten lip,
   The cold and sweating brow,
Later may yearn for fellowship—
   Not now, you ass, not now!

Time, not thy ne'er so timely speech,
   Life, not thy views thereon,
Shall furnish or deny to each
   His consolation.

Or, if impelled to interfere,
   Exhort, uplift, advise,
Lend not a base, betraying ear
   To all the victim's cries.

Only the Lord can understand,
   When those first pangs begin,
How much is reflex action and
   How much is really sin.

E'en from good words thyself refrain,
   And tremblingly admit
There is no anodyne for pain
   Except the shock of it.

So, when thine own dark hour shall fall,
   Unchallenged canst thou say:
"I never worried *you* at all,
   For God's sake go away!"

The Song Of The Little Hunter

("The King's Ankus"—*The Second Jungle Book*)

Ere Mor the Peacock flutters, ere the Monkey People cry,
   Ere Chil the Kite swoops down a furlong sheer,
Through the Jungle very softly flits a shadow and a sigh—
   He is Fear, O Little Hunter, he is Fear!
Very softly down the glade runs a waiting, watching shade,
   And the whisper spreads and widens far and near.
And the sweat is on thy brow, for he passes even now—
   He is Fear, O Little Hunter, he is Fear!

Ere the moon has climbed the mountain, ere the rocks are ribbed with
    light,
   When the downward-dipping trails are dank and drear,

Comes a breathing hard behind thee—*snuffle-snuffle* through the night—
  It is Fear, O Little Hunter, it is Fear!
On thy knees and draw the bow; bid the shrilling arrow go;
  In the empty, mocking thicket plunge the spear!
But thy hands are loosed and weak, and the blood has left thy cheek—
  It is Fear, O Little Hunter, it is Fear!

When the heat-cloud sucks the tempest, when the slivered pine-trees fall,
  When the blinding, blaring rain-squalls lash and veer,
Through the war-gongs of the thunder rings a voice more loud than all—
  It is Fear, O Little Hunter, it is Fear!
Now the spates are banked and deep; now the footless boulders leap—
  Now the lightning shows each littlest leaf-rib clear—
But thy throat is shut and dried, and thy heart against thy side
  Hammers: Fear, O Little Hunter—this is Fear!

Gow's Watch

(Enlarged from various sources including "The Prophet and the Country" and "A Madonna of the Trenches"—Debits and Credits)

ACT II.   SCENE 2
The Pavilion in the Gardens.   Enter FERDINAND *and the* KING

FERDINAND.   Your tiercel's too long at hack, Sir.   He's no eyass
But a passage-hawk that footed ere we caught him,
Dangerously free o' the air.   'Faith were he mine
(As mine's the glove he binds to for his tirings)
I'd fly him with a make-hawk.   He's in yarak—
Plumed to the very point.   So manned, so weathered!
Give him the firmament God made him for
And what shall take the air of him?

THE KING.   A young wing yet.
Bold—overbold on the perch, but think you, Ferdinand,
He can endure the raw skies yonder?   Cozen
Advantage out of the teeth of the hurricane?
Choose his own mate against the lammer-geier?
Ride out a night-long tempest, hold his pitch
Between the lightning and the cloud it leaps from,
Never too pressed to kill?

FERDINAND.   I'll answer for him.
Bating all parable, I know the Prince.
There's a bleak devil in the young, my Lord;
God put it there to save 'em from their elders

And to break their fathers' hearts, but bear them scatheless
Through mire and thorns and blood if need be.   Think
What our prime saw!   Such glory, such achievements
As now our children, wondering at, examine
Themselves to see if they shall hardly equal.
But what cared we while we wrought the wonders?   Nothing!
The rampant deed contented.

THE KING.   Little enough, God knows!   But afterwards—after—
Then comes the reckoning.   I would save him that.

FERDINAND.   Save him dry scars that ache of winter nights,
Worn-out self-pity and as much of knowledge
As makes old men fear judgment?   Then loose him—loose him
A' God's name loose him to adventure early!
And trust some random pike, or half-backed horse,
Besides what's caught in Italy, to save him.

THE KING.   I know.   I know.   And yet . . . What stirs in the garden?

Enter GOW *and a* GARDENER *bearing the Prince's body*

FERDINAND.   (Gods give me patience!) Gow and a gardener
Bearing some load along in the dusk to the dunghill.
Nay—a dead branch— But as I said, the Prince—

THE KING.   They've laid it down.   Strange they should work so late.

GOW (*setting down the body*).   Heark, you unsanctified fool, while I set out
our story.   We found it, this side the North Park wall which it had climbed
to pluck nectarines from the alley.   Heark again!   There was a nectarine in
its hand when we found it, and the naughty brick that slipped from the coping
beneath its foot and so caused its death, lies now under the wall for the King
to see.

THE KING (above).   The King to see!   Why should he?   Who's the man?

GOW   That is your tale.   Swerve from it by so much as the breadth of my
dagger and here's your instant reward. You heard not, saw not, and by the
Horns of ninefold-cuckolded Jupiter you thought not nor dreamed not anything
more or other!

THE KING.   Ninefold-cuckolded Jupiter.   That's a rare oath!   Shall we
look closer?

FERDINAND.   Not yet, my Lord!   (I cannot hear him breathe.)

GARDENER.   The North Park wall?   It was so.   Plucking nectarines.   It
shall be.   But how shall I say if any ask why our Lady the Queen—

Gow. (*stabs him*).   Thus!   Hie after the Prince and tell him y'are the first fruits of his nectarine tree.   Bleed there behind the laurels.

The King.   Why did Gow buffet the clown?   What said he?   I'll go look.

Ferdinand (*above*).   Save yourself!   It is the King!

Enter the King *and* Ferdinand *to* Gow

Gow.   God save you!   This was the Prince!

The King.   The Prince!   Not a dead branch?   (*Uncovers the face.*)   My flesh and blood!   My son!   My son!

Ferdinand (*to* Gow).   I had feared something of this.   And that fool yonder?

Gow.   Dead, or as good.   He cannot speak.

Ferdinand.   Better so.

The King.   "Loosed to adventure early!"   Tell the tale.

Gow.   Saddest truth alack!   I came upon him not a half hour since, fallen from the North Park wall over against the Deerpark side—dead—dead!—a nectarine in his hand that the dear lad must have climbed for, and plucked the very instant, look you, that a brick slipped on the coping.   'Tis there now.   So I lifted him, but his neck was as you see— and already cold.

The King.   Oh, very cold.   But why should he have troubled to climb?   He was free of all the fruit in my garden, God knows! . . . What, Gow?

Gow.   Surely, God knows!

The King.   A lad's trick.   But I love him the better for it . . . True, he's past loving . . . And now we must tell our Queen.   What a coil at the day's end!   She'll grieve for him.   Not as I shall, Ferdinand, but as youth for youth.   They were much of the same age.   Playmate for playmate.   See, he wears her colours.   That is the knot she gave him last—last . . . Oh, God!   When was yesterday?

Ferdinand.   Come in!   Come in, my Lord.   There's a dew falling.

The King.   He'll take no harm of it.   I'll follow presently . . .
He's all his mother's now and none of mine—
Her very face on the bride-pillow.   Yet I tricked her.
But that was later—and she never guessed.
I do not think he sinned much—he's too young—
Much the same age as my Queen.   God must not judge him
Too hardly for such slips as youth may fall in.
But I'll entreat that Throne.
    (*Prays by the body*)

Gow.   The Heavens hold up still.   Earth opens not and this dew's mere water. What shall a man think of it all? (*To* GARDENER.) Not dead yet, sirrah? I bade you follow the Prince. Despatch!

GARDENER. Some kind soul pluck out the dagger. Why did you slay me? I'd done no wrong. I'd ha' kept it secret till my dying day. But not now—not now!—I'm dying. The Prince fell from the Queen's chamber window. I saw it in the nut-alley. He was—

FERDINAND. But what made you in the nut-alley as that hour?

GARDENER. No wrong. No more than another man's wife. Jocasta of the still-room. She'd kissed me good-night too; but that's over with the rest . . . I've stumbled on the Prince's beastly loves, and I pay for all. Let me pass!

GOW. Count it your fortune, honest man. You would have revealed it to your woman at the next meeting. You fleshmongers are all one feather. (*Plucks out the dagger.*) Go in peace and lay your death to Fortune's door. He's sped—thank Fortune!

FERDINAND. Who knows not Fortune, glutted on easy thrones,
Stealing from feasts as rare to coney-catch
Privily in the hedgerows for a clown,
With the same cruel-lustful hand and eye,
Those nails and wedges, that one hammer and lead
And the very gerb of long-stored lightnings loosed
Yesterday 'gainst some King!

THE KING. I have pursued with prayers where my heart warns me
My soul shall overtake—

Enter the QUEEN

THE KING. Look not! Wait till I tell you, dearest. . . Air! . . .
"Loosed to adventure early" . . . I go late. (*Dies.*)

GOW. So! God hath cut off the Prince in his pleasures. Gow, to save the King, hath silenced one poor fool who knew how it befell, and, now the King's dead, 'needs only that the Queen should kill Gow and all's safe for her this side o' the Judgment . . . Señor Ferdinand, the wind's easterly. I'm for the road.

FERDINAND. My horse is at the gate. God speed you. Whither?

GOW. To the Duke, if the Queen does not lay hands on me before. However it goes, I charge you bear witness, Señor Ferdinand, I served the old King faithfully. To the death, Señor Ferdinand—to the death!

ACT IV.   SCENE 4

The Head of the Bargi Pass—in snow.   GOW *and* FERDINAND *with their Captains*

GOW (*to* FERDINAND).   The Queen's host would be delivered me to-day—but that these Mountain Men have sent battalia to hold the Pass.   They're shod, helmed and torqued with soft gold.   For the rest, naked.   By no argument can I persuade 'em their gilt carcasses against my bombards avail not.   What's to do, Fox?

FERDINAND.   Fatherless folk go furthest.   These loud pagans
Are doubly fatherless.   Consider; they came
Over the passes, out of all man's world—
Adullamites, unable to endure
Its ancient pinch and belly-ache—full of revenges,
Or wilfully forgetful.   The land they found
Was manless—her raw airs uncloven by speech,
Earth without wheel-track, hoof-mark, hearth or ploughshare
Since God created; nor even a cave where men,
When night was a new thing, had hid themselves.

GOW.   Excellent.   Do I fight them, or let go?

FERDINAND.   Unused earth, air and water for their spoil,
And none to make comparison of their deeds.
No unbribed dead to judge, accuse 'em or comfort—
Their present all their future and their past.
What should they know of reason—litters of folk—
New whelped to emptiness?

GOW.   Nothing.   They bar my path.

FERDINAND.   Turn it, then—turn it.
Give them their triumph.   They'll be wiser anon—
Some thirty generations hence.

GOW.   Amen!   I'm no disposed murderer.   (*To the Mountain Men*) Most magnificent Señors?   Lords of all Suns, Moons, Firmaments—Sole Architects of Yourselves and this present Universe?   Yon Philosopher in the hairy cloak bids me wait only a thousand years, till ye've sorted yourselves more to the likeness of mankind.

THE PRIEST OF THE MOUNTAIN MEN.   There are none beside ourselves to lead the world!

GOW.   That is common knowledge.   I supplicate you, allow us the head of the Pass, that we may better reach the Queen's host yonder.   Ye will not?   Why?

THE PRIEST.   Because it is our will.   There is none other law for all the earth.

Gow.   (That a few feet of snow on a nest of rocky mountains should have
hatched this dream-people!)   (*To* Priest) Ye have reason in nature—all you've
known of it. . . . But—a thousand years—I fear they will not suffice.

The Priest.   Go you back!   We hold the passes into and out of the
world.   Do you defy us?

Ferdinand.   (*To* Gow) I warned you.   There's none like them under
Heaven.   Say it!

Gow.   Defy your puissance, Señors?   Not I.   We'll have our bombards
away, all, by noon; and our poor hosts with them.   And you, Señors, shall
have your triumph upon us.

Ferdinand.   Ah!   That touches!   Let them shout and blow their horns half
a day and they'll not think of aught else!

Gow.   Fall to your riots then!   Señors, ye have won.   We'll leave you the
head of the Pass—for thirty generations.   (*Loudly*) The mules to the bombards
and away!

Ferdinand.   Most admirably you spoke to my poor text.

Gow.   Maybe the better, Fox, because the discourse has drawn them to the
head of the Pass.   Meantime, our main body has taken the lower road, with
all the Artillery.

Ferdinand.   Had you no bombards here, then?

Gow.   None, Innocence, at all!   None, except your talk and theirs!

Act V.   Scene 3

After the Battle.   The Princess *by the Standard on the Ravelin.*

Enter Gow, *with the Crown of the Kingdom.*

Gow.   Here's earnest of the Queen's submission.   This by her last
herald—and in haste.

Princess.   'Twas ours already.   Where is the woman?

Gow.   Fled with her horse.   They broke at dawn.   Noon has not
struck, and you're Queen questionless.

Princess.   By you—through you.   How shall I honour *you*?

Gow.   Me?   But for what?

Princess.   For all—all—all—
Since the realm sunk beneath us!   Hear him!   "For what?"
Your body 'twist my bosom and her knife,
Your lips on the cup she proffered for my death;

Your one cloak over me, that night in the snows,
We held the Pass at Bargi. Every hour
New strengths, to this most unbelievable last.
"Honour him?" I will honour—will honour you—
'Tis at your choice.

Gow. Child, mine was long ago.

Enter FERDINAND, *as from horse*

But here's one worthy honour. Welcome, Fox!

FERDINAND. And to you, Watchdog. This day clenches all.
We've made it and seen it.

Gow. Is the city held?

FERDINAND. Loyally. Oh, they're drunk with loyalty yonder
A virtuous mood. Your bombards helped 'em to it . . .
But here's my word for you. The Lady Frances—

PRINCESS. I left her sick in the city. No harm, I pray.

FERDINAND. Nothing that she called harm. In truth, so little
That (*to* GOW) I am bidden to tell you, she'll be here
Almost as soon as I.

Gow. She says it?

FERDINAND. Writes.
This. (*Gives him letter.*) Yester eve 'twas given me by the priest—
He with her in her hour.

Gow. So? (*Reads*) So it is.
She will be here. (*To* FERDINAND) And all is safe in the city?

FERDINAND. As thy long sword and my lean wits can make it.
You've naught to stay for. Is it the road again?
Gow. Ay. This time, not alone . . . She will be here?

PRINCESS. I am here. You have not looked at me awhile.

Gow. The rest is with you, Ferdinand . . . Then free.

PRINCESS. And at my service more than ever. I claim—
(Our wars have taught me)—being your Queen, now, claim
You wholly mine.

Gow. Then free . . . She will be here? A little while—

PRINCESS. (*to* FERDINAND). He looks beyond, not at me.

FERDINAND. Weariness.

We are not so young as once was.   Two days' fight—
A worthy servitor—to be allowed
Some freedom.

    PRINCESS.   I have offered him all he would.

    FERDINAND.   He takes what he has taken.

                  The Spirit of the LADY FRANCES *appears to* GOW

    GOW.   Frances!

    PRINCESS.   Distraught!

    FERDINAND.   An old head-blow, maybe.   He has dealt in them.

    GOW   (*to the Spirit*).   What can the Grave against us, O my Heart,
Comfort and light and reason in all things
Visible and invisible—my one God?
Thou that wast I these barren unyoked years
Of triflings now at end!   Frances!

    PRINCESS.   She's old.

    FERDINAND.   True.   By most reckonings old.
They must keep other count.

    PRINCESS.   He kisses his hand to the air!

    FERDINAND.   His ring, rather he kisses.   Yes—for sure—the ring.

    GOW.   Dear and most dear.   And now—those very arms!   (*Dies.*)
    PRINCESS.   Oh, look!   He faints.   Haste, you!   Unhelm him!   Help!

    FERDINAND.   Needless.   No help avails against that poison.   He is sped.

    PRINCESS.   By his own hand?   *This* hour?   When I had offered—

    FERDINAND.   He had made other choice—an old, old choice,
Ne'er swerved from, and now patently sealed in death.

    PRINCESS.   He called on—the Lady Frances, was it?
Wherefore?

    FERDINAND.   Because she was his life.   Forgive, my friend—(*covers* GOW's
face).
God's uttermost beyond me in all faith,
Service and passion—that I unveil at last
The secret.   (*To the* PRINCESS) Thought—dreamed you, it was for *you*
He poured himself—for you resoldered the Crown?
Struck here, held there, amended, broke, built up
His multiplied imaginings for *you*?

PRINCESS.   I thought—I thought he—

FERDINAND.   Look beyond.   *Her* wish
Was the sole Law he knew.   *She* did not choose
Your House should perish.   Therefore he bade it stand.
Enough for him when she had breathed a word:
'Twas his to make it iron, stone, or fire,
Driving our flesh and blood before his ways
As the wind straws.   Her one face unregarded
Waiting you with your mantle or your glove—
That is the God whom he is gone to worship.

Trumpets without.   Enter the Prince's Heralds

And here's the craft of Kingship begun again.
These from the Prince of Bargi—to whose sword
You owe such help as may, he thinks, be paid . . .
He's equal in blood, in fortune more than peer,
Young, most well favoured, with a heart to love—
And two States in the balance.   Do you meet him?

PRINCESS.   God and my Misery!   I have seen Love at last.
What shall content me after?

The Wishing-Caps

(Enlarged from "Kim")

Life's all getting and giving,
I've only myself to give.
What shall I do for a living?
I've only one life to live.
End it?   I'll not find another.
Spend it?   But how shall I best?
Sure the wise plan is to live like a man
And Luck may look after the rest!
Largesse!   Largesse, Fortune!
Give or hold at your will.
If I've no care for Fortune,
Fortune must follow me still.

Bad Luck, she is never a lady
But the commonest wench on the street,
Shuffling, shabby and shady,
Shameless to pass or meet.
Walk with her once—it's a weakness!
Talk to her twice—it's a crime!

Thrust her away when she gives you "good day"
And the besom won't board you next time.
Largesse!   Largesse, Fortune!
What is Your Ladyship's mood?
If I've no care for Fortune,
My Fortune is bound to be Good!

Good Luck she is never a lady
But the cursedest quean alive!
Tricksy, wincing and jady,
Kittle to lead or drive.
Greet her—she's hailing a stranger!
Meet her—she's busking to leave.
Let her alone for a shrew to the bone,
And the hussy comes plucking your sleeve!
Largesse!   Largesse, Fortune!
I'll neither follow nor flee.
If I don't run after Fortune,
Fortune must run after me!

"By the Hoof of the Wild Goat"

("To be Filed for Reference"—*Plain Tales from the Hills*)

By the Hoof of the Wild Goat uptossed
From the cliff where she lay in the Sun
Fell the Stone
To the Tarn where the daylight is lost,
So she fell from the light of the Sun
And alone!

Now the fall was ordained from the first
With the Goat and the Cliff and the Tarn,
But the Stone
Knows only her life is accursed
As she sinks from the light of the Sun
And alone!

O Thou Who hast builded the World,
O Thou Who has lighted the Sun,
O Thou Who has darkened the Tarn,
Judge Thou
The sin of the Stone that was hurled
By the goat from the light of the Sun,
As she sinks in the mire of the Tarn,
Even now—even now—even now!

Song of the Red War-Boat

(A.D. 683)

("The Conversion of St. Wilfrid"—*Rewards and Fairies*)

Shove off from the wharf-edge!   Steady!
Watch for a smooth!   Give way!
If she feels the lop already
She'll stand on her head in the bay.
It's ebb—it's dusk—it's blowing—
The shoals are a mile of white,
But (snatch her along!) we're going
To find our master to-night.

For we hold that in all disaster
Of shipwreck, storm, or sword,
A Man must stand by his Master
When once he has pledged his word.

Raging seas have we rowed in
But we seldom saw them thus,
Our master is angry with Odin—
Odin is angry with us!
Heavy odds have we taken,
But never before such odds.
The Gods know they are forsaken
We must risk the wrath of the Gods!

Over the crest she flies from,
Into its hollow she drops,
Cringes and clears her eyes from
The wind-torn breaker-tops,
Ere out on the shrieking shoulder
Of a hill-high surge she drives.
Meet her!   Meet her and hold her!
Pull for your scoundrel lives!

The thunders bellow and clamour
The harm that they meant to do!
There goes Thor's own Hammer
Cracking the dark in two!
Close!   But the blow has missed her,
Here comes the wind of the blow!
Row or the squall'll twist her
Broadside on to it!—*Row!*

Heark'ee, Thor of the Thunder!
We are not here for a jest—
For wager, warfare, or plunder,
Or to put your power to test.
This work is none of our wishing—
We would house at home if we might—
But our master is wrecked out fishing.
We go to find him to-night.

For we hold that in all disaster—
As the Gods Themselves have said—
A Man must stand by his Master
Till one of the two is dead.

That is our way of thinking,
Now you can do as you will,
While we try to save her from sinking
And hold her head to it still,
Bale her and keep her moving,
Or she'll break her back in the trough . . .
Who said the weather's improving,
Or the swells are taking off?

Sodden, and chafed and aching,
Gone in the loins and knees—
No matter—the day is breaking,
And there's far less weight to the seas!
Up mast, and finish baling—
In oars, and out with the mead—
The rest will be two-reef sailing . . .
That was a night indeed!

But we hold that in all disaster
(And faith, we have found it true!)
If only you stand by your Master,
The Gods will stand by you!

Mine Sweepers

1914–18

(Sea Warfare)

Dawn off the Foreland—the young flood making
    Jumbled and short and steep—
Black in the hollows and bright where it's breaking—
    Awkward water to sweep.

"Mines reported in the fairway,
"Warn all traffic and detain.
"Sent up *Unity, Claribel, Assyrian, Stormcock,* and *Golden Gain.*"

Noon off the Foreland—the first ebb making
  Lumpy and strong in the bight.
Boom after boom, and the golf-hut shaking
  And the jackdaws wild with fright!
  "Mines located in the fairway,
  "Boats now working up the chain,
"Sweepers—*Unity, Claribel, Assyrian, Stormcock,* and *Golden Gain.*"

Dusk off the Foreland—the last light going
  And the traffic crowding through,
And five damned trawlers with their syreens blowing
  Heading the whole review!
  "Sweep completed in the fairway.
  "No more mines remain.
"Sent back *Unity, Claribel, Assyrian, Stormcock,* and *Golden Gain.*"

Morning Song in the Jungle

("Letting in the Jungle"—*The Second Jungle Book*)

One moment past our bodies cast
  No shadow on the plain,
Now clear and black they stride our track,
  And we run home again.
In morning-hush, each rock and bush
  Stands hard, and high, and raw:
Then give the Call: "*Good rest to all
  That keep the Jungle Law!*"

Now horn and pelt our peoples melt
  In covert to abide;
Now, crouched and still, to cave and hill
  Our Jungle Barons glide.
Now, stark and plain, Man's oxen strain,
  That draw the new-yoked plough;
Now, stripped and dread, the dawn is red
  Above the lit *talao.*[1]

[1] Pond or lake.

Ho!　Get to lair!　The sun's aflare
　Behind the breathing grass:
And creaking through the young bamboo
　The warning whispers pass.
By day made strange, the woods we range
　With blinking eyes we scan;
While down the skies the wild duck cries:
　"*The Day—the Day to Man!*"

The dew is dried that drenched our hide,
　Or washed about our way;
And where we drank, the puddled bank
　Is crisping into clay.
The traitor Dark gives up each mark
　Of stretched or hooded claw:
Then hear the Call: "*Good rest to all
　That keep the Jungle Law!*"

Blue Roses

(*The Light that Failed*)

Roses red and roses white
Plucked I for my love's delight.
She would none of all my posies—
Bade me gather her blue roses.

Half the world I wandered through,
Seeking where such flowers grew.
Half the world unto my quest
Answered me with laugh and jest.

Home I came at wintertide,
But my silly love had died
Seeking with her latest breath
Roses from the arms of Death.

It may be beyond the grave
She shall find what she would have.
Mine was but an idle quest—
Roses white and red are best!

A Ripple Song

("The Undertakers"—*The Second Jungle Book*)

Once a ripple came to land
    In the golden sunset burning—
Lapped against a maiden's hand,
    By the ford returning.

Dainty foot and gentle breast—
Here, across, be glad and rest.
"Maiden, wait," the ripple saith;
"Wait awhile, for I am Death!"

"Where my lover calls I go—
    Shame it were to treat him coldly—
'Twas a fish that circled so,
    Turning over boldly."

Dainty foot and tender heart,
Wait the loaded ferry-cart.
"Wait, ah, wait!" the ripple saith;
"Maiden, wait, for I am Death!"

"When my lover calls I haste—
    Dame Disdain was never wedded!"
Ripple-ripple round her waist,
    Clear the current eddied.

Foolish heart and faithful hand,
Little feet that touched no land.
Far away the ripple sped,
Ripple—ripple running red!

Butterflies

(" 'Wireless' "—*Traffics and Discoveries*)

Eyes aloft, over dangerous places,
The children follow the butterflies,
And, in the sweat of their upturned faces,
Slash with a net at the empty skies.

So it goes they fall amid brambles,
And sting their toes on the nettle-tops,

Till, after a thousand scratches and scrambles,
They wipe their brows and the hunting stops.

Then to quiet them comes their father
And stills the riot of pain and grief,
Saying, "Little ones, go and gather
Out of my garden a cabbage-leaf.

"You will find on it whorls and clots of
Dull grey eggs that, properly fed,
Turn, by way of the worm, to lots of
Glorious butterflies raised from the dead." . . .

"Heaven is beautiful, Earth is ugly,"
The three-dimensional preacher saith;
So we must not look where the snail and the slug lie
For Psyche's birth . . . And that is our death!

My Lady's Law

(Enlarged from "The Naulahka")

The Law whereby my lady moves
Was never Law to me,
But 'tis enough that she approves
Whatever Law it be.

For in that Law, and by that Law,
My constant course I'll steer;
Not that I heed or deem it dread,
But that she holds it dear.

Tho' Asia sent for my content
Her richest argosies,
Those would I spurn, and bid return,
If that should give her ease.

With equal heart I'd watch depart
Each spicèd sail from sight;
Sans bitterness, desiring less
Great gear than her delight.

Though Kings made swift with many a gift
My proven sword to hire—
I would not go nor serve 'em so—
Except at her desire.

With even mind, I'd put behind
Adventure and acclaim,
And clean give o'er, esteeming more
Her favour than my fame.

Yet such am I, yea, such am I—
Sore bond and freest free,
The Law that sways my lady's ways
Is mystery to me!

The Nursing Sister

(Maternity Hospital)

(The Naulahka)

Our sister sayeth such and such,
And we must bow to her behests.
Our sister toileth overmuch,
Our little maid that hath no breasts.

A field untilled, a web unwove,
A flower withheld from sun or bee,
An alien in the Courts of Love,
And—teacher unto such as we!

We love her, but we laugh the while,
We laugh, but sobs are mixed with laughter;
Our sister hath no time to smile,
She knows not what must follow after.

Wind of the South, arise and blow,
From beds of spice thy locks shake free;
Breathe on her heart that she may know,
Breathe on her eyes that she may see!

Alas! we vex her with our mirth,
And maze her with most tender scorn,
Who stands beside the Gates of Birth,
Herself a child—a child unborn!

Our sister sayeth such and such,
And we must bow to her behests.
Our sister toileth overmuch,
Our little maid that hath no breasts.

The Love Song Of Har Dyal

("Beyond the Pale"—*Plain Tales from the Hills*)

Alone upon the housetops to the North
I turn and watch the lightnings in the sky—
The glamour of thy footsteps in the North.
Come back to me, Beloved, or I die.

Below my feet the still bazar is laid—
Far, far below the weary camels lie—
The camels and the captives of thy raid.
Come back to me, Beloved, or I die!

My father's wife is old and harsh with years,
And drudge of all my father's house am I—
My bread is sorrow and my drink is tears.
Come back to me, Beloved, or I die!

A Dedication

(To "Soldiers Three")

And they were stronger hands than mine
That digged the Ruby from the earth—
More cunning brains that made it worth
The large desire of a king,
And stouter hearts that through the brine
Went down the perfect Pearl to bring.

Lo, I have wrought in common clay
Rude figures of a rough-hewn race,
Since pearls strew not the market-place
In this my town of banishment,
Where with the shifting dust I play,
And eat the bread of discontent.

Yet is there life in that I make.
O thou who knowest, turn and see—
As thou hast power over me
So have I power over these,
Because I wrought them for thy sake,
And breathed in them mine agonies.

Small mirth was in the making—now
I lift the cloth that cloaks the clay,
And, wearied, at thy feet I lay

My wares, ere I go forth to sell.
The long bazar will praise, but thou—
Heart of my heart—have I done well?

Mother O' Mine

(Dedication to "The Light that Failed")

If I were hanged on the highest hill,
Mother o' mine, O mother o' mine!
I know whose love would follow me still,
Mother o' mine, O mother o' mine!

If I were drowned in the deepest sea,
Mother o' mine, O mother o' mine!
I know whose tears would come down to me,
Mother o' mine, O mother o' mine!

If I were damned of body and soul,
I know whose prayer would make me whole,
Mother o' mine, O mother o' mine!

The Only Son

(Enlarged from "Many Inventions")

She dropped the bar, she shot the bolt, she fed the fire anew,
For she heard a whimper under the sill and a great grey paw came
   through.
The fresh flame comforted the hut and shone on the roof-beam,
And the Only Son lay down again and dreamed that he dreamed a dream.
The last ash fell from the withered log with the click of a falling spark,
And the Only Son woke up again, and called across the dark:—
"Now was I born of womankind and laid in a mother's breast?
For I have dreamed of a shaggy hide whereon I went to rest.
And was I born of womankind and laid on a father's arm?
For I dreamed of clashing teeth that guarded me from harm.

And was I born an Only Son and did I play alone?
For I have dreamed of comrades twain that bit me to the bone.
And did I break the barley-cake and steep it in the tyre?
For I have dreamed of a youngling kid new-riven from the byre:
For I have dreamed of a midnight sky and a midnight call to blood
And red-mouthed shadows racing by, that thrust me from my food.
'Tis an hour yet and an hour yet to the rising of the moon,

But I can see the black roof-tree as plain as it were noon.
'Tis a league and a league to the Lena Falls where the trooping blackbuck
   go;
But I can hear the little fawn that bleats behind the doe.
'Tis a league and a league to the Lena Falls where the crop and the
   upland meet,
But I can smell the wet dawn-wind that wakes the sprouting wheat.
Unbar the door. I may not bide, but I must out and see
If those are wolves that wait outside or my own kin to me!"

She loosed the bar, she slid the bolt, she opened the door anon,
And a grey bitch-wolf came out of the dark and fawned on the Only Son!

Mowgli's Song Against People

("Letting in the Jungle"—*The Second Jungle Book*)

I will let loose against you the fleet-footed vines—
I will call in the Jungle to stamp out your lines!
   The roofs shall fade before it,
     The house-beams shall fall;
   And the *Karela*,[1] the bitter *Karela*,
     Shall cover it all!

In the gates of these your councils my people shall sing.
In the doors of these your garners the Bat-folk shall cling;
   And the snake shall be your watchman,
     By a hearthstone unswept;
   For the *Karela*, the bitter *Karela*,
     Shall fruit where ye slept!

Ye shall not see my strikers; ye shall hear them and guess.
By night, before the moon-rise, I will send for my cess,
   And the wolf shall be your herdsman
     By a landmark removed;
   For the *Karela*, the bitter *Karela*,
     Shall seed where ye loved!

I will reap your fields before you at the hands of a host.
Ye shall glean behind my reapers for the bread that is lost;
   And the deer shall be your oxen

[1] A wild melon.

On a headland untilled;
For the *Karela*, the bitter *Karela*,
   Shall leaf where ye build!

I have untied against you the club-footed vines—
I have sent in the Jungle to swamp out your lines!
   The trees—the trees are on you!
   And the *Karela*, the bitter *Karela*,
      Shall cover you all!

Romulus And Remus

(*Canadian*)

Oh, little did the Wolf-Child care—
   When first he planned his home,
What City should arise and bear
   The weight and state of Rome.

A shiftless, westward-wandering tramp,
   Checked by the Tiber flood,
He reared a wall around his camp
   Of uninspired mud.

But when his brother leaped the Wall
   And mocked its height and make,
He guessed the future of it all
   And slew him for its sake.

Swift was the blow—swift as the thought
   Which showed him in that hour
How unbelief may bring to naught
   The early steps of Power.

Foreseeing Time's imperilled hopes
   Of Glory, Grace, and Love—
All singers, Caesars, artists, Popes—
   Would fail if Remus throve,

He sent his brother to the Gods,
   And, when the fit was o'er,
Went on collecting turves and clods
   To build the Wall once more!

Chapter Headings

THE JUNGLE BOOKS

Now Chil the Kite brings home the night
    That Mang the Bat sets free—
The herds are shut in byre and hut,
    For loosed till dawn are we.
This is the hour of pride and power,
    Talon and tush and claw.
Oh, hear the call!—Good hunting all
    That keep the Jungle Law!

                                 Mowgli's Brothers.

His spots are the joy of the Leopard: his horns are the Buffalo's pride,
Be clean, for the strength of the hunter is known by the gloss of his hide.
If ye find that the bullock can toss you, or the heavy-browed Sambhur can
    gore;
Ye need not stop work to inform us.   We knew it ten seasons before.
Oppress not the cubs of the stranger, but hail them as Sister and Brother,
For though they are little and fubsy, it may be the Bear is their mother.
"There is none like to me!" says the Cub in the pride of his earliest kill;
But the Jungle is large and the Cub he is small.   Let him think and be
    still.

                                 Kaa's Hunting.

The stream is shrunk—the pool is dry,
And we be comrades, thou and I;
With fevered jowl and dusty flank
Each jostling each along the bank;

And, by one drouthy fear made still,
Forgoing thought of quest or kill.
Now 'neath his dam the fawn may see
The lean Pack-wolf as cowed as he,
And the tall buck, unflinching, note
The fangs that tore his father's throat.
The pools are shrunk—the streams are dry,
And we be playmates, thou and I,
Till yonder cloud—Good Hunting!—loose
The rain that breaks our Water Truce.

                               How Fear Came.

What of the hunting, hunter bold?
Brother, the watch was long and cold.
What of the quarry ye went to kill?

Brother, he crops in the jungle still.
Where is the power that made your pride?
Brother, it ebbs from my flank and side.
Where is the haste that ye hurry by?
Brother, I go to my lair to die!

"Tiger-Tiger!"

Veil them, cover them, wall them round—
    Blossom, and creeper, and weed—
Let us forget the sight and the sound,
    The smell and the touch of the breed!
Fat black ash by the altar-stone,
    Here is the white-foot rain,
And the does bring forth in the fields unsown,
    And none shall affright them again;
And the blind walls crumble, unknown, o'erthrown,
    And none shall inhabit again!

Letting in the Jungle.

These are the Four that are never content, that have never been filled
    since the Dews began—
Jacala's mouth, and the glut of the Kite, and the hands of the Ape, and
    the Eyes of Man.

The King's Ankus.

For our white and our excellent nights—for the nights of swift running,
    Fair ranging, far seeing, good hunting, sure cunning!
For the smells of the dawning, untainted, ere dew has departed!
For the rush through the mist, and the quarry blind-started!
For the cry of our mates when the sambhur has wheeled and is standing
    at bay!
            For the risk and the riot of night!
            For the sleep at the lair-mouth by day!
        It is met, and we go to the fight.
            Bay! O bay!

Red Dog.

Man goes to Man! Cry the challenge through the Jungle!
    He that was our Brother goes away.
Hear, now, and judge, O ye People of the Jungle,—
    Answer, who can turn him—who shall stay?

Man goes to Man! He is weeping in the Jungle:
    He that was our Brother sorrows sore!
Man goes to Man! (O, we loved him in the Jungle!)
    To the Man-Trail where we may not follow more.

The Spring Running.

At the hole where he went in
Red-Eye called to Wrinkle-Skin.
Hear what little Red-Eye saith:
"Nag, come up and dance with death!"

Eye to eye and head to head,
   (*Keep the measure, Nag.*)
This shall end when one is dead;
   (*At thy pleasure, Nag.*)

Turn for turn and twist for twist—
   (*Run and hide thee, Nag.*)
Hah! The hooded Death has missed!
   (*Woe betide thee, Nag!*)

Rikki-Tikki-Tavi.

Oh! hush thee, my baby, the night is behind us,
   And black are the waters that sparkled so green.
The moon, o'er the combers, looks downward to find us
   At rest in hollows that rustle between.

Where billow meets billow, there soft be thy pillow;
   Ah, weary wee flipperling, curl at thy ease!
The storm shall not wake thee, nor shark overtake thee,
   Asleep in the arms of the slow-swinging seas.

The White Seal.

You mustn't swim till you're six weeks old,
   Or your head will be sunk by your heels;
And summer gales and Killer Whales
   Are bad for baby seals.
Are bad for baby seals, dear rat,
   As bad as bad can be.
But splash and grow strong,
And you can't be wrong,
   Child of the Open Sea!

The White Seal.

I will remember what I was. I am sick of rope and chain—
   I will remember my old strength and all my forest-affairs.
I will not sell my back to man for a bundle of sugar-cane.
   I will go out to my own kind, and the wood-folk in their lairs.

I will go out until the day, until the morning break,
   Out to the winds' untainted kiss, the waters' clean caress,
I will forget my ankle-ring and snap my picket-stake.
   I will revisit my lost loves, and playmates masterless!

Toomai of the Elephants.

The People of the Eastern Ice, they are melting like the snow—
They beg for coffee and sugar; they go where the white men go.
The People of the Western Ice, they learn to steal and fight;
They sell their furs to the trading-post; they sell their souls to the white.
The People of the Southern Ice, they trade with the whaler's crew;
Their women have many ribbons, but their tents are torn and few.
But the People of the Elder Ice, beyond the white man's ken—
Their spears are made of the narwhal-horn, and they are the last of the
    Men!

Quiquern.

When ye say to Tabaqui, "My Brother!" when ye call the Hyaena to
    meat,
Ye may cry the Full Truce with Jacala—the Belly that runs on four feet.

The Undertakers.

> The night we felt the earth would move
>   We stole and plucked him by the hand,
> Because we loved him with the love
>   That knows but cannot understand.
>
> And when the roaring hillside broke,
>   And all our world fell down in rain,
> We saved him, we the Little Folk;
>   But lo! he does not come again!
>
> Mourn now, we saved him for the sake
>   Of such poor love as wild ones may.
> Mourn ye! Our brother will not wake,
>   And his own kind drive us away!

The Miracle of Purun Bhagat.

The Egg-Shell

(Enlarged from "Traffics and Discoveries")

The wind took off with the sunset—
The fog came up with the tide,
When the Witch of the North took an Egg-shell
With a little Blue Devil inside.
"Sink," she said, "or swim," she said,
"It's all you will get from me.
And that is the finish of *him!*" she said,
And the Egg-shell went to sea.

The wind fell dead with the midnight—
The fog shut down like a sheet,
When the Witch of the North heard the Egg-shell
Feeling by hand for a fleet.
"Get!" she said, "or you're gone," she said,
But the little Blue Devil said "No!
The sights are just coming on," he said,
And he let the Whitehead go.

The wind got up with the morning—
The fog blew off with the rain,
When the Witch of the North saw the Egg-shell
And the little Blue Devil again.
"Did you swim?" she said. "Did you sink?" she said,
And the little Blue Devil replied:
"For myself I swam, but I *think*," he said,
"There's somebody sinking outside."

"The Trade"

1914-18

(*Sea Warfare*)

They bear, in place of classic names,
   Letters and numbers on their skin.
They play their grisly blindfold games
   In little boxes made of tin.
    Sometimes they stalk the Zeppelin,
Sometimes they learn where mines are laid,
   Or where the Baltic ice is thin.
That is the custom of "The Trade."

Few prize-courts sit upon their claims.
   They seldom tow their targets in.
They follow certain secret aims
   Down under, far from strife or din.
    When they are ready to begin
No flag is flown, no fuss is made
   More than the shearing of a pin.
That is the custom of "The Trade."

The Scout's quadruple funnel flames
   A mark from Sweden to the Swin,
The Cruiser's thund'rous screw proclaims
   Her comings out and goings in:
    But only whiffs of paraffin

Or creamy rings that fizz and fade
    Show where the one-eyed Death has been.
That is the custom of "The Trade."

Their feats, their fortunes and their fames
    Are hidden from their nearest kin;
No eager public backs or blames,
    No journal prints the yarn they spin
    (The Censor would not let it in!)
When they return from run or raid.
    Unheard they work, unseen they win.
That is the custom of "The Trade."

"Tin Fish"

1914-18

(Sea Warfare)

The ships destroy us above
    And ensnare us beneath.
We arise, we lie down, and we move
    In the belly of Death.

The ships have a thousand eyes
    To mark where we come . . .
But the mirth of a seaport dies
    When our blow gets home.

The King's Task

1902

(Enlarged from "Traffics and Discoveries")

After the sack of the City, when Rome was sunk to a name,
In the years that the lights were darkened, or ever St. Wilfrid came,
Low on the borders of Britain (the ancient poets sing)
Between the Cliff and the Forest there ruled a Saxon King.
Stubborn all were his people from cottar to overlord—
Not to be cowed by the cudgel, scarce to be schooled by the sword;
Quick to turn at their pleasure, cruel to cross in their mood,
And set on paths of their choosing as the hogs of Andred's Wood.
Laws they made in the Witan—the laws of flaying and fine—
Common, loppage and pannage, the theft and the track of kine—
Statutes of tun and of market for the fish and the malt and the meal—

The tax on the Bramber packhorse and the tax on the Hastings keel.
Over the graves of the Druids and under the wrecks of Rome,
Rudely but surely they bedded the plinth of the days to come.
Behind the feet of the Legions and before the Norseman's ire
Rudely but greatly begat they the framing of State and Shire.
Rudely but deeply they laboured, and their labour stands till now,
If we trace on our ancient headlands the twist of their eight-ox plough . . .
There came a king from Hamtun, by Bosenham he came,
He filled Use with slaughter, and Lewes he gave to flame.
He smote while they sat in the Witan—sudden he smote and sore,
That his fleet was gathered at Selsea ere they mustered at Cymen's Ore.
Blithe went the Saxons to battle, by down and wood and mere,
But thrice the acorns ripened ere the western mark was clear.
Thrice was the beechmast gathered, and the Beltane fires burned
Thrice, and the beeves were salted thrice ere the host returned.
They drove that king from Hamtun, by Bosenham o'erthrown,
Out of Rugnor to Wilton they made his land their own.
Camps they builded at Gilling, at Basing and Alresford,
But wrath abode in the Saxons from cottar to overlord.
Wrath at the weary war-game, at the foe that snapped and ran,
Wolf-wise feigning and flying, and wolf-wise snatching his man.
Wrath for their spears unready, their levies new to the blade—
Shame for the helpless sieges and the scornful ambuscade.
At hearth and tavern and market, wherever the tale was told,
Shame and wrath had the Saxons because of their boasts of old.
And some would drink and deny it, and some would pray and atone;
But the most part, after their anger, avouched that the sin was their own.
Wherefore, girding together, up to the Witan they came,
And as they had shouldered their bucklers so did they shoulder their
    blame;
(For that was the wont of the Saxons, the ancient poets sing),
And first they spoke in the Witan and then they spoke to the King:
"Edward King of the Saxons, thou knowest from sire to son,
"One is the King and his People—in gain and ungain one.
"Count we the gain together. With doubtings and spread dismays
"We have broken a foolish people—but after many days.
"Count we the loss together. Warlocks hampered our arms.
"We were tricked as by magic, we were turned as by charms.
"We went down to the battle and the road was plain to keep,
"But our angry eyes were holden, and we struck as they strike in sleep—
"Men new shaken from slumber, sweating, with eyes a-stare,
"Little blows uncertain, dealt on the useless air.
"Also a vision betrayed us and a lying tale made bold,
"That we looked to hold what we had not and to have what we did not
    hold:

"That a shield should give us shelter—that a sword should give us
   power—
"A shield snatched up a venture and a hilt scarce handled an hour:
"That being rich in the open, we should be strong in the close—
"And the Gods would sell us a cunning for the day that we met our foes.
"This was the work of wizards, but not with our foe they bide,
"In our own camp we took them, and their names are Sloth and Pride.
"Our pride was before the battle, our sloth ere we lifted spear,
"But hid in the heart of the people, as the fever hides in the mere,
"Waiting only the war-game, the heat of the strife to rise
"As the ague fumes round Oxeney when the rotting reed-bed dries.
"But now we are purged of that fever—cleansed by the letting of blood,
"Something leaner of body—something keener of mood.
"And the men new-freed from the levies return to the fields again,
"Matching a hundred battles, cottar and lord and thane;
"And they talk loud in the temples where the ancient war-gods are;
"They thumb and mock and belittle the holy harness of war.
"They jest at the sacred chariots, the robes and the gilded staff.
"These things fill them with laughter, they lean on their spears and laugh.
"The men grown old in the war-game, hither and thither they range—
"And scorn and laughter together are sire and dam of change;
"And change may be good or evil—but we know not what it will bring;
"Therefore our King must teach us. That is thy task, O King!"

Poseidon's Law

("The Bonds of Discipline"—*Traffics and Discoveries*)

When the robust and Brass-bound Man commissioned first for sea
His fragile raft, Poseidon laughed, and "Mariner," said he,
"Behold, a Law immutable I lay on thee and thine,
That never shall ye act or tell a falsehood at my shrine.

"Let Zeus adjudge your landward kin whose votive meal and salt
At easy-cheated altars win oblivion for the fault,
But you the unhoodwinked wave shall test—the immediate gulf
   condemn—
Except ye owe the Fates a jest, be slow to jest with them.

"Ye shall not clear by Greekly speech, nor cozen from your path
The twinkling shoal, the leeward beach, or Hadria's white-lipped wrath;
Nor tempt with painted cloth for wood my fraud-avenging hosts;
Nor make at all, or all make good, your bulwarks and your boasts.

"Now and henceforward serve unshod, through wet and wakeful shifts,
A present and oppressive God, but take, to aid, my gift—
The wide and windward-opening eye, the large and lavish hand,
The soul that cannot tell a lie—except upon the land!"

In dromond and in catafract—wet, wakeful, windward-eyed—
He kept Poseidon's Law intact (his ship and freight beside),
But, once discharged the dromond's hold, the bireme beached once more,
Splendaciously mendacious rolled the Brass-bound Man ashore . . .

The thranite now and thalamite are pressures low and high,
And where three hundred blades bit white the twin-propellers ply.
The God that hailed, the keel that sailed, are changed beyond recall,
But the robust and Brass-bound Man he is not changed at all!

From Punt returned, from Phormio's Fleet, from Javan and Gadire,
He strongly occupies the seat about the tavern fire,
And, moist with much Falernian or smoked Massilian juice,
Revenges there the Brass-bound Man his long-enforcèd truce!

The Lowestoft Boat

(East Coast Patrols of the War)

1914-18

In Lowestoft a boat was laid,
    Mark well what I do say!
And she was built for the herring-trade,
    But she has gone a-rovin', a-rovin', a-rovin',
    The Lord knows where!

They gave her Government coal to burn,
And a Q.F. gun at bow and stern,
And sent her out a-rovin', etc.

Her skipper was mate of a bucko ship
Which always killed one man per trip,
So he is used to rovin', etc.

Her mate was skipper of a chapel in Wales.
And so he fights in topper and tails—
Religi-ous tho' rovin', etc.

Her engineer is fifty-eight,
So *he's* prepared to meet his fate.
Which ain't unlikely rovin', etc.

Her leading-stoker's seventeen,
So he don't know what the Judgments mean,
Unless he cops 'em rovin', etc.

Her cook was chef in the Lost Dog's home,
    Mark well what I do say!
And I'm sorry for Fritz when they all come
    A-rovin', a-rovin', a-rovin', and a-rovin',
    Round the North Sea rovin',
    The Lord knows where!

A Truthful Song

("The Wrong Thing"—*Rewards and Fairies*)

THE BRICKLAYER:
I tell this tale, which is strictly true,
Just by way of convincing you
How very little, since things were made,
Things have altered in the building trade.

A year ago, come the middle of March
We was building flats near the Marble Arch,
When a thin young man with coal-black hair
Came up to watch us working there.

Now there wasn't a trick in brick or stone
Which this young man hadn't seen or known;
Nor there wasn't a tool from trowel to maul
But this young man could use 'em all!

Then up and spoke the plumbyers bold,
Which was laying the pipes for the hot and cold:
"Since you with us have made so free,
Will you kindly say what your name might be?"

The young man kindly answered them:
"It might be Lot or Methusalem,
Or it might be Moses (a man I hate),
Whereas it is Pharaoh surnamed the Great.

"Your glazing is new and your plumbing's strange,
But otherwise I perceive no change;
And in less than a month if you do as I bid
I'd learn you to build me a Pyramid!"

THE SAILOR:

I tell this tale, which is stricter true,
Just by way of convincing you
How very little, since things was made,
Things have altered in the shipwright's trade.

In Blackwall Basin yesterday
A China barque re-fitting lay,
When a fat old man with snow-white hair
Came up to watch us working there.

Now there wasn't a knot which the riggers knew
But the old man made it—and better too;
Nor there wasn't a sheet, or a lift, or a brace,
But the old man knew its lead and place.

Then up and spoke the caulkyers bold,
Which was packing the pump in the afterhold:
"Since you with us have made so free,
Will you kindly tell what your name might be?"

The old man kindly answered them:
"It might be Japheth, it might be Shem,
Or it might be Ham (though his skin was dark),
Whereas it is Noah, commanding the Ark.

"Your wheel is new and your pumps are strange,
But otherwise I perceive no change;
And in less than a week, if she did not ground,
I'd sail this hooker the wide world round!"

BOTH:

We tell these tales, which are strictest true,
Just by the way of convincing you
How very little, since things was made,
Anything alters in any one's trade!

A Smuggler's Song

("Hal o' the Draft"—*Puck of Pook's Hill*)

If you wake at midnight, and hear a horse's feet,
Don't go drawing back the blind, or looking in the street,
Them that asks no questions isn't told a lie.
Watch the wall, my darling, while the Gentlemen go by!
  Five and twenty ponies
  Trotting through the dark—

Brandy for the Parson,
'Baccy for the Clerk;
Laces for a lady, letters for a spy,
And watch the wall, my darling, while the Gentlemen go by!

Running round the woodlump if you chance to find
Little barrels, roped and tarred, all full of brandy-wine,
Don't you shout to come and look, nor use 'em for your play.
Put the brishwood back again—and they'll be gone next day!

If you see the stable-door setting open wide;
If you see a tired horse lying down inside;
If your mother mends a coat cut about and tore;
If the lining's wet and warm—don't you ask no more!

If you meet King George's men, dressed in blue and red,
You be careful what you say, and mindful what is said.
If they call you "pretty maid," and chuck you 'neath the chin,
Don't you tell where no one is, nor yet where no one's been!

Knocks and footsteps round the house—whistles after dark—
You've no call for running out till the house-dogs bark.
Trusty's here, and *Pincher's* here, and see how dumb they lie—
They don't fret to follow when the Gentlemen go by!

If you do as you've been told, likely there's a chance,
You'll be give a dainty doll, all the way from France,
With a cap of Valenciennes, and a velvet hood—
A present from the Gentlemen, along o' being good!
    Five and twenty ponies
    Trotting through the dark—
    Brandy for the Parson,
    'Baccy for the Clerk.
Them that asks no questions isn't told a lie—
Watch the wall, my darling, while the Gentlemen go by!

King Henry VII. And The Shipwrights

(A.D. 1487)

("The Wrong Thing"—*Rewards and Fairies*)

Harry, our King in England, from London town is gone,
And comen to Hamull on the Hoke in the Countie of Suthampton.
For there lay the *Mary of the Tower*, his ship of war so strong,
And he would discover, certaynely, if his shipwrights did him wrong.

He told none of his setting forth, nor yet where he would go,
(But only my Lord of Arundel) and meanly did he show,
In an old jerkin and patched hose that no man might him mark.
With his frieze hood and cloak above, he looked like any clerk.

He was at Hamull on the Hoke about the hour of the tide,
And saw the *Mary* haled into the dock, the winter to abide,
With all her tackle and habiliments which are the King his own;
But then ran on his false shipwrights and stripped her to the bone.

They heaved the main-mast overboard, that was of a trusty tree,
And they wrote down it was spent and lost by force of weather at sea.
But they sawen it into planks and strakes as far as it might go,
To maken beds for their own wives and little children also.

There was a knave called Slingawai, he crope beneath the deck,
Crying: "Good felawes, come and see! The ship is nigh a wreck!
For the storm that took our tall main-mast, it blew so fierce and fell,
Alack! it hath taken the kettles and pans, and this brass pott as well!"

With that he set the pott on his head and hied him up the hatch,
While all the shipwrights ran below to find what they might snatch;
All except Bob Brygandyne and he was a yeoman good.
He caught Slingawai round the waist and threw him on to the mud.

"I have taken plank and rope and nail, without the King his leave,
After the custom of Portesmouth, but I will not suffer a thief.
Nay, never lift up thy hand at me—there's no clean hands in the trade.
Steal in measure," quo' Brygandyne. "There's measure in all things
made!"

"Gramercy, yeoman!" said our King. "Thy counsel liketh me."
And he pulled a whistle out of his neck and whistled whistles three.
Then came my Lord of Arundel pricking across the down,
And behind him the Mayor and Burgesses of Merry Suthampton town.

They drew the naughty shipwrights up, with the kettles in their hands,
And bound them round the forecastle to wait the King's commands.
But "Sith ye have made your beds," said the King, "ye needs must lie
thereon.
For the sake of your wives and little ones—felawes, get you gone!"

When they had beaten Slingawai, out of his own lips
Our King appointed Brygandyne to be Clerk of all his ships.
"Nay, never lift up thy hands to me—there's no clean hands in the trade.
But steal in measure," said Harry our King. "There's measure in all
things made!"

God speed the Mary of the Tower, *the* Sovereign, *and* Grace Dieu,
The Sweepstakes *and the* Mary Fortune, *and the* Henry of Bristol *too!*
All tall ships that sail on the sea, or in our harbours stand,
That they may keep measure with Harry our King and peace in Engeland!

The Wet Litany

("Their Lawful Occasions"—*Traffics and Discoveries*)

When the waters' countenance
Blurs 'twixt glance and second glance;
When our tattered smokes forerun
Ashen 'neath a silvered sun;
When the curtain of the haze
Shuts upon our helpless ways—
   Hear the Channel Fleet at sea:
   Libera nos Domine!

When the engines' bated pulse
Scarcely thrills the nosing hulls;
When the wash along the side
Sounds, a-sudden, magnified;
When the intolerable blast
Marks each blindfold minute passed;

When the fog-buoy's squattering flight
Guides us through the haggard night;
When the warning bugle blows;
When the lettered doorways close;
When our brittle townships press,
Impotent, on emptiness;

When the unseen leadsmen lean
Questioning a deep unseen;
When their lessened count they tell
To a bridge invisible;
When the hid and perilous
Cliffs return our cry to us;

When the treble thickness spread
Swallows up our next-ahead;
When her siren's frightened whine
Shows her sheering out of line;
When—her passage undiscerned—
We must turn where she has turned,
   Hear the Channel Fleet at sea:
   Libera nos Domine!

The Ballad Of Minepit Shaw

("The Tree of Justice"—*Rewards and Fairies*)

About the time that taverns shut
  And men can buy no beer,
Two lads went up to the keepers' hut
  To steal Lord Pelham's deer.

Night and the liquor was in their heads—
  They laughed and talked no bounds,
Till they waked the keepers on their beds
  And the keepers loosed the hounds.

They had killed a hart, they had killed a hind,
  Ready to carry away,
When they heard a whimper down the wind
  And they heard a bloodhound bay.

They took and ran across the fern,
  Their crossbows in their hand,
Till they met a man with a green lantern
  That called and bade 'em stand.

"What are ye doing, O Flesh and Blood,
And what's your foolish will,
That you must break into Minepit Wood
  And wake the Folk of the Hill?"

"Oh, we've broke into Lord Pelham's park,
  And killed Lord Pelham's deer,
And if ever you heard a little dog bark
  You'll know why we come here.

"We ask you let us go our way,
  As fast as we can flee,
For if ever you heard a bloodhound bay
  You'll know how pressed we be."

"Oh, lay your crossbows on the bank
  And drop the knives from your hand,
And though the hounds be at your flank
  I'll save you where you stand!"

They laid their crossbows on the bank,
  They threw their knives in the wood,
And the ground before them opened and sank
  And saved 'em where they stood.

"Oh, what's the roaring in our ears
    That strikes us well-nigh dumb?"
"Oh, that is just how things appear
    According as they come."

"What are the stars before our eyes
    That strike us well-nigh blind?"
"Oh, that is just how things arise
    According as you find."

"And why's our bed so hard to the bones
    Excepting where it's cold?"
"Oh, that's because it is precious stones
    Excepting where 'tis gold.

"Think it over as you stand,
    For I tell you without fail,
If you haven't got into Fairyland
    You're not in Lewes Gaol."

All night long they thought of it,
    And, come the dawn, they saw
They'd tumbled into a great old pit,
    At the bottom of Minepit Shaw.

And the keeper's hound had followed 'em close;
    And broke her neck in the fall;
So they picked up their knives and their crossbows
    And buried the dog.   That's all.

But whether the man was a poacher too
    Or a Pharisee[1] so bold—
I reckon there's more things told than are true,
    And more things true than are told!

Heriot's Ford

(Enlarged from "The Light that Failed")

What's that that hirples at my side?"
The foe that you must fight, my lord.
"That rides as fast as I can ride?"
The shadow of your might, my lord.

[1] A fairy.

"Then wheel my horse against the foe!"
He's down and overpast, my lord.
You war against the sunset-glow,
The judgment follows fast, my lord!

"Oh, who will stay the sun's descent?
King Joshua he is dead, my lord.
"I need an hour to repent!"
'Tis what our sister said, my lord.

"Oh, do not slay me in my sins!"
You're safe awhile with us, my lord.
"Nay, kill me ere my fear begins!"
We would not serve you thus, my lord.

"Where is the doom that I must face?"
Three little leagues away, my lord.
"Then mend the horses' laggard pace!"
We need them for next day, my lord.

"Next day—next day!   Unloose my cords!"
Our sister needed none, my lord.
You had no mind to face our swords,
And—where can cowards run, my lord?

You would not kill the soul alive?"
'Twas thus our sister cried, my lord.
"I dare not die with none to shrive."
But so our sister died, my lord.

"Then wipe the sweat from brow and cheek."
It runnels forth afresh, my lord.
"Uphold me—for the flesh is weak."
You've finished with the Flesh, my lord!

Frankie's Trade

("Simple Simon"—*Rewards and Fairies*)

Old Horn to All Atlantic said:
(*A-hay O!   To me O!*)
"Now where did Frankie learn his trade?
For he ran me down with a three-reef mains'l."
    (*All round the Horn!*)

Atlantic answered:—"Not from me!
You'd better ask the cold North Sea,
For he ran me down under all plain canvas."
    (*All round the Horn!*)

The North Sea answered:—"He's my man,
For he came to me when he began—
Frankie Drake in an open coaster.
   (*All round the Sands!*)

"I caught him young and I used him sore,
So you never shall startle Frankie more,
Without capsizing Earth and her waters.
   (*All round the Sands!*)

"I did not favour him at all.
I made him pull and I made him haul—
And stand his trick with the common sailors.
   (*All round the Sands!*)

"I froze him stiff and I fogged him blind,
And kicked him home with his road to find
By what he could see in a three-day snow-storm.
   (*All round the Sands!*)

"I learned him his trade o' winter nights,
'Twixt Mardyk Fort and Dunkirk lights,
On a five-knot tide with the forts a-firing.
   (*All round the Sands!*)

"Before his beard began to shoot,
I showed him the length of the Spaniard's foot—
And I reckon he clapped the boot on it later.
   (*All round the Sands!*)

"If there's a risk which you can make,
That's worse than he was used to take
Nigh every week in the way of his business;
   (*All round the Sands!*)

"If there's a trick that you can try,
Which he hasn't met in time gone by,
Not once or twice, but ten times over;
   (*All round the Sands!*)

"If you can teach him aught that's new,
   (*A-hay O! To me O!*)
I'll give you Bruges and Niewport too,
And the ten tall churches that stand between 'em!"
   Storm along, my gallant Captains!
   (*All round the Horn!*)

The Juggler's Song

(Enlarged from "Kim")

When the drums begin to beat
Down the street,
When the poles are fetched and guyed,
When the tight-rope's stretched and tied,
When the dance-girls make salaam,
When the snake-bag wakes alarm,
When the pipes set up their drone,
When the sharp-edged knives are thrown,
When the red-hot coals are shown,
To be swallowed by-and-by—
Arré Brethren, here come I!

Stripped to loin-cloth in the sun,
Search me well and watch me close!
Tell me how my tricks are done—
Tell me how the mango grows!

Give a man who is not made
To his trade
Swords to fling and catch again,
Coins to ring and snatch again,
Men to harm and cure again,
Snakes to charm and lure again—
He'll be hurt by his own blade,
By his serpents disobeyed,
By his clumsiness bewrayed,
By the people laughed to scorn—
So 'tis not with juggler born!

Pinch of dust or withered flower,
Chance-flung nut or borrowed staff,
Serve his need and shore his power,
Bind the spell or loose the laugh.

The North Sea Patrol

1914-18

(Sea Warfare)

Where the East wind is brewed fresh and fresh every morning,
   And the balmy night-breezes blow straight from the Pole,
I heard a Destroyer sing: "What an enjoya-
   ble life does one lead on the North Sea Patrol!

"To blow things to bits is our business (and Fritz's)
    Which means there are mine-fields wherever you stroll.
Unless you've particular wish to die quick, you'll a-
    void steering close to the North Sea Patrol.

"We warn from disaster the mercantile master
    Who takes in high Dudgeon our life-saving role,
For every one's grousing at Docking and Dowsing[1]
    The marks and the lights on the North Sea Patrol."

[*Twelve verses omitted.*]

So swept but surviving, half drowned but still driving,
    I watched her head out through the swell of the shoal,
And I heard her propellers roar: "Write to poor fellers
    Who run such a Hell as the North Sea Patrol!"

Thorkild's Song

("The Knights of the Joyous Venture"—*Puck of Pook's Hill*)

There's no wind along these seas,
    Out oars for Stavanger!
Forward all for Stavanger!
So we must wake the white-ash breeze,
    Let fall for Stavanger!
A long pull for Stavanger!

Oh, hear the benches creak and strain!
(A long pull for Stavanger!)
She thinks she smells the Northland rain!
(A long pull for Stavanger!)

She thinks she smells the Northland snow,
And she's glad as we to go.

She thinks she smells the Northland rime,
And the dear dark nights of winter-time.

She wants to be at her own home pier,
To shift her sails and standing gear.

She wants to be in her winter-shed,
To strip herself and go to bed.

Her very bolts are sick for shore,
And we—we want it ten times more!

So all you Gods that love brave men,
Send us a three-reef gale again!

[1]Shoals and lights on the East Coast.

Send us a gale, and watch us come,
With close-cropped canvas slashing home!

But—there's no wind on all these seas,
A long pull for Stavanger!
So we must wake the white-ash breeze.
A long pull for Stavanger!

"Angutivaun Taina"

Song of the Returning Hunter (Esquimaux)

("Quiquern"—*The Second Jungle Book*)

Our gloves are stiff with the frozen blood,
  Our furs with the drifted snow,
As we come in with seal—the seal!
  In from the edge of the floe.

Au jana! Aua! Oha! Haq!
  And the yelping dog-teams go;
And the long whips crack, and the men come back,
  Back from the edge of the floe!

We tracked our seal to his secret place,
  We heard him scratch below,
We made our mark, and we watched beside,
  Out on the edge of the floe.

We raised our lance when he rose to breathe,
  We drove it downward—so!
And we played him thus, and we killed him thus,
  Out on the edge of the floe.

Out gloves are glued with the frozen blood,
  Our eyes with the drifting snow;
But we come back to our wives again,
  Back from the edge of the floe!

Au jana! Aua! Oha! Haq!
  And the loaded dog-teams go;
And the wives can hear their men came back,
  Back from the edge of the floe!

Hunting-Song Of The Seeonee Pack

("Mowgli's Brothers"—*The Jungle Book*)

As the dawn was breaking the Sambhur belled—
Once, twice and again!
And a doe leaped up, and a doe leaped up
From the pond in the wood where the wild deer sup.
This I, scouting alone, beheld,
    Once, twice and again!

As the dawn was breaking the Sambhur belled—
    Once, twice and again!
And a wolf stole back, and a wolf stole back
To carry the word to the waiting pack,
And we sought and we found and we bayed on his track
    Once, twice and again!

As the dawn was breaking the Wolf-Pack yelled
    Once, twice and again!
Feet in the jungle that leave no mark!
Eyes that can see in the dark—the dark!
Tongue—give tongue to it! Hark! O Hark!
    Once, twice and again!

Song Of The Men's Side

(Neolithic)

("The Knife and the Naked Chalk"—*Rewards and Fairies*)

Once we feared The Beast—when he followed us we ran,
    Ran very fast though we knew
It was not right that The Beast should master Man;
    But what could we Flint-workers do?
The Beast only grinned at our spears round his ears
    Grinned at the hammers that we made;
But now we will hunt him for the life with the Knife—
    And this is the Buyer of the Blade!

> *Room for his shadow on the grass—let it pass!*
>   *To left and right—stand clear!*
> *This is the Buyer of the Blade—be afraid!*
>   *This is the great god Tyr!*

Tyr thought hard till he hammered out a plan,
  For he knew it was not right
(And it *is* not right) that The Beast should master Man;
  So he went to the Children of the Night.
He begged a Magic Knife of their make for our sake.
  When he begged for the Knife they said:
"The price of the Knife you would buy is an eye!"
  And that was the price he paid.
Tell it to the Barrows of the Dead—run ahead!
  Shout it so the Women's Side can hear!
This is the Buyer of the Blade—be afraid!
  This is the great god Tyr!

Our women and our little ones may walk on the Chalk,
  As far as we can see them and beyond.
We shall not be anxious for our sheep when we keep
  Tally at the shearing-pond.
We can eat with both our elbows on our knees, if we please,
  We can sleep after meals in the sun,
For Shepherd-of-the-Twilight is dismayed at the Blade,
  Feet-in-the-Night have run!
Dog-without-a-Master goes away (Hai, Tyr, aie!),
  Devil-in-the-Dusk has run!

Then:
  Room for his shadow on the grass—let it pass!
    To left and right—stand clear!
  This is the Buyer of the Blade—be afraid!
    This is the great god Tyr!

The Runes On Weland's Sword

1906

("Old Men at Pevensey"—*Puck of Pook's Hill*)

A Smith makes me
To betray my Man
In my first fight.

To gather Gold
At the world's end
I am sent.

The Gold I gather
Comes into England
Out of the deep Water.

Like a shining Fish
Then it descends
Into deep Water.

It is not given
For goods or gear,
But for The Thing.

The Gold I gather
A king covets
For an ill use.

The Gold I gather
Is drawn up
Out of deep Water.

Like shining Fish
Then it descends
Into deep Water.

It is not given
For goods or gear,
But for The Thing.

Darzee's Chaunt

Sung in honour of Rikki-tikki-tavi

(" 'Rikki-Tikki-Tavi' "—*The Jungle Book*)

Singer and tailor am I—
    Doubled the joys that I know—
    Proud of my lilt to the sky,
        Proud of the house that I sew—
Over and under, so weave I my music—so weave I the house that I sew.

Sing to your fledglings again,
        Mother, O lift up your head!
    Evil that plagued us is slain,
        Death in the garden lies dead.
Terror that hid in the roses is impotent—flung on the dung-hill and dead!

Who hath delivered us, who?
        Tell me his nest and his name.
    Rikki, the valiant, the true,
        Tikki, with eyeballs of flame,
Rik-tikki-tikki, the ivory-fangèd, the Hunter with eyeballs of flame.

Give him the Thanks of the Birds,
  Bowing with tail-feathers spread!
Praise him in nightingale-words—
  Nay, I will praise him instead.
Hear! I will sing you the praise of the bottle-tailed Rikki, with eyeballs of
  red!

(Here Rikki-tikki interrupted, and the rest of the song is lost.)

Song Of The Galley-Slaves

(" 'The Finest Story in the World' "—*Many Inventions*)

We pulled for you when the wind was against us and the sails were low.
  Will you never let us go?
We ate bread and onions when you took towns, or ran aboard quickly
  when you were beaten back by the foe.
The Captains walked up and down the deck in fair weather singing songs,
  but we were below.
We fainted with our chins on the oars and you did not see that we were
  idle, for we still swung to and fro.
  Will you never let us go?
The salt made the oar-handles like shark-skin; our knees were cut to the
  bone with salt-cracks; our hair was stuck to our foreheads; and our
  lips were cut to the gums, and you whipped us because we could not
  row.
  Will you never let us go?
But, in a little time, we shall run out of the port-holes as the water runs
  along the oar-blade, and though you tell the others to row after us
  you will never catch us till you catch the oar-thresh and tie up the
  winds in the belly of the sail.   Aho!
  Will you never let us go?

The Four Angels

("With the Night Mail"—*Actions and Reactions*)

As Adam lay a-dreaming beneath the Apple Tree
The Angel of the Earth came down, and offered Earth in fee;
    But Adam did not need it,
    Nor the plough he would not speed it,
  Singing:—"Earth and Water, Air and Fire,
    What more can mortal man desire?"
      (The Apple Tree's in bud.)

As Adam lay a-dreaming beneath the Apple Tree
The Angel of the Waters offered all the Seas in fee;
    But Adam would not take 'em,
    Nor the ships he wouldn't make 'em,
  Singing:—"Water, Earth and Air and Fire,
    What more can mortal man desire?"
      (The Apple Tree's in leaf.)

As Adam lay a-dreaming beneath the Apple Tree
The Angel of the Air he offered all the Air in fee;
    But Adam did not crave it,
    Nor the flight he wouldn't brave it,
  Singing:—"Air and Water, Earth and Fire,
    What more can mortal man desire?"
      (The Apple Tree's in bloom.)

As Adam lay a-dreaming beneath the Apple Tree
The Angel of the Fire rose up and not a word said he;
    But he wished a flame and made it,
    And in Adam's heart he laid it,
  Singing:—"Fire, Fire, burning Fire!
    Stand up and reach your heart's desire!"
      (The Apple Blossom's set.)

As Adam was a-working outside of Eden-Wall,
He used the Earth, he used the Seas, he used the Air and all;
    Till out of the black disaster
    He arose to be the master
      Of Earth and Water, Air and Fire,
      But never reached his heart's desire!
        (The Apple Tree's cut down!)

The Beginnings

1914-18

("Mary Postgate"—*A Diversity of Creatures*)

    It was not part of their blood,
      It came to them very late
    With long arrears to make good,
      When the English began to hate.

    They were not easily moved,
      They were icy-willing to wait
    Till every count should be proved,
      Ere the English began to hate.

Their voices were even and low,
　　Their eyes were level and straight.
There was neither sign nor show,
　　When the English began to hate.

It was not preached to the crowd,
　　It was not taught by the State.
No man spoke it aloud,
　　When the English began to hate.

It was not suddenly bred,
　　It will not swiftly abate,
Through the chill years ahead,
　　When Time shall count from the date
　　That the English began to hate.

The Prayer

(Kim)

My brother kneels, so saith Kabir,
To stone and brass in heathen wise,
But in my brother's voice I hear
My own unanswered agonies.
His God is as his fates assign,
His prayer is all the world's—and mine.

The Muse Among The Motors
1900 – 1930

Sepulchral

(FROM THE GREEK ANTHOLOGIES)

Swifter than aught 'neath the sun the car of Simonides moved him.
Two things he could not out-run—Death and a Woman who loved him.

Arterial

(EARLY CHINESE)

I

Frost upon small rain—the ebony-lacquered avenue
   Reflecting lamps as a pool shows goldfish.
The sight suddenly emptied out of the young man's eyes
   Entering upon it sideways.

II

In youth by hazard, I killed an old man.
   In age I maimed a little child.
Dead leaves under foot reproach not:
But the lop-sided cherry-branch—whenever the sun rises,
   How black a shadow!

Carmen Circulare

(Q. H. FLACCUS)

Dellius, that car which, night and day,
   Lightnings and thunder arm and scourge—
Tumultuous down the Appian Way—
   Be slow to urge.

Though reckless Lydia bid thee fly,
   And Telephus o'ertaking jeer,
Nay, sit and strongly occupy
   The lower gear.

They call, the road consenting, "Haste!"—
   Such as delight in dust collected—
Until arrives (I too have raced!)
   The unexpected.

What ox not doomed to die alone,
   Or inauspicious hound, may bring
Thee 'twixt two kisses to the throne
   Of Hades' King,

I cannot tell; the Furies send
   No warning ere their bolts arrive.
'Tis best to reach our chosen end
   Late but alive.

The Advertisement

(IN THE MANNER OF THE EARLIER ENGLISH)

Whether to wend through straight streets strictly,
Trimly by towns perfectly paved;
Or after office, as fitteth thy fancy,
Faring with friends far among fields;
There is none equal in action.
Sith she is silent, nimble, unnoisome,
Lordly of leather, gaudily gilded,
Burgeoning brightly in a brass bonnet,
Certain to steer well between wains.

The Justice's Tale

(CHAUCER)

With them there rode a lustie Engineere
Wel skilled to handel everich waie her geere,
Hee was soe wise ne man colde showe him naught
And out of Paris was hys learnynge brought.
Frontlings mid brazen wheeles and wandes he sat,
And on hys heade he bare an leathern hat.
Hee was soe certaine of his gouvernance,
That, by the Road, he tooke everie chaunce.
For simple people and for lordlings eke
He wolde not bate a del but onlie squeeke
Behinde their backés on an horné hie
Until they crope into a piggestie.
He was more wood than bull in chine-shoppe,
And yet for cowes and doggés wolde hee stop,
Not out of Marcie but for Preudence-sake—
Than hys dependaunce ever was hys brake.

The Consolations Of Memory

(*Circa* 1904)

(*Done out of Boethius by Geoffry Chaucer*)

Blessèd was our first age and morning-time. Then were no waies tarren, ne
no cars numberen, but each followed his owne playinge-busyness to go about
singly or by large interspaces, for to leden his viage after his luste and layen
under clene hedge. Jangling there was not, nor the over-taking wheele, and all
those now cruel clarions were full-hushed and full-still. Then nobile horses, lest
they should make the chariots moveable to run by cause of this new feare, we
did not press, and were apayed by sweete thankes of him that drave. There
was not cursings ne adventure of death blinded bankes betweene, but good-
fellowship of yoke-mates at ignorance equal, and a one pillar of dust covered
all exodus . . . But, see now how the blacke road hath strippen herself of hearte
and beauty where the dumbe lampe of Tartarus winketh red, etc.

The Four Points

(THOMAS TUSSER)

Ere stopping or turning, to put foorth a hande
Is a charm that thy daies may be long in the land.

Though seventy-times-seven thee Fortune befriend,
O'ertaking at corners is Death in the end.

Sith main-roads for side-roads care nothing, have care
Both to slow and to blow when thou enterest there.

Drink as thou canst hold it, but *after* is best;
For Drink with men's Driving makes Crowners to Quest.

To A Lady, Persuading Her To A Car

(BEN JONSON)

Love's fiery chariot, Delia, take
Which Vulcan wrought for Venus' sake.
Wings shall not waft thee, but a flame
Hot as my heart—as nobly tame:
Lit by a spark, less bright, more wise
Than linkèd lightnings of thine eyes!

Seated and ready to be drawn
Come not in muslins, lace or lawn,
But, for thy thrice imperial worth,
Take all the sables of the North,
With frozen diamonds belted on,
To face extreme Euroclydon!
Thus in our thund'ring toy we'll prove
Which is more blind, the Law or Love;
And may the jealous Gods prevent
Our fierce and uncontrolled descent!

The Progress Of The Spark

(XVIth Circuit)

(DONNE)

This spark now set, retarded, yet forbears
To hold her light however so he swears
That turns a metalled crank and, leather-cloked,
With some small hammers tappeth hither and yon;
Peering as when she showeth and when is gone;
For wait he must till the vext Power's evoked
That's one with the lightnings. Wait in the showers soaked;
Or by the road-side sunned. She'll not progress.
Poor soul, here taught how great things may be less
Be stayed, to file contacts doth himself address!

The Braggart

(MAT. PRIOR)

Petrolio, vaunting his Mercedes' power,
Vows she can cover eighty miles an hour.
I tried the car of old and know she can.
But dare he ever make her? Ask his man!

"When The Journey Was Intended To The City"

(MILTON)

When that with meat and drink they had fulfilled
Not temperately but like him conceived
In monstrous jest at Meudon, whose regale
Stands for exemplar of Gargantuan greed,
In his own name supreme, they issued forth
Beneath new firmaments and stars astray,
Circumvoluminant; nor had they felt
Neither the passage nor the sad effect
Of many cups partaken, till that frost
Wrought on them hideous, and their minds deceived.
Thus choosing from a progeny of roads,
That seemed but were not, one most reasonable,
Of purest moonlight fashioned on a wall,
Thither they urged their chariot whom that flint
Buttressed received, itself unscathed—not they.

To Motorists

(HERRICK)

Since ye distemper and defile
Sweet Herè by the measured mile
Nor aught on jocund highways heed
Except the evidence of speed;
And bear about your dreadful task
Faces beshrouded 'neath a mask;
Great goblin eyes and gluey hands
And souls enslaved to gears and bands;
Here shall no graver curse be said
Than, thou y'are quick, that ye are dead!

The Tour

(BYRON)

Thirteen as twelve my Murray always took—
  He was a publisher. The new Police
Have neater ways of bringing men to book,
  So Juan found himself before J.P.'s

Accused of storming through that placid nook
  At practically any place you please.
The Dogberry, and the Waterbury, made
It fifty mile—five pounds. And Juan paid!

The Idiot Boy

(WORDSWORTH)

He wandered down the mountain grade
  Beyond the speed assigned—
A youth whom Justice often stayed
  And generally fined.

He went alone, that none might know
  If he could drive or steer.
Now he is in the ditch, and Oh!
  The differential gear!

The Landau

(PRAED)

There was a landau deep and wide,
  Cushioned for Sleep's own self to sit on—
The glory of the country-side
  From Tanner's End to Marlow Ditton.
John of the broad and brandied cheek
  (Well I recall its eau-de-vie hues!)
Drove staid Sir Ralph five days a week
  At speeds which we considered Jehu's ...

But now poor John sleeps very sound,
  And neither hears nor smells the fuss

Of the young Squires nine-hundred-pound—
   Er—*Mors communis omnibus.*
And I who in my daily stroll
   Observe the reckless chauffeur crowd her,
Laudator temporis, extol
   The times before the Act allowed her.

Contradictions

(LONGFELLOW)

The drowsy carrier sways
   To the drowsy horses' tramp.
His axles winnow the sprays
Of the hedge where the rabbit plays
   In the light of his single lamp.

He hears a roar behind,
   A howl, a hoot, and a yell,
A headlight strikes him blind
And a stench o'erpowers the wind
   Like a blast from the mouth of Hell.

He mends his swingle-bar,
   And loud his curses ring;
But a mother watching afar
Hears the hum of the doctor's car
   Like the beat of an angel's wing!

So, to the poet's mood,
   Motor or carrier's van,
Properly understood,
Are neither evil nor good—
   Ormuzd nor Ahriman!

Fastness

(TENNYSON)

This is the end whereto men toiled
   Before thy coachman guessed his fate,—
   How thou shouldst leave thy 'scutcheoned gate
On that new wheel which is the oiled—

To see the England Shakespeare saw
   (Oh, Earth, 'tis long since Shallow died!
   Yet by yon farrowed sow may hide
Some blue deep minion of the Law)—

To range from Ashby-de-la-Zouch
   By Lyonnesse to Locksley Hall,
   Or haply, nearer home, appal
Thy father's sister's staid barouche.

The Beginner

(After he has extemporising on an instrument not of his own invention)

(BROWNING)

Lo! what is this that I make—sudden, supreme, unrehearsed—
  This that my clutch in the crowd pressed at a venture has raised?
Forward and onward I sprang when I thought (as I ought) I reversed,
  And a cab like a martagon opes and I sit in the wreckage dazed.
And someone is taking my name, and the driver is rending the air.
  With cries for my blood and my gold, and a snickering newsboy brings
My cap, wheel-pashed from the kerb. I must run her home for repair,
  Where she leers with her bonnet awry—flat on the nether springs!

Lady Geraldine's Hardship

(E. B. BROWNING)

I turned—Heaven knows we women turn too much
To broken reeds, mistaken so for pine
That shame forbids confession—a handle I turned
(The wrong one, said the agent afterwards)
And so flung across your English street
Through the shrill-tinkling glass of the shop-front—paused,
Artemis mazed 'mid gauds to catch a man,
And piteous baby-caps and christening-gowns,
The worse for being worn on the radiator.

My cousin Romney judged me from the bench:
Propounding one sleek forty-shillinged law
That takes no count of the Woman's oversoul.
I should have entered, purred he, by the door—

The man's retort—the open obvious door—
And since I chose not, he—not he—could change
The man's rule, not the Woman's, for the case.
Ten pounds or seven days . . . Just that . . . I paid!

The Bother

(CLOUGH)

Hastily Adam our driver swallowed a curse in the darkness—
Petrol nigh at end and something wrong with a sprocket
Made him speer for the nearest town, when lo! at the cross-ways
Four blank letterless arms the virginal signpost extended.
"Look!" thundered Hugh the Radical. "This is the England we boast of—
Bland, white-bellied, obese, but utterly useless for business.
They are repainting the signs and have left the job in the middle.
They are repainting the signs and traffic may stop till they've done it,
Which is to say till the son-of-a-gun of a local contractor,
Having laboriously wiped out every name for
Probably thirty miles round, be minded to finish his labour!
Had not the fool the sense to paint out and paint in together?"

Thus, not seeing his speech belied his Radical Gospel
(Which is to paint out the earth and then write "Damn" on the shutter),
Hugh embroidered the theme imperially and stretched it
From some borough in Wales through our Australian possessions,
Making himself, reformer-wise, a bit of a nuisance
Till, with the help, we cast him out on the landscape.

The Dying Chauffeur

(ADAM LINDSAY GORDON)

Wheel me gently to the garage, since my car and I must part—
     No more for me the record and the run.
That cursèd left-hand cylinder the doctors call my heart
     Is pinking past redemption—I am done!
They'll never strike a mixture that'll help me pull my load.
     My gears are stripped—I cannot set my brakes.
I am entered for the finals down the timeless untimed Road
     To the Maker of the makers of all makes!

The Inventor

(R. W. EMERSON)

Time and space decreed his lot,
    But little Man was quick to note:
When Time and Space said Man might not,
    Bravely he answered, "Nay! I mote."

I looked on old New England.
    Time and Space stood fast.
Men built altars to Distance
    At every mile they passed.

Yet sleek with oil, a Force was hid
Making mock of all they did,
Ready at the appointed hour
    To yield up to Prometheus
The secular and well-drilled Power
    The Gods secreted thus.

And over high Wantastiquet
    Emulous my lightning ran,
Unregarded but afret,
    To fall in with my plan.

I beheld two ministries,
    One of air and one of earth—
At a thought I married these,
    And my New Age came to birth!

For rarely my purpose errs
    Though oft it seems to pause,
And rods and cylinders
    Obey my planet's laws.

Oil I drew from the well,
    And Franklin's spark from its blue;
Time and Distance fell,
    And Man went forth anew.

On the prairie and in the street
    So long as my chariots roll
I bind wings to Adam's feet,
    And, presently, to his soul!

The Ballad Of The Cars

(Wardour Street Border Ballad)

"Now this is the price of a stirrup-cup,"
   The kneeling doctor said.
And syne he bade them take him up,
   For he saw that the man was dead.

They took him up, and they laid him down
   (And, oh, he did not stir),
And they had him into the nearest town
   To wait the Coroner.

They drew the dead-cloth over the face,
   They closed the doors upon,
And the cars that were parked in the market-place
   Made talk of it anon.

Then up and spake a Daimler wide,
   That carries the slatted tank:—
"'Tis we must purge the country-side
   And no man will us thank.

"For while they pray at Holy Kirk
   That souls should turn from sin,
We cock our bonnets to the work,
   And gather the drunken in.—

"And if we spare them for the nonce,—
   Or their comrades jack them free,—
They learn more under our dumb-irons
   Than they learned at their mother's knee."

Then up and spake an Armstrong bold,
   And Siddeley was his name:—
"I saw a man lie stark and cold
   By Grantham as I came.

"There was a blind turn by a brook,
   A guard-rail and a fall:
But the drunken loon that overtook
   He got no hurt at all!

"I ha' trodden the wet road and the dry—
   But and the shady lane;
And why the guiltless soul should die,
   Good reason find I nane."

Then up and spake the Babe Austin—
   Had barely room for two—
"'Tis time and place that make the sin,
   And not the deed they do.

"For when a man drives with his dear,
   I ha' seen it come to pass
That an arm too close or a lip too near
   Has killed both lad and lass.

"There was a car at eventide
   And a sidelings kiss to steal—
The God knows how the couple died,
   But I mind the inquest weel.

"I have trodden the black tar and the heath—
   But and the cobble-stone;
And why the young go to their death,
   Good reason find I none."

Then spake a Morris from Oxenford,
   ('Was kin to a Cowley Friar):—
"How shall we judge the ways of the Lord
   That are but steel and fire?

"Between the oil-pits under earth
   And the levin-spark from the skies,
We but adventure and go forth
   As our man shall devise:

"And if he have drunken a hoop too deep,
   No kinship can us move
To draw him home in his market-sleep
   Or spare his waiting love.

"There is never a lane in all England
   Where a mellow man can go,
But he must look on either hand
   And back and front also.

"But he must busk him every tide,
   At prick of thorn, to leap
Either to hide in ditch beside
   Or in the bankès steep.

"And whether he walk in drink or muse,
   Or for his love be bound,
We have no wit to mark and chuse,
   But needs must slay or wound."

They drew the dead-cloth from its face.
 The Crowner looked thereon;
And the cars that were parked in the market-place
 Went all their ways anon.

A Child's Garden

(R. L.STEPHENSON)

Now there is nothing wrong with me
Except—I think it's called T.B.
And that is why I have to lay
Out in the garden all the day.

Our garden is not very wide,
And cars go by on either side,
And make an angry-hooty noise
That rather startles little boys.

But worst of all is when they take
Me out in cars that growl and shake,
With charabancs so dreadful-near
I have to shut my eyes for fear.

But when I'm on my back again,
I watch the Croydon aeroplane
That flies across to France, and sings
Like hitting thick piano-strings.

When I am strong enough to do
The things I'm truly wishful to,
I'll never use a car or train
But always have an aeroplane;

And just go zooming round and round,
And frighten Nursey with the sound,
And see the angel-side of clouds,
And spit on all those motor-crowds!

The Moral

(AUTHOR UNKNOWN)

You mustn't groom an Arab with a file.
  You hadn't ought to tension-spring a mule.
You couldn't push a brumby fifty mile
  And drop him in a boiler-shed to cool.
I'll sling you through six counties in a day.
  I'll hike you up a grade of one in ten.
I am Duty, Law and Order under way,
  I'm the Mentor of banana-fingered men!
I will make you know your left hand from your right.
  I will teach you not to drink about your biz.
I'm the only temperance advocate in sight!
  I am all the Education Act there is!

The Marred Drives of Windsor

PREFACE BY SAMUEL JOHNSON

*It is to be observed of this play that, though its plan is irregular, it has been made
instrumental to the production of many discriminate characters who deliver themselves
with candour and propriety, as they approach towards, or recede from, the operation of
Justice.   The juxtaposition of Hamlet and Falstaff may be questioned by the learned
or the delicate, but the conjectural critic of an author neither systematic nor consequential
can affirm that those same forces of natural genius, which expatiate in splendour and
passion, demand for their refreshment and sanity an abruptness of release and a lawlessness
of invention, proportioned to precedent constrictions.   He only who hath never toiled in
the anfractuous mines of Philosophy or Letters, nor subdued himself to the ignoble needs
of the Stage, will dispute the proposition.*

*There is a tradition that this play was composed after a drinking bout.   I would
prefer to credit that it owed its birth to some such concatenation of circumstances as I
have adumbrated.   The more so since, amid much that is ill-considered, or even depraved,
our author has assigned to the crafty and careless Falstaff an awful, if fleeting, visitation
of self-knowledge.   Let us now be told no more of the illegitimacy of this play.*

ACT I

Argument.   FALSTAFF, NYM, POINS, BARDOLPH *and* FLUELLEN *having accompanied*
PRINCE HENRY *in a motor drive through the city of London, their car breaks down, and*
FALSTAFF *returns to the Boar's Head Tavern in Eastcheap, where he is followed by the*
PRINCE *and* FLUELLEN.

Enter FALSTAFF, *Habited as a motorist*

Here's all at an end between us, or I'll never taste sack again. Prince or no Prince, I'll not ride with him to Coventry on the hinder parts of a carbonadoed stink, not though he call her all the car in Christendom.   Sack!   Sack!   Sack!

HOSTESS.   I spied her out of the lattice.   A' fizzled and a' groaned and a' shook from the bones out, Sir John, and a' ran on her own impulsidges back and forth o' Chepe, and I knew that there was but one way to it when I saw them fighting at the handles.   She died of a taking of pure wind on the heart, and they be about her body now with tongs. A marvellous searching perfume, Sir John!

FALSTAFF.   He hath called me ribs; he hath called me tallow.   There is no name in the extremer oiliness of comparisons which I have not borne meekly.   But to go masked at midday; to wrap my belly in an horse-hide cloak of ten thousand buttons till I looked like a mushroomed dunghill; to be smoked over burnt oils; to be enseamed, moreover, with intolerable greases; and thus scented, thus habited, thus vizarded, to leap out—for I leaped, mark you . . . Another cup of sack!   But there's vengeance for my case! These eyes have seen the Lord's Anointed on his knees in Chepe, foining with the key of Shrewsbury Castle, which Poins had bent to the very crook of Nym's theftuous elbow, to wake the dumb devil in the guts of her.   "Sweet Hal," said I, "are all horses sold out of England, that thou must kneel before the lieges to any petrol-piddling turnspit?" Then he, Poins, and Bardolph whose nose blanched with sheer envy of her bodywork, begged a shoulder of me to thrust her into some alley, the street being full of Ephesians of the old Church.   Whereat I . . .

Enter PRINCE *and* FLUELLEN

PRINCE.   Whereat thou, hearing her once or twice tenderly backfire——

FALSTAFF.   Heaven forgive thee, Hal!   She thundered and lightened a full half-hour, so that Jove Himself could not have bettered the instruction.   There's a pit beneath her now, which she blew out of thy father's highway the while I watched, where Sackerson could stand to six dogs.

PRINCE.   Hearing, I say, her gentle outcry against Poins' mishandling, thou didst flee up Chepe, calling upon the Sheriff's Watch for a red flag.

FALSTAFF.   I?   Call me Jack if I were not jack to each of her wheels in turn till I am stamped like a butter-pat with the imprint of her underpinnings.   I seek a red flag?

PRINCE.   Ay, roaring like a bull.

FALSTAFF.   Groans, Hal, groans such as Atlas heaved. But she overbore me at the last.   Why has thou left her?—Faugh, that a King's son should ever reek like a smutty-wicked lamp upon the wrong side of the morning!

PRINCE.   There was Bardolph in the buckbasket behind, nosing fearfully overside like a full-wattled turkey-poult from Norfolk.   There was Poins upon his belly beneath her, thrice steeped in pure plumbago, most despairfully clanking of chains like the devil in Brug's Hall window; and there were some four thousand 'prentices at her tail, crying, "What ho!" and that she bumped.   Methought 'twas no place for my father's son.

FALSTAFF.   Take any man's horses and hale her to bed! The laws of England are at thy commandment, that the Heir should not be made a common stink in the nostrils of the lieges.

PRINCE.   She'd not stir for all Apollo's team—not though Phaeton himself, drunk with nectar, lashed 'em stark mad.   Poor Phaeton!

HOSTESS.   A' was a King's son, was a' not, and came to's end by keeping of bad company?

FALSTAFF.   No more than a little horseflesh.   I tell thee, Hal, this England of ours has never looked up since the nobles fell to puking over oil-buckets by the side of leather-jerkined Walloons.

PRINCE.   He that drives me now is French as our princely cousin.

FALSTAFF.   Dumain? Hang him for a pestilent, poke-eyed, chicken-chopping, hump-backed, leather-hatted, muffle-gloved ape!   He hath been fined as often as he hath broken down; and that is at every tavern 'twixt here and York.   Dumain!   He's the most notorious widow-maker on the Windsor road.   His mother was a corn-cutter at Ypres, and his father a barber at Rouen, by which beastly conjunction he rightly draws every infirmity that damns him in his trade.   Item: He cuts corners niggardly and upon the wrong side.   Item: He'll look behind him after a likely wench in the hottest press of Holborn, though he skid into the kennel for it.   Item: He depends upon his brake to save him at need—a death-bed repentance, Hal, as hath been proved ere this, since grace is uncertain.   Item: He is too proud to clean the body of her, but leaves the care of that which should be the very cote-armour of his mechanic knighthood to an unheedful ostler.   Thus, at last, he comes to overlook even the oiling; and so it falls that she's where she must be, and not where thou wouldst have her.   Ay, laugh if thou wilt, Hal, but a round worthy knight need not fire himself through three baronies in eight hours to know the very essence of the petrol[1] that fumes him.   Dumain will one day clutch thee into Hell upon the first speed.

PRINCE.   Strange that clear knowledge should so long outlive mere nerve! I'll dub Dumain knight when I come to the throne, if he be hanged first for murder on the highway.   'Twill save the state a pension.

FALSTAFF.   So the lean vice goes ever before the solid virtue.   (*Confused noise without.*)   What riot's afoot now?

[1]Petard, which is almost synonymous.   HORNE TOOKE: First Folio; *private notes upon.*

FLUELLEN.   Riots, look you, by my vizaments, make one noise, but murders
another.   There's riots in Monmouth; but, by my vizaments, look you, there's
murders in Chepe.   Pabes and old 'oomen—they howl so tamnably.

FALSTAFF.   Rebellion rather!   Half London's calling on thy name, Hal, and
half on thy father's.   Well, if it be successful, forget not who was promised
the reversion of the Chief Justiceship.   Ha!   Unquestioned rebellion, if broken
crowns signify aught.

Enter HERALDS (*wounded*)

Most gracious lord, the car that bore thy state,
Too long neglected and adjudged acold,
Hath, without warning or advertisement,
Risen refreshed from her supposed stand
In unattended revolution.

PRINCE.   This it is to be a King's son!   That a pitiful twelve-horse touring-
car[1] cannot jar off her brakes but they must rehearse it me in damnable
heroics.   Your pleasure, gentlemen?

HERALDS.   The blood upon our boltered brow attests
'Twas Bardolph's art that waked her, whereat she
Skipped thunderously before our mazèd eyes,
Drew out o'er several lieges (all with God!),
Battered a house or so to laths, and now
Fumes on her side in Holborn.   Please you, come!

PRINCE.   Anon!   Seek each a physician according to his needs and
revenues.   I'll be with you anon.   (*To* FALSTAFF) The third in three
weeks!   These whoreson German clock-cases no sooner dint honest English
paving-stone than they incontinent lay their entrails on the street.   Five hundred
and seventy pounds!   I'll out and pawn the Duchy!

HERALDS.   The Lord Chief Justice waits thy princely will, In thy dread
father's Court at Westminster.

FALSTAFF.   A Star Chamber matter, Hal—a Star Chamber matter!   Glasses,
Doll!   We'll drink to his deliverance.

HERALDS.   You, too, Sir John, as party to these broils
And breakings-forth, in like attainder stand
For judgment: wherein fail not at your peril!

FALSTAFF.   I do remember now to have had some dealings with this same
Chief Justice.   An old feeble man, drawn abroad in a cart by horses.   We
must enlighten—enlighten him, Hal.   (*Exeunt.*)

---

[1] Touraine-cart (*conjectural*).—WARBURTON

Act II

Argument. Prince Henry, Poins, Fluellen, Nym, *and* Sir John Falstaff (Bardolph *having escaped*) *are charged on* Dogberry's *evidence, before the* Lord Chief Justice *at Westminster, with exceeding the speed-limit and leaving their car unattended in the street.* Portia *defends them.* Justice Shallow *has been accommodated with a seat on the Bench.*

Prince. Where's our red rear-lamp? Where's Bardolph?

Poins. Shining over Southwark if he be not puffed out by now. He ran when the watch came. The Chief Justice looks sourly. Is any appointed to speak for us, Hal?

Prince. Thy notorious innocence, my known virtue, and if these fail, Sir John's big belly. I have fed my father's exchequer here twice since Easter.

Ch. Justice. Intemperate, rash, and ill-advisèd men—
Yoke-fellows at unsavoury enterprise—
Harry, and you, Sir John, stand forth for sentence!

Fluellen. Put—put there is no indictments discharged upon us yet. T pronounce sentences, look you, pefore the indictments is discharged is ropperies and oppressions.

Nym. Ay, that's the humour of it. When they cry Budget we must cry mum.

Falstaff. Cram the Welsh flannel down his throat, or we are imprisoned after the fine. I know the Chief Justice is sick of me.

Shallow (*to* Ch. Justice). My lord, my lord, if you suffer yon fat knight to talk, he'll cozen the teeth out of your lordship's head, while his serving-man steals the steeped crust you'd mumble to. I lent him a thousands pounds, my lord.

Falstaff. I deny it not. For the which I promised thee advancement. Art thou not now visibly next the Chief Justice himself?

Shallow. Not on my merits, Sir John. I sit here simple of courtesy as visiting-justice. I'd do as much for my lord if he came to Gloucestershire, 'faith!

Falstaff. Shallow! Shallow! I say I gave thee occasion and opportunity to rise. Promotion is in thy hands. (*To* Ch. Justice) Have a care, my lord! He fingers his dagger already.

Shallow. My dagger? My ink-horn, la! I'll sit further off. I told you how he'd talk, my lord. But I'll sit further off. My dagger, 'faith!

Ch. Justice. Sir John! Sir John! The licence of inveterate humour overstretched rends like an outworn garment—with like shame to the

enduer.   Answer me roundly, what defence make you to the charge you have
run through Chepe at ten leagues the hour?

FALSTAFF.   Roundly, my lord, my shape—my evident shape.

CH. JUSTICE.   But 'tis so charged, and will be so witnessed.

DOGBERRY.   Yes, and by one that hath a stopped watch and everything
forsworn about him.   Write it down fifteen leagues, my lord.

PRINCE (*to* CH. JUSTICE).   We knights of the road have ever been fair quarry
for your knights of the post to bind to, but this passes endurance.   We left
our car, my lord, extinct and combust in the kennel, while we sought an engineer
to hoist her.   In which stay she would have continued but for the prying vulgar
who found on her some handle to their curiosity, which, doubtless, they
turned.   For in such a car as this——

CH. JUSTICE.   In such a car as this
The enfranchised 'prentices of London quash
Our harmless babes and necessary wives
At morning to the sound of Sabbath bells
Through panicked Huntingdon.

PORTIA.   In such a car as this,
Slides young Desire athwart the mountain-tops,
Drinking the airs that part him from his dear
'Twixt Berwick and Glamorgan.

CH. JUSTICE.   In such a car as this,
The lecherous Israelite to Brighthelmstone
Convoys his Jessica.

PORTIA.   In such a car as this,
The lean chirurgeon burns the midnight oil
Impetuous over England.   Where his lamp
Strikes pale the hedgerow, all the affrighted fays,
Their misty revels in the dew divulged,
Flee to the coney's burrow, or divide
His antre with the squirrel—whom that ministrant
Marks not, his eyes being bent to thrid the dark,
Indifferent beneath the morning star,
To the poor cot that summoned him, and the life—
Some hour-old, mother-naked life, scarce held
By the drowsy midwife but it yarks and squeaks
Batlike, and batlike, would to the void again.
This he forbids, and yet not he, whose art,
His car unaiding, else had ne'er o'erleaped
The largess of a county in an hour.

SHALLOW.   Neat, faith, la!   For how a brace of twins now, the far side
Cotsall, of a snowy night, my lord?

FALSTAFF.   A pregnant wit.   Which of thy misdeeds, Hal, hath raised this
angel to help us?   I'll ask Doll.

PRINCE.   Peace, dunghill, peace!   She was never of Doll's company.

PORTIA.   And I charge you, my lord, if ever need,
Extreme and urgent need hath, visited you,
Or, in the unprobeable decree of Time,
May visit and masterfully constrain, think well
Ere your abhorrence of new enginery
Seal up the avenues of mercy here!

CH. JUSTICE.   I sealed no avenues.   They sealed the King's
(Albeit it was called Northumberland)
With hellish engines drawn across the street
In an opposed and desperate barrier
Unto the lieges' progress.

PORTIA.   Not by their will, nor their intent, my lord!
It was a passing humour of the car—
Gusty incontinence which, overlooked,
As unregard oft cows pretension,
May well not chance again.

CH. JUSTICE.   But if it chance?

PORTIA.   If the deep-brooding vault of Heaven retain
Memory and record of miracle.
Vouchsafed, like this your prayed-for mercy, once,
And, in default of quail, rain from her gate
Heaven's sweetest choristers—then it may fall,
But not till then!

FLUELLEN.   Put—put—look you, she is telling the old shentlemans to wait
till the sky shall rain larks!   It is open contempts of Courts!

NYM.   Ay, there's humours in them all.   But I think the old man's humour
is sweeter.

CH. JUSTICE.   Yet, bating miracle, how if mercy breed
Not gratitude, but livelier insolence,
And through my softened verdict after years
Grow bold to break the law?   How if our England—
Loverly, temperate, the midmost close of peace—
Dissolve in smoke and oils along the green,
Till sickened memory conceive no minute

Unharried, unpollutable, unhooted?
If I loose these, what do I loose on England?

PORTIA. Too late! Too late! That babe is viable!
The hour we dread o'ertops us while we wonder,
Not asking sufferance, but imposing change,
Most multitudinously. Hark, it sings i' the wind!

ARIEL (*invisible*) *sings:*
   Where the car slips there slip I—
   In a sunbeam's path I lie!
   There I crouch while crowds do cry,
   After somersaults muddily!
   Where I lie, where I lie, shall I live now
   Under the bonnet that bangs on my brow?

FALSTAFF (*to* PRINCE). The Chief Justice is mazed by the fairies. He hath
great motions towards virtue. He'll let us go.

CH. JUSTICE. Ourselves have snuffed some savour of these changes,
And more our horses who, poor winkered fools,
Hearing their dooms outstrip them, cast aside
And pole the all-shattered house-fronts.
                                         We ourselves,
Of purpose to repair to Westminster,
Infirmity and age consenting, signalled
From her hot lair an horseless chariot
Which, in the recorded twelfth part of an hour,
Bore our inviolate ermines half a league.
It is, and woe it is, the chill refuge,
The lean, unenvied privilege of Age,
To meet new changes with old courtesy,
Not as averting change but sparing souls
Worn weak, and bodies extenuate with the years
That heed nor never heeded! Set them free.
What has been was, and what will be, must be!

ACT III
*Argument. A room in the Boar's Head Tavern set for a banquet to celebrate the
discharge of the motorists from the King's Justice. Enter* PRINCE HENRY *with* PORTIA
and several others. Also FALSTAFF *drunk.*

FALSTAFF. "When that I had and a little tinny car—
With a heigh-ho, the wind and the screen—"
Empty the radiator!

HOSTESS. Sir John, there's one without says he's your twin-brother.

FALSTAFF. I'll be the wise child. Have him in! (*Enter* HAMLET *drunk*.)
Ha! Begot a night's ride the cooler side o' the blanket! But if I be knight,
he's Blood-Royal. (*To* PRINCE HENRY) Here's thy meat, Hal. I stay by our
commons.

PRINCE. Lions know lions, tho' they pride apart,
And Princes Princes. (*To* HAMLET) For these, my companions
Rejoicingly from Justice, your pardon, Brother,
And, if it so far please, your title.

HAMLET. Prince. Hamlet of Denmark. Your pardon too. 'Tis the
Rhenish . . . But conceive, sirrah, how it comes about 'neath the unjust stars,
that by a few ink-spirts and frail pretences of the plays, a bald-pated ostler
to Pegasus conjures life into such as we. In which continuance, mark you, we
live and inextinguishably shake spheres: he having left the globe—how
long? But I'll go find my double.[1]

PRINCE. Rumour wrongs not the Danes. They drink too deep.
He is full proof. (*To* HAMLET) Welcome, distracted Sir.
We have a foolish feast in hand, whereat,
Wine and our near escapes making familiar,
You shall be richer by a score of brothers
Before the score is paid. Seek and make merry.
(*To* NYM) When the fat gentleman stumbles, lay him against the arras, head
highest. There's a crown waiting.

NYM. For him—not me. That's an old humour.

PRINCE (*to* PORTIA). Lovely lady,
To whom we go in bondage, first, of beauty,
And next of golden advocacy, snatching
Us from deservèd Bridewells,—name thy fee.

PORTIA. I here confess I never owned a car;
Never, in all my life, have driven car;

---

[1] . . . After the transparent reference to "the unjust stars," the word "ink-spirts" leaps to the eye
of the initiated as the simplest anagram of "*scripsit*" (the "k" being used, of course, for the desiderated
"c" and the apparently superfluous "n", for the initial of Nicholas, Bacon's father). "Frail pretences"
(taking the first three letters of the first, and the last four of the second, word) reveals, beyond negation,
the same "Frances" who wrote to his King (Mar. 25, 1631) that he might be "frail and partake,
etc." The "*ba*ld-pated ostler" who "*con*jures life into, etc.," is even more palpable and needs not the
additional "*con*-tinuance" which follows. Nor does this exhaust the category. Miss Nessa Droenbergh
acutely explains Hamlet's opening remark to Prince Henry as a well-bred man's apology for phenomena
due to liquor-excess—briefly a hiccough. But we must remember that Bacon, where possible, always
"doubles his clues," on the principle of the British railroads' "distant" and "home" signals. Thus
after "Your pardon too," comes " 'Tis the Rhenish," a German wine long traded into Britain and
the Baltic, and later known as "hoc(k)." So we have, all but *en clair*, the author of "Shakespeare's"
plays proclaiming, "*Hoc scripsit Frances Bacon.*" (Francis Bacon wrote this.) What more, in the name
of sanity, is needed to convince anyone who is not delivered over to the "man of Stratford" complex?—
From PROFESSOR O. P. CALLOWITZ'S *William the World-Impostor*.

And, touching any uses of a car,
From airiest hearsays[1] were my pleadings drawn.
Therefore, I ask no guerdon but a car,
To experience on the heels of phantasy.

PRINCE. A car? A car?

HAMLET (*to* FALSTAFF). Women have dread affections, for their spirit,
Out-plumbing ours, their easier sympathies
Frame both the passion and the appurtenance;
Else they go mad.

FALSTAFF. True! Doll's a she-kite of the same feather.
But moulting—moulting!

PRINCE (*to* PORTIA). Nay, entertain conjecture of a time
When, horses fed to hounds, the thrice-stuffed streets
Ring, reek and rumble with opprobrious wains
Inveterately unheedful. Straw between
Their bulks the rash and pillioned amorists
Whose so mis-tamed embracements on the wood[2]
Sling hose and cap[3] to inquest.

BEATRICE. Signor Prince, spare thyself a dry mouth and us drier
discourse. The world moves, for all man's owlings, and we women in the
va'ward.[4]

NYM. That's the new humour. To over-run the law and lieges and say "I
am a maid!"

BENEDICK. To have at a man sideways out of a blind lane, and if he give
natural vent on some broken head, arm, or running-board,[5] her husband or
lover must challenge him as though he were Claudio.

BEATRICE. That, Signor Benedick, shall never be. For when I drive you
shall stay at home.

SHYLOCK. I have a bond! I have a bond in my office,
Whose virtue is—for every pound of flesh,
Or drop of blood, on such mistakings drawn,
Or push or market-bestial—being signed
(And some poor ducats paid) assures the holder
'Gainst every act and charge of law or leech.

---

[1] Hearses.—WARBURTON (*conject.*)

[2] The text is corrupt. It is impossible to imagine a street paved with wood. But mis-timed
embracements might well be "untoward."—JOHNSON.

[3] At this epoch the London 'prentices wore cloth caps, and their female companions stockings,
which had then been largely discovered by the vulgar.—THEOBALD.

[4] "Ford" (*conjectural*).—STEEVENS.

[5] Running aboard—in the sense of vessels falling "foul" of each other at sea. (*Conjectural.*)—JOHNSON.

PORTIA.   We made sweet composition long ago,
Shylock and I.   He pays upon such bonds,
As, in mine office, I can well avouch;
Having prepared the like for Jessica
Whose paths are wayward.   Let them see it, Jew.

SHYLOCK *shows the company a Third Party Risks Policy.* HAMLET *and* FALSTAFF *talk apart*

FALSTAFF (*to* HAMLET).   Unconfined truth!   Cowards natural, both of us, with each some huddled deliverance of jest or philosophy to piece out the skirts of 'voided occasion. 'You drive?

HAMLET.   For action to be taken on the instant?   I'd liever!   But, oh, God—I have no choice, being what I am and informed of myself past endurance.

FALSTAFF.   I have some same cause.   How, now, of drink and lechery to drown self-knowledge?

HAMLET.   Serves me not.   There's a mad woman whom I drowned floats in my every cup, like borage.[1]   But I am not brave.

FALSTAFF.   Women   in   liquor!   Double   damnation   and   half satisfaction.   Think you, Ham, that he who made us twins knew his work?

HAMLET.   I set no limit, being born of that soul—
One spark in all its hells.   Flesh, canst thou tremble?

FALSTAFF.   I am too young to 'scape the cold fit o' mornings.

HAMLET.   Shake to thy core, contemplating what vasts
Unlawful, and what darkness, whereto ours
Is the sun's targe, had he adventured down
(Holding the poised brain ice) till he arraigned[2]
A murderess, a Moor, a mad King—me!
For ensample of all uttermosts of woe
Man bears or shall be designate to suffer
Inly or of the Gods!

FALSTAFF.   True enough.   But the sack's here, and I have 'scaped Justice an hour.   What a plague does the Jew with his papers?

---

[1] An allusion to the old distich:—

'I, Borage,
Give Courage.'

This herb is not included in the Queen's category of those used by Ophelia previous to her suicide, nor does Ophelia herself mention it.   (*Conjectural.*)—STEEVENS.

[2] Mr. Malone says that this word should be "arrayed," in the sense of displaying before the public; but considering that each one of the characters enumerated is, in various forms, arraigned by Conscience, that most dreadful of judges, I incline towards the former reading.—M. MASON.

PRINCE (*taking Insurance Policy from* SHYLOCK).
Thus furnished, and with knowledge of the wealth
Behind the bond, are well my doubts resolved.
My fears?   (*To* PORTIA) Fair lady, warn me of thy comings
When that car rolls its fifty roystering steeds
Which is our instant, grateful, deadly gift!

SIR A. AGUECHEEK.   There's simply no back-alley left in Illyria now where
a man may let 's liquor out of him, but he must stand ready to leap into either
hedge.

PRINCE.   To-morrow be his own klaxon.[1]   Till he call,
Put cars away, and revel comrades all!

FESTE.   When all about the joiners thrive—
          And coffins quick as man can saw;—
     When learning lady-owners drive,
          And beaks sit brooding on the Law;
     When roasting cabs hiss on the grass,
     Then lightly brays the headlong ass:—
          "*Where to?   To Hell!*"   Oh, word of fear,
     Unpleasing to the charioteer!

---

[1] "Sexton."   This word, through corruption, has been lost, and is now restored to its original
meaning.—SIR T. HANMER.

Songs Written for
C. R. L. Fletcher's
"A History of England"
1911

The River's Tale

(PREHISTORIC)

Twenty bridges from Tower to Kew—
(Twenty bridges or twenty-two)—
Wanted to know what the River knew,
For they were young and the Thames was old,
And this is the tale that the River told:—

"I walk my beat before London Town,
Five hours up and seven down.
Up I go till I end my run
At Tide-end-town, which is Teddington.
Down I come with the mud in my hands
And plaster it over the Maplin Sands.
But I'd have you know that these waters of mine
Were once a branch of the River Rhine,
When hundreds of miles to the East I went
And England was joined to the Continent.

I remember the bat-winged lizard-birds,
The Age of Ice and the mammoth herds,
And the giant tigers that stalked them down
Through Regent's Park into Camden Town.
And I remember like yesterday
The earliest Cockney who came my way,
When he pushed through the forest that lined the Strand,
With paint on his face and a club in his hand.
He was death to feather and fin and fur.
He trapped my beavers at Westminster.
He netted my salmon, he hunted my deer,
He killed my heron off Lambeth Pier.
He fought his neighbour with axes and swords,
Flint or bronze, at my upper fords,
While down at Greenwich, for slaves and tin,
The tall Phoenician ships stole in,
And North Sea war-boats, painted and gay,
Flashed like dragon-flies, Erith way;
And Norsemen and Negro and Gaul and Greek
Drank with the Britons in Barking Creek,
And life was gay, and the world was new,
And I was a mile across at Kew!
But the Roman came with a heavy hand,
And bridged and roaded and ruled the land,
And the Romans left and the Danes blew in—
And that's where your history-books begin!"

The Roman Centurion's Song

(ROMAN OCCUPATION OF BRITAIN, A.D. 300)

Legate, I had the news last night—my cohort ordered home
By ship to Portus Itius and thence by road to Rome.
I've marched the companies aboard, the arms are stowed below:
Now let another take my sword. Command me not to go!

I've served in Britain forty years, from Vectis to the Wall.
I have none other home than this, nor any life at all.
Last night I did not understand, but, now the hour draws near
That calls me to my native land, I feel that land is here.

Here where men say my name was made, here where my work was done;
Here where my dearest dead are laid—my wife— my wife and son;
Here where time, custom, grief and toil, age, memory, service, love.
Have rooted me in British soil. Ah, how can I remove?

For me this land, that sea, these airs, those folk and fields suffice.
What purple Southern pomp can match our changeful Northern skies,
Black with December snows unshed or pearled with August haze—
The clanging arch of steel-grey March, or June's long-lighted days?

You'll follow widening Rhodanus till vine and olive lean
Aslant before the sunny breeze that sweeps Nemausus clean
To Arelate's triple gate; but let me linger on,
Here where our stiff-necked British oaks confront Euroclydon!

You'll take the old Aurelian Road through shore-descending pines
Where, blue as any peacock's neck, the Tyrrhene Ocean shines.
You'll go where laurel crowns are won, but—will you e'er forget
The scent of hawthorn in the sun, or bracken in the wet?

Let me work here for Britain's sake—at any task you will—
A marsh to drain, a road to make or native troops to drill.
Some Western camp (I know the Pict) or granite Border keep,
Mid seas of heather derelict, where our old messmates sleep.

Legate, I come to you in tears—My cohort ordered home!
I've served in Britain forty years. What should I do in Rome?
Here is my heart, my soul, my mind—the only life I know.
I cannot leave it all behind. Command me not to go!

The Pirates in England

(SAXON INVASION, A.D. 400–600)

When Rome was rotten-ripe to her fall,
  And the sceptre passed from her hand,
The pestilent Picts leaped over the wall
  To harry the English land.

The little dark men of the mountain and waste.
  So quick to laughter and tears,
They came panting with hate and haste
  For the loot of five hundred years.

They killed the trader, they sacked the shops,
  They ruined temple and town—
They swept like wolves through the standing crops
  Crying that Rome was down.

They wiped out all that they could find
  Of beauty and strength and worth,
But they could not wipe out the Viking's Wind
  That brings the ships from the North.

They could not wipe out the North-East gales,
  Nor what those gales set free—
The pirate ships with their close-reefed sails,
  Leaping from sea to sea.

They had forgotten the shield-hung hull
  Seen nearer and more plain,
Dipping into the troughs like a gull,
  And gull-like rising again—

The painted eyes that glare and frown
  In the high snake-headed stem,
Searching the beach while her sail comes down,
  They had forgotten them!

There was no Count of the Saxon Shore
  To meet her hand to hand,
As she took the beach with a grind and a roar,
  And the pirates rushed inland!

Dane-Geld

(A.D. 980–1016)

It is always a temptation to an armed and agile nation
    To call upon a neighbour and to say:—
"We invaded you last night—we are quite prepared to fight,
    Unless you pay us cash to go away."

And that is called asking for Dane-geld,
    And the people who ask it explain
That you've only to pay 'em the Dane-geld
    And then you'll get rid of the Dane!

It is always a temptation to a rich and lazy nation,
    To puff and look important and to say:—
"Though we know we should defeat you, we have not the
    time to meet you.
    We will therefore pay you cash to go away."

And that is called paying the Dane-geld;
    But we've proved it again and again,
That if once you have paid him the Dane-geld
    You never get rid of the Dane.

It is wrong to put temptation in the path of any nation,
    For fear they should succumb and go astray;
So when you are requested to pay or be molested,
    You will find it better policy to say:—

"We never pay *any*-one Dane-Geld,
    No matter how trifling the cost;
For the end of that game is oppression and shame,
    And the nation that plays it is lost!"

The Anvil

(NORMAN CONQUEST, 1066)

England's on the anvil—hear the hammers ring—
    Clanging from the Severn to the Tyne!
Never was a blacksmith like our Norman King—
    England's being hammered, hammered, hammered into line!

England's on the anvil!   Heavy are the blows!
    (But the work will be a marvel when it's done.)
Little bits of Kingdoms cannot stand against their foes.
    England's being hammered, hammered, hammered into one!

There shall be one people—it shall serve one Lord—
   (Neither Priest nor Baron shall escape!)
It shall have one speech and law, soul and strength and sword.
   England's being hammered, hammered, hammered into shape!

Norman and Saxon

(A.D. 1100)

"My son," said the Norman Baron, "I am dying, and you will be heir
To all the broad acres in England that William gave me for my share
When we conquered the Saxon at Hastings, and a nice little handful it is.
But before you go over to rule it I want you to understand this:—

"The Saxon is not like us Normans.   His manners are not so polite.
But he never means anything serious till he talks about justice and right.
When he stands like an ox in the furrow with his sullen set eyes on your
   own,
And grumbles, 'This isn't fair dealing,' my son, leave the Saxon alone.

"You can horsewhip your Gascony archers, or torture your Picardy spears;
But don't try that game on the Saxon; you'll have the whole brood round
   your ears.
From the richest old Thane in the county to the poorest chained serf in
   the field,
They'll be at you and on you like hornets, and, if you are wise, you will
   yield.

"But first you must master their language, their dialect, proverbs and
   songs.
Don't trust any clerk to interpret when they come with the tale of their
   wrongs.
Let them know that you know what they're saying; let them feel that you
   know what to say.
Yes, even when you want to go hunting, hear 'em out if it takes you all
   day.

"They'll drink every hour of the daylight and poach every hour of the
   dark.
It's the sport not the rabbits they're after (we've plenty of game in the
   park).
Don't hang them or cut off their fingers.   That's wasteful as well as
   unkind,
For a hard-bitten, South-country poacher makes the best man-at-arms you
   can find.

"Appear with you wife and the children at their weddings and funerals
and feasts.
Be polite but not friendly to Bishops; be good to all poor parish priests.
Say 'we,' 'us' and 'ours' when you're talking, instead of 'you fellows' and
'I.'
Don't ride over seeds; keep your temper; and *never you tell 'em a lie!*"

The Reeds of Runnymede

(MAGNA CHARTA, JUNE 15, 1215)

At Runnymede, at Runnymede,
   What say the reeds at Runnymede?
The lissom reeds that give and take,
That bend so far, but never break.
They keep the sleepy Thames awake
   With tales of John at Runnymede.

At Runnymede, at Runnymede,
   Oh, hear the reeds at Runnymede:—
"You mustn't sell, delay, deny,
A freeman's right or liberty.
It wakes the stubborn Englishry,
   We saw 'em roused at Runnymede!

"When through our ranks the Barons came,
With little thought of praise or blame,
But resolute to play the game,
   They lumbered up to Runnymede;
And there they launched in solid line
The first attack on Right Divine—
The curt, uncompromising 'Sign!'
   That settled John at Runnymede.

"At Runnymede, at Runnymede."
Your rights were won at Runnymede!
No freeman shall be fined or bound,
   Or dispossessed of freehold ground,
Except by lawful judgment found
And passed upon him by his peers.
Forget not, after all these years,
   The Charter signed at Runnymede."

And still when Mob or Monarch lays
Too rude a hand on English ways,

The whisper wakes, the shudder plays,
  Across the reeds at Runnymede.
And Thames, that knows the moods of kings,
And crowds and priests and suchlike things,
Rolls deep and dreadful as he brings
  Their warning down from Runnymede!

My Father's Chair

(PARLIAMENTS OF HENRY III., 1265)

There are four good legs to my Father's Chair—
Priest and People and Lords and Crown.
I sits on all of 'em fair and square,
And that is the reason it don't break down.

I won't trust one leg, nor two, nor three,
To carry my weight when I sets me down.
I wants all four of 'em under me—
Priest and People and Lords and Crown.

I sits on all four and I favours none—
Priest, nor People, nor Lords nor Crown:
And I never tilts in my chair, my son,
And that is the reason it don't break down.

When your time comes to sit in my Chair,
Remember your Father's habits and rules.
Sit on all four legs, fair and square,
And never be tempted by one-legged stools!

The Dawn Wind

(THE FIFTEENTH CENTURY)

At two o'clock in the morning, if you open your window and listen,
  You will hear the feet of the Wind that is going to call the sun.
And the trees in the shadow rustle and the trees in the moonlight glisten,
  And though it is deep, dark night, you feel that the night is done.

So do the cows in the field. They graze for an hour and lie down,
  Dozing and chewing the cud; or a bird in the ivy wakes,
Chirrups one note and is still, and the restless Wind strays on,
  Fidgeting far down the road, till, softly, the darkness breaks.

Back comes the wind full strength with a blow like an angel's wing.
   Gentle but waking the world, as he shouts: "The Sun! The Sun!"
And the light floods over the fields and the birds begin to sing,
   And the Wind dies down in the grass. It is day and his work is done.

So when the world is asleep, and there seems no hope of her waking
   Out of some long, bad dream that makes her mutter and moan,
Suddenly, all men arise to the noise of fetters breaking,
   And every one smiles at his neighbour and tells him his soul is his own!

The King's Job

(THE TUDOR MONARCHY)

Once on a time was a King anxious to understand
What was the wisest thing a man could do for his land.
Most of his population hurried to answer the question,
Each with a long oration, each with a new suggestion.
They interrupted his meals—he wasn't safe in his bed from 'em—
They hung round his neck and heels, and at last His Majesty fled from
   'em.
He put on a leper's cloak (people leave lepers alone),
Out of the window he broke, and abdicated his throne.
All that rapturous day, while his Court and his Ministers mourned him,
He danced on his own highway till his own Policemen warned him.
Gay and cheerful he ran (lepers don't cheer as a rule)
Till he found a philosopher-man teaching an infant-school.
The windows were open wide, the King sat down on the grass,
And heard the children inside reciting "Our King is an ass."
The King popped in his head:"Some people would call this treason,
But I think you are right," he said; "Will you kindly give me your
   reason?"
Lepers in school are as rare as kings with a leper's dress on,
But the class didn't stop or stare; it calmly went on with the lesson:
'The wisest thing, we suppose, that a man can do for his land,
Is the work that lies under his nose, with the tools that lie under his hand."
The King whipped off his cloak, and stood in his crown before 'em.
He said: "My dear little folk, *Ex ore parvulorum—*
(Which is Latin for "Children know more than grown-ups would credit")
You have shown me the road to go, and I propose to tread it."
Back to his Kingdom he ran, and issued a Proclamation,
"Let every living man return to his occupation!"
Then he explained to the mob who cheered in his palace and round it,
"I've been to look for a job, and Heaven be praised I've found it!"

With Drake in the Tropics
(A.D.1580

South and far south below the Line
  Our Admiral leads us on,
Above, undreamed-of planets shine—
  The stars we knew are gone.
Around, our clustered seamen mark
  The silent deep ablaze
With fires, through which the far-down shark
  Shoots glimmering on his ways.

The sultry tropic breezes fail
  That plagued us all day through;
Like molten silver hangs our sail,
  Our decks are dark with dew.
Now the rank moon commands the sky.
  Ho!   Bid the watch beware
And rouse all sleeping men that lie
  Unsheltered in her glare.

How long the time 'twixt bell and bell!
  How still our lanthorns burn!
How strange our whispered words that tell
  Of England and return!
Old towns, old streets, old friends, old loves,
  We name them each to each,
While the lit face of Heaven removes
  'Them farther from our reach.

Now is the utmost ebb of night
  When mind and body sink,
And loneliness and gathering fright
  O'erwhelm us, if we think—
Yet, look, where in his room apart,
  All windows opened wide,
Our Admiral thrusts away the chart
  And comes to walk outside.

Kindly, from man to man he goes,
  With comfort, praise, or jest,
Quick to suspect our childish woes,
  Our terror and unrest.
It is as though the sun should shine—
  Our midnight fears are gone!
South and far south below the Line,
  Our Admiral leads us on!

"Together"

(ENGLAND AT WAR)

When Horse and Rider each can trust the other everywhere,
It takes a fence and more than a fence to pound that happy pair;
For the one will do what the other demands, although he is beaten and
blown,
And when it is done, they can live through a run that neither could face
alone.

When Crew and Captain understand each other to the core,
It takes a gale and more than a gale to put their ship ashore;
For the one will do what the other commands, although they are chilled to
the bone,
And both together can live through weather that neither could face alone.

When King and People understand each other past a doubt,
It takes a foe and more than a foe to knock that country out;
For the one will do what the other requires as soon as the need is shown;
And hand in hand they can make a stand which neither could make
alone!

This wisdom had Elizabeth and all her subjects too,
For she was theirs and they were hers, as well the Spaniard knew;
For when his grim Armada came to conquer the Nation and Throne.
Why, back to back they met an attack that neither could face alone!

It is not wealth, nor talk, nor trade, nor schools, nor even the Vote
Will save your land when the enemy's hand is tightening round your
throat.
But a King and a People who thoroughly trust each other in all that is
done
Can sleep on their bed without an dread—for the world will leave 'em
alone!

James I.

(1603–25)

The child of Mary Queen of Scots,
    A shifty mother's shiftless son,
Bred up among intrigues and plots,
    Learnèd in all things, wise in none.
Ungainly, babbling, wasteful, weak,
    Shrewd, clever, cowardly, pedantic,

The sight of steel would blanch his cheek.
   The smell of baccy drive him frantic.
He was the author of his line—
   He wrote that witches should be burnt;
He wrote that monarchs were divine,
   And left a son who—proved they weren't!

Edgehill Fight

(CIVIL WARS, 1642)

Naked and grey the Cotswolds stand
   Beneath the autumn sun,
And the stubble-fields on either hand
   Where Stour and Avon run.
There is no change in the patient land
   That has bred us every one.

She should have passed in cloud and fire
   And saved us from this sin
Of war—red war—'twixt child and sire,
   Household and kith and kin,
In the heart of a sleepy Midland shire,
   With the harvest scarcely in.

But there is no change as we meet at last
   On the brow-head or the plain,
And the raw astonished ranks stand fast
   To slay or to be slain
By the men they knew in the kindly past
   That shall never come again—

By the men they met at dance or chase,
   In the tavern or the hall,
At the justice-bench and the market-place,
   At the cudgel-play or brawl—
Of their own blood and speech and race,
   Comrades or neighbours all!

More bitter than death this day must prove
   Whichever way it go,
For the brothers of the maids we love
   Make ready to lay low
Their sisters' sweethearts, as we move
   Against our dearest foe.

Thank Heaven!   At last the trumpets peal
  Before our strength gives way.
For King or for the Commonweal—
  No matter which they say,
The first dry rattle of new-drawn steel
  Changes the world to-day!

The Dutch in the Medway

(1664–72)

If wars were won by feasting,
  Or victory by song,
Or safety found in sleeping sound,
  How England would be strong!
But honour and dominion
  Are not maintainèd so.
They're only got by sword and shot,
  And this the Dutchmen know!

The moneys that should feed us
  You spend on your delight,
How can you then have sailor-men
  To aid you in your fight?
Our fish and cheese are rotten
  Which makes the scurvy grow—
We cannot serve you if we starve,
  And this the Dutchmen know!

Our ships in every harbour
  Be neither whole nor sound,
And when we seek to mend a leak,
  No oakum can be found;
Or, if it is, the caulkers,
  And carpenters also,
For lack of pay have gone away,
  And this the Dutchmen know!

Mere powder, guns, and bullets,
  We scarce can get at all;
Their price was spent in merriment
  And revel at Whitehall,
While we in tattered doublets
  From ship to ship must row,
Beseeching friends for odds and ends—
  And this the Dutchmen know!

No King will heed our warnings,
   No Court will pay our claims—
Our King and Court for their disport
   Do sell the very Thames!
For, now De Ruyter's topsails
   Off naked Chatham show,
We dare not meet him with our fleet—
   And this the Dutchmen know!

"Brown Bess"

(THE ARMY MUSKET—1700–1815)

In the days of lace-ruffles, perukes and brocade
   Brown Bess was a partner whom none could despise—
An out-spoken, flinty-lipped, brazen-faced jade,
   With a habit of looking men straight in the eyes—
At Blenheim and Ramillies fops would confess
They were pierced to the heart by the charms of Brown Bess.

Though her sight was not long and weight was not small,
   Yet her actions were winning, her language was clear;
And everyone bowed as she opened the ball
   On the arm of some high-gaitered, grim grenadier.
Half Europe admitted the striking success
Of the dances and routs that were given by Brown Bess.

When ruffles were turned into stiff leather stocks,
   And people wore pigtails instead of perukes,
Brown Bess never altered her iron-grey locks.
   She knew she was valued for more than her looks.
"Oh, powder and patches was always my dress,
And I think I am killing enough," said Brown Bess.

So she followed her red-coats, whatever they did,
   From the heights of Quebec to the plains of Assaye,
   From Gibraltar to Acre, Cape Town and Madrid,
   And nothing about her was changed on the way;
   (But most of the Empire which now we possess
Was won through those years by old-fashioned Brown Bess.)

In stubborn retreat or in stately advance,
   From the Portugal coast to the cork-woods of Spain,
She had puzzled some excellent Marshals of France
   Till none of them wanted to meet her again:
But later, near Brussels, Napoleon—no less—
Arranged for a Waterloo ball with Brown Bess.

She had danced till the dawn of that terrible day—
    She danced till the dusk of more terrible night,
And before her linked squares his battalions gave way,
    And her long fierce quadrilles put his lancers to flight:
And when his gilt carriage drove off in the press,
"I have danced my last dance for the world!" said Brown Bess.

If you go to Museums—there's one in Whitehall—
    Where old weapons are shown with their names writ beneath,
You will find her, upstanding, her back to the wall,
    As stiff as a ramrod, the flint in her teeth.
And if ever we English had reason to bless
Any arm save our mothers', that arm is Brown Bess!

The American Rebellion

(1776)

BEFORE

'Twas not while England's sword unsheathed
    Put half a world to flight,
Nor while their new-built cities breathed
    Secure behind her might;
Not while she poured from Pole to Line
    Treasure and ships and men—
These worshippers at Freedom's shrine
    They did not quit her then!

Not till their foes were driven forth
    By England o'er the main—
Not till the Frenchman from the North
    Had gone with shattered Spain;
Not till the clean-swept oceans showed
    No hostile flag unrolled,
Did they remember what they owed
    To Freedom—and were bold!

AFTER

The snow lies thick on Valley Forge,
    The ice on the Delaware,
But the poor dead soldiers of King George
    They neither know nor care.

Not though the earliest primrose break
  On the sunny side of the lane,
And scuffling rookeries awake
  Their England's spring again.

They will not stir when the drifts are gone,
  Or the ice melts out of the bay:
And the men that served with Washington
  Lie as still as they.

They will not stir though the mayflower blows
  In the moist dark woods of pine,
And every rock-strewn pasture shows
  Mullein and columbine.

Each for his land, in a fair fight,
  Encountered, strove, and died,
And the kindly earth that knows no spite
  Covers them side by side.

She is too busy to think of war;
  She has all the world to make gay;
And, behold, the yearly flowers are
  Where they were in our fathers' day!

Golden-rod by the pasture-wall
  When the columbine is dead,
And sumach leaves that turn, in fall,
  Bright as the blood they shed.

The French Wars

(NAPOLEONIC)

The boats of Newhaven and Folkestone and Dover
To Dieppe and Boulogne and to Calais cross over;
And in each of those runs there is not a square yard
Where the English and French haven't fought and fought hard!

If the ships that were sunk could be floated once more,
They'd stretch like a raft from the shore to the shore,
And we'd see, as we crossed, every pattern and plan
Of ship that was built since sea-fighting began.

There'd be biremes and brigantines, cutters and sloops,
Cogs, carracks and galleons with gay gilded poops—

Hoys, caravels, ketches, corvettes and the rest,
As thick as regattas, from Ramsgate to Brest.

But the galleys of Caesar, the squadrons of Sluys,
And Nelson's crack frigates are hid from our eyes,
Where the high Seventy-fours of Napoleon's days
Lie down with Deal luggers and French *chasse-marées*.

They'll answer no signal—they rest on the ooze,
With their honey-combed guns and their skeleton crews—
And racing above them, through sunshine or gale,
The Cross-Channel packets come in with the Mail.

Then the poor sea-sick passengers, English and French,
Must open their trunks on the Custom-house bench,
While the officers rummage for smuggled cigars
And nobody thinks of our blood-thirsty wars!

Big Steamers

1914–18

"Oh, where are you going to, all you Big Steamers,
    With England's own coal, up and down the salt seas?"
"We are going to fetch you your bread and your butter,
    Your beef, pork, and mutton, eggs, apples, and cheese."

"And where will you fetch it from, all you Big Steamers,
    And where shall I write you when you are away?"
"We fetch it from Melbourne, Quebec, and Vancouver—
    Address us at Hobart, Hong-Kong, and Bombay."

"But if anything happened to all you Big Steamers,
    And suppose you were wrecked up and down the salt sea?"
"Then you'd have no coffee or bacon for breakfast,
    And you'd have no muffins or toast for your tea."

"Then I'll pray for fine weather for all you Big Steamers,
    For little blue billows and breezes so soft."
"Oh, billows and breezes don't bother Big Steamers,
    For we're iron below and steel-rigging aloft."

"Then I'll build a new lighthouse for all you Big Steamers,
    With plenty wise pilots to pilot you through."
"Oh, the Channel's as bright as a ball-room already,
    And pilots are thicker than pilchards at Looe."

"Then what can I do for you, all you Big Steamers,
    Oh, what can I do for your comfort and good?"
"Send out your big warships to watch your big waters,
    That no one may stop us from bringing you food.

"For the bread that you eat and the biscuits you nibble,
    The sweets that you suck and the joints that you carve,
They are brought to you daily by all us Big Steamers—
    And if any one hinders our coming you'll starve!"

The Secret of the Machines

(MODERN MACHINERY)

We were taken from the ore-bed and the mine,
    We were melted in the furnace and the pit—
We were cast and wrought and hammered to design,
    We were cut and filed and tooled and gauged to fit.
Some water, coal, and oil is all we ask,
    And a thousandth of an inch to give us play:
And now, if you will set us to our task,
    We will serve you four and twenty hours a day!

We can pull and haul and push and lift and drive,
We can print and plough and weave and heat and light,
We can run and race and swim and fly and dive,
We can see and hear and count and read and write!

Would you call a friend from half across the world?
    If you'll let us have his name and town and state,
You shall see and hear your crackling question hurled
    Across the arch of heaven while you wait.
Has he answered?   Does he need you at his side?
    You can start this very evening if you choose,
And take the Western Ocean in the stride
    Of seventy thousand horses and some screws!

The boat -express is waiting your command!
You will find the *Mauretania* at the quay,
Till her captain turns the lever 'neath his hand,
And the monstrous nine-decked city goes to sea.

Do you wish to make the mountains bare their head
    And lay their new-cut forests at your feet?
Do you want to turn a river in its bed,
    Or plant a barren wilderness with wheat?

Shall we pipe aloft and bring you water down
    From the never-failing cisterns of the snows,
To work the mills and tramways in your town,
    And irrigate your orchards as it flows?

It is easy!   Give us dynamite and drills!
Watch the iron-shouldered rocks lie down and quake,
As the thirsty desert-level floods and fills,
And the valley we have dammed becomes a lake.

But remember, please, the Law by which we live,
    We are not built to comprehend a lie,
We can neither love nor pity nor forgive.
    If you make a slip in handling us you die!
We are greater than the Peoples or the Kings—
    Be humble, as you crawl beneath our rods!—
Our touch can alter all created things,
    We are everything on earth—except The Gods!

Though our smoke may hide the Heavens from your eyes,
It will vanish and the stars will shine again,
Because, for all our power and weight and size,
We are nothing more than children of your brain!

The Bells and Queen Victoria

1911

"Gay go up and gay go down
   To ring the Bells of London Town."
When London Town's asleep in bed
You'll hear the Bells ring overhead.
   In excelsis gloria!
   Ringing for Victoria,
Ringing for their mighty mistress—ten years dead!

The Bells:
Here is more gain than Gloriana guessed—
   Than Gloriana guessed or Indies bring—
Than golden Indies bring.   A Queen confessed—
   A Queen confessed that crowned her people King.
Her people King, and crowned all Kings above,
Above all Kings have crowned their Queen their love—
Have crowned their love their Queen, their Queen their love!

Denying her, we do ourselves deny,
  Disowning her are we ourselves disowned.
Mirror was she of our fidelity,
  And handmaid of our destiny enthroned;
The very marrow of Youth's dream, and still
Yoke-mate of wisest Age that worked her will!

Our fathers had declared to us her praise—
  Her praise the years had proven past all speech.
And past all speech our loyal hearts always,
  Always our hearts lay open, each to each—
Therefore men gave the treasure of their blood
To this one woman—for she understood!

Four o' the clock!   Now all the world is still.
Oh, London Bells, to all the world declare
The Secret of the Empire—read who will!
The Glory of the People—touch who dare!

THE BELLS:
Power that has reached itself all kingly powers,
  St. Margaret's: By love o'erpowered—
  St. Martin's: By love o'erpowered—
  St. Clement Danes: By love o'erpowered,
    The greater power confers!

THE BELLS:
For we were hers, as she, as she was ours,
  Bow Bells: And she was ours—
  St. Paul's: And she was ours—
  Westminster: And she was ours,
    As we, even we, were hers!

THE BELLS:
As we were hers!

The Glory of the Garden

Our England is a garden that is full of stately views,
Of borders, beds and shrubberies and lawns and avenues,
With statues on the terraces and peacocks strutting by;
But the Glory of the Garden lies in more than meets the eye.

For where the old thick laurels grow, along the thin red wall,
You find the tool- and potting-sheds which are the heart of all;
The cold-frames and the hot-houses, the dungpits and the tanks,
The rollers, carts and drain-pipes, with the barrows and the planks.

And there you'll see the gardeners, the men and 'prentice boys
Told off to do as they are bid and do it without noise;
For, except when seeds are planted and we shout to scare the birds,
The Glory of the Garden it abideth not in words.

And some can pot begonias and some can bud a rose,
And some can hardly fit to trust with anything that grows;
But they can roll and trim the lawns and sift the sand and loam,
For the Glory of the Garden occupieth all who come.

Our England is a garden, and such gardens are not made
By singing:—"Oh, how beautiful!" and sitting in the shade,
While better men than we go out and start their working lives
At grubbing weeds from gravel-paths with broken dinner-knives.

There's not a pair of legs so thin, there's not a head so thick,
There's not a hand so weak and white, nor yet a heart so sick,
But it can find some needful job that's crying to be done,
For the Glory of the Garden glorifieth every one.

Then seek your job with thankfulness and work till further orders,
If it's only netting strawberries or killing slugs on borders;
And when your back stops aching and your hands begin to harden,
You will find yourself a partner in the Glory of the Garden.

Oh, Adam was a gardener, and God who made him sees
That half a proper gardener's work is done upon his knees,
So when your work is finished, you can wash your hands and pray
For the Glory of the Garden, that it may not pass away!
And the Glory of the Garden it shall never pass away!

Verses from
"Land and Sea Tales"
1919–1923

A Preface

To all to whom this little book may come—
  Health for yourselves and those you hold most dear!
Content abroad, and happiness at home,
  And—one grand Secret in your private ear:—
  Nations have passed away and left no traces,
And History gives the naked cause of it—
  One single, simple reason in all cases;
They fell because their peoples were not fit.

Now, though your Body be mis-shapen, blind,
  Lame, feverish, lacking substance, power or skill,
Certain it is that men can school the Mind
  To school the sickliest Body to her will—
  As many have done, whose glory blazes still
Like mighty flames in meanest lanterns lit:
  Wherefore, we pray the crippled, weak and ill—
Be fit—be fit! In mind at first be fit!

And, though your Spirit seem uncouth or small,
  Stubborn as clay or shifting as the sand,
Strengthen the Body, and the Body shall
  Strengthen the Spirit till she take command;
  As a bold rider brings his horse in hand
At the tall fence, with voice and heel and bit,
  And leaps while all the field are at a stand,
Be fit—be fit! In body next be fit!

Northing on earth—no Arts, no Gifts, nor Graces—
  No Fame, no Wealth—outweighs the want of it.
This is the Law which every law embraces—
  Be fit—be fit! In mind and body be fit!

The even heart that seldom slurs its beat—
  The cool head weighing what that heart desires—
The measuring eye that guides the hands and feet—
  The Soul unbroken when the Body tires—
  These are the things our weary world requires
Far more than superfluities of wit;
  Wherefore we pray you, sons of generous sires,
Be fit—be fit! For Honour's sake be fit.

There is one lesson at all Times and Places—
  One changeless Truth on all things changing writ,
For boys and girls, men, women, nations, races—
  Be fit—be fit! And once again, be fit!

The Junk and the Dhow

("An Unqualified Pilot")

Once a pair of savages found a stranded tree.
  (One-piecee stick-pidgen—two-piecee man.
Straddle-um—paddle-um—push-um off to sea.
  That way Foleign Debbil-boat began.)
But before, and before, and ever so long before
  Any shape of sailing-craft was known,
The Junk and Dhow had a stern and a bow,
  And a mast and a sail of their own—ahoy! alone!
  As they crashed across the Oceans on their own!

Once there was a pirate-ship, being blown ashore—
  (Plitty soon pilum up, s'posee no can tack.
Seven-piecee stlong man pullum sta'boa'd oar.
  That way bling her head alound and sail-o back.)
But before, and before, and ever so long before
  Grand Commander Noah took the wheel,
The Junk and the Dhow, though they look like anyhow,
  Had rudders reaching deep below their keel—ahoy! akeel!
  As they laid the Eastern Seas beneath their keel!

Once there was a galliot yawing in a tide.
  (Too much foolee side-slip.   How can stop?
Man catchee tea-box lid—lasha longaside.
  That way make her plenty glip and sail first-chop.)
But before, and before, and ever so long before
  Any such contrivances were used,
The whole Confucian sea-board had standardised the lee-board,
  And hauled it up or dropped it as they choosed—or chose—or chused!
  According to the weather, when they cruised!

Once there was a caravel in a beam-sea roll—
  (Ca'go shiftee—alla dliftee—no can livee long.
S'posum' nail-o boa'd acloss—makee ploper hol'?
  That way, ca'go sittum still, an' ship mo' stlong.)
But before, and before, and ever so long before
  Any square-rigged vessel hove in sight,
The Canton deep-sea craft carried bulkheads fore and aft,
  And took good care to keep 'em water-tight—atite—atite!
  From Amboyna to the Great Australian Bight!

Once there was a sailor-man singing just this way—
  (Too muchee yowl-o, sickum best flend!

Singee all-same pullee lope—haul and belay!
  Hully up and coilum down an'—bite off end!)
But before, and before, and ever so long before
  Any sort of chanty crossed our lips,
The Junk and the Dhow, though they look like anyhow,
  Were the Mother and the Father of all Ships—ahoy!—a'ships!
  And of half the new inventions in our Ships!
  From Tarifa to Formosa in our Ships!
    From Socotra to Sel*ank*hor of the windlass and the anchor.
  And the Navigators' Compass in our Ships—ahoy!—our Ships!
(O, hully up and coilum down and—bite—off—end!)

The Master-Cook

("His Gift")

With us there rade a Maister-Cook that came
From the Rochelle which is neere Angoulême.
Littel hee was, but rounder than a topp,
And his small berd hadde dipped in manie a soppe.
His honde was smoother than beseemeth mann's,
And his discoorse was all of marzipans,[1]
Of tripes of Caen, or Burdeux snailés swote,[2]
And Seinte Menhoulde where cooken piggés-foote.[3]
To Thoulouse and to Bress and Carcasson
For pyes and fowles and chesnottes hadde hee wonne;[4]
Of hammés of Thuringie[5] colde hee prate,
And well hee knew what Princes hadde on plate
At Christmas-tide, from Artois to Gascogne.

Lordinges, quod hee, manne liveth nat alone
By bred, but meatés rost and seethed, and broth,
And purchasable[6] deinties, on mine othe.
Honey and hote gingere well liketh hee,
And whalés-flesch mortred[7] with spicerie.
For, lat be all how man denie or carpe,[8]

[1] A kind of sticky sweetmeat.
[2] Bordeaux snails are specially large and sweet.
[3] They grill pigs'-feet still at St. Menehoulde, not far from Verdun, better than anywhere else in all the world.
[4] Gone—to get pâtés of ducks' liver at Toulouse; fatted poultry at Bourg in Bresse, on the road to Geneva; and very large chestnuts in sugar at Carcassonne, about forty miles from Toulouse.
[5] This would probably be some sort of wild-boar ham from Germany.
[6] Expensive.   [7] Beaten up.   [8] Sneer or despise.

Him thries a daie his honger maketh sharpe,
And setteth him at boorde[1] with hawkés eyne,
Snuffing what dish is set beforne to deyne,
Nor, till with meate he all-to fill to brim,
None other matter nowher mooveth him.
Lat holie Seintés sterve[2] as bookés boast,
Most mannés soule is in his bellie most.
For, as man thinketh in his hearte is hee,
But, as hee eateth so his thought shall bee.
And Holie Fader's self[3] (with reveraunce)
Oweth to Cooke his port and his presaunce.
Wherbye it cometh past disputison[4]
Cookes over alle men have dominion,
Which follow them as schippe her gouvernail.[5]
Enoff of wordes—beginneth heere my tale:—

The Hour of the Angel

("Stalky")

Sooner or late—in earnest or in jest—
    (But the stakes are no jest) Ithuriel's Hour
Will spring on us, for the first time, the test
    Of our sole unbacked competence and power
    Up to the limit of our years and dower
Of judgment—or beyond.   But here we have
Prepared long since our garland or our grave.
    For, at that hour, the sum of all our past,
    Act, habit, thought, and passion, shall be cast
In one addition, be it more or less,
    And as that reading runs so shall we do;
Meeting, astounded, victory at the last,
    Or, first and last, our own unworthiness.
And none can change us though they die to save!

[1]Brings him to table.   [2]Starve.
[3]The Pope himself, who depends on his cook for being healthy and well-fed.
[4]Dispute or argument.
[5]Men are influenced by their cooks as ships are steered by their rudders.

The Last Lap

("The Burning of the *Sarah Sands*")

How do we know, by the bank-high river,
  Where the mired and sulky oxen wait,
And it looks as though we might wait for ever,
  How do we know that the floods abate?
There is no change in the current's brawling—
  Louder and harsher the freshet scolds;
Yet we can feel she is falling, falling,
  And the more she threatens the less she holds.
Down to the drift, with no word spoken,
  The wheel-chained wagons slither and slue. . . .
Achtung! The back of the worst is broken!
  And—lash your leaders!— we're through—we're through!

How do we know, when the port-fog holds us
  Moored and helpless, a mile from the pier,
And the week-long summer smother enfolds us—
  How do we know it is going to clear?
There is no break in the blindfold weather,
  But, one and another, about the bay,
The unseen capstans clink together,
  Getting ready to go up and away.
A pennon whimpers—the breeze has found us—
  A headsail jumps through the thinning haze.
The whole hull follows, till—broad around us—
  The clean-swept ocean says: "Go your ways!"

How do we know, when the long fight rages,
  On the old, stale front that we cannot shake,
And it looks as though we were locked for ages,
  How do we know they are going to break?
There is no lull in the level firing,
  Nothing has shifted except the sun.
Yet we can feel they are tiring, tiring—
  Yet we can tell they are ripe to run.
Something wavers, and, while we wonder,
  Their centre-trenches are emptying out,
And, before their useless flanks go under,
  Our guns have pounded retreat to rout!

A Departure

("The Parable of Boy Jones")

Since first the White Horse Banner blew free,
  By Hengist's horde unfurled,
Nothing has changed on land or sea
  Of the things that steer the world.
(As it was when the long-ships scudded through the gale
  So it is where the Liners go.)
Time and Tide, they are both in a tale—
  "Woe to the weaker—woe!"

No charm can bridle the hard-mouthed wind
  Or smooth the fretting swell.
No gift can alter the grey Sea's mind,
  But she serves the strong man well.
(As it is when her uttermost deeps are stirred
  So it is where the quicksands show,)
All the waters have but one word—
  "Woe to the weaker—woe!"

The feast is ended, the tales are told,
  The dawn is overdue,
And we meet on the quay in the whistling cold
  Where the galley waits her crew.
Out with the torches, they have flared too long,
  And bid the harpers go.
Wind and warfare have but one song—
  "Woe to the weaker—woe!"

Hail to the great oars gathering way,
  As the beach begins to slide!
Hail to the war-shields' click and play
  As they lift along our side!
Hail to the first wave over the bow—
  Slow for the sea-stroke!   Slow!—
All the benches are grunting now:—
  "Woe to the weaker—woe!"

The Nurses

("The Bold 'Prentice")

When, with a pain he desires to explain to his servitors, Baby
Howls himself black in the face, toothlessly striving to curse;
And the six-months-old Mother begins to inquire of the Gods if it may be
Tummy, or Temper, or Pins—what does the adequate Nurse?

See!   At a glance and a touch his trouble is guessed; and, thereafter,
She juggles (unscared by his throes) with drops of hot water and spoons,
Till the hiccoughs are broken by smiles, and the smiles pucker up into
    laughter,
And he lies o'er her shoulder and crows, and she, as she nurses him,
    croons! . . .

When, at the head of the grade, tumultuous out of the cutting
Pours the belated Express, roars at the night, and draws clear,
Redly obscured or displayed by her fire-door's opening and shutting—
Symbol of strength under stress—what does her small engineer?

Clamour and darkness encircle his way.   Do they deafen or blind him?
No!—nor the pace he must keep.   He, being used to these things,
Placidly follows his work, which is laying his mileage behind him,
While his passengers placidly sleep, and he, as he nurses her, sings! . . .

When, with the gale at her heel, the ship lies down and recovers—
Rolling through forty degrees, combing the stars with her tops,
What says the man at the wheel, holding her straight as she hovers
On the summits of wind-screening seas; steadying her as she drops?

Behind him the blasts without check from the Pole to the Tropic, pursue
    him,
Heaving up, heaping high, slamming home, the surges he must not
    regard:
Beneath him the crazy wet deck, and all Ocean on end to undo him:
Above him one desperate sail, thrice-reefed but still buckling the yard!

Under his hand fleet the spokes and return, to be held or set free again;
And she bows and makes shift to obey their behest, till the master-wave
    comes
And her gunnel goes under in thunder and smokes, and she chokes in the
    trough of the sea again—
Ere she can left and make way to its crest; and he, as he nurses her,
    hums! . . .

These have so utterly mastered their work that they work without thinking;
Holding three-fifths of their brain in reserve for whatever betide.
So, when catastrophe threatens, of colic, collision or sinking,
They shunt the full gear into train, and take that small thing in their stride.

A Counting-Out Song

("An English School")

What is the song the children sing
When doorway lilacs bloom in Spring,
And the Schools are loosed, and the games are played
That were deadly earnest when Earth was made?
Hear them chattering, shrill and hard,
After dinner-time, out in the yard,
As the sides are chosen and all submit
To the chance of the lot that shall make them "It."
    (Singing) *"Eenee, Meenee, Mainee, Mo!*
                Catch a nigger by the toe!
                If he hollers let him go!
                Eenee, Meenee, Mainee, Mo!
                You—are—It!"

Eenee, Meenee, Mainee, and Mo
Were the First Big Four of the Long Ago,
When the Pole of the Earth sloped thirty degrees,
And Central Europe began to freeze,
And they needed Ambassadors staunch and stark
To steady the Tribes in the gathering dark:
But the frost was fierce and flesh was frail,
So they launched a Magic that could not fail.
    (Singing) *"Eenee, Meenee, Mainee, Mo!*
                Hear the wolves across the snow!
                Some one has to kill 'em—so
                Eenee, Meenee, Mainee, Mo
                Make—you—It!"

Slowly the Glacial Epoch passed,
Central Europe thawed out at last;
And, under the slush of the melting snows,

The first dim shapes of the Nations rose.
Rome, Britannia, Belgium, Gaul—
Flood and avalanche fathered them all;
And the First Big Four, as they watched the mess,
Pitied Man in his helplessness.
    (Singing) *"Eenee, Meenee, Mainee, Mo!*
                Trouble starts when Nations grow.
                Some one has to stop it—so
                Eenee, Meenee, Mainee, Mo
                Make—you—It!"

Thus it happened, but none can tell
What was the Power behind the spell—
Fear, or Duty, or Pride, or Faith—
That sent men shuddering out to death—
To cold and watching, and, worse than these,
Work, more work, when they looked for ease—
To the day's discomfort, the night's despair,
In the hope of a prize that they never could share.
    (Singing) *"Eenee, Meenee, Mainee, Mo!*
                Man is born to Toil and Woe.
                One will cure the other—so
                Eenee, Meenee, Mainee, Mo
                Make—you—It."

Once and again, as the Ice went North
The grass crept up to the Firth of Forth.
Once again, as the Ice came South
The glaciers ground over Lossiemouth.
But, grass or glacier, cold or hot,
The men went out who would rather not,
And fought with the Tiger, the Pig and the Ape,
To hammer the world into decent shape.
    (Singing) *"Eenee, Meenee, Mainee, Mo!*
                What's the use of doing so?
                Ask the Gods, for we don't know;
                But Eenee, Meenee, Mainee, Mo
                Make—us—It!"

Nothing is left of that terrible rune
But a tag of gibberish tacked to a tune
That ends the waiting and settles the claims
Of children arguing over their games;

For never yet has a boy been found
To shirk his turn when the turn came round;
Nor even a girl has been known to say
"If you laugh at me I shan't play."
    For—   "Eenee, Meenee, Mainee, Mo,
            (Don't you let the grown-ups know!)
            You may hate it ever so,
            But if you're chose you're bound to go,
            When Eenee, Meenee, Mainee, Mo
            Make—you—It!"

Verses from
"Debits and Credits"
1919 – 1926

The Changelings

(R.N.V.R.)

("Sea Constables")

Or ever the battered liners sank
    With their passengers to the dark,
I was head of a Walworth Bank,
    And you were a grocer's clerk.

I was a dealer in stocks and shares,
    And you in butters and teas;
And we both abandoned our own affairs
    And took to the dreadful seas.

Wet and worry' about our ways—
    Panic, onset, and flight—
Had us in charge for a thousand days
    And a thousand-year-long night.

We saw more than the nights could hide—
    More than the waves could keep—
And—certain faces over the side
    Which do not go from our sleep.

We were more tired than words can tell
    While the pied craft fled by,
And the swinging mounds of the Western swell
    Hoisted us Heavens-high ...

Now there is nothing—not even our rank—
    To witness what we have been;
And I am returned to my Walworth Bank,
    And you to your margarine!

The Vineyard

("Sea Constables")

At the eleventh hour he came,
But his wages were the same
As ours who all day long had trod
The wine-press of the Wrath of God.

When he shouldered through the lines
Of our cropped and mangled vines,

His unjaded eye could scan
How each hour had marked its man.

(Children of the morning-tide
With the hosts of noon had died;
And our noon contingents lay
Dead with twilight's spent array.)

Since his back had felt no load,
Virtue still in him abode;
So he swiftly made his own
Those last spoils we had not won.

We went home, delivered thence,
Grudging him no recompense
Till he portioned praise or blame
To our works before he came.

Till he showed us for our good—
    Deaf to mirth, and blind to scorn—
How we might have best withstood
    Burdens that he had not borne!

"Banquet Night"

(" 'In the Interests of the Brethren' ")

"Once in so often," King Solomon said,
    Watching his quarrymen drill the stone,
"We will club our garlic and wine and bread
    And banquet together beneath my Throne.
And all the Brethren shall come to that mess
As Fellow-Craftsmen—no more and no less.

"Send a swift shallop to Hiram of Tyre,
    Felling and floating our beautiful trees,
Say that the Brethren and I desire
    Talk with our Brethren who use the seas.
And we shall be happy to meet them at mess
As Fellow-Craftsmen—no more and no less.

"Carry this message to Hiram Abif—
    Excellent Master of forge and mine:—
I and the Brethren would like it if
    He and the Brethren will come to dine
(Garments from Bozrah or morning-dress)
As Fellow-Craftsmen—no more and no less.

"God gave the Hyssop and Cedar their place—
    Also the Bramble, the Fig and the Thorn—
But that is no reason to black a man's face
    Because he is not what he hasn't been born.
And, as touching the Temple, I hold and profess
We are Fellow-Craftsmen—no more and no less."

So it was ordered and so it was done,
    And the hewers of wood and the Masons of Mark,
With foc'sle hands of the Sidon run
    And Navy Lords from the *Royal Ark*,
Came and sat down and were merry at mess
As Fellow-Craftsmen—no more and no less.

The Quarries are hotter than Hiram's forge,
    No one is safe from the dog-whips' reach.
It's mostly snowing up Lebanon gorge,
    And it's always blowing off Joppa beach;
But once in so often, the messenger brings
Solomon's mandate: "Forget these things!
Brother to Beggars and Fellow to Kings,
Companion of Princes—forget these things!
Fellow-Craftsman, forget these things!"

To the Companions

HORACE, Bk. V. Ode 17.

("The United Idolaters")

How comes it that, at even-tide,
    When level beams should show most truth,
Man, failing, takes unfailing pride
    In memories of his frolic youth?

Venus and Liber fill their hour;
    The games engage, the law-courts prove;
Till hardened life breeds love of power
    Or Avarice, Age's final love.

Yet at the end, these comfort not—
    Nor any triumph Fate decrees—
Compared with glorious, unforgot-
    ten innocent enormities

Of frontless days before the beard,
    When, instant on the casual jest,

The God Himself of Mirth appeared
    And snatched us to His heaving breast.

And we—not caring who He was
    But certain He would come again—
Accepted all He brought to pass
    As Gods accept the lives of men . . .

Then He withdrew from sight and speech,
    Nor left a shrine. How comes it now,
While Charon's keel grates on the beach,
    He calls so clear: "Rememberest thou?"?

The Centaurs

("The United Idolaters")

Up came the young Centaur-colts from the plains they were fathered in—
    Curious, awkward, afraid.
Burrs on their hocks and their tails, they were branded and gathered in
    Mobs and run up to the yard to be made.

Starting and shying at straws, with sidlings and plungings,
    Bucking and whirlings and bolts;
Greener than grass, but full-ripe for their bridlings and lungings,
    Up to the yards and to Chiron they bustled the colts . . .

First the light web and the cavesson; then the linked keys
    To jingle and turn on the tongue. Then, with cocked ears,
The hours of watching and envy, while comrades at ease
    Passaged and backed, making naught of these terrible gears.

Next, over-pride and its price at the low-seeming fence,
    Too oft and too easily taken—the world-beheld fall!
And none in the yard except Chiron to doubt the immense,
    Irretrievable shame of it all! . . .

Last, the trained squadron, full-charge—the sound of a going
    Through dust and spun clods, and strong kicks, pelted in as they went,
And repaid at top-speed; till the order to halt without slowing
    Showed every colt on his haunches—and Chiron content!

"Late Came the God"

("The Wish House")

Late came the God, having sent his forerunners who were not regarded—
    Late, but in wrath;
Saying: "The wrong shall be paid, the contempt be rewarded
    On all that she hath."
He poisoned the blade and struck home, the full bosom receiving
The wound and the venom in one, past cure or relieving.

He made treaty with Time to stand still that the grief might be fresh—
Daily renewed and nightly pursued through her soul to her flesh—
Mornings of memory, noontides of agony, midnights unslaked for her,
Till the stones of the street of her Hells and her Paradise ached for her.

So she lived while her body corrupted upon her.
    And she called on the Night for a sign, and a Sign was allowed,
And she builded an Altar and served by the light of her Vision—
    Alone, without hope of regard or reward, but uncowed,
Resolute, selfless, divine.
    These things she did in Love's honour . . .
What is a God beside Woman?   Dust and derision!

Rahere

("The Wish House")

Rahere, King Henry's Jester, feared by all the Norman Lords
For his eye that pierced their bosoms, for his tongue that shamed their
    swords;
Feed and flattered by the Churchmen—well they knew how deep he stood
In dark Henry's crooked counsels—fell upon an evil mood.

Suddenly, his days before him and behind him seemed to stand
Stripped and barren, fixed and fruitless, as those leagues of naked sand
When St. Michael's ebb slinks outward to the bleak horizon-bound,
And the trampling wide-mouthed waters are withdrawn from sight and
    sound.

Then a Horror of Great Darkness sunk his spirit and anon,
(Who had seen him wince and whiten as he turned to walk alone)
Followed by Gilbert the Physician, and muttered in his ear,
"Thou hast it, O my brother?" "Yea, I have it," said Rahere.

"So it comes," said Gilbert smoothly, "man's most immanent distress.
'Tis a humour of the Spirit which abhorreth all excess;
And, whatever breed the surfeit—Wealth, or Wit, or Power, or Fame
(And thou hast each) the Spirit laboureth to expel the same.

"Hence the dulled eye's deep self-loathing—hence the loaded leaden brow;
Hence the burden of Wanhope that aches thy soul and body now.
Ay, the merriest fool must face it, and the wisest Doctor learn;
For it comes—it comes," said Gilbert, "as it passes—to return."

But Rahere was in his torment, and he wandered, dumb and far,
Till he came to reeking Smithfield where the crowded gallows are,
(Followed Gilbert the Physician) and beneath the wry-necked dead,
Sat a leper and his woman, very merry, breaking bread.

He was cloaked from chin to ankle—faceless, fingerless, obscene—
Mere corruption swaddled man-wise, but the woman whole and clean;
And she waited on him crooning, and Rahere beheld the twain,
Each delighting in the other, and he checked and groaned again

"So it comes,—it comes," said Gilbert, "as it came when Life began.
'Tis a motion of the Spirit that revealeth God to man.
In the shape of Love exceeding, which regards not taint or fall,
Since in perfect Love, saith Scripture, can be no excess at all.

"Hence the eye that sees no blemish—hence the hour that holds no
    shame.
Hence the Soul assured the Essence and the Substance are the same.
Nay, the meanest need not miss it, though the mightier pass it by;
For it comes—it comes," said Gilbert, "and, thou seest, it does not die!"

The Survival

HORACE, Bk. V. Ode 22.

("The Janeites")

Securely, after days
    Unnumbered, I behold
Kings mourn that promised praise
    Their cheating bards foretold.

Of earth-constricting wars,
    Of Princes passed in chains,
Of deeds out-shining stars,
    No word or voice remains.

Yet furthest times receive,
    And to fresh praise restore,
Mere breath of flutes at eve,
    Mere seaweed on the shore.

A smoke of sacrifice;
    A chosen myrtle-wreath;
An harlot's altered eyes;
    A rage 'gainst love or death;

Glazed snow beneath the moon;
    The surge of storm-bowed trees—
The Caesars perished soon,
    And Rome Herself: But these

Endure while Empires fall
    And Gods for Gods make room. . . .
Which greater God than all
    Imposed the amazing doom?

Jane's Marriage

("The Janeites")

Jane went to Paradise:
    That was only fair.
Good Sir Walter followed her,
    And armed her up the stair.
Henry and Tobias,
    And Miguel of Spain,
Stood with Shakespeare at the top
    To welcome Jane—

Then the Three Archangels
    Offered out of hand
Anything is Heaven's gift
    That she might command.
Azrael's eyes upon her,
    Raphael's wing above,
Michael's sword against her heart,
    Jane said: "Love."

Instantly the under-
    standing Seraphim
Laid their fingers on their lips
    And went to look for him.

Stole across the Zodiac,
    Harnessed Charles's Wain,
And whispered round the Nebulae
    "Who loved Jane?"

In a private limbo
    Where none had thought to look,
Sat a Hampshire gentleman
    Reading of a book.
It was called *Persuasion*,
    And it told the plain
Story of the love between
    Him and Jane.

He heard the question
    Circle Heaven through—
Closed the book and answered:
    "I did—and I do!"

Quietly but speedily
    (As Captain Wentworth moved)
Entered into Paradise
    The man Jane loved!

Jane lies in Winchester, blessèd be her shade!
Praise the Lord for making her, and her for all she made.
And, while the stones of Winchester—or Milsom Street—remain,
Glory, Love, and Honour unto England's Jane!

The Portent

HORACE, Bk. V. Ode 20.

("The Prophet and the Country")

Oh, late withdrawn from human-kind
    And following dreams we never knew!
Varus, what dream has Fate assigned
    To trouble you?

Such virtue as commends the law
    Of Virtue to the vulgar horde
Suffices not. You needs must draw
    A righteous sword;

And, flagrant in well-doing, smite
   The priest of Bacchus at their fane,
Lest any worshipper invite
   The God again.

Whence public strife and naked crime
   And—deadlier than the cup you shun—
A people schooled to mock in time,
   All law—not one.

Cease, then, to fashion State-made sin,
   Nor give thy children cause to doubt
That Virtue springs from iron within—
   Not lead without.

Alnaschar and the Oxen

("The Bull that Thought")

There's a pasture in a valley where the hanging woods divide.
   And a Herd lies down and ruminates in peace;
Where the pheasant rules the nooning, and the owl the twilight-tide,
   And the war-cries of our world die out and cease.
Here I cast aside the burden that each weary week-day brings
   And, delivered from the shadows I pursue,
On peaceful, postless Sabbaths I consider Weighty Things—
   Such as Sussex Cattle feeding in the dew!

At the gate beside the river where the trouty shallows brawl,
   I know the pride that Lobengula felt,
When he bade the bars be lowered of the Royal Cattle Kraal,
   And fifteen miles of oxen took the veldt.
From the walls of Bulawayo in unbroken file they came
   To where the Mount of Council cuts the blue . . .
I have only six and twenty, but the principle's the same
   With my Sussex Cattle feeding in the dew!

To a luscious sound of tearing, where the clovered herbage rips,
   Level-backed and level-bellied watch 'em move—
See those shoulders, guess that heart-girth, praise those loins, admire those
    hips
   And the tail set low for flesh to make above!
Count the broad unblemished muzzles, test the kindly mellow skin,
   And, where yon heifer lifts her head at call,
Mark the bosom's just abundance 'neath the gay and clean-cut chin,
   And those eyes of Juno, overlooking all!

Here is colour, form and substance!   I will put it to the proof
    And, next season, in my lodges shall be born
Some very Bull of Mithras, flawless from his agate hoof
    To his even-branching, ivory, dusk-tipped horn.
He shall mate with block-square virgins—kings shall seek his like in vain,
    While I multiply his stock a thousandfold,
Till an hungry world extol me, builder of a lofty strain
    That turns one standard ton at two years old!

There's a valley, under oakwood, where a man may dream his dream,
    In the milky breath of cattle laid at ease,
Till the moon o'ertops the alders, and her image chills the stream,
    And the river-mist runs silver round their knees!
Now the footpaths fade and vanish;   now the ferny clumps deceive;
    Now the hedgerow-folk possess their fields anew;
Now the Herd is lost in darkness, and I bless them as I leave,
    My Sussex Cattle feeding in the Dew!

Gipsy Vans

("A Madonna of the Trenches")

Unless you come of the gipsy stock
    That steals by night and day,
Lock your heart with a double lock
    And throw the key away.
Bury it under the blackest stone
    Beneath your father's hearth,
And keep your eyes on your lawful own
    And your feet to the proper path.
        Then you can stand at your door and mock
            When the gipsy vans come through . . .
        For it isn't right that the Gorgio stock
            Should live as the Romany do.

Unless you come of the gipsy blood
    That takes an never spares,
Bide content with your given good
    And follow your own affairs.
Plough and harrow and roll your land,
    And sow what ought to be sowed;
But never let loose your heart from your hand,
    Nor flitter it down the road!

Then you can thrive on your boughten food
    As the gipsy vans come through . . .
For it isn't nature the Gorgio blood
    Should love as the Romany do.

Unless you carry the gipsy eyes
    That see but seldom weep,
Keep your head from the naked skies
    Or the stars'll trouble your sleep.
Watch your moon through your window-pane
    And take what weather she brews;
But don't run out in the midnight rain
    Nor home in the morning dews.
        Then you can huddle and shut your eyes
            As the gipsy vans come through . . .
        For it isn't fitting the Gorgio ryes
            Should walk as the Romany do.

Unless you come of the gipsy race
    That counts all time the same,
Be you careful of Time and Place
    And Judgment and Good Name:
Lose your life for to live your life
    The way you ought to do;
And when you are finished, your God and your wife
    And the Gipsies'll laugh at you!
        Then you can rot in your burying-place
            As the gipsy vans come through . . .
        For it isn't reason the Gorgio race
            Should die as the Romany do.

The Birthright

("The Propagation of Knowledge")

The miracle of our land's speech—so known
And long received, none marvel when 'tis shown!

We have such wealth as Rome at her most pride
Had not or (having) scattered not so wide;
Nor with such arrant prodigality
Beneath her any pagan's foot let lie . . .
Lo! Diamond that cost some half their days
To find and t'other half to bring to blaze:
Rubies of every heat, wherethrough we scan

The fiercer and more fiery heart of man:
Emerald that with the uplifted billow vies,
And Sapphires evening remembered skies:
Pearl perfect, as immortal tears must show,
Bred, in deep waters, of a piercing woe;
And tender Turkis, so with charms y-writ,
Of woven gold, Time dares not bite on it.
Thereafter, in all manners worked and set,
Jade, coral, amber, crystal, ivories, jet,—
Showing no more than various fancies, yet
Each a Life's token or Love's amulet. . . .
With things, through timeless arrogance of use,
We neither guard nor garner, but abuse;
So that our scholars—nay, our children—fling
In sport or jest treasure to arm a King;
And the gross crowd, at feast or market, hold
Traffic perforce with dust of gems and gold!

A Legend of Truth

("A Friend of the Family")

Once upon a time, the ancient legends tell,
Truth, rising from the bottom of her well,
Looked on the world, but, hearing how it lied,
Returned to her seclusion horrified.
There she abode, so conscious of her worth,
Not even Pilate's Question called her forth,
Nor Galileo, kneeling to deny
The Laws that hold our Planet 'neath the sky.
Meantime, her kindlier sister, whom men call
Fiction, did all her work and more than all,
With so much zeal, devotion, tact, and care,
That no one noticed Truth was otherwhere.

Then came a War when, bombed and gassed and mined,
Truth rose once more, perforce, to meet mankind,
And through the dust and glare and wreck of things,
Beheld a phantom on unbalanced wings,
Reeling and groping, dazed, dishevelled, dumb,
But semaphoring direr deeds to come.
Truth hailed and bade her stand; the quavering shade
Clung to her knees and babbled, "Sister, aid!
I am—I was—Thy Deputy, and men

Besought me for my useful tongue or pen
To gloss their gentle deeds, and I complied,
And they, and thy demands, were satisfied.
But this—" she pointed o'er the blistered plain,
Where men as Gods and devils wrought amain—
"This is beyond me!   Take thy work again."

Tablets and pen transferred, she fled afar,
And Truth assumed the record of the War . . .
She saw, she heard, she read, she tried to tell
Facts beyond precedent and parallel—
Unfit to hint or breathe, much less to write,
But happening every minute, day and night.
She called for proof.   It came.   The dossiers grew.
She marked them, first, "Return.   This *can't* be true."
Then, underneath the cold official word:
"This is not really half of what occurred."

She faced herself at last, the story runs,
And telegraphed her sister: "Come at once.
Facts out of hand.   Unable overtake
Without your aid.   Come back for Truth's own sake!
Co-equal rank and powers if you agree.
They need us both, but you far more than me!"

We and They

("A Friend of the Family")

Father, Mother, and Me,
    Sister and Auntie say
All the people like us are We,
    And every one else is They.
And They live over the sea,
    While We live over the way,
But—would you believe it?—They look upon We
    As only a sort of They!

We eat pork and beef
    With cow-horn-handled knives.
They who gobble Their rice off a leaf,
    Are horrified out of Their lives;
While They who live up a tree,
    And feast on grubs and clay,

(Isn't it scandalous?) look upon We
   As a simply disgusting They!

We shoot birds with a gun
   They stick lions with spears.
Their full-dress is un-.
   We dress up to Our ears.
They like Their friends for tea.
   We like Our friends to stay;
And, after all that, They look upon We
   As an utterly ignorant They!

We eat kitcheny food.
   We have doors that latch.
They drink milk or blood,
   Under an open thatch.
We have Doctors to fee.
   They have Wizards to pay.
And (impudent heathen!) They look upon We
   As a quite impossible They!

All good people agree,
   And all good people say,
All nice people, like Us, are We
   And every one else is They:
But if you cross over the sea,
   Instead of over the way,
You may end by (think of it!) looking on We
   As only a sort of They!

Untimely

("The Eye of Allah")

Nothing in life has been made by man for man's using
But it was shown long since to man in ages
Lost as the name of the maker of it,

Who received oppression and shame for his wages—
Hate, avoidance, and scorn in his daily dealings—
Until he perished, wholly confounded.

More to be pitied than he are the wise
Souls which foresaw the evil of loosing
Knowledge or Art before time, and aborted
Noble devices and deep-wrought healings,
Lest offence should arise.

Heaven delivers on earth the Hour that cannot be thwarted,
Neither advanced, at the price of a world nor a soul, and its Prophet
Comes through the blood of the vanguards who dreamed—too soon—it
    had sounded.

The Last Ode

NOV. 27, 8 B.C.

HORACE, Bk. V. Ode 31.

("The Eye of Allah")

As watchers couched beneath a Bantine oak,
    Hearing the dawn-wind stir
Know that the present strength of night is broke
    Though no dawn threaten her
Till dawn's appointed hour—so Virgil died,
Aware of change at hand, and prophesied

Change upon all the Eternal Gods had made
    And on the Gods alike—
Fated as dawn but, as the dawn, delayed
    Till the just hour should strike—

At Star new-risen above the living and dead;
    And the lost shades that were our loves restored
As lovers, and for ever.   So he said;
    Having received the word . . .

Maecenas waits we on the Esquiline:
    Thither to-night go I. . . .
And shall this dawn restore us, Virgil mine,
    To dawn?   Beneath what sky?

The Burden

("The Gardener")

One grief on me is laid
    Each day of every year,
Wherein no soul can aid,
    Whereof no soul can hear:
Whereto no end is seen

Except to grieve again—
Ah, Mary Magdalene,
  Where is there greater pain?

To dream on dear disgrace
  Each hour of every day—
To bring no honest face
  To aught I do or say:
To lie from morn till e'en—
  To know my lies are vain—
Ah, Mary Magdalene,
  Where can be greater pain?

To watch my steadfast fear
  Attend mine every way
Each day of every year—
  Each hour of every day:
To burn, and chill between—
  To quake and rage again—
Ah, Mary Magdalene,
  Where shall be greater pain?

One grave to me was given—
  To guard till Judgment Day—
But God looked down from Heaven
  And rolled the Stone away!
One day of all my years—
  One hour of that one day—
His Angel saw my tears
  And rolled the Stone away!

The Supports

("On the Gate")

Song of the Waiting Seraphs

Full Chorus.
To Him Who bade the Heavens abide, yet cease not from their motion,
To Him Who tames the moonstruck tide twice a day round Ocean—
Let His Names be magnified in all poor folks' devotion!

Powers and Gifts.
Not for Prophecies or Powers, Visions, Gifts, or Graces,
But the unregardful hours that grind us in our places
With the burden on our backs, the weather in our faces.

Toils.
Not for any Miracle of easy Loaves and Fishes,
But for doing, 'gainst our will, work against our wishes—
Such as finding food to fill daily-emptied dishes.

Glories.
Not for Voices, Harps or Wings or rapt illumination,
But the grosser Self that springs of use and occupation,
Unto which the Spirit clings as her last salvation.

Powers, Glories, Toils, and Gifts.
(He Who launched our Ship of Fools many anchors gave us,
Lest one gale should start them all—one collision stave us.
                    Praise Him for the petty creeds
                    That prescribe in paltry needs
Solemn rites to trivial deeds and, by small things, save us!)

Services and Loves.
Heart may fail, and Strength outwear, and Purpose turn to Loathing,
But the everyday affair of business, meals, and clothing,
Builds a bulkhead 'twixt Despair and the Edge of Nothing.

Patiences.
(Praise Him, then, Who orders it that, though Earth be flaring
                    And the crazy skies are lit
                    By the searchlights of the Pit,
Man should not depart a whit from his wonted bearing.)

Hopes.
He Who bids the wild-swans' host still maintain their flight on
                    Air-roads over islands lost—
                    Ages since 'neath Ocean lost—
Beaches of some sunken coast their fathers would alight on—

Faiths.
He shall guide us through this dark not by new-blown glories.
But by every ancient mark our fathers used before us,
Till our children ground their ark where the proper shore is.

Services, Patiences, Faiths, Hopes, and Loves.
He Who used the clay that clings on our boots to make us,
Shall not suffer earthly things to remove or shake us:
                    But, when Man denies His Lord,
                    Habit without Fleet or Sword
                    (Custom without threat or word)

Sees the ancient fanes restored—the timeless rites o'ertake us!

Full Chorus.
For He Who makes the Mountains smoke and rives the Hills asunder,
                    And, to-morrow, leads the grass—
                    Mere unconquerable grass—
Where the fuming crater was, to heal and hide it under,
                    He shall not—He shall not—
Shall not lay on us the yoke of too long Fear and Wonder!

Verses from
"Limits and Renewals"
1932

Gertrude's Prayer

("Dayspring Mishandled")

That which is marred at birth Time shall not mend
   Nor water out of bitter well make clean;
All evil thing returneth at the end,
   Or elseway walketh in our blood unseen.
Whereby the more is sorrow in certaine—
Dayspring mishandled cometh not againe.

To-bruizèd be that slender, sterting spray
   Out of the oake's rind that should betide
A branch of girt and goodliness, straightway
   Her spring is turnèd on herself, and wried
And knotted like some gall or veiney wen.—
Dayspring mishandled cometh not again.

Noontide repayeth never morning-bliss—
   Sith noon to morn is incomparable;
And, so it be our dawning goth amiss,
   None other after-hour serveth well.
Ah! Jesu-Moder, pitie my oe paine—
Dayspring mishandled cometh not againe!

Dinah in Heaven

("The Woman in his Life")

She did not know that she was dead
   But, when the pang was o'er,
Sat down to wait her Master's tread
   Upon the Golden Floor,

With ears full-cock and anxious eyes,
   Impatiently resigned;
But ignorant that Paradise
   Did not admit her kind.

Persons with Haloes, Harps, and Wings
   Assembled and reproved;
Or talked to her of Heavenly things,
   But Dinah never moved.

639

There was one step along the Stair
   That led to Heaven's Gate;
And, till she heard it, her affair
   Was—she explained—to wait.

And she explained with flattened ear,
   Bared lip and milky tooth—
Storming against Ithuriel's Spear
   That only proved her truth!

Sudden—far down the Bridge of Ghosts
   That anxious spirits clomb—
She caught that step in all the hosts,
   And knew that he had come.

She left them wondering what to do,
   But not a doubt had she.
Swifter than her own squeal she flew
   Across the Glassy Sea;

Flushing the Cherubs everywhere,
   And skidding as she ran,
She refuged under Peter's Chair
   And waited for her man.

There spoke a Spirit out of the press,
   Said:—"Have you any here
That saved a fool from drunkenness,
   And a coward from his fear?

"That turned a soul from dark to day
   When other help was vain;
That snatched it from Wanhope and made
   A cur a man again?"

"Enter and look," said Peter then,
   And set The Gate ajar.
"If I know aught of women and men
   I trow she is not far."

"Neither by virtue, speech nor art
   Nor hope of grace to win;
But godless innocence of heart
   That never heard of sin:

"Neither by beauty nor belief
   Nor white example shown.
Something a wanton—more a thief—
   But—most of all—mine own."

"Enter and look," said Peter then,
  "And send you well to speed;
But, for all that I know of women and men
  Your riddle is hard to read."

Then flew Dinah from under the Chair,
  Into his arms she flew—
And licked his face from chin to hair
  And Peter passed them through!

Four-Feet

("The Woman in his Life")

I have done mostly what most men do,
And pushed it out of my mind;
But I can't forget, if I wanted to,
Four-Feet trotting behind.

Day after day, the whole day through—
Wherever my road inclined—
Four-Feet said, "I am coming with you!"
And trotted along behind.

Now I must go by some other round—
Which I shall never find—
Somewhere that does not carry the sound
Of Four-Feet trotting behind.

The Totem

("The Tie")

Ere the mother's milk had dried
  On my lips, the Brethren came—
Tore me from my nurse's side,
  And bestowed on me a name

Infamously overtrue—
  Such as "Bunny," "Stinker," "Podge";—
But, whatever I should do,
  Mine for ever in the Lodge.

Then they taught with palm and toe—
  Then I learned with yelps and tears—

All the Armoured Man should know
  Through his Seven Secret Years . . .

Last, oppressing as oppressed,
  I was loosed to go my ways
With a Totem on my breast
  Governing my nights and days—

Ancient and unbribeable,
  By the virtue of its Name—
Which, however oft I fell,
  Lashed my back into The Game.

And the World, that never knew,
  Saw no more beneath my chin
Than a patch of rainbow-hue,
  Mixed as Life and crude as Sin.

The Disciple

("The Church that was at Antioch")

He that hath a Gospel
  To loose upon Mankind,
Though he serve it utterly—
  Body, soul and mind—
Though he go to Calvary
  Daily for its gain—
It is His Disciple
  Shall make his labour vain.

He that hath a Gospel
  For all earth to own—
Though he etch it on the steel,
  Or carve it on the stone—
Not to be misdoubted
  Through the after-days—
It is His Disciple
  Shall read it many ways.

It is His Disciple
  (Ere Those Bones are dust)
Who shall change the Charter,
  Who shall split the Trust—
Amplify distinctions,

Rationalise the Claim;
Preaching that the Master
 Would have done the same.

It is His Disciple
 Who shall tell us how
Much the Master would have scrapped
 Had he lived till now—
What he would have modified
 Of what he said before.
It is His Disciple
 Shall do this and more. . . .

He that hath a Gospel
 Whereby Heaven is won
(Carpenter, or cameleer,
 Or Maya's dreaming son),
Many swords shall pierce Him,
 Mingling blood with gall;
But His Own Disciple
 Shall wound Him worst of all!

The Playmate

("Aunt Ellen")

She is not Folly—that I know.
Her steadfast eyelids tell me so
When, at the hour the lights divide,
She steals as summonsed to my side.

When, finger on the pursèd lip
In secret, mirthful fellowship,
She, heralding new-framed delights,
Breathes, "This shall be a Night of Nights!"

Then, out of Time and out of Space,
Is built an Hour and a Place
Where all an earnest, baffled Earth
Blunders and trips to make us mirth;

Whence, from the trivial flux of Things,
Rise unconceived miscarryings,
Outrageous but immortal, shown,
Of Her great love, to me alone. . . .

She is not Wisdom, but, maybe,
Wiser than all the Norns is She:
And more than Wisdom I prefer
To wait on Her,—to wait on Her!

Naaman's Song

("Aunt Ellen")

"Go, wash thyself in Jordan—go, wash thee and be clean!"
Nay, not for any Prophet will I plunge a toe therein!
For the banks of curious Jordan are parcelled into sites,
Commanded and embellished and patrolled by Israelites.

There rise her timeless capitals of Empires daily born,
Whose plinths are laid at midnight, and whose streets are packed at
    morn;
And here come hired youths and maids that feign to love or sin
In tones like rusty razor-blades to tunes like smitten tin.

And here be merry murtherings, and steeds with fiery hooves;
And furious hordes with guns and swords, and clamberings over rooves;
And horrid tumblings down from Heaven, and flights with wheels and
    wings;
And always one weak virgin who is chased through all these things.

And here is mock of faith and truth, for children to behold;
And every door of ancient dirt reopened to the old;
With every word that taints the speech, and show that weakens thought;
And Israel watcheth over each, and—doth not watch for nought. . . .

But Pharpar—but Abana—which Hermon launcheth down—
They perish fighting desert-sands beyond Damascus-town.
But yet their pulse is of the snows—their strength is from on high—
And, if they cannot cure my woes, a leper will I die!

The Mother's Son

("Fairy-kist")

I have a dream—a dreadful dream—
    A dream that is never done.
I watch a man go out of his mind,
    And he is My Mother's Son.

They pushed him into a Mental Home,
    And that is like the grave:
For they do not let you sleep upstairs,
    And you aren't allowed to shave.

And it was *not* disease or crime
    Which got him landed there,
But because They laid on My Mother's Son
    More than a man could bear.

What with noise, and fear of death,
    Waking, and wounds and cold,
They filled the Cup for My Mother's Son
    Fuller than it could hold.

They broke his body and his mind
    And yet They made him live,
And They asked more of My Mother's Son
    Than any man could give.

For, just because he had not died,
    Nor been discharged nor sick,
They dragged it out with My Mother's Son
    Longer than he could stick. . . .

And no one knows when he'll get well—
    So, there he'll have to be:
And, 'spite of the beard in the looking-glass,
    I know that man is me!

The Coiner

(*Circa* 1611)

*(To be sung by the unlearned to the tune of "King John and the Abbot of
Canterbury," and by the learned to "Tempest-a-brewing.")*

("A Naval Mutiny")

Against the Bermudas we foundered, whereby
This Master, that Swabber, yon Bo'sun, and I
(Our pinnace and crew being drowned in the main)
Must beg for our bread through old England again.

For a bite and a sup, and a bed of clean straw,
We'll tell you such marvels as man never saw,
On a Magical Island which no one did spy
Save this Master, that Swabber, yon Bo'sun, and I.

Seven months among Mermaids and Devils and Sprites,
And Voices that howl in the cedars o' nights,
With further enchantments we underwent there.
Good Sirs, 'tis a tale to draw guts from a bear!

'Twixt Dover and Southwark it paid us our way,
Where we found some poor players were labouring a play;
And, willing to search what such business might be,
We entered the yard, both to hear and to see.

One hailed us for seamen and courteous-ly
Did guide us apart to a tavern near by
Where we told him our tale (as to many of late),
And he gave us good cheer, so we gave him good weight.

Mulled sack and strong waters on bellies well lined
With beef and black pudding do strengthen the mind;
And seeing him greedy for marvels, at last
From plain salted truth to flat leasing we passed.

But he, when on midnight our reckoning he paid,
Says, "Never match coins with a Coiner by trade,
Or he'll turn your lead pieces to metal as rare
As shall fill him this globe, and leave something to spare. . . ."

We slept where they laid us, and when we awoke
Was a crown or five shillings in every man's poke.
We bit them and rang them, and, finding them good,
We drank to the Coiner as honest men should!

For a cup and a crust, and a truss, etc.

Akbar's Bridge

("The Debt")

Jelaludin Muhammed Akbar, Guardian of Mankind,
Moved his standards out of Delhi to Jaunpore of lower Hind,
Where a mosque was to be builded, and a lovelier ne'er was planned;
And Munim Khan, his Viceroy, slid the drawings 'neath his hand.

(High as Hope upsheered her out-works to the promised Heavens above.
Deep as Faith and dark as Judgment her unplumbed foundations dove.
Wide as Mercy, white as moonlight, stretched her forecourts to the dawn;
And Akbar gave commandment, "Let it rise as it is drawn.")

Then he wearied—the mood moving—of the men and things he ruled,
And he walked beside the Goomti while the flaming sunset cooled,
Simply, without mark or ensign—singly, without guard or guide,
Till he heard an angry woman screeching by the river-side.

'Twas the Widow of the Potter, a virago feared and known,
In haste to cross the ferry, but the ferry-man had gone.
So she cursed him and his office, and hearing Akbar's tread,
(She was very old and darkling) turned her wrath upon his head.

But he answered—being Akbar—"Suffer me to scull you o'er."
Called her "Mother," stowed her bundles, worked the clumsy scow from
    shore,
Till they grounded on a sand-bank, and the Widow loosed her mind;
And the stars stole out and chuckled at the Guardian of Mankind.

"Oh, most impotent of bunglers!   Oh, my daughter's daughter's brood
Waiting hungry on the threshold; for I cannot bring their food,
Till a fool has learned his business at their virtuous grandam's cost,
And a greater fool, our Viceroy, trifles while her name is lost!

"Munim Khan, that Sire of Asses, sees me daily come and go
As it suits a drunken boatman, or this ox who cannot row.
Munim Khan, the Owl's Own Uncle—Munim Khan, the Capon's seed,
Must build a mosque to Allah when a bridge is all we need!

"Eighty years I eat oppression and extortion and delays—
Snake and crocodile and fever, flood and drouth, beset my ways.
But Munim Khan must tax us for his mosque whate'er befall;
Allah knowing (May He hear me!) that a bridge would save us all!"

While she stormed that other laboured and, when they touched the shore,
Laughing brought her on his shoulder to her hovel's very door.
But his mirth increased her anger, for she thought he mocked the weak;
So she scored him with her talons, drawing blood on either cheek. . . .

Jelaludin Muhammed Akbar, Guardian of Mankind,
Spoke with Munim Khan his Viceroy, ere the midnight stars declined—
Girt and sworded, robed and jewelled, but on either cheek appeared
Four shameless scratches running from the turban to the beard.

"Allah burn all Potters' Widows!   Yet, since this same night was young,
One has shown me by sure token, there was wisdom on her tongue.
Yes, I ferried her for hire.   Yes," he pointed, "I was paid."
And he told the tale rehearsing all the Widow did and said.

And he ended, "Sire of Asses—Capon—Owl's Own Uncle—know
I—most impotent of bunglers—I—this ox who cannot row—
I—Jelaludin Muhammed Akbar, Guardian of Mankind—
Bid thee build the hag her bridge and put our mosque from out thy
    mind."

So 'twas built, and Allah blessed it; and, through earthquake, flood, and
    sword,
Still the bridge his Viceroy builded throws her arch o'er Akbar's Ford!

At His Execution

("The Manner of Men")

(*St. Paul*)

I am made all things to all men—
    Hebrew, Roman and Greek—
    In each one's tongue I speak,
Suiting to each my word,
That some may be drawn to the Lord!

I am made all things to all men—
    In City or Wilderness
    Praising the crafts they profess
That some may be drawn to the Lord—
By any means to my Lord!

Since I was overcome
    By that great Light and Word,
I have forgot or forgone
The self men call their own
(Being made all things to all men)
    So that I might save some,
    At such small price, to the Lord,
As being all things to all men.

I was made all things to all men,
But now my course is done—
And now is my reward . . .
Ah, Christ, when I stand at Thy Throne
With those I have drawn to the Lord,
Restore me my self again!

The Threshold

("Unprofessional")

In their deepest caverns of limestone
  They pictured the Gods of Food—
The Horse, the Elk, and the Bison
  That the hunting might be good;
With the Gods of Death and Terror—
  The Mammoth, Tiger, and Bear.
And the pictures moved in the torchlight
  To show that the Gods were there!
    But that was before Ionia—
    (Or the Seven Holy Islands of Ionia)
    Any of the Mountains of Ionia,
    Had bared their peaks to the air.

The close years packed behind them,
  As the glaciers bite and grind,
Filling the new-gouged valleys
  With Gods of every kind.
Gods of all-reaching power—
  Gods of all-searching eyes—
But each to be wooed by worship
  And won by sacrifice.
    Till, after many winters, rose Ionia—
    (Strange men brooding in Ionia)
    Crystal-eyed Sages of Ionia
    Who said, "These tales are lies.

"We dream one Breath in all things,
  "That blows all things between.
"We dream one Matter in all things—
  "Eternal, changeless, unseen.
"That the heart of the Matter is single
  "Till the Breath shall bid it bring forth—
"By choosing or losing its neighbour—
  "All things made upon Earth."
    But Earth was wiser than Ionia
    (Babylon and Egypt than Ionia)
    And they overlaid the teaching of Ionia
    And the Truth was choked at birth.

It died at the Gate of Knowledge—
  The Key to the Gate in its hand—

And the anxious priests and wizards
   Re-blinded the wakening land;
For they showed, by answering echoes,
   And chasing clouds as they rose,
How shadows should stand for bulwarks
   Between mankind and its woes.
      It was then that men bethought them of Ionia
      (The few that had not allforgot Ionia)
      Or the Word that was whispered in Ionia;
      And they turned from the shadows and the shows.

They found one Breath in all things,
   That moves all things between.
They proved one Matter in all things—
   Eternal, changeless, unseen;
That the heart of the Matter was single
   Till the Breath should bid it bring forth—
      Even as men whispered in Ionia,
      (Resolute, unsatisfied Ionia)
      Ere the Word was stifled in Ionia—
      All things known upon earth!

Neighbours

("Beauty Spots")

The man that is open of heart to his neighbour,
   And stops to consider his likes and dislikes,
His blood shall be wholesome whatever his labour,
   His luck shall be with him whatever he strikes.
The Splendour of Morning shall duly possess him,
   That he may not be sad at the falling of eve.
And, when he has done with mere living—God bless him!—
   A many shall sigh, and one Woman shall grieve!

But he that is costive of soul toward his fellow,
   Through the ways, and the works, and the woes of this life,
Him food shall not fatten, him drink shall not mellow;
   And his innards shall brew him perpetual strife.
His eye shall be blind to God's Glory above him;
   His ear shall be deaf to Earth's Laughter around;
His Friends and his Club and his Dog shall not love him;
   And his Widow shall skip when he goes underground!

The Expert

("Beauty Spots")

Youth that trafficked long with Death,
    And to second life returns,
Squanders little time or breath
    On his fellow-man's concerns.
Earnèd peace is all he asks
To fulfil his broken tasks.

Yet, if he find war at home
    (Waspish and importunate),
He hath means to overcome
    Any warrior at his gate;
For the past he buried brings
Back unburiable things—

Nights that he lay out to spy
    Whence and when the raid might start;
Or prepared in secrecy
    Sudden blows to break its heart—
All the lore of No-Man's Land
Steels his soul and arms his hand.

So, if conflict vex his life
    Where he thought all conflict done,
He, resuming ancient strife,
    Springs his mine or trains his gun;
And, in mirth more dread than wrath,
Wipes the nuisance from his path!

The Curé

("The Miracle of Saint Jubanus")

Long years ago, ere R—lls or R—ce
    Trebled the mileage man could cover;
When Sh—nk's Mare was H—bs—n's Choice,
    And Bl—r—ot had not flown to Dover:
When good hoteliers looked askance
    If any power save horse-flesh drew vans—
Time was in easy, hand-made France,
    I met the Curé of Saint Juvans.

He was no babbler, but, at last,
   One learned from things he left unspoken
How in some fiery, far-off past,
   His, and a woman's, heart were broken.
He sought for death, but found it not,
   Yet, seeking, found his true vocation,
And fifty years, by all forgot,
   Toiled at a simple folk's salvation.

His pay was lower than our Dole;
   The piteous little church he tended
Had neither roof nor vestments whole
   Save what his own hard fingers mended:
While, any hour, at every need
   (As Conscience or La Grippe assailed 'em),
His parish bade him come with speed,
   And, foot or cart, he never failed 'em.

His speech—to suit his hearers—ran
   From pure Parisian to gross peasant,
With interludes North African
   If any Légionnaire were present:
And when some wine-ripe atheist mocked
   His office or the Faith he knelt in,
He left the sinner dumb and shocked
   By oaths his old Battalion dealt in.

And he was learned in Death and Life;
   And he was Logic's self (as France is).
He knew his flock—man, maid, and wife—
   Their forebears, failings, and finances.
Spite, Avarice, Devotion, Lies—
   Passion ablaze or sick Obsession—
He dealt with each physician-wise;
   Stern or most tender, as Confession . . .

To-day? God knows where he may lie—
   His Cross of weathered beads above him:
But one not worth to untie
   His shoe-string, prays you read—and love him!

Song of Seventy Horses

("The Miracle of Saint Jubanus")

Once again the Steamer at Calais—the tackles
Easing the car-trays on to the quay. Release her!

Sign—refill, and let me away with my horses.
(Seventy Thundering Horses!)
Slow through the traffic, my horses!   It is enough—it is France!

Whether the throat-closing brick-fields by Lille, or her pavés
Endlessly ending in rain between beet and tobacco;
Or that wind we shave by—the brutal North-Easter,
Rasping the newly dunged Somme.
(Into your collars, my horses!) It is enough—it is France!

Whether the dappled Argonne, the cloud-shadows packing
Either horizon with ghosts; or exquisite, carven
Villages hewn from the cliff, the torrents behind them
Feeding their never-quenched lights.
(Look to your footing, my horses!)   It is enough—it is France!

Whether that gale where Biscay jammed in the corner
Herds and heads her seas at the Landes, but defeated
Bellowing smokes along Spain, till the uttermost headlands
Make themselves dance in the mist.
(Breathe—breathe deeply, my horses!)   It is enough—it is France!

Whether the broken, honey-hued, honey-combed limestone,
Cream under white-hot sun; the rosemary bee-bloom
Sleepily noisy at noon and, somewhere to Southward,
Sleepily noisy, the Sea.
(Yes, it is warm here, my horses!)   It is enough—it is France!

Whether the Massif in Spring, the multiplied lacets
Hampered by slips or drifts; the gentians, under
Turbaned snow, pushing up the heavens of Summer
Though the stark moors lie black.
(Neigh through the icicled tunnels:—"It is enough—it is France!")

Hymn to Physical Pain

("The Tender Achilles")

Dread Mother of Forgetfulness
    Who, when Thy reign begins,
Wipest away the Soul's distress,
    And memory of her sins.

The trusty Worm that dieth not—
    The steadfast Fire also,
By Thy contrivance are forgot
    In a completer woe.

Thine are the lidless eyes of night
    That stare upon our tears,
Through certain hours which in our sight
    Exceed a thousand years:

Thine is the thickness of the Dark
    That presses in our pain,
As Thine the Dawn that bids us mark
    Life's grinning face again.

Thine is the weariness outworn
    No promise shall relieve,
That says at eve, "Would God 'twere morn!"
    At morn, "Would God 'twere eve!"

And when Thy tender mercies cease
    And life unvexed is due
Instant upon the false release
    The Worm and Fire renew.

Wherefore we praise Thee in the deep,
    And on our beds we pray
For Thy return that Thou may'st keep
    The Pains of Hell at bay!

The Penalty

("The Tender Achilles")

Once in life I watched a Star;
    But I whistled, "Let her go!
There are others, fairer far,
    Which my favouring skies shall show."
Here I lied, and herein I
Stood to pay the penalty.

Marvellous the Planets shone
    As I ranged from coast to coast;
But beyond comparison
    Rode the Star that I had lost.
I had lied, and only I
Did not guess the penalty! . . .

When my Heavens were turned to blood,
    When the dark had filled my day,
Furthest, but most faithful, stood
    That lone Star I cast away.
I had loved myself, and I
Have not lived and dare not die!

Azrael's Count

("Uncovenanted Mercies")

Lo! the Wild Cow of the Desert, her yeanling estrayed from her—
Lost in the wind-plaited sand-dunes—athirst in the maze of them.
Hot-foot she follows those foot-prints—thrice-tangled ways of them.
Her soul is shut save to one thing—the love-quest consuming her.
Fearless she lows past the camp, our fires affright her not.
Ranges she close to the tethered ones—the mares by the lances held.
Noses she softly apart the veil in the woman's tent.
Next—withdrawn under moonlight, a shadow afar off—
Fades. Ere men cry, "Hold her fast!" darkness recovers her.
She the all-crazed and forlorn, when the dogs threaten her,
Only a side-tossed horn, as though a fly troubled her,
Shows she hath heard, till a lance in the heart of her quivereth.
—Lo, from that carcass aheap—where speeds the soul of it?
Where is the tryst it must keep? Who is her pandar? Death!

Men I dismiss to the Mercy greet me not willingly;
Crying, "Why seekest Thou *me* first?   Are not my kin unslain?"
Shrinking aside from the Sword-edge, blinking the glare of it,
Sinking the chin in the neck-bone. How shall that profit them?
Yet, among men a ten thousand, few meet me otherwise.

Yet, among women a thousand, one comes to me mistress-wise.
Arms open, breasts open, mouth open—hot is her need on her.
Crying, "Ho, Servant, acquit me, the bound by Love's promises!
Haste Thou! He waits! I would go! Handle me lustily!"
Lo! her eyes stare past my wings, as things unbeheld by her.
Lo! her lips summonsing part. *I* am not whom she calls!
Lo! My sword sinks and returns. At no time she heedeth it
More than the dust of a journey, her garments brushed clear of it.
Lo! Ere the blood-gush has ceased, forward her soul rushes.
She is away to her tryst.   Who is her pandar   Death!

Miscellaneous Verse

The Gods of the Copybook Headings

1919

As I pass through my incarnations in every age and race.
I make my proper prostrations to the Gods of the Market-Place.
Peering through reverent fingers I watch them flourish and fall,
And the Gods of the Copybook Headings, I notice, outlast them all

We were living in trees when they met us.   They showed us each in turn
That Water would certainly wet us, as Fire would certainly burn:
But we found them lacking in Uplift, Vision and Breadth of Mind,
So we left them to teach the Gorillas while we followed the March of
  Mankind.

We moved as the Spirit listed.   *They* never altered their pace,
Being neither cloud nor wind-borne like the Gods of the Market-Place;
But they always caught up with our progress, and presently word would
  come
That a tribe had been wiped off its icefield, or the lights had gone out in
  Rome.
With the Hopes that our World is built on they were utterly out of touch,
They denied that the Moon was Stilton; they denied she was even Dutch.
They denied that Wishes were Horses; they denied that a Pig had Wings.
So we worshipped the Gods of the Market Who promised these beautiful
  things.

When the Cambrian measures were forming, They promised perpetual
  peace.
They swore, if we gave them our weapons, that the wars of the tribes
  would cease.
But when we disarmed They sold us and delivered us bound to our foe,
And the Gods of the Copybook Headings said: *"Stick to the Devil you
  know."*

On the first Feminian Sandstones we were promised the Fuller Life
(Which started by loving our neighbour and ended by loving his wife)
Till our women had no more children and the men lost reason and faith,
And the Gods of the Copybook Headings said: *"The Wages of Sin is
  Death."*

In the Carboniferous Epoch we were promised abundance for all,
By robbing selected Peter to pay for collective Paul;
But, though we had plenty of money, there was nothing our money could
  buy,
And the Gods of the Copybook Headings said: *"If you don't work you die."*

Then the Gods of the Market tumbled, and their smooth-tongued wizards withdrew,
And the hearts of the meanest were humbled and began to believe it was true
That All is not Gold that Glitters, and Two and Two make Four—
And the Gods of the Copybook Headings limped up to explain it once more.

As it will be in the future, it was at the birth of Man—
There are only four things certain since Social Progress began:—
 That the Dog returns to his Vomit and the Sow returns to her Mire,
And the burnt Fool's bandaged finger goes wabbling back to the Fire;

And that after this is accomplished, and the brave new world begins
When all men are paid for existing and no man must pay for his sins,
As surely as Water will wet us, as surely as Fire will burn,
The Gods of the Copybook Headings with terror and slaughter return!

The Scholars

1919

"Some hundreds of the younger naval officers whose education was interrupted by the War are now to be sent to various colleges at Cambridge to continue their studies. The experiment will be watched with great interest."—DAILY PAPERS.

"Oh, Show me how a rose can shut and be a bud again!"
Nay, watch my Lords of the Admiralty, for they have the work in train.
They have taken the men that were careless lads at Dartmouth in
   'Fourteen
And entered them at the landward schools as though no war had been.
They have piped the children off all the seas from the Falklands to the
   Bight,
And quartered them on the Colleges to learn to read and write!

Their books were rain and sleet and fog—the dry gale and the snow,
Their teachers were the hornèd mines and the hump-backed Death below.
Their schools were walled by the walking mist and roofed by the waiting
   skies,
When they conned their task in a new-sown field with the Moonlight
   Sacrifice.
They were not rated too young to teach, nor reckoned unfit to guide
When they formed their class on Helles' beach at the bows of the "River
   Clyde."

Their eyes are sunk by endless watch, their faces roughed by the spray,

Their feet are drawn by the wet sea-boots they changed not night or day
When they guarded the six-knot convoy's flank on the road to Norroway.
Their ears are stuffed with the week-long roar of the West-Atlantic gale
When the sloops were watching the Irish Shore from Galway to Kinsale.
Their hands are scored where the life-lines cut or the dripping funnel-stays
When they followed their leader at thirty knot between the Skaw and the
    Naze.
Their mouths are filled with the magic words they learned at the collier's
    hatch
When they coaled in the foul December dawns and sailed in the
    forenoon-watch;
Or measured the weight of a Pentland tide and the wind off Ronaldshay,
Till the target mastered the breathless tug and the hawser carried away.

They know the price to be paid for a fault—for a gauge-clock wrongly
    read,
Or a picket-boat to the gangway brought bows-on and full-ahead,
Or the drowsy second's lack of thought that cost a dozen dead.
They have touched a knowledge outreaching speech—as when the cutters
    were sent
To harvest the dreadful mile of beach after the *Vanguard* went.
They have learned great faith and little fear and a high heart in distress,
And how to suffer each sodden year of heaped-up weariness.
They have borne the bridle upon their lips and the yoke upon their neck,
Since they went down to the sea in ships to save the world from wreck—
Since the chests were slung down the College stair at Dartmouth in
    'Fourteen,
And now they are quit of the sea-affair as though no war had been.
Far have they steamed and much have they known, and most would they
    fain forget;
But now they are come to their joyous own with all the world in their
    debt.

Soft—blow soft on them, little East Wind! Be smooth for them, mighty
    stream!
Though the cams they use are not of your kind, and they bump, for
    choice, by steam.
Lightly dance with them, Newnham maid—but none too lightly believe.
They are hot from the fifty-month blockade, and they carry their hearts on
    their sleeve.
Tenderly, Proctor, let them down, if they do not walk as they should:
For, by God, if they owe you half a crown, you owe 'em your four years'
    food!

Hallowed River, most gracious Trees, Chapel beyond compare,
Here be gentlemen sick of the seas—take them into your care.

Far have they come, much have they braved.   Give them their hour of
   play,
While the hidden things their hands have saved work for them day by
   day:
Till the grateful Past their youth redeemed return them their youth once
   more,
And the Soul of the Child at last lets fall the unjust load that it bore!

The Clerks and the Bells

(OXFORD IN 1920)

The merry clerks of Oxenford they stretch themselves at ease
Unhelmeted on unbleached sward beneath unshrivelled trees.
For the leaves, the leaves, are on the bough, the bark is on the bole,
And East and West men's housen stand all even-roofed and whole . . .
(Men's housen doored and glazed and floored and whole at every turn!)
And so the Bells of Oxenford ring:—"Time it is to learn!"

The merry clerks of Oxenford they read and they are told
Of famous men who drew the sword in furious fights of old.
They heark and mark it faithfully, but never clerk will write
What vision rides 'twixt book and eye from any nearer fight.
(Whose supplication rends the soul?   Whose night-long cries repeat?)
And so the Bells of Oxenford ring:—"Time it is to eat!"

The merry clerks of Oxenford they sit them down anon
At tables fair with silver-ware and naperies thereon,
Free to refuse or dainty choose what dish shall seem them good;
For they have done with single meats, and waters streaked with blood . . .
(That three days' fast is overpast when all those guns said "Nay"!)
And so the Bells of Oxenford ring:—"Time it is to play!"

The merry clerks of Oxenford they hasten one by one
Or band in companies abroad to ride, or row, or run
By waters level with fair meads all goldenly bespread,
Where flash June's clashing dragon-flies—but no man bows his head,
(Though bullet-wise June's dragon-flies deride the fearless air!)
And so the Bells of Oxenford ring'—"Time it is for prayer!"

The pious clerks of Oxenford they kneel at twilight-tide
For to receive and well believe the Word of Him Who died.
And, though no present wings of Death hawk hungry round that place,
Their brows are bent upon their hands that none may see their face—

(Who set aside the world and died?   What life shall please Him best?)
And so the Bells of Oxenford ring:—"Time it is to rest!"

The merry clerks of Oxenford lie under bolt and bar
Lest they should rake the midnight clouds or chase a sliding star.
In fear of fine and dread rebuke, they round their full-night sleep,
And leave that world which once they took for older men to keep.
(Who walks by dreams what ghostly wood in search of play-mate slain?)
Until the Bells of Oxenford ring in the light again.

Unburdened breeze, unstricken trees, and all God's works restored—
In this way live the merry clerks,—the clerks of Oxenford!

A Rector's Memory

(ST. ANDREWS, 1923)

The Gods that are wiser than Learning
  But kinder than Life have made sure
No mortal may boast in the morning
  That even will find him secure.
With naught for fresh faith or new trial,
  With little unsoiled or unsold,
Can the shadow go back on the dial,
  Or a new world be given for the old?
    But he knows not what time shall awaken,
      As he knows not what tide shall lay bare,
      The heart of a man to be taken—
      Taken and changed unaware.

He shall see as he tenders his vows
  The far, guarded City arise—
The power of the North 'twixt Her brows—
  The steel of the North in Her eyes;
The sheer hosts of Heaven above—
  The grey warlock Ocean beside;
And shall feel the full centuries move
  To Her purpose and pride.
Though a stranger shall he understand,
  As though it were old in his blood,
The lives that caught fire 'neath Her hand—
  The fires that were tamed to Her mood.
And the roar of the wind shall refashion,
  And the wind-driven torches recall,

The passing of Time and the passion
  Of Youth over all!
    And, by virtue of magic unspoken
      (What need She should utter Her power?)
    The frost at his heart shall be broken
      And his spirit be changed in that hour—
      Changed and renewed in that hour!

Lollius

1920

HORACE, Bk. V. Ode 13

Why gird at Lollius if he care
  To purchase in the city's sight,
With nard and roses for his hair,
  The name of Knight?

Son of unmitigated sires
  Enriched by trade in Afric corn,
His wealth allows, his wife requires,
  Him to be born.

Him slaves shall serve with zeal renewed
  At lesser wage for longer whiles,
And school- and station-masters rude
  Receive with smiles.

His bowels shall be sought in charge
  By learned doctors; all his sons
And nubile daughters shall enlarge
  Their horizons.

For fierce she-Britons, apt to smite
  Their upward-climbing sisters down,
Shall smooth their plumes and oft invite
  The brood to town.

For these delights will he disgorge
  The State enormous benefice,
But—by the head of either George—
  He pays not twice!

Whom neither lust for public pelf,
  Nor itch to make orations, vex—
Content to honour his own self
  With his own cheques—

That man is clean. At least, his house
    Springs cleanly from untainted gold—
Not from a conscience or a spouse
    Sold and resold.

Time was, you say, before men knew
    Such arts, and rose by Virtue guided?
The tables rock with laughter—you
    Not least derided.

A Song of French Roads

1923

"The National Roads of France are numbered throughout, and carry their numbers upon each kilometre stone. By following these indications, comprehensible even to strangers, the tourist can see at a glance if he is on the correct road. For example, Route Nationale No. 20 conducts from Paris to the Spanish frontier at Bourg-Madame, in the Eastern Pyrenees; and No. 10 to the same frontier at Hendaye, on the Bay of Biscay."—GUIDE BOOK.

Now praise the Gods of Time and Chance
    That bring a heart's desire,
And lay the joyous roads of France
    Once more beneath the tyre—
So numbered by Napoleon,
    The veriest ass can spy
How Twenty takes to Bourg-Madame
    And Ten is for Hendaye.

Sixteen hath fed our fighting-line
    From Dunkirk to Péronne,
And Thirty-nine and Twenty-nine
    Can show where it has gone,
Which slant through Arras and Bapaume,
    And join outside Cambrai,
While Twenty takes to Bourg-Madame,
    And Ten is for Hendaye.

The crops and houses spring once more
    Where Thirty-seven ran,
And even ghostly Forty-four
    Is all restored to man.
Oh, swift as shell-hole poppies pass
    The blurring years go by,
And Twenty takes to Bourg-Madame,
    And Ten is for Hendaye!

And you desire that sheeted snow
    Where chill Mont Louis stands?
And we the rounder gales that blow
    Full-lunged across the Landes—
So you will use the Orleans Gate,
    While we slip through Versailles;
Since Twenty takes to Bourg-Madame,
    And Ten is for Hendaye.

Sou'-West by South—and South by West—
    On every vine appear
Those four first cautious leaves that test
    The temper of the year;
The dust is white at Angoulême,
    The sun is warm at Blaye;
And Twenty takes to Bourg-Madame,
    And Ten is for Hendaye.

Broad and unbridled, mile on mile,
    The last highway drops her line
Past Langon down that grey-walled aisle
    Of resin-scented pine;
And ninety to the lawless hour
    The kilometres fly—
What was your pace to Bourg-Madame?
    We sauntered to Hendaye.

Now Fontarabia marks our goal,
    And Bidassoa shows,
At issue with each whispering shoal
    In violet, pearl and rose,
Ere crimson over ocean's edge
    The sunset banners die . . .
Yes—Twenty takes to Bourg-Madame,
    But Ten is for Hendaye!

Oh, praise the Gods of Time and Chance
    That ease the long control,
And bring the glorious soul of France
    Once more to cheer our soul
With beauty, change and valiancy
    Of sun and soil and sky,
Where Twenty takes to Bourg-Madame,
    And Ten is for Hendaye!

Chartres Windows

1925

Colour fulfils where Music has no power:
   By each man's light the unjudging glass betrays
All men's surrender, each man's holiest hour
   And all the lit confusion of our days—
Purfled with iron, traced in dusk and fire,
   Challenging ordered Time who, at the last,
   Shall bring it, grozed and leaded and wedged fast,
   To the cold stone that curbs or crowns desire.
Yet on the pavement that all feet have trod—
   Even as the Spirit, in her deeps and heights,
Turns only, and that voiceless, to her God—
   There falls no tincture from those anguished lights.
And Heaven's one light, behind them, striking through
Blazons what each man dreamed no other knew.

London Stone

NOV. 11, 1923

When you come to London Town,
   (Grieving—grieving!)
Bring your flowers and lay them down
   At the place of grieving.

When you come to London Town,
   (Grieving—grieving!)
Bow your head and mourn your own,
   With the others grieving.

For those minutes, let it wake
   (Grieving—grieving!)
All the empty-heart and ache
   That is not cured by grieving.

For those minutes, tell no lie:
   (Grieving—grieving!)
"Grave, this is thy victory;
   And the sting of death is grieving."

Where's our help, from Earth or Heaven.
   (Grieving—grieving!)

To comfort us for what we've given,
    And only gained the grieving?

Heaven's too far and Earth too near,
    (Grieving—grieving!)
But our neighbour's standing here,
    Grieving as we're grieving.

What's his burden every day?
    (Grieving—grieving!)
Nothing man can count or weigh,
    But loss and love's own grieving.

What is, the tie betwixt us two
    (Grieving—grieving!)
That must last our whole lives through?
"As I suffer, so do you."
    That may ease the grieving.

The King's Pilgrimage

King George V's Visit to War Cemeteries in France

1922

Our King went forth on pilgrimage
    His prayers and vows to pay
To them that saved our heritage
    And cast their own away.

And there was little show of pride,
    Or prows of belted steel,
For the clean-swept oceans every side
    Lay free to every keel.

And the first land he found, it was shoal and banky ground—
Where the broader seas begin,
And a pale tide grieving at the broken harbour-mouth
Where they worked the death-ships in.

And there was neither gull on the wing
    Nor wave that could not tell
Of the bodies that were buckled in the life-buoy's ring
    That slid from swell to swell.

All that they had they gave—they gave; and they shall not return,
For these are those that have no grave where any heart may mourn.

And the next land he found, it was low and hollow ground—
Where once the cities stood,
But the man-high thistle had been master of it all,
Or the bulrush by the flood.

> And there was neither blade of grass,
>   Nor lone star in the sky,
> But shook to see some spirit pass
>   And took its agony.

And the next land he found, it was bare and hilly ground—
Where once the bread-corn grew,
But the fields were cankered and the water was defiled,
And the trees were riven through.

> And there was neither paved highway,
>   Nor secret path in the wood,
> But had borne its weight of the broken clay
>   And darkened 'neath the blood.

Father and mother they put aside, and the nearer love also—
An hundred thousand men that died whose graves shall no man know.

And the last land he found, it was fair and level ground
About a carven stone,
And a stark Sword brooding on the bosom of the Cross
Where high and low are one.

> And there was grass and the living trees,
>   And the flowers of the spring,
> And there lay gentlemen from out of all the seas
>   That ever called him King.

'Twixt Nieuport sands and the eastward lands where the Four Red Rivers spring,
Five hundred thousand gentlemen of those that served their King.

> All that they had they gave—they gave—
>   In sure and single faith.
> There can no knowledge reach the grave
>   To make them grudge their death
> Save only if they understood
>   That, after all was done,
> We they redeemed denied their blood
>   And mocked the gains it won.

A Song in the Desert

(P.L.   Ob. Jan. 1927)

Friend, thou beholdest the lightning? Who has the charge of it—
To decree which rock-ridge shall receive—shall be chosen for targe of it?
Which crown among palms shall go down, by the thunderbolt broken;
While the floods drown the sere wadis where no bud it token?

First for my eyes, above all, he made show of his treasure.
First in his ear, before all, I made sure of my measure.
If it were good—what acclaim! None other so moved me.
If it were faulty—what shame? While he mocked me he loved me.

Friend, thou hast seen in Rida'ar, the low moon descending,
One silent, swart, swift-striding camel, oceanward wending?
Browbound and jawbound the rider, his shadow in front of him,
Ceaselessly eating the distances? That was the wont of him.

Whether the cliff-walled defiles, the ambush prepared for him;
Whether the wave-crested dunes—a single sword bared for him—
Whether cold danger fore-weighed, or quick peril that took him
Alone, out of comfort or aid, no breath of it shook him.

Whether he feasted or fasted, sweated or shivered,
There was no proof of the matter—no sign was delivered.
Whatever this dust or that heat, or those fools that he laboured with,
He forgot and forbore no observance towards any he neighboured with.

Friend, thou hast known at Rida'ar, when the Council was bidden,
One face among faces that leaped to the light and were hidden?
One voice among night-wasting voices of boasting and shouting?
And that face and that voice abide with thee? His beyond doubting!

Never again in Rida'ar, my watch-fire burning,
That he might see from afar, shall I wait his returning;
Or the roar of his beast as she knelt and he leaped to unlade her,
Two-handedly tossing me jewels. *He* was no trader!

Gems and wrought gold, never sold—brought for me to behold them;
Tales of far magic unrolled—to me only he told them,
With the light easy laugh of dismissal 'twixt story and story—
As a man brushes sand from his hand, or the great dismiss glory.

Never again in Rida'ar! My ways are made black to me!
Whether I sing or am silent, he shall not come back to me!
There is no measure for trial, nor treasure for bringing.
Allah divides the Companions. *(Yet he said—yet he said:—*
  "Cease not from singing.")

Brazilian Verses

1927

THE FRIENDS

I had some friends—but I dreamed that they were dead—
Who used to dance with lanterns round a little boy in bed;
Green and white lanterns that waved to and fro:
But I haven't seen a Firefly since ever so long ago!

I had some friends—their crowns were in the sky—
Who used to nod and whisper when a little boy went by,
As the nuts began to tumble and the breeze began to blow:
And I haven't seen a Cocoa-palm since ever so long ago!

I had a friend—he came up from Cape Horn,
With a Coal-sack on his shoulder when a little boy was born.
He heard me learn to talk, and he helped me thrive and grow:
But I haven't seen the Southern Cross since ever so long ago!

I had a boat—I out and let her drive,
Till I found my dream was foolish, for my friends were all alive.
The Cocoa-palms were real, and the Southern Cross was true:
And the Fireflies were dancing—so I danced too!

A Song of Bananas

Have you no Bananas, simple townsmen all?
    "Nay, but we have them certainly.
"We buy them off the barrows, with the vegetable-marrows
    "And the cabbage of our own country,
    "(From the costers of our own country.)"

Those are not Bananas, simple townsmen all.
    (Plantains from Canaryward maybe!)
For the true are red and gold, and they fill no steamer's hold
    But flourish in a rare country,
    (That men go far to see.)

Their stiff fronds point the nooning down, simple townsmen all,
    Or rear against the breezes off the sea;
Or duck and loom again, through the curtains of the rain
    That the loaded hills let free—
    (Bellying 'twixt the uplands and the sea.)

Little birds inhabit there, simple townsmen all—
  Jewelled things no bigger that a bee;
And the opal butterflies plane and settle, flare and rise,
  Through the low-arched greenery,
  (That is malachite and jade of the sea.)

The red earth works and whispers there, simple townsmen all,
  Day and night in rank fecundity,
That the Blossom and the Snake lie open and awake,
  As it was by Eden Tree,
  (When the First Moon silvered through the Tree) . . .

But you must go to business, simple townsmen all,
  By 'bus and train and tram and tube must flee!
For your Pharpars and Abanas do not include Bananas
  (And Jordan is a distant stream to drink of, simple townsmen),
  Which leaves the more for me!

Song of the Dynamo

How do I know what Order brings
  Me into being?
I only know, if you do certain things,
  I must become your Hearing and your Seeing;
Also your Strength, to make great wheels go round,
And save your sons from toil, while I am bound!

What do I care how you dispose
  The Powers that move me?
I only know that I am one with those
  True Powers which rend the firmament above me,
And, harrying earth, would save me at the last—
But that your coward foresight holds me fast!

"Such as in Ships"

Such as in Ships and brittle Barks
  Into the Seas descend
Shall learn how wholly on those Arks
  Our Victuals do depend.
For, when a Man would bite or sup,
  Or buy him Goods or Gear,
He needs must call the Oceans up,
  And move an Hemisphere.

Consider, now, that Indian Weed
    Which groweth o'er the Main,
With Teas and Cottons for our Need,
    And Sugar of the Cane—
Their Comings We no more regard
    Than daily Corn or Oil:
Yet, when Men waft Them Englandward,
    How infinite the Toil!

Nation and People harvesteth
    The tropique Lands among,
And Engines of tumultuous Breath
    Do draw the Yield along—
Yea, even as by Hecatombs
    Which, presently struck down
Into our Navies' labouring Wombs
    Make Pennyworths in Town.

"Poison of Asps"

(*A Brazilian Snake-Farm*)

"Poison of asps is under our lips"?
    Why do you seek us, then?
Breaking our knotted fellowships
    With your noisy-footed men?

Time and time over we let them go;
    Hearing and slipping aside;
Until they followed and troubled us—so
    We struck back, and they died.

"Poison of asps is under our lips"?
    Why do you wrench them apart?
To learn how the venom makes and drips
    And works its way to the heart?

It is unjust that when we have done
    All that a serpent should,
You gather our poisons, one by one,
    And thin them out to your good.

"Poison of asps is under our lips."
    That is your answer?   No!
Because we hissed at Adam's eclipse
    Is the reason you hate us so.

The Open Door

England is a cosy little country,
   Excepting for the draughts along the floor.
And that is why you're told,
When the passages are cold:
   "Darling, you've forgot to shut the Door!"

The Awful East Wind blows it—
Pussy on the Hearthrug shows it,
Aunty at the Writing-table knows it—
   "Darling, you've forgot to shut the Door!"

Shut—shut—shut the Door, my darling!
   Always shut the Door behind you, but
You can go when you are old
Where there isn't any cold—
   So there isn't any Door that need be shut!
      And—
The deep Verandah shows it—
The pale Magnolia knows it—
And the bold, white Trumpet-flower blows it:—
   There isn't any Door that need by shut!

The piping Tree-toad knows it—
The midnight Firefly shows it—
And the Beams of the Moon disclose it:—
   There isn't any Door that need be shut!

The milky Beaches know it—
The silky Breezes blow it—
 And the Shafts of the Sunrise show it—
   There isn't any Door that need be shut!

Two Races

I seek not what his soul desires.
   He dreads not what my spirit fears.
Our Heavens have shown us separate fires.
   Our dooms have dealt us differing years.

Our daysprings and our timeless dead
   Ordained for us and still control
Lives sundered at the fountain-head,
   And distant, now, as Pole from Pole.

Yet, dwelling thus, these worlds apart,
  When we encounter each is free
To bare that larger, liberal heart
  Our Kin and neighbours seldom see.

(Custom and code compared in jest—
  Weakness delivered without shame—
And certain common sins confessed
  Which all men know, and none dare blame.)

E'en so it is, and well content
  It should be so a moment's space,
Each finds the other excellent,
  And—runs to follow his own race!

The Glories

1925

In Faiths and Food and Books and Friends
  Give every soul her choice.
For such as follow divers ends
  In divers lights rejoice.

There is a glory of the Sun
  (Pity it passeth soon!)
But those whose work is nearer done
  Look, rather, towards the Moon.

There is a glory of the Moon
  When the hot hours have run;
But such as have not touched their noon
  Give worship to the Suns.

There is a glory of the Stars,
  Perfect on stilly ways;
But such as follow present wars
  Pursue the Comet's blaze.

There is a glory in all things;
  But each must find his own,
Sufficient for his reckonings,
  Which is to him alone.

"Very Many People"

1926

On the Downs, in the Weald, on the Marshes,
   'I heard the Old Gods say:
"Here come Very Many People:
   "We must go away.

"They take our land to delight in,
   "But their delight destroys.
"They flay the turf from the sheep-walk.
   "They load the Denes with noise.

"They burn coal in the woodland.
   "They seize the oast and the mill.
"They camp beside Our dew-ponds.
   "They mar the clean-flanked hill.

"They string a clamorous Magic
   "To fence their souls from thought,
"Till Our deep-breathed Oaks are silent,
   "And Our muttering Downs tell nought.

"They comfort themselves with neighbours.
   "They cannot bide alone.
"It shall be best for their doings
   "When We Old Gods are gone."

Farewell to the Downs and the Marshes,
   And the Weald and the Forest known
Before there were Very Many People,
   And the Old Gods had gone!

Supplication of the Black Aberdeen

1928

I pray!   My little body and whole span
Of years is Thine, my Owner and my Man.
For Thou hast made me—unto Thee I owe
This dim, distressed half-soul that hurt me so,
Compact of every crime, but, none the less,
Broken by knowledge of its naughtiness.
Put me not from Thy Life—'tis all I know.
If Thou forsake me, whither shall I go?

Thine is the Voice with which my Day begins:
Thy Foot my refuge, even in my sins.
Thine Honour hurls me forth to testify
Against the Unclean and Wicked passing by.
(But when Thou callest they are of Thy Friends,
Who readier than I to make amends?)
I was Thy Deputy with high and low—
If Thou dismiss me, whither shall I go?

I have been driven forth on gross offence
That took no reckoning of my penitence.
And, in my desolation—faithless me!—
Have crept for comfort to a woman's knee!
Now I return, self-drawn, to meet the just
Reward of Riot, Theft and Breach of Trust.
Put me not from Thy Life—though this is so.
If Thou forsake me, whither shall I go?

Into The Presence, flattening while I crawl—
From head to tail, I do confess it all.
Mine was the fault—deal me the stripes—but spare
The Pointed Finger which I cannot bear!
The Dreadful Tone in which my Name is named.
That sends me 'neath the sofa-frill ashamed!
(Yet, to be near Thee, I would face that woe.)
If Thou reject me, whither shall I go?

Can a gift turn Thee?   I will bring mine all—
My Secret Bone, my Throwing-Stick, my Ball.
Or wouldst Thou sport?   Then watch me hunt awhile,
Chasing, not after conies, but Thy Smile,
Content, as breathless on the turf I sit,
Thou shouldst deride my little legs and wit—
Ah!   Keep me in Thy Life for a fool's show!
If Thou deny me, whither shall I go? . . .

Is the Dark gone?   The Light of Eyes restored?
The Countenance turned meward, O my Lord?
The Paw accepted, and—for all to see—
The Abject Sinner throned upon the Knee?
The Ears bewrung, and Muzzle scratched because
He is forgiven, and All is as It was? . . .
Now am I in Thy Life, and since 'tis so—
That Cat awaits the Judgment.   May I go?

"His Apologies"

1932

Master, this is Thy Servant.   He is rising eight weeks old.
He is mainly Head and Tummy,   His legs are uncontrolled.
But Thou hast forgiven his ugliness, and settled him on Thy knee . . .
Art Thou content with Thy servant?   He is *very* comfy with Thee.

Master, behold a Sinner!   He hath committed a wrong.
He hath defiled Thy Premises through being kept in too long.
Wherefore his nose has been rubbed in the dirt, and his self-respect has been
    bruisèd.
Master, pardon Thy Sinner, and see he is properly loosèd.

Master—again Thy Sinner!   This that was once Thy Shoe,
He has found and taken and carried aside, as fitting matter to chew.
Now there is neither blacking nor tongue, and the House-maid has us in tow.
Master, remember Thy Servant is young, and tell her to let him go!

Master, extol Thy Servant, he has met a most Worthy Foe!
There has been fighting all over the Shop—and into the Shop also!
Till cruel umbrellas parted the strife (or I might have been choking him yet).
But Thy Servant has had the Time of his Life—and now shall we call on the vet?

Master, behold Thy Servant!   Strange children came to play,
And because they fought to caress him Thy Servant wentedst away.
But now that the Little Beasts have gone, he has returned to see
(Brushed—with his Sunday collar on) what they left over from tea.

Master, pity Thy Servant!   He is deaf and three parts blind.
He cannot catch The Commandments.   He cannot read Thy Mind.
Oh, leave him not to his loneliness; nor make him that kitten's scorn.
He hath none other God than Thee since the year that he was born.

Lord, look down on Thy Servant!   Bad things have come to pass
There is no heat in the midday sun, nor health in the wayside grass.
His bones are full of an old disease—his torments run and increase.
Lord, make haste with Thy Lightnings and grant him a quick release!

Hymn of the Triumphant Airman

(FLYING EAST TO WEST AT 1000 M.P.H.)

1929

Oh, long had we paltered
　With bridle and girth
Ere those horses were haltered
　That gave us the Earth—

Ere the Flame and the Fountain
　The Spark and the Wheel,
Sank Ocean and Mountain
　Alike 'neath our keel.

But the Wind in her blowing,
　The bird on the wind,
Made naught of our going,
　And left us behind.

Till the gale was outdriven,
　The gull overflown,
And there matched us in Heaven
　The Sun-God alone.

He only the master
　We leagued to o'erthrow,
He only the faster
　And, therefore, our foe!

Light steals to uncurtain
　The dim-shaping skies
That arch and make certain
　Where he shall arise.

We lift to the onset.
　We challenge anew.
From sunrise to sunset,
　Apollo, pursue!

What ails thee, O Golden?
　Thy Chariot is still?
What Power has withholden
　The Way from the Will?

Lo, Hesper hath paled not,
　Nor darkness withdrawn.

The Hours have availed not
　　To lead forth the Dawn!

Do they flinch from full trial,
　　The Coursers of Day?
The shade on our dial
　　Moves swifter than they!

We fleet, but thou stayest
　　A God unreleased;
And still thou delayest
　　Low down in the East—

A beacon faint-burning,
　　A glare that decays
As the blasts of our spurning
　　Blow backward its blaze.

The mid-noon grows colder,
　　Night rushes to meet,
And the curve of Earth's shoulder
　　Heaves up thy defeat.

Storm on at that portal,
　　We have thee in prison!
Apollo, immortal,
　　Thou hast not arisen!

Fox-Hunting

1933

(The Fox Meditates)

When Samson set my brush afire
　　To spoil the Timnites' barley,
I made my point for Leicestershire
　　And left Philistia early.
Through Garth and Rankesborough Gorse I fled,
　　And took the Coplow Road, sir!
And was a Gentleman in Red
　　When all the Quorn wore woad, sir!

When Rome lay massed on Hadrian's Wall,
　　And nothing much was doing,
Her bored Centurions heard my call
　　O' nights when I went wooing.

They raised a pack—they ran it well
    (For I was there to run 'em)
From Aesica to Carter Fell,
    And down North Tyne to Hunnum.

When William landed hot for blood,
    And Harold's hosts were smitten,
I lay at earth in Battle Wood
    While Domesday Book was written.
Whatever harm he did to man,
    I owe him pure affection;
For in his righteous reign began
    The first of Game Protection.

When Charles, my namesake, lost his mask,
    And Oliver dropped his'n,
I found those Northern Squires a task,
    To keep 'em out of prison.
In boots as big as milking-pails,
    With holsters on the pommel,
They chevied me across the Dales
    Instead of fighting Cromwell.

When thrifty Walpole took the helm,
    And hedging came in fashion,
The March of Progress gave my realm
    Enclosure and Plantation.
'Twas then, to soothe their discontent,
    I showed each pounded Master,
However fast the Commons went,
    I went a little faster!

When Pigg and Jorrocks held the stage,
    And Steam had linked the Shires,
I broke the staid Victorian age
    To posts, and rails, and wires.
Then fifty mile was none too far
    To go by train to cover,
Till some dam' sutler pupped a car,
    And decent sport was over!

When men grew shy of hunting stag,
    For fear the Law might try 'em,
The Car put up an average bag
    Of twenty dead *per diem*.

Then every road was made a rink
    For Coroners to sit on;
And so began, in skid and stink,
    The real blood-sport of Britain!

Memories

1930

"The eradication of memories of the Great War."—SOCIALIST GOVERNMENT ORGAN.

The Socialist Government speaks:

Though all the Dead were all forgot
    And razed were every tomb,
The Worm—the Worm that dieth not
    Compels Us to our doom.
Though all which once was England stands
    Subservient to Our will,
The Dead of whom we washed Our hands,
    They have observance still.

We laid no finger to Their load.
    We multiplied Their woes.
We used Their dearly-opened road
    To traffic with Their foes
And yet to Them men turn their eyes,
    To Them are vows renewed
Of Faith, Obedience, Sacrifice,
    Honour and Fortitude!

Which things must perish.   But Our hour
    Comes not by staves or sword
So much as, subtly, through the power
    Of small corroding words.
No need to make the plot more plain
    By any open thrust;
But—see Their memory is slain
    Long ere Their bones are dust!

Wisely, but yearly, filch some wreath—
    Lay some proud rite aside—
And daily tarnish with Our breath
    The ends for which They died,
Distract, deride, decry, confuse—
    (Or—if it serve Us—pray!)
So presently We break the use
    And meaning of Their day!

The English Way

1929

After the fight at Otterburn,
  Before the ravens came,
The Witch-wife rode across the fern
  And spoke Earl Percy's name.

"Stand up—stand up, Northumberland!
  I bid you answer true,
If England's King has under his hand
  A Captain as good as you?"

Then up and spake the dead Percy—
  Oh, but his wound was sore!
"Five hundred Captains as good," said he,
  "And I trow five hundred more.

"But I pray you by the lifting skies,
  And the young wind over the grass,
That you take your eyes from off my eyes,
  And let my spirit pass."

"Stand up—stand up, Northumberland!
  I charge you answer true,
If ever you dealt in steel and brand,
  How went the fray with you?"

"Hither and yon," the Percy said;
  "As every fight must go;
For some they fought and some they fled,
  And some struck ne'er a blow.

"But I pray you by the breaking skies,
  And the first call from the nest,
That you turn your eyes away from my eyes,
  And let me to my rest."

"Stand up—stand up, Northumberland!
  I will that you answer true,
If you and your men were quick again,
  How would it be with you?"

"Oh, we would speak of hawk and hound,
  And the red deer where they rove,
And the merry foxes the country round,
  And the maidens that we love.

"We would not speak of steel or steed,
    Except to grudge the cost;
And he that had done the doughtiest deed
    Would mock himself the most.

"But I pray you by my keep and tower,
    And the tables in my hall,
And I pray you by my lady's bower
    (Ah, bitterest of all!)

"That you lift your eyes from outen my eyes,
    Your hand from off my breast,
And cover my face from the red sun-rise,
    And loose me to my rest!"

She has taken her eyes from out of his eyes—
    Her palm from off his breast,
And covered his face from the red sun-rise,
    And loosed him to his rest.

"Sleep you, or wake, Northumberland—
    You shall not speak again,
And the word you have said 'twixt quick and dead
    I lay on Englishmen.

"So long as Severn runs to West
    Or Humber to the East,
That they who bore themselves the best
    Shall count themselves the least.

"While there is fighting at the ford,
    Or flood along the Tweed,
That they shall choose the lesser word
    To cloke the greater deed.

"After the quarry and the kill—
    The fair fight and the fame—
With an ill face and an ill grace
    Shall they rehearse the same.

"Greater the deed, greater the need
    Lightly to laugh it away,
Shall be the mark of the English breed
    Until the Judgment Day!"

The Storm Cone

1932

This is the midnight – let no star
Delude us—dawn is very far.
This is the tempest long foretold—
Slow to make head but sure to hold.

Stand by!   The lull 'twixt blast and blast
Signals the storm is near, not past;
And worse than present jeopardy
May our forlorn to-morrow be.

If we have cleared the expectant reef,
Let no man look for his relief.
Only darkness hides the shape
Of further peril to escape.

It is decreed that we abide
The weight of gale against the tide
And those huge waves the outer main
Sends in to set us back again.

They fall and whelm.   We strain to hear
The pulses of her labouring gear,
Till the deep throb beneath us proves,
After each shudder and check, she moves!

She moves, with all save purpose lost,
To make her offing from the coast;
But, till she fetches open sea,
Let no man deem that he is free!

The King and the Sea

(17th July 1935)

After His Realms and States were moved
To bare their hearts to the King they loved,
Tendering themselves in homage and devotion,
The Tide Wave up the Channel spoke
To all those eager, exultant folk:—
"Hear now what Man was given you by the Ocean!

"There was no thought of Orb and Crown
When the single wooden chest went down
To the steering-flat, and the careless Gunroom haled him
To learn by ancient and bitter use,
How neither Favour nor Excuse,
Nor aught save his sheer self henceforth availed him.

"There was no talk of birth or rank
By the slung hammock or scrubbed plank
In the steel-grated prisons where I cast him;
But niggard hours and a narrow space
For rest—and the naked light on his face—
While the ship's traffic flowed, unceasing, past him.

"Thus I schooled him to go and come—
To speak at the word—at a sign be dumb;
To stand to his task, not seeking others to aid him;
To share in honour what praise might fall
For the task accomplished, and—over all—
To swallow rebuke in silence.   Thus I made him.

"I loosened every mood of the deep
On him, a child and sick for sleep,
Through the long watches that no time can measure,
When I drove him, deafened and choked and blind,
At the wave-tops cut and spun by the wind;
Lashing him, face and eyes, with my displeasure.

"I opened him all the guile of the seas—
Their sullen, swift-sprung treacheries,
To be fought, or forestalled, or dared, or dismissed
    with laughter.
I showed him Worth by Folly concealed,
And the flaw in the soul that a chance revealed
(Lessons remembered—to bear fruit thereafter.

"I dealt him Power beneath his hand,
For trial and proof, with his first Command—
Himself alone, and no man to gainsay him.
On him the End, the Means, and the Word,
And the harsher judgment if her erred,
And—outboard—Ocean waiting to betray him.

"Wherefore, when he came to be crowned,
Strength in Duty held him bound,
So that no Power misled nor ease ensnared him
Who had spared himself no more than his seas had
    spared him!"

After His Lieges, in all His Lands,
Had laid their hands between His hands,
And His ships thundered service and devotion,
The Tide Wave, ranging the Planet, spoke
On all Our foreshores as it broke:—
"Know now what Man I gave you—I, the Ocean!"

The Appeal

IF I HAVE GIVEN YOU DELIGHT
    BY AUGHT THAT I HAVE DONE,
LET ME LIE QUIET IN THAT NIGHT
    WHICH SHALL BE YOURS ANON:

AND FOR THE LITTLE, LITTLE, SPAN
    THE DEAD ARE BORNE IN MIND,
SEEK NOT TO QUESTION OTHER THAN
    THE BOOKS I LEAVE BEHIND.

INDEX TO FIRST LINES